International Computer Music Conference (ICMC 2023)

Shenzhen, China
15 – 20 October 2023

ISBN: 978-1-7138-8477-4

Printed from e-media with permission by:

Curran Associates, Inc.
57 Morehouse Lane
Red Hook, NY 12571

CURRAN ASSOCIATES INC. proceedings.com

Some format issues inherent in the e-media version may also appear in this print version.

International Computer Music Association
1819 Polk Street #330
San Francisco, CA
94109

Phone: (734) 878-3031

www.computermusic.org

Additional copies of this publication are available from:

Curran Associates, Inc.
57 Morehouse Lane
Red Hook, NY 12571 USA
Phone: 845-758-0400
Fax: 845-758-2633
Email: curran@proceedings.com
Web: www.proceedings.com

ICMC 2023
THE SOUND OF CHANGER

ICMC 2023
THE SOUND OF CHANGER
声易·声息
International Computer Music Conference

OCT. 15-20

Proceedings

香港中文大学（深圳）音乐学院
深圳音乐学院（筹）
School of Music
The Chinese University of Hong Kong, Shenzhen
Shenzhen Conservatory of Music (Provisional)

International Computer Music Association

2023 International Computer Music Conference

THE SOUND OF CHANGES

School of Music, The Chinese University of Hong Kong, Shenzhen
International Computer Music Association

CONTENTS

WELCOME

In this beautiful season, I am honored to welcome composers, artists and scholars from across the globe to gather in Shenzhen, to embrace the vitality of the city and the charm of life-changing technology.

In the era of rapid development of science and technology, computer technology, as the core of science and technology, is playing a bigger role in music and culture. The integration of musical culture and technology, has an impact on music creation, music performance and other areas, from various dimensions, offering more diversified choices and possibilities for human to enjoy music, and this is where human civilization heads for in the future.

Founded in 1974,ICMA has played an irreplaceable and crucial role in all aspects of computer music and music technology development while ICMC,the largest and the most important international academic conference in the field of computer music, is held annually in different countries, which provides a platform for demonstrating the achievements of creation, performance and research in music technology, and opportunities for knowledge and experiences sharing.

Shenzhen today is being referred to as the Silicon Valley of China, where high-tech enterprises and young talents gather, full of momentum to actively explore the unknown world in the future. And this year, ICMC is held in Shenzhen, which indicates that the city gradually shifting its development model from technology-intensive to development of culture and arts, highlighting the innovation of the city, and its potential to develop culture and education. In fact, there are many industries in Shenzhen that are closely related to musical and cultural development, such as sensors for computer music, vinyl records, accounting for 70% of the global market, all of which are manufactured in Shenzhen and be shipped to the rest of the world, help provide high-quality products for artists and build up a close relationship with music technology.

School of Music, CUHK-Shenzhen is located in the Greater Bay Area, which is the most dynamic region in China and the place where China has the most frequent exchanges with the rest of the world in science and culture. The geographical advantage propels us to utilize the opportunity and take up the responsibility to serve as a window for international exchanges.

This year's event aims to promote mutual understanding of civilizations through the medium-music, and to explore the in-depth role music technology plays in art, culture, society and people's lives, to bring together various cultures of different backgrounds, enhance mutual understanding through the exchanges of ideas, technology, culture and arts. We also expect Shenzhen to contribute more to future technological innovation and artistic creation with this year's event as the new starting point.

In closing, I wish ICMC 2023 a full success and wish you all enjoy your stay in the city. Thank you.

叶小钢
Xiaogang YE

2023 国际计算机音乐大会组委会主席
香港中文大学（深圳）音乐学院院长
中国文联副主席
中国音乐家协会主席
美国艺术与科学院院士

ICMC 2023 Organizing Committee Chair
Dean of School of Music, the Chinese University of Hong Kong, Shenzhen
Vice Chairman of the China Federation of Literary and Art Circles
Chairman of the China Musicians Association
International Honorary Member of the American Academy of Arts and Sciences

叶小钢
Xiaogang YE

叶小钢，香港中文大学（深圳）音乐学院创院院长、中央音乐学院教授、音乐教育家。第十届全国政协委员、第十一、十二、十三届全国政协常委。现任中国文联副主席、中国音乐家协会主席、美国艺术与科学院院士、英国北方皇家音乐学院国际作曲主席、上海音乐学院特聘教授、星海音乐学院特聘教授、乌克兰柴可夫斯基音乐学院名誉教授、天津茱莉亚学院顾问，北京现代音乐节、深圳“一带一路”国际音乐季、青岛海洋国际音乐季、“粤港澳大湾区”国际音乐季艺术总监，以及哈尔滨音乐比赛艺委会主任。他是中宣部首届“四个一批”人才入选者、享受国务院特殊津贴专家。叶小钢是我国当代著名作曲家，是中国当代音乐领域的领军和代表人物。

他的主要作品包括交响乐、室内乐、歌剧、舞剧、影视音乐等多体裁的大量音乐作品。其代表作有《英雄颂》《地平线》《最后的乐园》《大地之歌》《喜马拉雅之光》《青芒果香》《峨眉》《鲁迅》《英雄》《美丽乡村》《林泉》《羊卓雍错》《深圳故事》《澳门新娘》《永乐》等。其影视音乐《玉观音》《大国崛起》等广受好评。2008 年北京奥运会开幕式上，全球共计有 30 亿观众聆听由郎朗演奏，叶小钢创作的钢琴协奏曲《星光》。从 1995 年起，他的作品被世界著名的音乐出版公司 Schott 所出版和代理。

其作品在世界各地被众多乐团广泛演出，包括纽约爱乐、费城交响乐团、底特律交响乐团、克利夫兰交响乐团、英国皇家爱乐乐团、皇家苏格兰国家管弦乐团、爱尔兰国家交响乐团、新西兰交响乐团、柏林德意志交响乐团、班贝格交响乐团、慕尼黑爱乐、汉堡爱乐、赫尔辛基爱乐乐团、意大利斯卡拉爱乐乐团、俄罗斯国家交响乐团、东京交响乐团、新日本爱乐、新加坡交响乐团、香港管弦乐团、澳门乐团、中国爱乐、中国交响乐团、上海交响乐团，以及国内外众多其他乐团。其作品曾在香港国际艺术节、澳门艺术节、北京国际音乐节、上海之春国际音乐节、上海当代音乐周、德国萨尔州艺术节、波兰华沙之秋国际现代音乐节、罗马尼亚乔治・恩斯库音乐节等众多国内外音乐节和艺术节上演出。

叶小钢曾在美国纽约林肯中心、德国柏林、萨布吕肯和慕尼黑、英国伦敦、爱丁堡和格拉斯哥、俄罗斯莫斯科、印度加尔各答、哥斯达黎加圣何塞、秘鲁利马、法国南特、爱尔兰都柏林等地分别举办《中国故事》专场音乐会，演出获得极大成功，为中国当代音乐在国际上的展示和传播做出了巨大的贡献。

叶小钢荣获过众多国内外奖项和荣誉，包括中宣部“五个一工程”奖、文化部“文华音乐奖”、中国音乐家协会“金钟奖”一等奖、2012 年美国古根海姆基金作曲家大奖、2013 年第二届“中华艺文奖”等。其电影音乐《惊涛骇浪》获中国电影华表奖“最佳音乐奖”，《刮痧》《太行山上》和《开罗宣言》荣获中国电影金鸡奖“最佳音乐奖”，《人约黄昏》获上海国际电影节“最佳音乐奖”。叶小钢本人还获得过上海国际电影节颁发的“杰出电影音乐贡献奖”。

在担任全国政协常委期间，叶小钢一直为音乐普及、全国范围的美育教育呼吁，敦促国家加大对艺术的投入。他在促进中外文化交流，尤其是促进中德两国之间的音乐交流，加强国际音乐版权保护，向政府提出了众多议案。他曾多次在全国性会议上做重点发言，强调保护知识版权的重要意义。在他的大力有效的推动下，中国对外文化交流、国际知识版权在中国的保护工作有了很大的推进。

Xiaogang YE is is the founding dean of School of Music, The Chinese University of Hong Kong, Shenzhen, a professor of the Central Conservatory of Music, and a music educator. YE was a member of the National Committee of 10th Chinese People's Political Consultative Conference (CPPCC) and a member of the Standing Committee of the 11th, 12th, and 13th CPPCC. He is currently vice chairman of the China Federation of Literary and Art Circles, chairman of the China Musicians Association, an international honorary member of the American Academy of Arts and Sciences, international chair in composition at the Royal Northern College of Music, distinguished professor of the Shanghai Conservatory of Music and the Xinghai Conservatory of Music in Guangzhou, honorary professor of the Ukrainian National Tchaikovsky Academy of Music, and a consultant to the Tianjin Juilliard School. YE is the founder and artistic director of the Beijing Modern Music Festival, Shenzhen Belt & Road International Music Festival, Tsingtao International Music Festival, Guangdong-Hongkong-Macao Greater Bay Area Music Season, and International Music Competition Harbin. He is one of the members of Talents Project selected by the Publicity Department of the Communist Party of China, and an expert who enjoys a special allowance from the State Council. YE is a representative figure of contemporary Chinese music and one of the most well-known composers in the country.

YE has composed a large number of works in a variety of genres, including symphonic music, chamber music, dance drama and opera, as well as film and TV music. YE's important symphonic works include Ode to Heroes, Horizon, The Last Paradise, Song of the Earth, Twilight of the Himalayas, Scent of Green Mango, Mount E'mei, Lu Xun (Symphony No.5), The Heroes (Symphony No.7), The Backyard of the Village, Springs in the Forest, Yangzhuoyong Cuo, Shenzhen Story, Macau Bride Suites and Yong Le. The Jade Goddess of Mercy and The Rise of the Great Nations, two of his film scores, were very well received. YE's piano concerto Starry Sky, written for Lang Lang, was viewed by an audience of around three billion people worldwide when it was performed as part of the opening ceremony concert of the Beijing Olympics in 2008. Since 1995, the world-renowned publisher Schott has published and served as an agent for YE's works.

YE's works have been widely performed by orchestras in China and abroad, including the New York Philharmonic, Philadelphia Orchestra, Detroit Symphony Orchestra, Cleveland Orchestra, Royal Philharmonic Orchestra, Royal Scottish National Orchestra, RTÉ National Symphony Orchestra of Ireland, New Zealand Symphony Orchestra, Deutsches Symphonie-Orchester Berlin, Bamberger Symphoniker, Munchner Philharmoniker, Philhamoniker Hamburg, Helsinki Philharmonic Orchestra, Orchestra Del Teatro Alla Scala, Russian National Orchestra, Tokyo Symphony Orchestra, New Japanese Philharmonic, Singapore Symphony Orchestra, Hong Kong Philharmonic Orchestra, Macao Orchestra, China Philharmonic Orchestra, China National Symphony Orchestra, and Shanghai Symphony Orchestra. His works have been presented in the Hong Kong Arts Festival, Macau Arts Festival, Beijing Music Festival, Shanghai Spring International Music Festival, Shanghai New Music Week, Musikfestspiele Saar, Warsaw Autumn International Festival of Contemporary Music, and George Enescu International Festival.

Beginning in 2013, the "China Story" concert series featuring YE's music has been presented in venues all over the world, including Avery Fisher Hall at Lincoln Center (New York), and concert halls in Berlin, Saarbrücken, Münich, Edinburgh, Glasgow, Moscow, Kolkata, San Jose (Costa Rica), Lima (Peru), Nates (France), Dublin, and Bydgoszcz (Poland). The events have constituted a significant contribution to the propagation of Chinese contemporary music on the international stage, receiving wide acclaim and gaining great success.

YE has been the recipient of many prestigious honors in China and abroad, including a Five Distinguished Project Award by the Publicity Department of the Communist Party of China, a Wenhua Music Award by the China Ministry of Culture, a first prize of the Golden Bell Award by the China Musicians Association, a 2012 Guggenheim Fellowship Award, and a 2013 China Arts Award, among others. YE has composed music for more than 30 important Chinese movies and TV series, and won "The Best Score Award" five times for his efforts in this area.

As a member of the Standing Committee of the 11th, 12th, and 13th CPPCC, YE has been enthusiastic in the promotion of music and of national arts education. He has made strong appeals to increase government funding for the arts and has proposed motions concerning cross-cultural exchanges and the protection of musical copyright. At many national meetings, YE has called relentlessly for increasing public attention to the protection of intellectual property, and for the promotion of cultural exchanges with the rest of the world. There has been dramatic progress in both of these areas as a result of his vigorous efforts.

Peer Reviewers

Jay	Afrisando
Miriam	Akkermann
Christopher	Anderson
Xiaomo	BAI
Marc	Battier
Mariam	Bergloff
Marco	Bidin
Guillaume	Boutard
Sabine	Breitsameter
Courtney	Brown
George	Brunner
Ivica	Bukvic
Shane	Byrne
Anıl	Çamcı
Rodrigo	Cadiz
Vincent	Caers
YIBIN	CAI
Jean-Michaël	Celerier
Paulo	Chagas
Chin Ting	Chan
Qiangbin	CHEN
Si	CHEN
Ka Hei	CHENG
Yibing	CHENG
Cathy	Cox
Patti	Cudd
Kevin	Dahan
Roger	Dannenberg
Anthony	De Ritis
Domenico	DE SIMONE
James	Dooley
David	Dow
Xiaohu	DU
Ruilei	DUAN
Frédéric	Dufeu
David	Durant
Arne	Eigenfeldt
Tom	Erbe
Çağrı	Erdem
Hongshuo	FAN
Jinshuo	FENG
Jian	FENG
Iván	Ferrer-Orozco
Martim	Galvão
Richard	Garrett
Travis	Garrison
Jason	Geistweidt
Giampiero	Gemini
Marta	Gentilucci
Karl	Gerber
Michael	Gogins
Matthew	Goodheart
Benoit	Granier
Liqiong	Guan
Peng	GUAN
Kerry	Hagan
Yanmin	HAN
Henry James	Harkins
G. Blake	Harrison-Lane
Akiko	Hatakeyama
Christopher	Hawarth
Mara	Helmuth
Eric	Honour
Hubert	Howe, Jr.
Xiao	HU
Fan	Huang
Chih-Fang	HUANG
Simon	Hutchinson
Hiromi	Ishii
Anqing	JIANG
Chaoqian	JIANG
Fan	JIN
Ping	JIN
Jeyong	Jung
Julien	Junod
Elsa	Justel
Dragica	Kahlina
Howie	Kenty
John	Keston
Yuriko Hase	Kojima
Panayiotis	Kokoras
Tomas	Koljatic
Mikel	Kuehn
Leigh	Landy
Kun	LEE
Censong	LENG
Yong	LI
Zijin	LI
Yunpeng	LI
Jia	LI
Pengyun	LI
Huizi	LI
Qiuxiao	LI
Hongqi	LIANG
Elainie	Lillios
PerMagnus	Lindborg
Annie Yen-Ling	Liu
Shuming	LIU
Hau Man	Lo
Patrick	Long
Minjie	LU
Eric	Lyon
Dave	O Mahony
Shihua	MA
Anthony	Marasco
Dariusz	Mazurowski
Kieran	McAuliffe
Scott	Miller
Adam	Mirza
Daichi	Misawa
Mikako	Mizuno
Barry	Moon

Takeyoshi	Mori
Jeff	Morris
Timothy	Moyers
Yunze	Mu
Chryssie	Nanou
Jon	Nelson
Robert	Newcomb
Ken	Paoli
Joo Won	Park
Juan	Parra Cancino
Kevin	Patton
Sean	Peuquet
Stephen	Pope
Mengjie	QI
Raphael	Radna
Takayuki	Rai
Todd	Reed
David	Reeder
Michael	Rhoades
Felipe	Ribeiro
Bradley	Robin
Stephen	Roddy
Anna	Rubin
Marcel Zaes	Sagesser
Jacob	Sandridge
Robert	Seaback
Ambrose	Seddon
Serkan	Sevilgen
Seth	Shafer
Kyle	Shaw
Lin	SHEN
Liwei	SHI
Jia lin	Song
Blake	Stevens
Jeffrey	Stolet
Martin	Supper
Lukasz	Szalankiewicz
Akira	Takaoka
Xu	TAN
Seth	Thorn
Zhenzi	TIAN
Massimiliano	Tonelli
Pierre Alexandre	Tremblay
Kari	Vakeva
Annette	Vande Gorne
Kyle	Vanderburg
Juan	Vasquez
Mark	Volker
Dmitri	Volkov
Jack	Walker
Fang	WAN
Gang	WANG
Xinyu	WANG
Chi	WANG
Rodney	Waschka
Zhizheng	WU
Jiayue	WU
BingYuan	XIE
Liumeng	XUE
Kai	YANG
Wanjun	YANG
TIAN	YE
Ji Won	Yoon
Masatsune	Yoshio
Xiangguo	YU
Dezhi	YU
Ruibin	Yuan
Guo	Yuan
Ruibin	YUAN
Chao	ZHANG
Zhaoyu	ZHANG
Zhiliang	ZHANG
Chao	ZHANG
Di	ZHANG
Xiaofu	ZHANG
Da	ZHENG
Tiange	ZHOU
Qian	ZHOU
Jiaxing	ZHU
Yao	ZHUANG
Lidia	Zielinska

2023 国际计算机音乐大会组织委员会
Organizing Team

组织委员会主席：叶小钢
Organizing Committee Chair: Xiaogang YE

副主席：Kerry Hagan 陈永华 张立萍 袁芳 王兆玉
Joint Committee Vice Chairs: Kerry Hagan, CHAN Wing Wah, ZHANG Liping, YUAN Fang, WANG Zhaoyu

大会主席：金平
Conference Chair: Ping JIN

论文与音乐奖项评审委员会
Committee on Paper and Music Awards:
* 按照姓氏首字母排序 Alphabetically

论文奖项评审委员会：
Miriam Akkermann, 陈仰平 , Eric Honour, PerMagnus Lindborg, Anthony De Ritis, 申林 , 周倩
Paper Award:
Miriam Akkermann, Yeung-ping Chen, Eric Honour, PerMagnus Lindborg, Anthony De Ritis, SHEN Lin, ZHOU Qian

中文论文奖项评审委员会：
陈强斌，付晓东，关鹏，黄枕宇，宁佐良，吴粤北，杨万钧，袁昊昱，张伯瑜
Honorary Chinese Paper Award:
CHEN Qiangbin, FU Xiaodong, GUAN Peng, HUANG Zhenyu, NING Zuoliang, WU Yuebei, YANG Wanjun, YUAN Haoyu, ZHANG Boyu

音乐奖项评审委员会:
Music Award:
优秀音乐作品评审委员会： Marc Battier, 程伊兵，李鹏云，钱琦，金平，Tae Hong Park, 于阳
Best Music Award: Marc Battier, CHENG Yibing, LI Pengyun, QIAN Qi, Ping JIN, Tae Hong Park, YU Yang

优秀学生音乐作品评审委员会： 黄志方，李秋筱，李彦汶，李云鹏，陆敏捷，亓梦婕，王铉
Best Student Music Award: Chih-Fang Huang, LI Qiuxiao, LI Yanwen, LI Yunpeng, LU Minjie, QI Mengjie, WANG Xuan

工作委员会
Operating Committee

主任：金平
Director: Ping JIN

行政总监：王兆玉
Administrative Director: WANG Zhaoyu

项目统筹：亓梦婕
Coordinator: QI Mengjie Maggie

协调：苏虹
Executive Coordinator: Sue SU

项目协调：齐磊
Sectional Coordinator: QI Lei

经费协调：王宇涛
Finance Executive: WANG Yutao

会务 Conference Affairs:

项目总监：苏虹
Director: Sue SU
项目执行：李嘉俊
Operational Executive: LI Jiajun
协助执行：齐磊 许雪芹 李静贤 陈丽芳 洪玲 蒋娟娟 窦晓晨 彭艺娑
Operational Team: QI Lei, XU Xueqin, LI Jingxian, CHEN Lifang, HONG Ling, JIANG Juanjuan, DOU Xiaochen, PENG Yisuo
项目支持：沈亚学 冀宇婷 苏扬 汤芷莹 陈慧妍 朱明中 黄煜玉 周绮雯 郭若涵 王萱 权怡桦 黄丽莎 柯寒
Support Team: SHEN Yaxue, JI Yuting, SU Yang, TANG Zhiting, CHEN Huiyan, ZHU Mingzhong, HUANG Yuyu, ZHOU Qiwen, GUO Ruohan, WANG Xuan, QUAN Yihua, HUANG Lisha, KE Han

音乐会 Concerts:

项目总监：亓梦婕
Director: QI Mengjie Maggie

龙岗文化中心：
Longgang Cultural Center:
项目总监：阮思思
Director: RUAN Sisi
项目执行：齐磊 巫静 许雪芹 李静贤 陈丽芳 李冰 刘濒月
Operational Team: QI Lei, WU Jing, XU Xueqin, LI Jingxian, CHEN Lifang, LI Bing, LIU Binyue

时空胶囊黑匣子剧场下午场：
Black Box Theatre (afternoon sessions):
项目总监：潘行紫旻 虞鹏飞 李嘉俊
Director: PAN Xingzimin, YU Pengfei, LI Jiajun
项目执行：贾煪博 朱丹 丁龙
Operational Team: JIA Yubo, ZHU Dan, DING Long

时空胶囊黑匣子剧场晚场：
Black Box Theatre (late night sessions):
项目总监：金卓晟 李嘉俊
Director: JIN Zhuosheng, LI Jiajun
项目执行：陈曦 丁龙
Operational Team: CHEN Xi, DING Long

论文主席：Miriam Akkermann
Paper Chair: Miriam Akkermann

音乐主席：亓梦婕
Music Chair: QI Mengjie Maggie

装置主席：卢厚敏
Installation Chair: LO Hau Man

工作坊主席：武执正
Workshop Chair: WU Zhizheng

主旨演讲嘉宾：Mari Kimura, Pamela Z
Keynote Speakers: Mari Kimura, Pamela Z

论文 Paper Sessions:

项目总监：Miriam Akkermann, Anthony Paul De Ritis
Director: Miriam Akkermann, Anthony Paul De Ritis
项目执行：齐磊 韩宇哲
Operational Team: QI Lei, HAN Yuzhe

装置 Installations:

项目总监：卢厚敏
Director: LO Hau Man
项目执行：李嘉俊 张旭 王爱文 窦晓晨 彭艺娑
Operational Team: LI Jiajun, ZHANG Xu, WANG Aiwen, DOU Xiaochen, PENG Yisuo

工作坊 Workshops:

项目总监：武执正
Director: WU Zhizheng
项目执行：罗苑君 韩宇哲 陈玥彤 房子皓 郑奕然
Operational Team: LUO Wanjun, HAN Yuzhe, CHEN Yuetong, FANG Zihao, ZHENG Yiran

音乐产业讲座 Lectures:

项目执行：许雪芹
Operational Team: XU Xueqin

宣传 Publicity:

宣传总监：史润胜
Director: SHI Runsheng
宣传执行：成美玲 王萱 柯寒 苏虹 彭艺娑 Patrick Gunawan Hartono
Publicity Executive: CHENG Meiling, WANG Xuan, KE Han, Sue SU, PENG Yisuo, Patrick Gunawan Hartono
项目执行：学生志愿者
Operational Team: Student Volunteers

演出 Performance:

项目总监：余乐
Director: YU Le
项目执行：苏虹 齐磊 许雪芹 权怡桦 汤芷莹 袁冰昕 学生志愿者
Operational Team: Sue SU, QI Lei, XU Xueqin, QUAN Yihua, TANG Zhiying, YUAN Binxin, Student Volunteers

技术团队 Audio Technical Team:

项目总监：张巍 于得智 申坤 罗梓畅 苏虹
Director: ZHANG Wei, YU Dezhi, SHEN Kun, LUO Zichang, Sue SU
项目执行：杨若婷 王家悦 马晓睿 张鹤 苑裕东 彭艺娑
Operational Team: YANG Ruoting, WANG Jiayue, MA Xiaorui, ZHANG He, YUAN Yudong, PENG Yisuo

会议接待及后勤支持
Conference Reception & Logistical Support：

项目总监：苏虹 李嘉俊 齐磊 洪玲 李静贤
Director: Sue SU, LI Jiajun, QI Lei, HONG Ling, LI Jingxian
项目执行：许雪芹 蒋娟娟 窦晓晨
Operational Team: XU Xueqin, JIANG Juanjuan, DOU Xiaochen

志愿者团队统筹 Volunteer Coordinating:

项目总监：李静贤
Director: LI Jingxian
项目执行：陈丽芳
Operational Team: CHEN Lifang

网络支持 Internet Support:

丰冬 杨焕强
FENG Dong, YANG Huanqiang

官网运营及票务 Website Operations and Ticketing：

项目总监：苏虹 齐磊 李嘉俊
Director: Sue SU, QI Lei, LI Jiajun
项目执行：虞鹏飞 窦晓晨 许雪芹 李静贤 彭艺娑 学生志愿者
Operational Team: YU Pengfei, DOU Xiaochen, XU Xueqin, LI Jingxian, PENG Yisuo, Student Volunteers

大会手册及论文集编辑
Conference Program and Proceedings Editing:

项目总监：亓梦婕
Director: QI Mengjie Maggie
项目执行：李冰 刘濒月 贾熇博 朱丹 陈曦 韩宇哲 穆韵泽
Operational Team: LI Bing, LIU Binyue, JIA Yubo, ZHU Dan, CHEN Xi, HAN Yuzhe, MU Yunze

纪念品 Souvenirs:

项目总监：苏虹
Director: Sue SU
项目执行：彭艺娑
Operational Team: PENG Yisuo

前期申报及筹备委员会 Bid Committee:

主席：叶小钢
Committee Chair: Xiaogang YE
成员：陈永华 金平 张立萍 袁芳 王兆玉 石倚洁 Krzysztof Jablonski 胡咏言 徐惟聆 石慧斌 亓梦婕
Committee Members: CHAN Wing Wah, Ping JIN, ZHANG Liping, YUAN Fang, WANG Zhaoyu, SHI Yijie, Krzysztof Jablonski, HU Yongyan, XU Weiling, SHI Huifu, QI Mengjie
工作人员：李嘉俊 苏虹 毛成华 许雪芹 侯蓓莎
Staff: LI Jiajun, Sue SU, MAO Chenghua, XU Xueqin, Hou Beisha

List of Previous Conferences

ICMC 2022, Limerick, Ireland
ICMC 2020-2021, Santiago, Chile
ICMC 2019, New York University, New York, USA
ICMC 2018, Daegu, South Korea
ICMC 2017, Shanghai, China
ICMC 2016, Utrecht, The Netherlands
ICMC 2015, Denton (Texas), USA
ICMC 2014, Athens, Greece
ICMC 2013, Perth, Australia
ICMC 2012, Ljubljana, Slovenia
ICMC 2011, Huddersfield, UK
ICMC 2010, New York, USA
ICMC 2009, Montreal, Quebec, Canada
ICMC 2008, Sarc, Belfast, N. Ireland
ICMC 2007, Copenhagen, Denmark
ICMC 2006, New Orleans, USA
ICMC 2005, Barcelona, Spain
ICMC 2004, Miami, USA
ICMC 2003, Singapore
ICMC 2002, Gothenburg, Sweden
ICMC 2001, Havana, Cuba
ICMC 2000, Berlin, Germany
ICMC 1999, Beijing, China
ICMC 1998, Univ. of Michigan, Ann Arbor, USA
ICMC 1997, Aristotle University, Thessaloniki, Greece
ICMC 1996, Hong Kong University of Science and Technology, China
ICMC 1995, Banff Centre for the Arts, Canada
ICMC 1994, Diem, Danish Institute of Electroacoustic Music, Denmark
ICMC 1993, Waseda University, Japan
ICMC 1992, San Jose State University, USA
ICMC 1991, McGill University, Canada
ICMC 1990, Univ. of Glasgow, Scotland
ICMC 1989, Ohio State University, USA
ICMC 1988, Gmimik, Kologne, Germany
ICMC 1987, University of Illinois at Champaign/Urbana, USA
ICMC 1986, Royal Conservatory of Music, Den Haag, Netherlands
ICMC 1985, Simon Frasier University, Canada
ICMC 1984, Ircam, France
ICMC 1983, Eastman School of Music, USA
ICMC 1982, The Venice Biennial, Italy
ICMC 1981, North Texas State University, USA
ICMC 1980, Queens College, New York City, USA
ICMC 1978, Northwestern University, Illinois, USA
ICMC 1977, Univ. of California, San Diego, USA
ICMC 1976, Massachusetts Institute of Technology, USA
ICMC 1975, Univ. of Illinois at Champaign/Urbana, USA
ICMC 1974, Michigan State University, East Lansing, USA

ICMA Board

Officers

President:	Kerry L Hagan
Vice President for Membership:	QI Mengjie (Maggie)
Vice President for Conferences:	Rodrigo Cádiz
Vice President for Asia/Oceania:	PerMagnus Lindborg
Vice President for the Americas:	Eric Honour
Vice President for Europe:	Nikos Stavropoulos
Vice President for Preservation:	Tae Hong Park
Treasurer/Secretary:	Chryssie Nanou
Publications Coordinator:	Juan Parra Cancino
Research Coordinator:	Anthony De Ritis
Music Coordinator:	Ping JIN
Array Editor:	Miriam Akkermann
Social Media Office:	Patrick Hartono

Directors 2023

At Large Directors:
Cecilia Wu
QI Mengjie (Maggie)
Henrik Von Coler
John Thompson

Americas Regional Directors:
Paulo C. Chagas
Steven Leffue

Asia/Oceania Regional Directors:
Marc Battier
Mikako Mizuno

Europe Regional Directors:
Miriam Akkermann
Juan Parra Cancino

Ex Officio

ICMA Administrative Assistant & Bookkeeper:
Sandra Ferrell

Keynote Speakers

Mari Kimura

Mari Kimura is a violinist/composer, entrepreneur, and a leading figure in interactive computer music. She is world-renowned for Subharmonics—the production of pitches that sound up to an octave below the violin' s lowest string—and her dynamic performances as an interpreter as well as an improviser. She received numerous awards including the Guggenheim Fellowship, the Fromm Commission Award from Harvard University, a residency award at IRCAM in Paris, and from the Rockefeller Brothers Fund. Educated at Toho School of Music, Boston University and The Juilliard School, Mari is a Professor of Music at UC Irvine and at Juilliard. In 2017, She developed a motion sensor prototype MUGIC®, a small WIFI device which can be worn as a 'wearable tech' or attached to objects. MUGIC® is intended to eliminate the disciplinary divide and enable new forms of art to emerge and flourish. Commercialized in 2020, MUGIC® is now used by musicians, artists and beyond and in numerous conservatories and universities around the world such as Harvard, Juilliard, Univ. of Toronto and University of Arts in Berlin. As an entrepreneur, Mari received the Certificate of Recognition from the House of Representatives and the California State Assembly in 2020.

Pamela Z

Pamela Z is a composer/performer and media artist working primarily with voice, live electronics, sampled sound, and video. A pioneer of live looping, she processes her voice to create complex sonic layers. Her solo works combine experimental extended vocal techniques, operatic bel canto, found objects, text, digital processing, and wireless MIDI controllers that allow her to manipulate sound with physical gestures. In addition to her solo work, she has been commissioned to compose scores for dance, theatre, film, and chamber ensembles including Kronos Quartet, Eighth Blackbird, the Bang on a Can All Stars, Julia Bullock with SF Symphony, and the LA Philharmonic New Music Group. Her interdisciplinary performances have been presented at venues including The Kitchen (NY), Yerba Buena Center for the Arts (SF), REDCAT (LA), and MCA (Chicago), and her installations have been presented at such exhibition spaces as the Whitney (NY), Savvy Contemporary (Berlin), and the Krannert (IL). Pamela Z has toured extensively throughout the US, Europe, and Japan. She has performed in numerous festivals including Bang on a Can (NY), Interlink (Japan), Other Minds (San Francisco), La Biennale di Venezia (Italy), Dak' Art (Sénégal) and Pina Bausch Tanztheater Festival (Wuppertal). She' s a recipient of numerous awards including the Rome Prize, Foundation for Contemporary Arts Dorothea Tanning Award, United States Artists, Robert Rauschenberg Foundation, the Guggenheim, Doris Duke Artist Impact Award, Herb Alpert Award, an Ars Electronica honorable mention, and the American Academy of Arts and Letters Award. She holds a music degree from the University of Colorado, Boulder.

Paper Session Schedule

Oct. 16 Monday
10 月 16 日 周一

论文宣读 1

Paper Session 1: Instrument(s) + Electronics
Moderator: Miriam Akkermann

Location:

W201 Governing Board Room, West-wing, Administration Building, CUHK-Shenzhen

香港中文大学（深圳）行政楼西翼 201 教室

9:30-10:00

Nolan A Hildebrand

Saxophone Controlled No-Input Mixer and Generative Digital Scores: An Exploration of Electroacoustic Improvisation with the NIMB+ 18

10:00-10:30

Julie Zhu

Sum and Difference: Compositional Techniques for Sheng and Electronics 22

10:30-11:00

Nicolas Brochec, Tsubasa Tanaka

Toward Real-Time Recognition of Instrumental Playing Techniques for Mixed Music: A Preliminary Analysis 27

论文宣读 2

Paper Session 2: Computer Music Tools
Moderator: QI Mengjie Maggie

Location:

301 Multi-function Hall, Student Centre, CUHK-Shenzhen

香港中文大学（深圳）学生中心 301 多功能厅

9:30-10:00

Kieran McAuliffe, Mara M Helmuth

The New StochGran: Expanded Granular Synthesis Tools 96

10:00-10:30

Bill Manaris, Anna Forgette

Meta-Xenakis: Developing Style-Agnostic, Stochastic Algorithmic Music 102

10:30-11:00

Paul Lascabettes, Elaine Chew, Isabelle Bloch

Characterizing and Interpreting Music Expressivity through Rhythm and Loudness Simplices 110

11:00-11:30

Gaël Navard

Elektronizza Orkestra: Developing a new kind of Digital Music Instruments Symphony Orchestra 118

Oct. 17 Tuesday
10 月 17 日 周二

论文宣读 3

Paper Session 3: MIR&DSP
Moderator: Paulo C. Chagas

Location:

W201 Governing Board Room, West-wing, Administration Building, CUHK-Shenzhen

香港中文大学（深圳）行政楼西翼 201 教室

9:30-10:00

Ka Ho Leung, Chuck-jee Chau

Enhancing Parameter Efficiency for Music Source Separation Models 35

10:00-10:30

Hong HUANG, Yuyi WANG, Luyao LI, Jun LIN

Music Style Transfer with Diffusion Model 39

10:30-11:00

Zhishu CHANG

The Heterogeneity of The Narrative Role In Kaija Saariaho's Émilie 47

Paper Session Schedule

14:00-14:30
Jonathan Bell
Networked Music Performance in PatchXR and FluCoMa 125

14:30-15:00
Paulo C Chagas, Cassia Carrascoza
I hear you breathe: Extended Techniques and Narratives in Telematic Audiovisual Immersion 133

15:00-15:30
Goni Peles, Yuval Adler
Game Live Streaming as a Model for Networked Music Performance 138

15:30-16:00
Jiayue Cecilia Wu, Rebecca Nie
Heart Sutra: A Network Audio Technology-Assisted Visual Music Composition 146

Oct. 19 Thursday
10 月 19 日 周四

论文宣读 8

Paper Session 8: NIME
Moderator: Marc Battier

Location:

W201 Governing Board Room, West-wing, Administration Building, CUHK-Shenzhen

香港中文大学（深圳）行政楼西翼 201 教室

9:30-10:00
David Kim-Boyle
Immersive Musical Notations in AR/VR 153

10:00-10:30
Greg Beller
Spatial Sampling in Mixed Reality 159

10:30-11:00
Steven Lewis
The Cybernetic "Trap" Kit:
Interface Design Considerations for Virtual Augmentation 166

论文宣读 9

Paper Session 9: Chinese Papers
Moderator: YANG Wanjun

Location:

301 Multi-function Hall, Student Centre, CUHK-Shenzhen

香港中文大学（深圳）学生中心 301 多功能厅

9:30-10:00
Ruolun WENG, YI Qin
基于 Max/MSP 的中国古代乐律学音律计算及可听化平台搭建 175

10:00-10:30
Ning LI
基于计算机技术的中国传统乐器数字化转型案例与对中国传统音乐发展的意义：以古琴为例 182

10:30-11:00
Chunlin ZHU, TIAN Xuhang
基于大规模预训练模型（GPT）和迁移学习的 AI 音乐生成 186

论文宣读 10

Paper Session 10: DSP & Music
Moderator: PerMagnus Lindbord

Location:

W201 Governing Board Room, West-wing, Administration Building, CUHK-Shenzhen

香港中文大学（深圳）行政楼西翼 201 教室

11:30-12:00
Fernando Hurtado, Patricio De La Cuadra, Miguel Attilio Torres
A robotic environment for flute music performance and creation 194

12:00-12:30
Philip Liu, Youngjun Choi, JINJOON LEE
Micro-variation of Sound Objects Using Component Separation and Diffusion Models 199

Oct. 20 Friday
10 月 20 日 周五

论文宣读 11

Paper Session 11: Generative Music/ Visuals
Moderator: Anthony De Ritis

Location:

W201 Governing Board Room, West-wing, Administration Building, CUHK-Shenzhen

香港中文大学（深圳）行政楼西翼 201 教室

论文宣读 12

Paper Session 12: Perception
Moderator: Paulo C. Chagas

Location:

W201 Governing Board Room, West-wing, Administration Building, CUHK-Shenzhen

香港中文大学（深圳）行政楼西翼 201 教室

Saxophone Controlled No-Input Mixer and Generative Digital Scores: An Exploration of Electroacoustic Improvisation with the NIMB+

Nolan Hildebrand
University of Toronto
nolanahildebrand@gmail.com

ABSTRACT

This short paper considers the practice of using acoustic instruments as controllers for no-input mixing board (NIMB). Developed in the Japanese noise music scene, no-input mixing is a technique where the inputs of a mixer are routed back into its outputs to create feedback loops. The sounds created from the feedback loops can be manipulated via the mixer's faders and dials. When an acoustic instrument's microphone is routed into a no-input mixer, its amplitude and musical gestures can control the behavior of the electronic sounds. These sounds can be further manipulated by another performer on the no-input mixer. The author has dubbed this live interactive electronics setup the NIMB+. This paper summarizes a recent NIMB+ composition by the author entitled "generative open graphic score #1" created in the software program TouchDesigner.

1. INTRODUCTION & BACKGROUND

This paper discusses the practice of using acoustic instruments as controllers for a no-input mixer, a practice that I call NIMB+. After a brief historical contextualization, a technical description of using acoustic instruments as no-input mixer controllers will be given followed by a case study of a performance of the author's composition *generative open graphic score #1* which will be used to discuss the NIMB+ set up.

The practice of using acoustic instruments as controllers for no input mixing grows out of the tradition of feedback-based music and sound art. Composers in the late 20th century began to experiment with feedback-based music and installations with works like *Rainforest I* (1968) by David Tudor, *Empty Vessels* (1997) by Alvin Lucier, and *The Wolfman* (1964) by Robert Ashley. In *Rainforest I,* Tudor first designed "input free" setups where feedback loops are generated without any external input [1]. This feedback was then sent to contact microphones placed on different resonant objects to reinforce the acoustic sound. As the setup for *Rainforest* developed, Tudor gradually added different input sources (e.g., a voice) to further manipulate the feedback. In *Empty Vessels,* Lucier placed microphones in small resonate glass vessels and placed speakers directly across the microphones to create a field of feedback. When people enter the feedback field in the installation, they create new sounds and unexpected frequencies. *The Wolfman* is a work written "for amplified voice and tape using acoustic feedback as one of its principal sounds" [2]. Because the tape is played through the loudspeaker at a high volume, the performer can control and manipulate the feedback with their voice similar to how an acoustic instrument can control the feedback created on a NIMB.

Although the no-input mixer connects with the tradition of feedback compositions in Western art music, it most notably came into popularity in the Japanese noise music scene and has slowly gained traction since its first official documented use in 2000 by Toshimaru Nakamura.

Figure #1 Example of a no-input mixer with three feedback loops (channel 1 input to headphone output, channel 2 input to aux send output, and channel 3 input to control room/submix output [on back of board).

2. THE NO-INPUT MIXER

By routing a mixer's inputs back into its outputs, a feedback loop is created (see figure #1). Because mixers contain amplifiers and because audio hardware is inherently noisy, the mixer amplifies its own system noise to create a unique electronic instrument. Although the mixer's voice can be manipulated by its faders and dials, no-input mixers are generally unpredictable and difficult to control adding a level of spontaneity, excitement, and danger to performance. Because of this, performances on no-input mixers are inherently improvisatory. This is echoed by Toshimaru Nakamura who states that, "the unpredictability of the instrument requires an attitude of obedience and resignation to the system and the sounds it produces. Bringing a high level of indeterminacy and surprise to the music" [3]. Although this is generally true, the virtuosic NIMB performances of Marco Ciciliani seen from a 2005 live performance of "Metronome" in Barcelona, illustrates that it is possible to tame (at least partially) the instrument's unpredictable nature and create repeatable, consistent performances [4].

The earliest officially documented use of no-input mixing can be seen by Nakamura on his 2000 album "No-Input Mixing Board". It is no coincidence that no-input mixing performance practice evolved extensively in the Japanese noise music scene: notable artists such as Merzbow, Mondes Brutis, and Filth the Sleep perform(ed) extensively on no-input mixers together with a slew of guitar pedals, cheap synthesizers, home-made instruments, and amplified scrap metal. These Japanese noise artists represent the range of sounds that are possible on a NIMB. The music on Nakamura's "No-Input Mixing Board" is a calm, subtle, and nuanced with pleasant timbres while many albums by Merzbow ("Noisembryo" (1994), Pulse Demon" (1996), "Noise Mass" (2019)) and Mondes Brutis ("Selected Noise Works 93-94" (1994)) use the same instrument to create harsh, noisy, and abrasive sounds. Cut to the 21st century and we can see examples of compositions written and notated exclusively for NIMB such as Ciciliani's album "Metronome" and *mixtape* (2013) by Hannes Seidl. More recently composers such as Kelley Sheehan, Louis Pino, and the author have experimented with acoustic instruments together with NIMB.

3. ACOUSTIC INSTRUMENTS AS NO-INPUT MIXER CONTROLLERS (NIMB+)

The practice of using acoustic instruments as controllers for a no-input mixer is a relatively unexplored area of live electronics. Although Nakamura coined the term NIMB and is regarded as the first artist to utilize the NIMB exclusively, in an interview, Masami Akita AKA Merzbow reveals that, as early as 1990, he was using "mixer feedback" (a no-input mixer) as his main sound together with "contact mics, delay, distortion, ring modulator, and bowed metal instruments" [5, pp 59]. Japanese noise artist Kohei Nakagawa AKA Filth the Sleep also use metal plates with contact microphones to trigger chains of guitar pedals that loop back into a mixer [6]. These examples illustrate that the practice of combining amplified acoustic instruments with mixer feedback is rooted in Japanese noise music.

Despite a growing body of research and work on no-input mixing as a solo performance practice (Tom Mudd (2023) [7] and Alan Chamberlain (2018) [8]), there is very little literature that discusses the practice of using acoustic instruments as controllers for no-input mixers. Although pieces like *Talk Circus* (2018) by Kelly Sheehan also route acoustic instrument's microphones into a no input mixer played by another performer, the acoustic instruments do not act as controllers for the NIMB. The NIMB+ set up is therefore unique in that it can not only morph the acoustic input, but the acoustic instrument can also control the feedback created by the no input mixer. This is achieved through specific routing and gain staging.

3.1 NIMB+ Setup

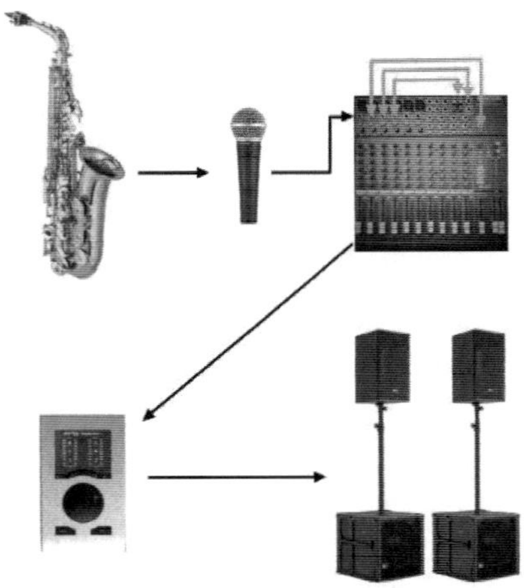

Figure #2 Signal path example for NIMB+ setup.

In performance the acoustic instrument needs to be first in the signal chain and the gain knob and volume fader must also be set very high to function as a controller for the NIMB. The set up in *generative open graphic score #1* consisted of four channel strips, one for the saxophone and three feedback loops with the following settings:

- The saxophone is routed to channel 1with the gain knob and volume fader set very high.
- Feedback loop 1 (channel 2 input to headphone output) is set as a high voice with the high and mid EQ knobs are turned 65%-100% up and the low EQ knob turned to 0%.
- Feedback loop 2 (channel 3 input to aux. send output) is set as a middle voice with the high EQ knob 50%, mid 60-80%, low 20-50%.
- Feedback loop 3 (channel 4 input to control room/submix output) is set as a low voice with the high EQ knob set to 0%, mid 40-70%, low 50-80%.

In performance, the open graphic score serves as generative material for the acoustic instrumentalist. The open, improvisatory nature of the score mirrors the way the performer reacts to the feedback from the no input mixer and vice versa. In performance, the NIMB player reacts to the sounds of the acoustic instrumentalist and does not interpret the score. This approach aligns with the improvisatory NIMB practices of artists like Merzbow, Mondes Brutis, and Filth the Sleep.

4. GENERATIVE OPEN GRAPHIC SCORE #1

In my recent composition *generative open graphic score #1*, I routed a saxophone (performed by Stef Haynes) through a no-input mixer that was being manipulated by a second performer (the author). An open graphic score is a graphic score where there is no legend given and the interpretation of the symbols is left mostly, if not entirely, to the performer's discretion. Open graphic scores are an ideal method for experimenting with the NIMB+ setup as it gives the performers freedom to explore different gestures and techniques. This allows them to listen to the way the live electronics respond without worrying too much about a "correct" execution of notation.

The generative digital score was created in the graphic software program TouchDesigner. In performance, the NIMB player controls the digital score's rate of change and how it morphs over time by interacting with the TouchDesigner patch network. The TouchDesigner patch uses basic instancing and post processing to create the score. The patch uses instancing to create copies of rectangles, circles, and triangles that can be placed in specific areas on a grid allowing users to endlessly generate new seeds/score pages. All post processing is controlled (by the NIMB performer) via changes with the preshrink and blur sliders in the Blur Texture Operator. The geometric shapes and grids can be hidden, blurred, and abstracted to create a multitude of generative shapes ranging from simple and smooth to complex and jagged (see figure #3). This morphology of the geometric shapes subsequently creates the form for the work.

Figure #3. Two seeds from *generative open graphic score #1* taken from the beginning and end of the recorded performance.

4.1 Performance Overview

Section	Saxophone	NIMB
A (0:00-1:40)	(1) high pass filter timbre, (2) distorted timbre, (3) breath sounds & squeaks,	(1) increase faders (Chnl 1+2) = mid-high electronic sound
B (1:40-2:14)	(1) distorted timbre, (2) multiphonics	(1) slowly turn up low voice (Chnl 4) (2) increase each fader to max = electronic voices combine
C (2:14-2:31)	(1) distorted timbre (2) flutter tongue	(1) gain knob twist (2) control room/sub mix fader = texture changes
D (2:31-3:21)	(1) distorted timbre (2) breath sounds (3) fast scalar gestures	(1) gain knob twist (2) control room/sub mix fader = texture changes
E (3:21-4:35)	(1) distorted timbre (2) fast scalar gestures (3) extreme high range	(1) gain knob twist (2) control room/sub mix fader = texture changes (multi-voice texture)

Figure #4. Form analysis of performance of *generative open graphic score #1.*

In section A the only active channel strip is the saxophone's (channel 1). For the saxophone to act as a controller, the gain/trim knob needs to be set very high. The result sounds like it has gone through a high pass filter with some light distortion. At the 1:00 mark, I slowly fade in the high voice and mid voice on channel 2 and channel 3. As the faders are increased, a sustained mid-high pitch in the electronic voice rises in volume. By 1:15 the channel 2 & 3 faders pass a threshold and the saxophone's input begins to control the sounds of the no-input mixer feedback. The mid-high electronic sound is affected by Haynes playing breath sounds which creates a harsh squeaky high-pitched sound like that of bowed styrofoam. At 1:30, a quick five note gesture is heard as the first pitched material to be processed by the no-input mixer, further distorting the saxophone's timbre. From 1:32-1:40, I increase the low tuned voice (channel 4) as Haynes experiments with singing into the saxophone. The singing gestures control the pitch contour of the NIMB feedback to create a crackling, garbled sound.

In section B, I turn up each fader to maximum, so all three electronic voices are sounding at once. This results in a gestalt timbre where the three feedback loops sum into a single monstrous electronic voice. As the faders increase, the saxophone's pitches become even more distorted and the electronic feedback's cries, squalls, and rumbles fill up any space between the saxophone's gestures. At 2:02 Haynes begins to experiment with multiphonics which are distorted by the sounds of the no-input mixer resulting in an even harsher more abrasive multiphonic.

From C and onward, all sound manipulation on the NIMB is controlled by the gain/trim knob of the three feedback loops, the control room/submix fader. At 2:29 I turn down the gain knob on the high voice to create a rumbling bass sound with slow oscillations (around 5-10 Hz). Haynes then matches this sound be playing a flutter tongue gesture which in turn controls the speed of the NIMB's slow oscillations.

From 2:31-3:14 (section D), Haynes further experiments with breath sounds and faster scalar melodic gestures. The breath sounds amplitude envelopes control and shape the rumbling bass, adding mids and highs to create a saturated noisy sound. The fast scalar passages engage with the high and mid feedback loops temporarily muting the low voice feedback loop.

Manipulating the EQ of the feedback loop channels in section E (3:21) results in a new interaction between the saxophone's extreme high range and the high electronic voice (channel 2) to create a piercing and intense sound. From 3:25-4:35 (end), Haynes continues to experiment with the extreme high range contrasted with fast scalar gestures. At 4:04, we can hear the saxophone controlling the high electronic voice, but this time the low rumbling bass is heard beneath resulting in a new multi-voice texture. The piece climaxes with two fast angular melodic gesture separated by a wall of electronic noise before ending with the same multiple voice gesture at 4:22.

Figure #5 Screenshot from recorded performance of *generative open graphic score #1.*

5. CONCLUSION

In summary, acoustic instruments used as controllers for no-input mixer presents exciting possibilities for live electroacoustic improvisation. The NIMB+ setup offers acoustic instrumentalists nuanced, interactive, and often unpredictable control over the electronic feedback soundsC created on a no input mixer and has the ability to bridge the gap between acoustic and electronic instruments in live improvisation. In short, the sound output from the NIMB+ setup is a combined collaboration between acoustic and electronic instruments.

This live electronics setup has had a significant impact on the author's collaborative compositional practices with an importance given to improvisation through open graphic digital scores. Combining the NIMB+ setup with the generative open graphic digital score provides both the musical aspects and the visual aspects of the score in real time.

5.1 Further Developments

Although the nature of no-input controllers is generally improvisatory, there is potential for its use in a more through composed environment. Another logical development for the NIMB+ set up would be to experiment with multiple controllers being used on a single no-input mixer or multiple groups of two (acoustic instrument performer and no-input mixer performer) performing together.

Acknowledgments

Thank you to the University of Toronto and Dr. Eliot Britton for the access and use of the University of Toronto's Electroacoustic Music Studio (UTEMS).

REFERENCES

[1] D. Sanfilippo and Andrea Valle. "Feedback Systems: An Analytical Framework." *Computer Music Journal* 37, no. 2 (2013): 12–27. http://www.jstor.org/stable/24265464.

[2] Eck, Cathy van, *Between Air and Electricity: Microphones and Loudspeakers as Musical Instruments.* New York, NY: Bloomsbury Academic, an imprint of Bloomsbury Publishing Inc, 2017.

[3] T. Nakamura, Bio (from personal website) accessed May 1st, 2023.

[4] M. Ciciliani, "Mask for no-input mixer," 2005. Youtube video. Accessed May 1st, 2023 https://www.youtube.com/watch?v=CoYE4QOWl3I.

[5] Cox, Christoph, and Daniel Warner, *Audio Culture : Readings in Modern Music*. Edited by Christoph Cox and Daniel Warner. Revised edition. New York, NY: Bloomsbury Academic, an imprint of Bloomsbury Publishing Inc, 2017.

[6] Novak, David. *Japanoise : Music at the Edge of Circulation*. Durham: Duke University Press, 2013.

[7] T. Mudd, "Playing with Feedback: Unpredictability, Immediacy, and Entangled Agency in the No-input Mixing Desk. In *Proceedings from the CHI Conference on Human Factors in Computing Systems*, article 243. pp 1-11. 2023.

[8] A. Chamberlain, "Surfing with Sound: An Ethnography of the Art of No-Input Mixing: Starting to Understand Risk, Control and Feedback in Musical Performance." In *Proceedings of the Audio Mostly 2018 on Sound in Immersion and Emotion*, 1–5. ACM, 2018.

Sum and Difference: Compositional Techniques for Sheng and Electronics

Julie Zhu
University of Michigan, Stanford University
julie@ccrma.stanford.edu

ABSTRACT

The sheng is a free-reed mouth organ that is commonly performed and taught through a Chinese musical idiom, playing a large role in the Chinese orchestral and folk music traditions. Additionally, because of its versatility, musicality, and expanded range thanks to modern developments in the 1950s, the sheng is increasingly invited into contemporary western classical music settings, where it is susceptible to appropriation and commodification. In this paper, I describe my personal compositional practice for extending the sheng into a 21st century practice through electronics as arising from the cultural history of the sheng and the embodied experience of the performer. Using five short pieces for sheng and electronics, titled SOMME ET DIFFÉRENCE *for Radio France's* CREATIÓN MONDIALE *as examples, I also discuss the enhancement of acoustic phenomena inherent to the sheng's musical meaning and normally only accessible to the performer, but that can be shared with the listener through electronics.*

1. INTRODUCTION

What does the harmonica, melodica, accordion, and harmonium have in common? All of these popular instruments arose from free-reed technology borrowed from the sheng, one of the oldest Chinese reed instruments [1]. Historical records of the sheng date back to 15th century B.C.E. describing its role in imperial court music. Yet it wasn't until the 17th century that it was first documented as an import to the West [2]. Free-reeds are flexible metal tongues that are attached to a plate inside of a wind chamber. When air is blown over the plate, the unattached end of the reed vibrates "freely" and produces sound that can be influenced expressively by the performer's breath or other means of wind production. Once introduction of this novel instrument-making technique began, popularity of free-reed instruments in the West exploded because of their inexpensive and portable nature, but their Chinese origin is often omitted. Amidst the political and racial context of the early nineteenth century, nationalistic opportunism—whether Christian Gottlieb Kratzenstein, Franz Kirsnick, and Joseph Vogler from Germany or Gabriel-Joseph Grenié from France or Charles Wheatstone from England, all claiming to have invented free-reed technology—subsumed correct attribution [1].

Today, free-reed instruments remain popular throughout the eastern and western world. Within that context, this history of the appropriation of free-reeds by the West can serve as an allegory for postcolonial methodologies when working with the sheng as an instrument performed in non-Chinese contexts [3]. Traditional ways of playing the sheng should not be omitted; rather, centering such techniques can lead to a more idiomatic approach to creating electronics with the sheng. An examination of the sheng's physical properties as a sound-producing object is inherently part of the composition process. However, a sole object-oriented ontological approach—focusing on waveforms rather than the humans making them—may obscure critical questions of intentionality and appropriation when composing for a traditional non-western instrument outside of its original context [4][5]. While the focus of this paper is not on cultural theory and ethics and aesthetics, my research rests on the foundational perspective that incorporating these questions in our interpretation and composition for sheng is valuable and necessary.

1.1 Cultural Context and Composition Process

Growing up watching ancient Chinese imperial court dramas with my mother, I have a specific and peculiar background for the sheng in historic Chinese music, but I am not an expert in traditional Chinese music nor the sheng. However, when I was presented with the opportunity to compose for sheng and electronics, I knew that I wanted to engage with the compositional process as a critical methodology [6] for working with traditional instruments and electronics through a lens of cultural integrity. As a Chinese-American composer, I feel a responsibility to model the synthesis of cultural heritage and novel techniques. The first tenet is to center the experience of the performer and have a dialogue before any compositional ideas are proposed. This is the pre-composition phase.

Proceeding from this commitment, for the development of *Somme et Différence*, five short pieces for sheng and electronics, at Radio France for the France Musique broadcast "Création Mondiale," I met three separate times with Wu Wei and Alexis Baskind prior to the final recording. This multi-iterative recording and pre-composition process was necessary to understand the cultural context of the sheng as well as the unique performative practice of Wu Wei, which felt essential to writing for the sheng and Wu Wei in an idiomatic and respectful way.

Importantly, the first recording session was not about my music and ideas at all. I reviewed musicological materials from PROJECT SEED, "an encyclopedia project that aims to promote diverse instrumentational and compositional techniques of Asian traditional instruments to music composers and those who are interested to learn Asian musical art forms" [7], and asked Wu Wei to demonstrate these different techniques of playing in their original Chinese idiomatic context. Only from there did we begin exploring using these techniques in a different context with electronics, and only after understanding how they arose and are used in common practice.

By the second recording session, I had come up with the narrative behind these five short pieces centered around the techniques that I learned from Wu Wei in the first recording session. Then, the conversation migrated primarily to the physical playing of the instrument, a discussion about how these notes felt in Wu Wei's hands and breath. Fingering for the sheng is complex not only because certain pitches can only be played by one particular finger, but also because in fast and complicated passages, the balance of the instrument has to be considered. This is because the player has to hold up the instrument as well as manipulate the keys and holes to sound pitches.

The narrative was based on a Chinese myth *Jing Wei Tian Hai* [8] that I grew up with as an American with Chinese-born parents which tells the story of a bird named Jing Wei who, after drowning in human form during an ocean crossing, is determined to take revenge on the sea. Every day, for thousands of years, Jing Wei flies back and forth from the mountain to the sea, dropping pebbles that one day may fill up the sea so that no one else may fall victim to the dark waves. The sound of the sheng embodies the characters of this famous myth about perseverance—Jing Wei, her fellow birds, the sea, the wind, its waves, and the beautiful mountainous setting—accompanied by electronics that help amplify the sound phenomenon known as difference tones that are so prominent and special in the sheng. This recorded musical material became the basis for the electronics, which I assembled before our next meeting.

Finally, at a week-long residency at GMEM – Centre National de Création Musicale (Group de Musique Expérimentale de Marseille), the rehearsal process necessary to any new musical collaboration brought together the live amplified sheng and the electronics. For each of the five pieces, Wu Wei, Baskind, and I rehearsed together as a trio. Even cuing the tape elements required deep knowledge of the musical material and a level of improvisation with the normal improvisational techniques in Wu Wei's practice when performing traditional sheng music. This engagement with traditional and contemporary musical practice simultaneously is what made the music come alive, which is precisely the compositional methodology that I argue should be celebrated and welcomed.

1.2 Microphone System

My compositional research relies upon the work by the aforementioned computer music designer Alexis Baskind, renowned sheng player Wu Wei, and musicologist and composer Lin-Ni Liao. In their project *Forêt de Bambous*, they designed an amplification method of the 37-reed modern sheng to reshape its spatial and timbral image, by close-mic'ing its bamboo pipes that are compactly bound together and not easily isolated, and capturing sounds which are normally not radiated and therefore not heard by the audience (Figure 1). Instead of presenting the sheng as an external sound source typically positioned frontally, in real or virtual space, *Forêt de Bambous* explores the sheng from inside and allows for an expanded set of possibilities, spectral and spatial, from the sound emanating from the sheng.[9]

Nine microphones are placed on and inside the sheng (4 DPA 4099, 1 DPA 4060, 1 DPA 4061, 2 AKG 411, 1 AKG 417). The sound of the sheng through the microphone system is mixed and spatialized live by Baskind, while the live cuing and spatialization of the tape electronics is performed by the author. The compositional methodologies discussed in the following section, however, mainly concerns the generation of electronic tape and the live electronics improvisation with with Wu Wei and Baskind rather than the technicalities of this particular amplification system.

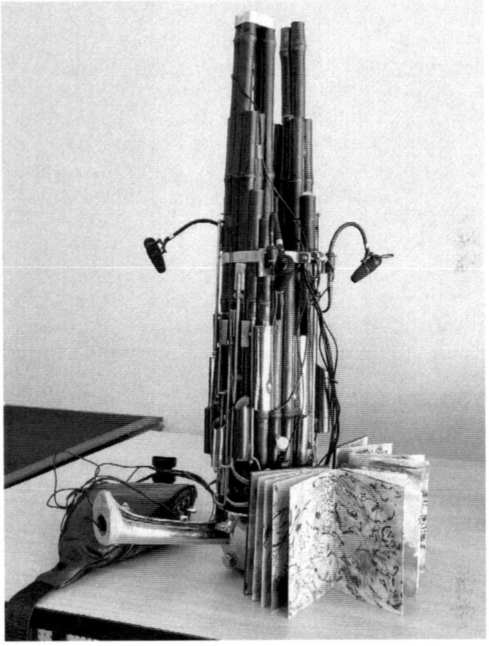

Figure 1. Wu Wei's 37-pipe sheng outfitted with the *Forêt de Bambous* microphone system with a graphic score of *Somme et Différence* beside it, photographed by the author.

2. COMPOSITIONAL METHODOLOGY

In ancient times, the sheng was also called *hé*, which means "with" or "harmony." This etymology is interesting because it not only describes the sheng's specialty among Chinese wind instruments as the only one that can play multiple notes together, but also its musical meaning, representing "harmony with other people, harmony with nature, and harmony with the universe."[10] In addition, the Chinese character *shēng* means life, or a kind of vitality, that rises from the earth. When the sheng plays chords, the resultant sound is active and vibrating, creating a kind of timbre that evokes the celestial. This special acoustic characteristic comes from the prominent difference tones in the sheng, which is featured in its traditional playing. For this reason, I focused on the combination tones in the sheng in my composition of the electronics as a natural growth from traditional practice.

2.1 Combination Tones

As is broadly known, when two tones are sounded at the same time, they produce combination tones: the sum tone and the difference tone (and the sum and difference tones of the new pairs of tones...). The effect is an expansion of the harmony. Specifically for the sheng, a soprano instrument, playing two notes at a close interval results in a lower heard tone, either pitched or a rumbling beating, also known as "tartini tones" or "missing fundamental" or "beating" [11]. This shimmering color of chords on the sheng has always been an attractive quality for the composer, as in the Chinese etymological history and meaning of the sheng as described, but also for contemporary composition [12]. For example, in a paper relating recent works for the shō and sheng, Christian Utz describes the ensemble supporting and imitating the sheng in Heinz Reber's *Music for Sheng*: "Winds and strings play fast repetitive figures which vibrate with the oscillation of the (amplified) sheng-chords to create a gossamer trembling texture, which the composer associates with the registrations of a baroque organ, among other possibilities" [13]. Such "oscillation" and "trembling" refers to the combination tones that are also present in older mechanical organs, which serves as the inspiration for the music writing of the entire ensemble. I am not alone in spotlighting the combination tones in the sheng.

2.1.1 Psychoacoustic Replication

Difference tones in the sheng are best heard when the two original tones are loud. The people who hear them best are the sheng players themselves, as they are closest to the instrument and there is bone conduction through contact with the instrument. The resultant tone is also more easily detected when the two tones are in isolation with minimal interference of other frequencies [14]. Musically, this presents a challenge, as composers would ideally not want to be limited to composing with only two notes played at an uncomfortable volume. Thus, in the **first piece** of *somme et différence*, I chose to live with a faint psychoacoustic effect for the listener regarding difference tones, and instead amplify those lower fundamentals using pitch shifting in the electronics. However, this is just an approximation of the psychoacoustic effect, as the frequencies that arise when playing pairs of notes depends on which specific dyad, since their physical location on the instrument is also a factor in other tones that arise. Physical coupling of proximate bamboo tubes has been observed to create frequencies not part of the calculated combination tones below [15].

In the 37-reed sheng, many pairs of notes have been recorded and analyzed for combination tones and their relative strength to the original pair, but since the sheng's tuning is susceptible to weather changes, these exact frequencies are not necessarily replicated in each performance [16]. This is the reason that for this first piece for sheng and electronics, I narrowed the electronic composition to the simple difference tone. An exciting future possibility, however, would be to explore in composed electronics, the myriad of combination tones that are present for each dyad in the sheng, in addition to the special other tones that arise from physical coupling.

2.1.2 Addition over Equalization

Another way to bring out the variation in the shimmering of difference tones is the use of glissando to get within a semitone difference between the two tones. Many of the lower notes of the sheng are played via keys, which then are not physically bendable, whereas the higher notes are played by covering holes with fingers, which can be bent by covering these holes partially. Bending pitches also requires a high velocity of breath and is sometimes difficult to control, depending on the note. In the diagram below (Figure 2), the difficulty of pitch-bending is indicated by the color: red is most difficult, green is least difficult, while no highlighting indicates that this note is played by a key and not by the finger.

Pitch	Hz	Finger
G3	197	R4
G#3	209	L1
A3	221	L4
A#3	234	L1/R1
B3	248	R4
C4	263	L1
C#4	278	L2/L3
D4	295	R2/L5
D#4	313	L1
E4	331	R3
F4	351	L2
F#4	372	R1
G4	394	L4
G#4	417	L3/L2/L4
A4	442	R4
A#4	468	R2/R5
B4	496	L1
C5	526	R1
C#5	557	L1/R1
D5	590	R4
D#5	625	L2
E5	662	R2
F5	702	L1
F#5	743	R2
G5	788	R1
G#5	834	R2
A5	884	L3
A#5	937	L1/L2
B5	992	L2
C6	1051	R3
C#6	1114	L2
D6	1180	L4
D#6	1250	R1
E6	1325	L1
F6	1403	R2
F#6	1487	R3
G6	1575	L1

Figure 2. Pitches of 37-pipe sheng with fingering and pitch-bend difficulty [17].

One solution to the difficulty of bending pitches acoustically on the sheng while playing another note simultaneously, is to have the sheng interact with a synthesized sound. The closest simple waveform to the sheng is a triangle wave, the combination of which similarly results in combination tones that produce the "shimmering" quality when multiple sheng notes are played, but synthesized waves can be finely controlled by the computer. Figure 3 is a zoomed-in waveform of Wu Wei playing approximately the dyad E6 and F6 without pitch bending—the rough triangle shape is present, as well as the large-form beating of the two pitches. As the large-form oscillation is around 17 milliseconds, the reciprocal of that is 59 Hz, which is slightly lower than the 78 Hz beating we would hear if the E6 and F6 dyad were of the exact frequencies in Figure 2.

Now, adding pitch bending for both the sheng and the synthesized triangle wave, there can be more nuance to the duet—the sheng player only has to worry about pitch-bending one note, and the computer performer can move with or against the sheng with fine-tooth adjustment, creating a pas de deux. The **third piece** of *somme et différence* has no tape and is only improvisation between Wu Wei on sheng and myself on a set of triangle waves that are being pitch-bent with knobs. Figure 4 is a spectrogram representing such an improvisation—Wu Wei is pitch-bending around E6 with an E6 triangle wave around 1325 Hz. In the lowest frequency band just above 1kHz, the triangle wave and the sheng look almost together, and going up the octaves, the separation and pitch-bending are more distinct. There is also a faint difference tone hovering just above 0 Hz in the zoomed-out figure.

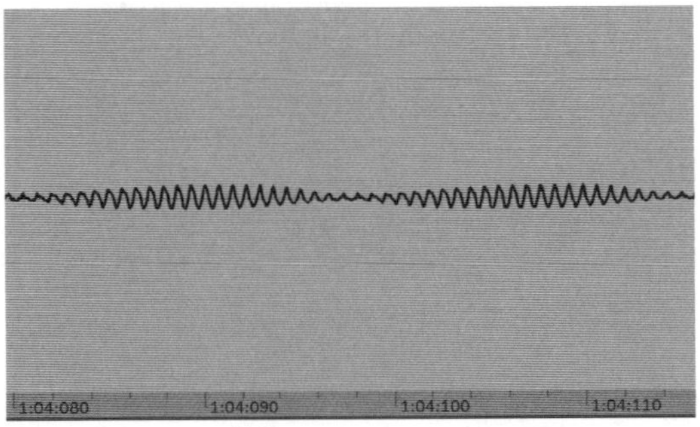

Figure 3. Screenshot of Ableton Live software showing E6-F6 played on the sheng [17].

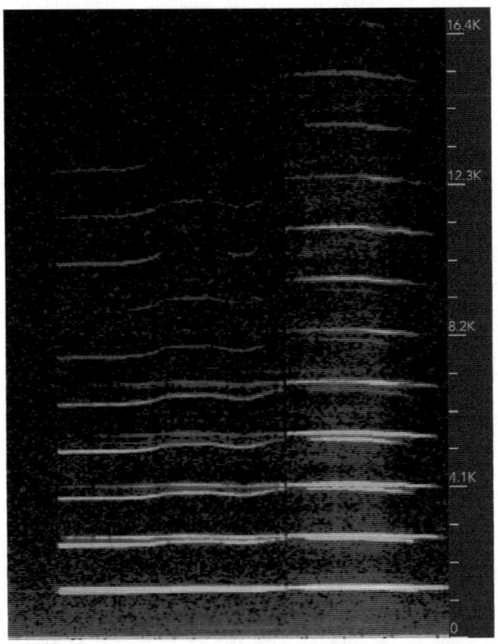

Figure 4. Screenshot of TS software showing the spectrogram of an E6 triangle wave interacting with a pitch-bending sheng [17].

2.2 Ring Modulation

Given that ring modulators output the sum and difference of the frequencies present and remembering that acoustic amplitude modulation naturally occurs in a sheng, for example when playing quick tremolos, ring modulation is a perfect electronic tool to use with the sheng that already produces a signal rich in partials so that the sound manipulation already fits in the sound world of the sheng. In the **fourth piece** of *somme et différence*, I utilized live ring modulation to add a timbral texture to the sheng. In the score, the thick vibrato line over cue sings indicates when to bring this effect (Figure 5).

Figure 5. Score of the beginning of the fourth piece.

As ring modulation or frequency shifting is very sensitive, I found that slight shifts in frequency was sufficient, as I only wanted to hint at a digital sound. In Figure 5, the sheng is already playing a specific acoustic tremolo technique called suìtù which is very rhythmically active. The effect of the ring modulation is then just a bit of distorted digitality that gives a little more crunch to a friction that is already part of the sheng.

2.3 Reverb

Because of the active difference tones, long or even infinite reverb can be especially interesting for an electronic effect on the sheng. When delaying and prolonging a sound, reverb can be very static. This can be the intended effect, but with the sheng, especially when playing clusters, long reverb can imitate a tremolo effect. The **first piece** of *somme et différence* uses electronics that are substantially made up of the infinite reverb part of IRCAM's Spat package. The rich partials of the ten different pairs of notes in the first five-note chord are constantly moving, so that the long reverb sounds more like a composed arpeggiation instead of a reflection of a certain space. Similar to working with ring modulation that enhances the difference tones inherent in the sheng, the electronic tape of long reverb starts with what the sheng already produces and points to a particular aspect that may be glossed over by a listener when listening to acoustic sheng.

2.4 Space

One of the revolutionary aspects of Baskind's system is that he can alter the position and distance of the sound of the sheng, relative to other sounds also sent to Spat. In the **fifth piece** of *somme et différence*, the sound of the sheng was positioned nearer distance-wise, and the sound of the tape was positioned further away, as a siren-call. Through the pieces, simple trajectories were used—circular, random, and left-right—to fit the musical material.

2.5 Granulation

Given the position of the microphones, there are two contact mics that can isolate key clicks, although the sound of the key clicks is not easily removed from the DPAs. The **second piece** of *somme et différence* takes advantage of the ubiquitous acoustic sound of key clicks when playing the sheng and maps trajectories for the fluttering granulated key clicks that are almost like bird wings fluttering around the audience. Again, the electronics start from the acoustic—key clicks that seem incidental to the instrument—and focuses on an overlooked aspect of the sheng to magnify for the listener.

3. CONCLUSIONS

The sheng is a rich instrument full of possibilities in collaboration with electronics. Its timbral color is already close to a digital sound given the omnipresent combination tones. From that one perspective—combination tones—a myriad of technical composition ideas arise: using tape to fill in the missing fundamental and simultaneously adding bass to a mostly soprano sound, live improvisation between single sheng tones and triangle waves to bring out the delicate flowering of changing difference tones born from glissandi, and live ring modulation that enhances the spectral quality of the sheng, all explored in *somme et différence*. But importantly, the electronic possibilities in conjunction with the sheng are shared within the framework of postcoloniality and subjective positionality. Through a hybrid approach that centers cultural practice, exploratory technical spokes such as spatial amplification or live filtering of combination tones can create novel and productive collaborations with the sheng. This role of the electronics—allowing deeper understanding the sheng from the performer's perspective—is a positive and inspiring compositional methodology for any instrument but especially one that has a traditional context. My hope is that there will be many more pieces for sheng and electronics that bring to light the unique and special qualities of the sheng.

Acknowledgments

Many thanks to Alexis Baskind, Wu Wei, Lin-Ni Liao, Julie Delisle, and Mikhail Malt for access to their research and for their support. This work is supported by Tout Pour la Musique Contemporaine (TPMC), GMEM – Centre National de Creation Musicale (Group de Musique Experimental de Marseille), IRCAM (Institut de Recherche et Coordination Acoustique/Musique), the Stanford-France Center, and Radio France - France Musique (Anne Montaron, Raffi Kevorkian, Delphine Baudet, Guillaume Leplege, and Nadege Antonini).

4. REFERENCES

[1] C. Raz, "How the sheng became a harp," *Sound Studies*, vol. 6, no. 2, pp. 239–256, 2020.

[2] C. Wang, J. Y. Chow, and S. Wong, *The Teng guide to the Chinese orchestra*. World Scientific, 2019.

[3] H.-L. Yang and M. Saffle, *China and the West: Music, representation, and reception*. University of Michigan Press, 2017.

[4] A. J. Chung, "Vibration, Difference, and Solidarity in the Anthropocene: Ethical Difficulties of New Materialist Sound Studies and Some Alternatives," *Resonance: The Journal of Sound and Culture*, vol. 2, no. 2, pp. 218–241, 2021.

[5] L. Whitesell, "White noise: Race and erasure in the cultural avant-garde," *American Music*, pp. 168–189, 2001.

[6] J. Impett, *Sound work: composition as critical technical practice*. Leuven University Press, 2021.

[7] J. Chow and C. Shimizu. SEED Project Virtual Academy. [Online]. Available: https://www.nyfa.org/nyfa-project/JC1722

[8] L. Yang and D. An, *Handbook of Chinese mythology*. Abc-clio, 2005.

[9] A. Baskind and W. Wei, "A Forest of Pipes: Presenting the 37-pipe Sheng from the Inside," *Circuit*, vol. 32, no. 1, pp. 37–51, 2022.

[10] W. Wu. Instrument: Sheng. [Online]. Available: https://www.youtube.com/watch?v=qkkA5yWrvww

[11] D. R. Chialvo, "How we hear what is not there: A neural mechanism for the missing fundamental illusion," *Chaos: An Interdisciplinary Journal of Nonlinear Science*, vol. 13, no. 4, pp. 1226–1230, 2003.

[12] H. Qin, "The Evolution of Sheng in Mainland China from 1949 to 2018," Ph.D. dissertation, Kent State University, 2021.

[13] C. Utz, "Beyond Cultural Representation: Recent Works for the Asian Mouth Organs Shō and Sheng by Western Composers," *the world of music*, pp. 113–134, 2005.

[14] R. Rasch and R. Plomp, "The perception of musical tones," in *The psychology of music*. Elsevier, 1999, pp. 89–112.

[15] M. Malt and J. Delisle. Spectral Characteristics of Sheng: Differential Tones. [Online]. Available: https://www.youtube.com/watch?v=h3nGT5Y7CMo

[16] ——. Sheng! L'orgue à la bouche #10 : Analyse acoustique de l'orgue à bouche. [Online]. Available: https://www.youtube.com/watch?v=m_nUmfWvuXc

[17] W. Wu and Y. Pei, "Layout of 37's discant Sheng," 1.2 Basic Instrumentation for the Sheng from SEED workshop, 2021, accessed: 2021-04-01.

Toward Real-Time Recognition of Instrumental Playing Techniques for Mixed Music: A Preliminary Analysis

Nicolas BROCHEC
Tokyo University of the Arts
nicolas.brochec@pm.me

Tsubasa TANAKA
Tokyo University of the Arts
tanaka.tsubasa@ms.geidai.ac.jp

ABSTRACT

In contemporary mixed music, real-time digital sound processing is often applied to live instrumental performances. However, switching between sound effects often relies on manual computer operation or the performer's foot pedal, burdening the operator. This research aims to develop a system that automatically classifies instrument playing techniques and switches sound effects according to the result of the classification, reducing the burden on the operator and expanding creative possibilities in contemporary mixed music. To realize such a system, the classification accuracy of existing research is not sufficient. In this study, we focused on the flute and tested various input data formats to improve the accuracy of the classification. The results show that using a number of frames of around 15 with the Log-Mel-Spectrogram (LMS) data format improves accuracy. Furthermore, we have measured the computational times of some classification algorithms to assure that the system can actually be used in real time. We found that Multi-Layer Perceptron (MLP) with LMS data format was the best choice among them because it had high accuracy and was fast enough, while other algorithms had concerns about computational speed.

1. INTRODUCTION

In the field of contemporary mixed music (*musique mixte*), real-time digital acoustic effects were applied to live instrumental performances circa 1980. This advancement was made possible thanks to increasing computer calculation speeds. Nevertheless, sound effects are usually fixed for each section of a piece, and switching between them is often done by computer operation or the performer's foot pedal, which places a burden on the operator. This is where automated score follower systems such as Antescofo [1] have been developed. These systems track the performer's temporal position on the score and automatically switch effects, reducing the burden on the operator. However, score followers require the score input information for each piece of music in order to estimate the performer's position, which adds an extra burden. Furthermore, instrumental techniques used in contemporary mixed music are nowadays various, and Antescofo, except for some, is not capable of identifying them all. This research proposes developing a system that automatically identifies instrument playing techniques (IPT) and switches sound effects in real time according to them. This would reduce the burden on the operator and the cost of music score input. If put to practical use, the creative possibilities of mixed music would expand to make better use of the real-time nature of sound effects.

There are some existing studies that tackle IPT identification based on principal component analysis [2] and onset detection [3]. These approaches require the design of a set of audio descriptors that detect only one IPT and cannot detect other IPTs. Hence, they are not sufficient for our task. Other research focusing on violin [4], cello [5, 6], electric guitar [7], Chinese bamboo flute [8], and drums [9] tackle IPT identification as a multiclass classification task using neural nets. To our knowledge, only the studies on cello [5, 6] have suggested using IPT classification for real-time performance. For this purpose, they attempted to discriminate various cello playing techniques using convolutional neural networks (CNN). Nonetheless, the proposed system has not yet reached sufficient accuracy and is not yet ready for practical application.

We think that one of the ways to improve the accuracy of IPT classification is to test different data dimensionalities and measure how they impact accuracy. In [5, 6], a number of frames of 60 have been employed as the data unit length. We did preliminary experiments with the flute instead of the cello, with different numbers of frames. It seemed that a smaller number of frames increased accuracy.

Therefore, the objective of this study is to find the most preferable data dimensionality to enhance the global accuracy of classifiers. In addition, we measure the maximum delay time to evaluate the real-time performance of the system. We selected the flute as the instrument for the experiments. This is because the first author of this paper is actually planning to compose a piece for flute that he is familiar with using this real-time classification system. To our knowledge, no research other than our own in the field of IPT classification has yet been conducted on the flute.

2. FLUTE PLAYING TECHNIQUES

There is a wide range of playing techniques for each type of instrument. In the case of the flute, different techniques such as *legato* and *staccato* articulations, *vibrato* and *flutter*, *slaps*, *key percussion* and other special techniques can

1	aeolian	11	play-and-sing
2	aeolian-and-ordinario	12	play-and-sing-unison
3	discolored-fingering	13	sforzando
4	flatterzunge	14	staccato
5	fortepiano	15	tongue-ram
6	harmonic-fingering	16	trill-major-second-up
7	key-click	17	trill-minor-second-up
8	multiphonics	18	whistle-tone
9	ordinario	19	whistle-tone-sweep
10	pizzicato		

Table 1. Flute playing techniques on 19 categories

be performed. The sound of the flute is mainly produced by the friction of air blown into the mouthpiece. Differences in the velocity and characteristics of the blown air cause changes in technique [10]. For example, the velocity of the air causes changes in volume and octave, and the adjustment of the airflow by the tongue produces differences in attack, such as *staccato*, *slap* and *flutter*. The flute can produce a chromatic scale thanks to the keys, from medium (C3 ≈ 261Hz) to treble pitch (C6 ≈ 2093Hz). Special techniques such as multiphonics and quarter tones can also be achieved by unusual fingering [11, 12]. The aim of this research is to automatically identify these various techniques as audio data in real time.

3. TRAINING DATASET

In this study, we perform an experiment that aims to investigate which data format is most adequate for flute playing technique classification. For this purpose, we create multiple training datasets with different data formats and test them on a set of algorithms.

3.1 Sound Bank

To form our training datasets, we use FullSOL [13], an existing sound bank of instrument solo recordings that include various IPTs of classical music instruments. This sound bank includes 27 different flute techniques, totaling 689MB and 1261 audio files for approximately 2 hours of sound.

3.2 Techniques Selection

Some techniques recorded in the FullSOL sound bank are not suitable for this task. For instance, transitional techniques (i.e. from ordinario sound to aeolian sound) could cause confusion for the classifiers, given their evolution over time. Such techniques will not be used in this study. Also, similar techniques that have been separated for audio sequencer needs (i.e *note-lasting* and *ordinario* techniques) are merged into one category. This study is then a 19-class problem and uses 388MB of data, comprising 837 audio files for approximately 1 hour of sound. The 19 categories of flute playing techniques are shown in the Table 1.

3.3 Data Formats

Following the methodology in [5, 14], we downsampled the audio file sample rate to 24kHz considering 12kHz (the Nyquist frequency) is sufficient to cover most flute harmonics. Additionally, reducing data dimensionality will decrease the prediction time. We then sliced the audio file into 60-frame-long sequences (∼1.28s). The sequences are analyzed with a Log-Mel-Spectrogram (LMS) analysis from the Librosa library [15] using the same parameters as in [5, 6]. The LMS is computed on 128 bins, the FFT window is fixed at 2048 samples, and the hop size is set to 512 samples (∼21.3ms). This is because the sensation of simultaneity between two different sound stimuli begins when the time gap between them is less than 20ms [16]. The data is then normalized.

n_frames	60	45	30	15	10	5
LMS	7680	5760	3840	1920	1280	640
FBA	128	128	128	128	128	128

Table 2. Data dimensionality for one sample

Each sound file is sliced into a maximum number of data samples according to the number of frames used. In cases of lack of length, as for *pizzicato*, *staccato* and *key clicks*, sample arrays are padded with zeros.

In order to investigate which data format is most suitable for our task, we propose reducing the data dimensionality using two methods. The first method consists of reducing the number of total frames from 60 frames to 5 frames. The second method consists of computing the average of each frequency bin (FBA) of a Log-Mel-Spectrogram over the number of frames. Table 2 shows the data dimensionality for both methods according to the number of frames.

4. METHODS OF CLASSIFICATION

4.1 Algorithms

To compare different algorithms, we chose three different types of them from the Scikit-learn library [17]. We have tested several parameter configurations and selected those that enhanced accuracy. Support Vector Machine Polynomial Kernel is set to default parameters, and the k-Nearest Neighbours algorithm is set to 1 neighbour (instead of 5). Multi-Layer Perceptron is set with two hidden layers of 400 neurons each because the default configuration didn't have sufficient layers to process large data dimensionalities. Also, *max_iter* parameter was set to 1000 instead of the default setting of 100.

4.2 Data Augmentation

To compensate for the lack of training data, data augmentation is often effective for audio classification tasks, and existing research has shown a substantial rise in accuracy [18]. The method consists of increasing the amount of data by making some modifications to the data we already have. For our experiments, we use three types of data augmentation methods: pitch shift, reverb addition, and noise addition, similar to those used in existing research [5, 6]. For the pitch shifting, the original recording tuning is shifted randomly within a range of ±20 Hz compared to the original tuning of 440 Hz. This is based on the assumption that the tuning of the instrument can change between performances. For reverb addition, a reverb of a fixed length is applied to the original sound source. This is based on the

n_frames	60	45	30	15	10	5
n_samples	10336	13832	21177	43165	65295	131937

Table 3. Total n_samples according to frames number

assumption that reverberation differs depending on the performance environment. For noise addition, white noise is added randomly to each file of the original recording. This is based on the assumption that noise is generated when a microphone is used to capture the sound of a musical performance. This data augmentation increases the number of training data points by a factor of four compared to the original data. As shown in the Table 3, the total training data samples are shown according to the number of frames after performing data augmentation.

5. EXPERIMENTS

We perform two experiments to find the best data format for accuracy score and prediction time. We first test our set of algorithms with different numbers of frames using the LMS and FBA data formats. Then, we measure the total prediction time for each data format, number of frames, and algorithm.

5.1 Test Data

In our experiments, we use *train_test_split* function from the Scikit-learn library to select 25% of our data for the test dataset. Because the amount of data for each class is not balanced, we use the parameter *stratify* of this function to select approximately the same percentage of samples from each target class as the complete dataset.

5.2 Accuracy Measure

As the train and test datasets are balanced, they may not vary much with different splits of train and test data. That is why, for SVM and KNN algorithms, we measure the accuracy only once. For MLP algorithm accuracy, we measure accuracy for each of the 500 epochs of training and then apply a moving average to the prediction score for each iteration. Computing the moving average helps filter out fluctuations in the prediction scores and represents overall performance rather than performance on specific tests.

5.3 Total Delay Time Calculation

The total delay time is composed of three different types of time. First, there is the time required to gather enough samples to process the spectrogram analysis. Since our system aims to make a prediction at each frame, this time is equal to the hop size value of the spectrogram analysis at 24kHz (512 samples $\approx$ 21.3ms).

Second, there is the time required to compute the spectrogram analysis. As the results may depend on CPU background task load, this was computed 10,000 times on the same audio sample, with any other application opened. From the 10,000 measurements, we computed the average, the standard deviation, and the maximum for a better understanding of the time required to compute the spectrogram analysis.

Third, there is the prediction time induced by the algorithm. We measured the prediction time on the first 500 test data samples and computed the average, the standard deviation, and the maximum.

The prediction time induced by each of the classification algorithms (SVM, kNN, MLP) must not exceed 21.3ms assuming that the predictions are done sequentially. If the time for a prediction for one frame is over 21.3ms, the next prediction is delayed for this, and the delays of the frames accumulate unlimitedly.Therefore, summing the time for gathering samples and the limit of the prediction time, the upper limit of the total maximum delay time for our system is two frames long, or 42.6 ms.

The time measurements are highly dependent on computer calculation speed. For these experiments, we used an i7-8700K CPU with 32.0 GB of RAM on a 64-bit Windows 10 operating system PC.

6. RESULTS

6.1 Accuracy

6.1.1 LMS Data Format

Results on Table 4 indicate that SVM is the best algorithm for our 19-class classification task. When using a frame number of 15, the accuracy reaches 77.50%.

n_frames	60	45	30	15	10	5
SVM	74,68	71,00	72,95	**77,50**	73,00	67,59
kNN	67,69	69,40	69,80	66,04	66,42	65,15
MLP	71,54	72,68	73,58	77,17	75,73	70,91

Table 4. Accuracy (%) on 19 classes, LMS data format

6.1.2 FBA Data Format

Results on Table 5 show that for the number of frames 60, 45, and 30, the MLP algorithm achieves higher accuracies with the FBA data format compared to the LMS data format. When using a frame number of 30, the accuracy reaches 75.40%.

n_frames	60	45	30	15	10	5
SVM	69,12	65,96	66,23	57,84	62,29	60,77
kNN	61,05	63,35	63,07	61,61	63,49	58,55
MLP	74,02	74,55	**75,40**	72,35	72,58	69,05

Table 5. Accuracy (%) on 19 classes, FBA data format

6.2 Confusion Matrices and Case Analysis

We computed confusion matrices to understand how well our set of algorithms identified different techniques. We provide confusion matrices for LMS and FBA data formats, with the number of frames corresponding to the best accuracy score for each algorithm.

6.2.1 LMS Data format

We can see in Figures 1, 2, and 3, that the majority of the techniques are well identified by SVM and MLP. In the case of kNN, we can see a lack of identification even

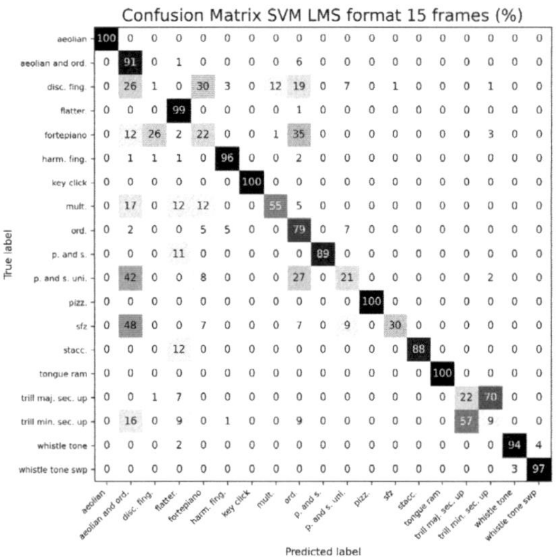

Figure 1. Confusion matrix, SVM, LMS data format, 15 frames

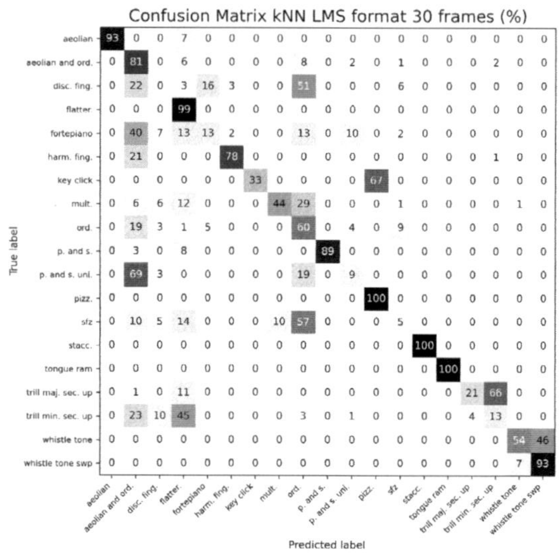

Figure 2. Confusion matrix, kNN, LMS data format, 30 frames

though some techniques of identification reach high accuracies (*aeolian*, *flatterzunge*, *play and sing unison*, *pizzicato*, *staccato*, *tongue ram*, *whistle tone sweep*). This may be attributed to the fact that some techniques are too similar. We can see for the three algorithms that *trill major second up* and *trill minor second up* techniques are misidentified. Also, *sforzando* is misidentified with *aeolian and ordinario* for SVM and *ordinario* for kNN. MLP is performing better than SVM and kNN, with fewer errors. All three algorithms do not accurately identify the *discolored fingering* technique. The *discolored fingering* technique consists of playing a note *ordinario* with an alternative fingering. This results in a soft detuning of the note. Because we are using pitch shifting as a data augmentation technique, it may be difficult for the algorithms to distinguish the augmented data of *ordinario*, *fortepiano*, and *aeolian and ordinario* techniques from the original data of the *discolored fingering* technique.

6.2.2 FBA Data format

Figures 4, 5 show that a lot of techniques are misidentified. The notably low accuracy score may be attributed to the small dimensionality of the data. For SVM, all short-length techniques, such as *key click*, *pizzicato*, *staccato*, *tongue ram* have been predicted as *staccato*. This may be attributed to data scarcity. Indeed, in the case of the *staccato* technique, there are in our dataset only 38 audio files, each approximately 400ms in length. Only a limited amount of training data can be generated from a single audio file (400ms $\approx$ 19 frames). Figure 6 shows that the performance of MLP is always better than that of SVM and kNN. Nevertheless, similar techniques such as *trill major second up* and *trill minor second up*, *whistle tone* and *whistle tone sweep* are misidentified.

6.3 Total Delay Time

To ensure that our system can be used for real-time performance, we measured the total delay time, the sum of the time required to gather enough samples to process the spectrogram analysis, the time required to compute the spectrogram analysis, and the time induced by the algorithms of predictions (see Section 5.3).

6.3.1 Log-Mel-Spectrogram Computation Time

Table 6 and Table 7 show the computation times for LMS and FBA data formats. The computation time of LMS data format is comparable to that of the FBA data format. Given that the maximum time is approximately 16.5μs, we can conclude that the Log-Mel-Spectrogram analysis computation time is negligible. Therefore, it will not be included in the total delay time calculation.

n_frames	60			45			30		
	mean	sd	max	mean	sd	max	mean	sd	max
LMS	7,3	0,4	12,8	6,2	0,4	16,5	4,7	0,3	9,6
FBA	7,3	0,4	13,9	6,2	0,4	16,1	4,7	0,3	9,7

Table 6. Log-Mel-Spectrogram calculation time (μs), computed 10,000 times.

n_frames	15			10			5		
	mean	sd	max	mean	sd	max	mean	sd	max
LMS	3,7	0,3	7,5	3,2	0,3	6,5	2,8	0,2	7,4
FBA	3,6	0,3	7,2	3,3	0,3	6,5	2,8	0,2	5,3

Table 7. Log-Mel-Spectrogram calculation time (μs), computed 10,000 times.

6.3.2 Algorithm's Prediction Time

Tables 9 to 14 show the prediction time induced by the algorithms according to the number of frames. The results show that prediction with FBA data format (Table 11, Table 12, Table 13) is performed much faster than LMS data format (Table 8, Table 9, Table 10) particularly for SVM and kNN algorithms. For kNN, the calculation time

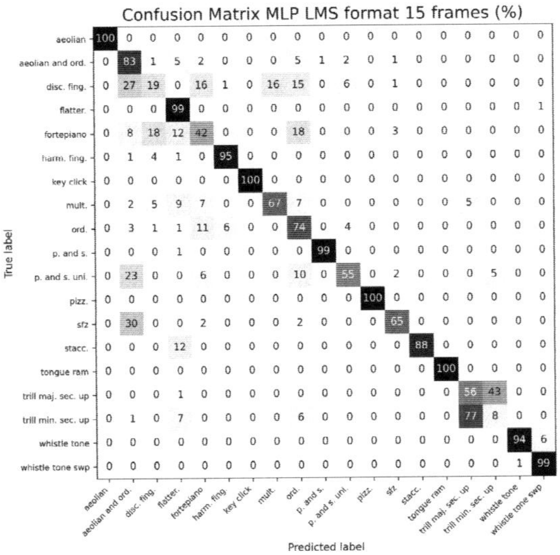

Figure 3. Confusion matrix, MLP, LMS data format, 15 frames

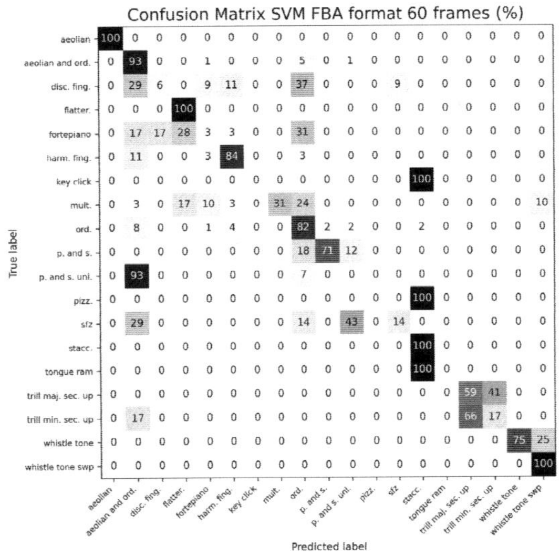

Figure 4. Confusion matrix, SVM, FBA data format, 60 frames

is related to the amount of data, whereas for SVM, the calculation is slower because the LMS data format has a wider data dimensionality than the FBA data format. Concerning the MLP algorithm, there is not much difference between the two data formats (time difference less than 2.0ms) even though prediction time with the FBA data format is still 50% quicker than the LMS data format. In summary, the FBA data format hastened prediction times significantly for SVM and kNN algorithms, taking only approximately a tenth of the time required by the LMS data format.

n_frames	60			45		
	mean	sd	max	mean	sd	max
SVM	17,62	2,09	25,71	15,79	2,10	23,63
kNN	60,57	2,48	70,61	60,50	2,17	68,67
MLP	1,49	0,32	2,58	1,22	0,23	1,88

Table 8. Prediction time (ms), LMS data format

n_frames	30			15		
	mean	sd	max	mean	sd	max
SVM	13,80	1,936	21,15	10,90	2,44	19,92
kNN	64,86	2,91	87,50	66,49	2,90	83,17
MLP	0,37	0,09	1,27	0,48	0,10	1,03

Table 9. Prediction time (ms), LMS data format

n_frames	10			5		
	mean	sd	max	mean	sd	max
SVM	8,60	1,56	13,80	6,90	1,40	10,35
kNN	66,49	2,90	83,17	67,16	2,68	84,56
MLP	0,48	0,10	1,03	0,80	0,09	1,15

Table 10. Prediction time (ms), LMS data format

n_frames	60			45		
	mean	sd	max	mean	sd	max
SVM	0,27	0,05	0,64	0,32	0,06	0,67
kNN	1,79	0,3	3,01	2,17	0,33	3,19
MLP	0,27	0,05	1,01	0,27	0,06	1,03

Table 11. Prediction time (ms), FBA data format

n_frames	30			15		
	mean	sd	max	mean	sd	max
SVM	0,41	0,11	0,89	0,67	0,18	1,44
kNN	2,83	0,41	4,07	4,91	0,60	3,39
MLP	0,28	0,06	1,05	0,32	0,04	0,72

Table 12. Prediction time (ms), FBA data format

n_frames	10			5		
	mean	sd	max	mean	sd	max
SVM	1,27	0,35	4,15	2,35	0,43	3,92
kNN	7,50	0,84	11,96	12,73	1,10	16,50
MLP	0,33	0,04	0,54	0,39	0,05	0,79

Table 13. Prediction time (ms), FBA data format

6.3.3 Total Maximum Delay Time

To represent worst-case scenarios, we calculated the total maximum delay time. As outlined in Section 5.3, the time to gather audio data is a fixed duration of approximately 21.3ms. This time is subsequently added to the algorithm's maximum prediction time. As mentioned in Section 6.3.1, the Log-Mel-Spectrogram analysis computation time is negligible and not included in the total maxi-

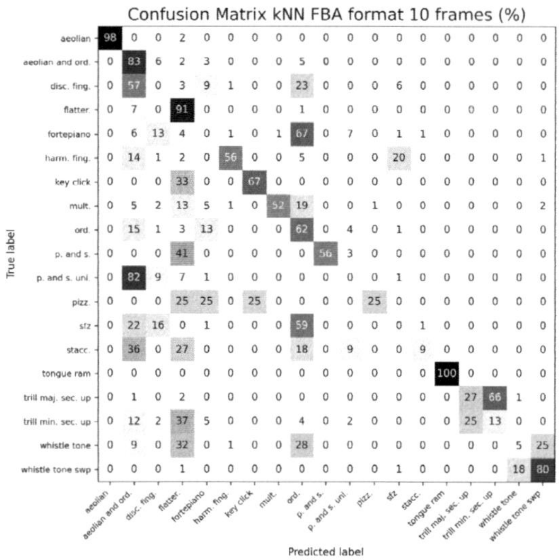

Figure 5. Confusion matrix, kNN, FBA data format, 10 frames

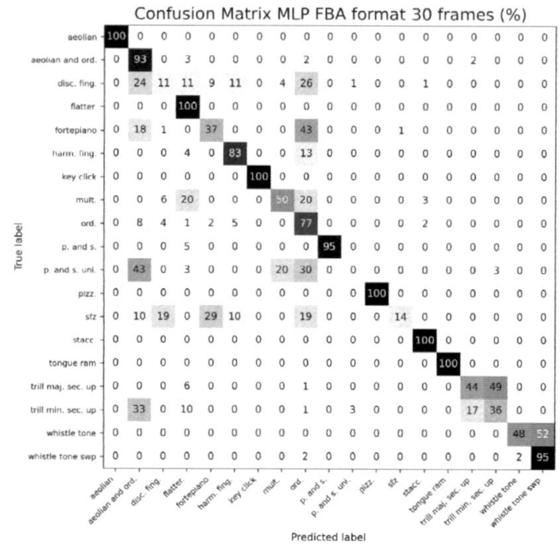

Figure 6. Confusion matrix, MLP, FBA data format, 30 frames

n_frames	60	45	30	15	10	5
SVM	47,01	44,93	42,45	41,22	35,10	31,65
kNN	91,91	89,97	108,8	104,47	104,47	105,86
MLP	23,88	23,18	22,57	22,33	22,33	22,45

Table 14. Total maximum delay time (ms), LMS data format

n_frames	60	45	30	15	10	5
SVM	21,94	21,97	22,19	22,74	25,45	25,22
kNN	24,31	24,49	25,37	24,69	33,26	37,80
MLP	22,31	22,33	22,35	22,02	21,84	22,09

Table 15. Total maximum delay time (ms), FBA data format

mum delay time calculation. A total maximum delay time near 21.3ms and below 42.6ms is necessary.

Table 14 and Table 15 show that MLP is much quicker to perform prediction than SVM and kNN on both LMS and FBA data formats (~22ms). With the LMS data format, SVM is usable only with a number of frames below 30. kNN is usable with the FBA data format (37.8ms at most), but unusable with the LMS data format (89.97ms at least).

7. DISCUSSION

The best accuracy we found overall was 77.50% with the SVM algorithm and LMS data format with 15-frame-long samples and a total maximum delay time of 41.22ms. For the MLP algorithm, we found that the FBA data format yields a little higher accuracy scores compared to the LMS data format for the numbers of frames 60, 45, and 30. For SVM and kNN algorithms, tables show a drop in accuracy for the FBA data format. LMS is a higher-dimensional format than FBA. With the LMS data format, when the data dimensionality becomes too large, performance drops. On the other hand, since FBA data format is an average of frames, the data dimensionality is always small, but the accuracy tends to decrease if the number of frames is too small.

We want to design a system capable of making a prediction at every frame (1 frame $\approx$ 21.3ms) for real-time responsiveness. We found that when using the LMS data format, the total maximum delay time of SVM (31.65ms at least) is near the maximum delay time upper limit (42.3ms) and exceeds it when using the number of frames of 60 and 45 (47.01ms, 44.93ms). For kNN, when using the LMS data format, we found that the total maximum delay time (89.97ms at least) exceeded the maximum delay time upper limit for any number of frames. When using the FBA data format, we can see an improvement in the total maximum delay time for SVM (25.45ms at most) and kNN (37.80ms at most), making them usable but not as fast as MLP. In the case of MLP, the total maximum delay time on both data formats is small (~22ms) and close to the 20ms threshold, which is the minimum duration required for perceiving the difference of timings [16]. That is why, MLP is the best choice considering both accuracy score and prediction time criteria.

In our experiments, we used three simple machine learning algorithms. For MLP, the prediction time does not change significantly between LMS and FBA data formats because it does not depend on the input dimension or the amount of training data (see Table 3). MLP has another advantage in that accuracy could be further increased by improving the neural network architecture, tuning hyperparameters, and using pre-trained models without impacting the prediction time very much.

Additionally, the confusion matrices revealed that the *staccato* and *key click* techniques were poorly identified. While other techniques, such as *sforzando* and *pizzicato*, demonstrated better identification, they still did not match the accuracies found with other techniques, such as *ordinario*. From this observation, we concluded that shorter-length techniques are less identifiable than others. As previously explained in Section 6.2.2, only a limited amount of data can be extracted from the short-length audio files. To enhance the classification of these techniques, we had better increase the data volume by using multiple sound banks and improving data augmentation methods.

We found that similar techniques, such as *trill major second up* and *trill minor second up*, and *whistle tone* and *whistle tone sweep* techniques, are misidentified. From this observation, we can guess that similar techniques are difficult to discriminate for the classification algorithms. To enhance the classification of these techniques, several similar techniques should be combined into one class in our future study.

The confusion matrices showed that the *discolored fingering* technique is not well recognized by the three algorithms with both LMS and FBA data formats. This may be caused by the similarity between the augmented data of other techniques and the original data of the *discolored fingering* technique (see Section 6.2.1 and Section 6.2.2). We consider that the *discolored fingering* technique should not be included in our future study.

8. CONCLUSIONS

In this article, we presented a preliminary analysis of real-time recognition of flute IPT for mixed music. Our study explored various algorithms and data formats to find the preferable data dimensionality to improve classification accuracy and measured the maximum delay time for real-time performance.

In our experiment, we found that reducing the number of frames around 15 improved accuracy and that SVM has the best accuracy with LMS data format. Concerning the prediction time, we made the following observations. The prediction time of MLP is smaller with the FBA data format than the LMS data format. When using the LMS data format, the total maximum delay time of kNN exceeds the maximum delay time upper limit, making kNN unusable with this data format. In the case of SVM, its total maximum prediction time is below but near the maximum delay time upper limit, making the SVM usable but not fully secured. When using the FBA data format, the total maximum delay time of kNN and SVM are below the maximum delay upper limit, making them usable but still slow compared to the MLP total maximum delay time. Therefore, based on both the accuracy score and delay time criteria, we conclude that MLP is the best choice as a comprehensive judgment for our task.

From the observation of the confusion matrices, we found that short-time techniques, such as *staccato*, *key click*, *sforzando*, and *pizzicato*, are less accurately identified when using the SVM and kNN algorithms. Even if MLP better identifies these techniques, accuracy still needs to be improved. The possible cause of this drop in accuracy could be due to training data scarcity, as the audio files for these techniques are short in length. Because of this, we will augment data quantity in our further study. Additionally, we found that techniques, such as *trill major second up* and *trill minor second up*, and *whistle tone* and *whistle tone sweep* techniques, are not well identified. The possible cause of this drop in accuracy could be the similarity of the techniques. To address this problem, we will combine similar techniques into the same class in our further study. We also found that the *discolored fingering* technique is poorly identified. The low accuracy scores may be caused by the similarity between the augmented data of other techniques and the original data of the *discolored fingering* technique. To handle this concern, we will not include this technique in our future study.

This study has some limitations. The train and test datasets originated from the same sound bank (homogeneous datasets). Consequently, the results in this experiment do not accurately represent real-time mixed music performance situations where the audio data from the circumstance of the live performance differs from that of training data. To deal with that, future research should evaluate the accuracy with different sound banks (heterogeneous datasets). Also, each data sample in our study only included delimited audio samples of one technique, where the first frame starts from the attack and the last ends at the release. This differs from real-time situations where the system analyzes audio on-the-fly where two techniques may be played successively. To address this concern, we should test the system in real time with a flutist. Given the time-critical nature of the real-time classification, Python may not be an optimal choice for ensuring time efficiency. Thus, we will consider using alternative high-performance languages such as C++ in our future research.

9. REFERENCES

[1] J.-M. Echeveste, "Un langage de programmation pour composer l'interaction musicale: la gestion du temps et des événements dans Antescofo," Ph.D. dissertation, Université Pierre et Marie Curie-Paris VI, 2015.

[2] M. Malt and E. Jourdan, "Real-time uses of low level sound descriptors as event detection functions using the max/msp zsa. descriptors library," in *Brazilian Symposium on Computer Music*, vol. 12, 2009, pp. 45–56.

[3] M. Malt and M. Gentilucci, "Real Time Vowel Tremolo Detection Using Low Level Audio Descriptors," *arXiv preprint arXiv:1511.07008*, 2015.

[4] L. Su, H.-M. Lin, and Y.-H. Yang, "Sparse modeling of magnitude and phase-derived spectra for playing technique classification," *IEEE/ACM Transactions on Audio, Speech, and Language Processing*, vol. 22, no. 12, pp. 2122–2132, 2014.

[5] J.-F. Ducher and P. Esling, "APPRENTISSAGE PROFOND POUR LA RECONNAISSANCE EN TEMPS REEL DES MODES DE JEU INSTRUMENTAUX," in *Journées d'Informatique Musicale*, 2019.

[6] ——, "FOLDED CQT RCNN FOR REAL-TIME RECOGNITION OF INSTRUMENT PLAYING TECHNIQUES," in *International Society for Music Information Retrieval*, Delft, Netherlands, Nov. 2019. [Online]. Available: https://hal.science/hal-02472560

[7] Y.-P. Chen, L. Su, Y.-H. Yang *et al.*, "Electric Guitar Playing Technique Detection in Real-World Recording Based on F0 Sequence Pattern Recognition." in *ISMIR*, 2015, pp. 708–714.

[8] C. Wang, E. Benetos, V. Lostanlen, and E. Chew, "Adaptive scattering transforms for playing technique recognition," *IEEE/ACM Transactions on Audio, Speech, and Language Processing*, vol. 30, pp. 1407–1421, 2022.

[9] P. Herrera, A. Yeterian, and F. Gouyon, "Automatic classification of drum sounds: a comparison of feature selection methods and classification techniques," in *Music and Artificial Intelligence: Second International Conference, ICMAI 2002 Edinburgh, Scotland, UK, September 12–14, 2002 Proceedings*. Springer, 2002, pp. 69–80.

[10] N. H. Fletcher and T. D. Rossing, *The physics of musical instruments*. Springer Science & Business Media, 2012.

[11] C. Levine and C. Mitropoulos-Bott, *The Techniques of Flute Playing I/Die Spieltechnik der Flöte I*. Bärenreiter-Verlag, 2019.

[12] P.-Y. Artaud and G. Geay, *Flûtes au présent: traité des techniques contemporaines sur les flûtes traversières à l'usage des compositeurs et des flutistes*. Editions Jobert & Editions musicales transatlantiques, 1980.

[13] C. E. Cella, D. Ghisi, V. Lostanlen, F. Lévy, J. Fineberg, and Y. Maresz, "OrchideaSOL: a dataset of extended instrumental techniques for computer-aided orchestration," *arXiv preprint arXiv:2007.00763*, 2020.

[14] Y. Han, J. Kim, and K. Lee, "Deep Convolutional Neural Networks for Predominant Instrument Recognition in Polyphonic Music," *IEEE/ACM Transactions on Audio, Speech, and Language Processing*, vol. 25, no. 1, pp. 208–221, jan 2017. [Online]. Available: https://doi.org/10.1109%2Ftaslp.2016.2632307

[15] B. McFee, C. Raffel, D. Liang, D. P. Ellis, M. McVicar, E. Battenberg, and O. Nieto, "librosa: Audio and music signal analysis in python," in *Proceedings of the 14th python in science conference*, vol. 8, 2015, pp. 18–25.

[16] I. J. Hirsh and C. E. Sherrick Jr, "Perceived order in different sense modalities." *Journal of experimental psychology*, vol. 62, no. 5, p. 423, 1961.

[17] F. Pedregosa, G. Varoquaux, A. Gramfort, V. Michel, B. Thirion, O. Grisel, M. Blondel, P. Prettenhofer, R. Weiss, V. Dubourg *et al.*, "Scikit-learn: Machine learning in Python," *the Journal of machine Learning research*, vol. 12, pp. 2825–2830, 2011.

[18] S. Wei, S. Zou, F. Liao *et al.*, "A comparison on data augmentation methods based on deep learning for audio classification," in *Journal of Physics: Conference Series*, vol. 1453, no. 1. IOP Publishing, 2020, p. 012085.

Enhancing Parameter Efficiency for Music Source Separation Models

Ka Ho Leung
Department of Computer Science and Engineering
The Chinese University of Hong Kong
markleung@link.cuhk.edu.hk

Chuck-jee Chau
Department of Computer Science and Engineering
The Chinese University of Hong Kong
chuckjee@cse.cuhk.edu.hk

ABSTRACT

Music source separation, referring to the task of decomposing music into its constituent components, has numerous valuable applications, such as home karaoke and music remixing. Recent approaches employ deep learning models based on the encoder-decoder architectures, taking spectrograms and/or waveforms of music as input. In this work, we introduce a novel approach that incorporates mel spectrogram encoders into the model architecture, resulting in a significant reduction of nearly 60% in the number of model parameters while preserving comparable performance, as measured by a novel Signal-to-Distortion Ratio (nSDR) metric [1]. In addition, we show that integrating a spectrogram reconstruction loss into the model can further enhance the nSDR. Our experiments are based on the Hybrid Demucs model [2], trained with MUSDB18 dataset [3], which comprises four music source categories: vocals, bass, drums, and other accompaniments. Audio samples are available at `https://radionic.github.io/efficient-demucs-demo`.

1. INTRODUCTION

The intriguing history of audio source separation can be traced back to the "cocktail party problem" [4], a term coined by the cognitive scientist Colin Cherry in the 1950s, referring to the challenge of isolating and focusing on a single speaker's voice in a noisy environment, such as a crowded party with multiple conversations happening simultaneously.

Over the years, various techniques have been proposed to address the audio source separation problem, ranging from classic methods, such as independent component analysis (ICA) [5] and non-negative matrix factorization (NMF) [6], to more recent advances in machine learning, including convolutional neural networks (CNNs) [7, 8, 9], recurrent neural networks (RNNs) [10, 11] and attention mechanisms [12]. Machine learning-based approaches have notably enhanced the results in the music source separation task. For instance, Huang et al. [13] have demonstrated that RNNs significantly outperform the NMF approach in this task.

In this work, we focus on enhancing the parameter efficiency of the machine learning models. Specifically, we experiment with incorporating mel spectrogram encoders and spectrogram reconstruction loss into the Hybrid Demucs model [2]. Although deep learning models are capable of learning the mapping from a spectrogram to a mel spectrogram, providing this information explicitly to the model may facilitate the training process and enhance the results. For instance, Cheuk et al. [14] have shown that, given a fixed model, using mel spectrograms as input outperforms using linear spectrograms as input for the music transcription task.

2. RELATED WORKS

2.1 U-Net

U-Net is an encoder-decoder convolutional neural network architecture initially developed for biomedical image segmentation [15]. In a subsequent study [16], the authors applied it to the music source separation task. They proposed using music spectrogram as input and training the U-Net to predict the spectrogram mask of the sources. The spectrogram mask is then element-wise multiplied with the music spectrogram, resulting in the source spectrogram. Finally, it is transformed back to the waveform with inverse short-time Fourier transform (iSTFT) and the phase information extracted from the STFT of the music waveform.

It is worth noting that the skip connections between layers allow the preservation of the fine-grained details extracted in the encoders, and hence significantly improved the quality of the predicted spectrogram mask, as shown in [16].

2.2 Hybrid Demucs

The Hybrid Demucs [2] is also a U-Net based model featuring two different branches: one operating in the spectral domain and the other in the temporal domain. Each branch consists of a series of encoders, decoders, and skip connections between them. This design enables the model to identify the most suitable domain for each source or even combine both domains to enhance source separation [2]. In addition, it eliminates the need to model the STFT and iSTFT functions for extracting information from the spectral or temporal domains, thus facilitating the training process.

The spectrogram encoder hyperparameters, such as the number of layers and kernel sizes, are carefully designed to ensure that the output shapes of the final spectrogram encoder and waveform encoder are the same and thus can be summed and fed to the decoders. After passing through the decoders, the spectral branch output is transformed back into the time domain using the iSTFT and then summed

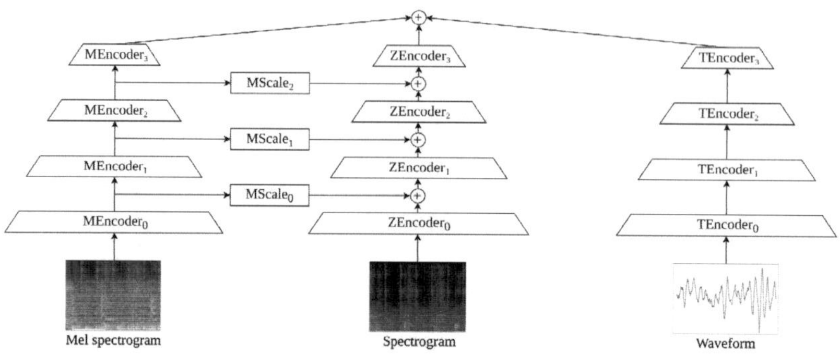

Figure 1. The proposed model architecture of the encoders. The decoders remain the same as the Hybrid Demucs [2].

with the temporal branch output, resulting in the final predicted waveform.

In [17], the authors enhance the Hybrid Demucs model by incorporating a Transformer encoder with self-attention mechanisms. While it outperforms the original Hybrid Demucs when trained on an additional 800 songs along with the MUSDB18 dataset, it performs poorly when trained exclusively on MUSDB18 [17].

3. METHODOLOGY

3.1 Model Architecture

We have incorporated the mel spectrogram encoders into the Hybrid Demucs. These encoders share the same building blocks as the Hybrid Demucs' spectrogram encoders: each block consists of convolution layers, activation function ReLU, and gated linear unit (GLU) [18]. We denote this block as *MEncoder*, as shown in Figure 1.

For the input of mel spectrogram encoders, we first transform the waveform into a spectrogram with STFT using window length 4096 and hop length 1024. Then we convert the spectrogram into mel-scale with 512 frequency bins.

We do not include the decoders for the mel spectrogram branch to avoid introducing additional model parameters. Besides, the waveform obtained by inverting the mel spectrogram is only an approximation of the original waveform, so it may not be appropriate to sum this to the final source waveform.

Instead, we integrate the mel spectrogram information into the spectrogram branch by summing the hidden representations of mel spectrogram and spectrogram, and then feeding it to the next spectrogram encoder. However, the height of the mel spectrogram representation differs from that of the spectrogram representation. To address this problem, we introduce an additional layer that adjusts the height of the mel spectrogram representation before summing them. We denote this layer as *MScale*, which is composed of a transposed convolution layer, group normalization, and GLU.

3.2 Loss Functions

Following [19], we use the L1 distance between the predicted source waveform $\hat{w}$ and ground truth source waveform w as the loss function. Furthermore, we introduce the spectrogram reconstruction loss, which is the L1 distance between the predicted source spectrogram $\hat{s}$ and ground truth spectrogram s. The predicted source spectrogram is obtained by applying STFT on the temporal branch output and then summing it with the spectral branch output. The two loss functions are defined as:

$$L_{waveform} = \frac{1}{N}\sum_{i=1}^{N}|w_i - \hat{w}_i| \quad (1)$$

$$L_{spectrogram} = \frac{1}{N}\sum_{i=1}^{N}|s_i - \hat{s}_i| \quad (2)$$

where N is the number of samples. The final loss function is the average of these two L1 losses. We minimize it using the AdamW optimizer [20] with two beta values set to 0.9 and 0.999.

4. EXPERIMENTS

4.1 Dataset

We have trained the models with MUSDB18 dataset [3], which comprises 150 music tracks, each containing isolated drums, bass, vocals, and other accompaniments. The dataset is split into 100 tracks for training and 50 tracks for testing. Each track is in stereo, with a sampling rate of 44.1 kHz, and is encoded in the WAV format. Notably, most songs in the dataset are rock or pop music, and English is the major language of the singing vocals, presenting in 141 out of the 150 songs [21].

4.2 Metrics

Three metrics were proposed by [22] to measure the quality of the separated sources: Source-to-Distortion Ratio (SDR), Source-to-Interference Ratio (SIR), and Source-to-Artifact Ratio (SAR). Later, a novel SDR metric is introduced in the music demixing challenge (MDX) [1], which provides a simpler definition and faster evaluation.

We denote this new metric as nSDR, as used in [2]. The nSDR is defined as:

$$nSDR = 10\log_{10}\frac{\sum_i ||w_i||^2 + \epsilon}{\sum_i ||w_i - \hat{w}_i||^2 + \epsilon} \quad (3)$$

	Model parameters	Ensemble size	Input duration	Batch size	Learning rate
Demucs (Paper)	84 millions	4	11 seconds	64	0.0003
Demucs (Reproduced)	84 millions	1	11 seconds	4	0.0001
Demucs (Weakened)	21 millions	1	8 seconds	12	0.0002
+MEL	34 millions	1	8 seconds	12	0.0002
+SPEC_LOSS	21 millions	1	8 seconds	12	0.0002

Table 1. The hyperparameters of different experiments.

	All	Vocals	Drums	Bass	Other
Demucs (Paper)	7.33	7.97	8.04	8.12	5.19
Demucs (Reproduced)	6.47	7.21	7.77	6.38	4.50
Demucs (Weakened)	6.03	6.80	7.19	5.95	4.17
+MEL	6.48	7.43	7.52	6.32	4.67
+SPEC_LOSS	6.21	6.94	7.25	6.33	4.34

Table 2. The nSDR metric of the last epoch of different experiments.

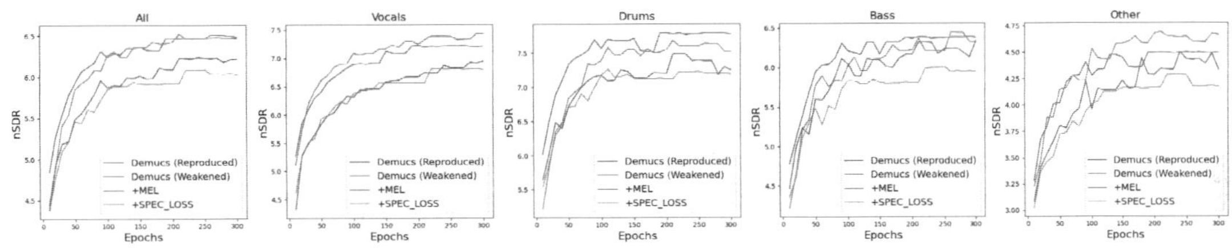

Figure 2. The nSDR metric of different experiments over training epochs.

where ϵ is a small constant to avoid division by zero. During training, we measure the model performance on the test set using the nSDR metric every 10 epochs.

4.3 Settings

We first try to reproduce the results of Hybrid Demucs [2], and their results are denoted as *Demucs (Paper)*. It is assumed that the authors followed the training settings defined in the code they released [1]. However, due to memory and time constraints, we reduce the batch size from 64 to 4, correspondingly lower the learning rate from 0.0003 to 0.0001 and train only 1 model for each experiment instead of 4 models for ensembling. We denote this experiment as *Demucs (Reproduced)*.

Next, we train a weakened version of Hybrid Demucs by halving the number of output feature channels in each layer, which reduces the total number of parameters from 84 millions to 21 millions. We denote this experiment as *Demucs (Weakened)*.

Finally, we add the mel spectrogram encoders and spectrogram reconstruction loss on top of the *Demucs (Weakened)*. We denote these two experiments as *+MEL* and *+SPEC_LOSS*, respectively. After adding the mel spectrogram encoders, the number of model parameters increases to 34 millions, which is still around 60% fewer parameters than *Demucs (Reproduced)*.

For each experiment, we train the model for 300 epochs in a single RTX 4090. The *Demucs (Reproduced)* takes around 6 days to complete, and for the rest of the experiments, each takes around 2.5 days to complete.

[1] https://github.com/facebookresearch/demucs

4.4 Results

Our experiments indicate that incorporating mel spectrogram encoders into *Demucs (Weakened)* shows comparable nSDR performance with *Demucs (Reproduced)*, while having 60% fewer model parameters. Moreover, *Demucs (Weakened)+MEL* requires only 12 minutes per epoch for training, which is half the time taken by *Demucs (Reproduced)*. This highlights the remarkable efficiency of our proposed approach in terms of both model parameter efficiency and training time.

Furthermore, incorporating the spectrogram reconstruction loss results in a modest improvement of the nSDR metric by 0.18, with more notable enhancements observed in the separation of bass and other accompaniments.

Figure 2 demonstrates that the nSDR scores of *Demucs (Weakened)+MEL* are consistently comparable to those of *Demucs (Reproduced)*. In addition, it shows that *Demucs (Weakened)+SPEC_LOSS* consistently achieves higher overall nSDR scores than *Demucs (Weakened)*.

5. CONCLUSIONS

Enhancing model parameters efficiency is crucial for reducing computational cost and waiting time during training and inferencing. In this work, we incorporated mel spectrogram encoders and spectrogram reconstruction loss into Hybrid Demucs model. As a result, the mel spectrogram encoders enhanced the model parameter efficiency that the number of model parameters is reduced by 60% and the training time is reduced by 50%, while maintaining comparable nSDR metric. In addition, the spectrogram reconstruction loss slightly improved the overall nSDR metric.

6. REFERENCES

[1] Y. Mitsufuji, G. Fabbro, S. Uhlich, F.-R. Stöter, A. Défossez, M. Kim, W. Choi, C.-Y. Yu, and K.-W. Cheuk, "Music Demixing Challenge 2021," *Frontiers in Signal Processing*, vol. 1, p. 808395, Jan. 2022, doi: 10.3389/frsip.2021.808395.

[2] A. Défossez, "Hybrid Spectrogram and Waveform Source Separation," 2021, doi: 10.48550/ARXIV.2111.03600.

[3] Rafii, Zafar, Liutkus, Antoine, Stöter, Fabian-Robert, Mimilakis, Stylianos Ioannis, and Bittner, Rachel, "MUSDB18-HQ - an uncompressed version of MUSDB18," Aug. 2019, doi: 10.5281/ZENODO.3338373.

[4] E. C. Cherry, "Some Experiments on the Recognition of Speech, with One and with Two Ears," *The Journal of the Acoustical Society of America*, vol. 25, no. 5, pp. 975–979, Sep. 1953, doi: 10.1121/1.1907229.

[5] A. Hyvärinen and E. Oja, "Independent component analysis: algorithms and applications," *Neural Networks*, vol. 13, no. 4-5, pp. 411–430, Jun. 2000, doi: 10.1016/S0893-6080(00)00026-5.

[6] D. D. Lee and H. S. Seung, "Learning the parts of objects by non-negative matrix factorization," *Nature*, vol. 401, no. 6755, pp. 788–791, Oct. 1999, doi: 10.1038/44565.

[7] Y. Lecun, L. Bottou, Y. Bengio, and P. Haffner, "Gradient-based learning applied to document recognition," *Proceedings of the IEEE*, vol. 86, no. 11, pp. 2278–2324, Nov. 1998, doi: 10.1109/5.726791.

[8] A. Krizhevsky, I. Sutskever, and G. E. Hinton, "ImageNet classification with deep convolutional neural networks," *Communications of the ACM*, vol. 60, no. 6, pp. 84–90, May 2017, doi: 10.1145/3065386.

[9] K. Simonyan and A. Zisserman, "Very Deep Convolutional Networks for Large-Scale Image Recognition," 2014, doi: 10.48550/ARXIV.1409.1556.

[10] S. Hochreiter and J. Schmidhuber, "Long Short-Term Memory," *Neural Computation*, vol. 9, no. 8, pp. 1735–1780, Nov. 1997, doi: 10.1162/neco.1997.9.8.1735.

[11] K. Cho, B. Van Merrienboer, C. Gulcehre, D. Bahdanau, F. Bougares, H. Schwenk, and Y. Bengio, "Learning Phrase Representations using RNN Encoder–Decoder for Statistical Machine Translation," in *Proceedings of the 2014 Conference on Empirical Methods in Natural Language Processing (EMNLP)*. Doha, Qatar: Association for Computational Linguistics, 2014, pp. 1724–1734, doi: 10.3115/v1/D14-1179.

[12] A. Vaswani, N. Shazeer, N. Parmar, J. Uszkoreit, L. Jones, A. N. Gomez, L. Kaiser, and I. Polosukhin, "Attention is All You Need," in *Proceedings of the 31st International Conference on Neural Information Processing Systems*, ser. NIPS'17. Red Hook, NY, USA: Curran Associates Inc., 2017, p. 6000–6010.

[13] Po-Sen Huang, Minje Kim, M. Hasegawa-Johnson, and P. Smaragdis, "Joint Optimization of Masks and Deep Recurrent Neural Networks for Monaural Source Separation," *IEEE/ACM Transactions on Audio, Speech, and Language Processing*, vol. 23, no. 12, pp. 2136–2147, Dec. 2015, doi: 10.1109/TASLP.2015.2468583.

[14] K. W. Cheuk, K. Agres, and D. Herremans, "The Impact of Audio Input Representations on Neural Network based Music Transcription," in *2020 International Joint Conference on Neural Networks (IJCNN)*. Glasgow, United Kingdom: IEEE, Jul. 2020, pp. 1–6, doi: 10.1109/IJCNN48605.2020.9207605.

[15] O. Ronneberger, P. Fischer, and T. Brox, "U-Net: Convolutional Networks for Biomedical Image Segmentation," in *Medical Image Computing and Computer-Assisted Intervention – MICCAI 2015*, N. Navab, J. Hornegger, W. M. Wells, and A. F. Frangi, Eds. Cham: Springer International Publishing, 2015, vol. 9351, pp. 234–241, doi: 10.1007/978-3-319-24574-4_28.

[16] A. Jansson, E. J. Humphrey, N. Montecchio, R. M. Bittner, A. Kumar, and T. Weyde, "Singing Voice Separation with Deep U-Net Convolutional Networks," in *International Society for Music Information Retrieval Conference*, 2017.

[17] S. Rouard, F. Massa, and A. Défossez, "Hybrid Transformers for Music Source Separation," 2022, doi: 10.48550/ARXIV.2211.08553.

[18] Y. N. Dauphin, A. Fan, M. Auli, and D. Grangier, "Language Modeling with Gated Convolutional Networks," in *Proceedings of the 34th International Conference on Machine Learning*, ser. Proceedings of Machine Learning Research, D. Precup and Y. W. Teh, Eds., vol. 70. PMLR, 06–11 Aug 2017, pp. 933–941.

[19] A. Défossez, N. Usunier, L. Bottou, and F. Bach, "Demucs: Deep Extractor for Music Sources with extra unlabeled data remixed," 2019, doi: 10.48550/ARXIV.1909.01174.

[20] I. Loshchilov and F. Hutter, "Decoupled Weight Decay Regularization," 2017, doi: 10.48550/ARXIV.1711.05101.

[21] K. Schulze-Forster, C. Doire, G. Richard, and R. Badeau, "Phoneme Level Lyrics Alignment and Text-Informed Singing Voice Separation," *IEEE/ACM Transactions on Audio, Speech, and Language Processing*, vol. 29, pp. 2382–2395, 2021, doi: 10.1109/TASLP.2021.3091817.

[22] E. Vincent, R. Gribonval, and C. Fevotte, "Performance measurement in blind audio source separation," *IEEE Transactions on Audio, Speech and Language Processing*, vol. 14, no. 4, pp. 1462–1469, Jul. 2006, doi: 10.1109/TSA.2005.858005.

Music Style Transfer With Diffusion Model

Hong Huang
Hunan University of Technology, China
alex_hh3344@163.com

Luyao Li
Hunan University of Technology, China
11753554929@163.com

Yuyi Wang*
CRRC Zhuzhou Institute, China
yuyiwang920@gmail.com

Jun Lin
CRRC Zhuzhou Institute, China
linj@163.com

ABSTRACT

Previous studies on music style transfer have mainly focused on one-to-one style conversion, which is relatively limited. When considering the conversion between multiple styles, previous methods required designing multiple modes to disentangle the complex style of the music, resulting in large computational costs and slow audio generation. The existing music style transfer methods generate spectrograms with artifacts, leading to significant noise in the generated audio. To address these issues, this study proposes a music style transfer framework based on diffusion models (DM) and uses spectrogram-based methods to achieve multi-to-multi music style transfer. The GuideDiff method is used to restore spectrograms to high-fidelity audio, accelerating audio generation speed and reducing noise in the generated audio. Experimental results show that our model has good performance in multi-mode music style transfer compared to the baseline and can generate high-quality audio in real-time on consumer-grade GPUs.

1. INTRODUCTION

The study of musical styles is important for the development of music. Incorporating different styles into compositions can lead to new and innovative music. Transferring musical styles can create works that pay homage to traditional styles while incorporating contemporary elements. By studying how different styles can be combined and transformed, musicians can create new forms of artistic expression.

When discussing the transfer of musical style, it is typically believed that music can be broken down into two elements: content and style. The goal of music style transfer is to maintain the content of the music while modifying the style. With the rapid development of deep generative models, various models such as autoregressive models, generative adversarial networks, variational autoencoders, and stream-based models have actively promoted the development of speech synthesis and music generation. Furthermore, many academics have used these models to research musical style transfer. MIDI-VAE, a neural network model based on variational autoencoders, was used by Brunner et al. [1] to convert the style of polyphonic music with several instrumental tracks. The same year, Brunner et al. [2] offered a different approach that involved converting midi format audio into a piano rolling matrix, training CycleGAN with the matrix, and then producing converted midi audio. However, this method can only transfer the style from the playing dimension. Huang et al. [3] proposed Timbretron by extracting CQT features of the audio, then converting them into timbre through CycleGAN, and finally synthesizing CQT features into original audio waveforms using pre-trained WaveNet. Their method can capture higher resolution at lower frequencies and maintain equal variance of pitch energy, but the generated audio quality is still inadequate. Donahue et al. [4] enhanced the effect of multi-instrument music generation through cross-domain training based on Transformer, but the quality of synthesized audio is still inadequate. Hung et al. [5] proposed a deep learning model for rearranging any music, resulting in a "stylistic shift" without much impact on the tonal substance. Bonnici et al. [6] used a variational autoencoder combined with a generative adversarial network to construct a meaningful representation of source audio and generate a realistic generation of the target audio. Noam et al. [7] proposed a general music translation network that achieves timbre conversion by training a WaveNet encoder and multiple WaveNet decoders. This method can convert from one timbre domain to multiple timbre domains, but it requires training multiple decoders to adapt to different styles, which is computationally expensive, and the synthesized audio speed is slow. Denoising Diffusion Probability Models (DDPMs) [8] and Score Matching (SM) [9] are recently proposed methods that have achieved good results in the fields of speech synthesis and music generation. The aforementioned studies have achieved promising results in their respective research directions, but they mainly focus on transferring a single attribute of music (timbre, performance style, composition style), and previous methods suffer from artifacts in the generated spectrograms. Considering many-to-many style migration, previous methods have suffered from complex design structures, high computational overhead, and slow generation of audio.

To overcome these limitations, this study uses DM, another type of generative model, whose synthesis process extracts the required generated samples from noise through

*Corresponding author

iterative steps. As the number of iterations increases, the quality of the synthesis improves. However, directly extending DMs to audio generation requires a large amount of computational resources [10] and cannot solve the problem of slow generation speed. To address these issues, this study proposes a general and efficient music style transfer framework based on the latent diffusion model (LDM) [11]. Specifically, the framework consists of two parts: style transfer and audio generation. In the style transfer part, a conditional mechanism is introduced to learn different types of input styles and transfer their information to the latent space for guiding the generation of target spectrograms. This approach avoids the need for designing complex, disentangled transfer frameworks and enables many-to-many style transfer. Moreover, the transfer process takes place in latent space, greatly reducing computational costs and improving generation speed. For the audio generation part, this study proposes GuideDiff, a waveform audio generator based on DMs. It compresses and encodes spectrograms into the latent space to control and guide waveform generation, achieving fast inference speed and high-quality audio generation compared to baseline vocoders. This has practical significance for the real-time generation of high-quality audio.

In summary, the main works are as follows:

(1) The paper introduces a music style transfer model that is based on DM and allows for many-to-many music styles to be transferred. This model is capable of performing real-time style transfer on audio, making it highly efficient and practical.

(2) This study proposes a novel audio generation method called GuideDiff, which is based on the diffusion model. The GuideDiff method is designed to generate high-quality audio waveforms by utilizing spectrogram restoration techniques.

(3) The experimental results show that the proposed model has good performance in both style transfer and audio quality compared to the baseline model. Moreover, it can achieve real-time conversion and generate target audio on consumer-grade GPUs.

In the remainder of this paper, we will organize the content as follows: Section 2 presents related work; Section 3 describes the architecture of the proposed method; Section 4 evaluates the effectiveness of the proposed method through experiments; and Section 5 provides the conclusion of this paper.

2. RELATED WORK

2.1 Music Style Transfer

Numerous studies on musical style transfer have taken cues from models for transferring image styles. Musical style transfer can be categorized into three types: timbral style transfer, performance style transfer, and compositional style transfer. Among these, timbral-style transfer has received the most attention in recent years. This type of transfer involves altering the timbre of a musical composition in the audio domain. However, relatively little study has been done on the latter two types of musical style transfer: performance and compositional. Further study on these types of musical style transfers could lead to new and innovative ways of creating and transforming music.

Researchers typically follow two different design patterns to achieve music style transfer. One involves symbolic music notation, and the other involves audio signals. For audio signals, researchers typically use time-frequency methods, which are more indirect and help reduce data complexity. They convert the abstract audio into spectrograms and use deep learning models for high-quality transfer. This method involves two deep learning models, with the first model involving the style transfer of the spectrogram of the audio and the second model involving the restoration of the generated spectrogram to real audio. Currently, researchers mainly use generative models such as CycleGAN [2], VAE [1], UNIT [12], and MusicVAE [13] for music style transfer. However, while these models have shown promising results, they also have limitations that hinder their practical application. Further research is needed to overcome these limitations and improve the effectiveness and efficiency of musical style transfer.

The focus of this study is to explore a new generic music style transfer model that employs a time-frequency approach. This model is designed to enable three types of music style transfer: timbral, performance, and compositional.

2.2 Diffusion Models

DM is a class of likelihood-based generative models, with its pioneering work being DDPM. Its core theoretical underpinnings are the Markov chain and Langevin dynamics. Due to its stable training and easy expansion, it has surpassed GANs [14] in image generation tasks and achieved higher sample quality. However, the sampling process is slow, and it needs to follow a Markov chain to generate a sample step by step. DDIM [15] accelerates the sampling process by iterative non-Markovian methods while keeping the training process unchanged. ADM [14] ultimately outperforms GAN-based methods through a well-designed architecture and classifier guidance. A latent diffusion model [11] has also been proposed recently for image synthesis. This model compresses the image from pixel space to latent space for diffusion, resulting in significantly reduced computational complexity while achieving high-quality image generation. However, the application of this model in the field of music generation has not been extensively studied. In this study, we propose a generic music style transfer framework based on the latent diffusion model, using spectrograms as an intermediate representation of music. In this respect, our work has something in common with riffusion [16], as both utilize Fourier transforms to process audio waveforms in order to obtain a spectrogram. This spectrogram is then diffused using a diffusion model.

2.3 Neural Vocoder

Deep generative models have achieved significant success in modeling audio generation, with common methods including autoregressive models, flow-based models, and diffusion models. WaveNet [17] is an autoregressive model that generates high-fidelity audio, but its synthesis is slow, and the synthesized audio contains audible noise. WaveRNN [18] is another autoregressive model that reduces computational complexity by using sparse recurrent neural networks. Stream-based models, such as WaveFlow [19], WaveGlow [20], and FloWaveNet [21], improve the quality of audio synthesis by maximizing the likelihood of training the model. Recently, DM-based audio generation models have been proposed, such as DiffWave [22] and WaveGrad [23], which are able to generate higher-quality audio and synthesize it faster than common models.

In this work, we propose a new neural vocoder called GuideDiff based on DM. This vocoder is mainly used in the style transfer model to restore high-quality audio from generated spectrograms. Moreover, its synthesis speed is several orders of magnitude faster than baseline models like WaveNet.

3. METHOD

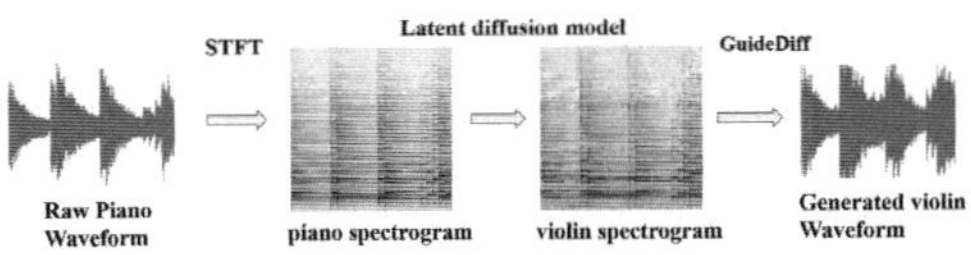

Figure 1. Piano to violin style transfer.

Music style transfer is accomplished in three steps in this work, as illustrated in Figure 1. Firstly, a spectrogram is obtained from the input audio waveform using the Short Time Fourier Transform (STFT), which represents time and frequency. The phase information is discarded, and only the amplitude is processed as an image. Secondly, the transfer of musical styles is performed by completing the domain conversion on the spectrogram using a latent diffusion model. Lastly, GuideDiff is utilized to convert the transformed spectrograms into audio waveforms.

The section following this introduction will focus on the second part of the music style transfer process, which involves the conversion of the input spectrogram to a target spectrogram using a latent diffusion model. The subsequent section will cover the third part of the process, which is the conversion of the target spectrogram into a high-quality audio waveform using the proposed neural coder, GuideDiff.

3.1 Time-Frequency Analysis

The audio signal is often more challenging to capture compared to image signals. As a result, an audio spectrogram, which provides a visual representation of the frequency content of sound, is commonly used. In Figure 2, the x-axis represents time, while the y-axis represents frequency. The color of each pixel corresponds to the frequency and volume of the audio in its corresponding rows and columns. To perform style transfer, we need to analyze the input audio in both the time and frequency domains to obtain a spectrogram.

One of the most commonly used techniques in this area is the Short Time Fourier Transform (STFT), which is often discretized for computer calculations. The discrete STFT operation can be abbreviated as

$$STFTx[n](m, \omega_k) = \sum_{n=-\infty}^{\infty} x[n]\omega[n-m]e^{-j\omega_k n} \quad (1)$$

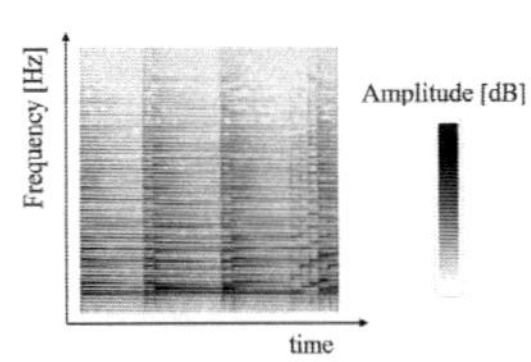

Figure 2. Spectrogram.

Where $x[n]$ is the input time domain signal, m is the step size, ω_k is the frequency, and ω is a window function.

The audio is divided into segments of 5 seconds for time-frequency analysis to make processing easier. By performing the STFT transform independently, the segmented audio is converted into a spectrogram. In this case, a Hanning window with a step size of 100 is used, and the phase information is discarded during processing because it is ambiguous and unpredictable.

3.2 Transfer Model

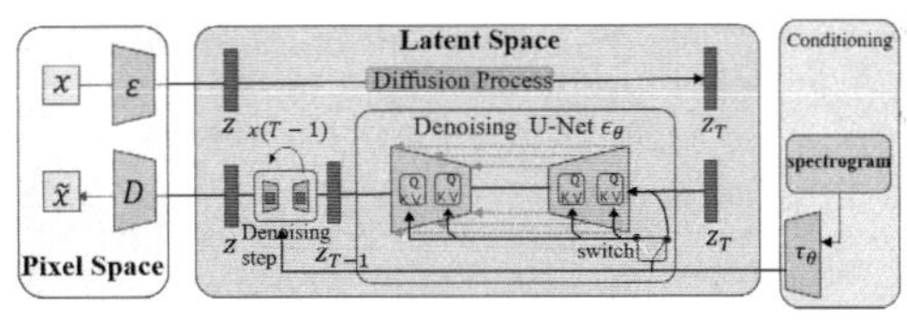

Figure 3. Models of transfer.

Figure 3 illustrates the three main components of the style transfer model: an autoencoder (AE) that compresses and restores the input and output spectrogram information in pixel space; a latent space diffusion model that is mainly used for style transfer, which incorporates a cross-attention mechanism that completes the domain transformation by transferring data from the conditional mechanism into the denoised UNet; the conditional mechanism is primarily used to convey information learned from various musical spectrograms into latent space.

3.2.1 Perceptual Compression

By drawing on the work of Robin Rombach et al. [11], we introduced perceptual compression to lower the computing needs of training DM for producing high-quality spectrograms. The sampling is carried out in a low-dimensional space, which increases the DM's computing efficiency.

A pre-trained self-encoder was employed for perceptual compression. This self-encoder is trained using a patch-based adversarial objective in conjunction with a perceptual loss. The blur created by relying simply on pixel space loss is effectively avoided, which enhances the reconstruction's realism. It offers a low-dimensional representation space that is analogous to the data space from a perceptual standpoint.

The self-encoder consists of an encoder ε and a generator D. They are both composed of three layers of three-dimensional convolution. Formally, given a sample spectrogram $x \in \mathbb{R}^{H \times W \times 3}$, the encoder ε encodes it into a potential representation $z = \varepsilon(x)$,where $z \in \mathbb{R}^{h \times w \times 3}$.

The encoder downsamples the spectrogram by a factor $f = H/h = W/w$ and the generator D reconstructs the potential representation back into a sample $\tilde{x}$,i.e. $\tilde{x} = D(z)$.

To avoid a high degree of dissimilarity in the potential representation space, we have adopted a KL-reg regularization, introducing a slight KL penalty term. A standard learning rate is obtained at the beginning, and the effect is very close to that of a variational autoencoder (VAE). The reconstruction loss $\mathcal{L}_{rec}$ consists of pixel-level mean squared error (MSE) and perceptual-level loss. In summary, the overall training objectives for encoder ε and generator D are

$$\mathcal{L}_{AE} = \min_{\varepsilon,D}(\mathcal{L}_{rec}(x, D(\varepsilon(x))) + KL_{reg}(x||(\varepsilon(x)))) \quad (2)$$

3.2.2 *Latent Diffusion Models*

With the perceptual compression model, we can obtain an effective, low-dimensional latent space in which high frequencies and some difficult-to-perceive details are abstracted. This is effective for the extraction of musical features such as pitch, loudness, timbre, etc. Recalling DM, we propose to diffuse and denoise the spectrogram in the latent space. Given a compressed latent code $z_0 \sim q(z_0)$. DM consists of a forward diffusion process and a backward denoising process. In the forward diffusion process, we train the diffusion model by iteratively adding T steps of diffusion Gaussian noise according to a fixed noise schedule, starting from data z_0 to produce a set of noisy latent variables, i.e. $z_1, ..., z_T$.

$$q(z_t|z_{t-1}) = \mathcal{N}(z_t; \sqrt{1-\beta_t} z_{t-1}, \beta_t I) \quad (3)$$

$$q(z_{1:T}|z_0) = \prod_{t=1}^{T} q(z_t|z_{t-1}) \quad (4)$$

where $\beta_1, \beta_2, ..., \beta_T$ is the noise scheduling that converts the data distribution z_0 into a potential z_T.

Ultimately, data points z_T are indistinguishable from pure Gaussian noise when mixed together. The diffusion model is employed in the reverse denoising process to recover z_T to z_0 by

$$p(z_{t-1}|z_t) = \mathcal{N}(z_{t-1}; \mu_\theta(z_t, t), \sigma_\theta(z_t, t)) \quad (5)$$

$$p_\theta(z_{0:T}) = p(z_T) \prod_{t=1}^{T} p_\theta(z_{t-1}|z_t) \quad (6)$$

where θ is a parameterized neural network that is defined by a Markov chain. The U-Net, commonly used in image synthesis, is used here to predict $\mu_\theta(z_t, t)$ and $\sigma_\theta(z_t, t)$. In actuality, σ_θ is set to a time-dependent constant that is untrained depending on a noise schedule of

$$\sigma_\theta(z_t, t) = \sigma_t = \frac{1-\bar{\alpha}_{t-1}}{1-\bar{\alpha}_t}\beta_t \quad (7)$$

Where $\alpha_t = 1 - \beta_t$,$\bar{\alpha}_t = \prod_{i=1}^{t} \alpha_i$, we parameterize $\mu_\theta = (z_t, t)$ by

$$\mu_\theta(z_t, t) = \frac{1}{\sqrt{\alpha_t}}(z_t - \frac{\beta_t}{\sqrt{1-\bar{\alpha}_t}}\epsilon_\theta(z_t, t)) \quad (8)$$

Final $\epsilon_\theta(z_t, t)$ was assessed.

In practice, we use simplified training objectives.

$$\mathcal{L}_{simple}(\theta) = \mathbb{E}_{\varepsilon(x),\epsilon\sim\mathcal{N}(0,1)}||\epsilon_\theta(z_t, t) - \epsilon||_2^2 \quad (9)$$

where $\epsilon \sim \mathcal{N}(0, 1)$. Since the forward process of the diffusion model is fixed, it can be efficiently obtained during training z_t and the $p(z)$ samples generated by the reverse process can be encoded once in perceptual space through the generator D into image space.

Style transfer module. To model the generation of spectrograms in the latent space and to accomplish style transfer. We used a 2-dimensional convolutional layer to build the underlying U-Net capabilities, specifically a 2×2 shaped convolutional layer. A cross-attention mechanism is added to augment the U-Net backbone, enabling it to generate spectrograms in the target domain conditional on the style transfer. And it ensures that style information can be shared across the potential space, which is essential for learning the style of audio and completing style transfer.

3.2.3 *Conditioning Mechanisms*

In this module, we employ a domain-specific encoder τ_θ to preprocess the input conditional style spectrogram y and project the encoded y onto an intermediate representation $\tau_\theta(y) \in \mathbb{R}^{M\times d_\tau}$, which is then mapped to the intermediate layer of the U-Net via a cross-attention layer to enable the generation of the spectrograms according to condition y. The following equation carries out the cross-attention mechanism.

$$Attention(Q, K, V) = softmax(\frac{QK^T}{\sqrt{d}}) \cdot V \quad (10)$$

where $Q = W_Q^{(i)} \cdot \varphi_i(z_t)$,$K = W_K^{(i)} \cdot \tau_\theta(y)$,$V = W_V^{(i)} \cdot \tau_\theta(y)$. $\varphi_i(z_t) \in \mathbb{R}^{d\times d_\epsilon^i}$ denotes the intermediate U-Net representation that implements ε_θ. $W_V^{(i)} \in \mathbb{R}^{d\times d_\epsilon^i}$,$W_K^{(i)} \in \mathbb{R}^{d\times d_\epsilon^i}$ and $W_Q^{(i)} \in \mathbb{R}^{d\times d_\epsilon^i}$ are projection matrices that are mainly used to learn and map styles from the target domain of the $\tau_\theta(y)$ representation, enabling style transfer. The objective function is rewritten as

$$\mathcal{L}_{CM}(\theta) = \mathbb{E}_{\varepsilon(x),y,\epsilon\sim\mathcal{N}(0,1)}||\epsilon - \epsilon_\theta(z_t, t, \tau_\theta(y))||_2^2 \quad (11)$$

Where τ_θ and ϵ_θ can be jointly optimized by means of an objective function.

3.3 Waveform Reconstruction

We propose a novel encoder, called GuideDiff, to convert the spectrogram output from the model into audio. It can restore the spectrogram to generate high-quality audio. As shown in Figure 4, a 3×3 encoder $\varepsilon = E_{\theta_{enc}}(m_w)$ is first used to encode the spectrogram into the latent space, and then the information x from the latent space is sent as conditional information into the U-Net's cross-attention

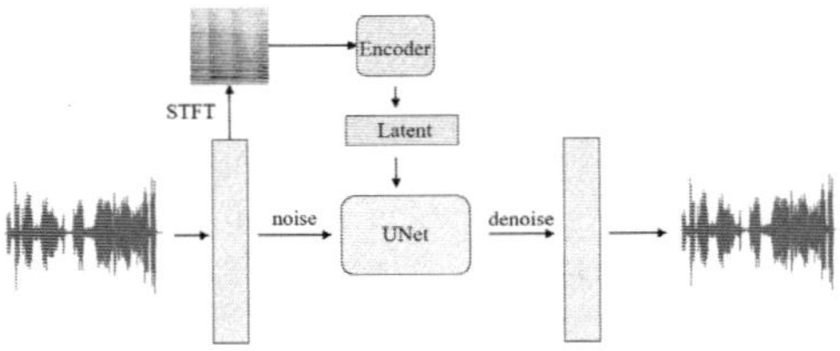

Figure 4. GuideDiff architecture.

mechanism for conditioning and directing the creation of waveforms. The original waveform is then recreated by using the diffusion decoder $D = D_{\theta_{dec}}(z, \alpha, s)$ to decode the latent signal, where $D_{\theta_{dec}}$ denotes the diffusion sampling method, α denotes the noise, and s denotes the sample pace length. Target diffusion is used to train Decoder D while conditioning the latent 2D U-Net, which is repeatedly invoked during the decoding procedure. Figure 5 displays the model's primary network diagram. Where y_n

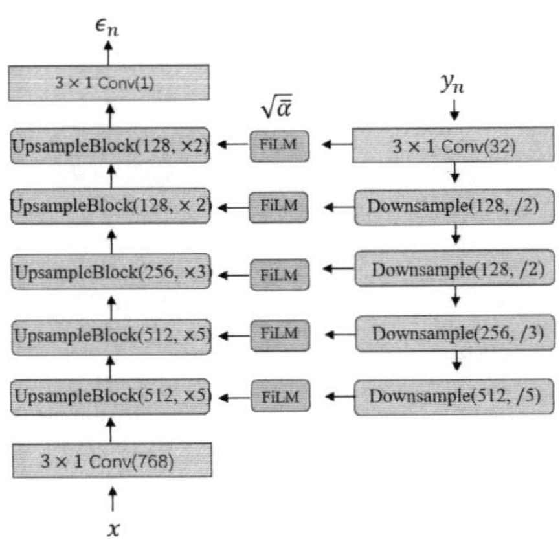

Figure 5. Model's primary network.

denotes the n th round of noisy audio input and ϵ_θ denotes the simulated generated noise. FiLM is the characteristic linear modulation module, consisting of two 3×1 convolutional layers and the Leaky ReLU function. Here we condition on noise level $\sqrt{\bar{\alpha}}$ and pass it to the position encoding function.

Compared to the DM objective function, we can write the objective function as

$$\mathcal{L}_{GuideDiff}(\theta) = \mathbb{E}_{\bar{\alpha},\varepsilon}[||\epsilon - \epsilon_\theta(\sqrt{\bar{\alpha}_n} y_0 + \sqrt{1-\bar{\alpha}_n}\epsilon, x, \sqrt{\bar{\alpha}})||_1] \quad (12)$$

where $\alpha = 1 - \beta_n, \bar{\alpha}_n = \sum_{s=1}^{n} \alpha_s$, in this case β_n, is an equivariant sequence from 0 to 1.

For the input spectrograms, we discarded the phase and used only the amplitude. By encoding the spectrograms in latent space, the computational load for the representation can be effectively reduced. Moreover, it enables the diffusion model to learn how to generate waveforms with true phase. The latent space obtained is used as the starting point for the next diffusion phase. The advantage of this is that our model only needs to be trained once. The latent trajectory space also allows for a large number of inference procedures to be performed without requiring retraining. Specifically, once this model is trained, it is only necessary to use a different number of iterations N in the inference process to determine the quality of the computational output. This is useful for rapidly bootstrapping the generation of high-quality raw audio. To ensure that the reduced latent space is available for latent diffusion, we apply the tanh function to the bottleneck, ensuring that the values remain within the range [-1, 1].

In summary, our overall objective function is

$$\mathcal{L} = \mathcal{L}_{AE} + \mathcal{L}_{simple}(\theta) + \mathcal{L}_{CM}(\theta) + \mathcal{L}_{GuideDiff}(\theta) \quad (13)$$

4. EXPERIMENTS

In Section 4.1, we provide details on the experimental setup, including data description and pre-processing, as well as evaluation metrics. Section 4.2 then provides a detailed description of the implementation.

4.1 Experimental Setup

4.1.1 Data Description And Preprocessing

The model consumes a large amount of memory when generating an entire song at once. To mitigate this issue, we employed the Demucs model to separate the music into its constituent sources, such as vocals, bass, and drums. Furthermore, each song was divided into smaller segments, which were modeled individually and then reassembled. However, rearranging the segments was challenging, as they differed in downbeat, key, and pace. To address this, we smoothly interpolated cues and seeds in the model's latent space. In a diffusion model, the latent space is a feature vector that encompasses the entire space of possibilities that can be generated by the model. Items that are similar to each other are approached in the latent space, and each value in the latent space is decoded into a feasible output. This makes the audio sound natural.

We require various types of music data to train our model to achieve music style migration. For all the experiments in this study, we used music datasets from multiple source domains collected from the web. This dataset includes over 100,000 WAV audio files of various instruments, genres, and compositional styles. The main instruments include piano, violin, guitar, and others, while the genres mainly consist of jazz, classical, and pop. The data was used for training (80%), testing (10%), and validation (10%).

4.1.2 Evalutaion Metrics

The following measures were used to evaluate and analyze the model's performance:

Fréchet Audio Distance (FAD) [24] The FAD calculates the Fréchet distance between the output generated audio samples and the real audio samples. The smaller the distance between the two data distributions, the more realistic the generated samples will be, which gives a reliable assessment of the difference between them.

Accuracy In this research, five independent style assessment classifiers were trained in order to test the efficacy of the model style transfer. The percentage of styles accurately predicted in each song bar served as a measure of the classifiers' accuracy.

Mean Opinion Score(MOS) In this work, a 5-scale mean opinion score is used to evaluate the proposed model. Where the MOS value suggests that a higher value is preferable. Subjects were asked to rate each of the three questions for each transfer version on a scale of 1 to 5.

1. Success in style transfer (ST): whether the target domain is migrated in the generated audio after transfer compared to the original audio.
2. Content preservation (CT): the extent to which the migrated-generated audio matches the original audio content.
3. Sound quality (SQ): the generated audio has high or poor sound quality.

A mean score will be used when comparing it to other baseline models. GuideDiff simply evaluates the quality of the generated sound.

Inception Score (IS) [25] To evaluate the level of diversity and quality of the sample generation. IS is an evaluation metric employing a ResNeXT classifier [26] trained on our dataset and a 10-dimensional logit based on a 1024-dimensional feature vector. To assess the effectiveness of the proposed audio generation model. IS is calculated as

$$IS = exp(E_{x \sim p_{gen}} KL(P\mathcal{F}(x) || E_{x' \sim p_{gen}} P\mathcal{F}(x'))) \tag{14}$$

Where $P\mathcal{F}(x)$ is a multinomial distribution and $E_{x' \sim p_{gen}} P\mathcal{F}(x')$ is an edge label distribution.

4.1.3 Implementation Details

This work uses a UNet architecture consisting of 14 layers of stacked convolution blocks and attention blocks as a combination of upsampling and downsampling for the diffusion model, which is based on the work of Robin Rombach et al [11]. For the downsampling factor, a downsampling factor of 4 was used. The same hidden size and skip connection layers were set between the layers in the UNet model. The first six layers of the UNet model use 512×512 input and output channels, followed by two 256×256 and $128x128$ input and output channels, respectively. After that, the input and output channels are halved layer by layer. The attention mechanism is used in this work at 16×16,8×8 and 4×4 resolutions. A ResBlock is also added to the UNet module, which receives two inputs: the image x and the embedding corresponding to the timestep. Two linear layers and the time_emb layer make up the time-step embedding layer. Our compression ratio for the latent space is 64. The audio samples were sampled at a frequency of 16000 Hz, with a channel size of 2, and an amplitude of -10 dB. The model was trained using the Adam optimizer with 500k steps, a learning rate of 5e-5, and a batch size of 100. The batch size for GuideDiff was set to 256. Approximately 1M steps were trained using the Adam optimizer.

The experiments in this research generated audio in less than 5 seconds, which can be regarded as real-time generation, and were trained on 3 NVIDA RTX3090Ti, a GPU capable of running 50 stable diffusion steps.

4.2 Experimental Analysis

Four primary musical style transfer tasks were taken into consideration in the trials:

1. Stylistic transfer of instrument timbres. Mainly consider piano to guitar (p2g) and piano to violin transitions (p2v). Each transition will do a bilateral transformation.
2. transfer of musical genres. Genre conversions from jazz to pop (j2p) and jazz to class (j2c) are mainly considered. Each transition will do a bilateral transformation.
3. Music composition style conversion. Beethoven to Chopin (B2C), and Chopin to Beethoven (C2B) conversions are mainly considered.
4. Many-to-many style conversions. Conversion of classical piano pieces played mainly by Beethoven to jazz violin in the Chopin style (Bcp2Cjv).

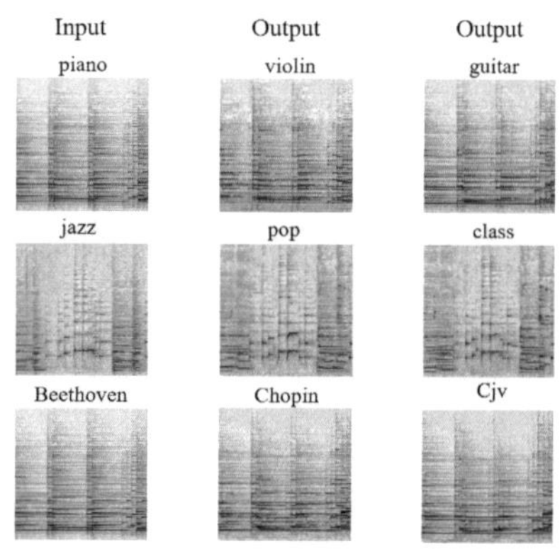

Figure 6. Style transitions for various tasks.

The spectrograms of our model's inputs and outputs for the various tasks are shown in Figure 6. From the plots, it is clear that the target domain is shifted while the contents are kept intact.

4.2.1 Style Conversion Evaluation

This study evaluates the proposed model through four different style transfer challenges. Subjective (MOS) and objective (FAD, accuracy) evaluations are used to compare the style conversions. Each score has its own limitations. Subjective measurements evaluate three main aspects of the model: the success of style transfer (ST), content preservation (CP), and sound quality (SQ). A 5-point scale is used for evaluation. Objective evaluations use FAD to measure individual aspects of the conversion, and accuracy is used to evaluate the accuracy of style transfer.

Subjective evaluation Mean opinion scores (MOS) were collected from 200 testers for the listening test. These testers included both music lovers and non-musicians. In each mid-round score, testers first listened to the original audio clip and then to the style-shifted version.

The results indicate that our model performs the best in the piano2violin task, which may be attributed to the relatively simple timbre conversion of a single instrument.

Task	ST	CP	SQ
piano2Violin	4.27	4.13	4.3
piano2guitar	4.02	4.05	4.2
jazz2pop	3.95	3.8	4.0
jazz2class	3.96	4.0	4.12
Beethoven2Chopin	4.05	4.1	4.15
Bcp2Cjv	4.1	4.23	4.3

Table 1. 5-scale MOS with style Transfer.

Model	Task				
	p2v	p2g	j2p	j2c	B2C
CycleGAN	3.98	3.96	4.17	4.12	4.0
UNIT	3.7	3.75	3.5	3.62	3.71
musicVAE	3.86	3.91	3.7	3.68	3.89
autoencoder	3.5	3.56	3.4	3.45	3.52
ours	4.23	4.09	3.91	4.02	4.07

Table 3. MOS with the baseline comparison model.

Our model's performance is slightly lower in the jazz2pop and jazz2class tasks, but it still achieves scores close to 4 in terms of successful style transfer and content retention. This suggests that our model is relatively successful in genre conversion. Additionally, the high scores for sound quality in all six tasks indicate that the proposed model is capable of generating high-quality music.

Objective review Measures how well the converted version matches the original version and the accuracy of the style transfer.

Task	FAD↓	Accuracy↑
piano2Violin	7.52	94.5%
piano2guitar	6.95	93.4%
jazz2pop	11.76	86.2%
jazz2class	10.55	87.2%
Beethoven2Chopin	6.19	95.3%
Bcp2Cjv	6.07	95.7%

Table 2. FAD&Accuracy for the tasks.

The accuracy of style transfer between the audio produced by the specified task and the original audio is presented in Table 2 along with the results of FAD calculations. The results indicate good performance in terms of the timbre transfer of instruments and the transfer of compositional styles. However, the performance is poor in terms of genre transfer, which is consistent with the results of the subjective evaluation. This is an area that requires improvement in future research.

4.2.2 *Comparison With Other Models*

Our model was compared against a number of baseline models, including CycleGAN [2], UNIT [12], musicVAE [13], and autoencoder [27], in order to show the validity of the model described in this work. Table 3 presents the outcomes.

Note that these baseline models for style transfer are all one-to-one mappings. In this work, the input transfers use the same music clip, and they are trained independently. Only the spectrogram form is considered for the intermediate representation of the music. The same model, GuideDiff, is used for the generation of the waveform.

The comparison of the baseline models indicates that CycleGAN performs the best in terms of genre migration, which may be related to the fact that cycle consistency loss is taken into account in its direct matching of target domains at the feature level. However, our model achieved a result that is only about 0.1 points lower than the best. Additionally, our model outperforms the other baseline models in terms of the migration of musical instrument timbre and compositional style. Therefore, it can be concluded that the proposed model demonstrates superior performance in terms of flexible many-to-many musical style migration compared to the other baseline models.

4.2.3 *Evaluation of the audio generating model*

To demonstrate the performance and high-quality audio generation capabilities of GuideDiff, the proposed audio generation model, examples are presented in this section. Comparisons are made between the proposed model and WaveNet [17], WaveRNN [18], and WaveGAN [28]. All models use the same training set and are tested using the same spectrograms to generate audio. Both subjective and objective evaluation techniques are used to assess the quality of the generated audio. Testers will rate the audio quality on a scale of 1 to 5 for subjective evaluation. The results are presented in Table 4.

Model	MOS(↑)	IS(↑)
WaveNet	3.02	2.84
WaveGAN	3.82	4.53
WaveRNN	4.40	5.38
GuideDiff	4.41	5.40

Table 4. Comparison of audio generation models.

The comparison demonstrates that our model performs similarly to the autoregressive model WaveRNN and surpasses the other baseline models. This suggests that the proposed model has excellent performance in producing high-quality audio.

5. CONCLUSIONS

In this work, we have designed an efficient DM-based framework for music style transfer. A latent layer was introduced into the framework, which effectively reduces the dimensionality of the data. A cross-attention mechanism is added to the latent layer. The transfer of styles is achieved by adding seed conditions to guide and complete the generation of transformations in the target domain. As for the generation of audio, this study proposes GuideDiff, a DM-based method for generating waveform audio. The method compresses the spectrogram into latent space via an encoder and transfers it to the U-Net. The potential signal is then decoded back into the waveform using diffusion guidance.

The experimental results demonstrate that the proposed model can achieve many-to-many style migration and generate high-quality music in comparison to previous approaches. Additionally, the model is capable of performing style migration and generating high-quality audio in real-time on a consumer-grade GPU. Given the excellent performance of this model, future work will utilize it to explore text-generated music.

6. REFERENCES

[1] G. Brunner, A. Konrad, Y. Wang, and R. Wattenhofer, "MIDI-VAE: Modeling dynamics and instrumentation of music with applications to style transfer," *arXiv preprint arXiv:1809.07600*, 2018.

[2] G. Brunner, Y. Wang, R. Wattenhofer, and S. Zhao, "Symbolic music genre transfer with cyclegan," in *2018 ieee 30th international conference on tools with artificial intelligence (ictai)*. IEEE, 2018, pp. 786–793.

[3] S. Huang, Q. Li, C. Anil, X. Bao, S. Oore, and R. B. Grosse, "Timbretron: A wavenet (cyclegan (cqt (audio))) pipeline for musical timbre transfer," *arXiv preprint arXiv:1811.09620*, 2018.

[4] C. Donahue, H. H. Mao, Y. E. Li, G. W. Cottrell, and J. McAuley, "LakhNES: Improving multi-instrumental music generation with cross-domain pre-training," *arXiv preprint arXiv:1907.04868*, 2019.

[5] Y.-N. Hung, I. Chiang, Y.-A. Chen, Y.-H. Yang *et al.*, "Musical composition style transfer via disentangled timbre representations," *arXiv preprint arXiv:1905.13567*, 2019.

[6] R. S. Bonnici, M. Benning, and C. Saitis, "Timbre transfer with variational auto encoding and cycle-consistent adversarial networks," in *2022 International Joint Conference on Neural Networks (IJCNN)*. IEEE, 2022, pp. 1–8.

[7] N. Mor, L. Wolf, A. Polyak, and Y. Taigman, "A universal music translation network," *arXiv preprint arXiv:1805.07848*, 2018.

[8] J. Ho, A. Jain, and P. Abbeel, "Denoising diffusion probabilistic models," *Advances in Neural Information Processing Systems*, vol. 33, pp. 6840–6851, 2020.

[9] Y. Song, J. Sohl-Dickstein, D. P. Kingma, A. Kumar, S. Ermon, and B. Poole, "Score-based generative modeling through stochastic differential equations," *arXiv preprint arXiv:2011.13456*, 2020.

[10] G. Mittal, J. Engel, C. Hawthorne, and I. Simon, "Symbolic music generation with diffusion models," *arXiv preprint arXiv:2103.16091*, 2021.

[11] R. Rombach, A. Blattmann, D. Lorenz, P. Esser, and B. Ommer, "High-resolution image synthesis with latent diffusion models," in *Proceedings of the IEEE/CVF Conference on Computer Vision and Pattern Recognition*, 2022, pp. 10 684–10 695.

[12] M.-Y. Liu, T. Breuel, and J. Kautz, "Unsupervised image-to-image translation networks," *Advances in neural information processing systems*, vol. 30, 2017.

[13] A. Roberts, J. Engel, C. Raffel, C. Hawthorne, and D. Eck, "A hierarchical latent vector model for learning long-term structure in music," in *International conference on machine learning*. PMLR, 2018, pp. 4364–4373.

[14] P. Dhariwal and A. Nichol, "Diffusion models beat gans on image synthesis," *Advances in Neural Information Processing Systems*, vol. 34, pp. 8780–8794, 2021.

[15] J. Song, C. Meng, and S. Ermon, "Denoising diffusion implicit models," *arXiv preprint arXiv:2010.02502*, 2020.

[16] S. Forsgren and H. Martiros, "Riffusion - Stable diffusion for real-time music generation." 2022. [Online]. Available: https://riffusion.com/about.

[17] A. v. d. Oord, S. Dieleman, H. Zen, K. Simonyan, O. Vinyals, A. Graves, N. Kalchbrenner, A. Senior, and K. Kavukcuoglu, "Wavenet: A generative model for raw audio," *arXiv preprint arXiv:1609.03499*, 2016.

[18] A. Gritsenko, T. Salimans, R. van den Berg, J. Snoek, and N. Kalchbrenner, "A spectral energy distance for parallel speech synthesis," *Advances in Neural Information Processing Systems*, vol. 33, pp. 13 062–13 072, 2020.

[19] W. Ping, K. Peng, K. Zhao, and Z. Song, "Waveflow: A compact flow-based model for raw audio," in *International Conference on Machine Learning*. PMLR, 2020, pp. 7706–7716.

[20] R. Prenger, R. Valle, and B. Catanzaro, "Waveglow: A flow-based generative network for speech synthesis," in *ICASSP 2019-2019 IEEE International Conference on Acoustics, Speech and Signal Processing (ICASSP)*. IEEE, 2019, pp. 3617–3621.

[21] S. Kim, S.-g. Lee, J. Song, J. Kim, and S. Yoon, "FloWaveNet: A generative flow for raw audio," *arXiv preprint arXiv:1811.02155*, 2018.

[22] Z. Kong, W. Ping, J. Huang, K. Zhao, and B. Catanzaro, "Diffwave: A versatile diffusion model for audio synthesis," *arXiv preprint arXiv:2009.09761*, 2020.

[23] N. Chen, Y. Zhang, H. Zen, R. J. Weiss, M. Norouzi, and W. Chan, "Wavegrad: Estimating gradients for waveform generation," *arXiv preprint arXiv:2009.00713*, 2020.

[24] K. Kilgour, M. Zuluaga, D. Roblek, and M. Sharifi, "Fr\'echet Audio Distance: A Metric for Evaluating Music Enhancement Algorithms," *arXiv preprint arXiv:1812.08466*, 2018.

[25] T. Salimans, I. Goodfellow, W. Zaremba, V. Cheung, A. Radford, and X. Chen, "Improved techniques for training gans," *Advances in neural information processing systems*, vol. 29, 2016.

[26] S. Xie, R. Girshick, P. Dollár, Z. Tu, and K. He, "Aggregated residual transformations for deep neural networks," in *Proceedings of the IEEE conference on computer vision and pattern recognition*, 2017, pp. 1492–1500.

[27] D. Bank, N. Koenigstein, and R. Giryes, "Autoencoders," *arXiv preprint arXiv:2003.05991*, 2020.

[28] R. Yamamoto, E. Song, and J.-M. Kim, "Parallel WaveGAN: A fast waveform generation model based on generative adversarial networks with multi-resolution spectrogram," in *ICASSP 2020-2020 IEEE International Conference on Acoustics, Speech and Signal Processing (ICASSP)*. IEEE, 2020, pp. 6199–6203.

The Heterogeneity Of The Narrative Role In Kaija Saariaho's *Émilie*

Zhishu Chang
China Conservatory of Music
guoyin_czs@163.com

ABSTRACT

As Kaija Saariaho's third opera but first monodrama, it is fascinating to witness how Saariaho recontextualizes a striking historical figure in Émilie. Written in 2008, the opera premiered in Lyon in March 2010; it contains nine scenes fitting into 75 minutes. The solo soprano character was originally sung by Finnish operatic soprano Karita Mattila. The libretto was written by Amin Maalouf, who arranged the libretto based on the biographies, books, and plays that have been written about Émilie du Châtelet's personal life and work since her death. Émilie du Châtelet (1706– 1749) is a French scientist, mathematician, physicist, philosopher, and, according to chronology, the first woman to establish an international scientific reputation.

By synthesizing a freaky but delicate sonic world combined with live electronics, visual staging, and acoustic orchestra, Saariaho utilizes more facets of tools to portray a female scientist vividly. Émilie evokes the expressivity of a theatrical world of a female role model and broadens the operatic subject variety regarding academic and female figures. In the following passages, I will unfold how the heterogeneity of the narrative role of the operatic figure was demonstrated by the thematic design and electronic configuration.

Primary Materials in *Émilie*

In nine scenes, Émilie's character's arias closely link to the birth of the child, her significant scholarship, and her persistence in pursuit of scholarship. Émilie makes a heavy amount of dialogue with Voltaire, Saint-Lambert, her unborn child, and even herself through time and space, also accompanying an evocative stream of subconsciousness and underlying subtext and emotions.

The composition starts with Émilie's anxiety and the scene she writes to Saint-Lambert to express the anxiety regarding foreseeing her pregnancy will lead to her death and conceiving new ideas of Newton's law's translation. The music begins with a sober and dispassionate entrance made by harpsichord among a very soft ambiance with a static nature.

The harpsichord paired with tam-tam and the bass drum's tremolo shaped an essential timbral definition. Afterward, ominous repeated unison notes with vibraphone and suspended cymbal attacks foreshadow a core element of the whole opera.

In detail, the harpsichord is chosen as a characteristic signal on purpose to lead constant development and transition between scenarios and dialogues. This is autobiographically partly because Émilie herself was a passable performer on the harpsichord. Thus, this appliance refers to historical context and brings more authenticity and a rich picture sense of the protagonist. Evidently, the characteristic showcase of the harpsichord gesture formed a pivotal motif that bridges the sentimental change between separate movements. Also, through the kinesthetic trigger and phrase conduction, the harpsichord complements the ensemble, which in turn resonates with the leading voice.

It is not uncommon to hear the pitch-class set (0,1,4) as a primary material, one of Saariaho's favorite harmony imprints. She has already used it in many pieces, including *Laterna Magica* (2008) and *Sept Papillons* (2000). She uses a highly recognizable harmonic language to make the key motif consistently linger in listeners' ears in various ways, where the core pitch class can be extended to pitch-class combinations like (0,1,4,5), (0,1,4,5,8), (0,1,4,7,8,11) and so forth. The first appearance of pitch-class (0,1,4,5) is introduced by harpsichord at the very beginning using tetrachord D-bE-#F-G, which is then shadowed in two measures by bassoon and clarinet using the same pitches but slightly longer duration. As such, the intervallic content of minor second, minor third, and major third are stressed. and the pitch-class set (0,1,4) harmony is more like a fragrance haunting different passages. Under additional textual employment and timbral design, this sound set produces different "scents."

Rhythmically, two overall pulsations drive the opera: the yearning, sustainable long line that expresses stillness and the fragmented but urgent and penetrating fast rhythms. Each of them has multiple variants. Likewise, underlying rhythmic propulsions also pass on between scenes. For instance, in Scene III, *Voltaire,* soprano is singing: "Dieu nous a donné d'un même geste La capacité d'éprouver la souffrance Et celle d'éprouver le plaisir." (God gave us with the same gesture, the ability to experience suffering). Then, vibraphone and marimba pick up the concealed rhythm made by eighth notes and irregular quarter notes, which are formerly utilized on the strings section in the first and second scenes. The percussive gesture ripples with long-pulsation hazy and sensuous phrases in wind and string instruments. Therefore, the reappeared rhythm takes on new pulsive meanings that also match the text-paining trope innately.

Gestural-based Thematic Configuration

Numerous passions constitute Émilie's life, and nine scenes are divided into two aspects: work and personal life. Each scene is based on its topic and, in general, represents characteristic thematic independence and gradually unfolds rhythmic patterns and developmental consistency.

The scenes regarding "Émilie's personal life are more gesture-based, carnal, and rhythmically capricious and the vocal wiring is more expressive, often nervous, and explosive even." [1]It applies to Scenes I, II, III, V, and VII.

The first scene is built on harpsichord and marimba ostinato, where the fragmented glitch-like notes occasionally disturb the vibe of stretchy lines of the ensemble by unbalanced phrasing, irregular appearance spot, and dynamic upheaval.

In Scene II, *Tombe*, the continuing marimba's inauspicious gesture becomes the foreground, and a gloomy tremolo-glissando of a large suspended cymbal placed on the drum conveys an obscure backdrop. The relentless downward minor-second gesture was emphasized with endless eighth-note beating, suggesting sighing and even indicating the minimalistic style. Interestingly, in the third scene Voltaire, both the psychoacoustic speed and pacing are fastened. It modifies the downward scale gesture and twists it into shortened exclamation punctuation. The entire chapter is dominated by rapid sixteenth-note figurations alternating between wood and string accompanied by one-single note fermata gesture to hold tensions.

Scene VII, *Enfant*, is the lengthiest rough scene which contains Émilie's dialogue with her unborn baby and Émilie's father. The tune is inspired by one of Scarlatti's themes which reveals itself progressively throughout the piece. "During the parts pertaining to Émilie's work, the music becomes more abstract, less rhythmic, the physical body is more absent" and vocal passages are less intense.[1]

While working at IRCAM and GRM[1], Saariaho experiments with slowing down recording samples to capture the nuances of sound that are undetectable at their regular speed. By zooming in on a sound, she concludes the quintessential compositional approach that she calls the "microscope for music."[1] It involves accentuating the sound's physical dimensions, revealing the microtonality domain, extending that timbre through electronic processing, or imitating these effects on acoustic instruments.[2]

For instance, in Scene IV, *Rayons*, a sense of the universe is depicted by shimmering slow-pacing streams of timbral reflections akin to a release of tension of the former three chapters. Tubular bells, Mark Tree, and Crotales add colorations, where strings are required to alternatively press light and normal, slowly swaying between normal and harmonic. Woodwinds wobble through different extents of vibratos. Decisive notation of open and closed brass plunger mutes combined with microtonality together transfigure an exquisite but fragile feeling.

The entire Scene IV is characterized by "unchanging consistency" and "self-containment via stasis or process" which represents the property of "vertical time."[3] It enables the sound- noise or harmony-timbre continuums to be integrated into a process of infinity. [3]

In Scene VI, *Feu*, the composer employs the opera's fastest tempo (q =84), shaping an unquiet ambiance, accumulating sentiment and frenzy for the next scene. Saariaho creatively uses amplified pre-recorded text from the soprano to draw threads of the plot and stress overall instrumental resonance.

Heterogeneity in Time and Narration

The narration of 9 scenes does not entirely follow a linear narration; prophecy and flashbacks co-exist across time and space, accompanied by the flashback of primary music gestures. The opera is set during the last night of Emilie's life, and she recalls various figures who have been significant in her life.[4] It is fascinating how Saariaho implies the duality on the female scientist's shoulder between life and work using musical forms. Indeed, Émilie's struggles are buried tremendously between the contradiction of science and personal life, through which the more rational and restrained request to pursue science research challenges her passion and desire for personal love.

The librettist Amin Maalouf and Saariaho mixed the timeline and set free more blocky juxtapositions between narrative contents. Starting with writing a letter to Monsieur de Saint-Lambert about the detestable presentiment, In particular, Émilie intrudes her conversations with Voltaire in Scene III, her love confession to Saint-Lambert in Scene V, and her heartfelt wishes to the unborn child in Scene VII. After the dialogical Scenes III, V, and VII, three contrasting theoretical scenes are set right after Scenes III, V, and VII correspondently. A scientific theme *Rayon* was connected behind Voltaire, which also takes on as the climax scene. Furthermore, Scene VIII, *Principia*, was inserted behind the Child scene. So, physical phenomenon and substance were captured and aroused huge spiritual contrast. Nevertheless, despite the fragments and cut-off of narrations, the dialogue between separate voices can be seen as the externalization of the inner monologue of Émilie herself, and the explanative scientific passages function as underlying bonds that connect spiritual reinforcement, forging a compound, overlapping idea.

Pressentiments	Tombe	Voltaire	Rayons	Reencontre	Feu	Enfant	Principia	Contre L'oubli
♩=48	♩=64	♩=72	♩=48	♩=48	♩=84	♩=66	♩=48	♩=54
present/future	future	past	present	past	present	future	present	presnet/future
life	life	life	work	life	work	life	work	work

Figure 1: the overall narrative layout by scene

Figure 1 illustrates a summary of the opera's narrative trajectory including the duality of work and life, tempo layout, and heterogeneity in time. In general, the

[1] Pierre Schaeffer founded Groupe de Recherches Musicales in 1958. It is a music research center in the field of sound and electroacoustic music.

sections reflecting Emilie's work employ a slower tempo whereas the tempo in sections narrating life is more agitated and self-generated. Threads between present, future, and past are often intertwined. However, work scenes IV, VI, VII, and VIII elucidate the essence of the present time. The dichotomy between the present time in work scenes and the future and past narration in life scenes gradually unfolds. Thus, the "reordered linearity" in time and "discontinuous" time arrangement shed light on "multiple time." [3]

Not only did narration reflect the juxtaposition, but the treatment of text applies it. Saariaho's fragmenting and reordering of words are known as a "fragmentary text collage."[5] She sometimes only sets fragmented parts of the original text, which confounds the linguistic meaning yet finally reveals the emotional undertone of the text. The text "J'aimais pour deux." (I loved for two) first appears toward the end of Scene III, *Voltaire* then shows in Scene IV, *Rayon*, as a thematic declamation which is ultimately illuminated in this scene's last phrase where "two principles" means self-love to urge, and reason, to restrain.

Similarly, the placement of the syllables is sometimes detached and disjoint. Following relatively intuitive vocal writing, the voice line is syllabic, kept in sheer and compact rhythm but most stay in a range lowering than G5 to ensure intelligibility. However, an instance in m.146 of scene VIII, the sopranos constantly repeat G5 with extensive halt and punctuate three words separately while the strings trigger frantic downward glissando reaching G5 simultaneously. This unusual syllabic disjunction foreshadows the advent of *Mathematical Principles of Natural Philosophy*.

More phenomenal, she also plays with diegetic time and musical time in Scene VIII, *Principia*. Diegetic time and location reflect and predict the "present." The text constantly shifts between Émilie's self-narration and the lunar and solar principles. The self-expression section narrates her daily work routine within the accurate diegetic clock in the text where a more agitated tempo (q= 96) is used. In comparison, in the more academic theoretical domain, the musical tempo is pulled back partly because of the implication of moon gravity towards the earth in the same way as text reference.

Multifaceted Configuration of Electronics

Saariaho's approach to electronics is various. As early as when she was working in IRCAM, she used a program called Iana[2] to analyze the FFT[3] of the sound material, which results in a position of a cent, amplitude, and perceptual weight where the physical and acoustical parameter data integrally construct a harmonic language and musical structure.

She is dedicated to the fusion between electronics and orchestra. She said, "The electronics are extensions of orchestration—an extension of instrumental writing." In *Émilie*, Saariaho continues using the synthesis concept of deviving from sound analysis and then utilizing orchestra to generate an ever-changing meta-instrument in which different sound envelops in combination with characteristical themes altogether form a dazzling soundscape. Meanwhile, "The [live] processing sometimes has to do with the dramaturgy of the piece, not only extending the voice or the instrument but in its own way contributing to the narration."[6]

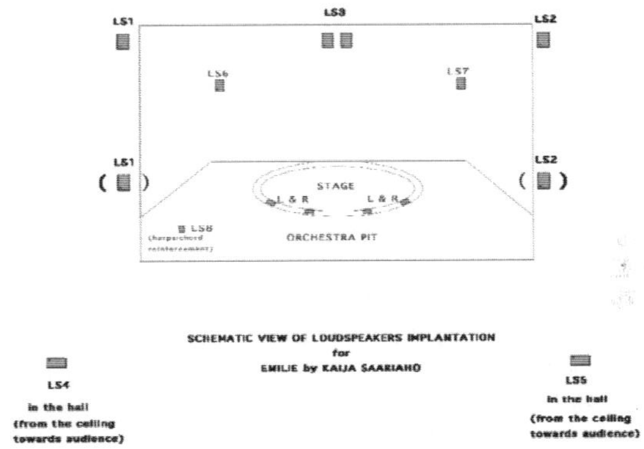

Figure 2: Schematic view of loudspeakers implantation

Saariaho's writing in electronic is detailed and precise. For sound field transmission, she designed a schematic view of loudspeaker implantation illustrated in Figure 2, where a total of 8 to 10 speakers makes a surrounding stereo system according to the hall's shape. Amid them, two speakers play the role of projecting sound from the ceiling toward audiences, alluring more multi-dimensional immersion. She uses Microphones to monitor the reverberation in the hall and add reverbs when too dry.

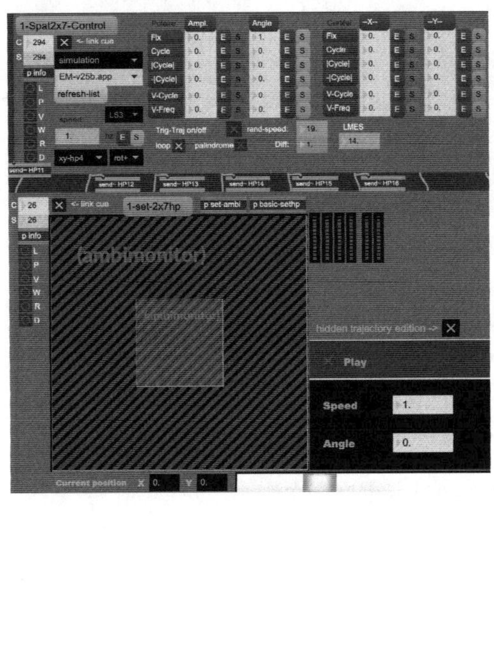

---

[2] Iana is a program implementing Ernst Terhardt's algorithms for determining the perceptual weights of spectral components for complex sounds), and compositional manipulations of the analysis data to control filtering, synthesis, and processing with Chant.

[3] The "Fast Fourier Transform" (FFT) is an important measurement method in the science of audio and acoustics measurement. It converts a signal into individual spectral components and thereby provides frequency information about the signal.

Figure 3: harpsichord spatialization setup in Max/MSP

Partly due to practicality, since applying live electronic to orchestra writing is so nerve-wracking and hard to control, Saariaho merely allocates live electronic to the soprano and harpsichord. After that, she set 56 electronics cues and sub-cues saved in the Max patch and triggered them from the mixer on the computer keyboard. Harpsichord's dominant role is undoubted. “It is consistently a soloist's voice and in a way is treated as another character of the story, or as Émilie's alter ego.”[7] Saariaho extends the harpsichord's sound projection by always sending it to a spatialization effect in output 11 to 16 and boosts its strength by putting local reinforcement with a loudspeaker in the orchestra pit. See Figure 3 above, the trajectory of sound sources is meticulously crafted. Specific coordinates along the x and y axes, as well as precise angles, are defined using azimuth. This allows the multi-channel sound resources to traverse in a horizontal, cyclical motion, altering both sound elevation and distance. The result is an emulation of a three-dimensional listening experience. Notably, the composer further refines spatialization by dynamically adjusting the speed parameter and introducing a “friction” effect, which mimics the resistance of physical forces on the motion of sound sources. In this process, the amplitude of sound is also carefully modulated, adding an additional layer of dynamic control to the spatialization. These adjustments contribute to a nuanced and immersive sonic landscape, adding depth and dimensionality.

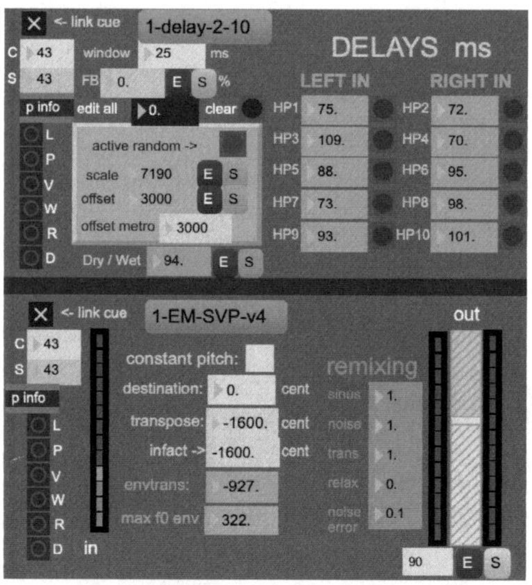

Figure 4: harpsichord delay and voice pitch shifting design in Max/MSP

In addition, the harpsichord's technical treatments are required by adding delay, feedback, and filters including lowpass, highpass, bandpass, bandstop, peaknotch, lowshelf, highshelf, and resonant and allpass. For instance, in Scene VII, *Infant,* the harpsichord's effect of delay, feedback, and high-pass filter was used to create a warmer sound quality and evocate motherhood and feminine beauty. Figure 4 provides a visual representation of the applied delay technique for the harpsichord. This involves a refined approach where output signals ranging from 1 to 10 are carefully distributed between the left and right channels. Through precise millisecond allocations, this method significantly enriches the sound's multilayered texture, resulting in a deeply immersive stereo delay experience.

As for live electronics for the voice, Saariaho utilizes parameters that define a specific voice timbre and quality and lets the soprano's voice change in real-time, into a child’s and into several men’s voices when Émilie was quoting these characters. This experience of the realtime transformations of human voice is carried into Saariaho’newest opera, *Only the Sound Remains* (2015), where, in particular, two kinds of real-time treatments for one of the two soloists in the opera, who represent two supernatural characters: a ghost and an angel.

By using pitch shifter that transposes the soprano's voice into a lower range and adding reverberation, in m.37 in Scene V, *Rencontre*, when singing: “Vous mériter, vous caresser, vous chanter, Emplira toute mon existence.” (To deserve you, to caress you, to sing you, will fill my whole existence), Émilie's voice transfers into a man's voice. It portrays a tone that is half nostalgic, half-mocking,”[1] so this dramatic changing of timbre expressive Émilie’s evoke desire and subconsciousness under the enunciation of another personality. In Scene VII, *Infant*, the soprano's original voice undergoes a mesmerizing transformation. At measure 106, her voice morphs into a male timbre when she utters: “le donne, i cavallier, L'arme, gliamori” (women, knights, weapons, love). This transformation, depicted in Figure 4, involves lowering the original pitch by 1600 cents using a pitch shifter. Subsequently, in measure 117, her voice adopts a childlike tonality as she sings: “le cortesie, l'audaci imprese io canto” (courtesy, bold adventure, I sing). Here, the pitch shifter reintroduces the singing pitch, which is elevated by 300 cents, creating a unique resonance. In tandem with these pitch variations, the envelope transformation is meticulously adjusted. This intricate interplay of electronic pitch shifting and resonance modeling gives rise to an uncanny amalgamation of breath resonances, evoking a multitude of characters in a truly fantastical manner. Later, the effect is off and the soprano adopts a whisper utterance, speaking in an intimate voice in m.126. Hence, the timbral metamorphosis and linguistic meaning sublimate through three electronic adjustments. Moreover, Saariaho uses different musical images to express Émilie’s self-internal mood and thoughts. The spoken sound, airy, breathy vocalization, and sprechstimme fit into distinctive contexts in the opera.

Apart from live electronics, Saariaho also takes advantage of pre-recorded material. A relatively long paragraph of the spoken text of the soprano Karita Mattila was pre-recorded in Scene VI and then triggered by a computer. It is a scenario where Émilie was flipping through the pages of her notes while reading the theory of fire and taking refuge through her reading. The speech is fantastical, using a clear, amplified voice in a free rhythm. Fulling exposed to the sound waves of strings and wind instruments, the pre-recorded sound was impressively distant and calm. Likewise, Karita's exhales and sighs were pre-recorded and released in Scene VII and VIII.

Multisensory sensations—which cast light on her musical world, bring Saariaho's work an encapsulation of multi-dimensional and coloristic attributes. Saariaho has also suggested how "[s]ounds, events, scents, colors, and dreams twist into each other—my world has been like this as long as I can remember."[2]

Saariaho keeps using the strong visual attachment to set *Émilie*. Unlike "Robert Lepage's dreamlike production in *L'Amour de Loin* with its thousands of twinkling LED lights stretching across the stage," Saariaho uses camera projection to show real-time interactions and images.[8] In the performance at the Lincoln Center Festival in 2012, Neal Wilkinson's set and Allen Hahn's lighting created a realistic background with a desk and chair, where "Émilie frantically scribbled her letters, work of translation, and a chaise longue where she reflected on her life."[9] The video canvases designed by Austin Switser "skillfully echoed the multiplicity of Émilie's experiences, showing mathematical equations and diagrams, a nude odalisque, her handwriting, leaping flames, and an obstetrical sonogram."[9] Undeniably, the video projection amplified the direct reaction toward an elevated but eccentric female character and aroused the piece's most primal, quintessential thoughtfulness. In Scene V, *Rencontre*, the pen is used as a prop but also as a carrier conveying sound and image. When Émilie was quickly writing a letter to Saint-Lambert on paper, the writing content "self-love, to urge, and reason, to restrain" was projected on video canvases.[1] Meanwhile, the soft, fricative sound of the pen was also amplified, blending the background of the orchestra. Therefore, audiences are initiated into not only sonic but visual interactive domains.

REFERENCES

[1] K. Saariaho and A. Maalouf, "Emilie: Opera in Nine Scenes. Full Score," *Chester Music*, pp. 97, 2013.

[2] S. P. Moisala, *Kaija Saariaho*, University of Illinois Press, 2009.

[3] J. D. Kramer, "New Temporalities in Music," *Critical Inquiry*, vol. 7, no. 3, pp. 539–556, 1981.

[4] E. Campion, "Dual Reflections: A Conversation with Kaija Saariaho and Jean-Baptiste Barrière on Music, Art, and Technology," *Computer Music Journal*, vol. 41, no. 3, pp. 9–20, 2017.

[5] T. Howell, J. Hargeaves, and M. Rofe, *Kaija Saariaho: Visions, Narratives, Dialogues*. Ashgate Publishing, 2011.

[6] K. Saariaho, "Work, Composition, What Role a Composer/Artist Should Play in Today's Society," *IRCAM Académie*, Paris, 2019.

[7] M. M. Diaz Garcia, "The Shaping of Time in Kaija Saariaho's Émilie: A Performer's Perspective," *Doctor of Musical Arts Dissertations*, 33, pp. 43, 2020.

[8] The Metropolitan Opera, "L'Amour de Loin"Accessed: Sep. 27, 2023. [Online]. Available: <https://www.metopera.org/Season/OnDemand/opera/?upc=811357018828>

[9] H. Waleson, "Love and a Life of the Mind," *The Wall Street Journal*, vol. 259, no. 20, pp. 3, 2012.

PdXR - the Evolution of Pure Data into the Metaverse

Damian Dziwis
TH Köln - University of Applied Sciences
Technische Universität Berlin
damian.dziwis@th-koeln.de

ABSTRACT

The Pure Data (Pd) visual programming language is among the most widely used real-time audio environments in computer music. Due to its open-source nature, Pd has undergone all sorts of transformations. As an embedded audio library (libpd), Pd has found its way into many programming languages, mobile apps, digital audio workstations, and other applications. Projects like WebPD, empd, Purr Data, and PdWebParty focus on bringing Pd to the web. The metaverse, as a network of immersive multiuser virtual environments, promises to become the next iteration of the Internet. With the "PdXR" project presented in this paper, Pure Data patches can be used not only in virtual, augmented and extended realities (XR), but also with others in shared web-based metaverse environments. In this way, solo and networked music performances with virtual instruments or interactive algorithms can be played in front of an online audience, virtual interactive installations can be realized, or procedural soundscapes for virtual worlds can be created. We describe the implementation, possibilities and limitations of PdXR, as well as its potential in combination with metaverse environments.

1. INTRODUCTION

1.1 The Evolution of Pure Data

Pure Data (Pd) is a Visual Programming Language (VPL) created by Miller S. Puckette [1]. Starting in the field of computer music with audio and MIDI objects, the functionality of Pd grew to include visual and other multimedia objects, and spread to other fields of application. This made it a popular environment for composers and media artists.

Since Pd is open-source software, it is possible to modify Pd [2], port it to different platforms (operating systems and hardware) [3], and integrate it outside the original functionality and application areas. The "libpd" project [4] embeds Pd as an audio library in numerous programming languages and brings it into various applications [5] such as mobile apps [6], game engines [7] or VST plug-ins for digital audio workstations [8, 9].

The Heavy compiler project (hvcc), transpiles audio and sound synthesis algorithms described in Pd source code (patches) into C/C++ code for integration into other environments [10, 11]. In this approach, patches are not interpreted directly by the Pd runtime environment, but translated into a code representation for the Heavy Lang and C/C++ Abstract Programming Interface (API). The actual Pd environment is therefore only used to describe the desired audio algorithms. Pd patches must be prepared for use with hvcc and only a subset of the Pd programming language is supported here. Using the generators built into Heavy, the resulting C/C++ code can be compiled for various operating systems and hardware architectures, frameworks and applications such as the Unity game engine, as well as into JavaScript and WebAssembly projects for use in the web.

Other projects focus exclusively on bringing Pd to the web so it can be used online in a browser. The "WebPd" project also transpiles Pd patches into JavaScript or AssemblyScript [12]. WebPd allows integrating resulting audio algorithms into other web projects but also converting interactive patches including a graphical user interface (GUI) as web applications. The "empd" [13], "Purr Data" [14] and "PdWebParty" [15] projects use libpd to bring Pd to the web. Instead of transpiling Pd patches, the Pd runtime environment using libpd, is translated into JavaScript and WebAssembly with emscripten. Pd patches are thus interpreted and executed the same way as with the Pd environment. With empd, Pd patches can be turned into web applications. Purr Data rebuilds the entire Pd programming environment as a web application, so that not only preprogrammed Pd patches can be executed, but also real-time programming can be done directly in an editor as with the usual Pd. Inspired by the Android and iOS apps PdDroidParty [16] and PdParty [6], PdWebParty lets you run Pd patches as interactive web applications in your browser. Besides audio processing, PdWebParty also supports WebMIDI and the GUI objects of a Pd patch are rendered as HTML elements.

Using the described projects, Pd patches can be put on the Internet with different representations (headless audio vs. interactive gui) and with different compatibility (transpiled patches vs. interpreted with libpd).

1.2 Music in the Metaverse

For the next iteration of the Internet, Web3, the "metaverse" is repeatedly brought into the conversation. The term "metaverse" was coined by Neal Stephenson in his dystopian science fiction novel "Snow Crash" [17]. He describes the metaverse as an immersive virtual parallel reality that blends into the physical world. Although it is partly used today as a marketing term for all kinds of extended, virtual and augmented reality (XR/VR/AR) appli-

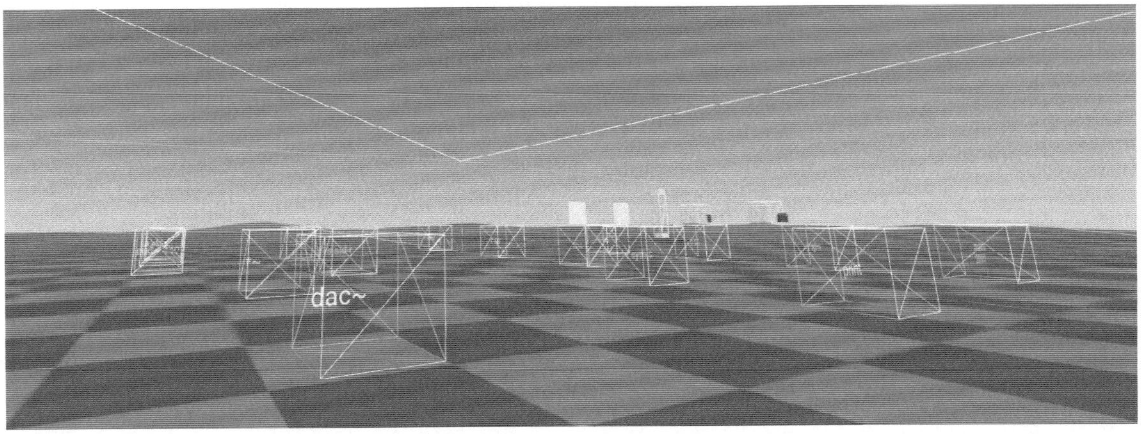

Figure 1. A screen capture of the PdXR template metaverse environment, showing how a Pd patch is represented in PdXR. While GUI objects (in the background) are rendered as interactive 3D objects, non-interactive objects in the patch are visually represented as connected boxes. This visual representation of the non-interactive parts of a Pd patch can be hidden by setting an argument flag.

cations, it is a suitable umbrella term for a specific type of virtual environments. There is a growing sentiment to define the metaverse as "an interconnected web of social, networked immersive environments in persistent multiuser platforms" [18], as a contrast to offline, single-user VR/AR applications.

However, classifying platforms as metaverse environments under such a definition is inherently fuzzy. Multiplayer games such as Fortnite are often used as examples of metaverse environments [19], but strictly speaking, they do not meet the criteria in the definition given before, as they are self-contained environments that also have a domain-specific purpose due to the included game mechanics. Higher immersion and more diverse social and interaction mechanisms can be found in social virtual worlds such as VRChat [20], Horizon Worlds [21], or the pioneering Second Life [22]. However, these are also self-contained platforms that cannot connect to each other. Thus, especially web-based virtual multiuser environments, as found in platforms like Mozilla Hubs [23] or STYLY [24], meet the definition of metaverse environments. They can be experienced through the browser on immersive VR/AR devices as well as computers or smartphones. Depending on the implementation, these applications can include a wide range of social and cultural interactions. Because they are web-based, connectivity between these environments can be enabled using existing web interfaces. As such, these web-based metaverse environments could be considered the current state of the metaverse.

As platforms for art practice, they offer new possibilities [19], specifically in a musical context [25]. As three-dimensional virtual environments that can also be experienced in XR/VR/AR, they offer special possibilities for virtual instruments [26] as well as for solo and networked music performances (NMPs) with geographically distributed musicians [27, 28]. Virtual environments not only offer numerous visual and architectural design possibilities, but also allow the integration of spatial composition techniques [29] or gamification concepts [30]. Since metaverse environments are online multiuser environments, they can also host live performances with a virtual audience. Unlike digital/virtual performances in the form of live streams with 2D audio and video, metaverse environments offer not only a more immersive presentation of the performance, but also expanded social and cultural participation between users and the environment [31]. While live performances in metaverse environments have been around for quite some time [32], they have come into wider public focus in recent years due to the restrictions imposed by the pandemic. The performances differ in the platforms used and thus in the degree of immersion and social interaction possible, as well as in the way the performance content is presented. Very common is the playback of audio to virtual avatars, having sometimes very detailed animations based on the motion capture of the performer [33]. A simpler and also common form, is 2D live streams from video streaming platforms placed as virtual screens in the environment. More advanced productions involve high-quality, but typically pre-recorded, volumetric audio and video [34]. Live streams, as well as pre-produced performances, using volumetric audio/video or motion-captured avatars, exclude performers from the virtual environment and thus do not allow interaction between the audience and performers.

1.3 Motivation & Related Work

The project "PdXR" presented here is not only intended for the integration of Pd into XR environments, but also for the integration into metaverse environments. In this way, interactive algorithms programmed in Pd can be used as virtual instruments for solo or networked music performances, or as interactive virtual installations.

By integrating Pd audio and sound synthesis algorithms through libpd or hvcc into game engines like Unity, such applications would already be possible. However, additional effort would be required to develop the virtual objects to interact with the algorithms and to extend them to shared multiuser metaverse environments. Out-of-the-box applications such as Patch World [35] enable the creation of musical instruments and environments in VR using a patching paradigm similar to Pd, and at the time of writing also multiuser possibilities are being developed. But

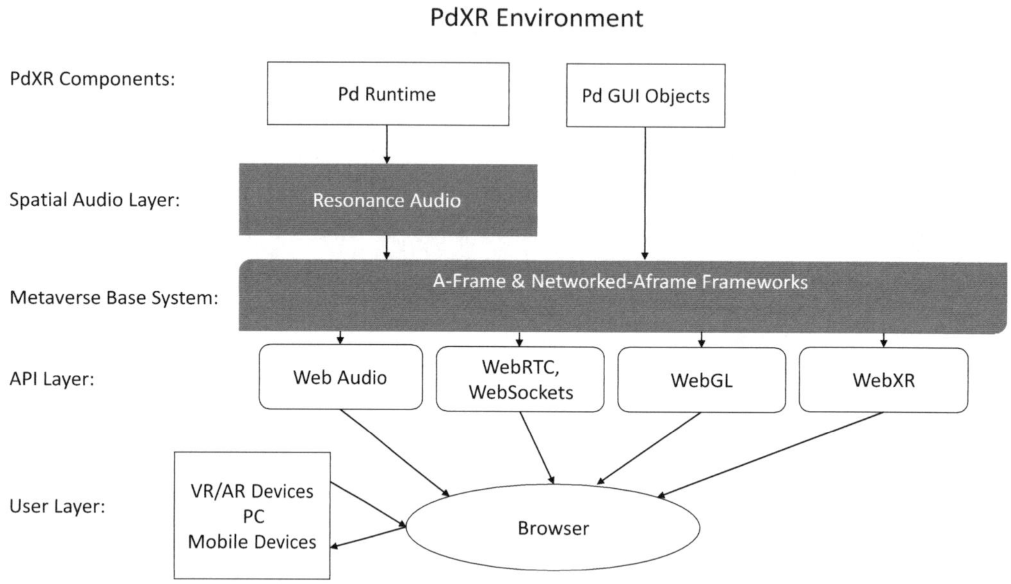

Figure 2. A diagram of the PdXR architecture, showing the involved frameworks, libraries, and programming interfaces.

although VPLs are particularly suited for programming in 3D/virtual environments, developing complex algorithms in 3D space with controllers or hand tracking can become complicated and confusing [36].

Thus, PdXR allows patches to be created in the (2D) Pd editor, and then be directly executed and used in metaverse environments (see Fig. 1). PdXR not only runs audio and sound synthesis algorithms, but also interprets GUI elements in the Pd patch as virtual interactive objects (see Fig. 3). Interactions and parameter changes by users in the metaverse environment are then shared with everyone in real-time. Thus, PdXR enables live performances and installations within metaverse environments where all users share the same experience and can interact with the Pd patches as well as with each other and the rest of the environment.

In the following, we describe the implementation of PdXR and the underlying metaverse environments and discuss the resulting use cases and artistic possibilities.

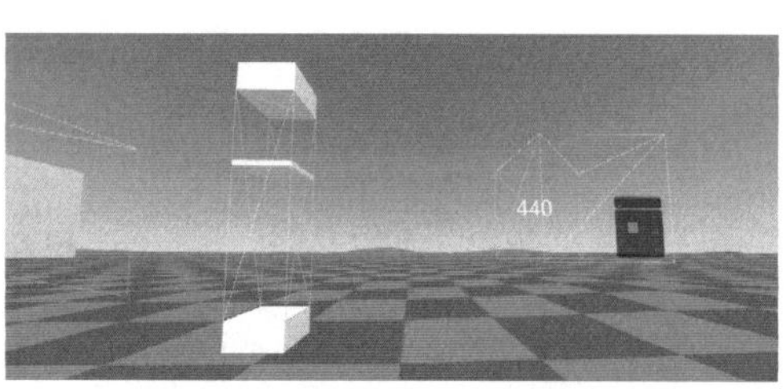

Figure 3. A screen capture of the PdXR template metaverse environment, showing how the Pd GUI objects 'vertical slider' and 'floatatom' are translated into 3D objects in PdXR.

2. IMPLEMENTATION

PdXR has been developed for web-based metaverse environments based on A-Frame [37] and Networked-Aframe [38]. These frameworks/libraries integrate numerous web-based APIs such as WebGL [39], Web Audio [40], WebXR [41], and WebRTC [42] to enable audiovisual rendering of 3D environments, presentation on VR and AR devices, and broadcasting of data and audio/video streams. To enhance the auditory rendering through room simulation, the Resonance Audio spatializer [43] has been integrated for PdXR, and the audio rendering adapted to it. The relationships between these technologies are shown schematically in Fig. 2 and described in the following.

2.1 Compatible Metaverse Environments

The A-Frame JavaScript framework abstracts the Three.js [44] library into an HTML-like syntax, enabling easy programming of virtual environments in WebGL. The WebXR integration allows for browser-based use with common VR/AR systems, including head-mounted displays (HMDs), controllers, and head and room tracking. At the same time, it also enables usage from PCs or smartphones with traditional interface devices. This allows people to use available WebXR-compliant hardware of their choice without the need to install additional software. For programming virtual environments, A-Frame provides various "components". With these components, 3D worlds can be programmed using virtual geometries and models, different materials, light and shadow, as well as multimedia content such as images, videos and sounds. The framework can be extended by developing your own JavaScript A-Frame components.

Networked-Aframe (NAF) is a library developed for A-

Figure 4. A screen capture of the PdXR template metaverse environment, showing a Pd patch with the interactive GUI objects 'bang', 'toggle', 'vertical slider', 'floatatom' and 'symbolatom'.

Frame that allows the development of shared multiuser environments. This combination is widely used, as it is also the basis of the well-known Mozilla Hubs metaverse environments. In the resulting metaverse environments, all users can move with 6 degrees of freedom (6-DoF) and interact with the environment and each other. To synchronize interactions and data, NAF provides different adapters for broadcasting via Web-RTC or WebSockets. Here, data is transferred from user to user in a peer-to-peer (P2P) network. Provided templates allow for the implementation of avatars using mentioned broadcasting technologies. The integration of the WebRTC standard also enables low-latency streaming of audio and video, allowing real-time audiovisual communication in addition to text chat. Further, the parameters of all A-Frame components, including custom ones, can be synchronized. This enables interactivity and persistence of the virtual world.
For the integration of PdXR, corresponding NAF templates are available for the virtual GUI components. Interactions with these are synchronized among all users in the environment, and since audio rendering is client-based, only the interaction needs to be transmitted instead of the audio. This enables live interaction with low latency and low bandwidth transmission between peers.

2.1.1 Spatial Audio Rendering

A particularly immersive experience of metaverse environments is possible through the use of HMDs and body tracking by VR and AR systems [45]. In addition to visual rendering, an important aspect is also the auditory representation of spatial sound through headphones. By integrating the Web Audio API, A-Frame already enables a three-dimensional sound experience through dynamic binaural rendering. Sound sources are convolved with head-related transfer functions in real-time and rendered depending on the user's head orientation and spatial position [46]. To further enhance the audiovisual coherence [47], a room simulation was also integrated for PdXR to add additional reverberation to the acoustic scene.
The Resonance Audio [43] spatializer is a suitable choice for web-based solutions [48], especially for A-Frame-based environments, as it is open-source and a port already exists here [49]. This A-Frame Resonance Audio component was extended as part of the development [50] and integrated for use with PdXR. The integration of Resonance Audio adds a room simulation to the binaural rendering that takes into account the material properties of reflective surfaces, with a ray-tracing-based model for early reflections and late reverberation filters for Ambisonics content [51].

2.2 PdXR Components

The PdXR system consists of a set of A-Frame components written in JavaScript. The core component is the "a-pdxr" component, which integrates the PdXR system into an A-Frame/NAF-based metaverse environment (see Sec. 2.1). As usual with A-Frame, the component is integrated into the virtual scene using an HTML-like tag and parameterized by attributes:

```
<a-pdxr visualize="true"
src="default.pd" position="0 1 0">
</a-pdxr>
```

The component reads and executes the Pd file specified by the user. A customized backend based on PdWebParty is used to execute the Pd patch. As described in Section 1.1, PdWebParty transpiles the PureData runtime into a WebAssembly and JavaScript-based application using libpd and emscripten. The generated backend uses the SDL2 Audio API with Web Audio API for audio rendering of the Pd patches. For PdXR this backend has been adapted for use with the Resonance Audio spatializer (see Sec. 2.1.1). The original Web Audio implementation, with a ScriptProcessorNode [52] and the resulting signal as a MediaStream, has been modified to be used as the source for a Resonance Audio Source (reseonance-audio-src) [53] of the spatializer. The resulting audio stream of the Pd patch, defined in the patch with the Pd "dac$\sim$" object, is binauralized and spatialized in the metaverse environment as a monaural sound source with Resonance Audio.
Furthermore, PdWebParty provides functions that handle the backend and parse the GUI objects of the Pd patch as HTML elements. For this purpose, an interface concept based on the message system in Pd is implemented for the communication and interaction between the HTML frontend and the Pd audio backend. Using this concept, the GUI objects in the Pd patch cannot be linked directly to

other objects in the patch, but have to communicate with sub-sequential objects by sending and receiving messages (see Fig. 5). For PdXR this parser was adapted accordingly. While the message-based interface concept has been retained, PdXR renders the Pd GUI objects not as plain HTML elements, but as A-Frame components consisting of three-dimensional interactive objects (see Fig. 4). For the implementation as a shared multiuser metaverse environment with NAF, templates for the GUI components are provided which ensure the synchronization of interactions and parameterization of objects between all users. Furthermore, the appearance of the GUI objects can be customized in the templates, so that they can be designed arbitrarily within the possibilities of A-Frame. At the time of writing, GUI components are implemented for the Pd objects bang, toggle, vertical/horizontal slider, number2, floatatom and symbolatom. While the backend is an implementation of the native Pd environment, the integration as a web application and the parsing of the patches for the front-end lead to limitations and incompatibilities. These are mainly related to the available GUI objects, data management and audio I/O. In addition to the GUI objects mentioned above, further ones are being developed. Some cannot be reasonably ported to virtual environments, e.g. patch design objects. Integration of the Web MIDI API [54], which is already integrated into PdWebParty, is also under development. Extended data management (e.g. to support external files such as samples) or I/O implementations such as microphone input or multi-channel audio are unlikely to be integrated in a useful way in the foreseeable future.

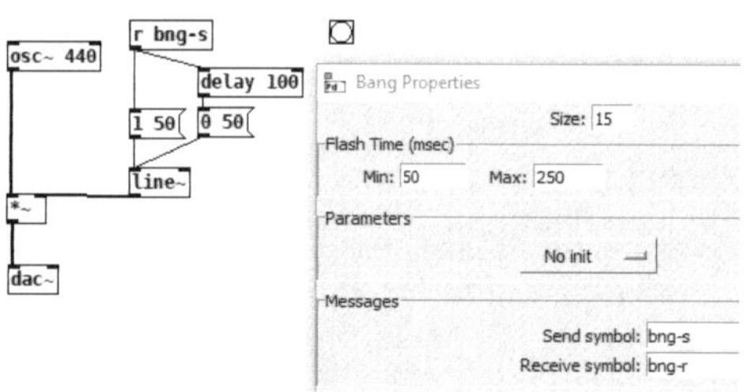

Figure 5. A screen capture from the Pd editor showing how to use the message properties of GUI objects for compatible patches for PdXR.

3. USE CASES

Pd is an open-source programming language that is not only flexible in its implementation for various purposes, but can also be used to realize almost countless and diverse results due to its ability to implement arbitrary algorithms. By extending Pd to PdXR, these algorithms can be implemented in metaverse environments in a similarly diverse manner, and also extended to include the possibilities of virtual environments: users can create a variety of virtual instruments and interaction concepts, as well as virtual worlds and art experiences, all of which would be difficult or impossible to realize in physical reality. Within the capabilities of A-Frame, artists can freely design virtual environments and also create experiences specifically for use with VR or AR systems. The multiuser capability using NAF in resulting metaverse environments allows all users in PdXR to interact with GUI objects, making it possible to play virtual instruments together or create interactive virtual installations. Live performances in metaverse environments, through immersive technologies and social participation, make it possible to experience concerts online in a way comparable to physical concerts, and artists and audiences from anywhere in the world can be connected in a cost-effective, environmentally friendly, and barrier-free manner. But it is primarily the possibilities of virtualization: such as the realization of specific artistic concepts, unique stage designs and entire virtual worlds, novel instruments and interaction possibilities; that make music-making and performance in the metaverse interesting. The potential lies not only in bringing existing works or practices online, but more importantly in realizing new kinds of art experiences and performance practices. Since the audio and visual components are represented in the 3D environment as virtual objects and spatial sound sources, spatial composition techniques such as trajectory creation and the addition of reverberation and echoes through acoustic simulation can be applied [29]. Sound sources can be selectively placed in virtual space or moved using the animation component in A-Frame. The Resonance Audio spatializer described in Sec. 2.1.1 can be used to shape the acoustic room according to the scene or artistic concept. As virtual environments are particularly present and widely used in video games, gamification concepts can be integrated into PdXR metaverse environments to develop new interactions and performance concepts [30]. With the capabilities of virtual environments, the behavior and characteristics of 3D objects can be designed and influenced at will. With the integration of physical simulation, not only can lifelike behavior of virtual instruments and objects be developed, but also artistic concepts for non-realistic physical behavior of interactive objects can be realized. The possibilities also go beyond the development of virtual instruments, installations, and solo or networked music performances. The sound resulting from the Pd algorithms can be combined with static sound sources from sound files in an A-Frame scene and used as a procedural soundscape for virtual scenes or games. The visualization of the Pd patches used in PdXR can also be disabled for this purposes. The first public presentation (Feb. 2023) of PdXR took place during a workshop for the "Pure Data coding camp" at the Academy of Media Arts Cologne (KHM) / Germany.

4. CONCLUSION & FUTURE WORK

PdXR is Pure Data's next step into the metaverse. It enables the use of Pd patches in virtual environments, even in VR or AR, and especially online with other users in shared metaverse environments. As outlined in Sec. 3, this opens up new possibilities for virtual performances and installations through immersive design, spatial composition techniques, and integration with gamification concepts. The web-based and open-source architecture allows virtual worlds and musical experiences to be easily implemented and made available to everyone. The code, as well as an online template implementation that artists can adapt for their own projects, can be found in the Github repository: `https://github.com/AudioGroupCologne/PdXR`

PdXR is under constant development to extend the range of available Pd objects and to improve compatibility as well as usability with different browsers and VR/AR devices. Limitations regarding the compatibility of Pd patches are described in Sec. 2.2, and since PdXR is browser-based, compatibility may also vary between browsers. In particular security mechanisms, such as disabling automatic playback of sound, or local settings may present additional hurdles. Through extensive testing and additional development, high compatibility with Mozilla Firefox and Chromium-based browsers (e.g. Google Chrome or Microsoft Edge) has been achieved.
PdXR is part of the Orchestra toolbox [55], which allows music experiences created with PdXR to be combined with other components for live coding [56] or volumetric audio and video streaming [57] in metaverse environments.

Acknowledgments

I would like to thank Christoph Pörschmann (TH Köln) for his guidance and support in the research and writing of this paper. And Zack Lee for the PdWebParty project on which the code of PdXR is based.

5. REFERENCES

[1] M. Puckette, "Pure Data : another integrated computer music environment," in *second intercollege computer music concerts*, 1997, pp. 37–41.

[2] I. I. Bukvic, A. Gräf, and J. Wilkes, "Meet the Cat : Pd-L2Ork and its New Cross-Platform Version " Purr Data "," in *Linux Audio Conference 2017*, 2017, pp. 1 – 8.

[3] I. I. Bukvic, "Pd-L2Ork Raspberry Pi Toolkit as a Comprehensive Arduino Alternative in K-12 and Production Scenarios," in *Proceedings of the International Conference on New Interfaces for Musical Expression*, 2014, pp. 163–166.

[4] P. Brinkmann, C. Mccormick, P. Kirn, M. Roth, and R. Lawler, "Embedding Pure Data with libpd," *Proceeding of the Fourth International Pure Data Convention*, pp. 291–301, 2011.

[5] P. Brinkmann, D. Wilcox, R. Eakin, and R. Alexander, "libpd : Past , Present , and Future of Embedding Pure Data," in *PdCon2016~*, 2016, pp. 1 – 6.

[6] D. Wilcox, "PdParty : An iOS Computer Music Platform using libpd," in *PdCon2016~*, 2016, pp. 1 – 7.

[7] L. J. Paul, "Using pure data as a game audio engine," in *139th Audio Engineering Society International Convention, AES 2015*, 2015, pp. 1 – 5.

[8] L. Cordiviola, PDVst. https://git.nubegris.com.ar/lucarda/pdvst-0.52. Accessed: 2023-05-04.

[9] T. Schoen, PlugData. https://plugdata.org/. Accessed: 2023-05-04.

[10] Wasted-Audio, Heavy Compiler. https://github.com/Wasted-Audio/hvcc. Accessed: 2023-05-04.

[11] giuliomoro, Heavy Compiler. https://github.com/giuliomoro/hvcc/. Accessed: 2023-05-04.

[12] S. Piquemal, WebPd. https://github.com/sebpiq/WebPd. Accessed: 2023-05-04.

[13] C. Heiland-Allen, empd. https://mathr.co.uk/empd/. Accessed: 2023-05-04.

[14] Z. Lee, Purr Data (Web). https://github.com/cuinjune/purr-data. Accessed: 2023-05-04.

[15] Z. Lee, PdWebParty. https://github.com/cuinjune/PdWebParty. Accessed: 2023-05-04.

[16] C. McCormick, PdDroidParty. https://droidparty.net/. Accessed: 2023-05-04.

[17] S. Neal, *Snow Crash*. New York: Bantam Books, 1992.

[18] S. Mystakidis, "Metaverse," *Encyclopedia*, vol. 2, no. 1, pp. 486–497, 2022. [Online]. Available: https://doi.org/10.3390/encyclopedia2010031

[19] L.-H. Lee, Z. Lin, R. Hu, Z. Gong, A. Kumar, T. Li, S. Li, and P. Hui, "When Creators Meet the Metaverse: A Survey on Computational Arts," *ACM Computing Surveys*, vol. 37, no. 4, p. 36, apr 2021. [Online]. Available: https://doi.org/10.48550/arXiv.2111.13486

[20] VRChat. https://hello.vrchat.com/. Accessed: 2023-02-06.

[21] Meta, Horizon Worlds. https://www.meta.com/horizon-worlds/. Accessed: 2023-02-06.

[22] Second Life. https://secondlife.com/. Accessed: 2023-02-06.

[23] Mozilla Hubs. https://hubs.mozilla.com/. Accessed: 2023-02-06.

[24] STYLY. https://gallery.styly.cc/. Accessed: 2023-02-06.

[25] L. Turchet, "Musical Metaverse: vision, opportunities, and challenges," *Personal and Ubiquitous Computing*, 2023. [Online]. Available: https://doi.org/10.1007/s00779-023-01708-1

[26] L. Turchet, R. Hamilton, and A. Camci, "Music in Extended Realities," *IEEE Access*, vol. 9, pp. 15 810–15 832, 2021. [Online]. Available: https://doi.org/10.1109/ACCESS.2021.3052931

[27] P. Oliveros, S. Weaver, M. Dresser, J. Pitcher, J. Braasch, and C. Chafe, "Telematic music: Six perspectives," *Leonardo Music Journal*, vol. 19, pp. 95–96, 2009. [Online]. Available: https://doi.org/10.1162/lmj.2009.19.95

[28] B. Loveridge, "Networked Music Performance in Virtual Reality: Current Perspectives," *Journal of Network Music and Arts*, vol. 2, no. 1, p. 2, 2020. [Online]. Available: https://commons.library.stonybrook.edu/jonma/vol2/iss1/2

[29] M. A. Baalman, "Spatial composition techniques and sound spatialisation technologies," *Organised Sound*, vol. 15, no. 3, pp. 209–218, 2010. [Online]. Available: https://doi.org/10.1017/S1355771810000245

[30] M. Ciciliani, "Virtual 3D environments as composition and performance spaces," *Journal of New Music Research*, vol. 49, no. 1, pp. 104–113, jan 2020. [Online]. Available: https://doi.org/10.1080/09298215.2019.1703013

[31] S. M. Park and Y. G. Kim, "A Metaverse: Taxonomy, Components, Applications, and Open Challenges," *IEEE Access*, vol. 10, pp. 4209–4251, 2022. [Online]. Available: https://doi.org/10.1109/ACCESS.2021.3140175

[32] R. Elen, "Music in the Metaverse," *Journal of the Audio Engineering Society*, April 2008.

[33] Travis Scott and Fortnite Present: Astronomical (Full Event Video). https://www.youtube.com/watch?v=wYeFAlVC8qU. Accessed: 2023-02-06.

[34] VRROOM, Oxymore 2 - Overview. https://vimeo.com/767098450/6fcf797c5a. Accessed: 2023-02-06.

[35] PatchXR, Patch World. https://patchxr.com/. Accessed: 2023-05-12.

[36] R. Castelo-Branco, A. Leitão, and G. Santos, "Immersive Algorithmic Design Live Coding in Virtual Reality," *Proceedings of the International Conference on Education and Research in Computer Aided Architectural Design in Europe*, vol. 2, no. September, pp. 455–464, 2019.

[37] A-Frame. https://aframe.io. Accessed: 2023-02-06.

[38] Networked-Aframe. https://github.com/networked-aframe. Accessed: 2023-02-06.

[39] Khronos, WebGL. https://www.khronos.org/webgl/. Accessed: 2023-02-06.

[40] W3C, Web Audio. https://www.w3.org/TR/webaudio/. Accessed: 2023-02-06.

[41] W3C, WebXR. https://immersiveweb.dev/. Accessed: 2023-02-06.

[42] Google Developer, WebRTC. https://webrtc.org/. Accessed: 2023-02-06.

[43] Resonance Audio. https://resonance-audio.github.io/resonance-audio/. Accessed: 2023-02-06.

[44] Three.js. https://www.khronos.org/webgl/. Accessed: 2023-02-06.

[45] M. Slater, B. Lotto, M. M. Arnold, and M. V. Sanchez-Vives, "How we experience immersive virtual environments: The concept of presence and its measurement," *Anuario de Psicologia*, vol. 40, no. 2, pp. 193–210, 2009.

[46] H. Møller, "Fundamentals of binaural technology," *Applied Acoustics*, vol. 36, no. 3-4, pp. 171–218, 1992. [Online]. Available: https://doi.org/10.1016/0003-682X(92)90046-U

[47] S. Werner, F. Klein, T. Mayenfels, and K. Brandenburg, "A summary on acoustic room divergence and its effect on externalization of auditory events," in *8th International Conference on Quality of Multimedia Experience (QoMEX)*. IEEE, 2016, pp. 1–6. [Online]. Available: https://doi.org/10.1109/QoMEX.2016.7498973

[48] A. McArthur, C. V. Tonder, L. Gaston-Bird, and A. Knight-Hill, "A survey of 3D audio through the browser: Practitioner perspectives," in *2021 Immersive and 3D Audio: From Architecture to Automotive, I3DA 2021*. Institute of Electrical and Electronics Engineers Inc., 2021. [Online]. Available: https://doi.org/10.1109/I3DA48870.2021.9610839

[49] M. Kungla, A-Frame Resonance Audio. https://github.com/mkungla/aframe-resonance-audio-component/. Accessed: 2023-02-06.

[50] D. Dziwis, A-Frame Resonance Audio. https://github.com/AudioGroupCologne/aframe-resonance-audio-component. Accessed: 2023-02-06.

[51] Resonance Audio, Web SDK Source Code. https://github.com/resonance-audio/resonance-audio-web-sdk/tree/master/src. Accessed: 2023-02-06.

[52] Mozilla, Web Audio ScriptProcessorNode. https://developer.mozilla.org/en-US/docs/Web/API/ScriptProcessorNode. Accessed: 2023-02-15.

[53] M. Kungla, Resonance Audio Source. https://github.com/mkungla/aframe-resonance-audio-component/blob/main/src/resonance-audio-src.js. Accessed: 2023-02-21.

[54] W3C, Web MIDI API. https://www.w3.org/TR/webmidi/. Accessed: 2023-02-15.

[55] D. Dziwis, H. von Coler, and C. Pörschmann, "Orchestra: a Toolbox for Live Music Performances in a Web-Based Metaverse," *Journal of the Audio Engineering Society*, pp. 1–11, 2023, (accepted for publication).

[56] D. Dziwis, "VERSNIZ - Audiovisual Worldbuilding through Live Coding as a Performance Practice in the Metaverse," in *the 16th International Symposium on Computer Music Multidisciplinary Research (CMMR)*, 2023, pp. 1 – 12, (accepted for publication).

[57] D. Dziwis and H. von Coler, "The Entanglement – Volumetric Music Performances in a Virtual Metaverse Environment," *Journal of Network Music and Arts*, vol. 5, no. 1, pp. 1–12, 2023.

ModPhy: System Design for Real-time Modular Sound Synthesis with Physically-Modeled Objects

Zehao Wang
UC San Diego
zehaowang@ucsd.edu

Han Zhang
UC San Diego
haz074@ucsd.edu

Yifan Guo
UC San Diego
yig020@ucsd.edu

ABSTRACT

We introduce ModPhy, a system aiming for real-time modular sound synthesis with physically-modeled objects realized as Max/MSP and Pure Data externals. With the accelerated implementation of the finite-difference time-domain simulation for partial-differential-equation-based physical models and a hierarchical design of control parameters, these physically-modeled objects can be efficiently incorporated with an abstract sound synthesis paradigm for flexible sound design while keeping their real-world physical meaning. The unity of oscillators and audio effects and the advantages of those physical models' controllability provide a unified way for sound design and music creation and they are also in line with the philosophy of some contemporary composition schools. With the implemented Max/MSP and Pure Data objects, a number of potential music applications are discussed. We believe such a system will become a powerful toolkit for modern composers and sound artists.

1. INTRODUCTION

Real-time sound synthesis has become an indispensable requirement in contemporary music production, empowering musicians to create and manipulate sounds instantaneously during live performances. Abstract sound synthesis techniques, such as frequency modulation (FM)[1], offer users the ability to manipulate a predefined set of parameters that abstractly define how sounds are shaped for their desired sonic. In addition to abstract synthesis techniques, physical models have revolutionized sound synthesis by simulating the behavior of acoustic instruments. This approach provides a different avenue for creating expressive sounds. Recent advancements in both theoretical understanding and algorithm design[2, 3, 4, 5, 6] have significantly accelerated sound synthesis based on numerical solutions of partial differential equations (PDEs), which have made sound synthesis based on such methods much better and faster than ever before.

One notable distinction between PDE-based models and other synthesis techniques is controlling sound by describing the physical characteristics beforehand or during the generation process, rather than relying solely on post-processing. However, a significant challenge in physical modeling sound synthesis relates to the control parameters used for these models. Typically, physical models incorporate tens of raw parameters, while still needing to adhere to stability constraints. This poses a difficulty in effectively utilizing a limited set of parameter combinations within extensive feasible domains to manipulate the resulting sound which is an important aspect of sound synthesis.

Exploring the integration of physical models and abstract sound synthesis for sound design is a significant topic of interest. However, one major challenge lies in the disparity between the raw parameters used in physical synthesis and the common dimensions utilized in sound design. While it is important to preserve the dimensions of control parameters, it is equally crucial to consider both the controllability and representativeness of the resulting sound. By adopting a modular system that combines physical models with the abstract synthesis paradigm, physically-modeled objects can function as modules, interacting with other objects connected through different means that describe the sound. Such a modular way enables users to create unique sonic architectures by combining and connecting various modules, such as oscillators, filters, and envelopes, in diverse configurations, and the advantages of different techniques can be harnessed, providing a flexible and expressive platform for sound designers: physical models will not be limited to only "mimicking" existing musical instruments , they can also be treated as relatively complex processes or oscillations with meaningful physical properties to be incorporated into the entire sound design workflow, especially in modular computer music systems like Max/MSP (Max) and Pure Data (Pd).

In this paper, we introduce ModPhy, a system for real-time modular sound synthesis with physically-modeled objects in Max/Pd. We first present the underlying physics of modeled systems and the fast implementation approach of finite-difference time-domain (FDTD) methods, a particular method for numerical simulation of PDEs. Then we briefly introduce our system design of ModPhy, including the hierarchy of control parameters, and the interaction between modules. Finally, we discuss our inspiration from contemporary composers and potential music applications of ModPhy.

2. TECHNICAL SETUP

2.1 Modeling vibrations using PDEs

The underlying physics of vibrating bodies can be modeled by partial differential equations, especially the wave equation which is widely used in musical acoustics[7]. In this

1-D	Mass-spring systems	$-\omega^2\mathbf{1}$
	Strings	$c^2\frac{\partial^2}{\partial x^2}$
	Tubes	$c^2\frac{1}{S(x)}\frac{\partial}{\partial x}\left(S(x)\frac{\partial}{\partial x}\right)$
	Bars	$-\kappa^2\frac{\partial^4}{\partial x^4}$
2-D	Membranes	$c^2\Delta$
	Plates	$-\kappa^2\Delta\Delta$

Table 1: $\mathcal{L}$ for different vibrating objects, where $\mathbf{1}$ is the identity operator and $\Delta = \frac{\partial^2}{\partial x^2} + \frac{\partial^2}{\partial y^2}$ is the Laplacian operator; $S(x)$ is the cross-sectional area of the tube at position x; ω, c, κ are scaled parameters derived from physical parameters mentioned in the last tier mentioned in Sec 3.2.

paper, we mainly consider several different types of vibrating objects shown in Table 1, whose equations share the following general form of second-order systems in time:

$$\frac{\partial^2 u}{\partial t^2} = \mathcal{L}u + f, \tag{1}$$

where u denotes the displacement (like strings) or pressure (like tubes) at each position of the object, $\mathcal{L}$ is a differential operator corresponding to the object's vibration mechanism which has both spatial and temporal differential operators, and f is an external force like excitation for the use of oscillators/instruments or an input waveform for the use of audio effects like reverb. For the sake of brevity, here we only show these systems in their simplest form, in our implementation, we also consider models like systems with loss [1], stiff strings, or nonlinear plate models, where extra computational costs are required.

2.2 Simulating vibrations by FDTD methods

FDTD methods have a long history in scientific computing[9] and there are a large number of papers applying these methods for sound synthesis[8]. The basic idea is to discretize both temporal and spatial domains to grids u_l^n on a given region [2] where n denotes the time step and l denotes the spatial coordinate , and then derive the corresponding update rules using difference operators as approximations for differential operators. For the discretization of temporal domain, $\frac{\partial^2 u}{\partial t^2}$ in Eq. (1) is approximated by $\left.\frac{\partial^2 u}{\partial t^2}\right|_{t=nk} \approx \frac{u^{n+1}-2u^n+u^{n-1}}{k^2}$, i.e., the forward Euler method, where k is the equally spaced time interval. For other temporal/spatial differential operators in $\mathcal{L}$, we can also apply the forward Euler method or backward/central Euler method for approximation which are well established in various textbooks[9, 8]. Thus, the numerical scheme of Eq. (1) should have the following matrix form

$$\hat{\mathbf{u}}^{n+1} = \mathbf{B}\hat{\mathbf{u}}^n + \mathbf{C}\hat{\mathbf{u}}^{n-1} + \mathbf{f}^n, \tag{2}$$

where $\mathbf{B}$ and $\mathbf{C}$ are sparse matrices derived from the discrete operators and boundary conditions, and $\mathbf{f}^n$ denotes a function of discretized external force and extra terms which may include nonlinearities. Note that some external forces may depend on u or its derivatives, like $f(t) = \delta(x-x_i)F(t)\phi\left(\frac{\partial u}{\partial t}(x_i) - v(t)\right)$ for bow-string interaction where δ is the Dirac function, F and v is the force and velocity of the bowing motion, and ϕ is some friction parameter. In this paper, implementations of several simple external forces or interactions like raised cosine, bow/hammer-string interaction, mallet/stick excitation are provided [3].

To guarantee the numerical stability of FDTD-based simulation, each system needs to satisfy some stability conditions derived from frequency-domain analysis or von Neumann analysis[8]. Recent studies about invariant energy quadratization and scalar auxiliary variable methods also provide another approach to derive the numerical scheme of nonlinear systems like nonlinear string vibrations and nonlinear plate vibrations[2] with relatively weak requirements for stability conditions compared to the previous simple FDTD schemes. In general, the stability condition can be given as $h \geq \psi(k;\theta)$, where h is the equally-spaced spatial interval for each axis and $\psi(k)$ is a monotonic increasing function w.r.t. k given θ which is the parameter set of the corresponding PDE.

2.3 Variable conversion for other synthesis approaches

In order to interact with other synthesis approaches like digital waveguide methods (DWG)[10], variable conversion might be required. Considering the equivalence between DWG and FDTD methods[11], the K/W converter between DWG's wave variables (u^+, u^-) and FDTD's Kirchhoff variables (u) can thus be given as follows[10],

$$\begin{bmatrix} W^+ \\ z^{-1}W \end{bmatrix} = \begin{bmatrix} 1 & -z^{-2} \\ 1 & (1-z^{-2}) \end{bmatrix} \begin{bmatrix} z^{-1}K \\ W^- \end{bmatrix}, \tag{3}$$

where K is the Kirchhoff variable in FDTD, and $W = W^+ + W^-$ is the wave variable in DWG. This converter can be implemented as a standalone object in Max and Pd to connect objects using these two types of variables in real-time, which will be discussed in Sec 3.3 and Sec 3.4.

2.4 Fast implementation for real-time synthesis

To implement these simulations as Max or Pd externals running on personal computers, efficient implementation approaches on CPUs are needed. Webb and Bilbao[3] show the limits of several systems' real-time simulation mentioned in Sec 2.1, and (multi-thread) single instruction, multiple data (SIMD) parallelization using instructions like advanced vector extensions (AVX) has the best performance . The basic idea of SIMD parallelization is to rewrite/unroll the matrix-form update rules (2) to individual update rules for each grid point in a matrix-free way, and then perform the operations for a consecutive series of grid points in parallel using SIMD instructions. Using these acceleration strategies, Wang et al.[5] shows that only 0.025 seconds are needed to run a Pd external for a 1-second linear plate sound synthesis at 44.1Khz; with fast algorithms and implementations for sparse linear system solution[4], a 1-second 44.1kHz simulation single nonlinear plate with a

[1] For example, in the form of $\frac{\partial}{\partial t}$ (frequency-independent) or $\Delta\frac{\partial}{\partial t}$ (frequency-dependent)[7, 8]. In most cases of sound synthesis, the order of temporal differential operators in $\mathcal{L}$ is not greater than 2.

[2] In this paper, we only consider rectangular regions for 2-D systems.

[3] Note that some excitation mechanisms are coupled with the systems, which cannot be explicitly added as extra terms, but can be implemented as a separate coupled model which is beyond the scope of this paper.

discretization of 13×27 only takes 0.15 seconds[6]. Those results show the possibility to run a number of physically-modeled objects simultaneously in a modular system.

3. SYSTEM DESIGN

3.1 Oscillator as reverberator, reverberator as oscillator: to think physical

The presented synthesis approach illustrates one crucial insight: the oscillator and the reverberator or other audio effects could be combined into a single entity. Essentially, both are responses of systems with respective inputs: a short impulse results in the creation of an acoustic sound, while a more extended waveform induces a wet output with the reverb of the object. Thanks to this principle, the control parameters are no longer limited by their conservative paradigm. Parameters for these two objects thus become interchangeable, which provides the creative works with more flexibility. Most importantly, due to the nature of physical models, one can easily imagine the real-time counterparts of the modeled objects. It could inspire sound design by putting a sound source into a physical object and controlling the reverb with its physical parameters, or reversely synthesizing a sound with terms of reverberation like decay time and room size. Not limited to mimicking real-world objects, the capability of manipulating the identity to provide a wide sounding scale allows artists to find the border between the abstract and concrete form of sound perception and provoke communication between the real and virtual. Moreover, the unity of these two types of objects also benefits the design of ModPhy to be more efficient and controllable, which could also lead to a unified paradigm for music creation and sound design[12].

3.2 Hierarchical design of control parameters

Here we briefly discuss our design of control parameters. We design a hierarchy of control parameters from the raw physical parameters at the bottom to upper-level parameters that are more semantically connected to the way that people understand a sound and its vibration. In the following three-tier structure:

(1) materials, vibration parameters, sound descriptors

(2) stiffness, flexural rigidity, ...

(3) Young's modulus, density, thickness, size, ...

we use only the bottom layer to implement the numerical calculation. The inputs of this most fundamental object are specifications and dimensions that are directly utilized in the physical model, such as Young's modulus, material density, size, etc. However, these parameters are not practically convenient to use, so we added two more layers on top of it. The layer in the middle comprises some parameters to describe the material of the sounding object, such as stiffness and flexural rigidity. This layer serves as a translator from the physical quantities to a level of interpretation that could be connected to the sound with the imagination of the object. The highest-level parameters have the closest association with real-world analogs. In this layer, users can manipulate the parameters of the chosen materials or parameters that describe the process of wave propagation on the object. The formation of the propagation involves multiple factors including the material itself and the boundary condition, therefore it is accomplished by adjusting the two lower layers. The last set of parameters in this layer is the sound descriptors. These descriptors are not as quantified as the timbre descriptors but are qualitatively aligned with the sound quality. This design makes the whole system scalable and also opens up opportunities for customization according to the users' control demands.

3.3 As Max or Pd objects

The hierarchical paradigm with real-time inputs and outputs will be natural for Max MSP and Pd users, and the implementation can also benefit from the design. In PureData, for instance, the bottom layer is realized as the parameters of a DSP object which contains all the computations according to update rules described in Sec 2.2 and can be excited by indicator messages like a bang or DSP objects of excitation or outputs from other synthesis modules. Those DSP objects (both vibrating objects and excitation mechanisms) are FDTD simulations of systems in Sec 2.1 which are implemented with acceleration strategies presented in Sec 2.4, and they support at most 8-channel outputs from single/scanned positions. An example of a bowed string with the external force mentioned in Sec 2.2 can be realized by inserting one outlet of string~ at a given bowing position to a moving-difference high-pass filter divided by the temporal interval for velocity approximation, then inserting its outlet to bow~'s inlet, finally inserting bow~'s outlet to string~'s inlet. The rest of ModPhy is simply realized as Pd abstractions with inputs and outputs.

To interact with other modules, especially DWG-based synthesis modules, DSP objects for variable conversion like the K/W converter described in Sec 2.3 are also required.

3.4 Advantages of modularization

In a modular system, particularly in realizations using Max MSP or Pd, the flexibility to connect various elements together is readily available. This allows for not only the simulation of musical instruments using pre-built backbone blocks representing vibrating objects but also experimentation with modules employing different synthesis methodologies to observe the resulting sound. Furthermore, these physically-modeled objects can be utilized for cross-synthesis with other objects or input waveforms. It is even possible to introduce feedback from the cross-synthesized sounds back into the input of the physically-modeled objects. However, it is important to exercise caution as there is a risk of numerical instabilities that may arise when implementing such feedback loops. Being mindful of these potential instabilities is crucial to ensure the stability and reliability of the overall system.

4. MUSIC INSPIRATIONS AND APPLICATIONS

From the early 20th century, an increasing number of Western composers embarked on a quest to explore and expand the potential of musical expression through scientific and technological means. Many of their endeavors involved investigating the physical properties of sounds or utilizing the acoustic attributes of sound to give auditory form to non-musical concepts. To provide a clearer demonstration of the acoustic-composition trajectory throughout the 20th century, a selection of notable instances is presented here.

Several composers contributed to the development of this path: Edgar Varèse, a pioneer in the realm of sound, created novel sounds and performance forms while emancipating them from old restrictions by using unusual instruments, non-musical objects, or electronic sounds; Giacinto Scelsi aimed to perceive the third dimension of sound, namely its depth, through the repetitive playing of a single note on the piano; Pierre Schaeffer, drawing inspiration from the study of subjective characteristics of natural sound, developed a quantitative classification system for its features, employed innovatively both gramophone and magnetic recordings of subjective sounds to establish a novel compositional methodology; Iannis Xenakis sonified formulas and concepts from mathematics, statistics, and physics into musical events[13]; spectral composers (e.g. Gérard Grisey, Jonathan Harvey, Tristan Murail, and Julian Anderson), by valuing the inherent nature and properties of sound as a prominent organizing principle for music, sought to take advantage of emerging technologies in order to expand their compositional toolkit.

Along the path of new sound exploration, numerous compelling ideas and remarkable compositions have emerged. Nevertheless, it is crucial to acknowledge the challenges that have arisen during this nearly century-long exploration. When it comes to unraveling the higher dimensions of a single audible sound, identifying new potentials seems impossible. Consequently, it has become increasingly rare to encounter compositions in recent years that are solely dedicated to the exploration of new sounds, let alone introducing novel sound control methods. When it comes to the realm of sound design, it is indeed challenging to see additional approaches for the real-time integration of acoustic and electronic sound, apart from manipulating acoustic sound through electronic devices or resonating physical objects via speakers. Furthermore, relatively few works effectively embody non-musical concepts through sound. While works like Stockhausen's *Gruppen* and Xenakis' *Metastasis* are renowned for their musical excellence, conveying the intended ideas through sound alone may not always be so intuitive - who can actually perceive them? Many composers encounter challenges in successfully sonifying non-musical concepts, resulting from limitations in musical practice, technology, or a lack of understanding regarding the conversion of these concepts into musical practice. These limitations can hinder the process of effective sonification, leading to potential shortcomings in expressing non-musical ideas through sound.

One important thing to note is that the notion of a shared sonic experience holds significant importance for both composers and audiences. Within the Western music canon, countless examples demonstrate the effectiveness of composing in relation to the common sonic experience. Conversely, deliberately challenging and defying that experience can also be impactful, as evidenced by notable instances such as the premiere of Igor Stravinsky's *The Rite of Spring* and John Cage's *4'33"*. In the current musical landscape, the potential for surprise only through the introduction of "new sound" has diminished. The exploration of new sound has become a commonplace practice in music creation, which can sometimes result in clichéd outcomes.

Therefore, adopting an approach that incorporates elements of the common or familiar sonic experience but also plays with and deviates from it can be more intriguing and persuasive as a compositional strategy. Working with ModPhy while composing or sound designing holds considerable potential in addressing longstanding issues through its distinctive insight into reconstructing sound, offering promising solutions to historical challenges in the field. ModPhy provides users with a pathway to interact with sound by manipulating the attributes of a sounding object, including material, shape, size, and more. By assuming the role of a designer of the sounding process, users can exercise control over the sound and bring their sonic ideas to fruition in a swift and efficient manner. ModPhy serves as an empowering tool, enabling users to transform their imaginative concepts in the aspect of acoustic instrument design into tangible sonic realities. When employing ModPhy, one can begin by mimicking the sound of a familiar instrument. By subtly altering factors such as its size, material, or various excitation and parameter settings, users may be able to achieve a comprehensive range of sonic characteristics within the category. When ModPhy is employed in a performance alongside acoustic instruments, it can serve as an extension of their sound, effectively transforming them into a truly innovative and powerful hyper-instrument. By integrating ModPhy's capabilities of modeling real-world physical objects, new sonic dimensions and possibilities emerge. Let's imagine a potential scenario: a percussionist, adorned with motion sensors, is playing a tremolo on a tam-tam while traversing its surface. Concurrently, the physically modeled bowing tam-tam sound produced by ModPhy comes into play. The motion sensors track the percussionist's hand positions and manipulate the excitation points, materials, and thickness of the modeled sound. The fusion of this composite auditory experience with the visual spectacle on stage creates a sonic realm that exists between reality and dream. ModPhy enhances and expands the expressive and sonic potential of the acoustic instruments, resulting in a symbiotic relationship where they collectively form a compelling and versatile hyper-instrument. In addition, taking it to a surrealistic level, users can transcend the limitations of physical reality and explore even more extraordinary possibilities. ModPhy enables users to explore their sonic imaginations with physical perspective, allowing for the creation of otherworldly and dynamically evolving soundscapes that transcend the limitations of traditional acoustic instruments, importantly, while still retaining a connection to the common sonic experience.

5. CONCLUSIONS AND DISCUSSION

In this paper, we present our design of the real-time modular sound synthesis system, ModPhy. With the implementation of physically-modeled objects and a properly designed hierarchy of control parameters, it is possible now to bring their advantages to other sound synthesis techniques in a modular form. Future directions may include analyzing feasible regions of control parameters, encapsulating the acceleration of FDTD schemes as a C/C++ library, and providing more music and sound examples.

6. REFERENCES

[1] J. M. Chowning, "The synthesis of complex audio spectra by means of frequency modulation," *Journal of the audio engineering society*, vol. 21, no. 7, pp. 526–534, 1973.

[2] S. Bilbao, M. Ducceschi, and F. Zama, "Explicit exactly energy-conserving methods for Hamiltonian systems," *Journal of Computational Physics*, vol. 472, p. 111697, 2023.

[3] C. J. Webb and S. Bilbao, "On the limits of real-time physical modelling synthesis with a modular environment," in *Proceedings of the international conference on digital audio effects*, vol. 65, 2015.

[4] Z. Wang and M. Puckette, "A Fast Algorithm for the Inversion of the Biharmonic in Plate Dynamics Applications," in *Proceedings of the 5th Stockholm Music Acoustic Conference*, Stockholm, Sweden, June 2023.

[5] Z. Wang, M. Puckette, T. Erbe, and S. Bilbao, "Real-Time Implementation of the Kirchhoff Plate Equation using Finite-Difference Time-Domain Methods on CPU," *2023 Sound and Music Computing Conference (SMC)*, 2023.

[6] S. Bilbao, C. Webb, Z. Wang, and M. Ducceschi, "Real-Time Gong Synthesis," *submitted to DAFx*, 2023.

[7] A. Chaigne and J. Kergomard, *Acoustics of musical instruments*. Springer, 2016.

[8] S. Bilbao, *Numerical sound synthesis: finite difference schemes and simulation in musical acoustics*. John Wiley & Sons, 2009.

[9] K. S. Kunz and R. J. Luebbers, *The finite difference time domain method for electromagnetics*. CRC press, 1993.

[10] M. Karjalainen and C. Erkut, "Digital waveguides versus finite difference structures: Equivalence and mixed modeling," *EURASIP Journal on Advances in Signal Processing*, vol. 2004, no. 7, pp. 1–12, 2004.

[11] J. O. Smith III, "On the equivalence of the digital waveguide and finite difference time domain schemes," *arXiv preprint physics/0407032*, 2004.

[12] C. Chafe, "Case studies of physical models in music composition," in *Proceedings of the 18th international congress on acoustics*, 2004.

[13] E. Childs, "ACHORRIPSIS: A SONIFICATION OF PROBABILITY DISTRIBUTIONS," 2002.

MadLib: Developing performative skills with live electronics through educational compositions

Louis Pino
TaPIR Lab
ljpino95@gmail.com

Jonny Smith
TaPIR Lab
jonny.smith@alum.utoronto.ca

Timothy Roth
TaPIR Lab
timothy.roth@mail.utoronto.ca

ABSTRACT

The proliferation of the visual programming language Max has yielded a number of educational resources for those looking to use the language. Max course curricula often revolve around projects in composition or sound design, but rarely focus on developing the skills that a performer would need to perform with a Max patch. This study explores the musical output and educational potential of the composition MadLib (2021) by Louis Pino, for solo performer and Max patch. MadLib is specifically designed to engage fundamental skills to help performers think about the application of technological concepts from an artistic, rather than a task-oriented, perspective.

This paper incorporates the work into a creative, experiential study involving eight participants from the Technology and Performance Integration Research (TaPIR) Lab at the University of Toronto. Participants performed and recorded their own interpretations of MadLib, participated in interviews, and completed surveys describing their preparation process and learning outcomes.

Most participants described positive learning outcomes from this experience, indicating that projects such as MadLib could be beneficial for those looking to develop performative skills with Max. Further performer-oriented educational resources for Max could help to both encourage performances of new works and further disseminate existing works for live electronics.

1. INTRODUCTION

Max is a well-established programming language and interface, adopted internationally by composers to create electroacoustic music [1]. Max courses offered at universities often adopt a compositional, project-based approach, asking students to build material in creative and unique ways. Although these projects normally focus on outcomes related to composition or sound design, the practice of live performance with interactive electronics generally is less explored. In these curricula, performers do not get the opportunity to develop and integrate the concepts required to musically interact with the technology they are building.

This paper presents a study of the musical and educational potential of *MadLib* (2021), a new concert piece for solo performer and Max patch[1]. *MadLib* engages the performer's Max skills and creativity by requiring them to "play" with the patch using a wide variety of objects[2], workflows, and methods considered fundamental to understanding the Max language.

Playful practice-based learning has been proven to be an effective method of learning new interfaces for musical expression, also resulting in more interesting and unique final products [2]. At ICMC 2021, Andrea Bareggi and Simonetta Sargenti presented a paper examining two short instrumental pieces with live electronics as potential educational tools by "reconsider[ing] the electroacoustic music teaching process in relation to modern pedagogical approaches, more practical and student centered (learning by practice)" [3]. Several elements of *MadLib* can be—or in some cases must be—chosen and/or adjusted by the performer in the process of creating their interpretation of the piece. Here, we use the term "interpretation" to encompass both the player's individual live performance of the work as well as all of the preparatory decisions made ahead of time when preparing the patch and the piece.

Learning to perform with Max also requires students to develop troubleshooting skills that will naturally arise with nearly every patch. Consider, for example, uploading and playing audio files in a Max patch. All-too-often, files played from a directory fail to play after uploading: users familiar with how Max interacts with files will be able to identify and solve the issue much more quickly than those without this experience. Similarly, with pitch tracking, it is critical to be able to understand the process of how Max objects–such as the fiddle~ external object [4]–identify pitches so that issues can be identified and addressed. A

1 Programs written in Max are referred to as patches. The user interface where a Max program is written and interacted with can also be referred to as the patch.

2 An object is a pre-built module that performs a specific task or function. Objects are the building blocks of Max patches.

performer using Max patches with these features must be able to troubleshoot them in dynamic and stressful settings such as rehearsals and concerts. Beyond troubleshooting, increased interaction with complex patches can familiarize the performer to various audio processing techniques and different methods of transitioning within a patch.

Oliver Hancock advocates for an approach to learning visual programming languages centered on interactivity and creative experimentation [5]. In order to test the efficacy of *MadLib* as a potential platform for constructionist learning, this study below follows eight participants with varying degrees of experience with Max as they learned and performed the piece for the first time. The aim of this study is to determine the extent to which a composition like *MadLib* can be an effective practice-based supplement for learning Max. By asking multiple people to perform the same work, we were able to observe how different performers navigate the patch, and in the process, learn the semantics of Max and general concepts related to performing with live electronics.

2. ORIGIN AND CONCEPT

Percussionist Jonny Smith commissioned Louis Pino to compose *MadLib* in order to practice performing with live electronics while also gaining a better understanding of Max. The concept was to create a piece that gives the performer creative agency and allows for a wide array of musical outcomes through patch customization, sample selection, and open instrumentation.

The piece is named after and inspired by the word game, Mad Libs, in which the reader is prompted to provide words that fit certain categories (nouns, verbs, colors, etc.) in a given order [6]. These words subsequently fill the blanks of a prewritten story, usually resulting in a comedic outcome. Similarly, in *MadLib,* the performer must record or import their own samples to be inserted into the patch while also deciding certain parameters for how these samples will be manipulated to construct the electronic accompaniment.

MadLib was premiered on April 29, 2022 at The Space Between Conference at McMaster University in Hamilton, Ontario, Canada. Smith and Pino performed their own versions of the piece back-to-back to demonstrate how personal customization results in unique performances.

Figure 1. Smith and Pino at their respective setups during the premiere of *MadLib.*

3. THE PIECE

MadLib was specifically designed to aid in the performer's practical learning of skills related to performing with Max patches and live electronics in general. The following description of the piece and the preparations one must make to perform it is meant to highlight the specific ways in which *MadLib* can be a useful educational tool.

MadLib gives the performer a chance to interact directly with the Max patching environment through a selection of musical features including granular synthesis[3] and looping control[4], as well as organizational methods such as file directories, signal flow, and in-patch data management. The piece intentionally employs standard electroacoustic techniques and Max-specific language (e.g., objects, messages, digital signal processing) covered in various Max course syllabi in order to introduce concepts and techniques generally considered to be fundamental to understanding Max [7] [8] [9]. Furthermore, the piece allows for the performer to practice interacting with standard live electronic processes such as pitch and amplitude tracking, live looping, and live audio processing (i.e., delay, modulation, live sampling, and pitch shifting).

Figure 2 shows the main interface of the *MadLib* patch. The performer is encouraged to explore the given possibilities and, if desired, use their own code to augment the patch.

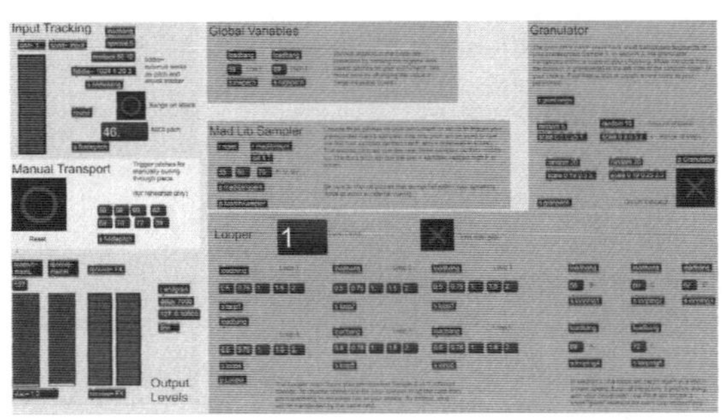

Figure 2. Screenshot of the main window within the *MadLib* Max patch.

3 An audio synthesis technique where a sound is cut into very short pieces (typically 5-100 milliseconds) and reconstituted based on various parameters into a longer piece of audio or continuous stream of sound.

4 The performer is able to preset the speed and pitch of a variety of sample loops used throughout the piece.

3.1 Preparation

The performer may choose any instrument or a collection of instruments for their performance of the piece. In order to accommodate the use of both traditionally pitched (e.g., piano, flute) and unpitched instruments (e.g., drum set, found sounds, non-western tuned instruments), the score is provided in both conventional and relative pitch notation (Figure3).

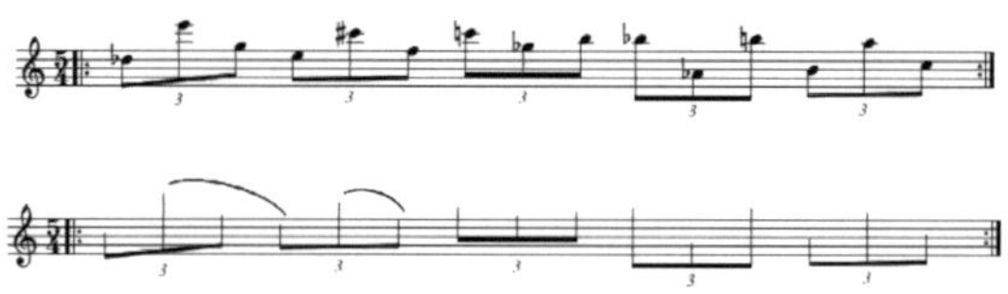

Figure 3. Excerpt of *MadLib* in conventional notation for pitched instruments (top) and relative pitch (bottom) notation for unpitched instruments.

They must also adjust certain pitch tracking values in the patch based on their instrument choice. The player sets two main cue pitches, the highest and lowest in their instrument range, along with five other arbitrary cue pitches that control various aspects of the electronics including moving between sections and triggering samples.

Furthermore, the performer must also source thirteen audio samples, as there are no default samples or pre-recorded materials included with the piece. Eleven samples are meant to be short, punctuative sounds that are played without alteration. The other two are longer samples of recorded music that are processed by the patch to generate much of the electronic material present throughout the work. In addition, an optional area of the patch allows the performer to select and customize a number of live audio effects:

- *Delay*: records sound and plays it back after a period of time
- *Pitch-shifted delay*: records sound and plays back a pitch-shifted version after a period of time
- *Amplitude modulator*: alters the volume of a sound by using another sound wave as a control signal
- *Harmonizer*: shifts the pitch of incoming sound by four different values
- *Reverse sampler*: records sound and plays it back in reverse at varying speeds and lengths

The performer also has access to a variety of low-frequency oscillators (LFOs), which allow the player to assign fluctuating streams of values to any parameter of the auxiliary effects. Using the "pattr" object, a common Max object that manages multiple parameters of a patch, the performer can choose to use certain effects in one section of the piece and forgo them in another. Understanding and controlling these mechanisms, which are embedded in many Max compositions, enhances the performer's ability to effectively present other composers' live electroacoustic music.

3.2 Form

MadLib has three main sections. The performer navigates the sections at their own pace using pitch and amplitude tracking provided by the fiddle~ external object.

In the first section, cued by the performer's first note, the patch loops a sample and gradually adds five more layers when triggered by designated cue pitches in the score. The performer chooses the speed of all six sample loops which determine the tempo and rhythmic framework for this section. The patch then listens for 5 seconds of silence, after which, any note played will cue the next section.

The middle section is a musical Mad Libs story. The performer speaks a text which is notated along with the music, while crucial words of the text are replaced by the performer's eleven short samples that are triggered by playing cue pitches. The performer also makes use of a granular synthesizer by cueing short bits of a sample with each note they play, resulting in a constant drone. After all of the short samples are played, slower versions of the loops from the first section are brought back one by one.

The last section is improvisatory, asking the performer to freely play in loose rhythmic conjunction with the slowed loops. The performer triggers cue pitches to briefly alter the speed of each loop, resulting in new composite rhythms with each speed change. After one minute in this section, the performer can choose when to end the piece by playing the highest pitch on their instrument.

4. OUR STUDY

The goal of the study is to test the effectiveness of *MadLib* as an opportunity for performers to develop skills and learn concepts about live electronics and Max and to observe the diversity of performance outcomes possible from the piece. In this creative, experiential study, eight participants were coached on and given resources to prepare performances of *MadLib*. There are two levels of preparation involved in learning *MadLib*: musical (i.e., playing the notation and improvising) and technical (i.e., patch customization). The majority of the participants spent most of their time modifying and customizing the patch. Therefore, the discussion below will describe the procedures that aided the participants in working with the patch and that most significantly affected the final results of the project.

The study involved eight research assistants, including seven graduate students and one recent graduate, with an average of sixteen years of musical training. There were seven percussionists and one accordion player, most of whom cited proficiency in other instruments: piano (3), woodwind (1), guitar (1), and brass (1). The participants demonstrated a wide range of experience working with Max and performing with live electronics (Table 1). All the participants are advanced performers with a high level of proficiency on their instruments.

Participant	Years of Max experience	Formal Max class completion	Frequency of performance with electronics
P1	0	Currently enrolled	Not often
P2	2	Currently enrolled	Not often
P3	0	No	Sometimes
P4	3	Yes	Often
P5	2	Yes	Often
P6	1	Currently enrolled	Often
P7	4	Yes	Often
P8	2	Yes	All the time

Table 1. Table showing participants' experience with Max and performance with live electronics.

This study, facilitated by TaPIR Lab, ran from October 4 to November 6, 2022. It consisted of the following steps:

1) An introductory workshop explaining the technical requirements for performing the piece, consisting of step-by-step instructions on how to customize the patch and prepare the work for performance.

2) Individual tutorials and independent experimentation with the piece between October 5 and November 4. Some participants who had very little to no experience felt more comfortable having the composer present as they recorded their samples and made their edits. For the participants who were already more comfortable with Max, these tutorials were a chance to go over their edits and gain a more thorough understanding of how the patch operates on a detailed level.

3) Final recorded performance and interview. Performers completed questionnaires before their recording sessions in order to collect background data on the participants' prior experience with live electronics. Immediately after recording, they were interviewed about their experiences of learning and preparing the piece.

Overall, including setup and troubleshooting, this process took approximately one hour per participant. The written questionnaire, video recordings of performances, and audio recordings of interviews were kept for later review by the authors.

5. PERFORMANCES

A diversity of interpretations and distinct performances resulted from this workshop. Table 2 shows participants' interpretive decisions regarding instrument selection, sample selection, and further auxiliary processing used in their preparation of the patch. The heterogeneity of these decisions, in addition to variation in each participant's musical interpretation, resulted in performances that sounded almost like different pieces of music entirely. Participants tended to stick to a particular theme for their *MadLib* sample selection, with some recording or designing their own sounds but the majority of participants sourcing audio clips from sources on the Internet.

The auxiliary effects tended to be either used individually per section or built up cumulatively throughout the piece, with many participants favoring the pitch-shifted feedback delay and the LFO. Given that participants were generally inexperienced with electronics, it was surprising that four out of the eight participants chose to experiment with these effects, as they were among the more complicated options for processing. We could infer that participants gravitated towards these specific effects because they offered the most immediate and drastic impact to the overall sound, motivating the performers to continue their experimentation and play, regardless of their technical facility.

Participant	Instrument	Mad Lib samples	Auxiliary effects used
P1	Vibraphone	Cantonese speaking clips	Pitch-shifted feedback delay, LFO
P2	Metal pipes and wood planks	Custom-made synthesized sounds	Feedback delay, pitch-shifted feedback delay, modulator
P3	voice	effects	Modulator
P4	Accordion	Various bird calls	Pitch-shifted feedback delay, harmonizer, reverse sampler
P5	Melodica	Vocal samples	None
P6	Vibraphone	Recorded tabla sounds	Pitch-shifted feedback delay, harmonizer, LFO
P7	Almglocken, gong and triangle	Ice and water sounds	Pitch-shifted feedback delay, modulator, reverse sampling, LFO
P8	Glockenspiel	Custom-made synthesized sounds	Pitch-shifted feedback delay, LFO

Table 2. Table showing participants' interpretive decisions.

Regarding instrumentation, the majority of participants chose pitched instruments; the three participants that chose un-pitched instruments were required to find creative solutions in order to set cue pitches. Participants 2 and 7 found specific instruments to act as cue pitches that seemed to work well with the pitch-tracking software, and Participant 3 sang pre-established high and low notes with their voice in order to trigger the cues. Each one of the participants described a process of trying out different combinations of things, listening to the results, and then going back to the patch to make alterations.

Not only did the participants produce vastly different musical results, but many stated that they had more ideas for what they would change if they ever performed the piece again. The comments below, from the participants' post-study interviews, indicate how the process of learning and preparing *MadLib* caused them to think critically about how they could engage with the electronics to create desired results:

- "If I were to perform it again I would probably go in and make my own user interface so I can get more information out of the patch by just looking over at my computer during performance." (Participant 8)
- "I would like to play around with the live effects a little bit more so that it doesn't sound so drastic but so that they feel unified through the whole thing." (Participant 2)
- "One thing I would do differently would be to refine the volume of the samples. That was one thing I noticed because one of the clips I got was a lot quieter and I felt like it might have gotten buried." (Participant 5)

These comments and the overall positive experiences of the study participants substantiate the idea that customizable repertoire such as *MadLib* can be a fulfilling creative outlet for performers that engages their imaginations and helps them to develop their skills with live electronics.

6. DISCUSSION

When discussing her view on why musicians are often hesitant to perform with unfamiliar technology, Elizabeth McNutt stated that "much of the schism that holds performers at bay may be repaired by simpler means: dialogue between composers and performers, education of performers in working with technology, and comprehension of performer's needs and expectations among composers" [10]. The learning experiences described by the participants of this study indicate that *MadLib* can be an effective tool to help bridge the schism described by McNutt because it addresses the specific needs of performers and allows them to engage directly with the technical aspects of the piece.

In the post-study interviews, the participants described learning about: A) troubleshooting problems when performing with a Max patch and live electronics in general (Participants 4, 6, 7, and 8), B) the fiddle~ object, how it interacts with live sound and tracks pitches (Participants 1, 2, and 5), and C) the possibilities of using live effects in Max such as delay, pitch-shifted delay, harmonizer, modulator, and reverse sampler (Participants 2, 3, 6, and 7). These are all transferable skills for performers who want to learn to play a variety of repertoire with Max and/or live electronics.

One of the most important phases of the study, especially for those with the least Max experience, was the workshops and one-on-one meetings led by the composer. Several of the performers mentioned that, while they had some degree of anxiety about preparing the piece, after meeting with Pino and being able to ask questions, their fears were alleviated. The comments listed below reinforce the need for quality instruction and interaction with a knowledgeable practitioner in order for this type of educational endeavor to be successful.

- "We had two workshops with Pino. That was really helpful, especially the second one, actually, because it really went into every detail of what I can customize and I did some of it. Then I looked at the playing part before I dove into the Max." (Participant 6)
- "Once I met with Pino... he explained to me what the different trigger points were. Once that was done, I was able to understand and figure out the rest." (Participant 2)

Although some of the study participants seemed initially intimidated by the *MadLib* patch, all were successful in presenting their own performances of the piece by the end of the study. With a sufficient amount of instruction and guidance, even novice Max users learned to play this piece, suggesting that *MadLib* could be a useful addition to a Max course where the student also receives direction from an instructor.

The hands-on experimentation and creative exploration required to prepare and perform *MadLib* were the main reasons that the participants of this study were able to develop and solidify their Max skills. There has been a wide range of published studies that advocate for this as a useful educational approach to music technology (e.g., Tomás, 2020; McPherson et al., 2016; Hancock, 2014) [2] [11] [5]. Hancock in particular advocates for constructivism/constructionism or learning through play: "Constructivism asserts that knowledge and understanding are constructed by learners. This is seen as an active process, distinct from models of passive reception associated with traditional instructionist methods.... Constructionism adds the notion that learning is aided by the manipulation of some tangible (not necessarily physical) object, possibly shared with other learners." [5]

Because the performer engages directly with the patch and electronic hardware by recording samples, establishing cue pitches and loop speeds, and setting levels for sound effects, it draws them into the process of exploration and experimentation. The requirement for the performer to venture below the surface level of the patch and engage with sub-patches and other features allows them to learn how to troubleshoot issues with the patch when they arise. Moreover, it provides an opportunity to apply one's skills with Max in a creative and personalized way. By providing a framework for the exploration of musical ideas, which is relatively user-friendly but also affords the user the artistic agency to make changes to and/or add to the existing framework, *MadLib* facilitates a form of constructivist learning that can complement other avenues for learning how to use Max software.

7. CONCLUSION

At ICMC 2016, Pete Furniss and Richard Dudas called for "the creation of a body of musical works that are technically straightforward enough to serve as an introduction to live electronic performance for musicians who might otherwise be daunted by the demands of the existing repertoire" [12]. This study demonstrates that, with some mentorship and oversight, *MadLib* can provide an effective and creative learning experience for both relative novices and more experienced performers working with Max. In their post-study interview, various participants expressed that their applied knowledge of Max and comfort level with the program increased through the experience of learning *MadLib*. More than just learning about various capabilities of the program, however, many of the participants stated that they gained "conceptual Max skills" or "inspiration about how to use Max" from learning and performing the piece. This higher-level thinking is a critical step towards regularly incorporating live electronics into one's artistic practice.

By examining the learned outcomes from the study participants and analyzing the aspects of interpreting and performing *MadLib* that facilitated that learning, this study demonstrates that creative interactivity with a pre-built patch can be a significant aid towards developing performance skills with Max. This kind of invited alteration of a patch can also produce highly individualized musical results that reflect the artistic choices and personality of the performer, far beyond what typical pre-composed material would allow.

Although *MadLib* is a concert piece, it can be thought of as an étude as it fosters the development of techniques relating to performance with live electronics [13]. *MadLib* covers a variety of concepts in Max, but the idea of performative Max études could be implemented on a smaller, more segmented scale. These etudes could then be used as a means to practice isolated live electronic performance techniques (e.g., pitch tracking, MIDI mapping, and amplitude reactivity). In *Making Music With Sounds,* Landy states "[t]here is an assumption regarding sound synthesis, namely, that the maker of such sounds is aware of what (s)he is doing. The need for detailed knowledge is in dire contrast to today's society in which instant gratification or at least understanding is almost assumed" [14]. The ability to "play" with performative, purposely customizable Max patches gives the learner the opportunity to explore the applied outcome of a particular concept in a top-down perspective (that is, with a fully-formed patch, rather than beginning with a blank canvas) that can inspire deeper and more diverse learning outcomes.

The syllabus for Oberlin Conservatory's Tech 170, an introductory electroacoustic performance course taught by Dr. Aurie Hsu, concludes with a call to "[c]ultivate a performance practice that integrates your personal style with a proficiency in electroacoustic performance techniques...and [to] have a heightened awareness of how musical elements function together in practice and performance" [7]. For many performers hoping to program works with Max patches, there is a general threshold after which works become too complicated to perform without direct, in-person involvement of the composer.

If implemented widely, however, further educational resources focused on familiarizing performers with the Max language could raise this overall threshold for complexity in contemporary works for live electronics resulting in the increased presence and dissemination of existing works. Just as instrumentalists need some time in the practice room and on stage to hone their abilities, those who want to perform with Max need a creative space and performance goal in order to practice and develop those skills.

Acknowledgments

This project was funded by the Social Sciences and Humanities Research Council of Canada (SSHRC) and the Technology and Performance Integration Research (TaPIR) Lab. The authors would like to thank Aiyun Huang, Christopher Dobrian, and Kristen Smith for their writing feedback and support.

REFERENCES

[1] Cycling '74, *Max, version 8.4,* 2018.

[2] E. Tomás, "A Playful Approach to Teaching NIME: Pedagogical Methods from a Practice-Based Perspective," in *Proceedings of the International Conference on New Interfaces for Musical Expression*, 2020.

[3] A. Bareggi and S. Sargenti, "Towards Accessible and Sustainable Learning of Real Time Electroacoustic Composition and Performance at Undergraduate Academic Level," in *13th International Conference on Computer Supported Education.*, 2021.

[4] M. Puckette, T. Apel and D. Zicarelli, "Real-time audio analysis tools for Pd and MSP," in *International Conference on Mathematics and Computing*, 1998.

[5] O. Hancock, "Play-based, constructionist learning of pure data: A case study," *Journal of Music, Technology & Education,* vol. 7, no. 1, pp. 93-112, 2014.

[6] L. Stern and R. Price, Mad Libs, Price Stern Sloan, 1962.

[7] A. Hsu, *TECH 170: Electroacoustic Interpretation and Performance Practice,* Oberlin, Ohio: Oberlin Conservatory, 2019.

[8] P. Whincop, *Composing with Computers I,* Cambridge, Massachusetts, 2008.

[9] N. C. Young, *ntroduction to Digital Media & Computer Music: Visual Programming with Max - MUCO 592,* Los Angeles, California: University of Southern California, 2020.

[10] E. McNutt, "Performing electroacoustic music: a wider view of interactivity," *Organised Sound,* vol. 8, no. 3, pp. 297-304, 2003.

[11] A. P. McPherson, A. Chamberlain, A. Hazzard, S. McGrath and S. Benford, "Designing for exploratory play with a hackable digital musical instrument," in *Proceedings of the 2016 ACM Conference on Designing Interactive Systems*, 2016.

[12] R. Dudas and P. Furniss, "Towards an Aesthetic of Instrumental Plausibility for Mixed Electronic Music," in *International Computer Music Conference (ICMC)*, 2016.

[13] T. Roth, A. Huang and T. Cunningham, "On Parallel Performance Practices: Some Observations on Personalizing DMIs as Percussionists," in *Proceedings of the International Conference on New Interfaces for Musical Expression*, 2021.

[14] L. Landy, Making music with sounds, Routledge, 2012.

SoundLab, first three years [studio report]

PerMagnus Lindborg
SoundLab, ACIM, School of Creative Media, City University of Hong Kong
pm.lindborg@cityu.edu.hk

Ryo Ikeshiro
SoundLab, ACIM, School of Creative Media, City University of Hong Kong
ryo.ikeshiro@cityu.edu.hk

ABSTRACT

This is a report on the development of SoundLab, a spatial audio research and practice unit at the School of Creative Media, City University of Hong Kong, co-directed by the authors. We outline how we have developed the lab's objectives in terms of research, artwork, teaching, and outreach. We give a brief account of the local context of electroacoustic music in Hong Kong, both in academia and in independent music and art scenes, to which SoundLab aims to contribute through its activities. We report the design of a hemispherical loudspeaker array dedicated to high spatial resolution audio, developed after consulting a number of academic institutions with comparable facilities and programmes. Recent activities in outreach and research are discussed, and future plans in relation to its objectives are given in closing.

1. SOUNDLAB

Space is key to audio and music. Effective design of sonic space is vital for achieving immersivity in most forms of creative media, such as performance, games, AR/VR/XR, 3D film, and installation. We are dedicated to developing SoundLab, a multifaceted laboratory hosted in a main space, the Multi-Media Theatre (M1060, here referred to as MMT) which we have fitted with a loudspeaker array for high spatial resolution audio. We are additionally developing other spatial audio technologies to augment and complement the main lab. SoundLab is a platform for spatial audio research, teaching, and outreach at City University of Hong Kong. The authors are its joint co-directors, and started to set it up in November 2020 thanks to a grant and facility support from the Applied Computing and Interactive Media Centre at the School of Creative Media. The ACIM grant was renewed two years later, in November 2021. We have previously reported the initial design work for SoundLab [1, 2] and the context of electroacoustic music and related sonic arts in Hong Kong [3].

2. OBJECTIVES

SoundLab is dedicated to establishing City University as the foremost institution within Hong Kong for spatial audio, significantly advancing the profile of the School of Creative Media within Asia and internationally. The team currently consists of three full-time faculty, ~10 fulltime PhD students (as of autumn of 2023), as well as MFA and undergraduate students working on creative projects and student-led concerts. Our work is guided by six research objectives, restated below with a brief statement of what has been achieved so far.

Lab space

The first and most important task for us was to design and develop a lab space for research in spatial audio perception and design. In early 2021 we contacted experts in spatial audio, including Eric Lyon, Tanner Upthegrove, Bill Brunson, Natasha Barrett, Franz Zotter, Matthias Frank, Simon Smith, Scott Wilson, and Craig Jackson, and we are deeply grateful for their advice. Considering needs and resources, we settled on designing a semi-permanent hemispherical rig with 25 equidistant point-source speakers at four levels (for design details see [2]). The installation was fully functional in late 2022. Ring One has 12 speakers on floor stands (see **Figure 1**), Ring Two has 8 speakers slightly below the trusses, and Ring Three has 4 speakers mounted at the upper edge of the trusses, with a time delay (it proved impossible to mount four speakers at the physically optimal positions, on a structure extending above the trusses, due to novel restrictions imposed after an unrelated incident at another stage in Hong Kong). All speakers are Genelec IP 4030a, connected via Cat5 cables on an AES65 digital audio network using high-powered routers and Dante software. Installing the remaining 25th 'zenith speaker' in the catwalk requires a special permit that is pending. Finally, we will be receiving two matching Genelec subwoofers in the autumn of 2023, to be augmented by another two, when funding allows.

Perception research

SoundLab supports empirical research in spatial auditory perception, through perceptual evaluation of soundscape recordings under different reproduction conditions, including headphones, 2ch stereo, surround, and higher-order Ambisonics (HOA). This is a large objective which we have only started to explore. Listening tests were carried out in the past year to support research by PhD candidate Manni Chen on AI-supported studio production tools [4] and the Open Ambisonics Toolkit [5]; this is a line of inquiry that we intend to pursue.

Technical research

SoundLab supports technical research through the creation of novel sonic artwork for spatial configurations i.e. soundscape composition, multichannel electroacoustic music, computer music, AR, VR. We have created new spatial audio compositions such as [6] or updated previous works [7, 8], and new media artworks [9, 10]. In addition to the faculty Start-Up grants that enable the loudspeaker array, we are currently working larger and multi-faceted granted projects. Lindborg is the Principle Investigator for *Multi-Modal Hong Kong* (2023-25), a three-year project funded by the Hong Kong Government which aims to create a multimodal database of places of culturally valued intangible heritage, specifically soundscape and smellscape. He also works on *Open Ambisonics Toolkit*, a hardware-software low-cost system [5, 11]. Meanwhile, Ikeshiro is the Principle Investigator for a project to investigate binaural audio for virtual environments, and has recently secured another grant to extend this work towards using Ambisonics. Our conference activities in the past 2.5 years include *ArtMachine2, CeReNeM, CMMR, ICAD, ICMC, ICMPC-ESCOM, International Conference Music and Sonic Art, ISEA, KEAMS,* and *Xenakis Centenary Symposium*.

Design research

We share a special interest in sonification. This has led to the creation of DACA, a conference on Data Art for Climate Science (dataclimate.org/) and the associated DAT/ACT Exhibition, both conducted in 2022; a Research Topic on data perceptualization [12], and workshops on spatial sonification of geodata (see below). Fundamental to our approach is to consider the interplay between aesthetic and utilitarian intentionalities, aka *ars musica* and *ars informatica* [13–15]. The cross-modal interaction between visual and auditory perception is another subject that has implications for design, and this is being explored by some of the PhD students.

Pedagogy

Since September 2022 we have conducted several workshops for graduate students, to relate spatial audio to data sonification, field recording, improvisation, and other key topics. Several invited guests, both Hong Kong-based and from abroad, have given workshops and concerts. In the past two years, they include: Christopher Keyes (composer, Baptist University HK), Giorgio Biancorosso (film music scholar, HKU), Yang Yeung (independent curator), Andras Blazsek (sound artist, EU), Mario de Vega (media/sound artist, Mexico), Fiona Lee (sound artist/performer), Sascia Pellegrini (composer, Singapore School of the Arts), Solomon Shiu (soundscape researcher), Andi Lai (machine/sound art), Edwin Lo (media art), and John D'Arcy (composer, UK). These activities are also effective for outreach, discussed further below.

The School of Creative Media offers several courses related to sound and music. Two classes by Lindborg have used the MMT space: in *Sound Installation and Spatialisation*, the acoustic space and loudspeakers enabled a range of teaching and learning activities, including the students' final class project, and in *Music for Film*, a movie screening highlighted surround sound and demonstrated upmixing of stereo to 5.1. A notable student graduation production was made in April 2023 by MFA graduate Longman Luk, supervised by Ikeshiro. The aforementioned Open Ambisonics Toolkit aims to support graduating students and practitioners outside of academia with a way to continue working with spatial audio in their own creative work. It is both an entry-point and a sustainable way of distributing the knowledge developed at SoundLab. First shown at ICAD in June 2023, we will be holding an OAT workshop at SCM in October this year.

Outreach

SoundLab is currently the only institution-based larger facility for spatial audio in Hong Kong. A snapshot image and analysis of the local Hong Kong scene is given in [1]. As we are building capacity for hosting events and concerts of different kinds, presenting sonic and media design and artwork by ourselves and student members of SoundTeam as well as by colleagues, collaboration with other institutions will be increasingly important. We aim to gradually develop outreach, in order to gain publicity and traction for SoundLab as much as to benefit the students and faculty at CityU, and the larger scene in Hong Kong.

3. FUTURE PLANS

Since 2020, SoundLab is an integral part of ACIM and SCM. We will be opening up for undergraduates to do their 4th year final project at SoundLab, related to spatial audio. In the future and subject to the funding situation, we hope to create and establish a creative residency scheme where composers can spend time at SoundLab to compose spatial audio works within the hemispheric loudspeaker rig. The number of PhD students has significantly increased. The two Co-Investigators together currently supervise ten PhD students who are attached to SoundLab, and have Research Assistants funded over grants. To conclude, we feel that SoundLab is approaching a certain 'critical mass', a level of activity that will be sustainable over longer term. For more information and to sign up for our newsletter, visit soundlab.scm.cityu.edu.hk/.

Figure 1. SoundLab: circle of twelve loudspeakers at floor level.

Acknowledgments

The authors thank all members of SoundTeam, invited guests, and collaborators for their contributions. The work presented in this paper was partially supported by grants from Hong Kong SAR Research Grants Council (Lindborg 11605622; Ikeshiro 21602822); Hong Kong Government Environmental Conservation Fund (Lindborg 9211241); CityU StartUp and Teaching StartUp grants (both authors).

4. REFERENCES

[1] R. Ikeshiro, D. Charrieras, & PM. Lindborg (2022/12). "Charting the scene(s) of sonic arts in Hong Kong. An overview based on 23 interviews with local practitioners and organisers". *Organised Sound*, https://doi.org/10.1017/S1355771822000450

[2] R. Ikeshiro & PM. Lindborg (2022/06). "SoundLab, a spatial audio research/practice unit in Hong Kong". 10 Jun 2022, *Proc. 27th International Symposium on Electronic Art (ISEA)*, https://isea2022.isea-international.org/

[3] R. Ikeshiro & PM. Lindborg (2021/10). "SoundLab and Electroacoustic Music in Hong Kong". *Proc. 2021 Conference of the Korean Electro-Acoustic Music Society*, Seoul, keams.org/emille/keamsac/

[4] M. Chen & PM. Lindborg (2023/01) "Observations on Guitar Music Produced by AI Reverberation and Professional Sound Engineers". *International Journal of Music Science, Technology and Art (IJMSTA)*, doi.org/10.48293/IJMSTA-93

[5] G. Pisano & PM Lindborg (2023/06). "Introducing the Open Ambisonics Toolkit". *Proceedings of the Conference of the International Community for Auditory Display (ICAD).*

[6] PM. Lindborg (2021/11). "Stairway to Helheim", *Soundislands 'Re:Sound'*, ArtScience Museum, Singapore.

[7] PM Lindborg (2022/2010). "Graviton Dance. Generative 3D sound composition". *Asia Composer League Festival*, Christchurch, New Zealand.

[8] R. Ikeshiro (2022/04). "Eternal Accelerando". *Sonorities Festival*, Belfast.

[9] R. Ikeshiro & MetaObjects (2023/06). Sonic Topologies: Hong Kong 地境：香港. With Jacklam Ho, Manni Chen, Cheng Yang Daniel Stempfer. *M+ at Night: Sensory Encounters M+夜不同：感官體驗,* Museum of Visual Culture, Hong Kong.

[10] PM. Lindborg, J. Xiao, F. Aletta, H. Cheung, R. Yue, N. Han, X. Xu. (2023/04). "The Dual City Multi-sensory Experience of Markets". *Symposium on Inclusive Design with Multi-senses*, STEAMhouse, Birmingham City University, UK.

[11] PM. Lindborg & G. Pisano (2023/09). "Learning spatial audio with the Open Ambisonics Toolkit" *Digitally Engaged Learning Conference* (DEL).

[12] PM. Lindborg, SS. Chopra, & K. Groß-Vogt (2023/08). *Data Perceptualization for Climate Science Communication. Frontiers in Psychology, Sec. Human-Media Interaction,* https://doi.org/10.3389/fpsyg.2023.1263971.

[13] P. Vickers & B. Hogg (2006). Sonification abstraite/sonification concrete: An 'aesthetic persepctive space' for classifying auditory displays in the ars musica domain. Proc. ICAD.

[14] D. Worrall (2019). Sonification Design. Springer.

[15] PM. Lindborg, S. Lenzi S & M. Chen (2023/01). "Climate Data Sonification and Visualisation: An Analysis of Aesthetics, Characteristics, and Topics in 32 Recent Projects". *Frontiers in Psychology, Human-Media Interaction,* 10.3389/fpsyg.2022.1020102

MTT Studio report

Juan Parra Cancino

Orpheus Institute
juan.parra@orpheusinstituut.be

Jonathan Impett

Orpheus Institute
jonathan.impett@orpheusinstituut.be

ABSTRACT

***Music, Thought and Technology** (MTT) is a research group at the Orpheus Institute, Ghent, an institution dedicated to artistic research in music. In this report we present our institutional statement, describe our current strands of work, the ongoing projects and case studies, and provide an overview of our members, outputs, and partners.*

1. INTRODUCTION

Music, Thought and Technology (MTT) is a research group at the Orpheus Institute, Ghent, an institution dedicated to artistic research in music. Members are drawn both from within Orpheus and from the wider artistic community. The foundational concepts of the group are articulated in their institutional statement:

Put simply, our common repertory of operational concepts is largely derived from technology; this therefore seems the natural place to look for constructive or explanatory models. Technology is fundamentally constitutive of music, its experience, practices and culture. Like all art, music could be seen to function in the context of a common sense of the possible, of the operations and relationships that it might embody, extend or reveal. This sense of the possible derives primarily from science, technology and their cognates such as natural philosophy or cosmology. Music is literally inconceivable without technologies. They participate in the imagining and apprehending of music, but in a bidirectional process also become part of the broader repertoire of conceptual operations that inform human thought at any given cultural moment. There is a continuum from the 'hard' technologies of instruments or reproduction through the materials of composition to the mental models we use to understand music. Engagement with music is thus also technical. The techniques of music are inseparably linked with its technologies of imagining, creation and production.

In our self-consciously technological age above all, technology provides a common set of ideas, metaphors and behaviours. It is the natural place to look for discourse that reaches across the many approaches to composition, sound art and improvisation that characterise contemporary musical activity irrespective of style or genre – including the vast body of inherited work for which we constantly search for new relevance.

At the same time, researchers investigating new areas of computer science and artificial intelligence are posing new questions about the nature of digital objects, concepts and experience. Musical works, we suggest, have much in common with virtual or digital objects. They exist in a unique state of materiality/immateriality: while they are intensely bound to direct experience, to technologies, techniques and materials, this physicality can exist in multiple instantiations, they can be manipulated, engaged with and acted upon as cultural abstractions. In cultural terms, music is the area of human activity in which we deal with the virtual, with the constructive relationship between human affect and abstract structures or formal systems. Digital humanities research and computer-based creation use the same repertory of tools; both are acts of musical imagination extended and explored through technology. The boundaries become increasingly blurred.

Orpheus was founded in 1996, and its research centre in 2007. MTT began work in 2015, since when the kind of questions and topics it investigates have become increasingly central to music research in general. Recent developments in AI, an increasing awareness of the new digital dynamics of knowledge and historical distance from 'conventional' understandings of art music are balanced by a keen sense of the ephemerality, materiality and performativity of music. These concerns serve to connect artist-researchers across different kinds of musical material. Impett's article 'Music, discourse and intuitive technology' (*AI & Society*, 2021)[1] sets out some ideas concerning the role of technology in thought and culture, as reflected in music. The increasing role of technology-related thought in general is also evident in infrastructural developments at Orpheus. We have a new 8-channel basement studio, along with a dedicated maker space. A mirror of the studio is installed as a performance space in the newly-converted 'Koetshuis' library building – the coach-house of the palace behind Orpheus. These and the larger concert hall are connected by a Dante system, allowing for flexible configurations of research and creation, performance, and recording and production.

Figure 1. MTT's basement studio and maker space

Figure 2. Performance space at 'Koetshuis' library building

The current members of MTT are:

Jonathan Impett (Orpheus Institute)
Juan Parra Cancino (Orpheus Institute)
Magno Caliman (Orpheus Institute)
Nicolas Collins (School of the Art Institute of Chicago)
Paulo Dantas (Orpheus Institute)
Simon Waters (Queen's University, Belfast)
Matt Wright (Canterbury Christchurch University)

The members of MTT are all practising artists for whom creation and research are inextricable. Within a vast range of work, specific strands have consolidated around the notions set out above, some of which we will outline in this paper:

2. CRITICAL TECHNICAL PRACTICE

A common theme through this period has been the idea of Critical Technical Practice (CTP), developed from the work of Philip Agre (1997)[2]. Discussion of composition had long been seen as problematic at Orpheus; composers would come and present on one hand their theory or techniques, and on the other their finished work. As Agre pointed out in early AI research, this is a closed system that tells us little. More important are the context and narrative of such development; it is there that the conflicts, decisions, values, leaps of imagination and underlying topics emerge. Following close-reading sessions with invited guests and an international seminar, an edited book of new retellings by composers - 'Sound Work: Composition as Critical Technical Practice' - was published in 2021.

3. *THREE STATES OF WAX*: ELECTRO-ACOUSTIC IMPROVISATION

As a genre, improvisation with extended instruments and live electronics may be a specialist interest. As a paradigm for the current and future state of music, however, the practice embodies the most urgent questions – the invention, performance, transmission and very ontology of the musical phenomenon. In its technicity this practice obliges us to confront such questions in practical ways. As with our 21st century understanding of mind, such a view sees music as situated, contingent, embodied, distributed and dynamic. Continuities and identities are not those of surface.

A particular property of contemporary technologically-facilitated music creation is its multiplicity of modes of representation (Vesely's 'divided representation')[3]: mimetic, symbolic, analogic, referential, processual. In a computational context, where operation across time and space (Lyotard's 'telegraphy')[4] brings together multiple levels of action, representation and contingency, what is our 'material'? What are appropriate operations? Luciano Floridi[5] has suggested that the natural mode of knowledge generation in an informational environment is poietic rather than mimetic-analytic; this is the model for our current work.

The title and approach of this project derive from Michel Serres'[6] investigation of the materials of physics. Developing Decartes' thought experiment of a piece of wax (always the same, always different), Serres identifies three views: the object as perceived, the object as described in terms of its properties, and the object as an informational nexus that not only embodies the entire history of its own genesis and interaction, but is further transformed in each encounter or interrogation. The latter, he suggests, is the appropriate view in an informational world; knowledge derives from the interference of such models.

Three States of Wax proceeds on two fronts. A core of Jonathan Impett and Juan Parra with a series of guests conduct experiments in regular performance. A broader set of challenges emerges from the notion of composing or structuring music for a larger ensemble of improvisers, each of whom brings not only their own improvising practice but also a custom, highly individual technological environment. On some levels these are incommensurable; in terms of protocols, communication, or behaviour with respect to live performance, for instance, they all work in very different ways. As well as being a creative research project in its own right, this work also addresses wider questions concerning the cult of individualism and perpetual novelty: how do we structure local music creation and experience in ways that at once respect the autonomy of individual practice and encourage the emergence of commonality, both phenomenological and of discourse. MTT has been working with network theory and agent-based models to encourage emergent form in such contexts. A new work written for MTT by George Lewis - *High Road, Low Road* – was premiered at the Concertgebouw, Bruges, using the methods of analog synthesis as relational operators between individual performers and systems without technological intervention. Frederic Rzewski's *Second Structure*, composed for MEV in the 1970s, has been revived by the group, also in telematic performance. It challenges distinctions between improvisatory 'freedom' and compositional 'planning', between individual autonomy and ensemble/personal dynamics, between remembered, present and future action.

4. PRESENCE AND RESONANCE

This sequence of works by Jonathan Impett explores the co-existence in contemporary culture of new music creation and the vast landscape of historical music – music that is at once de-historicised by participating in our contemporary culture and re-historicised by an ever-increasing awareness of practice and context. Works take their structure, material and performance dynamics (in the form of sound processing) from the music to which they refer:

- *Memoria colorata* - Messe de Notre-Dame (Machaut, Paris, c. 1300) - saxophone 4tet and percussion
- *Prado florido* – Prado verde y florido (Guerrero, Lisbon, late C16th) - saxophone 4tet, percussion and live electronics
- *Folto giardino I and II* – Le Nozze di Figaro (Mozart, Prague, 1786) - improvising ensemble / chamber orchestra, live electronics and long strings
- *Apollo e Marsyas* – Paeans of Athanaios, Limenios (Delphi, 128 BCE) - viola d'amore, computer and long tubes

In each, the performance is situated in both a physical and virtual environment (installation and sound processing) reflecting the use of the material as embodied in the score. Wave phenomena provide the common technique for manipulating material across its various modes of instantiation: score, physical gesture, sound processing, computational modelling.

5. OPAQUE TECHNOLOGIES

The socio-cultural assimilation of new technologies tends to proceed by initially employing them to facilitate and implement existing concepts and practices in some enhanced or optimised way; only subsequently does its transformational potential become evident, as appropriate new concepts emerge. This is as true in the case of music as in other areas of human activity. As examples, we might consider current laudable and sophisticated attempts to make the internet fully transparent as a means for enabling the remote co-performance of conventional scores.
In this project, MTT seeks rather to investigate the musical and sonic properties of technologies themselves – their *opacity* rather than their transparency. In many cases, this amounts to exploring the materiality of the very technologies that enable what we perceive as the virtual. Case studies for this subject include Juan Parra's series of telematic performances *Artifacts of 'not-here'* and Magno Caliman's *Machina.*

6. MATERIALITY

6.1 Technographical Imprints

Magno Caliman's musical practice is rooted in critical engagement with DIY electronics and the embracing of programming languages as art-making devices. This has steered his research towards *technologically-mediated creative processes* in experimental music.

His premise is that the material entities that are part of a given creative process, the actual objects manipulated during art making, are able to inform and dictate aspects of an artist's decision-making through their inherent characteristics and/or modes of operation. This symbolic grooves, or "technographical imprints" (*marca tecnográfica*) (Caesar 2009)[7] that a particular technical object can leave on a work, can be seen then as signs, byproducts even, of the non-transparent quality of technology.

An inquiry into the interplay between the materiality of instruments and composers' degrees of freedom is not the exclusive domain of musical practices making use of digital technologies: the affordances and constrains of a violin certainly play an integral role in writing a musical work for that instrument. Magno's research expands this discussion, by thinking in terms of the *reconfigurability* of our technological devices: what happens to the composer-apparatus negotiation, when that apparatus is reconfigurable by design? What does a compositional process look like, when choosing the constraints and affordances of our tools becomes part of that very act of composing? For that, his chosen areas of investigation (creative coding and the creation/manipulation of electronic circuits) serve as fertile ground, as they contain in their modes of operation a high degree of reconfigurability.

6.2 Vintage Materialities

With the concept of vintage materialities, Juan Parra Cancino seeks to frame creative initiatives aimed to rediscover the friction between artistic intention and technological affordance inherent to early pieces of electronic music, by presenting it, and exposing it, in performance. The goal is to draw comparisons between the frictions of the past and the present and to carry them into the future.

This experimental process opens questions: Ethical, technical, and compositional.

How can we trace back the performative actions inherent to sound production in early electronic music studios through the analysis and reproduction of the fixed media results, or the original technological setups? What kind of music does the re-enactment of those actions produce today? What was inherent to the tools used? What were the affordances and limitations, and how can we emulate and transcend them?

Some case studies developed in this context include experimental performances of

Karlheinz Stockhausen (*Solo(s)*), Bruno Maderna (*Hyperion*) and Eliane Radigue (*Usral*).

7. DISSEMINATION AND COMMUNITY

7.1 ECHO

Following much discussion of the appropriate vehicle for disseminating artistic research in our field, MTT launched the journal ECHO in 2020:

https://echo.orpheusinstituut.be/

Built on a bespoke platform that makes artwork foundational to its discussion (in both approach and architecture), this highly customisable, media-rich environment allows artists and researchers to present their ideas in the way most appropriate to them. Initial issues have been based on the 'tropes' of technology-informed culture that were central to the initial work of MTT. In addition to its range of modes of presentation, ECHO aspires to be inclusive in terms of contributors, materials and voices.

7.2 Sound Arguments - Electric Salon - Open Circuit

The range of artists and researchers engaged with sound and music through technology runs through many disciplines and farther into creative activities and initiatives beyond academic institutions. MTT has initiated a number of performance events, workshops and seminars that reach across borders to form new, dynamic communities. Our *Electric Salon* series invited artists engaged in sound-related to share work and learn new techniques. *Open Circuit* events have opened the doors of Orpheus, welcoming the public to share an MTT takeover of the building, to experience and interrogate our work at close hand. These performance-installation events have been repeated at Turner Contemporary, an art gallery in Margate, UK, and at the Concertgebouw Bruges.
Most recently, MTT has designed and convened a laboratory-atelier for all artists working with sound, *Sound Arguments*. In five two-day meetings, artists are invited to share work, acquire new skills from and discuss with guests, and develop new discourse across an enormous range of practices. *Sound Arguments* transcends the boundaries of art school or conservatory, art space or university to propose a new kind of creating-researching-learning community.

7.3 Study days

MTT regularly organises study days to encourage deep exchange with members of the community; in general, these study days are open to the wide range of researchers within Orpheus Institute. The aim in opening up these study days is to achieve a balance between facilitating the discourse developed around highly specialised research projects and topics, inviting healthy challenge and facilitating the broader dissemination of ideas. Among the guests we have welcomed, we include:

Germán Toro-Pérez (ICST, Zurich University of the Arts)
Michael Clarke (IRiMaS, Centre for Research in New Music, University of Huddersfield)
Roberto Trillo (Baptist University, Hong Kong) and
Marek Poliks (Berklee College of Music)
Jonathan de Souza (University of Western Ontario)
Alexandra Cárdenas (Independent researcher)
Laura Zattra (University of Bologna)
(CCRMA, Stanford University)
Zeynep Toraman (Harvard University)
Richard Scott (Catalyst/Berlin)
Andrew McPherson (Augmented Instruments Laboratory)
Sally Jane Norman (Victoria University of Wellington)

7.4 Partnerships

The project and researchers of MTT have established international collaborative partnerships that help both develop the discourse and expand the outreach of the experimental-natured work developed within the group.
NowNetArts (https://nownetarts.org), an organisation that works internationally in producing and presenting contemporary network arts works, technologies, education programs, and publications. Network arts utilises the Internet and related technologies as an artistic medium for works created for this platform.
Another partner of MTT is the Jacktrip Foundation (https://www.jacktrip.org/), which has the mission to drive continued innovation of network arts technologies and widespread adoption, by offering a wide array of technology, cultural, educational, and community services.

8. REFERENCES

1. J. Impett, "Music, discourse and intuitive technology," *AI & Society,* Springer, 2021, pp. 1-12.
2. P. Agre, *Computation and Human Experience.* Cambridge University Press, 1997.
3. D. Vesely, *Architecture in the Age of Divided Representation.* MIT Press, 2006.
4. J. F. Lyotard, "Logos and Techne, or Telegraphy," in *The Inhuman: Reflections on Time*, trans. Geoffrey Bennington and Rachel Bowlby. Stanford, CA: Stanford University Press, 1992, pp. 47–57.
5. L. Floridi, *The logic of Information: A theory of Philosophy as Conceptual Design.* Oxford University Press, 2019
6. M. Serres, *Hermès II, l'interférence,*. Editions de Minuit, Paris, 1972.
7. R. Caesar, *O Enigma do Lupe.* Zazie Edições, 2009.

The Computer Music Lab at Shenzhen University

Marc Battier
Shenzhen University
marc.battier@icloud.com

Yang Xiaoman
Shenzhen University
525407737@qq.com

ABSTRACT

We introduce the new computer music lab set up in the College of Arts of Shenzhen University (China). It was started before the arrival of the pandemic and its development was hampered by the sanitary situation which followed. Nevertheless, it became fully operational and this paper describes the various endeavours undertaken since its inception.

INTRODUCTION

In China, like in many other countries, computer music centers revolve around main conservatories. Since the mid 1980s, when electroacoustic music began to be practiced, musicians could find the necessary equipment in those establishments. This is why the blooming of that music took place in conservatories in Wuhan, Beijing, Shanghai...

Today, this situation has not changed much, except for two factors: one, there are additional conservatories, such as Guangzhou's Xinhai conservatory or Hanghzou's Zhejiang Conservatory; And other types of schools have begun to offer computer music facilities to students and professionals alike.

This is what happened at Shenzhen University. Even though this is a large school with multiple science and humanities departments, music has a rather small number of students and a compact faculty. It does not compete with conservatories, as it focuses mostly on musicology and music education, although it offers extensive composition courses as well.

A complete computer music lab was established in 2019 as a place for experimentation, composition and education.

In addition, Shenzhen University has a separate unit for popular music education. It is also housed in the College of Arts compound. It has a small but well-equipped recording studio with an adjacent control room. It is entirely devoted to recording students performing, and to the mixing and mastering of the sessions.

COMPUTER MUSIC AT SHENZHEN UNIVERSITY

Prior to 2019 and the foundation of the computer music lab which we are describing, an educational computer music room was operational. With its multiple stations working solely with MIDI equipment, it could not match the requirements of a complete computer music lab. It is still used today, but solely for general-purpose undergraduate introduction to digital equipment, such as music notation.

The computer music lab began in 2019 with a substantial grant provided by the university. Then came the need to find an adequate space, which was provided the same year. Architectural transformation began as soon as the space was made available and completed early the following year. Unfortunately, this coincided with the widespread Covid lockdown, so from then on, the development of the project slowed down. Nevertheless, the studio took shape across 2020. By the end of the year, it was completed.

INTENTION AND REALIZATIONS

1.1 Academic

The lab is able to accommodate a small group of students (up to 15). A Computer Music course takes place there, and several post-graduate seminars are held in the lab, taking advantage of the superb facilities, with an excellent listening system and a large 8k screen monitor.

The undergraduate course on computer music is geared towards composition, so all students have to create a piece of music, using the equipment. In the course, depending on the years, they learn how to use Max, Csound, and the analog synthesizers (and their software equivalents). Rather than creating an abstract composition, they mostly design a soundtrack to a short video, using their compositional skills, creative sound design and finding appropriate sound effects.

In the post-graduate courses, which have different batches of music and dance students, are taught OpenMusic, Max and Csound, in addition to musicology classes.

In order to solidify the teaching environment, a textbook has been written. It was published in 2023 by Sun Ya-Tsen University Press (中山大学 Zongshan University), a school located in Guangzou and a major Chinese education books publisher. A particularity of the book is that it came out with its text in English and in the same volume its translation in Chinese.

Figure 1. Cover of the book on computer music history and practice, 2023 [6].

1.2 Creative

The lab was established with the ambition of becoming a major creative hub for the university and beyond. However, the Covid crisis changed all that. The campus became locked down. For many months, even faculty had to make appointment to enter the campus, while classes were conducted remotely. During that time, the lab was out of reach. As a result, all invitations were cancelled. This fortunately, did not last too long, and progressively activities resumed. Nerveless, few pieces were realized since the inception of the lab. Here are some of them:
A piece for Chinese flutes and percussion, commissioned by the MUSICACOUSTIC-BEIJING festival, Rustle and Shimmer. It was performed by flutist Li Yue and percussionist Thierry Miroglio.

Figure 2. *Rustle and Shimmer,* performed in Beijing in October 2019.

Near the end of the Covid crisis was produced a piece for flute and tape made on the request of Italian flutist Gianni Trovalusci, *Nature morte avec sons (Still Life with Sounds).* It was performed in Rome in July 2022 during a festival organised by the Centro Richerche Musicali (CRM) of Laura Bianchini and Michelangelo Lupone. It was of course performed by Gianni Trovalusci, and all the sounds were produced with Csound, then mixed and produced in the lab using a large collection of mastering and imaging plugins and standalone software. Another piece was commissioned by the city of Fuzhou, a coastal town in the province of Fujian (also 2022). It was published in Fuzhou in a book with audio. All those compositions were composed by the founder of the lab.
Altogether, it is of course a rather disappointing result, after the efforts of putting together a well-equipped lab, but that was the reality between 2020 and 2022. Notably, students did not have access to the lab during those years, so the creative output expected from the student body was seriously hampered. Most of them were only able to work from home and could not take advantage of the lab facilities.

1.3 Community

One of the intentions of creating a computer music lab was to serve the community. To this effect, a project was undertaken to involve the whole of the music faculty. It consisted in publishing recordings of works on a double CD. The first CD gathered pieces made by the composers on the faculty (six of them). The music ranged from contemporary compositions to jazz. The second one was devoted to highlighting the work of seven faculty performers, plus a piece recorded by advanced students. The album was manufactured by a company in Guangzhou, Pacific Audio and Video.

Figure 3. Double CD produced in the lab in 2022.

In addition, the lab is regularly used by other classes for recordings, under the supervision of the lab staff.

1.4 Research

The principle axis of research implemented in the lab has been around the EMSAN project. Initiated at Sorbonne University but started in Beijing in 2008, EMSAN stands for "Electroacoustic Music Studies Asia Network". Its purpose has been to develop a number of actions to document the history and growth of electroacoustic music in East Asia since its inception in Japan in the mid 1950s up to today. It gathers scholars and composers who also felt the need to expose the development of this music to an international community.

Thus, EMSAN has fostered different types of activities. Amon them, and quite significant, are the EMSAN Day events, which are a one-day symposium. EMSAN Days notably took place in Beijing, in conjunction with the MUSICACOUSTICA-BEIJING festival at the Central Conservatory, during the WOCMAT conferences in Taipei, and in various locations in Japan. Its most recent occurrence was at Shenzhen University in 2021.

Another branch of EMSAN focuses on publications revolving around the practice of electroacoustic music in East Asia. For instance, a detailed analysis of a mixed piece by Beijing composer Zhang Xiaofu was published in 2020 [1]. That same year, the publisher Routledge published *Electroacoustic Music in East Asia,* a book compiled by Marc Battier and Kenneth Fields (the University of the Chinese Academy of Science and UC Santa Barbara) [3]. The originality of that book is that all chapters were written by Asian authors (contrary to the Western habit of writing *about* Asia). Thus, international readers are given the opportunity to grasp musical thought from Asia, mostly in an historical perspective of the development of electroacoustic music.

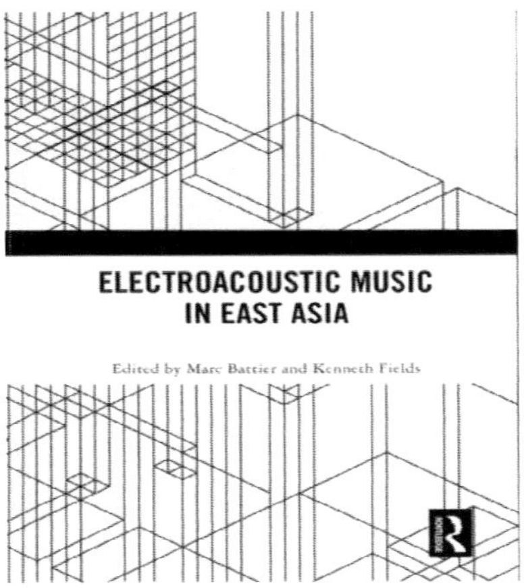

Figure 4. Book published by Routledge in 2020.

More recently, Ken and Marc plus Annie Yen-Ling Liu, a musicologist from Peking University and frequent author of texts on electronic music in China, edited an issue of *Organised Sound,* "Electronic Music in China Today". Contrary to the Routledge book, the issue was conceived to reflect on the recent issues of the development of electronic music in mainland China and Hong Kong. The majority of articles were written by Chinese authors, but there are some by Western authors as well. This is issue 27(3), which came out this year, 2023. Four authors from Shenzhen University were published in that issue: Marc Battier [2], Yang Ting and Zhou Ran [5], and Yang Mengchun [4].

Figure 5. Issue of *Organised Sound* devoted to "Electronic Music in China Today", 2023.

FACILITIES

The lab is housed in a part of the College of Arts building which is devoted to sculpture. In fact, it is a former sculpture studio, which has been completely overhauled. The large windows have been obliterated and covered with absorbent material The vicinity of devoted and energetic young artists is not a problem, as the lab is quite sound proof. Here is the layout of the lab and its auxiliary spaces.

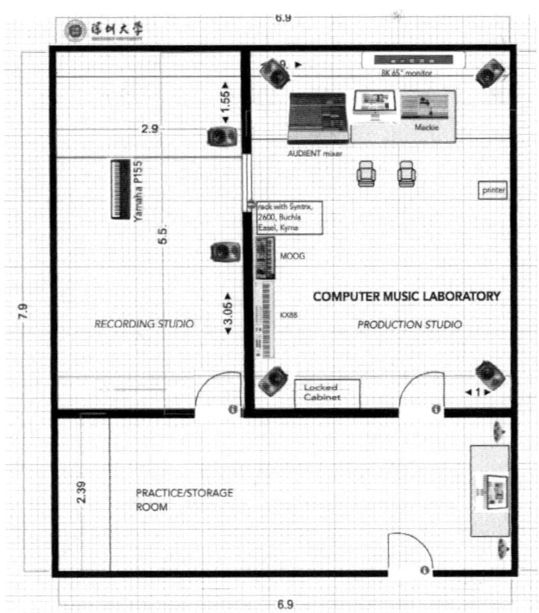

Figure 6. Plan of the Shenzhen University Computer Music Lab.

1.5 The Computer Music Lab

The lab offers a range of audio tools which blends analog equipment and various software as expected in a modern computer music studio. Some synthesizers are hybrid, with digital and analog components, like the Moog Matriarch semi-modular. There are also four analog synthesizers: an Erica Syntrx, based on the old EMS Synthi A, a VCS 300 from the British company Switchtrix, itself also a modern emulation of another EMS instrument, the widely loved VCS-3, a Behringer 2600, a device recreating on a reduced scale the old ARP 2600, and a modern Music Easel by Buchla, which came out in 2023.
A Pacarana system from Symbolic Sound, with its Kyma software, is also available in the lab. All those instruments are feeding an analog mixing board, an Audient ASP 4816 which came from England. The main computer is a Macintosh which is linked to a MOTU 828ES 8-channel audio and MIDI interface.
The MOTU is linked to a MIDI Solutions T8 thru box, capable of receiving up to 8 outputs from devices with MIDI out, such as the analog synthesizers.
The main Macintosh communicates with a Mackie control surface, the MCU Pro with its extender, so that 16 channels are available.
All around the lab are placed four Genelec 8340B monitors, themselves complemented by a Genelec subwoofer.

1.6 The Recording Studio

Next to the lab is a recording studio, with a window between the two spaces and a patch bay rack with 16 in and out XLRs. This is where the microphones are patched and, from there, connected to the Audient mixing board.
For recording, a number of high quality microphones are available, among them, two stereo pairs: a Schoeps MSTC 64-U ORTF Stereo and a Superlux S502 MKII ORTF Stereo; these can be used outdoors for recording with our Sound Devices 6 II digital recorder with 32-bit capability. In addition, there is a couple of Neumann KM 184, a Neumann TLM-103, a Superlux SE2300 multipolar large diaphragm, and a few others. All this equipment was inaugurated for the production of the two CDs mentioned above and is regularly put to use for student recordings.

Auxiliary spaces

The lab and the recording studio are complemented with two extra spaces: a practice room, with its own computer and stereo system, and a storage room for the large number of cables and other miscellaneous equipment.

CONCLUSION

When the construction of the lab was undertaken, no one could envision the problematic years which followed. The expectations to have a studio up and running were to be able to invite musicians from outside the university. It was supposed to become a living place for innovation, artistic creation and enrichment. Unfortunately, the following years saw a partial lockdown which prevented outside artists from using the lab. Now that this episode is finally behind us, hopes are coming back to put this well-equipped computer music lab and recording studio to full use.

Acknowledgments

The lab was entirely funded from generous grants provided by Shenzhen University, with the support of professor Liu Kun, Dean of the Music and Dance department at the College of Arts.

REFERENCES

[1] Battier, Marc, "*Nuo Ri Lang* by Zhang Xiaofu", in Kerry Hagan and Miller Puckette (eds), *Between the Tracks. Musicians on Selected Electronic Music*, Cambridge (MA): The MIT Press, 2020.

[2] Battier, Marc, "Crossing Lines: Stylistic gradients in Chinese electroacoustic music", *Organised Sound* 27(3), 2023, 284-293.

[3] Battier, Marc and Kenneth Fields (eds), *Electroacoustic Music in East Asia,* London: Routledge, 2020.

[4] Yang Mengchun and Xu Zhixin, "Liubai Technique in the Real-time Electroacoustic Chinese Art Song 'Lang Tao Sha' (浪淘沙)", *Organised Sound* 27(3), 2023, 338-335.

[5] Yang Ting and Zhou Ran, "Fusion and Application of Chinese Elements in Electroacoustic Music in *Mist on a Hill*", *Organised Sound* 27(3), 2023, 325-337.

[6] Battier, Marc, *Computer Music Creation in the 21st Century* / 21 世纪计算机音乐创作:历史与实践, Guangzhou, Sun Ya-Tsen/Zhongshan University Press, 2023.

The *ligeti center*: Ligeti and his vision of a center for computer music in Hamburg

Georg Hajdu
Hamburg University of Music and Drama
georg.hajdu@hfmt-hamburg.de

Christine Preuschl
Hamburg University of Music and Drama
christine.preuschl@hfmt-hamburg.de

Jacob Sello
Hamburg University of Music and Drama
jacob.sello@hfmt-hamburg.de

Manfred Stahnke
Hamburg University of Music and Drama
ms@manfred-stahnke.de

John Chowning
CCRMA
Stanford University
jc@ccrma.stanford.edu

ABSTRACT

When György Ligeti was appointed professor of composition to the Hamburg University of Music and Drama (HfMT) 50 years ago, he wished to see the establishment of an interdisciplinary computer music center of the kind he had encountered the year before at Stanford University. At the invitation of the young assistant professor John Chowning, Ligeti spent five months in the San Francisco Bay Area and was so taken with what he saw and heard at the Artificial Intelligence Lab that he visited several times. And indeed, for the planning of the Hamburg center, he managed to get Chowning, who had just received a DAAD fellowship for a stay in Berlin, as well as two of his Stanford colleagues on board. The University of Hamburg was also supposed to become a project partner while the money for the considerable investment was to come from the German Research Foundation. Unfortunately, to Ligeti's great disappointment, this center could not be realized. Instead, such centers were established elsewhere at Stanford University and in Paris. Yet, the development of computer music and later multimedia composition continued at the HfMT on a smaller scale until, in 2023, the transdisciplinary Ligeti Center was finally founded as a joint effort between the Hamburg University of Music and Drama, the Hamburg University of Applied Sciences, the Hamburg Technical University and the University Medical Center Hamburg-Eppendorf.

1. GYÖRGY LIGETI: HIS VISIONARY ABSTRACTION BECOMES CONCRETE

Invited by Stanford University's Department of Music, György Ligeti arrived in the winter of 1972, unaware of the system John Chowning and his colleagues had built at the Stanford Artificial Intelligence Laboratory beginning in 1964[1]. He accepted the invitation to find a calm atmosphere to "catch up on his commissions," far away from the pressures of Europe. But Ligeti's very nature was engagement, and he asked to visit the AI Lab for a demonstration of work being done there. Over the next five months, he made many visits to the lab, always probing for knowledge and learning of the *allure of their intrinsic abstraction*. He also visited the University of California in San Diego and the California Institute of the Arts, but he was most impressed with what was happening at Stanford's AI Lab. It was about six weeks after arriving that Ligeti asked to visit the lab, knowing only that Chowning and his colleagues were using a computer in connection with some aspect of music. Chowning demonstrated his spatialization work on the lab's quad system and played his first synthesized composition, *Sabelithe*. Never having heard music synthesized by a computer, Ligeti was astonished and immediately began asking questions, how computers work, and about programming. What was to have been a short visit became an entire afternoon. It was the first of several visits he made to the AI Lab.

How was it that this digital system for synthesizing music and research in signal processing, and perception, was unknown in Europe? In a conversation with musicologist/journalist Louis Christensen, Ligeti spoke at length about what he learned about computer music at Stanford — published in Numus-West, No.2, 1972 [2].

Chowning explained to Ligeti his spatialization strategy in 1972 which he was less interested in than in the FM synthesis of timbre. It was in searching for tones with internal dynamism for the distance cue that Chowning discovered FM Synthesis. But, beyond the AI Lab as well as Max Mathews, Jean-Claude Risset and colleagues at Bell Labs, no one knew of the work that had been accomplished at Stanford. That was about to change following Ligeti's presence at Stanford.

Chowning understood the importance of the diverse disciplines in the population of funded researchers at the AI Lab — computer scientists and electrical engineers, of

[1] https://lifeorange.com/writing/ChowningAnalysis_McGee.pdf

[2] https://ccrma.stanford.edu/sites/default/files/user/jc/conversation_with_ligeti_at_stanford_0.doc

course, also a philosopher, a linguist, a physicist and a psychiatrist.

Chowning, beginning in 1964, joined by his fellows in the Computer Music Project by 1970, were, in a sense, students. They found in these colleagues patient teachers who willingly answered their questions as they watched them build a new means for making and representing music.

"I think Chowning is the first who puts the two things together and composes directly with the computer and composes music which is entirely based on the thinking possibilities... (not of the computer; the computer is doing what you want it to)... but on this feedback effect that the use of computers has on the thinking of the composers. So, I think this is so important that you can compare it with the situation at the Cologne electronic studio in 1952-53, the beginning of a new thing. I had no information of it [the work at Stanford] in Europe. Nobody in Europe, I think, has information of just what is going on here at Stanford."[3]

On returning to Germany after his five months at Stanford, Ligeti told Boulez to "pay attention to what is going on at Stanford." Boulez did and invited Chowning to join the meetings of IRCAM planning committee beginning in 1973. In 1974, he invited Ligeti, and in 1975, the CCRMA team. IRCAM opened in 1977, with a PDP-10 computer running the CCRMA/AI Lab software/operating system. One of the Paris newspapers headlined "Stanford sur Seine!"

In 1973, Ligeti asked Chowning and computer scientist James A. Moorer help him set up a mirror system between the Computer Science at the University of Hamburg and the Hamburg State University of Music and Performing Arts (as it was called then), where he had just accepted a professorship of composition. Ligeti vigorously pursued his vision until the entire project was blocked because of the withdrawal of support from the City of Hamburg. He was greatly disappointed, of course[4]. They remained in close contact in the years following. He continued to learn, reading about scientific subjects, especially about computers. On a visit to Stanford in the early 1990s, he said to Jean-Claude Risset and Chowning, "I compose computer music, but I don't use computers."

Figure 1. Ligeti, Chowning, Silvia Fómina and Risset at Stanford's CCRMA.

[3] ibid

2. THE INTERIM

2.1 The Institute for Microtonal, Electronic and Computer Music

When György Ligeti came to Hamburg in 1973, he envisioned that computer equipment would be acquired with funds from the German Research Foundation (DFG) and that Chowning and Moorer would direct the center [1]. Ligeti donated the prize money of his Hamburg Bach Prize to this major project. Rooms for computer music were integrated into the new university building - and are still designated as such today, easily recognizable by the elevator labeling "Computer Music" for the ELA rooms (an abbreviation for electroacoustics) in the basement of "Green Wing". Unfortunately, all these efforts to establish electronics and an ensemble in Hamburg came to an end in the mid 1970s. Whatever may have stood in the way: the will was still there, especially with Werner Krützfeldt, who later became vice president and had already played a leading role in inviting Ligeti to Hamburg. Krützfeldt, himself a musicologist and theorist at the university, had a considerable interest in electronic music. Eckhard Maronn, sound engineer at the HfMT, who had achieved fame as Karajan's room acoustician in Berlin and at many opera houses, was also open to Ligeti's plans and, after the failure of the first large-scale plans, pursued the acquisition of analog technology. From the mid-1980s on, university president Hermann Rauhe repeatedly helped out with funds, although the amounts were rather symbolic. When Ligeti was joined by the Japanese student Kiyoshi Furukawa, who showed interest in computers, Krützfeldt, together with Rauhe and Stahnke, seized the opportunity to set up an environment that allowed initial research and composition by digital means. Krützfeldt and Furukawa first installed Atari PCs in the ELA rooms and soon thereafter Apple Macintosh computers. The machines used at CCRMA would have cost hundreds of thousands of Deutsche Marks (DM), yet for the Atari computers and their periphery, supplemented by four Yamaha DX7-II digital synthesizers, sponsored by Yamaha Music Europe in Rellingen (just outside of Hamburg), only a few thousand DM were sufficient.

Figure 2. Chowning with DX7 (1984)

[4] In a personal communication in August 2022, his widow Vera stated that he felt that he could have made significant contributions to the field, outside the canon of his works, had the center been built.

Furukawa soon learned to elicit sounds from the Atari computer. With his "cellular automata," programmed in C++, Furukawa created his interactive program "Small Fish" which was licensed by Sony[5]. It is remarkable that this all happened in Hamburg, of all places, where the companies Emagic and Steinberg soon started to dominate the sequencer market and thus revolutionized the pop music scene. And many composers of so-called 'serious music', including Stahnke, were also interested in the possibilities of trying out the precise rendering of complex rhythmic structures on the computers available to them. Klaus-Peter Dencker of the Hamburg authority of culture was extremely helpful and interested[6]. He organized the Interface symposium which also featured concerts and installations several times in the late 1980s and early 1990s cooperating with Furukawa, Stahnke and the HfMT. In 1988, Stahnke, previously a lecturer like Furukawa, was appointed part-time professor, at the instigation of Ligeti, who retired around the same time. The university leadership around Rauhe and Krützfeldt wanted to reconcile with Ligeti, who had never quite gotten over the failure of the computer music center he planned to establish 15 years prior. Krützfeldt was also eager to found an institute which he and Stahnke named "Institute for Microtonal, Electronic and Computer Music" (IMEC). Under the IMEC label, Stahnke and his collaborators organized a number of successful concerts and also attracted students from within and outside the university, Sascha Lino Lemke and Marko Ciciliani among them.

2.2 Multimedia Composition and ZM4

For the next years, and particularly after the departure of Furukawa who now is professor at the Tokyo National University of Fine Arts and Music, Stahnke pursued the establishment of a professorship in the field of computer music[7]. Considerable resistance had to be overcome, but finally in 2002, it was possible to get computer music specialist and composer Georg Hajdu to join the university [4]. The IMEC was ended and instead, in 2004, Germany's first master program in multimedia composition established at the instigation of Hajdu. The program has produced successful graduates (Konstantina Orlandatou, Alexander Schubert, Jacob Sello, Constantin Basica, Xiao Fu, Dong Zhou among them), In addition, Hajdu established the Center for Microtonal Music and Multimedia (ZM4) in 2010, and together with his colleagues, musicologists Beatrix Borchard, Reinhard Flender and Manfred Stahnke (also a musicologist by training) he initiated a doctoral program in Artistic Research—the first of its kind at a German music university.

Figure 3. The Hexenkesselchen developed by Jacob Sello

Between 2011 and 2020, various artistic and educational projects were realized in the multimedia department: Jacob Sello received an honorary mention in 2011 at the prestigious Guthman Musical Instrument Competition for his Hexenkessel, a timpani tripling as digital controller and score display to which he later added a smaller variant, the Hexelkesselchen, based on a tom-tom [2]. In the same year, a 288-channel wavefield synthesis system was installed in one of the ELA rooms which was used as a mobile system in various other contexts, most spectacularly in combination with the video wall for an audio-visual installation at the Internationales Bauforum which took place in August 2019 at the Hamburg Deichtorhallen[8].

In 2016, the university invited John Chowning as a keynote speaker to the Sound and Music Computing conference (SMC) hosted in Hamburg[9]. His keynote address was entitled *The Early Years of Computer Music and Ligeti's Dream - Stanford, Paris, CCRMA, Hamburg*, in which he detailed the original plans for the Hamburg computer music center. On this occasion, the university bestowed an honorary doctoral degree on him. Following the conference, he offered to write a letter of support should the need arise. Hajdu accepted his offer when it came to applying for funds for the *ligeti center*.

In 2016 and 2020, two editions of the ArtSearch symposium were organized by the multimedia department raising the bar for the discourse of artistic research in Germany[10]. In 2019, the Music Technology Online Repository (MUTOR) was revived with funds of the Hamburg Open Online University (HOOU) after an early attempt in the late 2000s – pursued by HfMT, the University of California, Berkeley and Northeastern University – had to be buried for lack of money. This

[5] https://zkm.de/en/artwork/small-fish

[6] https://vangoghtv.hs-mainz.de/?portfolio=baiba-ripa-3

[7] http://georghajdu.de/wp-content/uploads/MMM_Jubelschrift_17x24_170619.pdf

[8] https://youtu.be/j-0oFXyel_Q

[9] https://smc2016.hfmt-hamburg.de

[10] https://artsearch.hfmt-hamburg.de/wp-content/uploads/2020/01/abstracts_artsearch_druck.pdf

repository was created with the aim to turn David Wessel's Music Perception and Cognition class at Berkeley into an online course. A second course named History and Practice of Multimedia was added soon after the completion of the former[11].

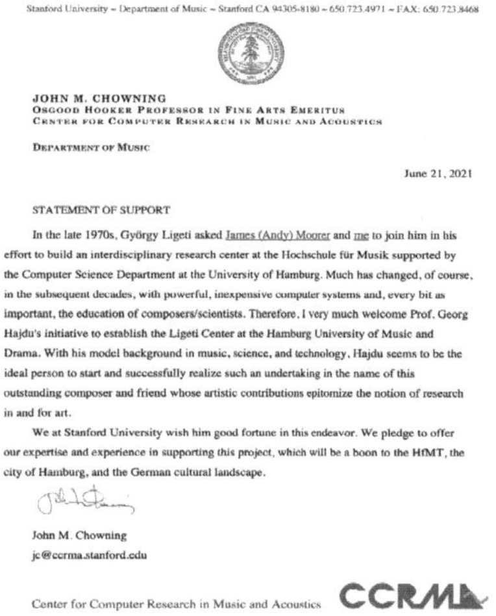
Stanford University ~ Department of Music ~ Stanford CA 94305-8180 ~ 650.723.4971 ~ FAX: 650.723.8468

JOHN M. CHOWNING
OSGOOD HOOKER PROFESSOR IN FINE ARTS EMERITUS
CENTER FOR COMPUTER RESEARCH IN MUSIC AND ACOUSTICS

DEPARTMENT OF MUSIC

June 21, 2021

STATEMENT OF SUPPORT

In the late 1970s, György Ligeti asked James (Andy) Moorer and me to join him in his effort to build an interdisciplinary research center at the Hochschule für Musik supported by the Computer Science Department at the University of Hamburg. Much has changed, of course, in the subsequent decades, with powerful, inexpensive computer systems and, every bit as important, the education of composers/scientists. Therefore, I very much welcome Prof. Georg Hajdu's initiative to establish the Ligeti Center at the Hamburg University of Music and Drama. With his model background in music, science, and technology, Hajdu seems to be the ideal person to start and successfully realize such an undertaking in the name of this outstanding composer and friend whose artistic contributions epitomize the notion of research in and for art.

We at Stanford University wish him good fortune in this endeavor. We pledge to offer our expertise and experience in supporting this project, which will be a boon to the HfMT, the city of Hamburg, and the German cultural landscape.

John M. Chowning
jc@ccrma.stanford.edu

Center for Computer Research in Music and Acoustics CCRMA

Figure 4. John Chowning's letter in support of the application for the *ligeti center*.

In the same year, the doctoral student artistic research project KiSS (Kinetics in Sound & Space) received funding for six part-time research assistantships (German Qualifikationsstellen) and the position of a coordinator. KiSS, which brought together people from such diverse areas such as multimedia composition, sound design, theater dramaturgy, musicology, and improvisation, was confidently steered by doctoral student Benjamin Helmer. In addition, KiSS was able to support a variety of projects including several full-scale music theater projects, installations, performances and a book release [3].

2.3 Multimedia Composition and ZM4

As certain areas at the HfMT are chronically underfunded, Hajdu repeatedly sought third-party funding. Hence, the university became part of the multi-year European Culture 2007 CO-ME-DI-A project on networked and telematic music, initiated the Healing Environment project together with music psychologist Clemens Wöllner of the University of Hamburg focusing on interactive sound installations in hospital waiting areas, and, in 2017, considerable funds were raised for the Stage_2.0 project as part of the Federal-State Innovative Hochschule initiative. In the application, Hajdu and co-author Jacob Sello set out to define the (music) stage of the 21st century. They came up with the following four categories:

- Real stages as dedicated performance spaces
- Virtual stages mediated by digital technologies
- Alternative stages as public places outside the established venues
- Hybrid stages as a combination of the previous three categories

Figure 5. Musicians performing in the Symphony in the St. Pauli Elbe Tunnel.

Between 2018 and 2022, the university thus embarked on numerous structural, strategic and translational projects some of which also took an unexpected turn during the Covid pandemic. Among them were (1) in 2019 the Symphony for the St. Pauli Elbe Tunnel[12] which placed 144 musicians in an elongated circle of a circumference of nearly 900m around the two tubes of this Hamburg landmark, synchronized by software developed at the HfMT [5], (2) the Moving Sound Pictures project which turned some of the classics of modern abstract painting such as *Der weiße Punkt* by Wassily Kandinsky into VR installations[13], (3) the *Remote Choir* at the 2021 online-only edition of the TENOR conference[14] which featured a choir of singers performing from their homes, controlled by animated notation (some of which used the same technology developed for the tunnel project) and (4) the large-scale multimedia project *A Space Journey – Perspectives of the Unknown* which brought together members of the HfMT multimedia and theater departments and astrophysicists from the university of Hamburg[15]. This two-hour production which premiered in October 2022 involved nearly 80 people (a 19-member Bohlen-Pierce ensemble with choir among them) and made use of the state of art technology installed in the main concert hall (a 146-speaker Meyer Sound constellation system[16] and a modular 600 square feet video wall mounted on a computer-controlled fly system).

3. THE LIGETI CENTER - A NEW PLACE FOR ARTS, SCIENCE AND TECHNOLOGY

Despite its obvious success—one of the sub project leaders was even invited for her work with seniors during the pandemic to a celebratory event organized by the president of the Federal Republic of Germany—neither the

[11] https://mutor-2.github.io/ScienceOfMusic/
[12] https://youtu.be/BXlaSBo0KXs
[13] https://youtu.be/zprjeT97RRI
[14] https://www.youtube.com/live/1sumbS_c8Y4?feature=share
[15] https://youtu.be/-2TCAVtklrQ
[16] https://meyersound.com/news/hfmt-hamburg/

university nor the City of Hamburg were able to allocate further funds to sustain the project. Concerned about a similar fate that Ligeti's first attempt at establishing a computer music center had endured, the HfMT decided to apply again together with the University of Applied Sciences, the Technical University and the University Medical Center to the same funding program in order to establish a Research and Transfer Center in the Harburg district of Hamburg. Searching for a suitable name that would also be suitable as an acronym. The choice fell on Ligeti, who would have turned 100 in 2023 and who 50 years earlier had made the founding of a center for computer music in Hamburg a condition of his appointment negotiations. The acronym stands for *Laboratorien für Innovation und Gesellschaftliche Entwicklung durch den Transfer von Ideen* (Laboratories for Innovation and Societal Development through the Transfer of Ideas). On May 5, 2022, the HfMT received the good news that its application had been successful. As mentioned before, the idea of transdisciplinarity was essential to Ligeti—connecting disciplines across the boundaries of music, fine arts, humanities, natural sciences, medicine, and technology. In this vein, the *ligeti center* will host twelve sub-projects in two clusters for a period of five years from 2023 to 2027: the cluster for music and health and the cluster for the transfer of ideas, knowledge, and technology. Especially against the backdrop of the Covid 19 pandemic, the field of work of the first cluster appears to be of particular societal relevance and aims to contribute to the exploration of the health-promoting effects of music and sound. The second cluster for the transfer of ideas, knowledge and technology brings together various laboratories in which cross-university and transdisciplinary cooperation takes place in working groups. The six labs (Artistic Research Lab, the XR Lab, the Innovation Lab, the Haptic Lab and the Sustainable Theater Lab) cover a wide range of topics which are expected to lead to synergies between the groups. As the core element of the *ligeti center*, the Production Lab will be established as a flexible production studio, serving as a platform to enable the members of both clusters as well as guest artists and scientists of the center's residency program to experiment with future technologies and enter into a dialogue with the public.

The opening of the *ligeti center* took place on May 3, 2023 in the presence of the second mayor of Hamburg, Katharina Fegebank, as well as John and Maureen Chowning who had flown in from Palo Alto to see the idea of a center finally come to fruition.

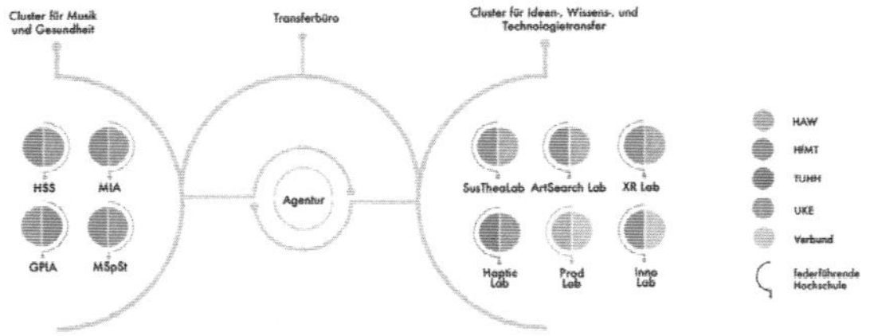

Figure 6. Overview of the 12 projects and work groups in the *ligeti center*. MIA = music therapy institute and teaching clinic; HSS = Healing Soundscapes; MSpSt = consultation hour for musicians with health concerns; GPIA = preventative healthcare for instrumental performers; Inno Lab = Innovations Lab; XR Lab = Extended Reality Lab; ArtSearch Lab = Artistic Research Lab; SusTheaLab = Sustainable Theater Lab; Prod Lab = Production Lab.

4. CONCLUSIONS

On the occasion of György Ligeti's 100 birthday and 50 years after his appointment as professor of composition, his vision of a transdisciplinary research center for art, science, health and technology is finally becoming reality. This center carries his name which can also be read as an acronym in line with its mission: innovation and societal impact through the transfer of knowledge.

Acknowledgments

We would like to acknowledge the Federal Ministry of Education and Research in Germany (BMBF), for their support of this research through the Innovative Hochschule initiative.

5. REFERENCES

[1] G. Hajdu (ed.), *13 Jahre: Masterstudiengang Multimediale Komposition an der Hochschule für Musik und Theater Hamburg*. HfMT Hamburg, 2017.

[2] J. Sello, "The Hexenkessel: A Hybrid Musical Instrument for Multimedia Performances," *NIME*, pp. 122–125, 2016.

[3] Th. Görne, G. Hajdu, B. Helmer, J. Richter (eds.), *KiSS, Kinetics in Sound & Space.* Wolke, 2022.

[4] G. Hajdu, "Von der Mövenstraße zum Ligeti Zentrum Mein Werdegang im Spiegel eines großen Komponisten," *György Ligeti im Spiegel seiner Hamburger Kompositionsklasse through a glass, and darkly, but face to face*, Manfred Stahnke, Sidney Corbett, Hubertus Dreyer, Wolfgang-Andreas Schultz, Hans Peter Reutter, Mari Takano (eds.), Hamburg, 2023, pp. 266-285.

[5] G. Hajdu and R. Gottfried, "Networked music performance in the St. Pauli Elbe Tunnel," in *Proceedings of the International Conference on Technologies for Music Notation and Representation (TENOR'19)*, Melbourne, 2019.

Developing Software for Digital Musicology: Inside an Experimental Laboratory

Pierre Couprie
RASM-CHCSC, Paris-Saclay University
pierre.couprie@univ-evry.fr

ABSTRACT

This article presents the concept of the experimental musicology laboratory through the development of several technologies (iAnalysis, EAnalysis, MotusLabTool). The aim is to consider musicological research as the result of an experimental empirical approach which combines methods (musicological methods and digital algorithms), tools (theoretical tools, technologies and software) and sources (traces or phonographic works) all in the same process. As an illustration of this musicological approach, we present three types of highly efficient visualization examples based on the superposition of several transparent colored representations and on the combination of several representations to facilitate the musicological interpretation of the data.

1. INTRODUCTION

The term "digital musicology" encompasses a wide range of scholarly practices, from the use of software to navigate and listen to digital audio files – which we refer to here as "weak digital musicology" – to the development of software or technologies for historical study or musical analysis – which we will call "strong digital musicology". In general, the practice of digital musicology reflects a desire to go beyond the traditional methods of musicology and towards a multidisciplinary or even interdisciplinary approach. One of the main goals is to find methods in other fields that overcome the dead ends confronting the musicologist. These impasses can have many origins: the study of a complex repertoire for its spectral richness, the analysis of structures that are dense and difficult to analyze (for example, long musical forms presenting heterarchical or rhizomic aspects), the study of creative processes involving a team of several people producing many files in different formats, the analysis of works based on algorithmic processes requiring an understanding of the computer developments made by the artists or the computer music assistants, the study of interpretation or improvisation processes on digital or hybrid musical instruments, and so on. These musicological practices are "outside-the-box" and often require the adaptation of methods from other fields (such as mathematics, computer science, or musical acoustics), or even the creation of new methods.

The practice of strong digital musicology remains a real challenge for the researcher. It requires going beyond one's musicological specialization and training in many other disciplines. It also often requires acquiring software development skills, a practice that is rarely covered by university musicology curricula. It is also challenging because strong digital musicology confronts the musicologist with difficulties unknown in other fields. The lack of musicological exchange formats between software programs is a striking example; how to work on the analysis of a certain musical form with various programs. In this practice of digital musicology, the researcher will usually be a composer who uses or develops research-creation methods for composing his works and developing related technologies.

A weak digital musicology has, however, been developing for about twenty years with the improvement of the multimedia capabilities of personal computers. The methods used in this new discipline of musicology are quite well known: support for the visualization of the audio signal, the use of semi-automatic techniques for the analysis of interpretation (for example, by comparing tempi and intensities), the annotation of scores, the study of digitized texts, the creation of databases for the classification of references, definitions, musical instruments, images, scores, etc. In these areas, there are many software programs that are widely used by musicologists [4].

The transition from a weak digital musicology to a strong digital musicology is not a simple change of scale but requires the acceptance of a real epistemological break by integrating digital methods into the more traditional methods of musicology. Nicholas Cook was one of the first to defend the need for an evolution towards digital musicology through the use of MIR technologies[1] [2]. One of the most profound breaks lies in the understanding of the relationship between technologies (software or hardware), data, and methods. Considering software use as a musicological research method is not obvious at first glance. In

[1] Music Information Retrieval (MIR) technologies are based on the extraction and analysis of information from digital sources (audio, text, image or data).

practice however, not only does technology provide methods that contribute to our knowledge of the data, but also to the workflow used in musicology. Bruno Latour, following Gilbert Simondon, has highlighted the way in which technologies construct our knowledge through specific scientific methods [16, 21]. In musicology, these methods are usually based on one or more theories that allow the study of a musical object. In digital musicology, technologies are combined with methods – practical, theoretical, and digital – and data – musical (e.g., score) and digital –to allow us to study the musical object in question. Technologies, methods, and data cannot be considered independently. This epistemological rupture can pose a problem by highlighting the strong dependence of methods on the digital domain itself. But this dependence also multiplies possibilities and offers new opportunities for the analysis of repertoires that have been little studied.

The aim of this article is to show how we have progressively integrated strong methods of digital musicology in the development of software, a true laboratory of experimentation in musical analysis.

2. TECHNOLOGIES

2.1. iAnalyse, EAnalysis, and MotusLabTools

The development of iAnalyse started in 2005 and the first public version was available in 2007 [6]. iAnalyse was intended to be the equivalent of a slide show software, but with features to synchronize graphical elements (slide, image, drawing, text, etc.) with an audio-visual file. iAnalyse 1 allowed the creation of listening guides with demonstrations of music analysis. The software was particularly well suited to instrumental music through the creation of annotated and animated scores. In 2011, Leigh Landy and Simon Emmerson from De Monfort University in Leicester asked us to create a version adapted to electroacoustic music and, more generally to non-notated music. We developed EAnalysis as part of the New Multimedia Tools for Electroacoustic Music Analysis project[2] [3, 11, 12]. The development of EAnalysis allowed us to move on from a type of software for interactive music presentation to one for music analysis support. We modularized the architecture to facilitate experimentation and the development of new analysis and presentation methods. In 2019, we integrated EAnalysis 2 into iAnalyse 5[3]. This latest version pursues the ideas of modularity and experimentation implemented using EAnalysis. Version 6 of iAnalysis, currently under development, is fully designed as a modular laboratory in which we experiment with new forms of data visualization and analysis.

Parallel to these two projects, in 2015 we started collaborating with the music company Motus[4] on the study of spatialized interpretation of acousmatic music [10]. In this context, we developed the first version of a program for synchronized MIDI, audio and video recordings of musical performances on loudspeaker orchestras (acousmoniums). The MotusLabTool[5] software has been used to record nearly 500 performances and is now being used with several acousmoniums in France, Belgium and Japan.

The next version of iAnalyse will integrate the recording and visualization functions of MotusLabTool.

2.2. Languages and Environments

Versions of this software have been developed for multiple languages and environments:

- The first versions of iAnalysis were developed using the REALbasic environment (now called Xojo).
- Versions 1 to 4 of iAnalyse and EAnalysis were developed in Objective-C using the Xcode environment.
- The MotusLabTool model (version 1) was developed in the Max environment.
- iAnalyse version 5 and MotusLabTool version 2 were developed in Swift using the Xcode environment.

Since we work mainly with MacOS, it seemed easier to develop these programs for this platform. This choice may be criticized (no version for Windows or Linux), but it has turned out to be the right one (especially since Swift language has come into use) as it enabled us to use a very rapid development flow to concretize our ideas and to use complex functions (for example the functions related to the Accelerate framework for the FFT calculation). Swift is often considered a modern language because it combines the simplicity of high-level scripting languages with the power of low-level languages, while integrating several types of programming (object-oriented, functional, protocol-oriented).

During the New Multimedia Tools for Electroacoustic Music Analysis project, we analyzed the development of many of the software tools used to support music analysis [4], and one of the main obstacles to development was the use of external libraries. A typical example is the Acousmograph[6], whose development is based on many libraries that are now obsolete, maintenance has become very difficult, and the software does not run on more recent systems. With iAnalyse, we have therefore gradually converted the functions realized in external libraries (such as SoX[7]) to native ones.

2.3. The iAnalyse Architecture

The architecture of iAnalysis has gradually moved towards a separation between the audiovisual player and the representations. Use in the context of music analysis requires the generation of representations from modified sources (file with audio channels mixed in monophony, multitrack file mixed in stereophony, filtered audio file, etc.). However, these sources are not optimal for audio playback during analysis. Playback must be performed from a reference

[2] https://www.dmu.ac.uk/research/research-faculties-and-institutes/technology/mtirc/projects.aspx.

[3] http://ianalyse5.pierrecouprie.fr.

[4] https://motus.fr.

[5] https://github.com/pierrecouprie/MotusLabTool.

[6] https://inagrm.com/fr/showcase/news/203.

[7] https://sox.sourceforge.net.

file that has been adapted for stereo listening. The architecture of iAnalysis is therefore organized in four separate parts:

1. Import of files in various formats. Some of them are converted to facilitate subsequent operations, such as data files, MIDI, MusicXML. A copy of the original file is also kept in the project.
2. The audiovisual player, which provides time synchronization between all the representations.
3. Computational tools to create or transform data and calculate representations.
4. The visualization interface of representations, temporal scrolling of which is synchronized with the audiovisual player.

3. A LABORATORY FOR DIGITAL MUSICOLOGY

3.1. Toward a Context-based Musicology

As well as the technological aspect, there are also questions and difficulties that are solely musicological [3, 7, 9]. As we have already shown, digital musicology is part of an epistemological rupture that has rarely been integrated in university instruction. The researcher thus faces several difficulties:

- Difficulty in learning the methods of computer science, mathematics, and musical acoustics. The online courses or books are designed for scientists in the exact sciences and not in the humanities, there is a lack of information that is part of the foundation of these scientific disciplines, but is often unknown to musicologists. For this reason, researchers are generally limited to using software that has already been developed, and the practice of digital musicology generally means simply using such software.
- Difficulty in using scripts or open-source code already developed in exact science projects that could be very useful in musicology. The compilation, maintenance, and use of such codes require a high level of computer literacy and are generally inaccessible to a musicologist.
- The lack of an exchange format for musical data also complicates the work of the musicologist. For example, the MEI[8] format often used in digital musicology is generally unsuitable for musical analysis.
- Difficulty in transferring methods between different scientific fields. Researchers do not generally speak the same language: for example, the distinction between a "singing voice" and a "speaking voice" is not the same in contemporary music, ethnomusicology, or musical acoustics.
- Difficulty using visualization or graphs formatted for other fields, such as musical acoustics or computer science that are not adapted to musicology.

Researchers in the exact sciences judge the "scientific quality" of a graph by the precision of the values displayed and the scales used on the axes and in the key. For example, for the musicologist, the precision in dB of an intensity curve is of limited importance, whereas the ability to easily compare amplitude evolution between two channels is essential when analyzing the spectromorphologies created by musicians. In this case, the usual waveform visualization is not sufficiently informative for a musicologist. It is preferable to superimpose the visualization of the channels (Figure 1).

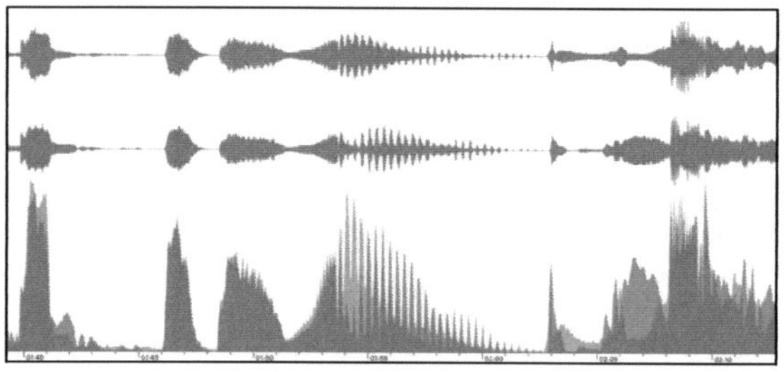

Figure 1: Two examples of amplitude visualization performed on an excerpt of *Ah Dulcinea* by Alain Savouret: (top) the waveform, (bottom) the RMS amplitude on two layers.

While some fields, such as the study of contemporary creation, have fully transitioned to the practice of digital musicology through the use of programming environments, this is still not the case for a large portion of musicologists, even though many of them work with digital sources. This shift requires a rethinking of methods of study and musical analysis in order to integrate digital methods. This is a practice I call "context-based musicology" because it requires

1. Taking into account the profound change in musical listening practices since the advent of digital technology [22]. This change can still barely be perceived in musicology, whereas it has been fully integrated into musical creation, for example with the development of concatenative synthesis techniques that extend fragmented listening.
2. Reconciling data, software and methods in musicological theory in order to take into account the way these technologies construct our knowledge [16].
3. Thinking of sources no longer as mere documents, but as data and media that are both human and digital constructions. This implies distinguishing between the "trace", the "document" and the "work", or speaking of these elements as "composite cultural beings" [15], i.e. objects that mix different types of realities.

With the consideration of these questions, we are moving from a "general musicology" [17] which is designed to encompass methods coming from various scientific domains (history, music theory, sociology, aesthetics, philosophy, etc.) to a "context-based musicology" centered on digital objects, including sources, software and methods.

[8] The Music Encoding Initiative (MEI) format is a more open version of the MusicXML format for encoding sheet music in XML.

3.2. A Digital Musicology Laboratory

Considering musicology in a digital regime requires profound changes in methods: the source no longer has a single reality, the document is no longer available on a single medium, the visualization of the document results from a translation process that can produce multiple representations, the software and tools build knowledge about the objects as much as the musicologist does, and the latter must take this knowledge into account through feedback, etc. For this reason, we first developed a framework [5] for our musicological research into the repertoire of music using technology, such as electroacoustic or computer music. At the heart of this framework were also methods of musical analysis based on various theories, as well as methods of representation produced in digital audio and musical acoustics. This first step helped us to structure the development of our software. Over the last few months, this framework has been gradually transformed to integrate the software itself. It became clear that we needed to bring together the sources, methods and tools of both musicology and digital musicology in a single entity: a digital musicology laboratory.

4. EXPERIMENTATION

In order to demonstrate how the experiments are carried out in this "laboratory" software, we present two types of representation developed with iAnalysis, which are not generally used in the fields of musical acoustics or computer science, while they have proven to be very useful in musicology.

4.1. Colored Layers of Spectrograms and Chromograms

The first group of representations consists of an overlay of colored, similar visualizations to facilitate the actual comparative musical analysis.

In 2019, we worked on a research project about the sheng instrument in contemporary musical creation[9]. We held a free improvisation session at Ircam with the musician Li Lin Chin on the sheng and Benjamin Levy on the automatic improvisation software OMax[10]. Our goal was to develop representations that show the behavior of the OMax software and its interactions with the sheng musician. The audio was recorded in multitrack[11]. Two visualizations were added to iAnalysis: the multilayered sonogram (Figure 2) and the multilayered chromogram (Figure 3).

The first figure (figure 2) simply consists of a superposition of transparent logarithmic sonograms. Each sonogram is tinted with a color enabling comparison of the musician's playing (in red) and the three iterations of OMax (in orange, green and blue). The processes used by the improvisation software are thus immediately recognizable: transposition, recording-playback with a time-lag, densification by duplication and their combinations.

The second figure (figure 3) uses the same principle of superposition from a chromogram[12]. In this case, as the sheng is principally a harmonic instrument[13], this type of representation proves to be most suitable for the recording. In order to improve readability, we decided to draw the dynamic profile (amplitude RMS) directly on the pitches, which permits correlation of data between the different tracks (red, green, blue and orange). Here also, the interaction between the sheng (in red) and the software (the other colors) is clearly visible whereas the spectral texture is a somewhat complex: response of the musician on some morphologies, morphological differentiation of pitches, improvisation strategies between the musician and each iteration of the software, software fragmentation of sounds, etc.

4.2. Self-Similarity Matrix (SSM)

SSM are particularly relevant in the analysis of musical form or microstructure [8, 13, 18, 19]. As macroscopies[14], they also facilitate the exploration or navigation of long audio files. Bruno Bachimont speaks of "laboratory objects" [1] to describe artistic objects that require an approach that is both precise and global to account for their complexity on multiple levels. SSM are perfectly suited to the study of this type of object. However, interpretation is difficult for the musicologist, which is why we have developed an interpretation-assistance system. This consists of 3 representations (figure 3):

1. (Top) A SSM computed from the FFT or multiple audio descriptors and a curve representing the novelty parameter.
2. Segmentation is extracted from the novelty parameter (yellow and blue graphs) using the Foote and Cooper technique based on peak detection [14].
3. A playback head (green) can be moved to display the result of a distance computation just below it (warm colors represent small distances). Finally, a main playback head (red) is used to navigate through the audio playback.

The musical work represented in this figure is *Burning bright* by Hugues Dufourt. This is a 64-minute piece for percussion composed in a single movement. Figure 3 also presents the segmentation (at the bottom) into tracks proposed in the recording. The aim is to facilitate the analysis of the musical form, which is difficult to grasp over such a long duration, but also to study concordances with the segmentation selected for the disc edition by the musicians and composer.

This interface is only in an experimental phase, but makes it possible to consider improvements for the analysis of long works or collections of works.

---

[9] The project is led by composer and musicologist Lin-Ni Liao (http://www.tpmc-paris.com/sheng-research-2019-2020/).

[10] OMax is an automatic improvisation software developed at Ircam, it has given rise to many variations such as SoMax or, more recently, DyCI2 (see : https://www.ircam.fr/projects/pages/omax/).

[11] One stereo track for the sheng and 3 stereo tracks for the 3 iterations of OMax spatialized around the musician.

[12] The chromogram represents the intensity of each note calculated from the FFT and plotted over a single octave.

[13] Some blowing effects and key noises were also used by the musician but they are not relevant in this extract.

[14] The term "macroscopy" is used here, in reference to the macroscope [20], to refer to representations that provide a global view of the information extracted from the signal while keeping track of the details.

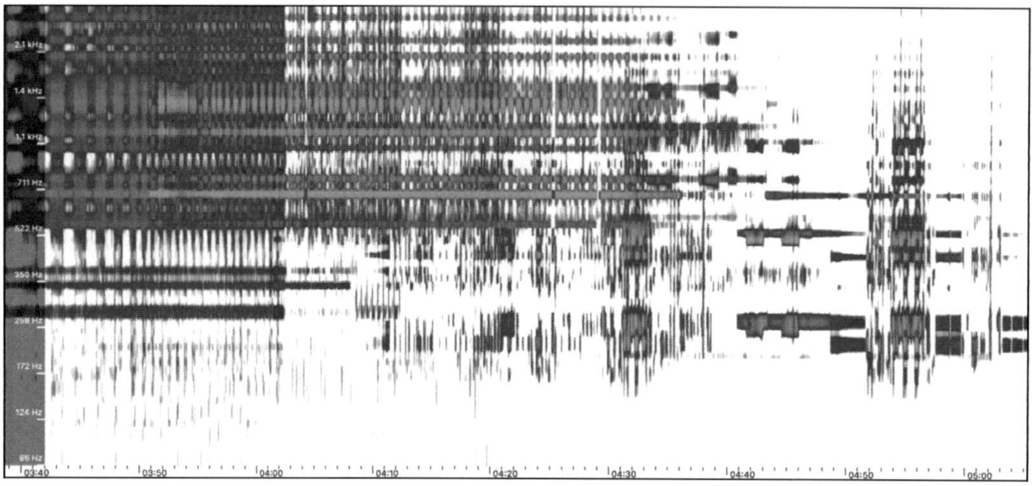

Figure 2. Multilayered sonogram to visualize correlations between recorded audio tracks.

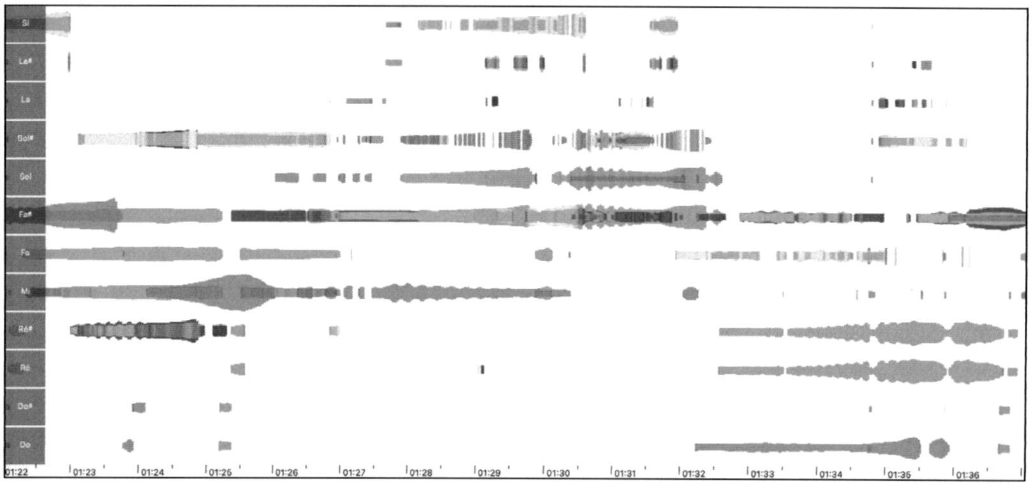

Figure 3. Multilayered chromagram to visualize correlations between recorded audio tracks.

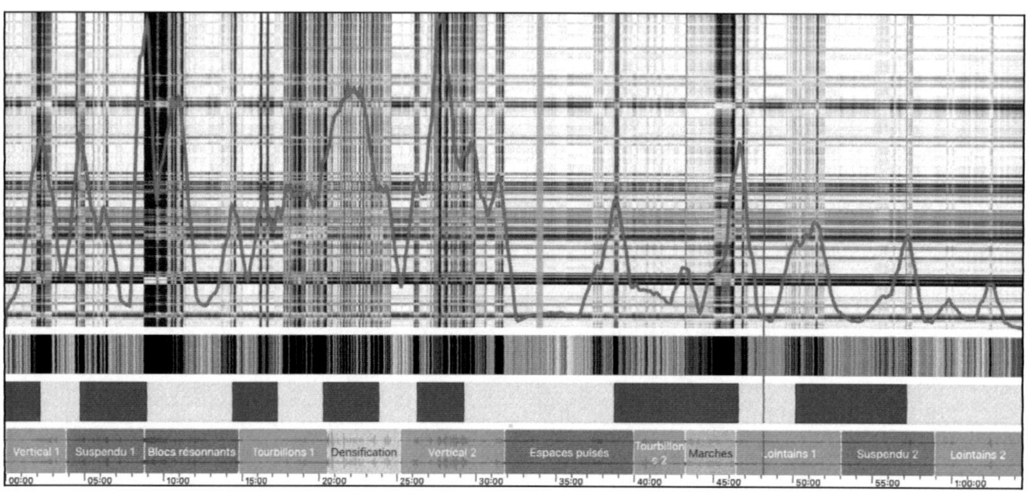

Figure 4. The interface is designed to assist in reading a self-similarity matrix (SSM) for the study of musical form in *Burning bright* by Hugues Dufourt.

4.3. Contribution to Digital Musicology

So what are the results of these two examples? First, the visualizations are not really new, but rather the result of an adaptation of already existing representations (spectrogram, chromogram, SSM). However, their use here is very different: the superposition of colored and transparent representations, the addition of the RMS amplitude in the chromogram and the association of several representations to facilitate the reading of a SSM. This approach is based on the use of the experimental laboratory in a contextual musicological approach. This transfer of methods makes it possible to create tools adapted to musicological research.

Figure 3 shows an example of representations in the process of experimentation. The interface is still far from being fully adapted. We borrow techniques from the similarity search. Although the acceptance of error (cost) is common in exact sciences, it is not common in musicology. Also, the development of an analysis method that does not produce a 100% reliable result is generally not considered valid. In this figure, the automatic segmentation obtained from the novelty parameter is still largely imperfect, but its association with a color gradient showing the probable similarities can become a valuable tool for musicology.

5. CONCLUSION

In this article we have presented technologies that we have been developing for several years for our musicological research on the repertoire of electroacoustic music. From software allowing the creation of listening guides with a musical mediation goal, we have progressively moved towards the development of an experimental laboratory for digital musicology. This concept of a digital laboratory is related to that of contextual musicology. Instead of using digital technology as a tool for musicology, it is a matter of considering methods (musicological methods and digital algorithms), tools (theoretical tools, technologies and software) with sources (traces or phonographic works). This synergy is strongly contextualized and the methods differ according to the repertoire studied. Moreover, contextual musicology is more respectful of the often hybrid sources used in the study of experimental repertoires. It is therefore also a question of taking their specificities into account, in particular, those of digital sources.

6. REFERENCES

[1] B. Bachimont, "Preface," *Performing Arts and Digital Humanities*. ISTE, 2021, pp. XXIII-XXXIV.

[2] N. Cook, "Towards the Compleat Musicologist," *International Conference on Music Information Retrieval*, London, 2005, http://ismir2005.ismir.net/documents/Cook-CompleatMusicologist.pdf

[3] P. Couprie, "EAnalysis: Developing a Sound Based Music Analytical Tool," *Expanding the Horizon of Electroacoustic Music Analysis*. Cambridge University Press, 2016, pp. 170-194.

[4] P. Couprie, "Le développement d'un outil d'aide à l'analyse musicale : bilan et perspectives musicologiques," Musiques électroacoustiques. Analyses – Écoutes, Delatour, 2016, pp. 157-169.

[5] P. Couprie, "Methods and Tools for Transcribing Electroacoustic Music," *Proceedings of the International Conference on Technologies for Music Notation and Representation*, Montréal, 2018, http://tenor-conference.org/proceedings/2018/02_Couprie_tenor18.pdf.

[6] P. Couprie, "iAnalyse 5 : le développement d'un logiciel pour la musicologie numérique," *Proceedings of Journées d'informatique musicale*, Bayonne, 2019, https://jim2019.sciencesconf.org/resource/page/id/3.

[7] P. Couprie, "Quelques propos sur les outils et les méthodes audionumériques en musicologie. L'interdisciplinarité comme rupture épistémologique," *Revue musicale OICRM*, vol. 6, no 2, pp. 25-44, 2020.

[8] P. Couprie, "Analytical Approaches to Taurhiphanie and Voyage absolu des Unari vers Andromède by Iannis Xenakis," *From Xenakis's UPIC to Graphic Notation Today*, Hatje Cantz Verlag/ZKM, 2020, pp. 434-456.

[9] P. Couprie, "Designing Sound Representations For Musicology," *Sound and Music Computing Conference*, Saint-Etienne, pp. 563-569, 2022.

[10] P. Couprie and N. Raboisson, "Acousmatic Music: Towards an Art of Performance," *acusfere – suoni_culture_musicologie*, no. 1, pp. 11-40, 2022.

[11] S. Emmerson and L. Landy, "The analysis of electroacoustic music, the differing needs of its genres and categories," *Proceedings of Electroacoustic Music Studies Network*, Stockholm, 2012, http://www.ems-network.org/spip.php?article343.

[12] S. Emmerson and L. Landy, *Expanding the Horizon of Electroacoustic Music Analysis*. Cambridge University Press, 2016.

[13] J. Foote, M. Cooper, "Visualizing Musical Structure and Rhythm via Self- Similarity," *Proceedings of the International Computer Music Conference*, Havana, 2001, pp. 419-422.

[14] J. T. Foote M. L. Cooper, M. L., "Media segmentation using self-similarity decomposition," *Storage and Retrieval for Media Databases*, vol. 5021, 2003, pp 167-175.

[15] Y. Jeanneret, *The Trace Factory*. ISTE, 2020.

[16] B. Latour, *An Inquiry into Modes of Existence: An Anthropology of the Moderns*. Harvard University Press, 2013[2012].

Sounds under control – interacting with technology

Miriam Akkermann
TU Dresden
miriam.akkermann@tu-dresden.de

ABSTRACT

Decisions taken along compositional ideas can be traced within different aspects of a composition, including a composition's instrumentation, its technical outline and its performance environment. For musical works that embed complex technical set-ups, this raises, amongst others, the basic question if technology should be considered as part of the instrumentation, as integral element to the composition – or as a composed technology-based instrument.
In the following, this question is explored starting from reflections on the concept of 'interactivity' and the associated role of the musician, and elaborated along the example of Iris ter Schiphorst's composition Dead Wire.

1. INTRODUCTION

The use of digital technologies in music has added a variety of new facets to both music compositions and musical performances, including, amongst others, a debate on possibly new ranges of interaction between musicians and performers, technology and audience. The engagement with electronics in musical works offers on the one hand the possibility to integrate processes that extend the compositional content, form or structure; on the other hand, the embedded technology can directly shape the sonic qualities of the audible outcome. The distinction between what is considered to be part of 'the composition' and what belongs to 'the instrument' starts to blur, especially, when the design of the technical set-up is directly related to the musical idea. This changes both, the way to compose and the requirements to be met by the technology in terms of its usability. The way technology is embedded in musical works can hence foster new forms of interactions between composer and adapted technology, performer and provided control units, musicians and emerging sound, as well as all partitioners and the (performance) environment.

In the following, the focus is set on the examination of the relationship between what is considered to be the compositional idea and the implementation of technology in terms of a musical instrument. Guiding questions are: How does the use of technology influence the implementation of compositional ideas in musical works and – in consequence – its performance setting? And how does the range of interaction between musician and technology shape the role technology is assigned to?

2. INTERACTING WITH TECHNOLOGY IN MUSIC

2.1 Interactivity in technology-based music

Interactions between humans and technology have mainly been discussed for specific compositions and their related technical set-ups. This is mirrored also in the existing literature. A central challenge in looking at 'interactivity' in computer music, is hereby according to Cathy Cox the fact that "[most] literature concerning interactive music is emic in nature" [1]. These publications provide a major emphasis on the technical design and the formal structures of exemplary artworks as they are often written by partitioners who create or perform (the) interactive musical works (examined in the respective paper). Cox, who is one of the few to address this personnel constellation, summarizes, based on descriptions of interactive computer music systems developed in the late 1980s and early 1990s, that music-related interactive systems are commonly either categorized by their input or their output (e.g. sonic events, gesture, physical motion). In addition, she highlights that the physical quality of the input, if applicable, as well as the type of performer can have a major impact on how the resulting (audio) output and the role distribution during a composition's performance is perceived by the audience: "whether the 'work' is considered to be the interactive musical system itself, or the realization of a performance using that system—or a blurred area in between" [1, with reference to 2]. This means, the musician's (physical) performance impacts the perceived range of interaction, which critically resonates with the debate on how performative aspects may influence the perception of technology in interactive systems.

It is hence not unlikely that the assigned range of interaction may differ from the actual possibilities to engage with the technology in use. Therefore, a performance setting can be designed in a way that allows to suggest more interaction than it technically provides, or, in contrast, hide interactions with(in) the system from the audience. Both approaches require a close mutual relationship between the implementation of a compositional idea, the development of the related technical setting, and the composition's performance. This is as ubiquitous as hardly reflected.

One of the few frameworks is by Joel Chadabe, who proposes the concept of 'interactive composing', in his terms "a method for using performable, real-time computer music systems in composing and performing music" [3]. Following his explanations, the creation process includes two steps: creating an interactive system, and composing and performing with the resulting set-up. The two steps are interlinked in two respects: the creation of the system and its use are interdependent and both steps can take place in parallel. This, as well as the fact that Chadabe is coming from a partitioner's perspective, may explain why he considers the emerging systems interactive by design, taking into account already the fact that they are designed for musicians interacting with technology.

It becomes clear that compositional decisions taken with regard to interactive musical works are always linked to the embedded technology. The way technology is embedded plays a central role for tracing the compositional idea; e.g., choosing or elaborating the interface, designing the signal flow, and integrating signal processing into the technical set-up can appear as both a part of the technical and the artistic decisions. This also applies to the design of the implemented sound synthesis, the development of specific sound combinations, and the way in which musicians (humans) are able to control these elements – in other words: to interact with(in) the system.

2.2 Reflections on the relationship between (technology-based) musical instrument and composition

The possibility of interactively engaging with technologies leads to constellations in which technology can take on a role equal to that of acoustic musical instruments. While in western music tradition, musical compositions are expected to consist of a specific sequence of sound combinations, musical instruments are expected to have a recognizable appearance and related sound qualities. This is true for most acoustic musical instruments used in western music tradition, but it may not necessarily apply to technology-based musical instruments. Neither exists a commonly shared (standardized) notation system for digital musical instruments or performance set-ups, nor is there a standard combination of technologies. However, Eduardo Miranda and Marcello Wanderley point out that the basic components of "musical instruments that use digital sound synthesis methods to generate sound" [4] can be subdivided into four elements: input gesture, gestural controller, mapping, and sound production. Hereby, two kinds of feedback facilitate the use of the instrument, a primary one resulting from the (gestural) controller, and a secondary one, resulting from the complete system (audio output) [4].

Despite acoustic systems, interfaces and sound generating units can operate and exist independently from each other. A central element in Miranda's and Wanderley's structure is hence the 'mapping': providing a reasonable, stable and understandable sound assignment from a (hard- or software) interface to a sound source in order to provide a consistent control of the created sounds. But mapping is not only a substantial part of an instrument's design, especially, when the design includes specific modes of interaction; sound mapping can also be an integral part of the compositional idea, e.g., when interactivity such as reacting on gestures or sounds are part of the compositional structure.

While each western acoustic musical instrument has a characteristic sound, and it is assumed that it is possible to identify the instrument by its specific sound characteristics, the sound produced by digital sound synthesis is, however, not limited to physical constraints. It can cover – and is not limited to – a broad range of sounds, timbres, and filters which are again programmable. That means on the one hand, that a technology-based musical instrument may not have an unchangeable characteristic sound; on the other hand, the possibility of creating specific sounds allows composers to create an instrument that matches their ideas: sounds can be completely composed for a specific work.

The same applies to the gesture controlling the interface: programmable by presets for every use, the gestures as well as the assigned control can change. Besides direct (gestural or physical) interaction, also other 'gestures' can be used for control, including, e.g., actions of the audience, the architectural space, as well as (additional) audio.

Hence, the design of the control gesture has a direct impact on the need and quality of the feedback. While audible and possibly visual/haptic feedback can help a performer or musician to interact with the interface in an instrument-like setting, e.g., in order to (re-play) given or intended sound sequences in a deliberate way, the control gesture can also be used to create wider interactions between one or more parties. This raises the question, if the possibility to deliberately control the sounds can enable the use of a musical instrument not only for performing one specific composition but also in other performances, which links back to very basic questions:

Is a composition developed in mutual relationship with a technological outline but intended to exist independently from the musical work? Or: Is a performance environment considered to be a set-up which is inevitably linked with a specific composition or an interchangeable technical outline? How does the range of interaction provided by the technical set-up influence this discussion? How does this relate to what can be considered a composed instrument? And which role does the performer play?

When examining compositions integrating technologies as fundamental elements of the artistic production, it becomes clear that the lines between digital musical instruments, composed set-ups and performance environments dissolve in various ways. Most technologies require – and hence enable – the setting(s) with which they operate. This means that each system implicitly defines itself to a certain range, depending on the complexity of the technology-based instrument. In consequence, the extent to what a set-up can be 'composed' varies with the technical outline – and vice versa: the more the technical outline is designed along compositional decisions, the more an instrument is connected to a specific composition. The question of what is considered to be 'the composition' is hence strongly and inevitably connected with the implemented technology. Asking for an embedded 'interactivity' can serve as a starting point for discussing the range within which elements are considered to be 'compositional' and 'instrumental'.

3. INBETWEEN CONCEPTS – PIECES AS COMPOSITION AND INSTRUMENT

The emergence of complex mutual relationships is not necessarily directly bound to the complexity of the technical set-up, even though it may increase proportional; multi-layered interactions can already emerge in seemingly simple settings such as, e.g., one performer with one acoustic instrument and electronics. This can be well observed in Iris ter Schiphorst's composition *Dead Wire*.

4.1 Iris ter Schiphorst "Dead Wire"

Dead Wire (2011) is a composition for piano and electronics by German-Dutch composer Iris ter Schiphorst. The composition was premiered on Feb 12, 2012, at Festival *eclat* in Stuttgart. The technical outline, loudspeaker set-up and electronics, were created in collaboration with the pianist Christoph Grund, and the SWR Experimentalstudio [5]. Soloist at the premiere, which is assigned with a performance duration of 19 minutes, was (despite the announcement in the concert program) Grund [6]. The composition's score is published by Boosey & Hawkes [7].

Dead Wire is written for "Solo-piano, Sampler and live-Electronics" [8], which are all played by the soloist who has to control at the same time three keyboards – the keyboard of the piano, one for the Sampler, one for controlling the live electronics – as well as two foot pedals. Hence, on the sound level, three layers are established: the live piano sound, pre-recorded samples, and live electronics consisting of live sampling and sound processing. Inspired by the concept of 'quivering' – an effect audible, e.g., in resonances within Clavichords – the composer creates a setting in which the appearing (live, sampled, and electronic) sounds stimulate surrounding elements to oscillate, which again produces new (acoustic) sounds. These resonances are produced by 'dead wires,' electronic devices with non-vibrating wires controlled and actuated by the soloist's actions. E.g., the intensity and duration of the effect keys being pressed changes the appearing microtonal vibrato allowing tiny glissandos, and microtonal quasi stepless up and down movements. These effects can also be carried on in chromatic scale via the very same keyboard – 'dead wires' are used to re-create an analog effect. Hence, the composition's main sound material derives from, or is based on the piano: played live at the keyboard and inside the piano – e.g., by plugging and hitting the piano strings or singing and screaming into the piano using the piano strings as an acoustic resonant space – as well as (live and pre-)recorded and played back as samples. According to ter Schiphorst [8], a set of the prerecorded samples used in *Dead Wire* were taken from the orchestral piece *Dislokationen* (2008-2009) she wrote for Grund at the time, a composition for solo-piano, orchestra, and sampler [9, 10].

On a technical level, the set-up of *Dead Wire* integrates a live acoustic piano, as well as a live electronics section consisting of a Max patch controlled by one MIDI-keyboard offering processing of the acoustic piano in real-time, sample playback and live sampling (triggered by one foot pedal), sound processing, and spatialization; and a Helicon sampler controlled by a second MIDI-keyboard. In addition, a second foot pedal allows to control the volume of the overall sound output played back via eight loudspeakers – two small ones placed near the piano and six speakers to be positioned throughout the performance space – in order to generate audio feed-backs depending on the architectural (performance) space. For capturing the sounds for the live electronics and amplification, ter Schiphorst assignes 4 microphones in the piano as well as a headset for the musician [8, 11, 12].

With this, ter Schiphorst creates an interactive set-up in which acoustic and electronic sounds are mutually interdependent, as is the design of instruments and compositional idea. The musician is assigned a central role as piano player and electronic musician. The composer claims that the electronics appears not as a direct extension of the piano, but as an element that allows a wider engagement with the appearing sound [8]. This may also derive from the composer's idea of the body as a central element of action through which a moment of physicality is inscribed in the piece – a complex interaction of musical and physical gestures, analog and electronic sounds, and electronic as well as acoustically evoked sound processing. Uli Aumüller describes this as a kind of 'experimental arrangement' in which the soloist navigates a system that is on the one hand under his control but is on the other hand not completely controllable as the soloist is both main interpreter and responsive actor [13]. The hereby caused overload for the soloist links back to another inherent compositional idea also hidden in the subtitle "Psychotechnics of Keyboards/a dissociative fugue" [8]. 'Dissociative' means here, according to the composer, setting out to behave in a way which is completely incomprehensible for others, then, for unknown reasons, changes plans and doing something completely different, and not have a memory of it at all [13].

4.2 Composed interaction beyond control

Dead Wire incorporates an interlaced approach concerning its inherent compositional ideas and the mutually created augmented instrument. While ter Schiphorst starts the description of her compositional idea with a phenomenon bound to an instrument (Clavichord) and by posing the main intention of creating an extended/augmented instrument that offers similar functions, she also states that she is much more interested in the sound result than in demonstrating technical possibilities. At the same time, the physical handling of the whole performance set-up by the soloist is highlighted as a major aspect of the composition. Hereby, the composition requires actions of the soloist that are clearly bound to the design of the instrumentation in order to address the composer's idea of dissociation.

In providing both, contrast and support for the sounds and actions, the piece comes along with a composed relationship between the musician, the (augmented) instrument and the performance space, as well as the appearing sound. What can be understood as interactive composing along Chadabe's terms hence includes for ter Schiphorst's piece also integrating the performance space. Are the piano samples on the one hand meant to evoke what the composer calls 'a resonance space' in which the pianist's playing takes place, the architectural performance space becomes on the other hand an interactive sound environment with specificities and sonic features creating resonances and feedback by amplification which can be seen as an extension to the instrumentation's effect processing. Selecting generic technical equipment for amplification such as microphones and loudspeakers as well as their positioning in space become a relevant part of both compositional and technical decisions, ranging on a comparable level with the selection of the three kinds of keyboards.

In this constellation, it is even more interesting to ask for the concept of 'interaction,' emphasizing especially its modes of expression. In *Dead Wire*, the human-machine relationship is characterized by two parallel confrontations: the real piano sound and the recorded/processed piano sound on the one hand, and the artistically enabling but at the same time overwhelming technical features on the other. While the augmented instrument opens up a great number of possibilities for shaping sounds, it is overburdening in its operation at the same time. This leads not to a complete loss of control, but to an insufficient capacity of the soloist to being able to control everything – an overload that cumulates in the requested control of the appearing (analog) feedback within space, which is hard to control in itself.

Ter Schiphorst wants the soloist to be physically in action, musically performing and latently surcharged. Following Cox's questions concerning the interaction inherent in the technical set-up in relation to the structure intended by the composer, the setup of *Dead Wire* complements the composition's instructions in establishing an interactively composed performance environment based on the hereby mutually developed augmentation of an acoustic piano. The audience's attention is drawn to the soloist and his (physical) gestures which provide correlations between the actions and the appearing sounds, while many other sounds or actions, e.g., the shifting resonances of the acoustic piano, are clearly audible but rather unassignable to interactions. The exposed soloist is counteracted with a seemingly not completely controllable set-up. Yet, there emerges no doubt of the soloist interacting with the instrument(s). This again chimes in with Cox's observation that the quality of a physical action/gestures helps a 'work' being considered interactive: the soloist's physical presence which is outlined by large gestures and significant actions (e.g. screaming [12, 14]) results in the impression of him being in active interaction with the system even though not all perceived sound changes can be traced or linked to gestures or (control) actions. The performance appears in control despite the fact that the piece itself contains intendedly a composed range of loss of control.

4. CONCLUSION

The exemplary examination of *Dead Wire* reveals that decisions taken along compositional ideas can influence the technical set-up which in parallel shapes the composition's performance. Whereas technology in performance settings often seems to be designed along practical requirements vaguely grounded in compositional ideas, it becomes clear that compositional decisions can have a significant impact on the outline of a technical set-up – and vice versa. Thinking about technology-based musical instruments is hereby one possible approach that can help to look at ongoing compositional (negotiation) processes. However, there exists not one generic structure, but a vast number of different approaches that can result in set-ups situated between instruments and compositions.

Within these new constellations, the role of the musician(s) and the range of interaction between humans, acoustic instruments, electronics/set-up, and performance space are subject to a new and ongoing negotiation process. Whether or not a technical outline can be considered part of a specific composition, does not only rely on the compositional process and the resulting set-up, it also strongly relates to its performance. Cox's considerations concerning the role of physical gestures making interactivity comprehensible can – to some extent – also be applied to the instrument-character of a performance set-up: the more it is visibly controlled e.g. by physical gestures, the more it appears as a technology-based musical instrument – independently from the relationship between artistic decisions and technological developments. The position of a 'soloist' or musician can hereby vary – with regard to, and depending on the importance of the (acoustic) music instrument and the electronics within a set-up. In *Dead Wire* the soloist is main actor for both, acoustic and electronic sounds, standing for a new group of musicians able to perform (at) the intersection of acoustic and electronic elements, creating some kind of an interactive 'new virtuosity.'

5. REFERENCES

[1] C. Cox, "Interactive Technologies in Music Composition: Towards a Theory of Interactivity." In: M. Ewans, R. Halton and J. Phillips (eds.). *Music Research: New Directions for a New Century*, Buckinghamshire: Cambridge Scholars Press; 2004, p. 332–43.

[2] J. Impett. "Situating the invention in interactive music." *Organised Sound* 2000 (5): 27–34.

[3] J. Chadabe. "Interactive Composing." *Computer Music Journal* 1983 (8): 22–7.

[4] E. R. Miranda and M. Wanderley, *New Digital Musical Instruments: Control And Interaction Beyond The Keyboard*. Middleton: A-R Editions; 2006.

[5] Musik der Jahrhunderte e.V. (ed.), "ECLAT Konzert 5 Teil 2" n.d., https://backup.eclat.org/terminleser-archiv-eclat/eclat-konzert-6.html (accessed May 15, 2023).

[6] IRCAM (ed.). "dead wire (2011-2012)." *Brahms* n.d. https://brahms.ircam.fr/en/works/work/50904/ (accessed May 12, 2023).

[7] Boosey&Hawkes (ed.). "Iris ter Schiphorst: DEAD WIRE (2011)." n.d., www.boosey.com/pages/cr/catalogue/cat_detail?site-lang=es&musicid=55526&langid=2 (accessed May 12, 2023).

[8] I. ter Schiphorst. "Dead Wire. I. Ter Schiphorst" n.d., www.iris-ter-schiphorst.de/kammermusik/articles/dead-wire-2011-psychotechnics-of-keyboards-a-dissociative-fugue.html (accessed September 18, 2022).

[9] "Programmhefttext von Rainer Pöllmann", in: I. ter Schiphorst. *Dead Wire*, Boosey & Hawkes, 2011, p. IV.

[10] I. ter Schiphorst. "Dislokationen. I. Ter Schiphorst" n.d., www.iris-ter-schiphorst.de/orchester/articles/dislokationen-fuer-orchester-solo-klavier-und-sampler-2008-2009.html (accessed September 18, 2022).

[11] SWR Experimentalstudio (ed.). *SWR Experimentalstudio 18/19*. Freiburg i. Br.: 2018.

[12] I. ter Schiphorst. *Dead Wire*, Boosey & Hawkes, 2011.

[13] U. Aumüller. "Nicht-Ich bin's: Die Komposition Dead-Wire von Iris ter Schiphorst", Radio feature 2013.

[14] o.a. "Iris ter Schiphorst: DEAD WIRE (2011) - Psychotechnics of Keyboards/a dissociative fugue." Youtube n.d., https://www.youtube.com/watch?v=Fwa-XtcpgVM (accessed September 22, 2022).

The New StochGran: Expanded Stochastic Granular Synthesis Tools

Kieran McAuliffe
College-Conservatory of Music
University of Cincinnati
bkieranmkcauliffe@gmail.com

Mara Helmuth
College-Conservatory of Music
University of Cincinnati
mara.helmuth@uc.edu

ABSTRACT

Kieran McAuliffe and Mara Helmuth have updated and expanded previous granular synthesis software instruments in the RTcmix music programming language and created MaxMSP externals for a new interface. The original non-real-time Cmix instruments by Helmuth allowed composers to create complex, changing timbres by specifying moving stochastic distributions of grains. The new instruments allow for much finer and real-time control of these distributions. This paper also introduces the multi-channel RTcmix instrument which generates stochastic grain clouds in up to 16 channels. In addition, two MaxMSP externals, based on the Cmix instruments, have been programmed for synthesis and sampling, with an expanded graphical user interface replacing the previous StochGran application. These tools provide expanded control options and facilitate more flexible and powerful performances and improvisations. Finally, compositions showcasing the new possibilities of the software are discussed, including McAuliffe's Jealousy...guilt, in eight channels, and Helmuth's Slither, Bursty Splat for laptop ensemble.

1. INTRODUCTION

Stochastic granular synthesis is a powerful compositional and sound-generating technique for creating unique sounds and families of related sounds. Stochastic generation of grain parameters allows composers to create complex granular sounds using probabilities, without having to go through the laborious process of specifying the details for each individual grain. For dense granular clouds there may be hundreds of thousands of parameters for a sound that lasts a matter of seconds. Mara Helmuth originally developed the stochastic granular instruments sgran() and stgran() as part of the non-real time CMIX music programming language [1], and has used these programs in many of her compositions. To allow for graphical parameter control, and algorithmic sound generation, she created the StochGran application [2, 3, 4] to run those instruments. Later. she programmed SGRANR() and STGRANR() in RTcmix and used them with live control in MaxMSP in two laptop ensemble works.

Our goal was to update the instruments to offer the control over grain parameters and their changes over time available in the non-real-time Cmix instruments, but in a real-time context. Other enhancements were added for multichannel grain panning, an adjustable limit on concurrent grains, and a buffer size control for STGRANR2() in RTcmix. Additionally, McAuliffe rewrote the instruments as MaxMSP externals and created useful interface tools for this environment.

2. BACKGROUND

2.1 Granular Synthesis

Iannis Xenakis envisioned granular synthesis [5] and the inspiration for this has been variously attributed to the theories of Einstein or work of mathematician Denis Gabor. In computer music, Barry Truax and Curtis Roads became pioneers in the technique with Truax developing the first real-time software for his piece *Riverrun* [6, 7], written in 1986. This piece and Xenakis's *Formalized Music* [8] inspired Helmuth to write her early stochastic instruments. Granular synthesis [9] is widely used today, and found in many plugins and applications.

2.2 RTcmix

RTcmix [10, 11] is a music programming language developed by Brad Garton, John Gibson, Dave Topper, Doug Scott and others as a real-time expansion of Paul Lansky's CMIX, which was written primarily in C. Instruments in RTcmix are inherited C++ classes, and scorefiles can be programmed in Minc, Perl or Python interfaces. Development continues to this day, including Brad Garton's embedded RTcmix plugins within MaxMSP (rtcmix~) and within Unity (urtcmix). The command line (standalone) RTcmix software currently only works on Linux and OSX, but the embedded versions work on any operating system the host software runs on.

2.3 Other Stochastic Granular Synthesizers

Dan Trueman and Luke Dubois included the granular external munger~ as part of the Percolate MaxMSP package. Ico Bukvic later upgraded this to munger1~ [12], improving performance and adding additional features such as cross platform usage with Pure Data. Unlike our instruments, this is a sort of "swiss army knife" with a wide array of granular capabilities. It can work with fixed buffers or live input. For stochastic control of pitch munger1~ requires discrete bins, though a jitter control allows variability around these pitch centers.

Similarly, the CREATE team's EmissionControl2 [13] offers a wide array of granular controls, but here in the form of a standalone program, where all granular parameters can be controlled by low frequency oscillators. It works with a fixed soundfile buffer and cannot operate on live signals. Though extremely powerful and controllable, its use case will be different as a standalone software.

Inspiration for multichannel granular spatialization comes from in part from Michael Norris's spindrift~ [14], which provides a variety of interesting capabilities including grains which move through multichannel space. It is also designed to work with a fixed buffer, and not for extremely dense grain clouds.

3. THE INSTRUMENTS

The instruments are two subclasses of the RTcmix Instrument class, and their shared libraries are loaded and run on the command-line or Terminal window with scripts or scorefiles containing parameter lists. We have also used them in both the Max and pd plugins, rtcmix~, which allows for RTcmix instruments to be controlled within those environments. SGRAN2() uses a wavetable for its source signal, as shown in Figure 1. STGRAN2() uses either a live input signal or sound file, shown in Figure 2.

3.1 Dense Stochastic Distributions

SGRAN2() and STGRAN2() stand out for allowing the user to precisely specify the stochastic distribution for each of their parameters, while other granular synthesizers with stochastic control generally rely on uniform distributions with equal probability of a parameter being chosen within the user provided bounds, shown in the middle example of Figure 3. This precision results in a variety of novel timbres especially with its dense polyphonic capabilities allowing tens of thousands of overlapping grains per second.

All iterations of the instrument have used the `prob` function for stochastic control. This function can sample a variety of distribution shapes with four intuitive parameters. The user provides low and high values which are hard limits of the range, along with a middle point, which values will cluster around or avoid according to the tightness control being greater or less than one, as shown in Figure 4. SGRAN2() uses four different prob distributions for determining grain duration, grain rate (period between successive grain attack points), pitch and panning as shown in Figure 1. As it works with sampled sound, STGRAN2() replaces the pitch control with a transposition control. STGRAN2() also adds a parameter controlling the size of the input circular buffer, shown in Figure 2. A short buffer allow for granulations which preserve the transients of the original material, while a long buffer blur them.

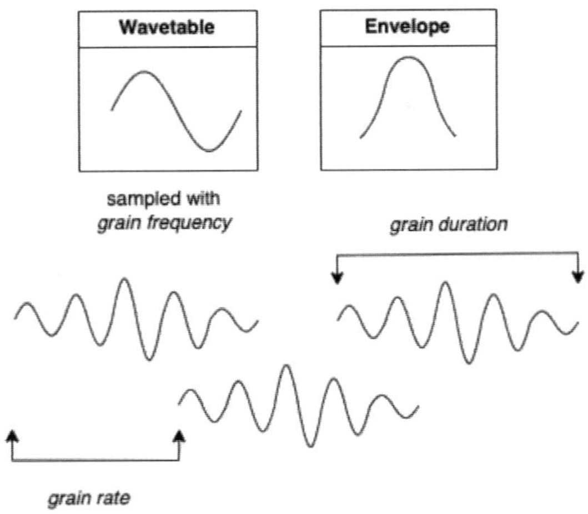

Figure 1. SGRAN2() algorithm: An envelope is applied to a waveform for each grain. Grain rate is time in seconds between grain starting points. (All graphs show time vs. amplitude.)

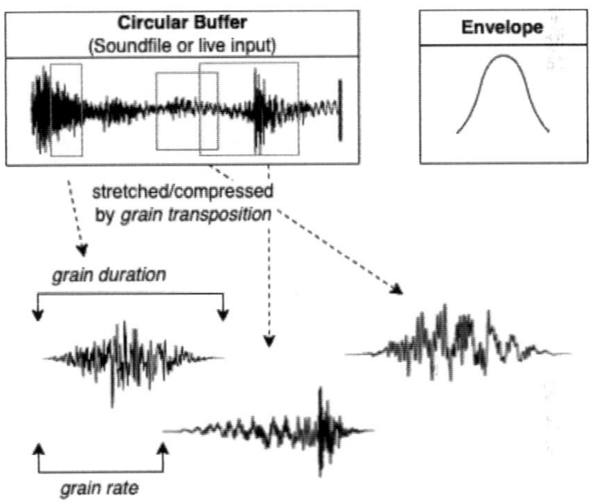

Figure 2. STGRAN2() algorithm: An envelope is applied to sound from the buffer for each grain. (All graphs show time vs. amplitude.)

3.2 Real-Time Control

Inn RTcmix, all parameters previously controlled by functions which could not be changed after initiating the scorefile, can now be programmed to accept input values, allowing them to be modified in real time by envelopes, LFOs or user control. This allows for a variety of complex timbral gestures from changing distribution shapes in real time, such as the sound produced by the script below in Figure 3.

```
rtsetparams(44100, 2)
load("./libSGRAN2.so")

outskip = 0
dur = 25

amp = maketable("line", 1000, 0, 0, 8, 0.8, 16, 1, 17, 0)

ratelo = 0.00004
ratemid = 0.00005
ratehi = 0.00007
rateti = 3

durlo = 0.000001
durmid = 0.000005
durhi = 0.0008
durti = 0.4

freqlo = 220
freqmid = 440
freqhi = 480
freqti = maketable("line", "nonorm", 200, 0, 6, 1, 1)

panlo = 0
panmid = 0.5
panhi = 1
panti = 0.4

wave = maketable("wave", 1000, "square")
env = maketable("window", 1000, "hanning")

SGRAN2(outskip, dur, 800 * amp, ratelo, ratemid, ratehi, rateti,
durlo, durmid, durhi, durti, freqlo, freqmid, freqhi, freqti,
panlo, panmid, panhi, panti, wave, env)
```

Figure 3. RTcmix script showing an SGRAN2() instance which starts as a narrow frequency band around 440 Hz. and spreads out into a wide band between 220 and 880 Hz. by use of the tightness control (freqti).

3.3 Max Externals

Although these instruments are accessible in the MaxMSP programming environment via the rtcmix~ external, McAuliffe also programmed MaxMSP externals, sgran~ and stgran~. The maketable() functions required for choosing waveforms and envelopes for sgran~ are replaced by user-specified buffer~ tables. Similarly, instead of using an internal buffer for storing granular source material, stgran~ relies on an external MaxMSP buffer for the source signal. stgran~ involves a fifth prob function controlled set of parameters for GrainHead, which gives more detailed stochastic control of the start point for grains in the buffer. In the absence of RTcmix pfield controls, the externals require the user to send new messages to live update the distributions, which is shown in the help patches. This may seem to go against MaxMSP design principles, and we considered the use of audio rate inlets for every stochastic parameter, but this would result in unwieldy objects with 12+ inlets. Both externals can be compiled for OSX or Windows.

3.4 Max Display Scripts

Additionally in MaxMSP, a Javascript script prob-visual.js can allow users to visualize the probability density of a set of parameters by attaching the script to a plot~ object to help understand the intuition behind the prob function, shown in Figure 4. Another script, prob-transition.js, allows users to linearly interpolate between the parameters of two prob distributions allowing for the easy creation of a moving distribution or sonically exploring timbral possibilities. Both of these are demonstrated in the help patches for the externals.

4. STOCHGRAN DISPLAY

Mara Helmuth previously developed a standalone software, StochGran to run the original pair of instruments. This graphical interface for creating moving granular textures with the original RTcmix instruments [5]. We have created a reimagining of this software in the form of a Max patch using the new Max externals which we call Stochgran Display, partially shown in Figure 4. Users can either craft or randomly generate two probability distributions for each parameter and edit a breakpoint function controlling interpolation between the two. Now with real time operation, StochGran can be used as either a tool for crafting fixed pieces, or an interactive patch for live improvisation.

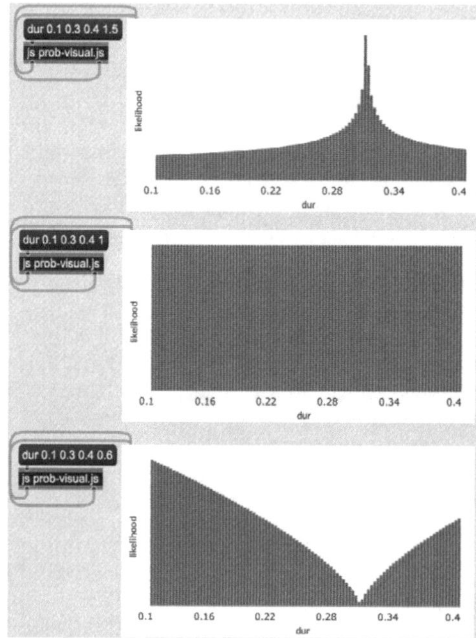

Figure 4. StochGran Panel. Various probability densities functions for grain duration created with the prob function with 0.1 low, 0.3 mid, 0.4 high and varying tightness. Higher vertical bars show a greater probability of choosing that duration value. Visualized using the prob-visual.js script and plot~ in MaxMSP.

4.1 Integration with NPAN()

The new SGRAN2MULTI and STGRAN2MULTI RTcmix instruments borrow John Gibson's code developed for the multichannel panning instrument NPAN [15] and apply it to each individual grain to create circular clouds or swarms of grains. Gibson based NPAN itself off a scheme described in F. R. Moore's *Elements of Computer Music* [16]. Instead of using prob() values to stereo pan each grain, with these instruments the user provides a location for a cloud center via polar or cartesian coordinates, and a radius, with which the instrument will use to randomly place grains as shown in Figure 5. These parameters can also be controlled in real time, allowing moving clouds which may change in shape.

4.2 Performance

The RTcmix SGRAN2() and STGRAN2() instruments

Figure 3. RTcmix script showing an SGRAN2() instance which starts as a narrow frequency band around 440 Hz. and spreads out into a wide band between 220 and 880 Hz. by use of the tightness control (freqti).

both performed well up to 1500 concurrent grains on a single core of a 2019 iMac with an Intel Core i9 processor, while with sgran~ and stgran~ MaxMSP externals

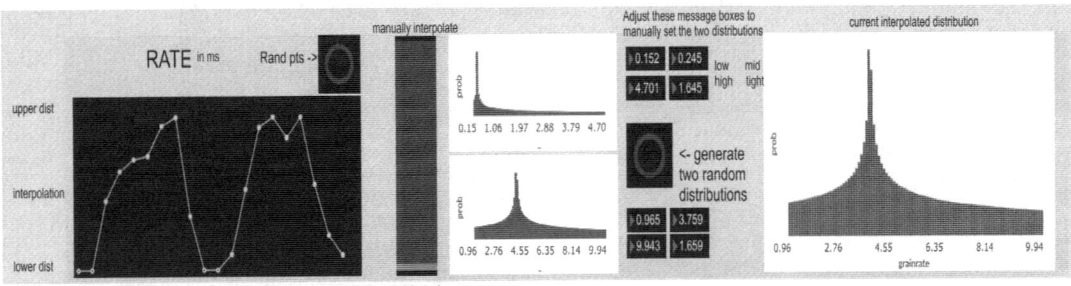

Figure 5. RTcmix script showing an SGRAN2() instance which starts as a narrow frequency band around 440 Hz. and spreads out into a wide band between 220 and 880 Hz. by use of the tightness control (freqti).

up to 1000 concurrent grains. In both software environments the user can specify a parameter for the maximum allowed overlapping grains, so they can freely experiment with parameters and distributions without having to worry about gapping artifacts from overloading CPU usage. Due to the instrument not allowing multiple grains to be started on the same sample frame, the sample rate is the current upper bound for the maximum grains per second. Using multiple copies of the instrument and a multithread enabled RTcmix build, or using the poly~ object with multithreading enabled in MaxMSP, the user can obtain densities and rates far higher than these.

4.3 Availability

All of the new instruments are open source. The RTcmix commandline versions and library for use with MaxMSP can be found at:

https://github.com/trian-gles/SGRAN

The multichannel instruments can be found at:

https://github.com/trian-gles/SGRANMULTI

The MaxMSP externals, prob-visual.js script, and StochGran remake can be found at:

https://github.com/trian-gles/stochgran-tilde

5. MUSIC

Kieran McAuliffe and Mara Helmuth have created several pieces using these newly-developed instruments.

5.1 *Jealousy...guilt*

Kieran McAuliffe's piece *Jealousy...guilt* uses the new SGRAN2MULTI() sent to an 8 channel speaker array. It uses 16 copies of the instrument within rtcmix~, spread out across cores with a multithreaded poly~. Each voice generates a granular cloud which fades in and out while orbiting the listener. The center of the frequency distribution for each cloud corresponds to a partial of the harmonic series, however for much of the piece this series is not heard. The piece heavily relies on various distortions of the harmonic spectrum, as shown in equation (1).

$$Partial_i = Fundamental \times i + shift \quad (1)$$

The extreme uses of granular parameters further disguises the spectrum. For example, the effect of raising the frequency tightness for each harmonic cloud is a gradual transition from pure harmonicity to scattered granular chaos. Additionally, a mean duration control allows individual grains to range from coherent pitches to noisy clicks. In the space between these textures lies a pitched yet transparent wind-like timbre. The compositional and recording process involved mapping all of these controls to physical MIDI controller sliders, and improvising with the sounds.

Combinations of parameters all yield different sound worlds which constitute the different sections of the piece. It opens with minimum grain duration combined with a super low fundamental, resulting in nothing more than a faint crackle. As the duration rises, a bubbling timbre emerges which rises in pitch and becomes the audible harmonic series. Halfway through the piece, the LFOs controlling the fading in and out of the various clouds jump to their fastest rates, turning into chaotic rhythmic chatter, heightened in intensity by rapidly changing granular parameters.

The piece can be either presented as a fixed piece or performed live with the MIDI controller operating the MaxMSP patch. With the intuitive nature of the controls, the patch can also function well in improvisatory settings.

5.2 *Burren Wind*

Mara Helmuth collaborated with Esther Lamneck to create together a piece for tarogato and fixed stereo audio in 2022-23, based largely on granular sampling of Lamneck's multiphonics played on the instrument. The piece was inspired by their experience of the rocky, sparse Burren landscapes on the Eastern coast of Ireland. Most of the processing was done with the new STGRAN2() instrument either in standalone RTcmix or in MaxMSP rtcmix~. A new version incorporates interactive video by composer Alfonso Belfiore.

5.3 *Slither, Bursty Splat*

Slither, Bursty Splat was created for the Cincinnati Composers Laptop Orchestra Project (CiCLOP) in a Live Electronic Music class at CCM by Mara Helmuth. Sonic gestures with identifying names such as slither, bursty, gloom, needle and splat and their combinations and fragments interact in various ways throughout the piece.

The compositional process for Slither, Bursty Splat was to choose three collections of descriptive words. The group of words describes the basic, unique, and variable sound gestures of the piece. Slither, bursty, splat, needle and gloom are examples of these sound gesture names. The second collection of words describes the extending processes which were applied to basic gestures, and includes corrugate, splinter, undulate, shiver, sway, twitch, and convulse. A final collection of one-word descriptors applies to the combination or breaking apart of multiple sound gesture types, including aggregate, amalgamate, squeeze, conspire, sunder and rupture. The various named sound gestures and their extensions were synthesized primarily with the new RTcmix granular synthesis instrument SGRAN2().

The piece can be improvised by laptop performers with MaxMSP patches, or played in an 8-channel fixed media format.

6. FUTURE DEVELOPMENT

6.1 LUAGRAN

Through the programming of these instruments, we realized that the most computationally expensive aspect was the polyphonic handling of many concurrent grains, and not the stochastic selection of parameters for new grains. We are currently developing a new instrument/external LUAGRAN()/luagran~ which takes advantage of this realization by delegating grain parameter generation to user provided Lua scripts, while leaving the CPU intensive polyphonic synthesis to C/C++ code. Code savvy users will get even finer granular control, and those not interested in learning Lua will still be able to use the instrument by modifying the many provided example scripts.

6.2 New Distributions

We plan on implementing additional distributions. The normal/Gaussian distribution has audibly different kurtosis, with higher density around the center, and lower density around the wings.

We are also exploring correlation between parameter distributions. For example, higher pitched grains tending to have shorter duration creates a different timbre than the inverse. A major challenge is making the required covariance matrix intuitive and controllable in real time.

Finally, we are researching options for non-independent calls for a particular distribution, such as random walks.

6.3 More Parameters

Though we do not intend to expand the capabilities of the instrument to the "swiss army knife" munger~ or EmissionControl2, we would like to try adding more parameters for user control. None of the updated instruments allow for stochastic control of grain amplitude, a feature of one of the original Cmix instruments, which should be included. STGRAN2() currently only produces grains that play forward, and the option to mix between forward and backward grains, such as in munger~, could create interesting textures. Finally, we would like to make a version of SGRAN2() which works with frequency modulated grains, offering stochastic control for carrier frequency, modulator frequency and modulator depth.

7. CONCLUSIONS

The new stochastic granular synthesis instruments SGRAN2() and STGRAN2() bring the parameter control and sound quality of their original Cmix versions into real time, encouraging new gestural exploration. The multichannel instruments and expanded interface implemented in MaxMSP also provide a powerful StochGran environment for original composition and improvisation.

Acknowledgments

We would like to acknowledge the RTcmix developer community for inspiration and responsiveness to questions.

8. REFERENCES

[1] P. Lansky, "The Architectural and Musical Logic of Cmix," *Proceedings of the 1990 International Computer Music Conference*, ICMA, 1990.

[2] M. Helmuth, "Patchmix and StochGran: Two Graphical Interfaces," *Proceedings of the 1991 International Computer Music Conference,* pp. 563-566, 1991.

[3] M. Helmuth, "Granular Synthesis with Cmix and Max" Proceedings of the 1993 International Computer Music Conf. ICMA, Tokyo, 1993, pp. 449-452.

[4] M. Helmuth, "StochGran on OSX" *Proceedings of the 2002 International Computer Music Conference.* ICMA, Gothenburg, 2002, pp. 77-78.

[5] M. Solomos, The Granular Connection (Xenakis, Vaggione, di Scipio…), Symposium: The Creative and Scientific Legacies of Iannis Xenakis International Symposium, 2006, Canada. ffhal-00770088.

[6] B. Truax, "Riverrun," *Digital Soundscapes.* Cambridge Street Records, 1987. Compact disk.

[7] M. Helmuth, "Barry Truax's Riverrun," *Analytical Methods of Electroacoustic Music.* Routledge: Taylor and Francis, 2006, *pp. 186-238.*

[8] I. Xenakis, *Formalized Music: Thought and Mathematics in Composition,* Bloomington and London, Indiana University Press, 1971.

[9] J. Haas, "Granular Synthesis and Granulation of Sampled Sound" in Introduction to Computer Music. cited 2023, Available from https://cmtext.indiana.edu/

[10] B. Garton, D. Topper, "RTcmix – Using CMIX in Real Time" *Proceedings of the 1997 International Computer Music Conference*, ICMA, 1997.

[11] RTcmix, "an open-source digital signal processing and sound synthesis language," cited 2023, Available from http://rtcmix.org/

[12] I. Bukvic, "munger1~: TOWARDS A CROSS-PLATFORM SWISSARMY KNIFE OF REAL-TIME GRANULAR SYNTHESIS," in Proc. Int. Computer Music Conf. (ICMC 2007), Copenhagen, 2007.

[13] EmissionControl2, cited 2023, Available from https://github.com/EmissionControl2/EmissionControl2

[14] M. Norris, "spindrift~ granular synthesis Max external," cited 2023, Available from https://www.michaelnorris.info/software/spindrift

[15] J. Gibson, "NPAN", cited 2023, Available from https://github.com/RTcmix/RTcmix/blob/1b04fd3f121a1c65743fde8ea37eb5d65f2cf35c/insts/jg/NPAN/NPAN.cpp

[16] F. R. Moore, Elements of Computer Music. Pearsons, 1990, pp. 353-359.

Meta-Xenakis: Developing Style-Agnostic, Stochastic Algorithmic Music

Bill Manaris
Computer Science Department
College of Charleston, USA
manarisb@cofc.edu

Anna Forgette
Computer Science Department
College of Charleston, USA
forgetteak@g.cofc.edu

ABSTRACT

Iannis Xenakis was a pioneer in algorithmic composition of music and art. He combined architecture, mathematics, music, and performance art to create avant-garde compositions and performances that are still being analyzed, performed widely, and discussed today. Xenakis's musical contributions are deeply algorithmic in nature, inspired by his appreciation and understanding of mathematics and controlled randomness, i.e., stochastic processes.

This paper argues that Xenakis's algorithmic approach is style-agnostic, as it may be used with different sonification choices to produce pieces with more traditional aesthetics, possibly bringing broader acceptance, appreciation, and application of his techniques and ideas to more traditional compositional spaces. Also, today's music technology has evolved tremendously, through the integration of artificial intelligence, advanced computing algorithms, and human-computer interaction – techniques and technology that were unavailable to Xenakis, but which would have been inline with his pioneering spirit.

We explore some of Xenakis's early works in algorithmic and stochastic music, and reimagine the types of music Xenakis could possibly be making today, having access to the modern technology of smartphones and computing devices. Examples include a retelling of Xenakis's "Concret PH" using smartphones for sound spatialization and audience interaction / participation; "Éolienne PH", an example piece which utilizes the same statistical distributions as "Concret PH" to produce a completely different sound aesthetic; "on the Fractal Nature of Being..." which combines Xenakis's stochastic / aleatoric techniques with traditional music theory and modern mathematics / fractal geometry; and, finally "Nereides / Νηρηΐδες", a piano miniature piece, which is made using statistical distributions from a cloudy sky. We close with some general ideas on the future of the Algorithmic Arts.

1. INTRODUCTION

Iannis Xenakis was a pioneer in algorithmic composition of music and art. He combined architecture, mathematics, music, and performance art to create avant-garde compositions and performances that are still being analyzed, performed widely, and discussed today [1-9]. The compositions and other artifacts created by him were primarily inspired by his deep appreciation and understanding of algorithms, mathematics, and the use of controlled randomness, i.e., stochastic processes.

Given the evolution of the field of Computer Science since that time, Xenakis's work now falls clearly within in the field of the Algorithmic Arts (AlgoArts).[1] Xenakis's many musical contributions are deeply algorithmic in nature. Therefore, his rich and influential output would not have been possible without the ability to implement his processes through computer programming languages, such as FORTRAN and BASIC [10, 11], and the formalization, standardization, and replicability that such programming languages provide.

This paper is based on an invited talk-performance at the Music Library of Greece, in the context of "Meta–Xenakis" – a year-long, transcontinental celebration of the life and work of Iannis Xenakis (1922-2001). The word "meta" comes from the Greek "μετά", which means:

- "transcending", in a theoretical (or structural) sense, i.e., "higher level"; and
- "after", in a temporal (or spatial) sense, i.e., "afterwards" or "beyond".

In what follows, we engage with both notions of "meta". First, we explore the algorithmic side of Xenakis, through some of his works in algorithmic and stochastic music. Then, we reimagine the types of music Xenakis could possibly be making today, having access to the modern technology of smartphones and computing devices. The paper includes musical examples that hopefully demonstrate the points made.

2. THE ALGORITHMIC XENAKIS

In music and art, algorithms appear as early as Guido d'Arezzo (ca. 1000 A.D.), and in compositions of J.S. Bach, Mozart, John Cage, and Iannis Xenakis, as well as in the visual works of M.C. Escher, Roman Verostko, Vera Molnár, and Ernest Edmonds, among others.

Many sources on Xenakis are written by and for musicologists, music composers, and performers, and as such focus on the musical output that Xenakis created, e.g. [8, 12]. This is reasonable, as Xenakis was primarily known as a music composer. Fewer works have been written on the meta-level, algorithmic side of Xenakis – i.e., the algorithms or processes he created to generate

[1] This work is co-sponsored by the US National Science Foundation and the National Endowment for the Arts (#2139786), "Computing in the Arts – The Algorithm is the Medium", see http://AlgoArts.org .

Figure 1. Example of the musical output of Xenakis's ST compositional process – first five measures of *ST/10-1, 080262* [11, p. 154].

musical artifacts. Notable examples of such meta-level analyses are included in [6, 11, 13].

This section focuses on Xenakis's algorithmic process. It discusses an example of mathematical modeling, sonification, and computer programming he used in musical compositions.

By focusing on the algorithms used to generate pieces, Xenakis clearly placed great importance on them, decades before algorithmic music composition became an established field.

For instance, Xenakis included the complete ST (Stochastic Music) program in his seminal book, written in FORTRAN – the state-of-the-art, high-level programming language, at the time. By doing so, he indicated the autonomy, and significance of algorithms in his compositional approach [11, p. 145-152]. The following section begins to explore this autonomy further.

2.1 Input → Process → Output

All artifacts surrounding us (chairs, computers, smartphones) may be analyzed in terms of:

- the *process* that created them;
- the *input* to this process; and
- the *output* of this process.

In the case of music and art, *the process is usually hidden* (or protected) behind a veil of mystery (or secrecy), as few artists share their process openly with the world. On the other hand, *the input to the process*, the source materials (or inspiration) are available to us, usually from conversations with the artists. For instance, Debussy created harmonic material from gazing at colorful landscapes. Finally, *the output of the process* – the actual artifacts – are always available to experience, inspect, interpret, and evaluate. It is by experiencing these artifacts that people are attracted to, or not – as the case may be with Xenakis, or say, Jackson Pollock – to a particular composer, or artist.[2]

In terms of *process* and *input*, Xenakis used algorithms and mathematical models to compose much of his music. For instance, he presents a thorough, eight-step process in [11, p. 22]. His process is clearly influenced by early

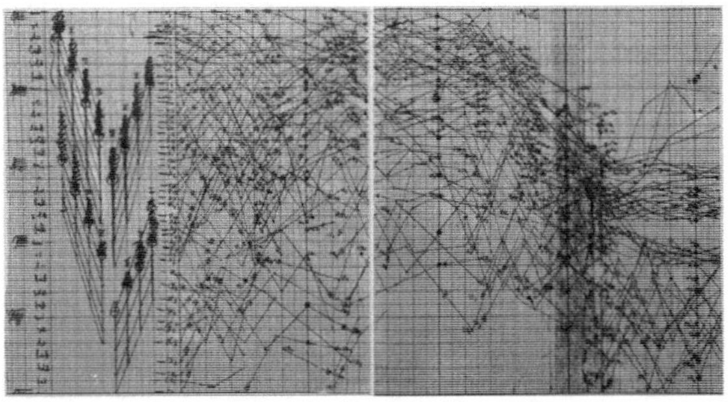

Figure 2. Example of sonification design to map the numerical output from the ST program to musical notation [11, p. 18–19]. The vertical axis represents solfege pitches, and the horizontal axis represents time.

software development processes, e.g., [14, p. 248-249]. However, it is his musical *output* that most people experience first. For example, Figure 1 shows the first few bars from *ST/10-1, 080262* (i.e., composed February 8, 1962). To compose this piece, Xenakis used his ST program (discussed above).

To fully appreciate this example, let us explore the input, process, and output:

- The *input* to the process consists of numerical data.
- The *process* is described by the program itself.
- The *output* generated by the program is just a sequence of numbers.

Given this *numerical output*, there are several possibilities, of course, for what to do with it:

- One possibility is *data visualization*, i.e., take the numerical output and convert it to visual drawings, or charts. Such visualizations may be information preserving, or focusing more on aesthetic or artistic outcome (i.e., without necessarily preserving accuracy). For example, consider visual charts for weather or stock-market reporting / forecasting.
- Another possibility is *data sonification,* i.e., take the numerical output and convert it to sounds or a musical composition. This is mainly what Xenakis did in his ST works.
- Yet another possibility is *data materialization*. The term is relatively recent [16], and refers to something Xenakis did do, i.e., take the numerical output and convert it to physical form.[3]

Figure 2 shows one of Xenakis's *sonification* designs, where he translates numerical data to sound. He uses solfege pitches on the Y (vertical) axis, and time on the X (horizontal) axis. The dots are actual numerical outputs, which are mapped to notes. Finally, he draws lines to connect the notes.

Xenakis uses an elaborate sonification design, to generate the *musical output*, by mapping the numerical output to musical notation. He chooses to sonify these numerical data as large masses of musical point-notes.

[2] Jackson Pollock's process generated artifacts with similar statistical properties to Xenakis's [15].

[3] This is the case, for example, with the architectural design of the Philips Pavilion [17, 18].

There are other possibilities, as will be shown later in the paper. These point-notes are mapped to string *pizzicati*, *glissandi*, and other aleatoric and stochastic microsound events, to be interpreted by – again – chosen orchestral instruments and performers (also, see section 3).

This mapping is stochastic, in that some aspects of the performance are approximate (and may even be unplayable); these aspects are left to be interpretated (or approximated by) the performers.[4]

The final piece is eventually performed by musicians, who interpret (or approximate) the musical score, adding subtle layers of breathing, hesitation, movement, simplification, and micro-textures to the sonic outcome.

The challenging nature of Xenakis's musical scores, generated through this compositional process, is captured in the following:[5]

> Of the many pianists who have performed and discussed *Evryali*, dedicatee Marie-Françoise Bucquet perhaps best expresses the performance issues Xenakis raised, writing, "Supreme challenge: he asks us to take risks and overwhelming responsibilities. I find it wonderful that instead of saying to the performer 'I have written this piece for you, and you are going to play it,' he said to me 'Here is the piece. Look at it, and if you think you can do something with it, play it'." [18, p. 74].

2.2 Style Agnosticism

Here, finally, it is important to emphasize that Xenakis chose the way his works sound – he meticulously crafted his *sound aesthetic*, through his sonification choices. In other words, his particular sound aesthetic is mainly the result of the *second part* of his compositional process – his sonification design.

The first part, i.e., his algorithmic approach is *style-agnostic*, and as such it can be used with other sonification choices, bringing possibly broader acceptance, and application of his techniques to other compositional spaces.

This is a significant point, which will be demonstrated further below with specific musical examples.

2.3 Authorship Attribution

Authorship attribution (or, "who is the composer?") is a significant question, often arising in the context of algorithmic music composition. Sometimes this may confuse even experts in computer science.

For example, given the above example (ST/10-1, 080262), let's explore who the composer is... Possible answers include:

- Carl Friedrich Gauss, the German mathematician who created the *probabilities* used for input in Xenakis's work.
- The computer – an IBM 7090 – which executed the ST program and produced the *output numbers*.
- Xenakis who created (a) the *process*, or *algorithm*, AND (b) the *sonification design* used to generate the final music score.

Interestingly, in the original talk (upon which this paper is based), from an audience of about 160 people, 3 identified Gauss as the composer, 3 identified the computer as the composer(!!), while the rest identified Xenakis as the composer. While this is not statistically significant by any means, it demonstrates the confusion general audiences may have with the question of authorship, when computers and algorithms are involved.

For the ICMC reader, of course, the answer is clear: The algorithm created the musical output. The computer (*blindly*) followed the algorithm. Xenakis wrote the algorithm – therefore, *Xenakis is the composer*.

However, the question of authorship becomes more nuanced when the input to the process becomes statistical probabilities derived from other composers' musical works, such as J.S. Bach, Mozart, or Beethoven – e.g., see [19-23].

Recently, this has become a controversial topic, given the availability of software systems trained with statistical probabilities from large language models (LLMs), such as ChatGPT and DALL·E [24, 25].

Regardless, this demonstrates the power of the algorithm as a creative medium, and strengthens our appreciation for Xenakis's vision and pioneering work.

3. STOCHASTIC MUSIC

Xenakis coined the term *stochastic music* (from the Greek stochos, "στόχος", or target), to describe music that evolves over time, within certain statistical tendencies and densities, and has points of origin and destination.

Xenakis created stochastic music to react to purely chaotic, random properties of 12-tone, or serialist music [11]. He believed the listener may be aesthetically overwhelmed by the complexity of serialist music – which, although deterministic due to its rules of creation, by definition, over time sounds utterly chaotic (i.e., uniformly distributed). He proposed to use statistical mathematics to produce compositional techniques, whose musical outcome is more controllable. This could produce music that is more aesthetically-pleasing – at least structurally, which he went on to demonstrate.

His first electroacoustic composition, *Concret PH* (1958), was composed intuitively (i.e., non-algorithmically, by ear) to demonstrate this.

Xenakis also created programs to assist in the compositional process. One major example is the *Unite Polygogique Informatique de CEMAMu (UPIC)* system. UPIC was constructed in 1977 by Xenakis and his associates to connect visual drawing (e.g., architectural drafting) with musical or sound design. This was done to achieve "sonic realization of drawn musical ideas by a computer" [26, p. 252].

We have reconstructed a simplified version of UPIC, in Python. To do so, we used *JythonMusic*, an environment

[4] For instance, in *Evryali* (1973), Xenakis overlooks the fact "that the two hands and ten fingers of the pianist can only reach so far ... and even includes a high C#, beyond the range of any piano" [18, p. 75].

[5] One may argue that this contributes to why he is admired by some musicians, while avoided by others.

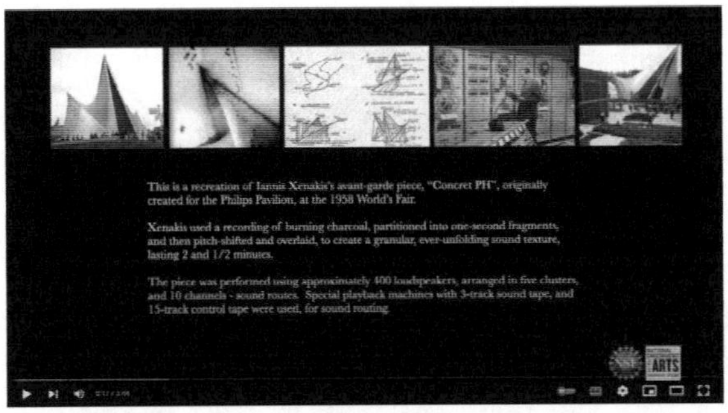

Figure 3. Performance of *Concret PH – A Retelling*, using smartphones, at the University of Maryland, College Park, USA, April 2022 – https://youtu.be/sCe2qQi_QBY

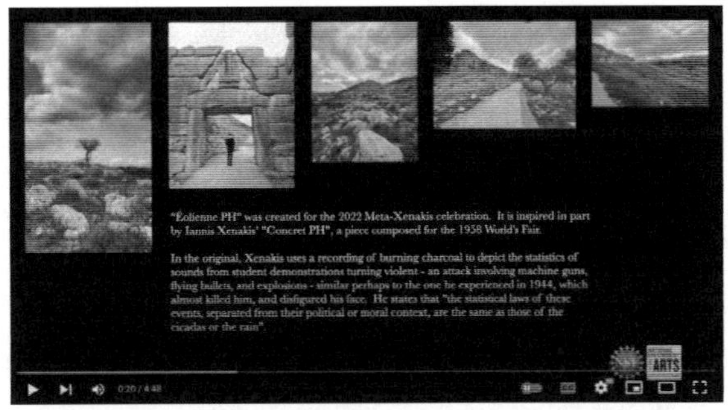

Figure 4. Performance of *Éolienne PH*, at the International Symposium on Electronic Art (ISEA 2022), Barcelona, Spain, June 2022. It includes photographs from the performance site of Mycenae Polytopon (1978) – https://youtu.be/mNBwNrpwdaA

for developing interactive musical experiences, and systems for computer-aided analysis, composition, and performance in music and art.[6] JythonMusic has been used for research in music information retrieval and computational musicology, as well as in modeling aesthetics and creativity, sound spatialization, and telematics.

Our UPIC implementation expands on the original to control various aspects of a musical piece through curves. Although we have implemented a simple graphical user interface for drawing curves and generating sounds in real-time, in our work, we find it more useful to simply output numerical sequences – x and y coordinates of graph points, and then incorporate them algorithmically into other programs.

In our approach, UPIC graphs may describe densities of *pitch*, *dynamic*, *harmonic probability* or *consonance*, *timbre* or *various instruments*, occurrence of *arbitrary sonic events* – as these unfold over time (or relative to each other). In fact, these graphs can model any musical attribute desired, as long as it can be controlled via algorithmic means. Since this is done in Python, such graphs can also control aspects of other algorithmic processes, including parameters of external sound engines (e.g., Ableton Live), visualizations, animation parameters, and arguments to arbitrary Python functions, thus tapping into the full power of a Turing Machine.[7]

4. CASE STUDIES

This section presents music examples, derived from Xenakis's work, suggesting a few possibilities of how to move forward (i.e., the "afterwards" or "beyond" meaning of "meta"). These demonstrate that it is possible to create *style-agnostic*, stochastic algorithmic music, based on Xenakis's original ideas and contributions. Also, they incorporate modern technology, more advanced algorithms, and use of smartphones for sound spatialization and audience interaction / participation.

4.1 *Concret PH – A Retelling* (2022)

Concret PH (1958) is an early and influential piece of stochastic music, composed by Xenakis intuitively, to capture mathematical probabilities he was deeply interested in. It was performed in the Philips Pavilion at the 1958 World's Fair, using approximately 400 loudspeakers – arranged in five clusters, and 10 channels, or sound routes. Special playback machines with a 3-track sound tape, and a 15-track control tape were used for sound routing. Unfortunately, the Pavilion was demolished soon thereafter, so we cannot experience the piece as it was originally intended / performed [5, 9, 17].

Our recreation of *Concret PH* utilizes speakers on audience smartphones, to recreate the multiplicity and apparent unpredictability of sound sources of the original, as well as audience movement through the performance space. We utilize our UPIC approach to control the density of sound events over time, in order to recreate the unfolding sound densities and textures of the original.

In the original, Xenakis used tape recordings of burning charcoal, partitioned into one-second fragments, pitch-shifted and overlaid, to create granular, unfolding sound textures. Our recreation uses sounds from the original, together with *hammer-on-anvil* sounds, to simulate individual charcoal sound events.

Our code distributes the required number of sound events across all participating audience smartphones. This works regardless of how many smartphones are participating. The piece may be reproduced using a single smartphone, as well as hundreds of them, always maintaining the desired density and sound texture. Participants are asked to move around freely, resembling people moving through the Philips Pavilion in 1958, to create a truly immersive experience [27].

Concret PH – A Retelling was first performed at the University of Maryland, College Park, USA in April 2022. A video link is available in Figure 3.[8]

[6] See http://jythonMusic.org .

[7] A great alternative, also inspired by UPIC, is the graphical environment *IanniX*, a 3D sequencer for digital art and real-time control (see https://www.iannix.org).

[8] This performance was captured via a high-quality 3D binaural microphone, so stereo headphones are recommended.

4.2 Éolienne PH (2022)

Éolienne PH (or *Be the Wind*) was composed in the context of the 2022 Meta-Xenakis transcontinental celebration. It was performed at the *International Symposium on Electronic Art (ISEA 2022)* in Barcelona, in June 2022. It was partially inspired by the ISEA 2022 conference themes of "exploring our relationship with nature" and "transforming / inhabiting our world".

Éolienne PH is based on Xenakis's *Concret PH* (see previous subsection). It demonstrates the importance of separating the two parts in Xenakis's compositional process:

(a) the *algorithmic process* used to generate numerical data, and
(b) the *sonification choices* mapping these data to sounds.

It should be emphasized that *Éolienne PH* utilizes the *same probability density function* as its sister piece, *Concret PH – A Retelling*. In fact, they share the exact same code.

However, the sonification design of *Éolienne PH* employs natural, soothing sounds, such as flowing water, and birdsong. The piece was composed during COVID-19, and given the ISEA 2022 conference theme, the sonification choices were meant to create a restorative, meditative, and potentially healing experience. Similarly to its sister piece, these sounds are partitioned into small fragments, and then pitch-shifted and overlaid, to create a granular, ever-unfolding sound texture.

Éolienne PH utilizes audience smartphones to deliver its sounds. Participants are asked to move around, creating independent, aleatoric sound trajectories. This is also inspired by Xenakis's *Mycenae Polytopon* (1978) [28]. This free movement creates infinite possibilities for sound texture and placement, as each person traverses a unique and unpredictable sound path.

Finally, the composition allows participants to generate high-quality, binaural sounds of wind-chimes – tuned in C *Aeolian* scale – by tapping on their screens. This makes them active contributors to the unfolding soundscape, and invites (but does not require) deep listening, and potentially collaboration.

While identical to *Concret PH* in terms of algorithmic design, the new sonification scheme produces a completely different (diametrically opposing?) aesthetic experience, and emotional outcome. This demonstrates the intrinsic value, and independence from sonic outcome, of Xenakis's algorithmic and stochastic contributions.[9]

A video link is available in Figure 4.

4.3 *on the Fractal Nature of Being…* (2022)

The piece *on the Fractal Nature of Being…* was also composed in the context of the 2022 Meta-Xenakis transcontinental celebration. It was performed at the Music Library of Greece, in May 2022. This piece brings together everything discussed so far, exploring how stochastic and aleatoric techniques introduced by Xenakis may be combined with traditional music theory and modern mathematics / fractal geometry. Similarly to the previous two pieces, audience members are invited to participate via their smartphones, contributing to the performance via their speakers and accelerometers.

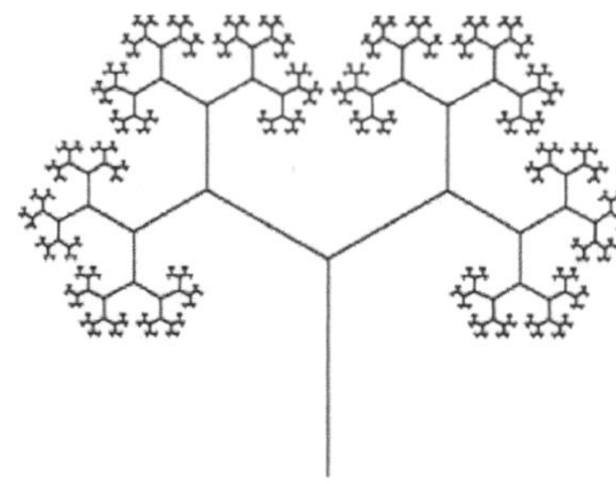

Figure 5. A golden tree is a fractal plant-like shape, incorporating the golden ratio, or φ (0.61803398…). The musical structure of *on the Fractal Nature of Being…* is based on this shape.

Figure 6. M.C. Escher's *Day and Night* (1938). The continuous transition between light and darkness, visually, best describes the sound transitions between consonance and dissonance in *on the Fractal Nature of Being…* (2022).

The piece is modeled after a fractal plant-like structure, or arborescence, known as the *golden tree*, which incorporates the golden ratio, or φ (0.61803398…), as shown in Figure 5. Following this structure, the piece is built from a one-minute-long harmonic theme, which serves as the "trunk" of the tree. This theme is expanded and embellished upon, at different levels of granularity, as the piece unfolds.

The fractal structure of the piece begins with the harmonic theme being introduced on the piano. As the piece unfolds, the theme is repeated at different levels of granularity, by different instruments – smartphones, cello, bassoon, and guitar – using tempo (faster), register (higher octaves), and randomness (improvised, aleatoric notes). This creates musical space for other instruments to enter, and the fractal to expand (i.e., become more detailed).

A UPIC-based probability density function controls the interplay between *consonance* and *dissonance*. This is a meta-Xenakian idea, as Xenakis mainly focused on the statistical interplay between sounds and silence.

---

[9] Also, this suggests that those who potentially dislike Xenakis's music, may only dislike his sonification choices.

Figure 7. Performance of *on the Fractal Nature of Being...* at the Music Library of Greece, Athens, Greece, May 2022. The piece utilizes audience smartphones for distributing sounds and controlling aspects of the performance – https://youtu.be/MG3l5v8FFbc

This idea is probably better communicated through M.C. Escher's *Day and Night* (1938), shown in Figure 6. Notice the continuous transition between light and darkness. This is similar to the continuous transition between consonance and dissonance in *on the Fractal Nature of Being...*

The piece moves through seven phases – each introducing a new instrument, while earlier instruments cyclically move to higher levels of detail (higher registers and faster tempi). The fifth phase introduces dissonance utilizing *stochastic probabilities* from the first 1½ minutes of Xenakis's *Metastaseis* (1953-4).[10] This phase also uses increased loudness of notes on smartphones, to highlight them – something that Xenakis was fond of (partially, due to his loss of hearing, caused by the tank shell explosion that almost took his life). Then, at the piece's golden ratio, the dissonance ends abruptly, and a new phase begins – with the bassoon entering to restore consonance. In the seventh and last phase, instruments go out one-by-one, ending the piece on an ambiguous interval (a major 2nd).

Smartphone sounds are aleatorically controlled via algorithm, while physical instruments improvise on the theme (in F minor scale), at different levels of granularity, based on their fractal level in the piece.

On the visual side, the performance includes fractal images displayed on a screen (see Figure 7), introducing a new image per phase, whose fractal properties (or entropy) are controlled by the accelerometers of participating audience smartphones. When the audience smartphones are still, the image's fractal structure is precisely the golden tree.[11]

A video link is available in Figure 7.[12]

4.4 *Nereides / Νηρηΐδες* (2022)

Xenakis was deeply interested in statistical properties of natural phenomena:

> [O]ther paths also led to the same stochastic crossroads—first of all, natural events such as the collision of hail or rain with hard surfaces, or the song of cicadas in a summer field. These sonic events are made out of thousands of isolated sounds; this multitude of sounds, seen here as a totality, is a new sonic event. This mass event is articulated and forms a plastic mold of time, which itself follows aleatory and stochastic laws. [11, pp. 8-9]

Interestingly, originating in a different (emotional, intuitive, non-mathematical) space, Claude Debussy makes a similar observation, in 1911:

> Who will discover the secret of musical composition? The sound of the sea, the curve of the horizon, the wind in the leaves, the cry of a bird, register complex impressions within us. Then suddenly, without any deliberate consent on our part, one of these memories issues forth to express itself in the language of music. It bears its own harmony within it. By no effort of ours can we achieve anything more truthful or accurate. ... No doubt, this simple musical grammar will jar some people. ... I foresee that and I rejoice in it. I shall do nothing to create adversaries, but neither shall I do anything to turn enmities into friendships (Debussy cited in [29, p. 226]).

It is intriguing to see how similar Xenakis and Debussy are – both being inspired by statistical properties of natural phenomena, and both being unapologetic about it. Still, they use different compositional tools and techniques – Xenakis, algorithmic and mathematical means, while Debussy, traditional (classical / impressionist) compositional processes [30].

Xenakis uses mathematical formulas to model natural phenomena. These formulas – being mathematical – are abstractions or generalizations, approximating trends in the actual data. They do not account for slight "imperfections" or noise, found in the original natural phenomena. Nature is never perfect, nor exactly ideal.[13]

This leads to the following compositional idea or "syllogism": What if, in an attempt to be more accurate in terms of natural imperfections, we bypassed the intermediate models of mathematical formulas (such as Gaussian or Poisson distributions) used by Xenakis (and others) to describe statistical tendencies of natural phenomena? Instead, what if we captured data directly from the natural phenomenon, since modern technology and computing allow us to do this relatively easily now? This way, we can use the exact distributions or fluctuations of densities in natural phenomena, for instance, through processing of *high-quality* audio recordings, or *high-resolution* digital images, among others.

Nereides / Νηρηΐδες is a four-hand, piano miniature piece, which demonstrates this approach. It explores the ever-unfolding interplay between sky and sea, or the evaporation-condensation-precipitation cycle. It is named

[10] See https://youtu.be/SZazYFchLRI .

[11] This can be seen later in the video of the piece's performance.

[12] This was on the last day of COVID-19 restrictions, so masks had to be worn. The following day, masks were removed.

[13] For example, Earth is not spherical, and its orbit is not a perfect ellipsis – there are small perturbations not captured by traditional geometrical or mathematical models, which tend to be ideal and approximate.

Figure 8. Source of thematic material for *Nereides / Νηρηΐδες*. Six trajectories, or curves, were selected intuitively (i.e., by ear) to capture the variety of white light distributions and densities – https://bit.ly/nereides1

after the female spirits of sea waters of Ancient Greece, the Nereides, that personify the cycle of water.

We used our UPIC approach to capture trajectories or curves of white light (luminosity) in the cloudy sky image, shown in Figure 8. We extracted the distributions of light straight from the source material (a high-resolution image), making deliberate choices where trajectories begin and end, and how they spread onto the piece's timeline – some lengthier, others shorter, some slower, others faster, some inverted, and so on. This is similar to Xenakis's own choices when using UPIC, i.e., where to draw shapes, how long to draw them, etc. Through this process, we selected six trajectories, or curves.

Nereides / Νηρηΐδες is then literally, and figuratively, a stochastic study of light in a cloudy sky. Moreover, it has a fractal, or self-similar structure. This is a direct result of the source material (i.e., cloud formations) being fractal [31]. The piece may sound deceptively simple. However, under the apparent musical simplicity, hides an intricate interweaving of pitches and rhythmic material that fit harmoniously together. The six musical trajectories, similarly to Xenakis's UPIC approach, were selected intuitively (i.e., non-algorithmically, by ear) to consist of reflective patterns. These patterns originated in the natural processes that produced these clouds.

A reduced, two-hand version of *Nereides / Νηρηΐδες* will be performed at the Megaron / The Athens Concert Hall in November 2023, as part of the celebration for the 70th anniversary of The Friends of Music Society of Greece.

An audio link is available in Figure 8.

5. CONCLUSIONS

The infusion of algorithms in the arts has increased dramatically since the greater availability of computers starting in the 1960s. All areas of art and entertainment, such as graphics, design, animation, sculpture, dance, theater, music, and film, to name a few, have been impacted greatly. At the same time, the inverse infusion of artistic creativity, design, and innovation into computing, engineering, and other scientific fields produces a creative tension, which leads to new ideas, and continues to produce new discoveries:

> Art and science are in a tension that is most fruitful when these disciplines observe and penetrate each other and experience how much of the other they themselves still contain. [32, p. 1]

As Xenakis similarly said:

> From here nothing prevents us from foreseeing a new relationship between the arts and the sciences, especially between the arts and mathematics: where the arts would consciously "set" problems which mathematics would then be obliged to solve through the invention of new theories. [33, p. 3]

We have finally reached a point where the algorithm has clearly been established as a very powerful, creative, and expressive medium, for artists and musicians. As we move forward into the 21st century, researchers, composers, artists, and educators are engaging algorithmically, and are interweaving algorithmic thinking and development of technological solutions, into their art theory and creative practice.

This raises a forward-thinking, yet inescapable question: Since algorithms have become such a powerful compositional tool, and a creative medium, when is the right time to begin teaching principles of algorithmic music composition (and computer programming), as part of a general, well-rounded music education curriculum?

The future demands "out-of-the-box" thinkers – people who will engage algorithmically to create new artifacts and techniques that have not been seen before. This is precisely what Xenakis did in a pioneering way, given how early he engaged with algorithms and computer programming, for musical and artistic purposes. His theoretical and artistic contributions continue to inspire and move us forward.

Acknowledgments

This work is partially funded by the US National Science Foundation and the National Endowment for the Arts (CNS-2139786). The first author would like to thank Sharon Kanach and Peter Nelson for providing in-depth comments to an extended version of this paper. We would like to thank Stephanie Merakos, director of the Music Library of Greece, for her invitation to give the talk, upon which this paper is based. Samantha Ramsden contributed significantly to the design, programming, and execution of some of the performances reported herein. Meghan Gillikin and Nick Moore provided additional help with the design, programming, and testing of these experiences. Finally, we thank the audiences of these experiences, for contributing to the performances, through interaction, physical movement, and use of their smartphone speakers.

6. REFERENCES

[1] A. Di Scipio, "Compositional Models in Xenakis's Electroacoustic Music", *Perspectives of New Music*, vol. 36, no. 2, pp. 201–243, 1998.

[2] S. Kanach, *Music and Architecture (Iannis Xenakis)*, Pendragon Press, 2008.

[3] S. Kanach, *Performing Xenakis*, Pendragon Press, 2010.

[4] S. Kanach, *Xenakis Matters: Contexts, Processes, Applications*, Pendragon Press, 2012.

[5] V. Lombardo, A. Valle, J. Fitch, K. Tazelaar, S. Weinzierl, and W. Borczyk, "A Virtual-Reality Reconstruction of Poème Électronique Based on Philological Research", *Computer Music Journal*, vol. 33, no 2, MIT Press, pp. 24–47, 2009.

[6] R. Reynolds, and K. Reynolds, *Xenakis Creates in Architecture and Music – The Reynolds Desert House*, Routledge, 2021.

[7] R.M. Schafer, *The Soundscape – Our Sonic Environment and the Tuning of the World*, Destiny Books, 1993.

[8] M. Solomos, *From Music to Sound – The Emergence of Sound in 20th- and 21st-Century Music*, Routledge, 2021.

[9] A. Valle, Andrea, K. Tazelaar, and V. Lombardo, "In a Concrete Space. Reconstructing the Spatialization of Iannis Xenakis' Concret PH on a Multichannel Setup", *Proceedings of the 7th Sound and Music Computing Conference (SMC 2010)*, Barcelona, Spain, pp. 271–278, 2010.

[10] P. Hoffmann, "The New GENDYN Program", *Computer Music Journal*, vol. 24, no 2, pp. 31–38, MIT Press, 2000.

[11] I. Xenakis, *Formalized Music: Thought and Mathematics in Composition*, Indiana University Press, 1971.

[12] C. Roads, *Microsound*, MIT Press, 2004.

[13] P. Hoffmann, *Music Out of Nothing? A Rigorous Approach to Algorithmic Composition by Iannis Xenakis*, Ph.D. Thesis, Technical University of Berlin, 2009.

[14] R. Page, and R. Didday, *FORTRAN 77 for Humans*, West Publishing, 1980.

[15] R.P. Taylor, A.P. Micolich, and D. Jonas, "Fractal Analysis of Pollock's Drip Paintings", *Nature*, vol. 399, 1999.

[16] C. Starrett, S. Reiser, and S. Pacio, "Data Materialization: A Hybrid Process of Crafting a Teapot", *Leonardo*, vol. 51, no. 4, pp. 381–385, MIT Press, 2018.

[17] L. Kalff, W. Tak, and S.L. de Bruin, "The 'Electronic Poem' Performed in the Philips Pavilion at the 1958 Brussels World Fair", *Philips Technical Review*, vol. 20, no. 2/3, pp. 37–84, 1958.

[18] J. Harley, *Xenakis: His Life in Music*, Routledge, 2004.

[19] D. Cope, *Virtual Music: Computer Synthesis of Musical Style*, MIT Press, 2001.

[20] B. Manaris, J. Romero, P. Machado, D. Krehbiel, T. Hirzel, W. Pharr, and R.B. Davis, "Zipf's Law, Music Classification and Aesthetics", *Computer Music Journal*, vol. 29, no. 1, MIT Press, pp. 55–69, Spring 2005.

[21] B. Manaris, P. Roos, P. Machado, D. Krehbiel, L. Pellicoro, and J. Romero, "A Corpus-Based Hybrid Approach to Music Analysis and Composition", *Proceedings of 22nd Conference on Artificial Intelligence (AAAI-07)*, Vancouver, BC, pp. 839–845, 2007.

[22] B. Manaris, P. Roos, D. Krehbiel, T. Zalonis, and J.R. Armstrong, "Zipf's Law, Power Laws and Music Aesthetics", in T. Li, M. Ogihara, G. Tzanetakis (eds.), *Music Data Mining*, pp. 169–216, CRC Press – Taylor & Francis, Jul. 2011.

[23] B. Manaris, D. Hughes, and Y. Vassilandonakis, "Monterey Mirror: An Experiment in Interactive Music Performance Combining Evolutionary Computation and Zipf's Law", *Evolutionary Intelligence*, vol. 8, no. 1, Springer-Verlag, pp 23–35, Mar. 2015.

[24] K. Roose, "The Brilliance and Weirdness of ChatGPT", *New York Times*, December 5, 2022.

[25] N. Vincent, and H. Li, "ChatGPT Stole Your Work. So What Are You Going to Do?", *Wired*, Jan. 20, 2023.

[26] R. Bourotte, and S. Kanach, "UPISketch: The UPIC idea and its current applications for initiating new audiences to music", *Organised Sound*, vol. 24, no. 3, p. 252–260, 2019.

[27] A. Forgette, B. Manaris, M. Gillikin, and S. Ramdsen, "Speakers, More Speakers!!! – Developing Interactive, Distributed, Smartphone-Based, Immersive Experiences for Music and Art", *Proceedings of the 28th International Symposium on Electronic Art (ISEA 2022)*, Barcelona, Spain, 2022.

[28] M. Kotzamani, "Greek History as Environmental Performance: Iannis Xenakis' Mycenae Polytopon and Beyond", *Gramma: Journal of Theory and Criticism*, vol. 22, no. 2, p. 163–178, 2014.

[29] L. Vallas, *Claude Debussy: His Life and Works*, Oxford University Press, 1933.

[30] D. Cope, *Techniques of the Contemporary Composer*, Cengage Learning, 1997.

[31] B. Spehar, C. Clifford, B. Newell, and R.P. Taylor, "Universal Aesthetic of Fractals", *Computers and Graphics*, vol. 27, pp. 813–820, 2003.

[32] M.C. Rillig, K. Bonneval, C. de Lutz, J. Lehmann, I. Mansour, R. Rapp, S. Spačal, and V. Meyer, "Ten simple rules for hosting artists in a scientific lab", *PLoS Computational Biology*, vol. 17, no 2, p. 1–5, 2001.

[33] I. Xenakis, and O. Messiaen (S. Kanach, translator), *Arts-Sciences: Alloys (Aesthetics in Music Series; no 2)*, Pendragon Press, 1985.

Characterizing and Interpreting Music Expressivity through Rhythm and Loudness Simplices

Paul Lascabettes
Sorbonne Université, Ircam,
CNRS, Ministère de la Culture,
STMS, Paris, France
paul.lascabettes@ircam.fr

Elaine Chew
King's College London,
London, United Kingdom
elaine.chew@kcl.ac.uk

Isabelle Bloch
Sorbonne Université,
CNRS, LIP6, Paris, France
isabelle.bloch@
sorbonne-universite.fr

ABSTRACT

Characterizing and interpreting expressivity in performed music remains an open problem. In this paper, we explore the novel representation of recorded performances of triple time music using a 2-simplex, a graphical representation used to visualize three-interval rhythms. We analyze the MazurkaBL dataset, which contains beat-level tempo and loudness data of over 2000 recorded performances of 46 Chopin Mazurkas. Mazurkas' triple time lends themselves well to the 2-simplex; the expressive features of each three-beat bar map directly to unique points in the 2-simplex. We extend the rhythm simplex designed for beat durations to the representation of loudness. Each recorded performance is thus reduced to a set of points in 2-simplices based on beat-level duration or loudness. We provide the transformation to convert three-interval information to points in the 2-simplex; prove that inter-beat intervals and tempo representations in the 2-simplex are equivalent when timing variations are small; and, explain how smoothing the data impacts the coordinates of the points in the simplex. We demonstrate that the use of simplices can facilitate the analysis and interpretation of expressive music features; the method enables the identifying of bars with notable expressive variations such as temporal suspensions that form tipping points, and characterizing of performance regularity.

1. INTRODUCTION

Characterizing and interpreting expressivity in performed music is a fundamental problem in fields such as musicology, music perception, and music analysis. Moreover, the emergence of computational models has produced significant advances in expressive music research [1]. Computational modeling of expressive music performance requires large-scale databases; to create such databases, it is more expedient to focus on piano music. We focus on the piano pieces of the romantic period, which allow for greater expressive variations. A significant amount of this repertoire has been written for solo instruments, which makes comparative analysis of performances more straightforward. Furthermore, with the existence of computer-controlled pianos such as the Bösendorfer Enspire PRO and Steinway Spirio, realistic piano performances can be readily captured with accuracy, which is not the case with other instruments. Therefore, the majority of performance research focuses on piano music.

Due to the resources amassed for and made available by the Mazurka Project [1], numerous studies have been based on Chopin's Mazurkas. A main purpose of the initial studies was to identify correlations between performed tempo and between performed loudness features [2, 3, 4, 5]. These analyses were based on selected Mazurka recordings. More recently, beat level tempo and loudness information of 2000 recorded Mazurkas have been extracted and made available for research [6]. Other studies have focused on generating Mazurka performances using machine learning models [7]. The two main expressive parameters considered are tempo and loudness variations [8]. Using these two parameters, trajectories in tempo-loudness space [9] were traced to represent the performance. Another representation of tempo and loudness curves for analysis is the arc model [10, 11]. Arc models have been successfully used to determine the segmentation of a piece based only on the loudness and tempo curves versus time [12, 13, 14].

In this paper, we propose to represent beat-level tempo and loudness information of a Mazurka performance in tempo and loudness simplices, a graphical representation used in music to analyze the perception of three-interval rhythms. This is the first time these simplices are applied to visualize Mazurka performances. This representation makes it straightforward to determine performance characteristics such as the accented beat in a bar or the regularity of a performance.

This paper is organized as follows: Section 2 introduces the rhythm simplex and reviews related work; Section 3 presents the dataset we used and explains why the 2-simplex representation is relevant to this dataset; Section 4 describes the proposed method, by first providing a transformation to convert a three-interval information into the 2-simplex, then proving that the choices of inter-beat intervals or tempo data are equivalent when timing variation are small, and explaining the impact of smoothing the data in the 2-simplex representation; and, Section 5 presents analyses and interpretations that can be made with the simplices, such as visualizing time suspensions, characterizing the notion of regularity of a performance, and identifying

[1] http://www.mazurka.org.uk/

the bars with notable expressive variations.

2. THE RHYTHM SIMPLEX

In this section, we introduce the rhythm simplex, a graphical representation used to visualize three-interval rhythms, and related work.

2.1 Presentation of the Rhythm Simplex

The *rhythm simplex*, also known as a *rhythm chart* or *chronotopological map*, is a graphical representation developed for visualizing three-interval rhythms. The idea of the rhythm simplex is that any three-interval rhythm can be represented in a 2-dimensional plot if the total duration of the rhythm is fixed (usually normalized to 1). For example, $A = [0.50, 0.25, 0.25]$ and $B = [0.33, 0.33, 0.33]$. By fixing the total duration, it is sufficient to know the first two intervals to deduce the third one. So a 2-dimensional plot can be used to visualize the rhythm. Thus, a three-interval rhythm is mapped to a unique point in the rhythm simplex. As illustrated in Figure 1(a), this 2-dimensional plot is a 2-simplex, i.e. a triangle. Figure 1(b) represents the rhythm simplex where each side of the triangle corresponds to one of the three intervals. In this figure, each three-interval rhythm is represented by a unique point. The rhythm A is located by the light blue arrows, while the rhythm B is in the middle of the rhythm simplex.

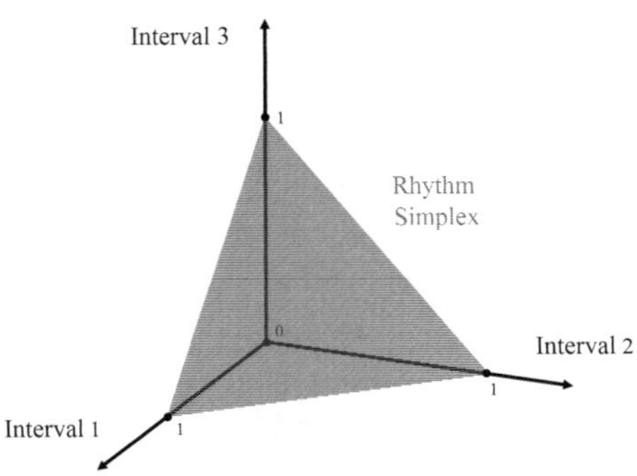

(a) The space of three-interval rhythms in the 2-simplex.

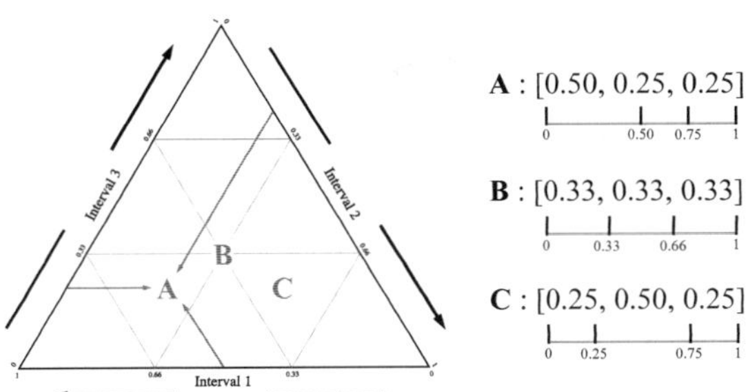

(b) Rhythm simplex where the three-interval rhythms A, B, and C are represented by unique points in the 2-simplex.

Figure 1. Three-interval rhythms in the rhythm simplex (adapted from Desain & Honing [15]).

2.2 Previous Work Related to the Rhythm Simplex

The use of the simplex representation in music was introduced by Desain and Honing [15, 16] to understand how listeners perceive rhythm categories. They asked the listeners to identify three-interval rhythms on a continuous scale to determine areas in the rhythm simplex representing equivalence classes. These rhythm equivalence classes can evolve according to parameters such as tempo [17], loudness or melodic structure [18]. Vaquero and Honing [19] created paths within these areas to generate performances. Based on a type of formal grammar called Lindenmayer systems [20], they defined paths in the rhythm simplex to generated expressivity in music. Bååth et al. [21] implemented a dynamical systems model to reproduce the categorical choices of listeners to retrieve these areas in the rhythm simplex. More recently, Jacoby and McDermott [22] ran a study where random rhythms in the rhythm simplex had to be reproduced by participants. Participants converged to rhythms having integer ratios after five iterations. They showed that the areas defined in [15] have little dependence on musical training but are highly dependent on cultural biases. For instance, listeners in the United States had different results than native Amazonian listeners. Nave et al. [23] conducted a similar experiment to the one in [22] with iterative reproductive tasks based on random rhythms in the rhythm simplex, but with children. They demonstrated the existence of rhythm priors in children, also related to cultural biases, which would develop in middle childhood.

Finally, these different studies used the rhythm simplex to understand the perception of three-interval rhythms, whether in populations of different cultures or of different ages. Only Vaquero and Honing have applied it to musical performances, but for generation rather than analysis. Here, we propose a new approach to use the rhythm simplex to represent musical performances in order to characterize and interpret music expressivity.

3. MAZURKA PERFORMANCES

In this section, we present the dataset that we use in this paper and explain how the rhythm simplex can be used to represent the essential expressive features of Mazurka performances.

3.1 The Dataset

To map a large number of Mazurka performances to the rhythm simplex for analysis, we used the MazurkaBL dataset [6]. This is currently by far the largest database of annotated performed classical music having multiple performances of each piece. The MazurkaBL contains beat level duration and loudness annotations for over 2000 recorded performances of 46 Chopin Mazurkas. There are, on average, more than 40 distinct performances per Mazurka. This dataset was made by manually annotating the beats of one recording of a Mazurka and automatically transferring these annotations to other recordings of the same piece through audio alignment. It is important to note that we used a smoothed version of the loudness data. Kosta et al. [6] filtered the loudness annotations by local regression using a weighted linear least squares and a 2nd degree polynomial model (the LOESS method of MATLAB's smooth function) with window sizes that are 1/30-th of the length of the recorded Mazurka while the tempo annotations are raw. It is therefore essential to take this into account, as it has an impact on the position of points in the 2-simplex and therefore on their interpretation, as explained in the following sections.

3.2 Representing Mazurka Performances in 2-Simplices

As described in Section 2.1, the rhythm simplex represents a three-interval rhythm as a unique point in a 2-dimensional plot. The use of the rhythm 2-simplex must therefore be applied to rhythm data that can be split into groups of three intervals, which is not the case for any general temporal data. However, Chopin's Mazurkas is particularly well suited to rhythm simplex representation because Mazurkas are folk dances mostly in triple meter, i.e., they are mostly pieces with three beats in each bar. On very rare occasions, some of Chopin's Mazurkas may contain bars that are not in triple meter, in which case these bars are removed from the analysis. Otherwise, the three beats can be seen as three intervals which have equal duration in the score but whose time is rendered differently in performance. Therefore, a bar of a performed Mazurka can be mapped into the rhythm simplex as a single point. By viewing the recording of a Mazurka as a sequence of performed three-beat bars, we can represent the recording by a set of points in the rhythm simplex. The rhythm simplex can show not only the timing variations in each bar, it can also display the beat accentuation because the loudness data of each beat of a three-beat bar can also be represented in a 2-simplex. For Mazurkas beginning with an anacrusis, we ignore the notes that come before the first full bar of music. Therefore, the essential expressive features of the musical performance of the Mazurkas can be visualized using 2-simplices because most of the bars have three beats.

4. THE METHOD TO REPRESENT MAZURKA PERFORMANCES IN 2-SIMPLICES

In this section, we give the transformation that we use to convert three-interval information into points in the 2-simplex. For the information related to rhythm, we prove that using inter-beat intervals or using tempo are equivalent in the 2-simplex representation. For the information related to loudness, we introduce the loudness simplex and explain how smoothing the data impacts the coordinates in the simplex.

4.1 Computing Points in the 2-Simplex

Previous articles on the rhythm simplex (see Section 2.2) have not explicitly provided the transformation to map a three-interval rhythm to a point in the rhythm simplex. Here, we provide the transformation we use to convert three-interval information to a point in 2-simplex.

First, we fix the vertices of the 2-simplex on the unit circle, i.e. the vertices are $(0, 1)$, $(\frac{\sqrt{3}}{2}, -\frac{1}{2})$, and $(-\frac{\sqrt{3}}{2}, -\frac{1}{2})$ (which are represented in Figure 1(b) by the top vertex, the bottom right vertex, and the bottom left vertex, respectively). In this case, the middle of the triangle is at the origin $(0, 0)$ (represented by point B in Figure 1(b)).

Let $B = (b_1, b_2, b_3)$ represent some properties of a three-beat bar such that $b_1 + b_2 + b_3 = 1$, where b_1, b_2, and b_3 are three positive numbers. The corresponding point (x, y) in the 2-simplex is defined by:

$$x = \frac{\sqrt{3}}{2} - \frac{\sqrt{3}}{2}b_3 - \sqrt{3}b_1, \quad (1)$$

$$y = \frac{3}{2}b_3 - \frac{1}{2}. \quad (2)$$

Reciprocally, given a point (x, y) in the 2-simplex, the corresponding bar $B = (b_1, b_2, b_3)$ is defined by:

$$b_1 = \frac{1}{3} - \frac{1}{\sqrt{3}}x - \frac{1}{3}y, \quad (3)$$

$$b_2 = \frac{1}{3} + \frac{1}{\sqrt{3}}x - \frac{1}{3}y, \quad (4)$$

$$\text{and} \quad b_3 = \frac{1}{3} + \frac{2}{3}y. \quad (5)$$

This defines a bijection between the 2-simplex and a normalized feature of the three-beat bars.

4.2 Inter-Beat Intervals and Tempo Data in the 2-Simplex

To represent a recorded Mazurka performance (or any performed piece in triple time) in the rhythm simplex, we compute inter-beat intervals from the beat onset information in the MazurkaBL. This gives us the duration of each beat, (d_1, d_2, d_3), in a bar. We scale this vector so that the elements sum to one to get (b_1, b_2, b_3), where $b_i = \frac{d_i}{d_1+d_2+d_3}$ for $i = 1, 2, 3$. The normalized durations in that bar then map to a point in the rhythm simplex according to Equations 1 and 2. In this way, we map the performed beat durations of all bars to the rhythm simplex. For example, in Figure 2, the different interpretations of the first four bars of Mazurka 6-1, obtained from the MazurkaBL dataset, are represented in the rhythm simplex. In this case, the first note is not considered, as Mazurka 6-1 begins with an anacrusis. Each point in a rhythm simplex corresponds to an interpretation of a bar, where the temporal deformation of the three beats (d_1, d_2, d_3) can be visualized. We can notice that all the performers follow a similar path. For instance, for the first bar, all points tend to be on the left in the simplex (meaning a long first beat and a short second beat). Whereas on the second and fourth bars, the points are on the right in the simplex (meaning a short first beat and a long second beat). Finally, for the third bar, interpretations are on average more regular as the points are concentrated in the middle of the simplex.

Previous studies on Mazurkas use tempo data rather than duration data. To generate comparable results, we can also compute the respective beat-to-beat tempo of a bar (t_1, t_2, t_3) with $t_i = 60/d_i$ for $i = 1, 2, 3$, and normalize the values for mapping to a 2-simplex. However, which data should we choose: inter-beat intervals or tempo? We show with the following proposition that the points in the 2-simplex based on inter-beat intervals or tempo data have approximately the same coordinates up to one symmetry

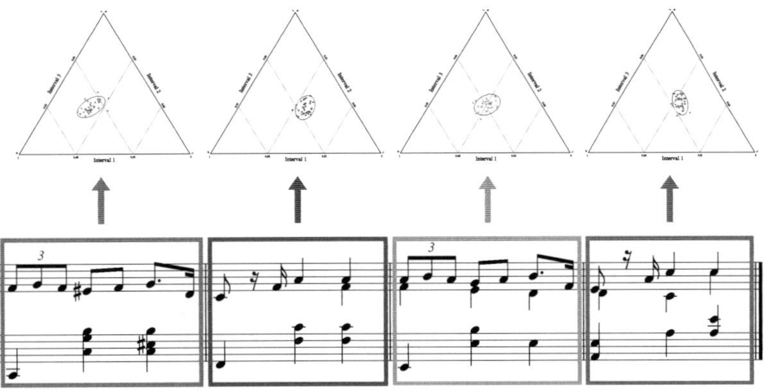

Figure 2. Visualization of different interpretations of the first four bars of Mazurka 6-1 in the rhythm simplex. Each point in a rhythm simplex corresponds to the interpretation of a bar by a performer, where the temporal deformation of the three beats of the bar is visualized.

with respect to the origin. This proposition shows that the choice of tempo or duration does not matter in the 2-simplex representation.

Proposition. Let (d_1, d_2, d_3) denote three inter-beat intervals of a bar and (x, y) the corresponding point in the 2-simplex. When (x, y) is close to the origin, the 2-simplex mapping of the beat-to-beat tempo of the same bar (t_1, t_2, t_3) is approximately $(-x, -y)$.

Proof. Let $d = d_1 + d_2 + d_3$ and $b_i = \frac{d_i}{d}$ for $i = 1, 2, 3$. Now, normalize the vector (t_1, t_2, t_3) and find its coordinates (x_T, y_T) in the 2-simplex.

$$\begin{aligned}
&\frac{1}{t_1 + t_2 + t_3}(t_1, t_2, t_3) \\
&= \frac{1}{\frac{60}{d_1} + \frac{60}{d_2} + \frac{60}{d_3}}(\frac{60}{d_1}, \frac{60}{d_2}, \frac{60}{d_3}) \\
&= \frac{1}{\frac{1}{d_1} + \frac{1}{d_2} + \frac{1}{d_3}}(\frac{1}{d_1}, \frac{1}{d_2}, \frac{1}{d_3}) \\
&= \frac{d}{d}\frac{1}{\frac{1}{d_1} + \frac{1}{d_2} + \frac{1}{d_3}}(\frac{1}{d_1}, \frac{1}{d_2}, \frac{1}{d_3}) \\
&= \frac{1}{\frac{d}{d_1} + \frac{d}{d_2} + \frac{d}{d_3}}(\frac{d}{d_1}, \frac{d}{d_2}, \frac{d}{d_3}) \\
&= \frac{1}{\frac{1}{b_1} + \frac{1}{b_2} + \frac{1}{b_3}}(\frac{1}{b_1}, \frac{1}{b_2}, \frac{1}{b_3}) \\
&= \frac{1}{b_2 b_3 + b_1 b_3 + b_1 b_2}(b_2 b_3, b_1 b_3, b_1 b_2)
\end{aligned}$$

with (b_1, b_2, b_3) expressed with x and y as shown in Equations 3, 4 and 5. The vector (d_1, d_2, d_3) represents the duration of each beat of a bar. In a performance without large timing variations, the b_i's are close to $\frac{1}{3}$ and (x, y) is close to $(0, 0)$ in the 2-simplex (i.e. close to point B shown in Figure 1(b)). When x and y are close to zero, x^2, y^2, and xy are negligible. In this case, we get:

$$b_1 b_2 \approx \frac{1}{9}(-2y + 1), \qquad b_1 b_3 \approx \frac{1}{9}(y - \sqrt{3}x + 1),$$

$$b_2 b_3 \approx \frac{1}{9}(y + \sqrt{3}x + 1), \qquad b_2 b_3 + b_1 b_3 + b_1 b_2 \approx \frac{1}{3}.$$

Applying the transformation in Equations 1 and 2 to the vector (t_1, t_2, t_3) normalized with the approximations (i.e. x^2, y^2, and xy are negligible), we have:

$$x_T \approx \frac{\sqrt{3}}{2} - \frac{\sqrt{3}}{2}(\frac{1}{3}(-2y+1)) - \sqrt{3}(\frac{1}{3}(y+\sqrt{3}x+1)) = -x,$$

and

$$y_T \approx \frac{3}{2}(\frac{1}{3}(-2y + 1)) - \frac{1}{2} = -y.$$

To illustrate this result, Mazurka 6-1 performed by Luisada is represented in a 2-simplex in Figure 3(a) based on inter-beat intervals, and in Figure 3(b) based on beat-to-beat tempo. We can see that the point sets are similar in both figures up to one symmetry with respect to the origin.

4.3 The Loudness Data in the 2-Simplex

Because loudness data are also available in the MazurkaBL dataset, we extend the rhythm simplex to the representation of loudness. We define the *loudness simplex* by considering the relative proportion of loudness for each beat in a three-beat bar. This is exactly the same idea as for rhythm; as we shall see later, it provides additional insights.

Because the loudness data have been smoothed with a LOESS filter by Kosta et al. [6], the loudness curves as a function of time tend to be smoother, involving fewer local maxima or minima. This has a direct consequence on the coordinates of the points in the loudness simplex. Figure 4 shows the triangle of the 2-simplex split into four regions: two areas, in blue, located at the top right and bottom left of the simplex; and, two areas, in red, located at the top left and bottom right. The two blue areas correspond to points in the simplex where the loudness increases or decreases with time within a bar. At the top right of the simplex, the elements are increasing, while at the bottom left they are decreasing. Musically, these areas translate to bars where the performer has an ascending (top right) or descending (bottom left) movement within that expressive property. Conversely, the points in the simplex are located in the red zone if the second beat is a local minimum or maximum, which is more seldom seen with loudness data because the data have been smoothed. Thus, as can be seen in Figures 6(a) and 6(b), when representing the loudness

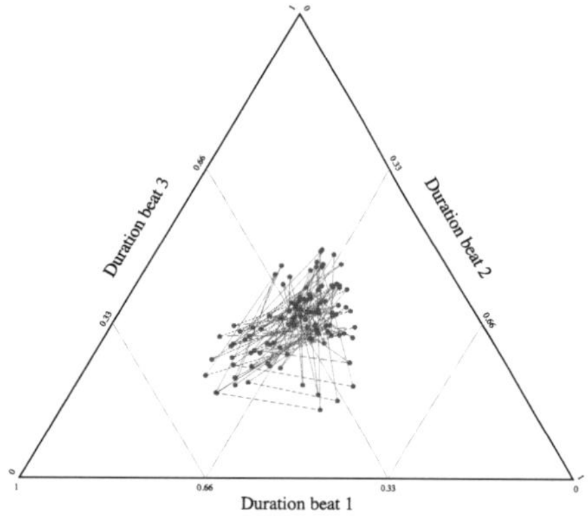

(a) Representation of Mazurka 6-1 performed by Luisada in the 2-simplex based on inter-beat intervals.

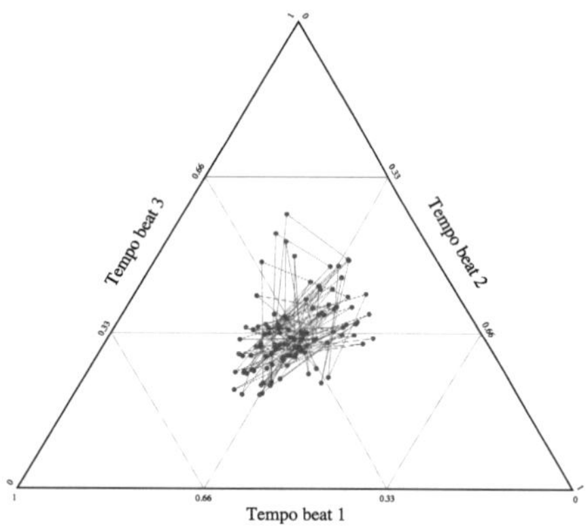

(b) Representation of Mazurka 6-1 performed by Luisada in the 2-simplex based on beat-to-beat tempo.

Figure 3. Inter-beat intervals and tempo data represented in a 2-simplex to illustrate the symmetry with respect to the origin between the two sets of points.

data in the 2-simplex, the points tend to stay in the blue area because the data have been smoothed. However, this does not exclude performance information as we will see in the rest of this paper. Note that this reasoning applies to any type of smoothed data projected into a 2-simplex.

5. ANALYSIS AND INTERPRETATION OF MUSICAL EXPRESSIVITY USING THE SIMPLICES REPRESENTATION

In this section, we present analyses and interpretations that can be derived from the simplices representation. This includes visualizing tipping points (here realized as time suspensions) introduced by the performer, defining the regularity of a performance, and identifying bars that exhibit notable expressivity.

5.1 Visualize Time Suspensions in the Simplex

Some recorded Mazurkas display musical tipping points [24] which present as significant temporal suspensions. These time elongations may be indicated in the score as fermatas or may simply be inserted by the performer. Representing these Mazurka performances in the rhythm simplex allows these temporal deformations to be visible. For example, in Mazurka 24-3, bars 10, 22, 46, and 70 are identical and have a fermata marked and executed on the second beat. Thus, the duration of the second beat of these bars is significantly longer than others, making them more important. Therefore, the points corresponding to these bars are situated at the bottom right of the rhythm simplex. For example, by representing Uninsky's interpretation of Mazurka 24-3 in the rhythm simplex, we can easily extract these bars as shown in Figure 5.

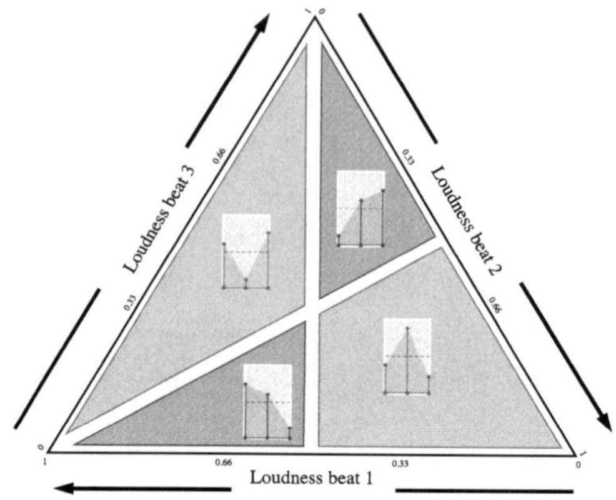

Figure 4. Area in the loudness simplex characterized by an increasing loudness curve (in blue) or local maxima or minima (in red) in the bar.

These temporal suspensions are present in most interpretations of Mazurka 24-3, so these four points in the bottom right of the simplex are seen in other interpretations as well. These tipping points [24] allow performers to pause to highlight certain notes or harmonies to create tension and anticipation [25]; in the case of Figure 5, it is the highest note of the bar on the second beat.

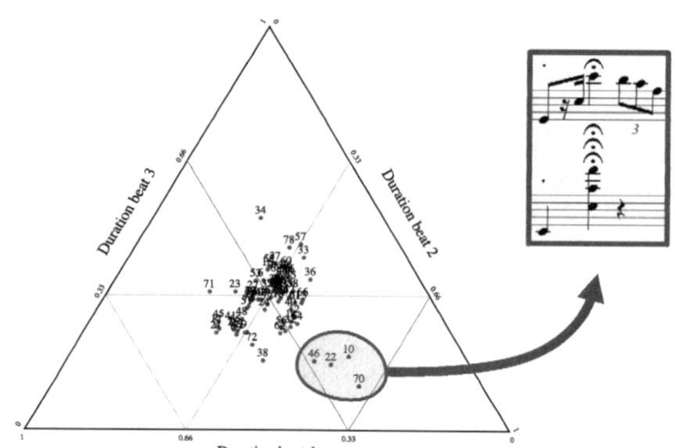

Figure 5. Temporal suspensions of the second beat of bar 10, 22, 46, and 70 of Mazurka 24-3 indicated as fermatas in the score (frame on the right) and visualized in Uninsky's interpretation by isolated points in the bottom right of the rhythm simplex.

5.2 Characterizing the Regularity of a Performance Using the Simplices Representation

During a music performance, some performers allow themselves greater latitude in their temporal and loudness variations than others. However, quantifying these variations to define the regularity of a performance is not easy [8]. If a performer chooses to always accentuate the first beat of each bar, the performance could be described as regular, even though the differences in tempo and volume per beat can be large during the piece. Therefore, it is not sufficient to characterize the regularity of a performance by the sum of the deviations per beat from the average of tempo and loudness. Hence, we propose to quantify the regularity of a performance using the 2-simplices. To get an intuition about this, see Figure 6(a) where the points are very dense in the loudness simplex meaning that the loudness variations are very regular. On the other hand, in Figure 6(b), the points are more spread out because the loudness varies less regularly.

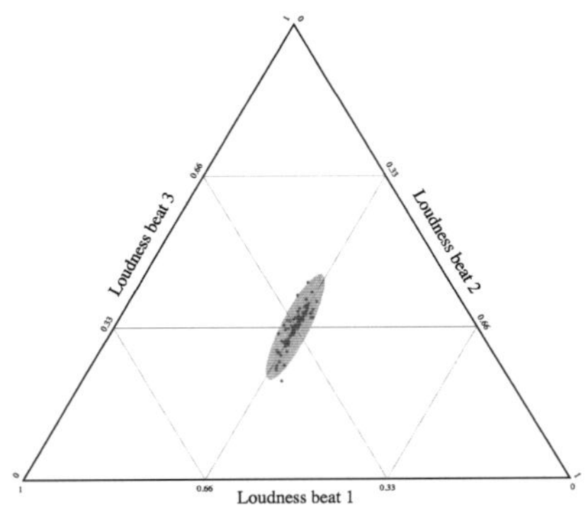

(a) Small area of the ellipse in the loudness simplex from Kapell's interpretation of Mazurka 6-2 indicating an interpretation with regular loudness.

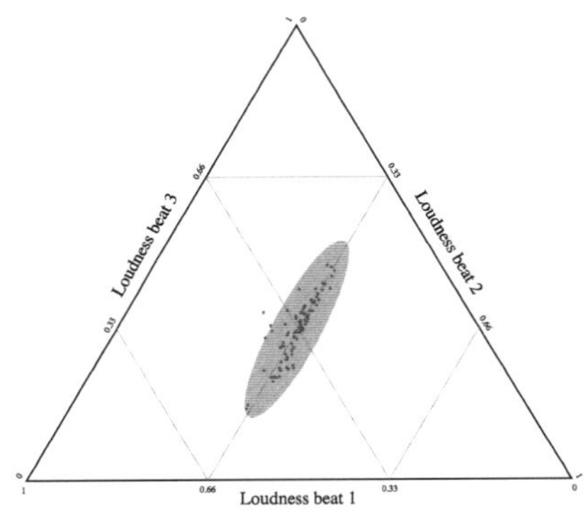

(b) Large area of the ellipse in the loudness simplex from Ohlsson's interpretation of Mazurka 6-2 indicating an interpretation with non-regular loudness.

Figure 6. Example of regular and non-regular performed loudness shown by a small and a large ellipse area in the loudness simplex. Kapell's ellipse area is three times smaller than Ohlsson's, pointing to greater loudness regularity.

We propose to define the regularity of a performance from the covariance matrix of the points in the 2-simplex as follows. Let $(x_i, y_i)_{1\leq i\leq n}$ denote the points in the simplex and Σ their covariance matrix:

$$\Sigma = \begin{pmatrix} \mathrm{Cov}(X,X) & \mathrm{Cov}(X,Y) \\ \mathrm{Cov}(Y,X) & \mathrm{Cov}(Y,Y) \end{pmatrix},$$

where $X = (x_i)_{1\leq i\leq n}$, $Y = (y_i)_{1\leq i\leq n}$,

$$\begin{aligned} \bar{x} &= \frac{1}{n}\sum_{i=1}^{n} x_i, \\ \bar{y} &= \frac{1}{n}\sum_{i=1}^{n} y_i, \\ \text{and} \quad \mathrm{Cov}(X,Y) &= \frac{1}{n}\sum_{i=1}^{n}(x_i - \bar{x})(y_i - \bar{y}). \end{aligned}$$

Let λ_1 and λ_2 denote the eigenvalues of Σ. They define an ellipse [2], whose semi-axes lengths are $\sqrt{\lambda_1}$ and $\sqrt{\lambda_2}$. The orientation is derived from Σ as well, but not involved in the regularity computation. We define the regularity value of a performance as the inverse of the area of that ellipse.

Since the area of an ellipse is equal to the multiplication of π by the length of the semi-major and the semi-minor axes, it is easy to compare the regularity of two performances in the 2-simplex. Using the example in Figure 5, Kappel (λ_1 and λ_2 as eigenvalues) is 2.995 times more regular than Ohlsson (λ'_1 and λ'_2 as eigenvalues) because $\sqrt{\lambda'_1\lambda'_2}/\sqrt{\lambda_1\lambda_2} = 2.995$. This reasoning can be applied across interpretations to other expressive features like beat-level tempo and duration.

5.3 The Most Distant Points in the Simplex Indicate Bars with Notable Musical Expressivity

The ellipses described in the previous section correspond to points having the same Mahalanobis distance to the center [26]. Distinct from Euclidean distance, the Mahalanobis distance takes into account the distribution of points in the simplex. Given two points (x_1, y_1) and (x_2, y_2) in the 2-simplex, the Mahalanobis distance is defined by:

$$d\left(\begin{pmatrix} x_1 \\ y_1 \end{pmatrix}, \begin{pmatrix} x_2 \\ y_2 \end{pmatrix}\right) = \sqrt{\begin{pmatrix} x_1 - x_2 \\ y_1 - y_2 \end{pmatrix}^T \Sigma^{-1} \begin{pmatrix} x_1 - x_2 \\ y_1 - y_2 \end{pmatrix}}.$$

This distance is useful in our case because there is often a correlation between the coordinates of the points in the simplex, in particular, for points in the loudness simplex, the x coordinate increases when the y coordinate increases (but the reasoning is also correct for the rhythm simplex). For example, in Figure 6, the points are aligned in the simplex because the loudness data have been smoothed, as detailed in Section 4.3. In this case, the Mahalanobis distance allows us to give more importance to the points that do not follow this alignment. Thus, the points with a high distance value compared to the average are the bars that present a strongly divergent musical expressivity according to the simplex feature. For example, we can identify the temporal elasticity in the interpretation of Mazurka 24-3 by Uninsky which is represented in the rhythm simplex in Figure 5.

[2] We used the matplotlib package `https://matplotlib.org/stable/gallery/statistics/confidence_ellipse.html`, with the default setting n_std=3.0, for the ellipses in Figure 6.

We computed the Mahalanobis distance between each simplex point and the mean and plotted the result in Figure 7. Bars that have an extreme time elongation on the second beat, i.e. bars 10, 22, 46, and 70 of Mazurka 24-3 represented by the four points at the bottom right of the rhythm simplex in Figure 5, are located almost at the end of each A section and have a high distance value due to their divergent interpretation as compared to other bars (Figure 7). Thus, by considering the maximum values of the Mahalanobis distance between the simplex points and their mean, we can detect the bars that have a notable expressive variation. For example, in Figure 7, bars 34 and 57 also have a high distance value because the first beat is considerably longer than the other two, which can be seen in the top corner of the rhythm simplex in Figure 5.

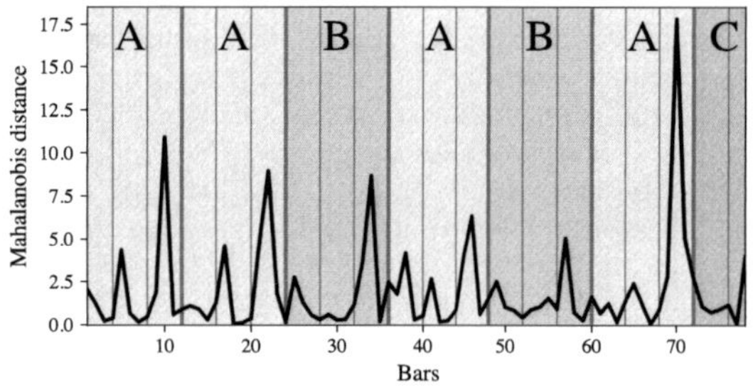

Figure 7. Mahalanobis distance between the points of Uninsky's interpretation of Mazurka 24-3 in the rhythm simplex shown in Figure 5. High distance values are bars with notable expressive variations. For example, bars 10, 22, 46, and 70 have high distance values because their second beats are elongated, while bars 34 and 57 have their first beats elongated.

6. CONCLUSION

In this paper, we proposed a novel method to represent performed music using beat duration, tempo and loudness simplices. We analyzed the MazurkaBL dataset using these simplices. MazurkaBL contains more than 2000 recorded performances of 46 of Chopin's Mazurkas with annotations of beat level tempo and loudness values. We provided the equations to map any bounded three-interval information into the 2-simplex. We proved that the choices of inter-beat intervals or tempo are nearly equivalent in the 2-simplex up to one symmetry with respect to the origin. We also explained the impact of smoothed data in the 2-simplex. Finally, we showed that the simplices facilitate the analysis and interpretation of music expressivity features. For example, by using the Mahalanobis distance, it is possible to identify bars with notable expressive variations such as temporal tipping points or to specify the regularity of a performance.

However, this method has some limitations. Firstly, the duration or loudness of each bar is normalized. As a result, information on the total duration or loudness of each bar is not available, i.e. only the proportional distribution of durations and loudness are shown. This means that two points with the same coordinates in the simplex might be two bars of completely different overall loudness or duration. For example, if the three beats of a bar are played equally fast or slow, the corresponding point is at the center of the rhythm simplex. Thus, this method is more appropriate for analyzing performance expressivity at the bar level. Nevertheless, we believe that variations on the scale of a musical phrase should also be considered. The bars corresponding to the beginning and end of the phrase are points distant from the center of the simplex, as they have increasing or decreasing tempo or loudness values. Whereas the bars in the middle of the phrase are bars with small variations in loudness or tempo, i.e. points in the center of the simplex. Another limitation of this method is that it can only be applied to three-interval data. While this approach is appropriate for the MazurkaBL dataset, which comprises of music pieces in triple time, it may not be suitable for more general types of data. However, since the MazurkaBL is the largest existing annotated dataset of performed music, we believe that developing tools like the 2-simplex, even if these methods are not applicable to all types of data, is crucial for analyzing and gaining a better understanding of music performances.

For future research, it would be valuable to study the movement of points within the simplex over time, in order to identify the trajectories of a section of music within the simplex and to capture the variation in interpretations amongst several performers. This would be useful to generate or modify performances by moving points in the 2-simplex and to identify the musical structure of a piece by knowing the trajectory patterns corresponding to the interpretation of sections. Finally, we expect that the development of methods based on formal mathematical representations, such as the 2-simplex in this paper, holds great promise for facilitating a more comprehensive analysis and understanding of musical performance.

Acknowledgments

P. Lascabettes is funded by a Contrat Doctoral Spécifique pour Normaliens (CDSN) scholarship. E. Chew is funded by a European Research Council (ERC) H2020 Advanced fellowship GA 788960 COSMOS. This work was partly supported by the chair of I. Bloch in Artificial Intelligence (Sorbonne Université and SCAI).

7. REFERENCES

[1] G. Widmer and W. Goebl, "Computational Models of Expressive Music Performance: The State of the Art," *Journal of New Music Research*, vol. 33, no. 3, pp. 203–216, 2004.

[2] N. Cook, "Performance Analysis and Chopin's Mazurkas," *Musicae Scientiae*, vol. 11, no. 2, pp. 183–207, 2007.

[3] C. S. Sapp, "Comparative Analysis of Multiple Musical Performances." in *International Society for Music Information Retrieval Conference (ISMIR)*, 2007, pp. 497–500.

[4] ——, "Computational Methods for the Analysis of Musical Structure," Ph.D. dissertation, Stanford University, 2011.

[5] N. Cook, "Between Art and Science: Music as Performance," *Journal of the British Academy*, vol. 2, pp. 1–25, 2014.

[6] K. Kosta, O. F. Bandtlow, and E. Chew, "MazurkaBL: Score-Aligned Loudness, Beat, Expressive Markings Data for 2000 Chopin Mazurka Recordings," in *Fourth International Conference on Technologies for Music Notation and Representation (TENOR)*, 2018, pp. 85–94.

[7] Z. Shi, "Computational Analysis and Modeling of Expressive Timing in Chopin's Mazurkas," in *22nd International Society for Music Information Retrieval Conference (ISMIR)*, 2021, pp. 650–656.

[8] C. E. Cancino-Chacón, M. Grachten, W. Goebl, and G. Widmer, "Computational Models of Expressive Music Performance: A Comprehensive and Critical Review," *Frontiers in Digital Humanities*, vol. 5, pp. 5–25, 2018.

[9] J. Langner and W. Goebl, "Visualizing Expressive Performance in Tempo-Loudness Space," *Computer Music Journal*, vol. 27, no. 4, pp. 69–83, 2003.

[10] N. P. M. Todd, "The Dynamics of Dynamics: A Model of Musical Expression," *Journal of the Acoustical Society of America*, vol. 91, no. 6, pp. 3540–3550, 1992.

[11] A. Gabrielsson, "Once Again: The Theme from Mozart's Piano Sonata in A Major," *Action and Perception in Rhythm and Music*, pp. 81–103, 1987.

[12] G. Widmer and A. Tobudic, "Playing Mozart by Analogy: Learning Multi-Level Timing and Dynamics Strategies," *Journal of New Music Research*, vol. 21, no. 1, pp. 259–268, 2003.

[13] D. Stowell and E. Chew, "Maximum a Posteriori Estimation of Piecewise Arcs in Tempo Time-Series," in *From Sounds to Music and Emotions*, M. Aramaki, M. Barthet, R. Kronland-Martinet, and S. Ystad, Eds. Berlin, Heidelberg: Springer Berlin Heidelberg, 2013, pp. 387–399.

[14] C. H. Chuan and E. Chew, "A Dynamic Programming Approach to the Extraction of Phrase Boundaries from Tempo Variations in Expressive Performances," in *8th International Society for Music Information Retrieval Conference (ISMIR)*, Vienna, Austria, 2007, pp. 305–308.

[15] P. Desain and H. Honing, "The Formation of Rhythmic Categories and Metric Priming," *Perception*, vol. 32, no. 3, pp. 341–365, 2003.

[16] H. Honing, "Structure and Interpretation of Rhythm and Timing," *Tijdschrift voor Muziektheorie*, vol. 7, no. 3, pp. 227–232, 2002.

[17] S. Handel, "The Effect of Tempo and Tone Duration on Rhythm Discrimination," *Perception & Psychophysics*, vol. 54, no. 3, 1993.

[18] H. G. Tekman, "Interactions of Perceived Intensity, Duration, and Pitch in Pure Tone Sequences," *Music Perception*, vol. 14, no. 3, pp. 281–294, 1997.

[19] C. V. Patricio and H. Honing, "Generating Expressive Timing by Combining Rhythmic Categories and Lindenmayer Systems," in *50th Anniversary Convention of the AISB*, London, UK, 2014, pp. 1–7.

[20] A. Lindenmayer, "Mathematical Models for Cellular Interactions in Development I. Filaments with One-Sided Inputs," *Journal of Theoretical Biology*, vol. 18, no. 3, pp. 280–299, 1968.

[21] R. Bååth, E. Lagerstedt, and P. Gärdenfors, "A Prototype-Based Resonance Model of Rhythm Categorization," *i-Perception*, vol. 5, no. 6, pp. 548–558, 2014.

[22] N. Jacoby and J. H. McDermott, "Integer Ratio Priors on Musical Rhythm Revealed Cross-Culturally by Iterated Reproduction," *Current Biology*, vol. 27, no. 3, pp. 359–370, 2017.

[23] K. Nave, C. Carrillo, N. Jacoby, L. Trainor, and E. Hannon, "The Development of Rhythmic Categories as Revealed Through an Iterative Production Task," *PsyArXiv*, 2021.

[24] E. Chew, "Playing with the Edge: Tipping Points and the Role of Tonality," *Music Perception*, vol. 33, no. 3, pp. 344–366, 2016.

[25] D. Herremans and E. Chew, "Tension Ribbons: Quantifying and Visualising Tonal Tension," in *Second International Conference on Technologies for Music Notation and Representation (TENOR)*, Cambridge, United Kingdom, 2016, p. 10.

[26] P. C. Mahalanobis, "On the Generalised Distance in Statistics," *Proceedings of the National Institute of Sciences of India*, vol. 2, no. 1, p. 49–55, 1936.

Elektronizza Orkestra: Developing a new kind of Digital Music Instruments Symphony Orchestra

Gaël Navard
Université Côte d'Azur
Conservatoire de Nice
gael.navard@univ-cotedazur.fr

ABSTRACT

This paper presents the different technological design stages of a Digital Music Instruments (DMIs) Orchestra similar in size and constitution to a traditional symphony orchestra. This ensemble has the particularity to include the digital equivalent of most of the traditional orchestral sections mixed with original interfaces. The choice was made to develop it without any laptop or screen on stage. The laptops are expensive, take space and tend to interfere with the musicians' performance and the audience's perception. This was made possible by using, on the one hand, wired audio and MIDI network technologies via IP, which allow the digital signal processing to be centralized in one or more computers in the FOH, and on the other hand, decentralized technologies with the use of Raspberry Pi single board computers embedded in 3D printed speakers with an amplified DAC, and a battery, all controlled wirelessly via an OSC network and a Web interface that run on any browser.

1. INTRODUCTION

1.1 Context

The Elektronizza project (initially titled MPEi - Multidimensional Polyphonic Expressive Digital Music Interfaces: From High-End Soloist Ensembles to Large Pedagogical Orchestras - Theoretical, Practical Studies and Developments on a New Class of Music Instruments) began in 2017 as part of the Université Côte d'Azur's IDEX (*Initiative d'Excellence*). This project was designed in partnership with several institutions and laboratories: Conservatoire de Nice, CTELA (Transdisciplinary Center for Epistemology of Literature and the Arts), CIRM (National Center for Musical Creation), LEAT (Laboratory of Electronics, Antennas and Telecommunications), IUT (University Institute of Technology), INRIA (National Institute for Research in Computer Science), XR^2C^2 (eXtended Reality Research and Creative Center), Studio Instrumental Association, and The Hublot (Digital Territory Factory).

The objective of this project was to create a research-creation-pedagogy ecosystem around the new DMIs (with a particular focus on "expressive" interfaces) by developing innovative devices allowing the deployment of all kinds of DMIs musical ensembles, from chamber music to the symphonic orchestra, intended for initiation in schools as well as for high level university students' musical practice.

1.2 Why a DMIs Symphonic Orchestra?

The beginning of the 21st century saw the tremendous emergence of laptop orchestras, primarily within institutions of higher education. Shelly Knotts listed nearly 160 such ensembles in 2014 [1]. Many of them are based on what we can call the "lorkian" model developed by the Plork (Princeton Laptop Orchestra) [2] in 2005. These ensembles are generally comprising up of an average of fifteen musicians, each with a laptop computer, often accompanied by interfaces from video games (Gamepads, Gametraks, Joysticks, Wiimotes, etc.) mostly used in a homogeneous way (each musician playing the same interface) thru omnidirectional loudspeakers associated with each station. For Dan Trueman [3], the symphonic orchestra is an incomplete model for laptop orchestras, and non-western orchestras have often more in common with this new type of ensemble. So why to revive this old institution?

In parallel with this movement of laptop orchestras, the progress of digital instrument making has allowed the emergence of a new class of interfaces giving the instrumentalist a fine expressivity, requiring assiduous practice and an advanced technique to be properly played. To motivate high level musicians to work and integrate these interfaces in their practice, it seemed relevant to constitute a DMIs orchestra directly stemming from the tradition of the symphonic orchestra, where the musicians and the public could find some familiar reference points while exploring new musical potentialities. This historical continuity, legibility and proximity to traditional instrumental music making allowed us to carry out a true transversal project with all the instrumental classes, taking this experimental practice out of the electroacoustic composition department.

As the two approaches can be seen as complementary, the lorkian model was also experimented in a pedagogical context with children, with the idea of eventually turning it into a kind of digital choir for the symphony orchestra. But this was done without the use of laptop, making the appellation laptop orchestra irrelevant for our project.

1.3 Why not use laptops?

While laptops have been essential since the beginning of the 21st century for real-time electroacoustic music creation, several reasons have led us not to use them.

A first reason is the cost. A Macbook Pro (by far the most used for live music) configured for sound usually costs around $2000, to which you must add an audio interface and various accessories and software. By switching to Linux and open-source software, the L^{2}ORK managed to go under the $750 per station in 2011 [4]. But this was still too much compared to the number of musicians planned to constitute our DMIs symphony orchestra. It was preferred to invest on high-end new interfaces for music expression rather than laptops.

A second reason is the lack of stability and the opacity in process management, especially in Windows and Mac OS, when musicians use the same computer as a home PC. In this case, the cost isn't a problem, but the use of devices primarily designed for office and multimedia tools has huge crash tendencies, hence the need for dedicated machines.

Finally, very often, the visual feedback from a screen on stage hinders the direct relationship between gestures and sounds for the instrumentalist and blurs the communication between the musician and the audience.

In 2012, Bruno Ruviaro [5] saw the possibility of changing this laptop architecture: *"(...) small pocket devices will soon have enough processing power to do anything a laptop can do today. At that point, the on-stage presence of an object such as a laptop may become completely unnecessary. The only hardware visible to the audience will be those the performer chooses to make visible, hopefully for an artistic reason. (...) The theater of a performance, then, may reappear in the actual human body. (...) The expression "laptop performance" may become as dated as the expression "tape music" today.*"

In 2014, the L^{2}Ork started using low-cost Raspberry Pi single board computers for initial music pedagogy [6]. After evaluating different solutions, we decided in 2018 to follow this path, which seemed very promising for the type of future orchestra planned to be developed.

2. DECENTRALIZED SYSTEMS

The initial idea was to create a decentralized system made of a wireless network of Raspberry Pi. But as we were not at that time familiar with these new terminals, we decided to start the first experimentations of the project with the technological elements we used to work with: laptops to work on the new expressive interfaces and smartphones and tablets to create a pedagogical proto-orchestra.

2.1 New expressive musical interfaces

At the time of the constitution of laptop orchestras appeared many DMIs whose potentialities for the expressivity of musical performance exceeded the previous generations (Haken Audio Continuum in 2002, Eigenlabs Eigenharp in 2009, Madrona Labs Soundplane in 2009, Roger Linn LinnStrument in 2015, Roli Seaboard in 2015, etc.). In 2018, the MIDI Manufacturers Association adopted the MIDI MPE (Multidimensional Polyphonic Expression) protocol suitable for their operation. A panel of these interfaces was thus acquired to explore their potential.

It was decided to work with the students of the coordinated Université Côte d'Azur-Conservatory Master's degree with the aim of creating small ensembles of soloists able to exploit their abilities. For this, I composed *Toccata in C++* for Sylphyo, Soundplane, and Boppads (2018) and Francis Faber composed *Slow Down* for Sylphyo, Seaboard, Malletstation and Boppads (2019). The project was integrated into Jean-François Trubert's Master seminar in 2021 and Gino Mariotti created an improvisation ensemble with eight students playing Seaboard, Linnstrument, Continuumini, Theremini, Handsonic, Vdrum and Malletstation (Figure 1).

Figure 1. At the top: *Slow Down* by Francis Faber. At the bottom: Master's degree's students improvisation ensemble conducted by Gino Mariotti.

This first phase of the project allowed us to master the use of these new interfaces, and it was a successful milestone for the next step of the development of an orchestra with a large number of musicians grouped in different sections.

2.2 Smartphone and tablet ensembles

To reach this goal, we decided, inspired by the projects MoPho [7] and Smartfaust [8], to start with the constitution of a pedagogical orchestra of smartphones with 22 students aged 13-14 from school Matisse (Nice), playing a composition of Yohan Brimicombe, *Electrons* (2018), conducted by Hélène Gaspérini (Figure 2). This piece mainly used the MobMuPlat app [9] allowing to load Pure Data patches on smartphones.

Figure 2. *Électrons* by Yohan Brimicombe for smartphone orchestra with Handsonic and Boppad. Conductor: Hélène Gaspérini.

A second experimentation was performed with Virginie Kracht's class of 18 students aged 13-14 in school Don Bosco (Nice) and a use of FAUST DSP to generate mobile apps in 2019 [10]. Finally, the same year, Bertrand Petit Hédelin used tablets and SKINI, a shared and non-linear composition system that he programmed during his PhD [11] with 15 students aged 11-12 from Frédéric Lacroix's class in school Nucéra (Nice)[1].

These experiences were very beneficial to figure out the different obstacles inherent in the technological constitution of DMIs orchestra. The conclusions reinforced the idea of changing the devices and no longer use non-dedicated peripherals and screens on stage, whether laptops, smartphones, or tablets [12]. Smartphones, for example, lack efficiency for music pedagogy: the embedded small speaker sound bad, the gestures that they allow are far from the subtility of a music instrument and, above all, the young students cannot detach themselves from the screen which hinders their musical listening.

As the COVID19 crisis arrived and momentarily stopped our orchestral activities, we decided to reallocate the large amount of Raspberry Pi we were working on to a partner project that was suffering from the global shortage of components: the *PrÉ* (*Présence Électroacoustique*) project, led by Camille Giuglaris, Bertrand Petit Hédelin and Jean-François Trubert [13], which was in the process of making small autonomous modules comprising a 3D printed speaker, a Raspberry Pi, an amplified DAC, a loudspeaker, and a battery. One of the goals of this project was to place 54 modules under the seats of the spectators in the Pierre Boulez concert hall in Paris for Jean-Luc Hervé's composition *Autre Nature* performed by the Radio France Philharmonic Orchestra (2022).

2.3 Gametrak ensemble

In 2022, thanks to the *PrÉ* project, the Raspberry Pi came back as 24 modules that we were able to use for the second phase of our project. Following the lorkian model, we acquired 24 gametrak interfaces [14] connected to the *PrÉ* modules via USB HID. We programmed an audio engine in Pure Data and a set of shell scripts to update the patches and sounds automatically on the whole devices. The Pure Data patch detected the MAC address of the raspberry and loaded the corresponding sub-patch specified in a JSON configuration file. Via a tablet interface initially created with Pure Data in MobMuPlat, we were able to control via OSC communication the volumes and cue changes of each module.

The gametrak allowing a large gestural amplitude, Elise Heinisch, who led these experiments in her class of 16 students aged 11-12 in the school Jean Rostand (Nice), decided to add a dancer and a choreography realized by Yaël Szwarcbaum. 8 students on music pedagogy at the university and the conservatory also took part in this project bringing the orchestra to 24 musicians (Figure 3).

Figure 3. Classroom work session and public performance of *Le Mouvement de l'Acanthe* by Elise Heinisch (2022).

The experiment was conclusive: this system was functional. Thanks to its lightness and its possible installation in a classroom facilitated by the battery powered *PrÉ* modules, it turned out to be perfectly adapted to orchestral teaching practice in schools. We decided to improve it and to add interfaces we were developing and specifically designing for the DMIs orchestral pedagogy.

2.4 New interfaces for musical pedagogy

The first idea was to develop a low-cost interface inspired by MPE interfaces like Linnstrument or Soundplane (Figure 4).

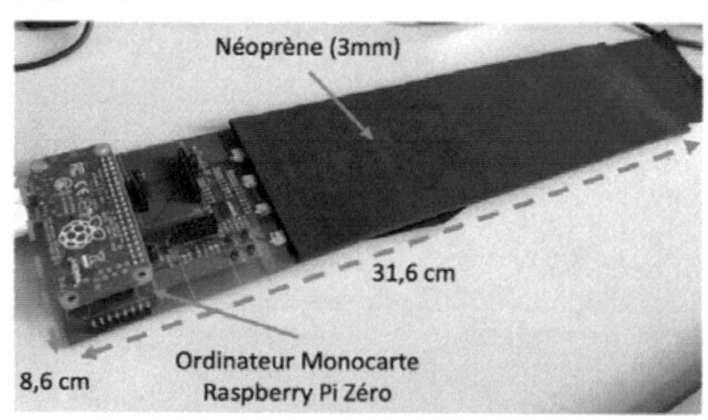

[1] This intervention was funded by the program *La Fabrique Musique Contemporaine* (SACEM).

Figure 4. Low cost MPE prototype. T. Louis, C. Andrieux, L. Zhuoer, A. Rochette and A. Pegatoquet, 2020.

But the result was far too complex and costly to build for this pedagogical context. We therefore oriented our development towards much simpler solutions (the Minimal Expressive Stick [12]), and after the realization of several other prototypes, we developed in 2023, with Patrice Colet and Wan Amira Syahirah Binti Wan Abdul Rahim, a pedagogical DMI named Hexapad (Figure 5). It was inspired by the Hang drum and the Roland Handsonic digital percussion. It is composed of a piezoelectric strike sensor, 7 capacitive sensors which allow to launch different sounds in a polyphonic way with aftertouch (resulting from the variations of contact surface with the capacitive sensors) and a Time-of-Flight distance sensor to modulate the sound. The microcontroller used is a Seeed Studio Xiao SAMD21 (which already has Atmel Qtouch inputs) and the ToF sensor a vl5310x.

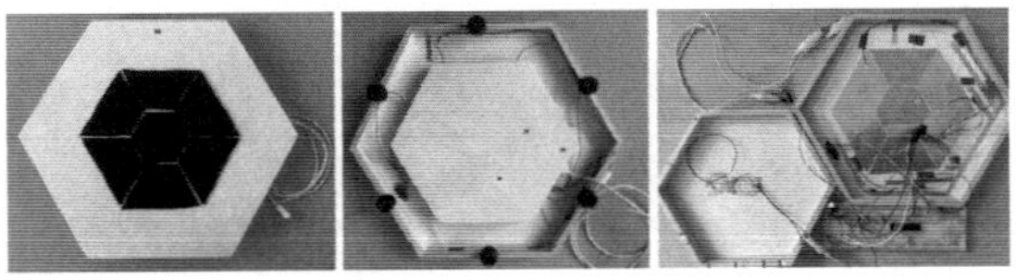

Figure 5. Hexapad first prototype.

The objective was to add an additional section of 16 expressive digital percussion instruments to the existing Gametrak section to allow the creation of full class DMIs orchestra (32 students), connected to the *PrÉ* modules and configurable in a network (Figure 6).

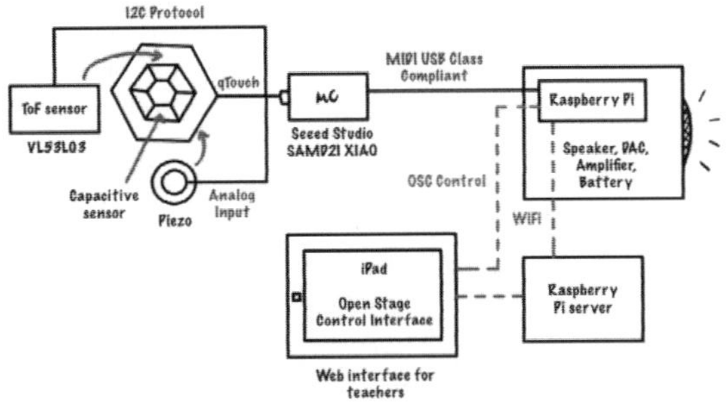

Figure 6. Hexapad orchestra architecture

But, while we were planning to experiment this new interface in an elementary school in spring 2023, a box ticked by mistake in a response to a call for projects[2] for the financing of school music assigned us to kindergarten classes. As these digital drums did not seem to be adapted to the awakening of the very young children, we decided, on the advice of Gilles Mottet, Professor at the Conservatoire de Nice specialized in school interventions, to make a simplified version. Only the hexagonal capacitive zone was kept and fixed on a plexiglass desk in order to slide in sheets with graphical illustrations (Figure 7).

Figure 7. Kindergarten prototype.

To change the sounds associated with the different illustrations (there were 6 different sheets during these interventions led by the composer Sarah Procissi at the kindergarten Madeleine Supérieure in Nice), and to manage the volumes of the *PrÉ* modules, our old Pure Data MobMuPlat interface was replaced by a much more practical Web interface (which does not require any installation) created by Patrice Colet with Open Stage Control (Figure 8).

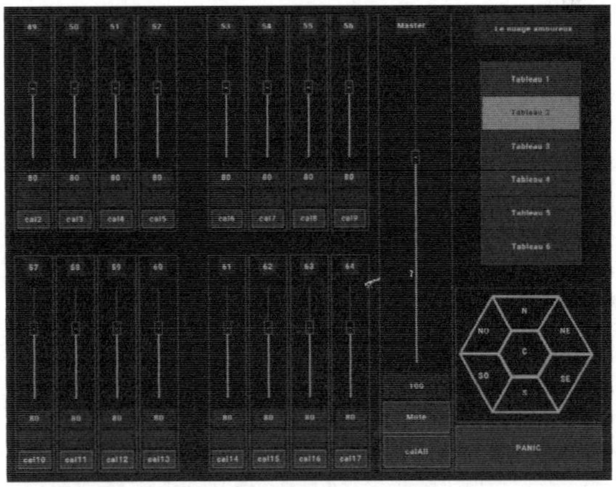

Figure 8. Open Stage Control OSC Web interface.

Playing this new prototype in kindergartens (children aged 3-6) showed that we were able to create digital orchestral tools for all types of ages. The Hexapad will be tested in school Jean Rostand (Nice), with students aged 11-12, in conjunction with Gametraks, as initially planned, between May and June 2023.

[2] This intervention was funded by the program *100% Culture à l'École* (city of Nice).

3. CENTRALIZED SYSTEMS

Experimentations in schools with decentralized battery-powered systems showed they are very efficient for educational interventions. But for working on high-end interfaces that require a lot of fine-tuning on the fly, it seemed to us more efficient to start on a more traditional centralized system.

3.1 Elektronizza Pedagogical Orkestra

Following the work we did with the students in small formations around the new expressive digital interfaces, we developed a first prototype of a heterogeneous DMIs orchestra (including sections inspired by the symphonic orchestra) with 22 musicians playing on a set of interfaces of the market: EWI, Sylphyo, Aerophones AE01, Linnstrument, Seaboard, Thereminis, Malletstations, Handsonics and Vdrums. For that ensemble, I composed the *ORK* study in 2021[3]. The orchestra was composed of 14 middle school students (aged 11-12) from the school Jean Rostand (Nice) and 6 university students in the context of an experimental music pedagogy workshop (Figure 9).

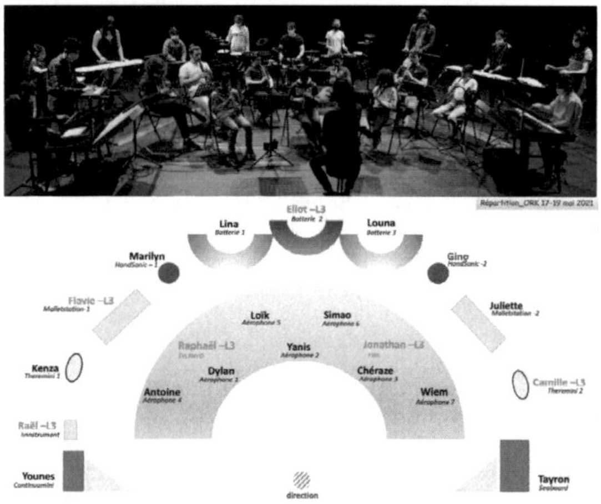

Figure 9. *ORK* by Gaël Navard. Conductor: Elise Heinisch. Espace Magnan, Nice, 2021.

The first test was to see if to hold such a DMI setup on a single Intel Mac Mini computer kept an acceptable latency in this context. We set the buffer size at 256 samples, and it was acceptable for this pedagogical experiment.

An encountered difficulty was the impossibility for the computer to recognize more than a dozen USB MIDI interfaces. This limitation, along with the desire to place the computer in the FOH (Front of House), led us to use an RTP-MIDI over IP network using several iConnectivity interfaces. This proved to be very efficient, and it allowed to plug and unplug the interfaces on the fly, without the need to rescan them with the Reaper DAW software used at the time. On the other hand, when having the same model of USB MIDI interface on the same MIDI interface (for example for the wind section) it was imperative to start the interfaces in the right order so that they would be routed to the right channels. This led to later use USB MIDI to MIDI DIN adapters to overcome this difficulty.

For the audio system, it was necessary to send the sound in multichannel to many speakers located on the back of the musicians, so that they could hear each other, and the audience could localize them. For this concert, 18 speakers, including 12 small 5″ speakers (5 on light 3m stands on the back, 3 on the percussion stand, and 4 on the keyboards stands), 4 small 8″ and 10″ subs and two omnidirectional wooden *Ondes* acoustic resonators from *La voix du luthier* (inspired by the work of Maurice Martenot) were used. An audio over IP system was used to simplify the wiring. After having tested the AVB protocol in another partner project (the Micadôme, a 32-channel immersive system installed at the Conservatoire de Nice and led by Michel Pascal) and having detected over time behaviors for a live context, we opted for an Audinate Dante system proved to be very robust with a small latency.

3.2 Elektronizza Symphony Orkestra

From this experience, we opened a series of workshops and courses offered by the department of electroacoustic composition at the Conservatoire de Nice and the Université Côte d'Azur, with the objective of training instrumentalists and composers of different levels in the handling of these new instruments. However, several sections of the symphony orchestra were still not represented in this digital instrument ensemble, which mainly includes woodwinds, percussion, keyboards, and other original interfaces. The choice was made to use electric string instruments (Guitar, Bass, Harp, Violin, Cello, Double Bass) and electrified brass instruments with Yamaha SilentBrass mutes (Trumpet, Trombone, French Horn, Euphonium) plugged into the Dante digital audio network and modified by digital effects.

2022 saw the launch of the development of this electroacoustic symphonic orchestra of 40 musicians interpreting Terry Riley's *In C* (1964). As a single central computer had not enough computing power for this large ensemble, 5 Mac Mini M1 were used in network, together with the Ableton Live software with Max4Live for more speed in the setting of the sounds of all these instruments. This also allowed us to lower the buffer size to 128 samples for having a better latency than the previous experiment.

This orchestra was installed on the whole stage of the auditorium of the Conservatoire de Nice behind the pedagogical orchestra of 24 Gametrak with the modules *Pré* on the proscenium, that was playing before on the same concert (Figure 10).

---

[3] This intervention was funded by the program *La Fabrique Musique Contemporaine* (SACEM).

Figure 10. Technical implementation for the May 5, 2022, concert: 40 musicians on stage (conductor: Gaël Navard) and 24 musicians on the proscenium (conductor: Elise Heinisch).

On stage, the 18 loudspeakers previously used together with loudspeakers of the Conservatoire de Nice's Acousmonium (loudspeaker orchestra dedicated to the spatial projection of acousmatic music) allowed to have more than 40 loudspeakers on stage in order to localize the sound of the musicians where they were physically on stage (Figure 11).

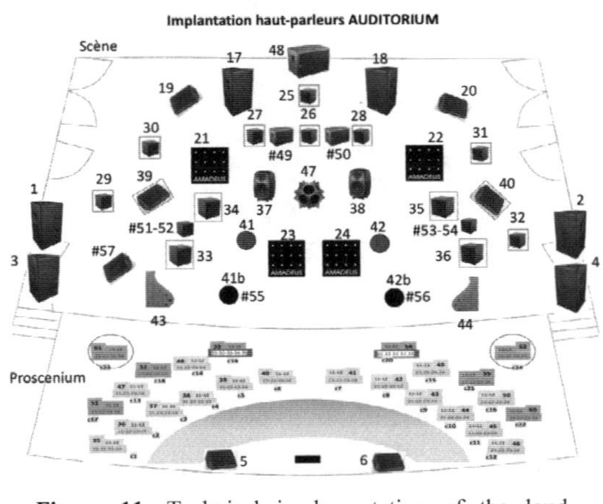

Figure 11. Technical implementation of the loudspeakers.

This orchestra played successfully May 5, 2022. The result was, for the first time since the beginning of this project, the installation of an electroacoustic orchestra of truly symphonic size and constitution.

There were several sections: 8 woodwinds, 8 plucked strings, 4 bowed strings, 4 brass, 4 keyboards, 6 percussions, 5 digital interfaces that have no link with traditional instruments and 1 modular synth (Figure 12).

Technically, the stage was divided into 3 zones (left, center and right) each one with a rack including an RTP-MIDI interface (iConnectivity mioXL) and a Dante audio network interface (Ferrofish Pulse16DX) for connecting the instruments and the loudspeakers. 3 Behringer X32 mixers with Dante cards was used on the FOH for controlling the speakers of these 3 zones, associate with 5 MIDI controllers Behringer X-Touch for controlling the 40 instruments inputs on the 5 Ableton Live sessions, synchronized via Ableton Link on the 5 computers.

Figure 22. Two general views of the stage and the FOH of the concert of May 5, 2022, at the auditorium of the Conservatoire de Nice. © Azur Photography

3.3 Elektronizza Big Band

In 2023, another type of digital instrument ensemble was experimented with students from the University and the Conservatory on a format inspired by pop music groups and jazz big bands, adapting compositions by Liam Chirico and Leo Morini.

As the required loudness was higher and the presence of microphones could cause some feedback problems, we mix our speaker system with a traditional Public Address configuration. The sound of the musicians was not only produced by a loudspeaker located near the musician as before, but also amplified in two main speakers on the front of the stage, with the use of wedges for the musicians, especially the singers. The absence of laptops on stage allowed to compact the set and to fit 20 musicians on a small 6x5m stage (Figure 13).

Technically, we simplified our system by using only the Behringer X32 mixer for inputs and outputs, without the need of the Behringer X-Touch MIDI controllers.

This concert allowed to test again our setup with many digital music interfaces in an audio and midi network, demonstrating once again its acceptable latency for musicians and its great robustness, since there were no technical crashes during the rehearsals and the concert.

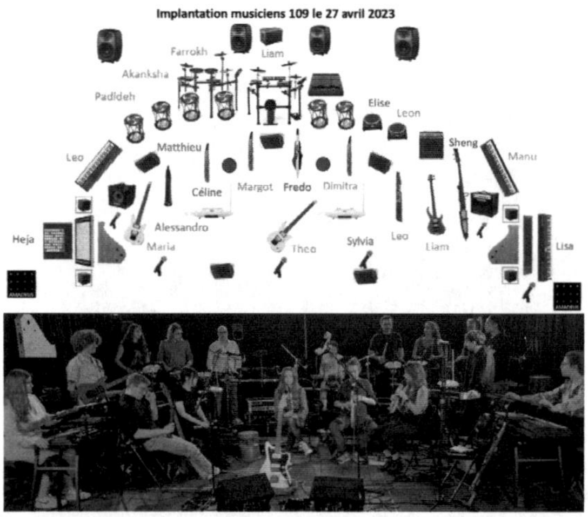

Figure 33. Technical implementation for the April 27, 2023, concert at the 109 (UCArts, Nice).

4. CONCLUSIONS

The aim of this paper was to describe the technological implementation of several non-laptop based DMI orchestras. The availability of reliable audio and MIDI networking technologies (RTP-MIDI in 2005, Dante in 2006) and low-cost single board computers (Raspberry Pi in 2012) are game changers for digital orchestras, and the joint use of these two technologies is very promising. The absence of screens on stage proved to be a great advantage in the setup, and the project allowed a very large number of instrumentalists from the Conservatory and the University to approach the new DMIs for the first time. Almost all the classes of the Conservatoire of Nice were involved in this project.

The first technological phase of the project described here lead to the installation of a functional and efficient DMI orchestral ensemble. The next step will be the creation of an original repertoire able to fully exploit the capabilities of these DMIs, an exciting challenge with many musical issues to explore.

Acknowledgments

This work was supported by the French government, through the UCA^{JEDI} Investments in the Future project managed by the National Research Agency (ANR) with the reference number ANR-15-IDEX-01.

5. REFERENCES

[1] S. Knotts and N. Collins, "The Politics of Laptop Ensembles: A Survey of 160 Laptop Ensembles and their Organisational Structures," *Proceedings of the 2014 International Conference on New Interfaces for Musical Expression*, 2014. p. 191-194.

[2] D. Trueman, P.R. Cook, S. Smallwood, and G., "PLOrk: the Princeton laptop orchestra, year 1," *Proceedings of the 2006 International Computer Music Conference,* 2006.

[3] D. Truman, "Why a laptop orchestra?" *Organised Sound*, vol. 12, no 2, pp. 171-179, 2007.

[4] I. Bukvic, T. Martin, and M. Matthews. "Moving Beyond Academia Through Open Source. Solutions–Introducing L2Ork, Virginia Tech's Linux Laptop Orchestra," *Proceedings of the 2011 Society for Electro-Acoustic Music in the United States Conference,* 2011.

[5] B. Ruviaro, B. Tucunduva, "From Schaeffer to *lorks: An expanded definition of musical instrument in the context of laptop orchestras," *Proceedings of the 1st Symposium on Laptop Ensembles & Orchestras*, 2012, pp. 23-26.

[6] I. Bukvic, "Pd-L2Ork Raspberry Pi Toolkit as a Comprehensive Arduino Alternative in K-12 and Production Scenarios," *Proceedings of the 2014 International Conference on New Interfaces for Musical Expression*, 2014, pp. 163-166.

[7] G. Wang, G. Essl, and H. Penttinen, "MoPho–A Suite for a Mobile Phone Orchestra," *Proceedings of the 8th International Conference on New Interfaces for Musical* Expression, 2008, p. 392.

[8] R. Michon, Y. Orlarey, S. Letz, *et al.* "Mobile music with the faust programming language" *Proceedings of the 14th International Symposium Perception, Representations, Image, Sound, Music,* Marseille, *2019,* pp. 307-318.

[9] D. Iglesia, I. Intermedia, "The mobility is the message: The development and uses of MobMuPlat," *Proceedings of the 2016 Pure Data Conference, New York*, 2016.

[10] V. Kracht, "Comment implémenter un orchestre numérique en collège ?" Master dissertation, musicology department, Université Côte d'Azur, 2019.

[11] B. Petit, M. Serrano, "Composing and Performing Interactive Music using the HipHop. js language," *Proceedings of the 2019 International Conference on New Interfaces for Musical Expression,* 2019.

[12] G. Navard, A. Pegatoquet, J.-F. Trubert, "Quels instruments pour un orchestre pédagogique électroacoustique?" *Proceedings of the 2020 Journées d'Informatique Musicale,* 2020.

[13] J.F. Trubert, B. Petit, C. Giuglaris, and J.-L. Hervé, "*PrÉ*: Connected Polyphonic Immersion," *Proceeding of the 2022 Web Audio Conference*, Cannes, France, 2022.

[14] A. Freed, D. McCutchen, A. Schmeder *et al.* "Musical applications and design techniques for the gametrak tethered spatial position controller," *Proceedings of the 6th Sound and Music Computing Conference*. Porto, 2009. pp. 23-25.

Networked Music Performance in PatchXR and FluCoMa

Jonathan Bell
PRISM-CNRS / XR2C2-CTEL
belljonathan50@gmail.com

ABSTRACT

The present study proposes to explore a sound corpus in VR, in which audio data is sliced and analysed in FluCoMa in order obtain relatively large collections of samples clustered by timbre similarity in a 3d room. The recent implementation of the multiplayer feature in PatchXR lets envisage wide variety of gesture-based control interfaces querying those corpora, and in which performers can interact remotely in order to simulate a chamber music situation.

1. INTRODUCTION

The recent emergence of multiplayer capabilities of a VR software such as patchXR [1] urges to find meaningful instrument design in order to remotely and collaboratively interact musically with a digital instrument, in multiplayer VR (or metaverse). In search of experiences that would relate to those found in traditional chamber music, the solution proposed here focuses on the exploration of a sound corpus projected on a 3d space, which the users can then navigate with his hand controllers (see Fig. 1): in an etude for piano and saxophone for instance [1], one musician plays blue buttons (the saxophone samples), and the other the yellow buttons (the piano samples).

An important reason here for using VR to explore a 3D dataset is that it allows users to interact with the data in a more natural and immersive way compared to a 2d plane (Chapter 3 will show how the present study derives from the CataRT 2d interface project), using the experience both as a tool for performance as well as data visualisation and analysis. Users can move around and explore the data from different angles, which can help them to better understand the relationships between different data points and identify patterns, which becomes more evident as the number of points increases. The use of machine learning (dimensionality reduction in our case) renders a world in which the absolute coordinates of each point has no more link to the descriptor space (the high sounds cannot be mapped to the y axis for instance), but offers compelling results for clustering information relating to the different playing styles of the instrument that is being analysed: as an example, in this extract [2] based on flute sounds, the opening shows a clear opposition between two types of gestures: 1/ (0'00) staccato notes and 2/ (0'05) legato scale-like type of material. This contrast in timbral quality is made explicit by a movement of the avatar which jumps from a cluster of buttons to another.

[1] https://youtu.be/kIi7YdzP2Nw?t=89
[2] https://youtu.be/777fqIIJCY4

Figure 1. A VR interface in which each button in the world corresponds to a slice of the sound file. Machine learning helps bringing closer sounds that share common spectral characteristics.

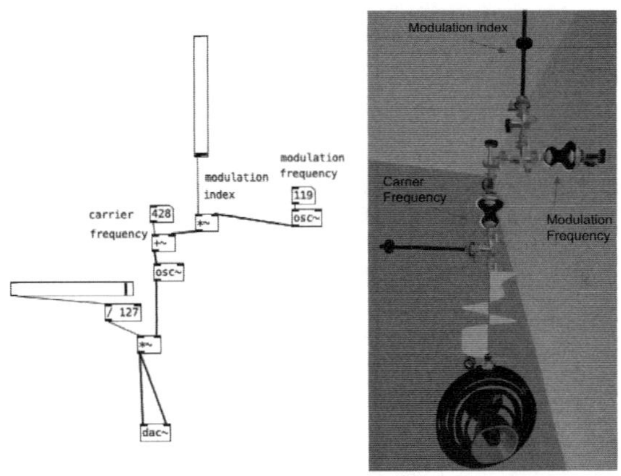

Figure 2. The implementation of the FM algorithm 1/ in Pure Data (left) 2/ in PatchXR (right).

2. VIRTUAL REALITY

2.1 Musical Metaverse

Turchet conducted a thorough study on what the musical metaverse means today [2], although the realm still is in its infancy. Berthaut [3] reviewed 3D interaction techniques and examined how they can be used for musical control. A survey of the emerging field of networked music performances in VR was offered by Loveridge [4]. Atherton and Wang [18] provided an overview of recent musical works in VR, while Çamcı and Hamilton [5] identified research trends in the Musical XR field through a set of workshops focusing on Audio-first VR.

Amongst a plethora of tools available today, PatchXR has caught our attention primarily because its ressemblance to Max/Pure Data environments (see Fig. 2).

2.2 PatchXR

PatchXR [1] is a tool for creating immersive virtual reality experiences in which users can design and build interactive worlds, games, and music experiences. At its core, Patch is a modular synthesis platform that allows users to create and connect different building blocks, or "patches" together to create complex systems. These building blocks can include everything from 3D models and textures to physics simulations, lighting controls, and, most importantly, audio digital signal processing.

One of the key features of Patch is its ability to enable collaboration between users. Patches can be shared and remixed, allowing multiple users to work together on a single project or create something entirely new. In addition, Patch has a robust library of resources for users to draw from, including tutorials, documentation, and sample patches. The community around Patch is also very active, with regular competitions, events, and meet ups happening around the world.

One of the most exciting aspects of Patch is its potential for use in music performance and composition. The modular design of the platform allows users to create complex audio and visual environments that can be controlled in real-time, opening up new possibilities for live music and audiovisual performances. Patch has been used in a variety of contexts, from creating interactive installations and exhibits to developing VR training simulations and games. Its flexibility and modular design make it a powerful tool for anyone interested in exploring the creative possibilities of VR.

3. CORPUS-BASED CONCATENATIVE SOUND SYNTHESIS (CBCS)

Corpus-Based Concatenative Sound Synthesis (CBCS) is a technique used in computer music that involves constructing a sound or music piece by concatenating (joining together) smaller units of sound, such as phonemes in speech synthesis or musical phrases in music synthesis. It is used in our case to model an improvising instrumental musician by creating a database of recorded musical phrases or segments that can be combined and rearranged in real-time to create a musical performance that sounds like it is being improvised.

Today nearly 20 years old if one refers to the first CataRT publications [6], CBCS today enjoys an increasing popularity. Various apps today are based on similar principals (AudioStellar, Audioguide, LjudMAP or XO). The democratisation of audio analysis and machine learning tools such as the FluCoMa package (for Max, SuperCollider and Pure Data) encourages computer music practitioners to engage in this field at the crux between music creation and data science/machine learning.

3.1 Timbre Space

In spite of promising advances in the domain of deep learning applied to sound synthesis [7] [8], CBCS tools may earn their popularity from a metaphor which leads back to the early days of computer music: the notion of timbre space, developed by Wessel [9] and Grey [10], according to which the multi-dimentional qualities of *timbre* may be better understood using spatial metaphors (e.g. the timbre of the English horn being closer to basson than is it of trumpet).

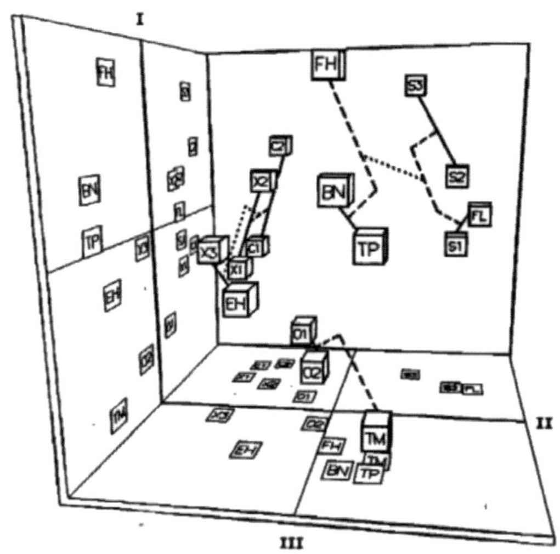

Figure 3. Multidimensional perceptual scaling of musical timbres (John M. Grey[10]). Sounds available at: https://muwiserver.synology.me/timbrespaces/grey.htm.

Pioneers in the perception of timbre studies such as Grey [10], J.C. Risset, D. Wessel, [11] or Stephen McAdams [12] [13] most often define timbre by underline what it is not. Risset and Wessel, for instance, define it as follow: *It is the perceptual attribute that enables us to distinguish among orchestral instruments that are playing the same pitch and are equally loud.* The co-variance such parameters (pitch, loudness and timbre), however, leads Schwarz to distinguish timbre space and CBCS notions: '*Note that this concept is similar but not equivalent to that of the timbre space put forward by Wessel and Grey [7, 24], since timbre is defined as those characteristics that serve to distinguish one sound from another, that remain after removing differences in loudness and pitch. Our sound space explicitly includes those differences that are very important to musical expression.*" [14]

The workflow described in Chapter 5 gave in practice strong evidence of inter-dependance between register, timbre and dynamics, particularly when the analysis run over a single instrument sound file (e.g. 30 minutes of solo flute), and chopped in short samples. The system will then precisely be able to find similarity between instrumental passages played in the same register, same dynamic, and same playing technique (e.g. a flute playing fast trills mezzo forte, in mid-low register, with air).

3.2 Corpus-Based Concatenative Synthesis - State of the art

A wide array of technologies today can be called corpus-based concatenative synthesis, in the sense that they allow, through segmentation and analysis, to explore large quantities of sound. Some of them are presented as "ready-made" solutions, such as the recent *Audiostellar* [15], or SCMIR [3] for SuperCollider. Hackbarth's AudioGuide [16] offers a slightly different focus because it uses the morphology/timeline of a soundfile to produce a concatenated output. Within the Max world finally, two environments appear as highly customizable: IRCAM's MuBu [17] and the more recent EU funded FluCoMa [18] project. CataRT is now fully integrated in MuBu, whose purpose encompasses multimodal audio analysis as well as machine for movement and gesture recognition [19]. This makes MuBu extremely general purpose, but also difficult to grasp. The data processing tools in MuBu are mostly exposed in the pipo plugin framework [20], which can compute for instance mfcc analysis on a given audio buffer [4] by embedding the pipo.mfcc plugin inside the mubu.process object.

FluComa also aims to be general purpose, but seems particularly suited to perform two popular specific tasks. With only limited knowledge of the framework nor of theory laying behind the algorithms it uses (such as those dimentionality reduction, mfcc analysis, or neural network training), the framework allows: 1/ to segment, analyse and represent/playback a sound corpus 2/ to train a neural network to control a synthesizer, in a manner reminiscent of Fiebrink's Wekinator [21].

Only the tools for segmentation, analysis, representation and playback (described in detail in Chapter 5) were used here, for they precisely fit the needs of corpus-based synthesis.

4. CONNECTING PATCHXR AND FLUCOMA

Porting analysis made in Max/FluCoMa to PatchXR consists in generating a world in which each sonic fragment's 3d position follows coordinates delivered by FluCoMa.

The structure of a .patch file (a patchXR world) follows the syntax of a .maxpat (for Max) or .pd file (for pure data) in the sense that it first declares the objects used, and then the connexions between them. This simple structure helped to generate a javascript routine generating a template world, taking as input 1/ dictionaries (json files) with each segment's 3d coordinates and 2/ each segment's temporal position in the sound file, and as output a new .patch file (a world accessible in VR, see general workflow on Fig. 4).

[3] A demo is available at: https://youtu.be/jxo4StjV0Cg

[4] MFCC stands for Mel-Frequency Cepstral Coefficients. It is a type of feature extraction method that is commonly used in speech and speaker recognition systems. MFCCs are used to represent the spectral characteristics of a sound in a compact form that is easier to analyze and process than the raw waveform. They are calculated by applying a series of transformations to the power spectrum of a sound signal, including a Mel-scale warping of the frequency axis, taking the logarithm of the power spectrum, and applying a discrete cosine transform (DCT) to the resulting coefficients. The resulting coefficients, which are called MFCCs, capture the spectral characteristics of the sound and are commonly used as features for training machine learning models for tasks such as speech recognition and speaker identification.

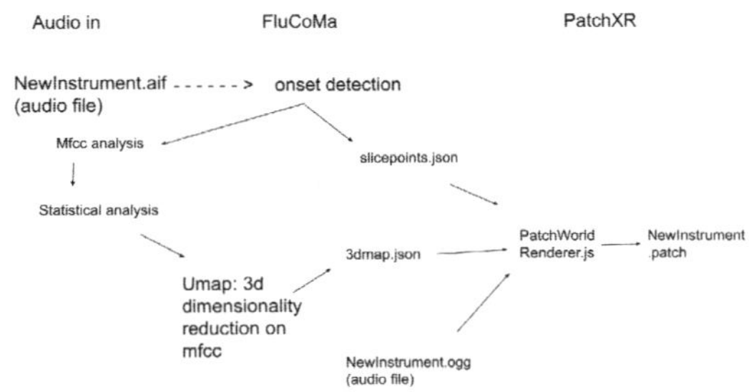

Figure 4. General workflow: from an input audio file to its .patch 3d representation in PatchXR.

After a few trials in which the x y z coordinates of a world directly represented audio descriptors such as loudness, pitch and centroid [5] , I more systematically used mfcc analysis and dimensionality reduction, as will be shown in section 5.

Section 6 will present different javascript programs and Max patches that were developed in order to diversify the ways in which FluCoMa analysis is represented in PatchXR, and how the user can interact with it.

5. WORKFLOW - ANALYSIS IN FLUCOMA

My experiments have focussed on musical instrument corpora almost exclusively [6] . The tools presented here can efficiently generate plausible virtuosic instrumental music but recent uses found more satisfying results in slower, quieter, "Feldman-like" types of textures. Various limitations on the playback side (either in standalone VR, or on a Pure Data sampler for RaspberryPi described in Section 6.2) have imposed restrictions in the first stages on the amount of data it could handle (less than 5 minutes in AIFF in PatchXR) or the number of slice the sample could be chunked into (256 because of limitation of lists in Max, a limitation that has also been surpassed since). Both limitations were later overcome (use of the compressed ogg format in PatchXR, and taking advantage of longer sound files since version 672, increase of internal buffer size in fluid.buf2list in FluCoMa), thus allowing for far more convincing models.

Using concatenative synthesis to model an improvising instrumental musician typically involves several steps:

1. Segmentation of a large soundfile: This involves dividing a large audio recording of the musician's performance into smaller units or segments.
2. Analysis: These segments are then organised in a database according to various descriptor data (mfcc in our case).
3. Scaling/pre-processing: scaling is applied for better visualisation.
4. Dimension reduction: Based on mfcc descriptors, the dimensionality of the data is reduced in order to

[5] https://youtu.be/1LHcbYh2KCI?t=19

[6] For cello: https://youtu.be/L-MiKmsIzjM For various instruments: https://www.youtube.com/playlist?list=PLc_WX6wY4JtnNqu4Lwe2YzEUq9S1IMvUk For flute: https://www.youtube.com/playlist?list=PLc_WX6wY4JtlbjLuLHDZhlx78sTDn

make it more manageable and easier to work with. This can be done using techniques such as principal component analysis (PCA) singular value decomposition (SVD), or Uniform Manifold Approximation and Projection (UMAP, preferred in our case).

5. Near neighbours sequencing: Once the segments have been organised and analysed, the algorythm selects and combines them in real-time based on certain input parameters or rules to create a simulated musical performance that sounds like it is being improvised by the musician. We use here a near neighbours algorithm, which selects segments that are similar in some way (e.g., in terms of pitch, loudness, or timbre - thanks to similarities revealed by umap on mfccs in our case) to the current segment being played.

We will now describe these steps in further detail:

5.1 Slicing

Slicing a sound file musically allow various possible exploitations in the realm of CBCS. In MuBu onset detection is done with pipo.onseg or pipo.gate. FluCoMa expose five different onset detection algorithms:

1. fluid.ampslice: Amplitude-based detrending slicer
2. fluid.ampgate: Gate detection on a signal
3. fluid.onsetslice: Spectral difference-based audio buffer slicer
4. fluid.noveltyslice: Based on self-similarity matrix (SSM)
5. fluid.transcientslice: Implements a de-clicking algorithm

Onsetslice only was extensively tested. The only tweaked parameters were a straight-forward "threshold" as well as a "minslicelength" argument, determining the shortest slice allowed (or minimum duration of a slice) in hopSize. This introduce a common limitation in CBCS: the system strongly biases the user to choose short samples for better analysis results, and more interactivity, when controlling the database with a gesture follower. Aaron Einbond remarks in the use of CataRT how short samples most suited his intention: "*Short samples containing rapid, dry attacks, such as close-miked key-clicks, were especially suitable for a convincing impression of motion of the single WFS source. The effect is that of a virtual instrument moving through the concert hall in tandem with changes in its timbral content, realizing Wessel's initial proposal.*"[22]

A related limitation of concatenative synthesis lies in the fact that short samples will demonstrate the efficiency of the algorithm [7], but at the same time moves away from the "plausible simulation" sought in the present study. A balance therefore must be found between the freedom imposed by large samples, and the refined control one can obtain with short samples.

A direct concatenation of slices clicks in most cases on the edit point, which can be avoided through the use of ramps. The second most noticeable glitch on concatenation concerns the interruption of low register resonances, which even a large reverb fails making sound plausible. Having a low threshold and large "minslicelenght" results in equidistant slices, all of identical durations, as would do the pipo.onseg object in MuBu.

Because we listen to sound in time, this parameter responsible for the *duration of samples* is of prior importance.

5.2 MFCC on each slice - across one whole slice/segment

Multidimensional MFCC analysis: MFCC (Mel-Frequency Cepstral Coefficient) analysis is a technique used to extract features from audio signals that are relevant for speech and music recognition. It involves calculating a set of coefficients that represent the spectral envelope of the audio signal, or decomposing a sound signal into a set of frequency bands and representing the power spectrum of each band with a set of coefficients. The resulting MFCC coefficients capture important spectral characteristics of the sound signal (albeit hardly interpretable by the novice user), such as the frequency and magnitude of the spectral peaks. We will see that combines with *umap*, it is able to capture the spectral characteristics of the musician's playing style.

5.3 Statistical Analysis Over Each Slice

BufStats is used to calculate statistical measures on data stored in a buffer channel. BufStats calculates seven statistics on the data in the buffer channel: mean, standard deviation, skewness, kurtosis, low, middle, and high values. These statistics provide information about the central tendency of the data and how it is distributed around that tendency. In addition to calculating statistics on the original buffer channel, BufStats can also calculate statistics on up to two derivatives of the original data, apply weights to the data using a weights buffer, and identify and remove outlier frames. These statistical measures can be useful for comparing different time-series data, even if they have different length, and may provide better distinction between data points when used in training or analysis. The output of BufStats is a buffer with the same number of channels as the original data, with each channel containing the statistics for its corresponding data in the original buffer.

5.4 Normalization

The FluCoMa package proposes several scaling or preprocessing tools, amongst which normalization and standardization were used. Standardization and normalization are techniques used to transform variables so that they can be compared or combined in statistical analyses. Both techniques are used to make data more comparable, but they work in slightly different ways.

Standardization scales a variable to have a mean of 0 and a standard deviation of 1, while normalization scales a variable to have a minimum value of 0 and a maximum value of 1. Normalization ccaling was found easier to use both in 2-D (in FluCoMa, the fluid.plotter object), as well as in the VR 3D world in which the origin corresponds to a corner of the world. The fluid.nomalize object features an "@max" attribute (1 by default), which then maps directly to the dimensions of the VR world.

[7] e.g. https://youtu.be/LD0ivjyuqMA?t=3032

Dimensionality reduction is a technique used in machine learning to reduce the number of features (dimensions) in a dataset. The goal of dimensionality reduction is to simplify the data without losing too much information. Various dimensionality reduction algorithms are presented in an early FluCoMa study [23], with interestingly no mention of UMAP, later favoured.

UMAP (Uniform Manifold Approximation and Projection) is a non-linear dimensionality reduction technique that is based on the principles of topological data analysis. It can be used to visualize high-dimensional data in a lower-dimensional space. When applied to sound data analysed with MFCC (Mel-Frequency Cepstral Coefficients), UMAP reduces the dimensionality of the data and creates a visual representation of the sound in a 2- or 3-dimensional space.

By applying UMAP to the MFCC coefficients of a sound signal, it is possible to create a visual representation of the sound that preserves the relationships between the different MFCC coefficients (see Fig. 5).

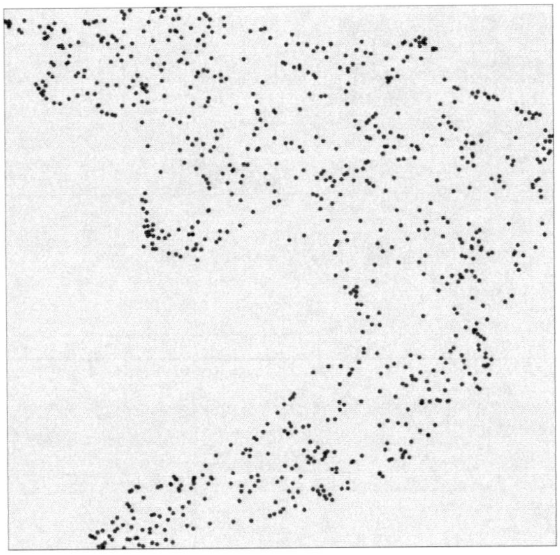

Figure 5. Dimensionality reduction of MFCCs help revealing spectral similarities. UMAP outputs coordinates in 2d or 3d.

UMAP is therefore used for its clustering abilities in the first place, helping for classification purposes. It helps identifying patterns or trends that may not be evident from the raw data. This can be useful for tasks such as exploring the structure of a sound dataset, identifying patterns or trends in the data, and comparing different sounds.

Most importantly, the non-linear dimensions proposed by UMAP (whether in 2d in Max or in 3 dimensions in PatchXR, and when compared to linear analyses in which, for instance, x, y and z correspond to pitch, loudness and centroid) gave far more "intelligent" clustering than more conventional parameter-consistent types of representations.

The neighbourhood retrieval function is based in FluCoMa on K-d trees and the knn algorythm. In MuBu, the mubu.knn object serves similar tasks. The ml.kdtree object in the ml.star library [24] gives comparable results.

K-d trees (short for "k-dimensional trees") and k-nearest neighbours (k-NN) are two algorithms that are related to each other, but serve different purposes, a k-d tree is a data structure that is used to store and efficiently query a set of points in a k-dimensional space, while the k-NN algorithm is a machine learning algorithm that is used for classification or regression. Both algorithms are often used in applications such as pattern recognition, image classification, and data mining.

6. WORKFLOW IN PATCHXR

I have most often used FluCoMa and PatchXR to generate monophonic instruments (one performer plays one instrument at a time), most typically in experiences where players the players face one another [8]. In the case of "button worlds" such as this one or those described in section 6.1, there is no need of nearest neighbour retrieval since the performer clicks exactly on the data point, and he (mediated by his avatar) reproduces what knn would do with an automated instrument: he will privilege in his choice the samples he can reach at hand, rather than constantly jump large distances between items (see Fig. 1).

In the worlds developed in Sections 6.2 and 6.3 on the other hand, data points are not explicitely represented and some near neighbour strategies need to be implemented. PatchXR exposes a wide range of blocks (a block corresponds to an object in Max or Pure Data) making it simple to access gesture data such as:

- The position/distance between hands/controllers and a reference.
- The rotation angles (x y z) of both hands' controllers
- 2-d touchscreen-like controllers, where the user moves the xy position of a selector across a plane by manually grabbing it.
- 2-d lazer-like controllers, where the user moves the xy position of a selector remotely, as if using a lazer pointer towards a remote screen or board.
- 2-d pads, which allow to access the velocity at which the pad is hit
- 3-d slider or theremine like controllers, where the user moves the xyz position of a selector across a plane by manually grabbing it.
- A block called "interaction box" similar to 3-d slider, with the main difference that the user does not grab the selector, but instead comes in and out of the interactive zone
- 1-d sliders, knobs, buttons...

One of the current challenges consists in diversifying the ways in which the corpus is queried.

[8] https://youtu.be/WhuqOOuzzBw

One to one mapping of UMAP results such as those of section 6.1 use buttons facing each other, in order to prompt the players to face each other [9].

When playing alone and controlling at the same time many instruments (the one-man-orchestra), encourages to use higher level type of control over automata, i.e. to implement the simple ability to concatenate automatically: play the next sample as soon as the previous one has stopped (see section 6.2).

6.1 One to one mapping between data points and buttons

The first javascript routine developed was designed to simply map a data point in the sonic space to a button in the virtual 3d space. By iterating over an array, the routine generates a world in which each button's coordinates are dictated by the FluCoMa umap analysis descripbed in section 5.5. Albeit simpler than the method that will be exposed later, this simple one to one to one mapping has several advantages, most importantly the haptic and visual feedback the performer gets when hitting each button.

6.2 Max/pd dependence

The second stage investigated the possibility to render the sounds on an array of raspberry pi computers [25]. While this method shows advantages in terms of patching (because of the convenience of using max and pure data), the main drawback is that patches designed in this way cannot be accessed by the PatchXR community. Documentation, similarly is harder to record since the sound is produced outside of PatchXR. The haptic and visual feedback is very different here in the sense that the user controls primarily the region of the space to be played, and when to start and stop playing (when his hand touches the interface or not). The way he plays is less rhythmical than in the button interface where the player "hits" [10] each sample (section6.1). Here on the contrary, the automat simply keeps playing as long as he touches the interface [11]

Flucoma exposes the fluid.kdtree that is able to find the k nearest number once it is given as input the coordinates of each data point (see Fig. 6). This method proved more suitable to control automata in which the player selects a region of a 2d plane together with the number of neighbours he wants the automate to improvise with.

Most satisfying results were achieved by sending messages to each RaspberriPi independently, according to its specific (static) IP address, with a simple syntax of a 2-integer list corresponding to: 1/which buffer to lookup 2/ which slice in this buffer to play, each Pi/speaker thus being able to play each sound in a pure data patch, in which each slice looks up an array with the corresponding slice points.

6.3 Nearest neighbour in PatchXR

The currently most frequently used program is a javascript routine that generates a world (a .patch file) in which the x y z coordinates of each data point are stored in a "knob

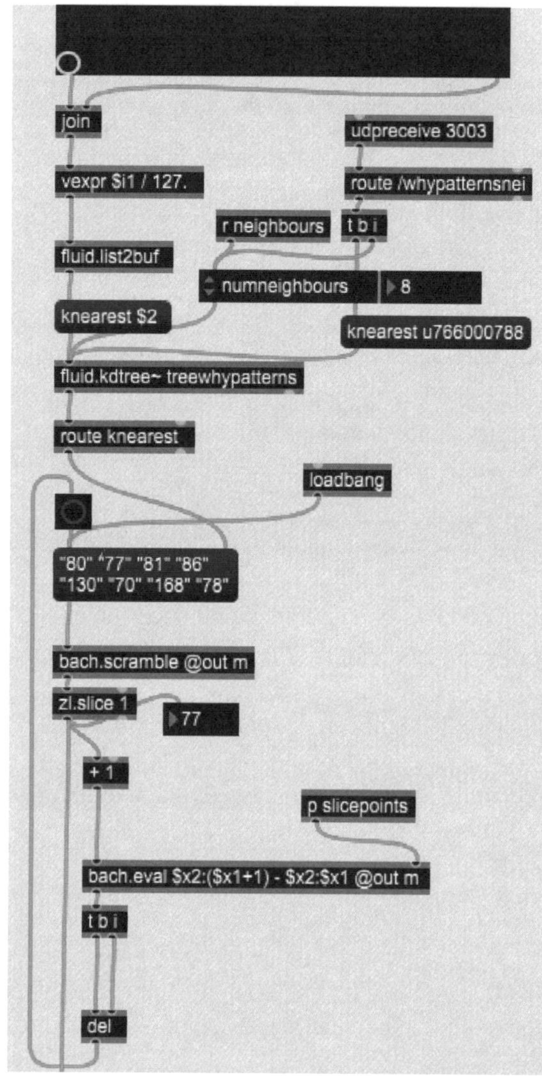

Figure 6. The *fluid.kdtree* object is used here to retrieve the 8 nearest neighbours of a point in a 2-d space.

board" block (the long rectangle in Fig.7). To measure the distance in 3D using Thales' theorem (or so called distance formula), we need to find the distance between two points in three-dimensional space, i.e find the diameter of the sphere that passes through both points.

$$\sqrt{(x_2 - x_1)^2 + (y_2 - y_1)^2 + (z_2 - z_1)^2}$$

Fig. 8 shows the corresponding implementation in patchXR.

This fragment of visual program (called "abstraction" or "subpatch" in Max, and called "group" in PatchXR) is then used in a more complex patch which iterates (100 times per second, for instance) over an array (the rectangular "knob-board" object in Fig.7, so as to output the index (the value 234 in the figure) of the point situated the closest to the controller.

[9] https://youtu.be/

[10] the opening of this video aptly conveys how the energy transfers form the player's gesture https://www.youtube.com/watch?v=glFdzbAJVRU

[11] https://youtu.be/vtob96F9cQw

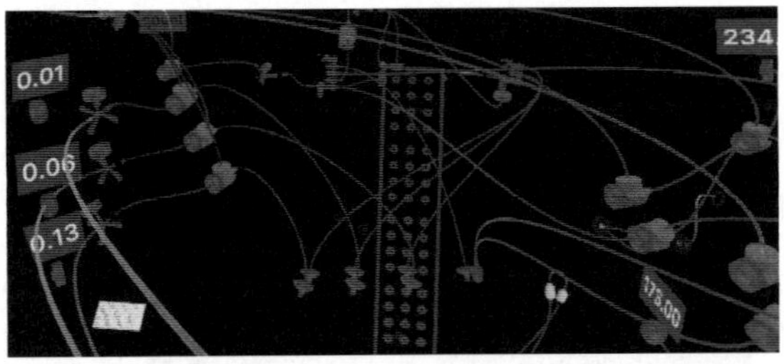

Figure 7. The coordinates of the player's controller (here 0.01, 0.06, 0.13) yield as a result index 234 as nearest neighbour (read from left to right).

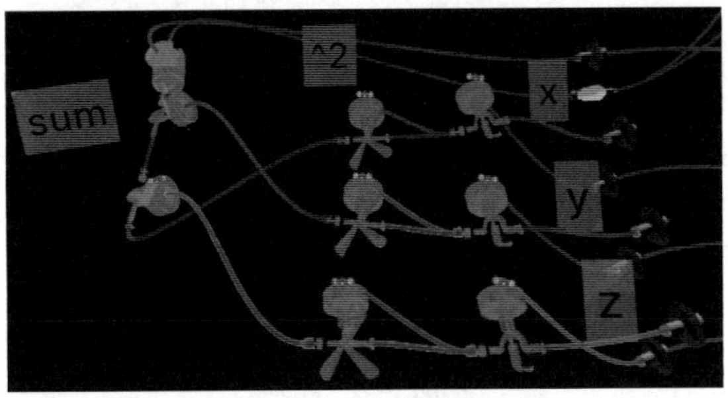

Figure 8. The implementation of Thales' theorem in patchXR (read from right to left).

7. NETWORKED MUSIC PERFORMANCE

The concept of online virtual collaboration has gained significant attention, notably through Meta's promotion in 2021. The application of this concept within the realm of "teleimprovisations" [26], most commonly referred to as Networked Music Performance (NMP) or holds the potential to overcome what was hitherto viewed as intrinsic limitation of the field, both from practitioners and from an audience point of view.

NMPs have indeed stimulated considerable research and experimentation whilst facing resistance at the same time. In his article "Not Being There", Miller Puckette argues that he finds "Having seen a lot of networked performances of one sort or another, I find myself most excited by the potential of networked "telepresence" as an aid to rehearsal, not performance." [27]. In *Embodiment and Disembodiment in NMP* [28], Georg Hajdu identifies an issue with a lack of readability from an audience perspective, who cannot perceive the gesture to sound relationship as would be the case in a normal concert situation: "These performances take machine–performer–spectator interactions into consideration, which, to a great deal, rely on embodied cognition and the sense of causality[...]. Classical cause-and-effect relationships (which also permeate the 'genuine' musical sign of the index) are replaced by plausibility, that is the amount to which performers and spectators are capable of 'buying' the outcome of a performance by building mental maps of the interaction." Performances of laptop orchestras, along with various other experiments using technology collaboratively, wether in local or distributed settings, have reported similar concerns, most commonly though in its infancy, a first live performance staged/composed by the author in Paris, with participants distributed across Europe, showed a promising potential for tackling these issues, most importantly through its attempt at dramatising the use of avatars.

- JIM 23: https://youtu.be/npyfwqN02qE

A lot remains to be improved in order to give the audience an experience aesthetically comparable to that of the concert hall. Carefully orchestrated movements of cameras around the avatars, and faithful translation the headset experience of spatial audio with immersive visuals need further exploration, but would go beyond the scope of the present article.

8. CONCLUSIONS

We've proposed a workflow for corpus-based concatenative synthesis CBCS in multiplayer VR (or metaverse), arguing that machine learning tools for data visualisation offer revealing and exploitable information about the timbral quality of the material that is being analysed. In a wider sense, the present approach can be understood as reflexive practice on new media, according to which the notion of data-base may be considered an art form [29]).

The discussed tools for "machine listening" (FluCoMa, MuBu) help building intelligent instruments with relatively small amounts of data, the duration of samples appear crucial in CBCS. A balance must be found between 1/ short duration sample analysis which are easier to process and categorise and 2/ long samples which sound more natural in the context instrument-based simulations.

Acknowledgments

I am grateful for the support of UCA/CTEL, whose artist residency research program has allowed to hold these experiments, and for the support of PRISM-CNRS.

9. REFERENCES

[1] Andersson, "immersive audio programming in a virtual reality sandbox," *journal of the audio engineering society*, march 2019.

[2] L. Turchet, "Musical Metaverse: vision, opportunities, and challenges," *Personal and Ubiquitous Computing*, 01 2023.

[3] F. Berthaut, "3D interaction techniques for musical expression," *Journal of New Music Research*, vol. 49, no. 1, pp. 60–72, 2020.

[4] B. Loveridge, "Networked music performance in virtual reality: current perspectives," *Journal of Network Music and Arts*, vol. 2, no. 1, p. 2, 2020.

[5] A. Çamcı and R. Hamilton, "Audio-first VR: new perspectives on musical experiences in virtual environments," *Journal of New Music Research*, vol. 49, no. 1, pp. 1–7, 2020.

[6] D. Schwarz, G. Beller, B. Verbrugghe, and S. Britton, "Real-Time Corpus-Based Concatenative Synthesis with CataRT," in *9th International Conference on Digital Audio Effects (DAFx)*, Montreal, Canada, Sep. 2006, pp. 279–282, cote interne IRCAM: Schwarz06c. [Online]. Available: https://hal.archives-ouvertes.fr/hal-01161358

[7] J.-P. Briot, G. Hadjeres, and F.-D. Pachet, *Deep Learning Techniques for Music Generation – A Survey*, Aug. 2019. [Online]. Available: https://hal.sorbonne-universite.fr/hal-01660772

[8] P. Esling, A. Chemla-Romeu-Santos, and A. Bitton, "Generative timbre spaces with variational audio synthesis," *CoRR*, vol. abs/1805.08501, 2018. [Online]. Available: http://arxiv.org/abs/1805.08501

[9] D. L. Wessel, "Timbre Space as a Musical Control Structure," *Computer Music Journal*, vol. 3, no. 2, pp. 45–52, 1979. [Online]. Available: http://www.jstor.org/stable/3680283

[10] K. Fitz, M. Burk, and M. McKinney, "Multidimensional perceptual scaling of musical timbre by hearing-impaired listeners," *The Journal of the Acoustical Society of America*, vol. 125, p. 2633, 05 2009.

[11] J.-C. Risset and D. Wessel, "Exploration of timbre by analysis and synthesis," *Psychology of Music*, pp. 113–169, 1999.

[12] S. Mcadams, S. Winsberg, S. Donnadieu, G. De Soete, and J. Krimphoff, "Perceptual scaling of synthesized musical timbres: Common dimensions, specificities, and latent subject classes," *Psychological research*, vol. 58, pp. 177–92, 02 1995.

[13] A. Caclin, S. Mcadams, B. Smith, and S. Winsberg, "Acoustic correlates of timbre space dimensions: A confirmatory study using synthetic tones," *The Journal of the Acoustical Society of America*, vol. 118, pp. 471–82, 08 2005.

[14] D. Schwarz, "The Sound Space as Musical Instrument: Playing Corpus-Based Concatenative Synthesis," in *New Interfaces for Musical Expression (NIME)*, Ann Arbour, United States, May 2012, pp. 250–253, cote interne IRCAM: Schwarz12a. [Online]. Available: https://hal.archives-ouvertes.fr/hal-01161442

[15] L. Garber, T. Ciccola, and J. C. Amusategui, "AudioStellar, an open source corpus-based musical instrument for latent sound structure discovery and sonic experimentation," 12 2020.

[16] B. Hackbarth, N. Schnell, P. Esling, and D. Schwarz, "Composing Morphology: Concatenative Synthesis as an Intuitive Medium for Prescribing Sound in Time," *Contemporary Music Review*, vol. 32, no. 1, pp. 49–59, 2013. [Online]. Available: https://hal.archives-ouvertes.fr/hal-01577895

[17] N. Schnell, A. Roebel, D. Schwarz, G. Peeters, and R. Borghesi, "MUBU and FRIENDS -ASSEMBLING TOOLS FOR CONTENT BASED REAL-TIME INTERACTIVE AUDIO PROCESSING IN MAX/MSP," *Proceedings of the International Computer Music Conference (ICMC 2009)*, 01 2009.

[18] P. A. Tremblay, G. Roma, and O. Green, "Enabling Programmatic Data Mining as Musicking: The Fluid Corpus Manipulation Toolkit," *Computer Music Journal*, vol. 45, no. 2, pp. 9–23, 06 2021. [Online]. Available: https://doi.org/10.1162/comj_a_00600

[19] F. Bevilacqua and R. Müller, "A Gesture follower for performing arts," 05 2005.

[20] N. Schnell, D. Schwarz, J. Larralde, and R. Borghesi, "PiPo, a Plugin Interface for Afferent Data Stream Processing Operators," in *International Society for Music Information Retrieval Conference*, 2017.

[21] R. Fiebrink and P. Cook, "The Wekinator: A System for Real-time, Interactive Machine Learning in Music," *Proceedings of The Eleventh International Society for Music Information Retrieval Conference (ISMIR 2010)*, 01 2010.

[22] A. Einbond and D. Schwarz, "Spatializing Timbre With Corpus-Based Concatenative Synthesis," 06 2010.

[23] G. Roma, O. Green, and P. A. Tremblay, "Adaptive Mapping of Sound Collections for Data-driven Musical Interfaces," in *New Interfaces for Musical Expression*, 2019.

[24] B. D. Smith and G. E. Garnett, "Unsupervised Play: Machine Learning Toolkit for Max," in *New Interfaces for Musical Expression*, 2012.

[25] *≪ PrÉ ≫ : connected polyphonic immersion*. Zenodo, Jul. 2022. [Online]. Available: https://doi.org/10.5281/zenodo.6806324

[26] R. Mills, "Tele-Improvisation: Intercultural Interaction in the Online Global Music Jam Session," in *Springer Series on Cultural Computing*, 2019. [Online]. Available: https://api.semanticscholar.org/CorpusID:57428481

[27] M. Puckette, "Not Being There," *Contemporary Music Review*, vol. 28, no. 4-5, pp. 409–412, 2009. [Online]. Available: https://doi.org/10.1080/07494460903422354

[28] G. Hajdu, "Embodiment and disembodiment in networked music performance," 2017. [Online]. Available: https://api.semanticscholar.org/CorpusID:149523160

[29] L. Manovich, "Database as Symbolic Form," *Convergence: The International Journal of Research into New Media Technologies*, vol. 5, pp. 80 – 99, 1999.

I hear you breathe: Extended Techniques and Narratives in Telematic Audiovisual Immersion

Cássia Carrascoza Bomfim
University of São Paulo, Brazil
cassiacarrascozabomfim@usp.br

Paulo C. Chagas
University of California, Riverside, USA
paulo.chagas@ucr.edu

ABSTRACT

Since 2020, Paulo C. Chagas and Cássia Carrascoza have been developing research of composition and performance based on the concept of telematic audiovisual immersion, which resulted in a series of works for flute(s), live-electronics and video. The duo has performed over 50 online concerts with Chagas works and also collaborated with other composers and performers in projects of telematic music in the US, China, Europe, and Brazil. This paper focuses on the work "I hear you breathe" (2022)[1] for bass flute, live-electronics and video. It discusses the development of extended techniques for bass flute in conjunction with electronic processing and the exploration of extended narratives of audiovisual immersion in the context of telematic music.

1. TELEMATIC MUSIC

The challenges of telematic music are numerous. Musicians must become familiar with the specific technologies developed for telematic music, as well as learn to use and improve sound possibilities mediated by technology. They must also work on specific performance aspects and, above all, find creative solutions for musically connecting with other musicians in a virtual environment. Telematic chamber music can unfold different acoustic instrument settings and be performed with digital technology such as electronic instruments, synthesizers, sound processing, and audiovisual devices. The unshared sound space in telematic performance alters the relationships of listening, visual communication, and sense of time between musicians. The physical distance imposes a different way of being together for musicmaking and performance.

Chagas advances a substantial reflection on telematic music in a number of texts [2], [3], [4], [5], [6], [7]. Drawing ideas from Flusser's model of telematic communication in the emerging digital information society, he proposes a definition of telematic music on the intersections of chamber music and electronic music:

> Flusser's model of telematic dialog is an attempt to make a synthesis of two different types of communication: (1) The communication of chamber music, which occurs in the physical medium with bodies producing gestures that are translated into sounds. (2) The communication of electronic music, which occurs in the virtual medium with apparatuses producing programs that are translated into sounds or images [4, p. 11].

2. TECHNICAL DETAILS

Chagas and Carrascoza performed *I hear you breathe* over internet from different locations, Carrascoza in São Paulo, Brazil and Chagas in Berlin, Germany. They rely on JackTrip software [8] for audio communication and Zoom platform for video communication. Ensuring high quality sound transmission is crucial to their artistic concept, as JackTrip allows transferring uncompressed audio over the network. The sound of the bass flute is captured by two microphones placed on the head joint and the bottom of the instrument. Chagas processes the audio with Max software and sends it back to Carrascoza and the virtual audience in Zoom. The audiovisual performance takes advantage of Zoom's background tool. Carrascoza performs in front of a green background (chromakey) and interacts in real-time with the video projection. Other streaming platforms may provide with a better video quality but, as for today, Zoom is the only viable option for real-time visual feedback. The video was specially created for the piece and processed with TouchDesigner. In the future, we plan to process to accomplish video processing in real time, in order to create a more "organic" relationship between sound and image and enhancing interactive performance.

3. FLUTE AMPLIFICATION AND ELECTRONIC PROCESSING

Sound amplification and electronic processing of the bass flute are fundamental aspects of the artistic concept of *I hear you breathe*, which takes advantage of a wide range of sonorities that are not perceivable in a "pure" acoustic environment. Along with sound production, the digitalization of the bass flute opens up new performing techniques and gestures. In a typical acoustic, non-amplified context, some sound phenomena such as residual tones, whistle tones, natural reverbs in the tube are almost inaudible due to their low dynamic. As Levine says, "[t]hrough the use of the amplification as well as electronics to modify the sound, the flute has experienced an almost limitless timbral expansion" [9, p. 51].

Exploring the sound possibilities of an instrument through the use of microphone requires from the performer broad knowledge that is at the intersections of performance, composition and sound engineering [10]. Anne La Berge, an American flutist and composer currently based in the Netherlands, is one artist who made significant contributions in this field. She is recognized by the digital magazine Paris Transatlantic for her enlargement to the development of sound modification techniques for the flute using microphones.

Important research on the amplification of the low instruments of the flute family and their specificities is "The Kingma System Bass Flute: A Practical Guide for Composers and Performers" by the English flutist specialized in the bass flutes Carla Rees. She wrote this guide on the basis of the bass flute developed by Eva Kingma[1], in 2007. The guide includes stage maps with suggestions from the author for the best situation of the amplification of the instrument and indications of the types of microphones that best suit the bass flute.

To play *I hear you breathe* we use two DPA microphones closed attached to the flute, one at the head joint and the other at the flute foot, in order to obtain a wider range of sound.[2]

4. EXTENDED TECHNIQUES

Throughout the 20th and 21st centuries, numerous flutists-composers have made significant contributions to the flute repertoire, publishing works and methods that serve as both reference manuals for composers and resources for flutists. These works have helped to disseminate extended techniques, which are basically new techniques for the flute, while also contributing to the creation of specific notations, generating a standardized vocabulary of sounds and gestures. Among the notable performers and composers in this field are István Matuz, Robert Dick, Pierre-Yves Artaud, Gergely Ittzés, Anne La Berge, Wil Offermans, Carin Levine, Christina Mitropoulos-Bott, Brian Ferneyhough, and many others. [10]

I hear you breathe makes use of different kinds of extended techniques that explore *breath* as expressive gesture. For instance: breath out, breath out in the flute, breath in, and breath in with sound. Additionally, it deploys a repertoire of established extended techniques for contemporary flute such as multiphonics, aeolian sounds, whistle tones, harmonics (overtones), bisbigliando, sounds with voice, frullato, glissandi, microtonal vibrato, microtonal tremolo, pizzicato, key click, and slap tongue.

5. COMBINED EXTENDED TECHNIQUES

A unique characteristic of *I hear you breathe* is the research on combined extended techniques, which was developed in collaboration between the interpreter and the composer. Several experiments were made seeking to create sound material that are amplified and enhanced with sound processing algorithms. Here are two examples of combined extended techniques.

The first example (Fig. 1) is a combination of bisbigliando and variation of whistle tones along the spectrum, which results in a very fragile sound that would not be audible without sound processing.

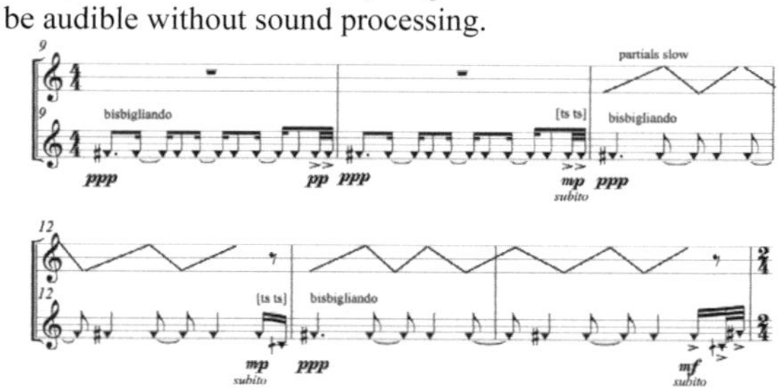

Figure 1. Combined extended technique: bisbigliando and whistle tones [1, p. 1].

In the second example (Fig. 2) the expanded techniques combined and associated with sound processing produce a very intense sonority with variations of register in the voice, resulting in ring modulation. We can see in bar 28 the change of reverb (marked as reverb 2 in the score). This is a moment of transition in the work. The latency of the telematic environment along with the use of a long reverb generate an expanded continuity, a sense of continuum in the time-space.

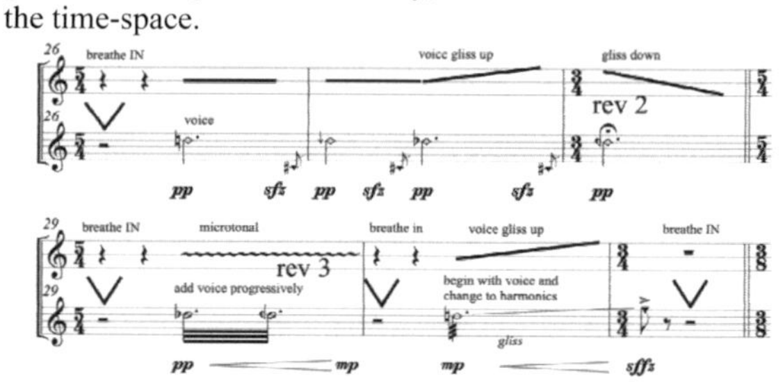

Figure 2. A sequence of several combined extended technique: aeolian sound + voice variations, glissandi up and down, microtonal tremolo, frullato and glissando [1, p. 1].

It is important to point out that these techniques are fully audible and expressive precisely due to the amplification of the flute and enhanced by the electronic sound processing of the flute with the Max software.

[1] Dutch flute builder who has developed a system of keys that simplifies the production of quarter-tones, which helps the production of trills and multiphonics in the family of flutes. http://www.bassflute.co.uk/ (accessed May 1, 2023).

[2] DPA 4009. https://www.dpamicrophones.com/instrument/4099-instrument-microphone. (accessed May 1, 2023).

6. ELECTRONIC SOUND PROCESSING

Compressed audio is a significant limitation of telematic music. Even when we use JackTrip for exchanging uncompressed audio over network, the audio that comes to the listener over streaming software is mostly compressed, not even to mention the "poor" quality of speakers from cell phone speakers and other mobile devices that are typically used for music listening over internet. Therefore, a huge challenge of telematic music is to create a "quality" audio that compensates this technical limitation and conveys the richness of the sound produced by the bass flute transformed through amplification and digital signal processing.

In the Max patches of *I hear you breathe* the signal of the bass flute, captured by the two microphones, is first treated with a compressor for reducing their dynamic range and shaping a sound with a balanced energy along the entire spectrum. It results in a sound that is quite different from the acoustic sound while compensating the loss of energy of the compressed audio of the streaming platforms. The ultimate goal is to recreate a sense of *presence*, which enhances the very fundamental concept of extended techniques.

A different patch was created for each of the three movements of *I hear you breathe*. The common feature of all three patches is to split the signal flow into multiple streams that are submitted to different kinds of processes and mixed at the end. A short description of the patches is provided in the following; an in-depth analysis would go beyond the scope of this article.

In the patch of the first movement (Fig. 3) the two input signals of the microphones are analyzed for pitch tracking; a structure of multiple sinusoidal signals is generated that follows the gestures of the bass flute and enhances the effect of the expanded techniques.

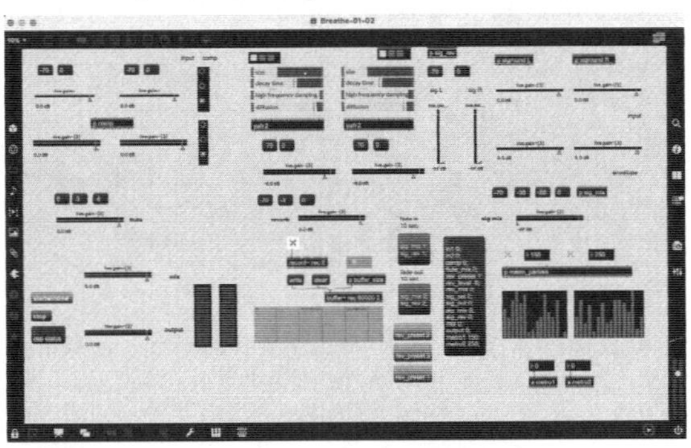

Figure 3. Max patch of the first movement.

The patch of the second movement (Fig. 4) is built upon an interpolating oscillator bank that is controlled and modulated by the signal received on both inputs. A continuous sonority of low frequencies underlies the whole movement, conferring to the music a drone and meditative character.

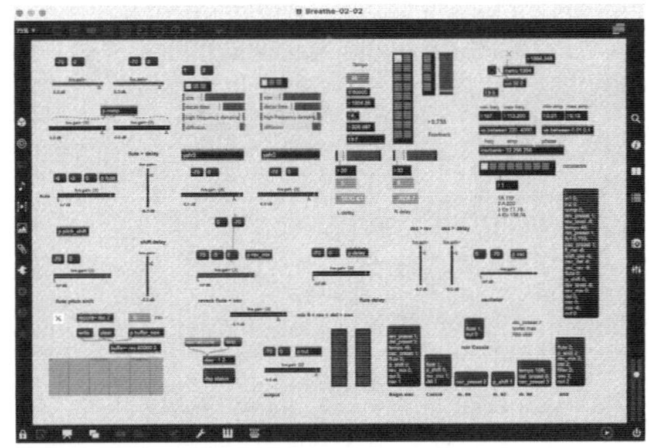

Figure 4. Max patch of the second movement.

The patch of the third movement (Fig. 5) unfolds a complexity of elements and events including several parallel processes of variable pitch shifting through delays, the degradation of the bass flute signals through sample rate and bit-depth reduction and the addition of a frequency modulation (FM) synthesizer on the second part of the movement. All these features exponentially increase the "noisy" character of the music.

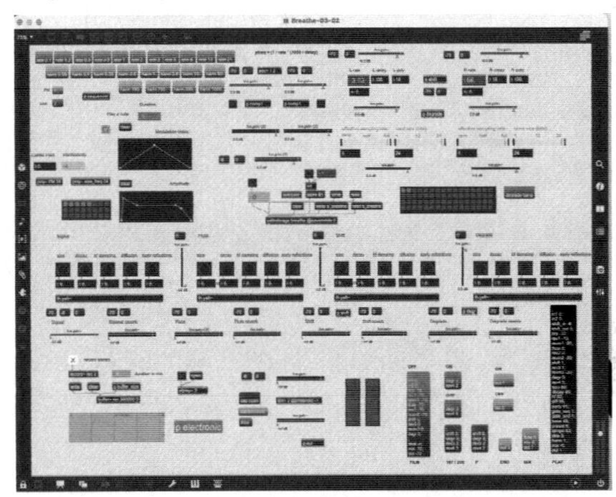

Figure 5. Max patch of the third movement.

7. SEMIOTIC SQUARE

The compositional concept of *I hear you breathe* was elaborated on the basis of the idea of telematic presence. As for previous Chagas' works such as *Mojave* (2020) [6] and *Virtual Studies* (2021) [11] the semiotic square proposed by Hayles [12] provides the conceptual framework. It reconstructs the distinction between *randomness* and *pattern* in the so-called posthuman society while emphasizing the role of embodiment and materiality in the processes of constituting meaning.

Hayles' semiotic square (Fig. 6) has two axes: the main axis is the distinction between *presence* and *absence*; the secondary axis is the distinction between *randomness* and *pattern*. Two diagonals that connect these two axes trigger a dynamic of signification. Presence and pattern are connected by a diagonal which is called *replication*. That is, presence and pattern are forms that reproduce themselves.

The diagonal that connects absence and randomness marks the *rupture*. That is, absence breaks the illusion of presence, revealing the lack of its original fullness. Randomness breaks the pattern, allowing the white noise of the world to come through.

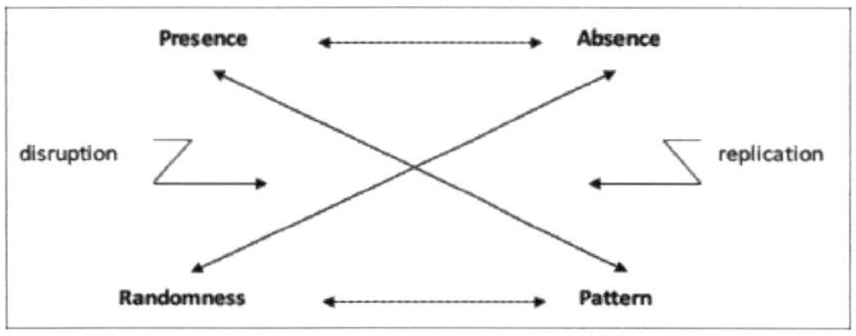

Figure 6. Hayles' semiotic square of the posthuman society [12, p. 249].

8. VISUAL COMPOSITION: TELEMATIC PRESENCE

For the online performance, we used Zoom's background tool to project the edited and processed black and white video. Additionally, we applied a black and white filter to create a visual homogeneity of the flutist represented in the video and performing live on the virtual stage. The visual composition was developed on the basis of four main ideas:

1) Exploring a very limited physical space to create images that bring together parts of the performer's body and bass flute with a dramaturgy based on minimal movements using the camera as a catalyst for proximity to the audience (Fig. 7).

Figure 7. Image of proximity to the camera.

2) Images of multiplied presence unfolding layers of time-space with overlays that depict the action of playing the bass flute in the present and the past. For instance, the proximity of the image of the mask's eye creates a vector of meaning that surpasses its boundary by seeming to directly gaze at the audience. It creates a dialogue between physical presence and absence in virtual space (Fig. 8)

Figure 8. Multiplication of presence.

3) Performing a kind of ritual painting of a mask, as if it ocurs on the stage in front of the audience, in order to create the metaphor of another layer over the physical distance that exists in telematics music (Fig. 9, 10).

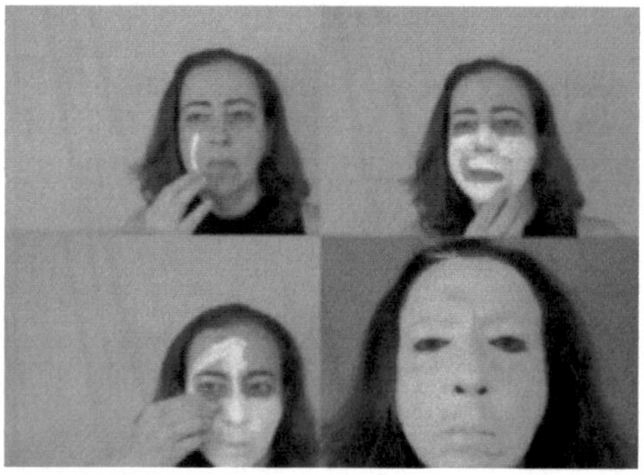

Figure 9. Pictures of the ritual of preparation of the mask..

Figure 10. Mask as it appears in the final movie.

4) Processing the video with the software TouchDesigner by applying a feedback algorithm that introduces a visual delay and creates a new visual narrative. It provides multiple combinations of bass flute and body and explores the different views and minimal movements recorded in the original videos (Fig. 11).

Figure 11. Visual delay of flute and mask.

9. CONCLUSIONS

I hear you breathe (2022) is a composition for bass flute, live-electronics and video that explores extended techniques and narratives in a vibrational search in the world of chaos beyond the limits of noise, voice and language. It thematizes the degradation of the environment and the contemporary existential feeling of breathlessness that is fueled by the chaos of financial capitalism The music explores rhythms of noise produced by breathing and other expanded techniques for bass flute in conjunction with different algorithms of electronic sound synthesis and visual narratives that configure the notions of presence/absence in the telematic virtual world.

The extension of the bass flute into noise is an act of escaping the technical automatism and reactivating the organic potency of the body. In summary, *I hear you breathe* (2022) proposes the opening to the ordered system of chaotic flows and vibrations, the surrendering to the vertigo and fascination of chaos and noise, seeking for rhythms that allow the organism to tune to the cosmos.

Acknowledgments

We appreciate the support given to this research by The São Paulo Research Foundation, FAPESP.

10. REFERENCES

[1] P. C. Chagas, *I hear you breathe*, 2022. [Manuscript]. Available: paulo.chagas@ucr.edu.

[2] P. C. Chagas, "A Música de Câmara Telemática: A Metáfora de Flusser e o Universo da Música Eletroacústica," *Revista Ghrebh,* vol. 11, pp. 26-49, Mar. 2008. [Online]. Available: https://www.cisc.org.br/portal/jdownloads/Ghrebh/Ghrebh-%2011/05_chagas.pdf.

[3] P. C. Chagas, *Unsayable Music: Six Essays on Musical Semiotics, Electroacoustic and Digital Music*. Leuven: Leuven University Press, 2014.

[4] P. C. Chagas, "Creativity with Apparatuses: from Chamber Music to Telematic Dialog," *Flusser Studies,* vol. 17, pp. 2-15, June, 2014. [Online]. Available: http://www.flusserstudies.net/sites/www.flusserstudies.net/files/media/attachments/paulo-chagas-creativity-with-apparatuses.pdf.

[5] P. C. Chagas, "Sound, Truth, and Paradigm," in *Sounds from Within: Phenomenology and Practice*, X. P. C. Chagas and J. C. Wu, Eds. Cham: Springer Nature Switzerland, 2021, pp. 1-28.

[6] P. C. Chagas, C. C. Bomfim, "With Love: Electroacoustic, Audiovisual, and Telematic Music," *Proc. of the 15^{th}Int. Symp. on Comput. Music Multidisciplinary Research (CMMR)*, Tokyo, 2021, pp. 269-278. [Online]. Available: https://cmmr2021.github.io/proceedings/pdffiles/CMMR2021_proceedings.pdf.

[7] P. C. Chagas, "Imaginações sonoras, imersão audiovisual telemática," in *Escrita, som, imagem: natureza em foco.* C. A. P. Figueiredo, C. N. Lima, E. L. L. Reis and T. F. N. Diniz, Eds. Belo Horizonte: Fino Traço, 2022, pp. 63-84. [Online]. Available: https://www.finotracoeditora.com.br/e-book-escrita-som-e-imagem.

[8] JackTrip. https://jacktrip.github.io/jacktrip/ (accessed May 1, 2023).

[9] C. Levine and C. Mitropoulos-Bott, *The Techniques of Flute Paying.* Kassel: Barenreiter, 2002.

[10] C. C. Bomfim, "O problema do tempo no repertório de obras mistas para flauta solista," Ph.D. dissertation, Dept. Mus. Univ. of São Paulo, São Paulo, 2016.

[11] C. C. Bomfim, "Telematic Immersion: Performance, Technology, and Audiovisual Work in Virtual Studies (2020) by Paulo C. Chagas." *Journal of Network Music and Arts*, vol. 4, no. 1, pp. 1-25, Mar. 2022. [Online]. Available: https://commons.library.stonybrook.edu/jonma/vol4/iss1/3.

[12] K. Hayles, *How We Became Posthuman: Virtual Bodies in Cybernetics, Literature, and Informatics*. Chicago: University of Chicago Press, 1999.

Game Live Streaming as a Model for Networked Music Performance

Goni Peles
Open Scores Lab, Bath Spa University
goni.pl@gmail.com

Yuval Adler
CIRMMT, McGill University
yuval.adler@mail.mcgill.ca

ABSTRACT

We propose a model of networked music performance to help musicians think through and evaluate their online music productions. First, we utilise a model of game live streaming by T. L. Taylor [1] to analyse several of our own productions of distanced networked music performances of ludified notation [2]. Building on Taylor's model and additional scholarship on music performance, both networked and not, we then extrapolate the insights gained to networked music performance in general and derive a list of key considerations for the analysis, critique, and creation of networked music performances. Online music production has become an important mode of musicking and continues to grow as a practice. We offer this model as a tool for both practice-based and scholarly work. [1]

1. INTRODUCTION

1.1 Motivation

For the past few years we have been developing and playing our own multiplayer music game and given opportunities to present this game in online performances. As these performances were presented entirely over the network, we wanted to think critically about what performing online entails. Focusing on the game aspect, we saw game live streaming as having interesting similarities to our situation. As such, we reviewed scholarship on game live streaming and found it to be a particularly rich perspective to consider. We believe what we have found can have value for other musicians and researchers thinking about online performances, whether of game-based music or not, and so developed the adapted model we present in this paper.

1.2 Background

Networked music performance has been defined as 'a musical performance that is conducted through the mobilization of telecommunication, electronic, and electromagnetic technologies to transmit musical signals across networks with more than one node' [4, p. 20]. Compared with previous definitions [5, 6], this definition deliberately avoids requiring musicians to be physically distanced, distinguishing it from a related term, *telematic music*, which not only requires that musicians are in different geographic locations, but is also associated with political ideas of cybernetics and globalisation [4, pp. 7–8]. Accordingly, telematic music has been considered a subcategory of the more general and technologically-oriented networked music performance [4, pp. 20–21] [7, pp. 5, 21–57]. [2]

The awareness of online music making as a possibility has spiked among a broad range of musical practitioners during the COVID-19 pandemic. During the pandemic lockdowns, performing music online suddenly became a forced mainstream mode of music performance—performances were distanced out of necessity rather than as an aesthetic position. Many musicians were trying to reproduce the offline experience of music performance, which they found to be highly frustrating given the technical limitations caused by the primary characteristics of the medium, that is, network latency and uncertainty, multi-located and multi-authorial participation, and digital mediation of presence, as noted by Rebekah Wilson [10, p. 3]. Wilson argued that 'rather than we should seek to reproduce offline experiences online, the Internet offers unique affordances for entirely new ways of performing together' [10, p. 2], proposing aesthetic approaches such as 'post-vertical harmony' and 'resonance and multi-located timbral fusion' [10, pp. 5–8]. Online music production has become an important mode of musicking and keeps growing as a practice, continuing a trend from before the pandemic.

One way to think about the unique affordances of performing online is to draw from game live streaming, a practice native to the Internet. T. L. Taylor, in her research on game live streaming, shows how it has evolved from esports broadcasting and recorded gameplay distributed online on platforms such as YouTube into a wide range of broadcast gameplay, from large-scale esports media events to 'variety' streamers (individual gamers transforming their 'private play to public entertainment') [1, pp. 3–6]. Like distanced networked music performance, game live streaming also utilises the Internet as a technological infrastructure, therefore, it has to similarly negotiate issues like those described by Wilson.

Further facilitating the translation between the two disciplines is the concept of *ludified notation*, 'a musical notation in which a game is used to direct musical action' [2]. Ludified notation can serve as an intermediary between the two disciplines, because a broadcast performance of ludified notation can be considered both game live streaming

[1] Parts of this work previously appeared in [3].

[2] Another characteristic of Lemmon's definition is that it does not limit networked music performance to computer networks, as for example, Gabrielli and Squartini's definition [8, p. 4]. This is to account for John Cage's *Imaginary Landscape No. 4* (1951) for 12 radios, which has been considered the first example of a networked music performance piece [9].

and networked music performance.

An example of ludified notation, ScoreCraft is a web-based multiplayer music game exploring online music making mediated through gameplay. [3] In ScoreCraft, each player produces sounds that are analysed in real time by the game engine, and this analysis is used to manipulate in-game parameters such as player avatar movement. Therefore—since players are required to make sounds in structured ways—by playing the game they are inherently making music. ScoreCraft is structured as a modular environment consisting of a collection of mini games and scenarios: mini games require the players to produce a particular set of sounds in order to interact with the game, shaping musical material; scenarios determine how the mini games are arranged, organising the musical material into larger musical forms.

1.3 Methodology

We will explore game live streaming as a model for networked music performance. Specifically, we will examine how a model of game live streaming production developed by Taylor [1, pp. 73–80] can be applied to distanced networked music performances of ludified notation, and then extrapolate the insights gained to networked music performance in general. We will use our own productions of ScoreCraft performances as cases situated at the overlap of networked music performance and game live streaming.

The following is an overview of the three productions discussed in this paper. For clarity and to save space, in the remainder of this paper we will use the abbreviations in square brackets instead of the full titles of the productions.

ScoreCraft@CIRMMT [Olympics] presented a game of 'ScoreCraft Olympics', produced for a special online edition of improv@CIRMMT. It featured five mini games played in a row, and four players competed for medals for each mini game. Each medal was worth a different number of points, and the player who earned the highest number of points by the end won. [4]

ScoreCraft: Show Biz @ NIME 2022 [Show Biz] was a mockumentary style interpretation of the ScoreCraft scenario Show Biz produced for NIME 2022. In the Show Biz scenario, players are grouped in teams of two, each made up of a talent and an agent. The teams try to complete challenges in 'venues' spread around the game board, and the first team to complete all the venues wins the game. [5]

ScoreCraft play session live [Live] is an ongoing series of public playtests streamed live on ScoreCraft's YouTube channel. The aim of the series is to explore relationships between the design and setup of ScoreCraft's mini games and scenarios and the resultant music. Each session we focus on a different mini game or scenario, and try out and discuss different features and configurations of it. The sessions present ScoreCraft as a work in progress, open to community feedback. [6]

2. LAYERS OF PRODUCTION

In this section, we apply a model of game live streaming production developed by Taylor [1, pp. 73–80] to the three ScoreCraft productions introduced above. Taylor breaks down live stream productions into six layers:

- Set design
- Performance
- Critique and evaluation
- Sociality
- Material and digital infrastructure
- Economic and commercial frameworks

These layers are apart from the game itself, which Taylor considers 'only one layer' of the overall production [1, p. 80]. A similar distinction, with regard to multimedia performance, has been made by Marko Cicliani, with the aim of expanding the discussion of artistic expression in multimedia performance to also include the entire technical manifestation and material conditions of the performance [11, p. 127]. Cicliani builds on film theorist Christian Metz's concept of *enunciation*, which is, in Metz's words, 'a trace that is concerned with the act of production and not the product' [11, p. 128]. Whereas the game layer concerns the enunciated, the production layers concern the enunciation.

In what follows, we devote a subsection to each layer as proposed by Taylor. In each subsection we follow a repeated structure. First, we introduce the layer by summarising from Taylor and adding further details as needed. [7] Second, we examine how the layer is manifested in each of the three ScoreCraft productions. And third, we look at how the layer applies to related work by other practitioners and scholars. ScoreCraft is used as an intermediary between game live streaming and networked music performance as it can be considered an instance of both.

2.1 Set Design

Set design refers to the arrangement of graphic and audio elements used by streamers to customise the default game view for spectatorship. Games already use HUDs [8] to convey information about the game to the players, and individual live streamers often extend that by using additional overlays, cameras, graphic/audio notifications of triggered events, a customised channel page, and a live chat [1, p. 73]. Esports broadcasts similarly augment the game view with a range of additional graphic and audio elements, for example, specialised HUDs designed to enhance the viewers' understanding of what is happening in the game [1, pp. 160–161], and an in-game camera showing varying player views to tell a story [1, p. 164–165].

ScoreCraft has a built-in audience mode, which, depending on the game, supports both manual control over which player to follow and an auto-follow option, for example,

[3] ScoreCraft is developed by Goni Peles as part of his PhD research project. Development is supported by ScoreCraft's community members who offer feedback and suggest development ideas in playtests.

[4] Available at https://youtu.be/GB2XCbQ61C4. Players: Alberto Acquilino, Meesh Fradkin, Oded Geizhals, Shoshana Klein.

[5] Available at https://youtu.be/tgk1iSrcuVY. Players: Shira Agmon, Jana De Troyer, Oded Geizhals, Elliot Simpson.

[6] Available at https://www.youtube.com/@scorecraft/streams. Each session there is a slightly different group of players.

[7] Taylor focuses on individual streamers in her model, but we also use it to discuss other types of game live streaming such as esports broadcasting.

[8] A HUD (heads-up display) is a 'a collection of persistent onscreen elements whose purpose is to indicate player status' [12]. It is called after modern aircraft's heads-up display used to show 'flight, navigation, attack, or other information superimposed upon the pilot's forward field of view' [13].

automatically following the leading player. In scenarios, which usually take place on a 2D board where multiple mini games can be played at the same time, the audience mode allows choosing which mini game to observe. In [Olympics] we used the auto-follow option to automatically follow the leading player in race-like mini games, whereas in [Show Biz] we recorded the game from the perspective of the two talents, then alternated between them according to the drama that emerged from the recorded gameplay. Of course, this is only possible when the video can be edited before streaming. [Live], on the other hand, often requires live, manual control of the in-game camera. [9]

ScoreCraft also has a range of built-in HUDs, such as an instruction text for each mini game, a leaderboard showing the status of each player, and an overview of the game board in scenarios. [Olympics] extends these with a specialised medals table screen showing the medals and points each player earned after each mini game. In [Show Biz], we overlaid scripted videos of the players commenting on the game as well as further clarifications of the rules we thought would make more sense if presented in context. Recent [Live] sessions feature camera videos of the players overlaid in the right bottom corner, as well as excerpts from previous play sessions played back in the introduction section, previewing the mini game/scenario to be played.

Moving beyond ludified notation to networked music performance more broadly, when substituting score for game, this layer translates well to networked music performances that use a distributed score system and/or present a score to the audience. [10] There is a growing body of works foregrounding the score by visually projecting it during performance, similarly offering 'an opportunity for the listener to develop a deeper understanding of the processes and structures underlying a musical work or performance' [15, p. 37]. In particular, projected scores can help the audience anticipate future events and relate them to current and past events [15, p. 49]. That said, projecting a score also imposes constraints on its visual design, such as limited informational density, difficulties in embedding multiple parts, and restricted speed of dynamic change. Various approaches to working around these constraints have been taken by practitioners [15, pp. 39–44]. For example, in Cat Hope's *Longing* (2013) the score consists of an image slowly scrolling from left to right. A vertical line serves as an indication for the part of the image being interpreted at any given moment [15, p. 40]. A similar example of how to consider the audience's view when presenting music can be seen in Donald Craig's YouTube video showcasing Ligeti's 1958 piece, *Artikulation*, with a synchronised scrolling scan of Rainer Wehinger's 1970 graphic listening score made for Ligeti's piece. [11] Craig added to Wehinger's graphic score a scrolling position indicator for the YouTube audience, much like the HUDs we discussed earlier. Game live streaming set design offers further approaches to be explored, especially when negotiating multiple perspectives of the score, as Wilson suggests is often the case in networked music performance characterised by multi-located and multi-authorial participation [10, pp. 10–11], such as parallel or alternating streams from differing points of view as in ScoreCraft. Of course, a networked music performance might also feature visuals other than the score, and even when the work presented does not intend to be visual, camera videos often still form part of a distanced networked music performance's digital stage, or at the very least the individual performers' setup.

2.2 Performance

Performance refers to the performative approach live streamers take to broadcasting their gameplay. Variety streamers think aloud while playing, externalising their thought processes via speech, but in an entertaining, theatrical way, using humour, frustration, and suspense to spice up their presentation. Esports streamers, on the other hand, talk much less and instead focus on showing their virtuosity and expertise as the performance [1, p. 75]. Note that by 'esports streamers' we mean professional gamers live streaming their practice time. Esports tournament broadcasts are rarely silent and usually involve commentators who draw heavily on traditional sportscasting, imitating commentary styles, narrative creation strategies, casting team structures, and even wardrobe conventions [16, pp. 47–57]. That said, it is worth noting that esports is not a one-to-one copy of traditional sports and framings can vary between games [17, pp. 57–59].

[Olympics] fits well into the 'esports as sports emulation' paradigm. Given the sports event framing ('ScoreCraft Olympics'), we both acted as sportscasters, following a traditional casting team structure: Adler played the role of the main commentator, and Peles played the role of the analyst. We introduced each mini game before it was played and pointed out dramatic moments as needed throughout. For example, before the last mini game we explained that three of the four contenders still stood a chance to win the whole tournament. Nevertheless, our commentary was deliberately sparse to keep the music in the foreground.

[Show Biz] is presented as a mockumentary telling the story of the Money-Man, an obscure tycoon who organised a fake talent show to launder money while on a cruise to the moon. The talent show was titled 'Galaxy's Got Talent' and realised as the Show Biz scenario. Two teams competed for a contract with the Money Man: Team 1 consisted of a classically trained guitarist (the Guitarist) and a successful impresario (the Impresario), and Team 2 consisted of a liberal, hippie shaman (the Shaman) and an alien hive-mind agent convinced they developed the perfect musical taste (Uni-Sonn). Each player role-played their character both while playing the game and in fictional interviews we interspersed with the recorded gameplay, borrowing conventions from popular reality gameshows [18, p. 30] and mockumentaries [19, p. 93].

[Live] echoes the growing practice of live streaming game development [20] but with a focus on playtesting rather than coding. In the sessions we alternate between playing and discussing. We do not narrate the gameplay, and except for very quick comments (or clarifications of the rules), we tend to save long discussions until the end of each game to avoid masking the music.

[9] For an example, see *ScoreCraft play session live #6 feat. Decibel New Music Ensemble*, which focused on the scenario Underworld: https://youtube.com/live/mXF9Ed48Tf0?t=1571.

[10] For an overview of browser-based distributed notation technologies from a user's point of view, see [14].

[11] Available at https://youtu.be/71hNl_skTZQ.

Connecting these ideas to networked music performance at large, we draw on Philip Auslander's theory of musical persona [21]. While a detailed discussion of Auslander's theory is beyond the scope of this paper, his core argument is worth considering: 'What musicians perform first and foremost is not music, but their own identities as musicians, their musical personae' [21, p. 88]. Importantly, by 'identity' Auslander does not mean the musician's personality but their role as performers within a social context [21, p. 89]. Musical personae are produced through interaction between performers and their audiences and are constrained by frames, a term Auslander borrows from sociologist Erving Goffman's *Frame Analysis* [22], defined as 'principles of organisation which govern events' [21, p. 91]. Accordingly, Auslander sees a musical performance as using at least four layered frames: the music frame, indicating that sound is to be perceived as music; the performance frame, determining that the event is not just music but a musical performance; the genre frame, establishing genre conventions; and the social frame, defining the overall social context surrounding the performance [21, pp. 91–92]. Networked music performances follow a similar structure, although distanced performances require at least one additional layer, a streaming frame, which is closely related to Auslander's 'recording frame' in that it enables understanding the experience as music being streamed [21, p. 93]. Whereas frames create sets of expectations, or a 'normative persona' [21, pp. 108–109], musical personae can also choose to break or playfully engage with them. Furthermore, Auslander notes that 'highly idiosyncratic personae function as something like frames' as their eccentric behaviour 'cannot be fully accounted for by reference to the general frames surrounding their performances', giving Glenn Gould's humming as an example [21, p. 110]. Idiosyncrasy is of particular relevance to networked music performance, as practitioners can create deeply intermedia presentations during performances. Such complex productions can bring about additional frames and hybrid personae to consider that go beyond conventions associated with offline music.

2.3 Critique and Evaluation

Critique and evaluation refers to variety streamers' tendency to analyse and reflect on aspects of the games they are playing, thereby offering their audience expert evaluation of the game, not just entertainment [1, p. 75]. More broadly, play itself can be critical. Subversive play is a prime example, as players push at the boundaries set by the rules of the game, looking for grey areas (or outright ignoring the expected rules of the game) in order to direct critique and work against the system [23, pp. 10–13].

[Live] sessions include discussion sections in which we analyse and reflect on the game we just played. The players offer feedback on their play experience, as well as development suggestions and ideas. This informs new features developed for the next session or even the setup of the next game we play in the same session. Additionally, players can also implicitly offer critique and evaluation through their spontaneous reactions to what is happening in the game. In [Live], we usually elaborate on these in the discussion sections, but evidence for such reactions can also be found in [Olympics] and [Show Biz] as the players vocally reacted to in-game action. In that regard, one of the players' numerous 'Fuck' interjections in [Olympics] are perhaps somewhat controversial. Although we earned the content warning 'explicit language' because of them, we decided not to censor them as we understood them not as insults but as authentic reactions to negative game outcomes indicating that the player was emotionally invested in the game.

[Show Biz] also directs critique beyond the game. As a mockumentary, it addresses issues such as funding and competition in the art music scene, classical training and open mindedness, and contemporary music aesthetics. It also features an example of subversive play. When Team 1 was about to enter their third and last venue, Uni-Sonn left the game as a 'spoil sport' and tried to mask the Impresario by playing musical samples continuously without stopping. Assuming that players should only produce sound to control the game, this was an act of subversive play. The Guitarist could not hear the Impresario and Team 1 was stuck until Uni-Sonn gave up and Team 1 won. [12] Another thing to note is that we potentially made the scenario more difficult for Uni-Sonn than for the Impresario, something we did not plan in advance. The scenario makes use of two different control schemes, pitch for the Guitarist and the Impresario and brightness for the Shaman and Uni-Sonn. The latter seemed harder for the musicians to conceptualise and control, and accordingly the game was more challenging for Team 2. Seemingly as a result, at the very end of the video the Shaman says: 'the game was fixed'.

Critique and evaluation of society are also ingrained in telematic music performance, for example, consider Pauline Oliveros' ending statement in 'Telematic Music: Six Perspectives': 'Musicians are leading the way to global development with a conscious way of connecting non-violently' [24, p. 43]. Another example is Scott Deal and Matthew Burtner's telematic opera, *Auksalaq*, which addresses global climate change as experienced in Alaska and the Arctic. The opera features interviews with people local to the region along with scientific commentary and data visualisation, interwoven into a fictional story about a man returning to his homeland in the Arctic after hearing about the drastic changes in the area. Deal and Burtner explain that the work should be performed on multiple distanced sites, each with an in-person audience influencing the other sites by interacting with a dedicated application called NOMADS. As such, the distributed nature of the performance serves to deliver the message that 'we are separate from some of the things we affect and that affect us' [25, p. 511], which illustrates a more implicit way of directing critique. Furthermore, this layer can also relate to event formats that already exist outside of networked music performances, such as lecture-concerts, masterclasses, or open rehearsals, where discussion of the music is part of these events.

2.4 Sociality

Sociality refers to the way in which live streaming involves audience and community engagement. Live stream-

[12] In the Show Biz scenario, each venue contains a Semiosis mini game, a kind of a musical charades in which one player chooses a word to sound out and the other tries to guess which one. This requires that players on a team can hear each other clearly.

ing platforms like Twitch and YouTube feature a live chat, which allows viewers to talk not only to one another but also the streamer. Viewers can comment and give input on the streamer's performance, and the streamer can solicit feedback from the viewers [1, p. 75]. The nature of this interaction and the fact that streamers often stream daily promote an intimate relationship between viewers and streamers, shifting viewers from audience to something more like a community or even a family [1, p. 91]. Accordingly, Taylor lists six motivations for spectatorship: aspirational, educational, inspirational, entertainment, community, and ambience [1, pp. 39–41]. In an earlier study focused on esports, she notes that before people become spectators, they usually first consider themselves players [26, p. 235]. N. T. Taylor similarly discussed the challenge of esports competitions to gain 'mainstream acceptance' and attract audiences beyond the player base, noting how the founders of the competitions looked at the success of televised poker as an inspiration [27, p. 298].

Both [Olympics] and [Show Biz] were streamed as part of online concerts consisting of pre-made videos. As such, the audience could comment on the videos and interact with other audience members, but not affect the performances themselves. [Live] sessions do feature a live chat, but because ScoreCraft's community is still small, we make little use of it. Moreover, the large majority of ScoreCraft's community members would rather play than watch if they can attend a session, which aligns well with Taylor's observation that game stream viewers are often first players. On the other hand, there were also a few cases of people without previous experience playing ScoreCraft who reached out to us after watching a session and asked to join as players.

Beyond ludified notation, focus on interaction and participation has been rooted in telematics since its very inception. Politically underpinned as a liberatory practice, it aimed from the start to connect individuals as active participants rather than passive receivers [4, p. 6]. Deal and Burtner's *Auksalaq*, discussed in the critique and evaluation subsection above, demonstrates this approach, as the audience can influence the work by interacting with a dedicated app. Maria Papadomanolaki's project, *A Certain Geography*, is another example, consisting of an ongoing series of telematic soundwalking performances. In her Parasol Unit performance (2014), Papadomanolaki live streamed herself soundwalking inside the Parasol Unity gallery in London to an audience seated in the main conference room. The audience listened to the sound transmitted from the soundwalk and watched a text-score video projected in the room. Throughout the performance, the audience could send Papadomanolaki text messages, sharing thoughts, asking questions, and prompting actions. In response, Papadomanolaki either read the messages out loud or performed actions according to the prompts given. Papadomanolaki describes the messages as playing 'a pivotal role in "freeing-up" the transmission chain' [28, p. 320] [13] and states that they 'constantly destabilised my prescribed trajectory and activated a more instinctive mode of conversation' [28, p. 322].

Audience participation is also common in networked music performance more generally and has been investigated from various perspectives, from the technical to the aesthetic [29, 30]. For example, *Chat Music* [WIP] (2022) by Sebastian Adams and Carl Ludwig Hübsch, allows the audience to influence a dynamic, generative score by sending messages in a live chat of a Twitch stream. The score blends traditional music notation with graphic notation as a framework for improvisation. Audience interaction is based on several command words that can impact the score, as well as an algorithmic approach to converting arbitrary messages into pitches and rhythms, among other techniques. Adams and Hübsch note that the work can produce diverse results, 'from an almost traditional improvisation, with audience carefully shaping the mood and pace of the performance, to a chaotic and exciting mess more redolent of the chat box of a Twitch gamer' [31].

With regard to growing an audience and building a community, there seems to be an issue with contemporary art music in general, which is also notorious for an audience constituted of a high percentage of practitioners [32, p. 5], similarly to game live streaming. Therefore, approaches to expanding the audience beyond the player-practitioner-base might be applicable across both disciplines.

2.5 Material and Digital Infrastructure

Material and digital infrastructure refers to the technological infrastructure that enables game live streaming. This includes a range of technical components, such as video codecs, storage, servers, and transmission nodes at the level of streaming platforms (Twitch, YouTube, etc.), and computers, A/V hardware and mixing boards, furniture, lighting, graphics and A/V processing software, bot and notification/trigger systems, and network functionality at the level of individual streamers [1, p. 78]. Notably, individual streamers follow a DIY approach to developing their broadcast setup, relying on self-taught technical skills and community knowledge [1, p. 79]. Esports broadcasting also started as a DIY practice, and sometimes it was only possible to produce a full broadcast by overlaying voice commentary after the fact. It took decades until esports broadcasts became live, rich media events as they are today [1, p. 158]. Nevertheless, early esports broadcasting practitioners focused on creating memorable, epic moments, not on delivering technically perfect experiences, which Taylor links to the practice of individual streamers current to her writing [1, pp. 168–169].

[Olympics] and [Show Biz] were both post-produced in a similar way to early esports broadcasts, that is, by overlaying recorded gameplay with commentary (audio and video). We used Discord for audio and video communication, OBS for recording, and DaVinci Resolve for post-production editing. [Live] is produced live, also using Discord and OBS, but in this case to stream directly on YouTube without editing.

Overall, in our productions of ScoreCraft, we embrace a rather casual approach to production. Performing ScoreCraft online involves playing the game in the browser while on a voice/video call using a third-party software for audio and video communication, as ScoreCraft does not capture and stream the audio input. As mentioned above,

[13] Papadomanolaki draws on Donatella Della Ratta's notion that sound in Zoom-like meetings has the 'potential for a freeing-up from the anxiety of the hyperconscious self-gaze, [which] might help create an opening for spaces of intimacy and in defiance of connectivity' [28, p. 317].

we use Discord, which we find to offer a good balance between ease of use, audio quality, and latency. Ease of use is particularly important for us as we cannot expect from all the players to go through an elaborate setup process. Furthermore, most of us use the built-in microphone of our laptop or headset. Latency is not typically a major issue as ScoreCraft does not require extremely accurate rhythmical synchronisation. When ScoreCraft does require synchronisation, it is possible to define the length of the synchronisation window. For example, when playing a Whac game in which the players need to hit two or more targets synchronously, the default synchronisation window is one second long. Of course, our choice to use Discord and built-in microphones instead of a specialised setup for networked music performance does compromise the overall audio quality. As such, distortion and streaming artifacts are common throughout the videos. Another type of potential technology failure involves the audio analysis algorithms. ScoreCraft uses Essentia.js [33, 34] for audio analysis, which is usually very accurate, but combined with low-end microphones can sometimes result in a false output (especially when using musical instruments other than voice). Moreover, the audio analysis can also fail if audio from other players leaks into the input, which makes it easier to perform ScoreCraft distanced rather than colocated. While a professional, seamless experience can be a worthy goal, we believe there is also merit to exposing and emphasising the imperfection of the virtual space within which we operate. This echoes Ciciliani's notion of letting the space itself 'generate presence' [11, p. 130].

More generally, game live streaming and networked music performance share similar technological infrastructure, most notably the Internet, but also broadcasting hardware and software such as microphones, cameras, recording and streaming apps, etc. As with game live streaming, approaches to technology in networked music performance vary. Oliveros, interviewed by Jason Robinson about her three-day 'Deep Listening Convergence' (2007), contrasts a 'low-tech' approach with 'university situations'. The latter refers to using the low-latency Internet2 network and professional audio and video equipment. The former represents a 'participatory technology' and refers to the bare minimum: a laptop, camera, and a working Internet connection [35, pp. 104–105]. Expanding on Oliveros' notion of participatory technology, we point to the ubiquity of mobile phones in participatory networked music performances [36, 37]. Technical requirements suggest a link between the material and digital infrastructure layer and the economic and commercial frameworks layer, as access to technology might be limited by the financial structures underlying the performance. Lemmon similarly considers the implicit social and political implications inscribed in such networking technologies, as even access to the Internet should not be taken for granted [4, p. 21]. Another consideration that is broadly applicable in any networked music performances where performers are distanced is latency. Carôt and Werner propose a categorisation of four main different musical interaction styles with respect to latency and rhythm synchronisation in networked music performance: a realistic interaction approach, assuming that the latency is below 25 ms; a centralised clock approach, [14] where one player maintains the rhythm while ignoring the incoming delayed signals, so that other players can rely on it; a latency accepting approach, which does not consider latency to be a problem but instead exploits it artistically; and a fake time approach, which introduces a deliberate delay locking the latency to musical tempo [39].

2.6 Economic and Commercial Frameworks

Economic and commercial frameworks refers to the financial structures that enable game live streaming. As mentioned above, game live streaming is linked with esports broadcasting, which started as a DIY practice. Early practitioners were hobbyists broadcasting because of a deep passion for gaming, dreaming it would eventually become their day job [1, p. 154]. This indeed happened to some, and large-scale esports production created by extensive professionalised teams are now a reality [1, p. 163]. For individual streamers, streaming platforms nowadays offer a range of ways to monetise live streams through partner and affiliate programs, and Taylor also lists donation-based systems, sponsorship deals, and Amazon affiliate links as mechanisms beyond the streaming platforms that individual streamers make use of [1, p. 77].

ScoreCraft is developed as part of an academic research project (Peles' doctoral work) and productions discussed in this paper were presented at academic and research-oriented events. [Olympics] was presented at a McGill University concert; [Show Biz] was presented at NIME, an international research conference; and [Live] forms a core part of Peles' research project. Apart from that, however, all work is voluntary. At present the project is not popular enough to qualify for any of the streaming platforms' affiliate and partner programs. Server costs are self-funded, and none of the players (some of whom are world-class professional musicians) receive remuneration for their participation. As such, as with ScoreCraft's material and digital infrastructure, also our economic and commercial frameworks can be said to resemble at present early esports practitioners. We are a small team of two organisers without formal training in many of the roles we undertake in production.

More broadly, there is a considerable difference between the financial structures of game live streaming and networked music performance. Crucially, game live streaming can comprise much larger communities, which opens up possibilities for financial support and profit unavailable to the typically smaller networked music performance productions. Platform-integrated means of monetisation and other donation-based systems in the spirit of game live streaming might be worth further investigation, however, given the financial complexities of the contemporary art music scene and their entanglement with wider economical and political issues, we have decided a more thorough examination and discussion of alternative revenue streams in networked music performance productions is beyond the scope of this paper.

[14] Carôt and Werner use the old 'master-slave' terminology, which has been identified as discriminatory and needlessly offensive [38]. Instead, we refer here to this approach as a 'centralised clock'.

3. TOWARDS A MODEL FOR NETWORKED MUSIC PERFORMANCE

Now that we have examined each of Taylor's layers of production in relation to ScoreCraft and networked music performance in general, we propose a derivation of Taylor's model as shown in Table 1.[15] For each layer, we propose key considerations and point to a range of possibilities for addressing them. The aim of the model is not to offer a comprehensive description of networked music performance but to present a nonexhaustive set of possible lenses through which networked music performance can be viewed and conceptualised. As these lenses are grounded in game live streaming rather than offline performance, they draw on the unique affordances of the Internet and can shed new light on aspects of networked music performance underemphasised by more music-focused approaches. As such, we believe this model can serve as a novel frame of reference to help guide the analysis, critique, and creation of networked music performances.

The model can be used in full, where the analytical/creative process aims to address all the listed considerations, or alternatively only a few specific considerations may be selected focusing on a more limited subset of the model. In that regard, it is important to note that the considerations are interrelated. Taylor notes about her model that the 'various layers interact with and impact each other in meaningful ways' [1, p. 79]. One example is the link between the material and digital infrastructure layer and the economic and commercial framework layer, where financial structures influence access to technology, and thus how professionalised the approach to production can be, as discussed above. Taylor gives further examples, such as interactions between economic and financial frameworks and sociality, and set design and sociality. The former concerns how the performance leverages engagement to generate commercial profit (ads, subscriptions, etc.); the latter addresses how engagement is facilitated by particular set designs (live chat, camera videos, etc.). Overall, this points towards a more holistic conception of performance, possible by taking into account multiple considerations simultaneously.

4. FUTURE WORK

Future work could follow three immediately apparent paths. First, assessing the utility of our current adaptation of Taylor's model as it applies to practising musicians outside of the ScoreCraft community, testing their attitudes towards the model and investigating their long term adoption of any of its ideas as practical conceptual tools. Second, using the model as a tool to investigate online productions of other artists, testing the model's applicability and utility as an analytical framework for comparison, critique, and evaluation. Third, in the same way that applying Taylor's model stemmed from the overlap of networked gameplay in ScoreCraft and game streamers on platforms such as Twitch, scholarship on other online performance practices (from poetry readings to guided meditations) and media content production and distribution modes (relating to environments such as TikTok or Metaverse) could be surveyed for additional considerations, best practices, and lessons learned. These three avenues of investigation can be used to inform further development and refinement of the model to increase its usefulness to a more diverse range of practitioners.

Acknowledgments

We would like to thank ScoreCraft community members for their feedback and insights during play sessions, as well as the players who participated in the ScoreCraft's productions discussed in this paper. Special thanks to the members of Open Scores Lab, led by James Saunders, for their valuable suggestions for improving this paper.

5. REFERENCES

[1] T. L. Taylor, *Watch Me Play: Twitch and the Rise of Game Live Streaming*. Princeton University Press, 2018.

[2] G. Peles, "On Ludified Notation and ScoreCraft," 2023, presented at SPIEL! Games as a Critical Practice, FHNW, Basel, Switzerland. [Online]. Available: https://youtu.be/UA4rW7gfCQg

[3] G. Peles and Y. Adler, "Streaming Digital Score Performances: What We Can Learn from Esports," 2023, presented at a research meeting on the impact of digital technology on instruments, performances, notations and compositions, CIRMMT, McGill University. [Online]. Available: https://www.cirmmt.org/en/events/workshops/research/impact-digital-technology

[4] E. C. Lemmon, "Telematic Music vs. Networked Music: Distinguishing Between Cybernetic Aspirations and Technological Music-Making," *Journal of Network Music and Arts*, vol. 1, no. 1, p. 2, 2019.

[5] J. Lazzaro and J. Wawrzynek, "A Case for Network Musical Performance," in *Proceedings of the 11th International Workshop on Network and Operating Systems Support for Digital Audio and Video*, 2001, pp. 157–166.

[6] C. Rottondi, C. Chafe, C. Allocchio, and A. Sarti, "An Overview on Networked Music Performance Technologies," *IEEE Access*, vol. 4, pp. 8823–8843, 2016.

[7] R. Mills, *Tele-Improvisation: Intercultural Interaction in the Online Global Music Jam Session*. Springer, 2019.

[8] L. Gabrielli and S. Squartini, *Wireless Networked Music Performance*. Springer Singapore, 2016.

[9] A. Carôt, P. Rebelo, and A. Renaud, "Networked Music Performance: State of the Art," in *Proceedings of the 30th AES International Conference on Intelligent Audio Environments*, 2007.

[10] R. Wilson, "Aesthetic and Technical Strategies for Networked Music Performance," *AI & Society*, pp. 1–14, 2020.

[15] Table 1 is only available in the online version of this paper.

[11] M. Ciciliani, "Token of Enunciation in Multimedia Performance," in *Proceedings of the International Computer Music Conference*, 2017.

[12] G. Wilson, "Off With Their HUDs!: Rethinking the Heads-Up Display in Console Game Design," *Game Developer*, Feb. 2006.

[13] Oxford Dictionaries, "head-up display," 2002. [Online]. Available: https://www.oxfordreference.com/view/10.1093/acref/9780199891580.001.0001/acref-9780199891580-e-3680

[14] J. Bell, "Distributed Notation in the Browser, an Overview," in *Proceedings of the International Conference on Technologies for Music Notation and Representation*, 2021.

[15] D. Kim-Boyle, "Reframing the Listening Experience through the Projected Score," *Tempo*, vol. 72, no. 284, pp. 37–50, 2018.

[16] J. Sell, "E-Sports Broadcasting," Master's thesis, Massachusetts Institute of Technology, 2015.

[17] E. M. H. Newbury, "The Case of Competitive Video Gaming and Its Fandom: Media Objects, Fan Practices, and Fan Identities," PhD dissertation, Cornell University, 2017.

[18] J. A. Mead, "Survivor and Other Reality T.V. Gameshows: The Uses and Gratifications Perspective on a Reality Sub-Genre," 2006.

[19] J. Roscoe and C. Hight, *Faking it: Mock-documentary and the subversion of factuality*. Manchester University Press, 2018.

[20] M. Consalvo and A. Phelps, "Game Development Live on Twitch: Observations of Practice and Educational Synergies," in *Game Production Studies*, O. Sotamaa and J. Svelch, Eds. Amsterdam University Press, 2021, pp. 123–140.

[21] P. Auslander, *In Concert: Performing Musical Persona*. University of Michigan Press, 2021.

[22] E. Goffman, *Frame Analysis: An Essay on the Organization of Experience*. Harvard University Press, 1974.

[23] M. Flanagan, *Critical Play: Radical Game Design*. The MIT Press, 2009.

[24] P. Oliveros, S. Weaver, M. Dresser, J. Pitcher, J. Braasch, and C. Chafe, "Telematic Music: Six Perspectives," *Leonardo Music Journal*, vol. 19, no. 1, 2009.

[25] S. Deal and M. Burtner, "Auksalaq, a Telematic Opera," in *Proceedings of the International Computer Music Conference*, 2011.

[26] T. L. Taylor, *Raising the Stakes: E-Sports and the Professionalization of Computer Gaming*. The MIT Press, 2012.

[27] N. T. Taylor, "Now You're Playing with Audience Power: The Work of Watching Games," *Critical Studies in Media Communication*, vol. 33, no. 4, pp. 293–307, 2016.

[28] M. Papadomanolaki, "Telematic Sound Body: A Trajectory of Intimacy and Defiance," *Organised Sound*, vol. 26, no. 3, pp. 317–326, 2021.

[29] D. Kim-Boyle, "Network Musics: Play, Engagement and the Democratization of Performance," *Contemporary Music Review*, vol. 28, no. 4-5, pp. 363–375, 2009.

[30] A. Xambó and G. Roma, "Performing Audiences: Composition Strategies for Network Music using Mobile Phones," in *Proceedings of the International Conference on New Interfaces for Musical Expression*, 2020.

[31] S. Adams, "Sebastian Adams' Works," https://www.sebastianadams.net/works.html, 2022.

[32] S. Chambers, "'You Don't go to These Kinds of Concerts for Fun': The Fluid and Emergent Performance of Taste in Contemporary Art Music," *Cultural Sociology*, 2023.

[33] A. A. Correya, D. Bogdanov, L. Joglar-Ongay, and X. Serra, "Essentia. js: A JavaScript library for music and audio analysis on the web," in *Proceedings of the 21st International Society for Music Information Retrieval Conference*, Montréal, Canada, 2020, pp. 605–612.

[34] A. A. Correya, J. Marcos Fernández, L. Joglar-Ongay, P. Alonso Jiménez, X. Serra, and D. Bogdanov, "Audio and Music Analysis on the Web using Essentia. js," *Transactions of the International Society for Music Information Retrieval*, vol. 4, no. 1, pp. 167–181, 2021.

[35] J. Robinson, "The Networked Body: Physicality, Embodiment, and Latency in Multisite Performance," in *Negotiated Moments: Improvisation, Sound, and Subjectivity*, G. Siddall and E. Waterman, Eds. Duke University Press, 2016, pp. 91–112.

[36] G. Essl and S. W. Lee, "Mobile Devices as Musical Instruments - State of the Art and Future Prospects," in *Music Technology with Swing*, M. Aramaki, M. E. P. Davies, R. Kronland-Martinet, and S. Ystad, Eds. Springer International Publishing, 2018, pp. 525–539.

[37] B. Taylor, "A History of the Audience as a Speaker Array," in *Proceedings of the International Conference on New Interfaces for Musical Expression*, 2017.

[38] R. Eglash, "Broken Metaphor: The Master-Slave Analogy in Technical Literature," *Technology and Culture*, vol. 48, no. 2, pp. 360–369, 2007.

[39] A. Carôt and C. Werner, "Network Music Performance – Problems, Approaches and Perspectives," in *Proceedings of the "Music in the Global Village" Conference*, vol. 162, Budapest, Hungary, 2007.

Heart Sutra: A Network Audio Technology-Assisted Visual Music Composition

Jiayue Cecilia Wu
University of Colorado Denver
cecilia.wu@ucdenver.edu

Rebecca Nie
Stanford University
rnie@stanford.edu

ABSTRACT

This research explicates the cultural background, creative process, and technical details of a network audio technology-assisted Visual Music composition named "Heart Sutra." Heart Sutra is an immersive audiovisual expression of one of the most widely recited Buddhist texts, integrating chanting traditions in Chinese, Japanese, and Korean, narrating in electroacoustic sounds, media arts, and technology. Heart Sutra is made possible by open-source network audio technology as well as real-time audio-driven visualization algorithms and high-precision 3D projection mapping, which enables the audiovisual composition to be precisely mapped onto the Western sacred art forms, such as mosaic, stained glass, and neoclassical architecture, in Stanford University's Memorial Church. Heart Sutra proves the efficiency of open-source network audio technology for remote music production and provides an economical solution for musicians to reimagine their future practices. It is the result of collaborative efforts among interdisciplinary scholars who seek to breathe new life into ancient Eastern contemplative cultural arts and inspire global society.

1. INTRODUCTION

Heart Sutra is an immersive Visual Music expression of one of the most widely recited East Asian liturgical texts [1], integrating chanting traditions in Chinese, Japanese, and Korean, as well as electroacoustic music, media arts, and network audio technology. It draws upon the sacred art traditions in vocalism, drumming, architecture, ink art, and figurative representations of the divine found throughout the world, and revives these ancient cultural art traditions with technology implementation.

1.1 Social Context

Heart Sutra was commissioned by Stanford University's Office for Religious & Spiritual Life and Ho Center for Buddhist Studies for their Sankofa World Music Concert [2], which is an invitation for the Stanford community to come together and collectively hold and process all they have been through in isolation and mental stress during and beyond the COVID-19 pandemic. It is an active call to care for ourselves and each other as we move beyond the pandemic to build a future with the power of humanity's collective imagination and resilience in daily life.

Open-source network audio technology was applied as a crucial vehicle for the music ensemble to remotely rehearse, record, perform, and produce the music part of the audiovisual composition without paying considerable studio rental fees and travel expenses. The composition premiered as an immersive audiovisual installation and was precisely mapped onto the Western sacred art in mosaic, stained glass, and neoclassical architecture at Stanford University's Memorial Church [3] during the concert. The installation event was then recorded, edited, and documented as a standalone Visual Music piece.

1.2 Visual Music

The music of *Heart Sutra* is an electroacoustic composition consisting of voice, percussion instruments, flute, electronic sounds, and Celletto [4], as well as precious field recording archives from one of the five "Palace of the Jewel of Nirvana" temples in South Korea–Tongdosa Monastery [5]. Hand-created paintings amplified by abstract audio-driven algorithmic art are created to evolve over time. Thet are linked with the musical structure, timbre, dynamics, rhythm, texture, and form.

Visual Music, as a broad and diverse multimedia art practice, has been giving public attention since the 18th century with Castel's Ocular Harpsichord [30]. There are many methods to realize a visual music composition from the perspectives of tempo, harmonics, colors, montages, and musical phrases [6]. We approach *Heart Sutra* through carefully controlling timing, movement (musical phrases), rhythm (tempo), and choreography of visual elements such as light and colors that are linked with the musical riffs and patterns. By purposefully emphasizing or neglecting certain aspects of audio signals, the visuals arrive as the non-hierarchical counterpoint of the music.

The synesthetic idea of *Heart Sutra* ties to an art movement that commenced in early twentieth century, in which visual artists such as Wassily Kandinsky and Georgia O'Keeffe were deeply interested in "the idea tha music could be translated into something for the eye [24]." Yet, the creative development of this work as a collaboration between musicians and media artists reflects the current practice of today's multimedia field. The work presented here can be perceived as an ongoing discourse involving interdisciplinary researchers, wherein computer technology assumes a crucial role as a contributing factor.

Figure 1: *Heart Sutra* during the immersive installation at Stanford University's architectural crown jewel — Memorial Church.

The audiovisual creative process spanning four months is interactive rather than linear. Through frequent communication and brainstorming between the composer and the artists, ideas are inspired, developed, reflected, and built upon. The final piece was realized through many iterations of such workflow. As Bill Alves well-stated, while music visualizers can "merely map the most elemental characteristics of one sensory mode to another create at best a naïve and predictable synesthesia," Visual Music provokes "the journey of emotions that music can awaken in an audience" which "does not automatically emerge when one characteristic (pitch, for example) is mapped to a characteristic in another sense (color, for example) [7]."

The media technology, computer, and most importantly, Memorial Church's sacred art and architecture also contribute to the creative chain via adding controlled randomness as well as materializing human-designed algorithms to produce the Visual Music outcome inconceivable prior to the immersive installation. Arguably, the computer and technology extend the artist's abilities in reasoning and envisioning, thus playing an essential role in realizing the Visual Music composition.

2. NETWORK MUSIC COMPOSITION

We collaborated with musicians from California, Colorado, and Minnesota, working across three states in the U.S.. The goal is to realize a three-movement music composition based on the inspirations from the structured improvisational sessions. We conducted nine remote sessions using open-sourced network audio technology, including Jacktrip/Jackaudio [12] and Netty-McNetface [13]. These tools allowed us to transmit and record high-fidelity multi-track audio during the collaboration. Musicians have been using this technology at an increasing rate to play tightly synchronized music with other musicians around the world. We engaged in musical collaborations, rehearsals, recordings, and improvisations across different geographical locations, all without incurring substantial transportation expenses.

The realm of Internet-based virtual music studio production poses several technical challenges, particularly concerning online network real-time multichannel recording, mixing, and production. A key question arised at the time of this research was conducted: How can one effectively implement multiple audio processing networks and record each location's audio input as separate tracks over the internet, considering factors such as low-speed home internet connections, prosumer hardware, and the varying quality of performance and recording spaces found in each unique home? Additionally, determining the most suitable musical style or compositional approach for performance and recording requires careful consideration. This research endeavors to shed light on these questions by presenting a case study.

2.1 Experimenting with Different Network Audio Technologies for Rehearsals and Recording

Our network music practice necessitated the use of software that treats all incoming signals from different geographical locations as independent audio channels, each of which can be routed to separate hardware outputs and tracks in a DAW. Software establishing multiple peer-to-peer connections especially met this requirement. While the initial motivation was to realise a particular approach to real-time interactive electroacoustic music performance, it naturally led to multitracking in a Digital Audio Workstation (DAW) for composition and postproduction.

The decision of which open-source applications to choose was based on the following criteria: 1) the highest quality of Internet audio transmission at the time; 2) low latency; 3) autonomy of choosing cloud servers by the users; 4) approachable and timely technical support from the technology developer; 5) ease of installation and use by participated musicians; 6) stability; and 7) discrete, multichannel routing of each node's signals. Commercial applications are beyond the scope of this research.

JackTrip met many of our criteria and we are using it in conjunction with Netty-McNetface at the time of the creation of this piece. JackTrip's long history, wide user base, the QJackTrip application, which provides an easy-to-use Graphical User Interface (GUI)—cross-platform stability and improved installation experience since 2021 make JackTrip an essential part of our toolkit going forward. Furthermore, the timely launch of JackTrip's "hub-mode" during the pandemic enables standing up a JackTrip server on a cloud-based virtual machine (VM), reducing bandwidth demands on users, and an approach to mixing and recording directly on the VM. Finally, the growth of third-party DIY and preconfigured kits make it easier than ever for musicians to work with JackTrip regardless of technical comfort level or access to the necessary technology.

With our goal of delivering a professional audio-engineered production that allows multi-channel network audio recordings that preserve each of the musicians' individual tracks for sophisticated mixing and editing in the postproduction process in mind, we also experimented with another open-source network audio application called Netty-McNetface, which uses the same Jackaudio for uncompressed internet audio connection that Jacktrip uses. Netty-McNetface was developed in PureData, and the GUI is easy-to-use and efficient for meeting our specific needs in multi-channel recording and mixing via home internet. The graphical virtual audio mixing console of Netty-McNetface is particulary user-friendly. We combined the two open-source network audio technologies and designed a network audio sulotion as shown in Figure 2:

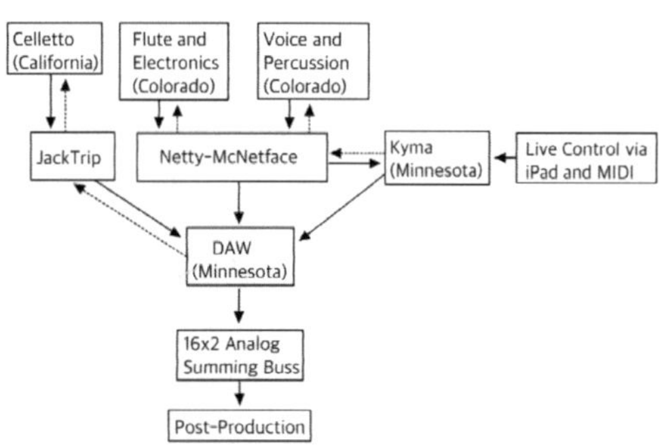

Figure 2. *Heart Sutra* Audio Signal Flow

Routing software was used to assign each incoming network audio signal to an independent channel on a multichannel audio interface, then routed to Pro Tools [11] (or any compatible DAW), where it is recorded on a unique track. Each channel is sent via the interface's hardware outputs to creative real-time Digital Signal Processing (DSP) systems, such as Kyma[15] and VCV Rack[16], for real-time audio sampling, analysis, and manipulation. Up to eight channels of audio output from Kyma are returned via hardware aux returns on the audio interface to the DAW and recorded to separate tracks.

Through connecting musicians using both Jacktrip/Jackaudio and Netty-McNetface on private cloud servers, each musician's individual stereo audio tracks were transmitted through the Internet to a local music studio and routed to a 32-channel audio interface and a costumed designed I/O path in the Pro-Tools [17], where all musicians' performances were recorded in their individual tracks, up to 12 tracks real-time at high-fidelity for uncompressed audio recording within 10-50 ms latency, depending on the network speed, stability, and geographical locations.

In both a live performance and recording session, two mixes are produced. The first is a cue mix for performer monitoring of the DSP output, returned to the performers via Netty-McNetface and Jacktrip. Each remote performer hears the results of the DSP processing on the studio Netty-McNetface or Jacktrip channel. Specifically, Netty-McNetface allows each participant to manage a mix of all participants, and a loopback of their input, albeit with noticeable latency since this is the result of a peer-to-peer connection between themselves and the server.

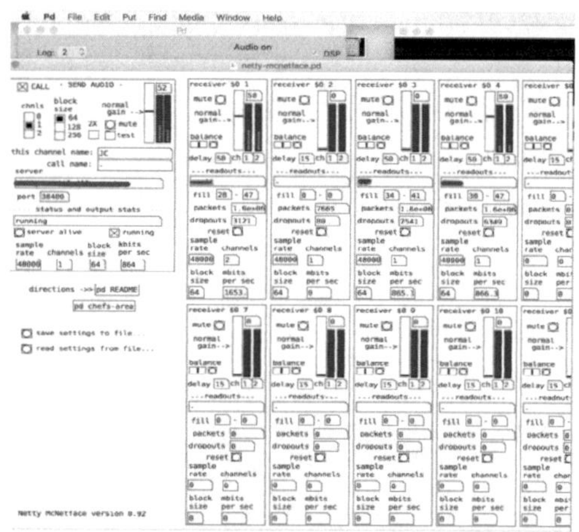

Figure 3. A multichannel recording session via Netty-McNetface GUI, with home internet and Jackaudio connection.

The second mix is for broadcast to the performance platform, typically via OBS [25]. In a recording session, this is the rough mix monitored in the studio. This mix includes all dry incoming signals, subjected to channel processing, spatialization (both stereo and 3D), and an analog summing buss. If being broadcast, it is synced with video in OBS, which is then streamed to the platform of choice.

The studio's computer used for networking and recording audio is a Mac Mini (2018) with OSX.11, Pro Tools Ultimate DAW, Antelope OrionIII routing and mixing software, Pure Data 0.52 and the Netty-McNetface 0.92 patch, with an Antelope Orion 32+ Gen. 3 audio interface, Universal Audio UAD-2 Octo DSP, and an analog summing buss (Roll Music Folcrom, A Designs Audio Pacifica mic pre-amplifier, TK BC1 compressor and Neve 8803 EQ). The home studio ISP offers 400 Mbps download and 20 Mbps upload speeds.

The hardware and software were used on hand in the studio for convenience. However, other open-source and shareware equivalents can minimise reliance on commercial software. The following open-source and shareware is a sampling of functionally equivalent software to that used in this research: 1) Ardour (DAW) [26]; 2) Blackhole (audio routing) [27]; and 3) VB-Audio Cable (audio routing) [28].

2.2 A New Aesthetics in Network Music Practice

Noticeably, the audio transmission latency for multi-channel synchronicity recording from different geographical locations' buffer underruns as well as the unstable internet speed and network issues contributing to the audio imperfections can be perceived and has intendedly become part of the composition itself. We used iZotope® RX9 to eliminate most of the unpleasant audio glitches and left the slightly mismatched vocal recitals of the chants, differentiating in milliseconds, to acknowledge the current technical state of the network music practices. Through this work, we have embraced a new aesthetic that includes noises, glitchy sounds, and "micro-rhythmic" timing mismatch. This unique sonic phenomenon defines technology-driven music collaboration in performance and recording arts during the COVID-19 era.

2.3 Combining Electroacoustic Music Vocabulary

For the collective electroacoustic music-making toolkit, Granular synthesis [14] is majorly implemented to process acoustic instruments such as voice, flute, and percussions. Specifically, precious field recordings of ancient chants from Tongdosa Monastery are granulized and deformalized to serve as drones in the background. The chants also come into the foreground with their original forms when articulating the musical structure. Graphical music programming languages Kyma [15] and VCV Rack [16] were used for electronic sound design, synthesis, and DSP. The signature electroacoustic instrument, celletto, structurally highlights each of the three movements from time to time. It has also grounded and solidified the low-middle range of the audio spectrum. A series of low-pass, high-pass, and band-pass filters were applied to avoid aliasing and tame the overly rich electric sounds in the final mix.

2.4 The Network Music Composition

The music piece was structured by the composer and then communicated with the other three virtuoso musicians who possess decades of experience in contemporary music improvisation practice. We had nine on-the-fly recording sessions as we rehearsed the piece together. These individual tracks were then hand-picked following the pre-defined compositional structure, remixed, and reorganized to serve the Visual Music narrative.

In the first movement, the voices of the sacred feminine are emphasized by empowering the women musicians to open up the sonic and spiritual space of the entire composition. The ancient chants in Chinese and Japanese represent two different East-Asian *Heart Sutra* traditions and serve as the backbone of the piece that has been sonically iterated, transformed, and mutated throughout the whole piece.

The second movement was an abstract sonic transcendental experience. The complex electroacoustic audio spectrums and compositional structure transform back and forth between high and low, dark and bright, tension and calm, dissonance and consonance, as well as harsh and smooth, illuminates the nondual view in "form is emptiness; emptiness is form [1]."

From 5'30" to 5'50" of the piece, with the companionship of the meditative drone sounds, the Heart Sutra mantra was recited: "*gate gate pāragate pārasaṃgate bodhi svāhā.*" This means "gone, gone, gone beyond, gone completely beyond to enlightenment, fulfilling all wishes. [1]" Then, the celletto and synthesizer duo gradually amplifies and eventually screams out of the ecstasy of Zen enlightenment with an interrupting stop by the percussions. This is the moment where the composer believes that singularity [18] and its new civilization will arrive with the realization of the collective intelligent minds.

The finale returns to the traditional Heart Sutra recital with an organized and concrete musical form. Led by the soprano's assertive yet relaxed voice and her calm and joyful feminine energy, the chant of the monks in the ancestral seat temple for the Jogye Order of Korean Buddhism, Tongdosa Monastery, concludes the piece.

3. ALGORITHMIC AUDIOVISUALS & MEDIA ARTS

As shown in Figure 4 (a), the digital painting and computer graphics featuring Avalokiteśvara [10] — the symbol of love, kindness, and compassion — This feminine visual presentation of Avalokiteśvara aims at inspiring women of color's spiritual leadership and attainment. We approach the core value of multifaith and cultural inclusion in *Heart Sutra* by carefully, respectfully, and aesthetically video mapping contemporary Buddhist art onto the Western sacred art and architecture in Stanford's Memorial Church, shown in Figure 1. Another multicultural example is the calligraphy featured throughout the piece and in Figure 4 (b). It is a tantric representation of the *Heart Sutra* in the Siddhaṃ script of ancient Indic languages [11], and we rendered it digitally with East Asian brushwork.

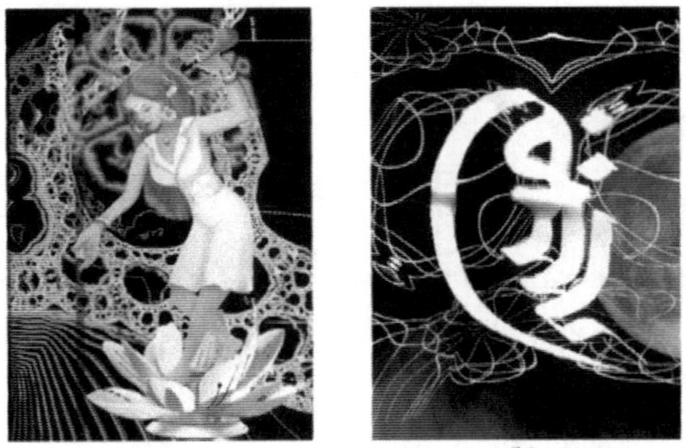

(a) (b)

Figure 4. (a) Avalokiteśvara in *Heart Sutra*; (b) Calligraphical work combining Indic script with East Asian brushwork.

These artworks range from texture-rich on-canvas paintings to 3D modeling. The concept of the *Heart Sutra* pervades each visual element and the algorithm-driven scenes at 30 frames per second. A series of GLSL algorithms were developed specifically for this piece. It is computationally intensive to combine the fractal algorithm, live audio processing, and multilayers of audio-driven filters at 30 frames per second and output the results into 5760 by 1080-pixel videos. This creative process is a showcase of the power of parallel computing at the GPU level. These custom-designed algorithms of fractal mathematics and trigonometry visually depict the evolutionary yet repetitive process of life in the state of Saṃsāra [19]. We developed a fractal deformation algorithm that steps down along the x-axis and steps up along the y-axis:

$$f_c\left(\begin{bmatrix}x_1\\x_2\end{bmatrix},\begin{bmatrix}y_1\\y_2\end{bmatrix}\right)=\begin{bmatrix}x_1y_1-x_2y_2\\x_1y_2+x_2y_1\end{bmatrix} \quad (1)$$

Then, the algorithm take real-time audio input through the A factor,

$$A=1.8\begin{bmatrix}Audio_1\\Audio_2\end{bmatrix}-1.75I \quad (2)$$

and iterates through with the following functions to calculate the colors pixel by pixel:

$$E^{R(t)}=\left[cos\left(\frac{t}{15.123}\right),sin\left(\frac{t}{15.123}\right)\right]^T \quad (3)$$

$$Z_{n+1}=\frac{|f_c(Z_n,R(t))|}{|Z_n|^2}+A \quad (4)$$

$$color_{n+1}=color_n+e^{-|Z_{n+1}|^2}+e^{-\frac{4}{|Z_n-Z_{n+1}|^2}} \quad (5)$$

Our trigonometric algorithm also takes the real-time audio data as input to create a visual representation of the rhythmic images through parallel computing. It calculates the color for each pixel in a twelve-step iteration:

$$\Delta(t)=\sin\left(\frac{1}{2}t+\sin(t)\right) \quad (6)$$

$$p_{n+1}=\begin{bmatrix}\cos(\cos(0.1t+\Delta(t))) & -\sin(\cos(0.1t+\Delta(t)))\\\sin(\cos(0.1t+\Delta(t))) & \cos(\cos(0.1t+\Delta(t)))\end{bmatrix}p_n \quad (7)$$

$$a=\arctan\left(\frac{p_{n+1_2}}{0.3\,p_{n+1_1}}\right)+0.2 \quad (8)$$

$$\varphi=\sin\left(sin\left(\frac{t}{10}\right)+a\right) \quad (9)$$

$$center=\begin{bmatrix}Audio_1\\Audio_2\end{bmatrix}-\begin{bmatrix}0.2a\\\varphi+0.3\,\Delta(t)\end{bmatrix} \quad (10)$$

$$color_{n+1}=color_n+color_i\big(smoothstep(0.35+0.05\,f+0.007.5,0.35+0.05\,\varphi,|p-center|)-smoothstep(0.35+0.05\,\varphi,0.35+0.05\,f-0.0075,|p-center|)\big)+[Audio_1,Audio_2,0,0]^T \quad (11)$$

In the last equation, *smoothstep* is GLSL's built-in function that performs Hermite Interpolation between the inputs [20].

4. THE IMMERSIVE INSTALLATION

The audio-driven computer graphic algorithms create a series of media art representations that can be real-time manipulated. Audio spectrums and frequencies are extracted from the network music composition. Then we feed the audio into a Fast Fourier analyzer. The audio data drives different parameters in the custom-designed algorithms and visual filters to real-time manipulate all the visual elements that reflects the piece's sonic narrative as detailed in Section 2. The results of the algorithm-driven audiovisual output raw footages for edit and render in Davinci Resolve [21]. The subsequent iteration is then mapped onto the Western sacred art wall at Stanford University's Memorial Church.

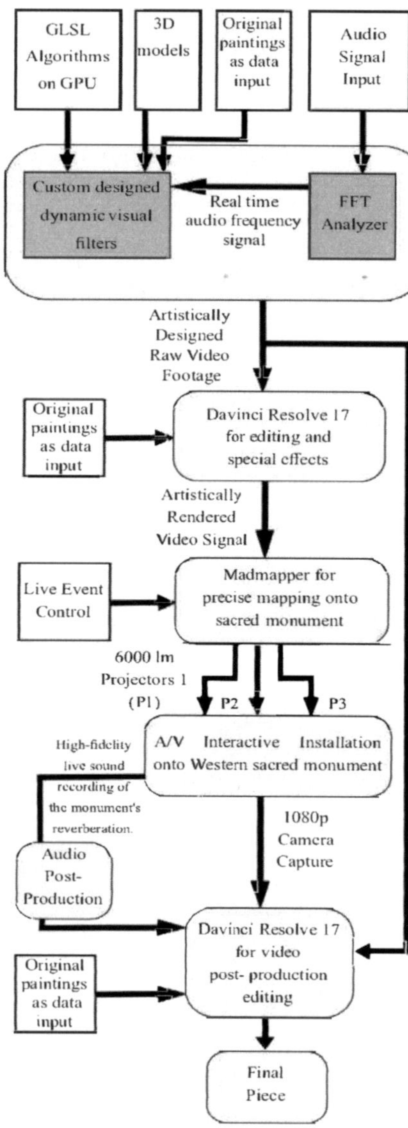

Figure 5. The system architecture of the *Heart Sutra*.

On October 10, 2021, at the Sankofa World Music Concert, *Heart Sutra's* immersive audiovisual installation was presented in front of 200 audience at the Memorial Church. The installation used three 6000 lumen projectors, each with 1080p output. At the installation site, we ported the video art into Madmapper [22] and used the software to calibrate and fine-tune the computer graphic elements and colors, so they are precisely mapped onto Memorial Church's architectural structures and existing Western sacred art. This final alignment was done with care and resepct to enable the positive impact of our multicultural Visual Music to account for the Memorial Church's grand scale.

The immersive installation harnesses the three-dimensionalities of the neoclassical monument at Stanford University. The reflective optical properties of Memorial Church's mosaic art and stained-glass windows added complexity that require us to intentionally consider in the compositional process. This multicultural and multifaith artistic expression creates depth and textural richness that would otherwise be impossible to achieve without the monumental space itself and the open-minded spiritual leadership at Stanford University. It also inspired the spiritual leaders at Stanford to reimagine their sacred space after the first viewing of our installation.

For immersive audio experience, the church's characteristic room acoustic reverberation [23] was also recorded by a Zoom H3-VR 360-degree ambisonic field recorder. This spatial reverberation was then mixed into the final Visual Music piece's audio postproduction to truthfully recreate the church's sacred soundscape. Figure 5 shows the system architecture of the entire immersive installation process, and a video documentation of this installation's premiere can be viewed at https://youtu.be/vSGVRu3mAiU.

5. DISCUSSIONS

Network audio technology has emerged as an essential tool for music ensembles, musicians, and institutions to engage in remote rehearsal, recording, performance, and music production, particularly during the pandemic. Notably, it facilitates a unique form of collaboration and fosters online music communities that span different cultures. Rather than replacing live performances or traditional studio recordings, it serves as an alternative platform [29]. Its versatility extends to various real-life applications such as online concerts, remote recording and audio production, and virtual music instruction, benefitting diverse cultural and socioeconomic groups. Essentially, this technology offers opportunities to overcome geographical barriers and foster meaningful connections among different cultures and communities.

On the other hand, the potential for the network audio solution described in Session 2.1 is to connect large ensembles and/or more than 12 nodes of performers. The JackTrip development community's work improving the installation and operation experience has been exceptional since 2020. JackTrip's user experience will continue to improve in the near future. For now, the advantage of this hybrid framework using Netty-McNetface and Jacktrip together is that the majority of first-time participants enjoy relative ease implementing the technology needed, and high musical satisfaction from the beginning. As the internet 2.0 technology has been rapidly developed, evolved and improved, some barriers and challenges in the next few years will be undoubtedly overcome.

6. CONCLUSIONS

From the philosophical perspective, *Heart Sutra* narrates the contemplative concept of "play of reality" in a multisensory way — understanding that mental events and our perception of life are illusory and fluid, just like the transformation of sounds and visuals, and the boundaries are not always firm and stable in our limited three-dimensional universe. This means that all such as suffering and happiness are passing, impermanent, and transformational. *Heart Sutra* beckons the audience to transcend their suffering by embracing the time-tested contemplative philosophy, experience this nondual wisdom through its artistic heritage, as well as computer music and media arts representation.

From the technological perspective, we leveraged current music and media arts technologies such as network audio, real-time algorithmic computer visuals, and 3D projection mapping in a complex system to achieve cross-state collaboration. This creative process is a statement of teamwork that is made possible only recently with the rapid improvement of network audio technology, high performance computing, algorithmic audiovisuals, and high precision 3D projection mapping systems.

By elaborating and analysing a detailed qualitative case study in multichannel high-fidelity network audio recording, mixing, and postproduction as evidence, we prove the significance and sufficiency of open-source network audio technology as well as provide effective, accessible, and economical solutions for musicians, composers, music educators, audio engineers, media artists, curators, and performing arts institutions to reimagine their future performance, composition, and teaching practices that lead to revolutionary institutional change in the post-COVID era. The technology successfully explores ways of connecting cultures and collaborative artistic partners over long distances.

Overall, the impact of *Heart Sutra* as a Visual Music piece and its immersive installation at Stanford's Memorial Church is multifold. At the time of this writing, the completed audiovisual production was officially selected by prestigious international music/film festivals and research venues such as the Berlin International Art Film Festival, Toronto International Women Film Festival, DAVAMOT Film Festival, New York City Electronic Music Festival (NYCFMF), MOXsonic Festival, the International Computer Music Conference (ICMC), Audio Engineering Society's 152 Convention, and the Seventh Computer Art Congress. An additional version of Heart Sutra's music production was realized for live concert performances with video projection and live electronics at the 2022 National Conference of the Society for Electro-Acoustic Music in the United States (SEAMUS) and the College of Music Society (CMS/ATMI) National Conference.

Last but not least, *Heart Sutra* initiates an open-ended dialogue of multi-faith and multiculturalism in computer music and media arts practice. By thoughtfully intertwining contemporary Buddhist art and electroacoustic music with sacred Christian imagery and neoclassical architectural space, the immersive installation achieves not only a heightened level of artistic quality and aesthetic refinement but also propels a visionary social impact. It amplifies the global faith-wisdom traditions and has inspired Stanford University's spiritual leaders as well as open-minded audience around the world.

Acknowledgments
We thank Stanford Office of Religious and Spiritual Life, The Ho Center for Buddhist Studies at Stanford, the University of Colorado Denver's Office of Research Services (ORS), College of Arts and Media (CU Denver-CAM), Center for Faculty Development and Advancement (CU Denver-CFDA), and Center for Excellence in Teaching and Learning (CU Denver-CETL), as well as Mahavajra Seon Sanctuary and Yuming Wang and Atman Partners for their funding support. We sincerely show gratitude to our collaborators Scott L. Miller, Jane Rigler, and Chris Chafe. Thanks to Miller S. Puckette for his consult in establishing Netty-McNetface cloud server.

REFERENCES

[1] R. E. Buswell and D. S. Lopez. *The Princeton Dictionary of Buddhism*, Princeton University Press. pp. 657, 2013.

[2] C. Adami, "Festival of Reflection and Renewal," Stanford Report, September 20, 2021, accessed May 15, 2023, https://news.stanford.edu/report/2021/09/30/stanford-festival-reflection-renewal-kicks-off-continues-oct-10

[3] Church, Stanford Memorial, Stanford Memorial Church *Stanford University Publications Service*, 1964.

[4] C. Chafe. "The celletto." Stanford University website, accessed 2000, http://ccrma.stanford.edu/~cc

[5] J. Kim. "Religious Rituals of Korea: Structure and Meaning." *The Review of Korean Studies*, Vol.10, No.01, pp. 5-9, 2007.

[6] B. Evans, "Foundations of a visual music." *Computer Music Journal*, Vol. 29(4), pp.11-24, 2005.

[7] B. Alves. "Consonance and dissonance in visual music." *Organised Sound*, Vol.17, No. 2, pp.114-119, 2012.

[10] R. E. Buswell and D. S. Lopez. *The Princeton Dictionary of Buddhism*, Princeton University Press, pp. 82, 2013.

[11] R. E. Buswell and D. S. Lopez. *The Princeton Dictionary of Buddhism*, Princeton University Press, pp. 816, 2013.

[12] C. Juan-Pablo, and C. Chafe. "JackTrip: Under the hood of an engine for network audio." Journal of New Music Research Vol.39, No. 03, pp. 183-187, 2010.

[13] M. S. Puckette, "Quacktrip and Netty NcNetface - network audio for musicians," accessed May 15, 2023. http://msp.ucsd.edu/tools/quacktrip/

[14] C. Roads, "Introduction to granular synthesis." *Computer Music Journal*, Vol.12, No. 2, pp. 11-13, 1988.

[15] C. A. Scaletti, and R. E. Johnson. "An interactive environment for object-oriented music composition and sound synthesis." *ACM SIGPLAN Notices* Vol. 23, No. 11, pp. 222-233, 1988.

[16] VCV Rack official website, https://vcvrack.com/

[17] F. Hoffmann, "PRO TOOLS." *In Encyclopedia of Recorded Sound*, Routledge Press, pp. 1709-1714, 2004.

[18] R. Kurzweil, *The singularity is near: When humans transcend biology*. Penguin Press, 2005.

[19] R. E. Buswell and D. S. Lopez. *The Princeton Dictionary of Buddhism*, Princeton University Press, pp. 757, 2013.

[20] S. A. Tavares, *Generation of Multivariate Hermite Interpolating Polynomials*. United States: CRC Press, 2005.

[21] Davinci Resolve 17, accessed May 15, 2023 https://www.blackmagicdesign.com/products/davinciresolve/

[22] Madmapper official website, accessed May 15, 2023, https://madmapper.com/

[23] J. S. Abel, N. J. Bryan, P. P. Huang, M. Kolar, and B. V. Pentcheva. "Estimating room impulse responses from recorded balloon pops." *In Audio Engineering Society Convention 129*. Audio Engineering Society, 2010.

[24] Leach, B.L., *Looking and Listening: Conversations Between Modern Art and Music*. Scarecrow Press. 2014.

[25] https://obsprojecct.com accessed May 15, 2023

[26] https://ardour.org accessed accessed May 15, 2023

[27] https://existential.audio accessed May 15, 2023

[28] https://vb-audio.com accessed May 15, 2023

[29] P. Oliveros, S. Weaver, M Dresser, J. Pitcher, J. Braasch, and C. Chafe, "Telematic music: six perspec tives." *Leonardo Music Journal*, Vol. 19, No. 1, pp. 95-96. 2009.

[30] F. Maarten, "The ocular harpsichord of louis-bertrand castel." *Tractrix, 3*(1991), pp.15-77. 1991.

Immersive Musical Notations in AR/VR

David Kim-Boyle
The University of Sydney
david.kim-boyle@sydney.edu.au

ABSTRACT

Augmented and virtual reality systems help facilitate an exploration of the aesthetic affordances of immersive performance scores. This paper describes several such applications in recent creative work by the author in which scores are generated in real-time and presented to performers via head-mounted displays. The historical context in which this work is situated is briefly described and various technical challenges and real-time performance constraints are discussed. Specific features of each application such as the visual transformation of scores through live audio signal analysis, the use of real-time natural language processing for dynamic updating of score parameters, and the anchoring of three-dimensional scores to real-world physical attributes are discussed and the paper concludes with a brief discussion of how these technical affordances offer exciting new possibilities for aesthetic and creative expression.

1. INTRODUCTION

Over the past ten years, there has been a significant renewal of interest in new forms of music notation and representation. Through the support of professional networks such as TENOR [1], a community of like-minded researchers and creative practitioners have explored how animated notations [2], three-dimensional notations [3], and reactive notations can provide new ways of thinking about musical form, new performance modalities, and offer fresh perspectives on aesthetic questions of engagement, creativity, embodiment, and temporal ontology.

In the creative practice and research of the author, a particularly exciting thread of this research has been greatly facilitated through the growing accessibility of VR and AR technologies. Through devices such as the HoloLens and the Oculus Quest 2, it has become possible to explore how notations can be developed which envelop performers in musical structure. Such immersive notations can be three-dimensional, static or dynamic, generative, or even responsive to the nuances of live performance. Before exploring such applications, it is helpful to briefly discuss the motivation behind this work and consider why one may want to immerse a performer in a musical score.

2. MOTIVATIONS AND CONTEXT

Given that common practice music notation is so widely used and understood, why might one wish to explore other ways of representing musical information? The question is by no means a new one as is evident in the often exquisitely designed scores produced during the fourteen-century Ars Subtilior movement, see Figure 1.

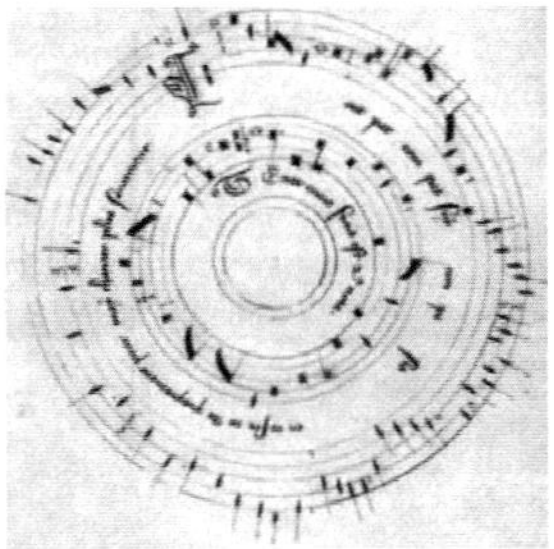

Figure 1. A circular score by Baude Cordier (1380-1440).

It was not until the 1950s however, when such questions were asked with greater force through the creative practice of composers such as John Cage, Earle Brown, Roman Haubenstock-Ramati, Cornelius Cardew, and Christian Wolff, amongst others. While the aesthetic trajectories of each of these composers was, of course, unique there are nevertheless common points of contact in their shared interest in non-conventional music notations. Firstly, and perhaps chief amongst these, is an exploration of non-linear temporal ontologies, i.e. musical forms that are not static but rather embrace variable orderings of musical material. Secondly, a desire to explore how performers can be engaged in the creative process by opening various formal aspects of the work to them which would ordinarily be fully prescribed in advance and thirdly, a desire to explore musical structures that are not based on pitch-time grids [4].

Many of these themes have continued to be explored in screen-based scores in the work of a new generation of contemporary composers such as Ryan Ross-Smith, Georg Hajdu, Cat Hope, Jason Freeman, and the author and new artistic areas of enquiry have emerged such as those involving extreme sight reading [5] and various other performance challenges related to reading information from a screen [6]. While the author has developed numerous screen-based scores in his own creative practice, the development of three-dimensional music notations has emerged as a key theme in much of his recent work and it has only been through the development of AR and VR technologies that the opportunity to explore new forms of creative expression has been afforded.

3. THREE-DIMENSIONAL AND IMMERSIVE NOTATION

For composers developing musical scores intended to be displayed on screens, one of the pressing challenges is how to overcome the limited display area in which information can be displayed. In traditional print media, while this is perhaps of tangential concern, it is addressed through the intuitive process of the page turn which allows new information to be presented. While the concept of a page turn still exists in screen scores, usually initiated by performers with a foot pedal, other more novel and perhaps idiomatic ways of updating information have been addressed through scrolling displays [7] or the animation of notational descriptors [8]. Neither of these techniques, however, are particularly useful when working with three-dimensional visualizations as the fundamental depth constraints of any two-dimensional display area remain. In works of the author such as *point studies no. 2* (2013), for any two pitched instruments, and computer, in which the work's score is represented by a three-dimensional node graph, see Figure 2, and displayed in OpenGL, the rotation of the score during performance is the only way in which depth-based information can be more easily discerned by the performers.

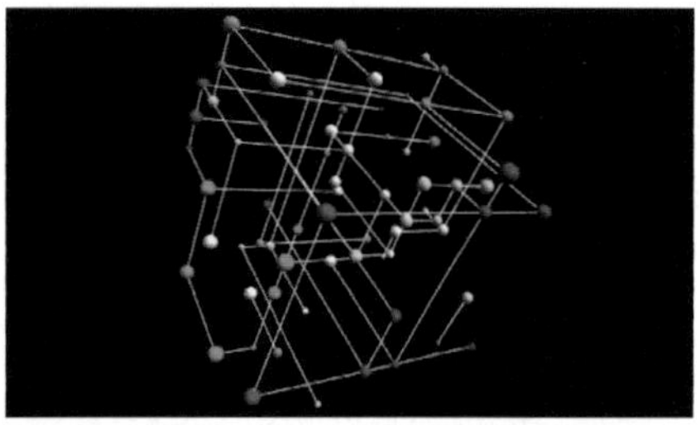

Figure 2. Screen snapshot from the score of the author's *point studies no. 2* (2013) for any two pitched instruments and computer. Each node represents the onset of a note with its color and size denoting pitch and dynamic respectively. The length of edges betwen nodes denotes the duration of a note.

With the growing development of VR and AR technologies, it is possible to create immersive, three-dimensional visualizations which more realisitically convey image depth and thus allow depth to be used as a formal determinant of musical structure. In the following discussion of three works, one of which is currently in progress, an exciting range of aesthetic possibilities have been opened which heretofore have been difficult if not impossible to investigate.

3.1 *5x3x3* (2019)

Written for the acclaimed Australian contemporary music ensemble ELISION and premiered in 2019, *5x3x3* for any three wind instruments, presents the three performers with a large three-dimensional graphic score which they each view through a Microsoft HoloLens. The physical exploration of the score's distribution in the performance space is a key aesthetic feature of the work, see Figure 3.

Figure 3. Performance of *5x3x3* (2019) at the Ian Potter Centre for the Performing Arts, Melbournw. Featuring Carl Rosman (clarinet), Ryan Williams (bass recorder), and Tamara Kohler (flute).

Employing a design aesthetic similar to *point studies no. 2*, the three-dimensional score for *5x3x3* presents a large node graph that is spatially distributed within the boundaries of the performance space. Each node represents the onset of a performed note with its color and size indicating different pitches and dynamic levels respectively, while the color and length of edges connecting nodes denote different pitches and their durations respectively, see Figure 4.

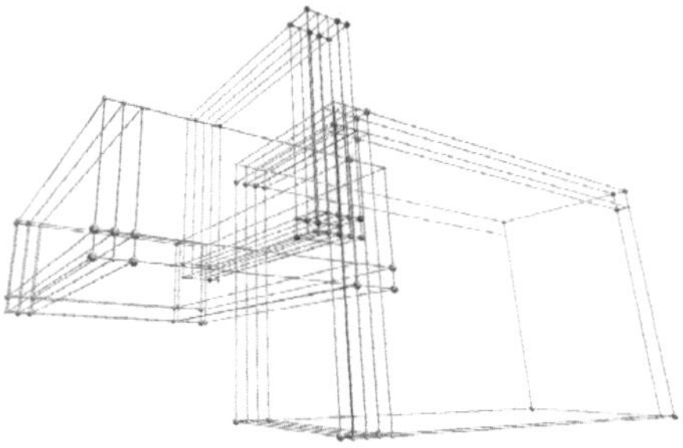

Figure 4. Static capture from the immersive score for *5x3x3*.

During performance the spatial position of the nodes is transformed, gradually filling the performance space, resulting in increasingly longer durations of performed notes. This transformation is mapped in advance and controlled through a Max patch, which sends information on node positions via UDP to each of the three HoloLenses [9]. In addition to the spatial remapping of nodes that takes place during performance, the curvature of edges connecting nodes is also transformed in response to the timbral fluctuations the performers elicit from their instruments. This is managed through a real-time FFT analysis within the same Max patch that determines the position of control points used in the Bezier curve generation, with wide timbral fluctuation generating greater edge curvatures. The position of control points is sent via UDP to each HoloLens with corresponding curvature calculated within the developed application. A schematic of the technical setup is presented in Figure 5.

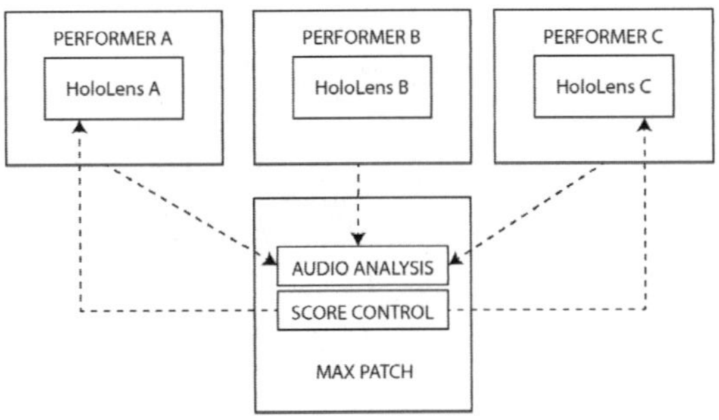

Figure 5. Technical schematic for *5x3x3*.

Given the real-world spatial positions of the score, the performers are required to physically move through the performance space in which the score is situated. This physical exploration, akin to a situationist dérive [10] is a critical aesthetic theme of the work and one which would have been extraordinarily difficult to emulate in any other form of score presentation. Clearly, given the need to maintain awareness of the real-world physical environment and ensure performer safety, it is a performance modality that could only be achieved in an AR space.

As the first work of the author's to feature AR technology, the development of *5x3x3* presented a number of unique and largely unforseen challenges ranging from the mundane, e.g. an inability of the HoloLens to connect to enterprise-based wireless networks, through to the more unexpected, e.g. how to ensure color mappings and hologram anchoring was not affected by performance lighting. Expected ergonomic issues related to the HoloLens did not prove to be particularly troubling for the performers but what was unexpected was a disconnect felt by some members of the audience in not knowing what the performers were experiencing as they physically traversed the performance space. While it is not customary for audience members to be able to view a performance score as it is being performed, it is hard to imagine how this experience could be satisfactorily conveyed.

3.2 *96 Postcards in Real Color* (2022)

96 Postcards in Real Color (2022), henceforth *96 Postcards*, was developed for the Neue Vocalsolisten of Stuttgart, one of the world's leading contemporary music vocal ensembles and was premiered in May 2022 in Stuttgart, see Figure 6. The work is for four to six vocalists each of whom wear an Oculus Quest 2 to view the performance score in which they are immersed. While the score for *96 Postcards* extends the node-edge design aesthetic developed in previous scores by the author, the design is somewhat unique in that its features are generated from data scraped from Instagram and subsequently analysed with various Python Natural Language Processing libraries. The title of the work is taken from French author Georges Perec's 1978 work *Deux Cent Quarante-Trois Cartes Postales en Coulers Veritables* [11], a series of postcard texts generated from simple combinatorial rules [12].

Figure 6. Rehearsal for *96 Postcards* with a score excerpt included beneath.

As a technology for presenting scores, virtual reality headsets have various constraints not least of which is that given the inability to see objects in the real-world performance space, there are serious potential safety issues. In *96 Postcards* each performer remains in a stationary position but turns around in a complete 360-degree rotation to read the score which encircles them in the VR scene. Given the work was developed for singers, there was no need to consider how hand-eye coordination issues might affect performance as they might if the work had been developed for a pianist, percussionist, or guitarist, for example.

The score for *96 Postcards* consists of a circular node graph which is uniquely instantiated for each performance. Nodes indicate the start of a sung pitch with a node's color and size denoting variations in pitch and dynamic respectively. Nodes are connected by thin white lines or edges which represent the duration of sung notes. Outside this ring of connected nodes in the VR scene, twelve panels are placed containing images collected from scrapes on Instagram locations from around the world. A unique Instagram text caption is positioned above each panel which provides information for the vocalists on how notes are to be articulated. During the performance, performers are instructed to freely read around the score from one node to another, musically exploring the myriad range of pathways presented as they traverse the full 360-degree node distribution. As in previous works of the author, the performance per se thus becomes an actualization of the latent possibilities presented by the non-linear, open form notational schema. A static snapshot from the VR scene in which the score is displayed is presented in Figure 7.

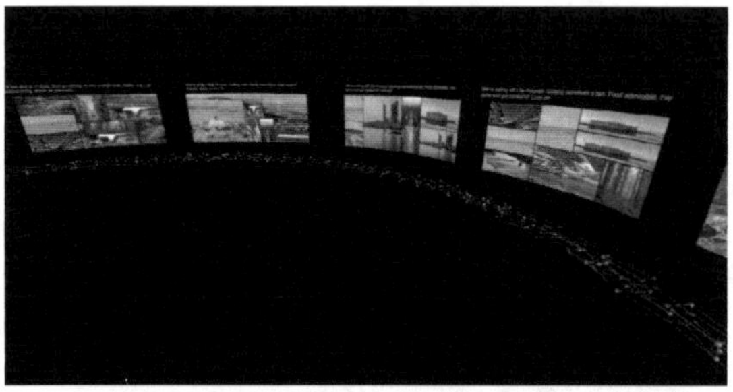

Figure 7. A static snapshot from the centre of the VR scene featuring a fragment of the performance score. An interconnected, three-dimensional grid of colored nodes is positioned in front of a panel containing various images gathered from Instagram with a single text caption positioned above.

Despite the unique instantiation of the node graph for each performance, the color distribution of nodes is predetermined in advance which ensures that there is a continuity of harmonic structure from one performance to another.

In addition to the use of NLP libraries to facilitate textual analysis, *96 Postcards* also uses the Photon Unity Networking (PUN) toolkit to ensure that the score, or VR scene, presented to each of the performers is consistent. Given that the performers do not interact with the score and merely passively observe and interpret it, the number of data synchronization calls made to the PUN network is minimized.

Vestibular effects commonly associated with VR were not an issue in performance. However, the speed with which singers turned around to read the score was certainly mitigated by issues of score readibility. Other UX issues related to scene design did, however, need to be considered most notably with respect to the use of text. While various notational representations of pitch articulations were considered in the development of *96 Postcards*, it was ultimately decided that performers were already expected to decode a significant amount of visual information and that the simple use of text would be the most natural way of indicating how pitches were to be articulated. The volume of text which could be displayed, was however limited by the display resolution of the Oculus Quest 2 at 1832 x 1920 per eye which resulted in the use of fonts no smaller than 40-point to remain legible.

3.3 *reTweets* (2023)

reTweets is a work for small ensemble currently being developed by the author. The work draws on many of the techniques developed for *5x3x3* and *96 Postcards* and features an immersive score displayed on VR head-mounted displays. The score presents real-time, three-dimensional visualizations of tweets scraped from Twitter. Tweet visualizations are progressively updated during performance of the work with all data sent from a Jupyter Notebook to the Oculus Quest via UDP.

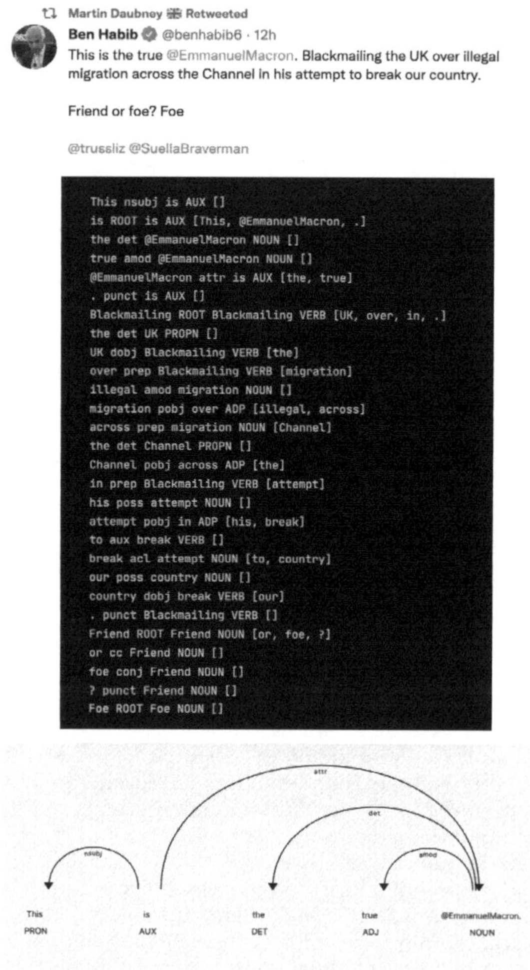

Figure 8. a) Original tweet, b) Tokenized with *spaCy*, c) Dependency parse of first five tokens with *spaCy*.

The process through which this is undertaken is somewhat complex and features the use of Python libraries *Tweepy* [13], *spaCy* [14], *Gensim* [15], and *sciKit* [16]. These four libraries provide access to the Twitter public API, allow tokenization and dependency parsing of a tweet text, determine word vectors for each word within a tweet, and perform dimensional reduction through Principal Component Analysis (PCA) respectively.

Tweets are scraped on keywords chosen in advance. To provide a diverse range of different tweets, it is best that these keywords are topical in nature. An example of one such returned tweet, on the keyword "Macron" is presented in Figure 8a with its tokenization and dependency structure shown in Figure 8b and 8c respectively.

Gensim returns word vectors on each token using a model pretrained on Google news. These vectors provide a mapping of a word within a multidimensional space and are commonly used in NLP to determine the similarity between words. By default, the dimensionality of these vectors is 100. Given the intent to develop visualizations of each tweet for use as performance scores, the dimensionality had to be reduced to three. This was achieved with *sciKit* and the corresponding visualization is shown in Figure 9.

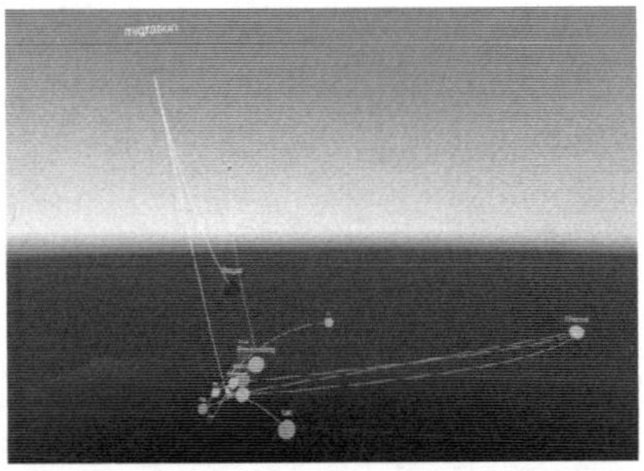

Figure 9. Three-dimensional visualization of the tweet from Figure 8a. Each node represents a word within a tweet with its spatial location derived from a dimensional reduction of its respective word vector. Edges connected nodes are determined through a dependency parse.

reTweets integrates responsiveness into its formal structure in a rather novel way. Like *5x3x3*, the musical nuances of each instrumentalist's performance is analyzed in Max with an FFT to extract certain key features from the incoming audio stream including measurements of pitch, intensity, harmonic complexity, and timbral fluctuation. These parameters are then applied as forces to the nodes within the visualization which generate new spatial coordinates. These transformed coordinates are subsequently mapped back through *sciKit* to generate new word vectors and *Gensim* to find the most closely mapped word before being posted through *Tweepy* as a new tweet to Twitter. The entire architecture of the work is outlined in Figure 10.

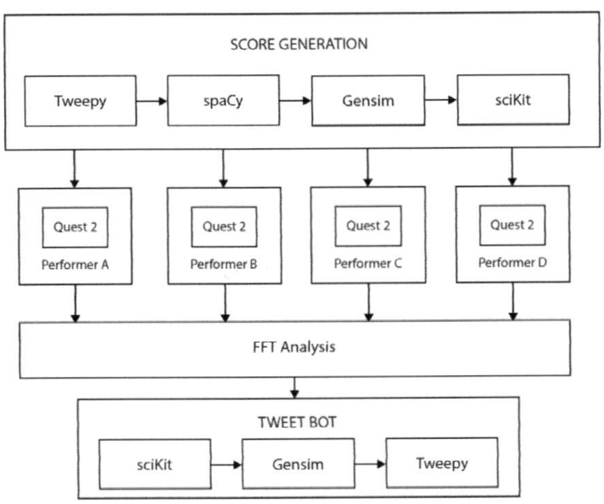

Figure 10. System architecture for *reTweets*.

4. FUTURE DIRECTIONS

Immersive performance scores for AR and VR technologies offer exciting possibilities for new forms of creative expression. One of these emerges from the correlation of the physical features of a performance space with a score's parameters. While the author has tentatively explored these possibilities in previous work where a three-dimensional performance score is aligned and anchored with a piano keyboard [16], the correlation of real-world spatial features with formal aspects of a musical structure is a unique affordance of AR technology. Aesthetically, the theme has been explored previously in the work of composers such as Xenakis [17], and more recently Rebecca Saunders, and Benedict Mason [18], with compositions that "sound-out" an architectural space but the ability to inscribe these properties into a score itself is somewhat unique. For the author's creative practice, this is most readily realized through the mapping of physical space to temporal properties of a score, as in *5x3x3*, where node locations, for example, might be mapped to vertices of the real-world space. Such possibilites do however, rely on an accurate way of spatially mapping a physical space and anchoring scores to those features. At present, this is a somewhat cumbersome and unreliable process with current AR hardware.

Another natural area in which this work would seem to lead is in the development of interactive scores for VR space. Such scores, which effectively become instruments, would help foster new paradigms of performance moving away from the traditional proscenium modes of performance towards ones in which collaboration and engagement become bearers of aesthetic value. Given the growing development of social VR, and software assets designed to facilitate multi-player gaming experiences, such a venture is perhaps timely.

5. CONCLUSION

While common practice notation has evolved to allow the salient features of a musical work to be described in a format suitable for performance, it is notable that these features have historically prioritized pitch and time. Dynamic and timbral nuance, for example, are poorly conveyed in such notation and musical forms foregrounding these qualities can only be approximated. The question of whether the dominance of pitch-time structures of musical form in the Western music tradition is purely due to the relative ease with which they can be notated is perhaps unanswerable. In any event, it is certainly the case that music notation goes well beyond simply conveying a set of instructions for performance but rather valorizes particular forms of aesthetic expression. In line with this argument, immersive scores offer new ways of thinking about musical structure and offer exciting possibilties for the aestheticization of collaborative, shared experiences. It is to be hoped that with the continual development of AR and VR technologies, new forms of creative expression exploring these possibilities will continue to be fostered which will in turn stimulate new areas of aesthetic enquiry.

6. REFERENCES

[1] https://network.tenor-conference.org/

[2] R. Ross-Smith, *A Practical and Theoretical Framework for Understanding Contemporary Animated Scoring Practices*. PhD Dissertation. Rensselsaer Polytechnic Institute, Troy, NY, 2016.

[3] D. Kim-Boyle. The 3D Score. In Proceedings of the 2017 International Conference on Technologies for Music Notation and Representation (TENOR 2017) (A Coruña, Spain, May 24-26).

[4] T. Wishart, *On Sonic Art*. Routledge, 1996.

[5] J. Freeman, "Extreme Sight Reading in Live Music Performance," *Computer Music Journal*, vol. 32, no. 3, pp. 25-41, Fall 2008.

[6] C. Hope and L. Vickery, "Visualising the Score: Screening Scores in Realtime Performance," *Proceedings of Diegetic Life Forms II: Creative Arts Practice and New Media Scholarship*. Edith Cowan University, Perth, Australia, 2011.

[7] L. Vickery, "The Evolution of Notational Innovations from the Mobile Score to the Screen Score," *Organised Sound*, 17(2), pp. 128-136, 2012.

[8] C. Fischer, "Understanding Animated Notation," *Proceedings of the 2015 International Conference on Technologies for Music Notation and Representation (TENOR 2015)*, Paris, 2015.

[9] D. Kim-Boyle and B. Carey. 3D Scores on the HoloLens. In *Proceedings of the 2019 International Conference on Technologies for Music Notation and Representation (TENOR 2019)* (Melbourne, Australia, July 23-27)

[10] G. Debord, "Théorie de la dérive," *La Lèvres Neus 9* (November 1956). Reprinted in *Internationale Situationniste* 2 (December 1958).

[11] G. Perec, "Deux Cent Quarante-Trois Cartes Postalles en Coulers Veritables," *Le Fou Parle*, 1978.

[12] T. Bonch-Osmolovskaya, "Combinatorial Greetings from Georges Perec," *Bridges 2018 Conference Proceedings*, Stockholm, 2018. Available: https://archive.bridgesmathart.org/bridges2018-253.pdf

[13] http://tweepy.org

[14] https://spacy.io

[15] https://radimrehurek.com/gensim/

[16] https://scikit-learn.org

[17] I. Xenakis, *Formalized Music: Thought and Mathematics in Composition*. Pendragon Press, 1992.

[18] D. Macleod, "Negotiating Space: A Composer's Perspective on Spatial Music," Unpublished conference paper from *Sounding out the Space: An International Conference on the Spatiality of Sound*. (Dublin, Ireland, November 2-4).

Spatial Sampling in Mixed Reality

Dr. Grégory Beller
Ligeti Zentrum, HfMT
Hamburg, Germany
gregory.beller@hfmt-hamburg.de
0009-0007-3553-4650

ABSTRACT

Spatial Sampler XR is a new musical instrument linking gesture capture to sound processing. In the same way that a sampler is an empty keyboard filled with sounds, Spatial Sampler XR uses gesture capture to transform the surrounding physical space into an area of keys for, recording, indexing and playing back samples. Spatial Sampler XR let the musician arrange the sound around him or her through gesture, creating a spatialized and interactive soundstage. A virtual reality headset adds to the instrument the ability to visualize the layout of sounds. The 3D immersion greatly facilitates their organization and increases the precision of the interaction. Several modes of play are possible and the interaction modalities vary according to the type of performance and the number of performers. This article first introduces the Synekine project, a ten-year research project from which the concept of spatial sampling is derived. It presents the technical devices used, the instruments created, the different modes of play in performative situations. The instrument relies on movement to link time and space. Thus, the Spatial Sampler XR is particularly suitable for movement artists as well as for extra-musical applications.

1. INTRODUCTION

For the past ten years, through residencies and artistic creations, *the Synekine Project*[1] has invited performers to question the intimate relationship between vocal gestures and manual gestures, through the manipulation of scenic devices based on new technologies. Metaphorically, the preeminent neuromotor link between voice and gesture is closed by "creative prostheses" joining the capture of movement to the transformation of the voice by artificial intelligence. Linking space and time through movement then transforms the search for sound into a scenic exploration.

[1] http://www.gregbeller.com/2014/01/synekine-project/

This paper presents the Synekine Project according to several dimensions. After the exhibition of the scientific basis and the genesis of the project, the new organology developed is described in chronological relation with the artistic works produced. Although it generates devices that can be used in other fields of application such as therapeutic rehabilitation, commercial signage or even dance and music education, these corollary results are not presented in this article for the sake of clarity of presentation.

Researches on the augmented voice in the theater [1, 2, 3, 4] led to the instinctive, expressive and pleonastic relationship between vocality and gesturality. The faculty of speaking with the hands would not only result from cultural origins, but would also result from a deep neuronal relation connecting the speech to the gestures of the hands [5]. By analogy to synesthesia, a phenomenon by which two or more senses of perception are associated, "synekinesia" would reflect our ability to associate two or more motor senses.

There is ample evidence for the ubiquitous link between manual motor and speech systems, in infant development, in deictic pointing, and in repetitive tapping and speaking tasks [6]. So, it is obvious to most people to clap their hands with every syllable spoken when we speak. Metaphorically, the Synekine Project proposes to "complete" this neuronal loop by artificially establishing an "external" link between vocal gesture and manual gesture.

The voice is conventionally captured by a microphone, while the positions and dynamics of the hands are informed by different movement capture processes, which have changed from one residence to another (glove-accelerometers, Genki Wave, LeapMotion, Kinect, Optitrack and Metaquest2, see Table 1).

Year	Work	Instrument	Gesture Sensor	Hand Button	Trans-mission	Hand tracking	Sound Recording	Visualisation
2011	Luna Park	SpokHands	XBEE V1	X	Wifi	X	Wireless headset	X
2013	Babil-on	Body Choir	XBEE V1	XBEE V1	Wifi	Kinect V1	Wireless headset	activity only
2014	TIIIME	Hand Sampling, Hyper Ball, Wired Gestures, Gesture Scape, Body Choir, Sound Space	XBEE V2	XBEE V2	Wifi	Kinect V2	Wireless headset	video for gesture scape
2015	Babil-on V2	Hand Sampling, Hyper Ball, Body Choir, Sound Space	XBEE V2	XBEE V2	Wifi	Kinect V2	Wireless headset	X
2017	TEDx Paris	Body Choir	X	X	X	Kinect V2	Wireless headset	X
2016	The Memory Palace - Installation	Sound Space	X	Kinect Gesture Recognition	X	Kinect V2	Ambient mic	Projected 3D space
2016	The Memory Palace - Performance	Sound Space	XBEE V2	XBEE V2	Wifi	Kinect V2	Wireless headset	X
2017	Fissures	Hand Sampling, Body Choir, Sound Space	XBEE V2	XBEE V2	Wifi	Kinect V2	Wireless headset	X
2020	Birth of a Tree	Spatial trigger, Spatial looper, Sound Space	Genki Wave	Genki Wave	BLE	Kinect V2	Wireless headset	X
2020	Air Sampling #001	Spatial trigger, Spatial looper, Sound Space	Genki Wave	Genki Wave	BLE	Kinect V2	Static mics	X
2021	Residency UME	Spatial trigger, Spatial looper, Sound Space	OptiTrack	Genki Wave	BLE	OptiTrack	Wireless headset	X
2022	Air Sampling #002	Spatial Sampler VR	Metaquest 2	Metaquest 2	Airlink	Metaquest 2	Static mics	VR + video
2022	The Vanishing Mirror	Spatial Sampler VR	Metaquest 2	Metaquest 2	Airlink	Metaquest 2	Static mics	VR only
2023	The Fault	Spatial Sampler VR	Metaquest 2	Metaquest 2	Airlink	Metaquest 2	Static mics	VR only
2023	Air Sampling #003 Macht macht macht	Spatial Sampler VR	Metaquest 2	Metaquest 2	Airlink	Metaquest 2	Wireless headset	VR + video
2023	Air Sampling #003 Touching Spirits	Spatial Sampler VR	Metaquest 2	Metaquest 2	Airlink	Metaquest 2	Static mics	VR + video
2024	TBA	Spatial Sampler XR	Hololens2	Hololens2	Wifi	Hololens2	Wireless headset	XR + video

Table 1. Chronology of the works realized within the framework of the Synekine project presenting the instruments elaborated from various technical devices.

Figure 1. Different hardware used to realize the instruments: Top left an XBEE sensor, bottom left a Genki Wave ring, top right a Kinect V2, bottom right two Optitrack cameras.

Between the two, different computer programs based on artificial intelligence, allow the direct manipulation of sound by gesture or the learning of temporal relationships between vocal and gestural. In both cases, the result is a new organology made up of different intangible musical instruments offering the user to spread the voice in space, to multiply it, to segment it and to manipulate it.
Taking advantage of the instinctive nature of the voice - gesture link, and taking advantage of new technologies allowing the joint capture of the sound of the voice and the coordinates of the gesture in real time, the Synekine Project has deployed across artistic productions and residencies, a new organology of sound, invisible and intangible instruments belonging to new Human-Computer Interactions. Motivated by artistic practice, the development of this organology is presented here in a genealogical form mixing innovations and creations.

2. GENESIS: EXPRESSIVITY, SENSORS AND LUNA *PARK*

On generative models of expressivity and their applications for speech and music, an artificial intelligence algorithm based on a corpus of expressive sentences, has been used to generate an "emotional" speech, by modulating the prosody of a "neutral" utterance [7, 8, 9, 10]. During the development of this synthesizer of the emotion in the voice came the desire to control the prosody by the gesture [11]. At the same time, instrumental gesture sensors were developed allowing the measurement of the dynamics of a bow by integrating small accelerometers and gyroscopes. The data related to movement is transmitted in real time by WIFI to a computer which triggers sounds and modulates effects according to the dynamics of the gesture [12]. In 2010, as part of the creation of *Luna Park*[2], a musical theater work by Georges Aperghis, these sensors have been integrated into gloves and a first instrument called *SpokHands* has been developed, which literally made it possible to speak with the hands [13, 14, 15, 16].

SpokHands[3] *allows the triggering and modulation of voice samples by aerial percussion and hand elevation. Like a vocal Theremin, the instrument offers the performer the option of three-voice polyphony (her.his own and both hands) or control of text-to-speech parameters.*

In this case, the natural division of a conductor's brain is used, the left brain (right hand) for the segmental part, and the right brain (left hand) for expressivity. The percussive gestures of the right-hand trigger pre-selected syllables whose pitch and intensity are modulated by continuous gestures of the left hand. A particular aerial percussion technique aimed at triggering sounds in a temporally precise manner without hurting the self has been practiced by a percussionist. Indeed, the absence of haptic feedback from a physical object could cause, in the long run, pain in the handles which acted as a stop to the percussive movement [17].

[2] http://www.gregbeller.com/2011/06/luna-park/
[3] http://www.gregbeller.com/2011/06/spokhands/

Figure 2. Gloves accelerometers allowing the capture of the gestural dynamics used in Babil-on, CMMR2013, Marseille, France.

3. *BABIL-ON*: FROM SPEECH TO TIME

Babil-on[4], for solo and electronic voice is an augmented musical theatre performance. Like a close-up, a "Speech" character discovers his own voice, cuts it up, superimposes it, spreads it around him, multiplies it, and reveals the emotional charge intrinsic to the language. A pair of button-rings have been added to the sensor-gloves allowing for the picking and erasing of voice samples on the fly. Thus, *SpokHands* and the triggering of pre-made sounds evolved into *Hand Sampling*, in which the vocal flow is cut and recombined in percussive gestures.

Hand Sampling[5] *allows the performer to cut her.his voice in real time, and recombine immediately by the gesture. It involves percussive gestures that will segment and trigger vocal fragments. The length of these fragments can vary from syllable to sentence. The order of the re-played segments can be sequential, random or palindromic, which allows different playing modes. In addition, the quality of the gesture influences the quality of the sound perceived, making the instrument expressive.*

To the fast capture of the dynamics of the gesture by the accelerometer gloves has been added the relatively slow capture of the absolute position of the hands in space, by the use of depth cameras of the Kinect type [18]. This made it possible to obtain, in addition to the fine temporal precision of the percussive type triggering, the continuous control of sound processes according to the posture and the spatial position of the hands. On the other hand, the sensor brought other constraints such as a reduction in the playing area, a single performer possible, the need for a phase of calibration and detection of the skeleton, the risk of infrared disturbance by lights. The *Body Choir* uses the hand position to control a choir effect and the *Hyper Ball* to control a granular synthesizer.

[4] The composition benefited from IRCAM's artistic research residency program and the piece was premiered by Richard Dubelski in Marseille, at the Théâtre des Bernardines, in 2013, as part of CMMR 2013: http://www.gregbeller.com/2013/10/babil-on/
[5] http://www.gregbeller.com/2014/02/hand-sampling/

*The **Body Choir**[6] transforms a singer into a choir. This virtual choir accompanies the singer according to her.his gestures and the postures s.he adopts. Singing involves movement of the body. This movement is captured and used to magnify the singer's musical intentions. The posture of the body and the sung note modulate in real time the harmony, the number of voices, or the spatial density of the choir.*

*The **Hyper Ball**[7] takes the form of a virtual sound ball, which the participant waters with her.his voice and modulates with her.his gesture. The position, size and orientation of the ball influence the height, density and volume of the sound generated. This type of musical activity, by its constitution, causes choreographic movements.*

Figure 3. Author performing with the Hyper Ball in Babil-on V2, ISEA2016, Vancouver, Canada.

In *Babil-on V2*[8] The Kinect V2 replaced the V1 offering better acuity in capturing movement, greater flexibility of use and the possibility of following the hands of several people at the same time. Another pair of button-rings have been added to the sensor gloves. From a compositional point of view, this second pair of button-rings offers free navigation in the structure of a work whose duration of each scene is flexible according to performer's own perception of time.

4. *TIIME*: FROM TIME TO MEMORY:

TIIME[9] stages three performers who play gestural, sound, visual and temporal mirror effects, in an apparent collective improvisation of which emerge from temporal themes: perception, memory, movement. the temporal relationship between vocal and manual gestures is modelled by artificial intelligence. On stage, a performer feeds a machine with his own vocal and gestural catalogue, then *Wired Gestures* restores fragments of this vocality in a way that is synchronous with the recognition and tracking of new gestures.

__Wired Gestures__[10] dynamically links voice to gesture, in an artificial way. The machine simultaneously records a voice gesture and a manual gesture [19]. *It learns the temporal relationship between the two. Then it reproduces the voice, when the performer repeats the same gesture. The nuances of timing in the gesture are then heard as prosodic variations of the voice, and it becomes possible to break down the expressivity.*

Visual extension, *Gesture Scape* records jointly and categorizes voice, gesture and video. Then new gestures, either manual or vocal will activate the visual and auditory archive. Video capture is introduced as a referential element of sound time. Not only does the manual gesture reproduce the sound of the voice, it can now also reproduce the image of the performer at the time of recording. Gesture Scape can be seen as the visual extension of Wired Gestures. The performer dances with her.his double, in a dialogue made of unison and counterpoint with the past, finding her.his inspiration in the lapsus of memory.

__Gesture Scape__[11] jointly records voice, gesture and video. Then, new gestures will activate this memory. The performer animates the video, by reproducing the same gesture, or by repeating the same associated sound.

Figure 4. Jean-Charles Gaume practicing the Gesture Scape, TIIIME 2014, Marseille, France

The performer dances with her.his double, in a dialogue made of unison and counterpoint, inspired by lapsus of memory. From the development of these two devices, based solely on the dynamics of the gesture and not on its location, was born the desire to be able to arrange and organize it in space. Symbolically, a wave of the hand, placed above the head, to say goodbye, differs from a refusal, however expressed by the same gesture, but located below the shoulder. From a performative point of view, the staging of learners manipulating learning machines has necessarily questioned the situation of memory.

5. *THE MEMORY PALACE*: FROM MEMORY TO PROCESS

The Memory Palace[12] is a mnemonic device practiced since antiquity allowing for memorizing long lists by arranging

[6] http://www.gregbeller.com/2014/05/body-choir/
[7] http://www.gregbeller.com/2014/03/hyper-ball/
[8] Babil-on V2 has been premiered in Vancouver, Simon Fraser University, ISEA2016: http://www.gregbeller.com/2015/08/babil-on-v2/
[9] TIIME, scene44, N + N Corsino, France, Marseille, 2014 with Richard Dubelski, Stéphany Ganachaud and Jean-Charles Gaume, in dialogue with Dr. Jennifer Coull, cognitive neuroscientist specializing in the study of the functional and neuronal substrates of temporal attention and synchronization: https://synekine.com/creation/tiiime/

[10] http://www.gregbeller.com/2014/02/wired-gestures/
[11] http://www.gregbeller.com/2014/04/gesture-scape/
[12] Three installations and a choreographic performance, all entitled *The Memory Palace*, were created during the FACTS - Bordeaux and EXPERIMENTA - Grenoble festivals in 2017, with the support of IRCAM and

the elements of these in imaginary places [20]. The construction of an interior architecture sensitive, has been realized with the *Sound Space*, a choreographic musical instrument linking space and time through movement. The surrounding space becomes a key zone in which the voice can be deposited and awakened by the gesture.

Sound Space[13] *is a choreographic musical instrument which links space and time, through movement. It transforms the physical space surrounding the performer, into a zone in which s.he can place her.his voice and awaken it by gesture. By drawing her.his voice, s.he creates a unique soundstage, while evolving within it, in a creative process. The space then vibrates with a sound quality in line with the quality of movement.*

Parable of the mnemonic, the installation transforms the place in which it is exhibited into a collective sound sculpture. Each participant is involved in the creation of a work of which s.he constitutes one of the many voices. Her.His gestures act as a reveler of the invisible sculpture. S.He can contribute to it by depositing elements of stories, sounds, or even songs that he can immediately recall in a creative process. A virtual but yet very audible forum, *The Memory Palace* acts as an indicator of the borders of the intimate, confronting the participant with the direct and immediate use of her.his voice imprint by others. In this mediation, the physical space, however empty, resonates with the different memories delivered by the participants in a temporal polyphony. Two sound installations based on the principle of *Sound Space* were presented.
One of the two installations uses a Kinect V2 for the localization and recognition of gestures, an ambient microphone as well as a video projection which materializes the sound traces of the participants on a screen. Two people were able to record sounds and play back the sounds of the others. The recording and erasing of sounds were controlled by gesture recognition (stone, leaf, scissors). The representation on a 2D screen of the 3D space was a great help for the audience and invite us to use a 3D visual representation using holography or mixed reality.
Within this setup, the dancer Valencia James delivers a musical choreography involving personal memories, ancestral traces and imaginary characters. The choreographic process consists of the progressive materialization of a memory palace by the deployment at different points of the stage of characters combining sound quality and quality of movement. Then, a free wandering generates by interpolation a new sound space which in turn provokes new states of the body. Everything happens as if the dancer were making an improvisation with herself and the traces of memory that she has just placed on the stage.

6. *BIRTH OF A TREE*: FROM PROCESS TO INSTRUMENT

As part of a Scientiarum Musicae doctorate[14] new technical gesture capture devices have been gradually being tested and integrated, such as the Genki Wave accelerometer rings, the Optitrack Motion Capture system, the Meta Quest 2 virtual reality headset and currently the Hololens 2. Spatial Sampling paradigm has been developed [21]. The constantly renewed interest in the device *Sound Space* in different artistic configurations stems from its adaptability. Indeed, it is an empty and silent box at the start, just like the musical sampler. So other instruments were derived from the hybridization of these two concepts and tested in the creation of *Birth of a Tree*[15]. They are the basis of the creative improvisation process of the *Air Sampling*[16] series.
Air Sampling is a series of improvised performances in which a sound source is sampled and distributed in space in real time. In the first performance #001, the sound source is given by Lin Chen on percussion and vocals. The author, playing the *Sound Space*, *Spatial Trigger* and *Spatial Looper* instruments, records and plays the samples in space. They perform with the percussionist an improvised musical choreography of which percussions are the only acoustic source. In the 1970s, the sampler revolutionized music production. This electronic music instrument, whose memory is empty at the beginning, allows the musician to create her.his own universe from percussion samples, ensembles, groups of instruments or orchestras and can also serve as a platform for musical creation.

Spatial Sampler[17] *substitutes the midi keyboard which classically indexes the samples, with spatial coordinates describing the positions of the hands.*

Spatial Trigger *allows the automatic segmentation of a sound and its distribution in space by the gesture, then the selection of one of these fragments according to its position and its triggering by aerial percussion.*

Spatial Looper *allows the mixing of several sound loops according to the proximity of the hands, as well as the generation of music from the fragments distributed in space. Many musicians are now familiar with the "looper" or live looping. One of the main difficulties in this art is dealing with multiple layers of samples (usually dealt with a guitar pedal). The Spatial Looper transforms the space surrounding the performer into a spatial sequencer and makes it easier to not only access the different layers but also to remember them.*

ADAMI. This work cycle benefited from an artistic research residency at IDEX - University of Bordeaux, in scientific companionship with the LaBRI: https://synekine.com/creation/le-palais-de-la-memoire/

[13] The Sound Space won the prize for technical excellence during the Guthman competition for new musical instruments: http://www.gregbeller.com/2014/05/sound-space/

[14] PhD in the framework of the KiSS program - Kinetics in Sound and Space - at the Hochschule für Musik und Theater Hamburg, Germany,

[15] http://www.gregbeller.com/2020/01/birth-tree/

[16] http://www.gregbeller.com/2020/10/air-sampling-001/

[17] http://www.gregbeller.com/2022/06/spatial-sampler-xr/

Figure 5. *Air Sampling #001*, with Lin Chen and video by Janina Luckow, 2020, Hamburg, Germany.

7. *AIR SAMPLING*: FROM INSTRUMENT TO EXPRESSION

For *Air Sampling #002*[18], VR versions of the *Sound Space*, the *Spatial Trigger* and the *Spatial Looper* instruments were created and tested in a performance situation[19]. An OpenGL representation allows the performer to visualize the position of the recorded sounds in a Meta Quest 2 headset, which greatly facilitates the organization of the session and allows for greater spatio-temporal accuracy.
The graphical representation of the recorded sounds also offers the possibility to draw 3D structures in the virtual space. The other performers and the audience can see the structure emerging from the gestures through video projection. Several performance situations have been explored with or without sharing the representation of the structure with the audience through video projection. Making it visible facilitates the understanding of the instrument by the audience but unbalances the performance if other musicians contribute. The other musicians only show the scores and their interpretation choices in front of them through the sound produced. In *Vanishing Mirror*, the performer is the only one to visualize the recording of the sounds produced by a piano-cello-vocal trio. Different modes of interaction with the sound sources have been explored, from the duet with a percussionist in *AirSampling #002*, to the live sampling of an ensemble of seven instruments in *The Fault*[20].
While Virtual Reality allows for a better organization of the sounds recorded and produced, it has the unfortunate side effect of visually cutting the performer off from the other musicians as well as the audience. Not only does it reduce the facial expression of the performer whose eyes are no longer visible, but the rupture of the visual contact of the performer with the others can generate complex situations for the synchronization in a comprovisation situation. In *AirSampling #003*[21] the strolling public interacts with the performer, who has a microphone. A protocol must then be established between the participating visitor and the performer in order to synchronize the production of sound on the one hand with the gesture of the other.
The total obstruction of the visual contact in situation of comprovisation can cause an interesting situation of performance, but can also harm the connivance between the public, the musicians and the perfomer made "blind". As holographic video is not yet mature enough, mixed reality seems to be the way to reduce the loss of visual contact. The evolution of the *Spatial Sampler VR* to the *Spatial Sampler XR* is currently being developed with the Hololens 2 mixed reality technology. This evolution implies the substitution of controllers by gesture recognition, thus reducing the playability of the instrument by decreasing its response time. Apart from the Optitrack system which operates at 120 frames per second, the other systems based on video or depth sensors do not offer a small enough latency to allow aerial percussion (latency lower than 20ms). Just as we added acceleration sensors to the data from the Kinect, the fusion of gesture recognition data with data from on-board accelerometers (Xbee sensors or Genki Wave rings) is being considered to improve gameplay in mixed reality.

Figure 6. *The Fault*, Opera composed by the g. Beller, 2023, Hamburg, Germany. In the background, a representation of a 3D sculpture elaborated from the sounds of the instrumentalists.

8. CONCLUSION

This article relates ten years of research and artistic production accompanied by technological development. In chronological form, it exposes the development of the research theme of spatial sampling, the new musical instruments elaborated through the evolution of the technologies of gesture capture as well as the artistic stakes approached in different works. From the link between gesture and voice, the research has evolved towards the manipulation of spatially situated media. From Hand Sampling or spatial sampler to sound space, different instruments make movement the link between time and space. The technical developments are based on the evolution of technologies for capturing gestures. The fusion of data from the capture of the dynamics of the gesture, the position of the hands in the space and the sound, allows the elaboration of an interactive sound scene. In performance, improvisation, comprovisation or composition situations, different modes of play are presented. The creation of about fifteen works with these instruments gives a context to the artistic stakes of spatial sampling.
Virtual reality allows to represent and manipulate "sounds located in space" in an environment comparable to that of a 3D painting software. The custom arrangement of media

[18] http://www.gregbeller.com/2022/06/air-sampling-002/
[19] http://www.gregbeller.com/2022/06/spatial-sampler-xr/
[20] http://www.gregbeller.com/2023/01/the-fault/
[21] http://www.gregbeller.com/2023/04/air-sampling-003/

whose recording and playback is done on the fly inaugurates the possibility of "spatially situated media" editing. Compared to modern sequencers whose organization of windows and sounds is constrained by 2D, the possibility of freely organizing media content in 3D space seems to accelerate the work of the editor, who joins spatial memory to content memory. The use of the memory palace in the audio-visual editing activity can greatly facilitate the access to the contents and accelerate the work steps without requiring any particular cognitive dispositions of the user.

Acknowledgments

The author would like to thank the supervisors of the KiSS program - Kinetics in Sound and Space, Prof. Dr. Georg Hajdu (HfMT Hamburg), Prof. Thomas Görne (HAW Hamburg), Prof. Dr. Jacob Sello (HfMT Hamburg) Nina Noeske (HfMT Hamburg), Prof. Sabina Dhein (HfMT Hamburg), Prof. Dr. Julius Heinicke (HfMT Hamburg), Dr. Rama Gottfried (HfMT Hamburg), as well as its coordinator Dr. Benjamin Helmer (HfMT Hamburg). This work is partially supported by the project "Stage_2.0: Alsterphilharmonie. Die Bühne als Ort des künstlerischen Wissenstransfers und der gesellschaftlichen Teilhabe" and "Ligeti Zentrum" and by the TransferBüro of the HfMT Hamburg. I would like to thank all those who have contributed to this artistic research.

REFERENCES

[1] G. Beller, "Arcane d'Un mage en été", *Théâtre Publique*, n° 200, 2011.

[2] G. Beller, "In-vivo: laboratoire de recherche et d'expérimentation autour du son pour le théâtre", *Towards a History of Sound in Theatre*, 2012.

[3] G. Beller, "L'IRCAM et la voix augmentée au théâtre: Les nouvelles technologies sonores au service de la dramaturgie", *L'Annuaire théâtral*, Numéro 56–57, p. 195–205, 2014.

[4] G. Beller, "Spectacle vivant: des voix imaginaires aux monstres vocaux", *InaGlobal*, 2017.

[5] J. M. Iverson, S. Goldin-Meadow, "Why people gesture when they speak", *Nature* 396, 228, 1998.

[6] B. Parrell, L. Goldstein, S. Lee, D. Byrd, "Spatiotemporal coupling between speech and manual motor actions". *Journal of Phonetics*, Volume 42, Pages 1-11, 2014.

[7] G. Beller, "Analyse et Modèle Génératif de l'Expressivité: application à la parole et à l'interprétation musicale", *PhD Sorbonne – IRCAM*, 2009.

[8] G. Beller, "Transformation of Expressivity in Speech", *The Role of Prosody in the Expression of Emotions in English and in French*, ed. Peter Lang, 2009.

[9] G. Beller, "Expresso: Transformation of Expressivity in Speech", *Speech Prosody*, Chicago, 2010

[10] P. Laukka, T. Eerola, N. Thingujam, T. S. Yamasaki, G. Beller, "Universal and Culture-Specific Factors in the Recognition and Performance of Musical Affect Expressions", *Emotion, American Psychological Association*, Vol 13(3), 434-449, 2013

[11] C. d'Alessandro, A. Rilliard and S. LeBeux, "Chironomic stylization of intonation", *JASA*, 129(3):1594-1604, 2011.

[12] F. Bevilacqua, N. Rasamimanana, E. Fléty, S. Lemouton, F. Baschet, "The augmented violin project: research, composition and performance report." *In 6th International Conference on New Interfaces for Musical Expression* (NIME 06), Paris, 2006

[13] G. Beller, G. Aperghis. "Contrôle gestuel de la synthèse concaténative en temps réel dans Luna Park", *IRCAM Internal Research Report*, 2011

[14] G. Beller, G. Aperghis, "Gestural Control of Real-Time Concatenative Synthesis in Luna Park", *P3S International Workshop on Performative Speech and Singing Synthesis*, Vancouver, pp. 23-28, 2011.

[15] G. Beller. "Gestural Control Of Real Time Concatenative Synthesis", *ICPhS*, Hong Kong, 2011

[16] G. Beller, "Gestural Control of Real-Time Speech Synthesis in Luna Park", *SMC*, Padova, 2011

[17] G. Beller, "The Synekine Project", *MOCO*, Paris, 2014

[18] S. Kean, J.C. Hall, P. Perry, "Microsoft's Kinect SDK. In: Meet the Kinect." *Apress. https://doi.org/10.1007/978-1-4302-3889-8_8,* 2011.

[19] J. Françoise, N. Schnell, R. Borghesi, F. Bevilacqua. "Probabilistic Models for Designing Motion and Sound Relationships". *NIME*, London, 2014.

[20] F. Yates, "The Art of Memory", *University of Chicago Press,* 1966

[21] G. Beller. "Sound Space and Spatial Sampler", *MOCO*, Vancouver, 2015

The Cybernetic "Trap" Kit: Interface Design Considerations for Virtual Augmentation

Steven Lewis
University of California, Irvine
smlewis2@uci.edu

ABSTRACT

The CV Drum Tracker is a cybernetic extension of the drumset that aims to reshape the performer's interaction and musical relationship with the acoustic instrument. It prompts users to embrace a systems-oriented, iterative method of design and performance, to explore the gestural and musical potentialities in a space where they serve as mediators between the physical instrument and its virtual components. In digital design, affordances actualized by the end-user correspond to the inherent constraints integrated within the system. The establishment of these constraints transpires through parameter mapping, and the perceptual affordances of a given system manifest as the user scrutinizes and navigates its predetermined boundaries. Each design phase culminating in the current iteration is presented and discussed through an analytical framework centered on constraints and affordances. This framework serves to highlight the dynamic relationship existing between these two crucial components in any interactive digital music software, and the procedural nature by which these design relationships formulate for both the programmer and performer of the system.

1. INTRODUCTION

In response to the rapid expansion of technological progress during the nineteenth and mid twentieth centuries in the United States, the "contraption kit," underwent a process of standardization into the modular assemblage of mechanized devices and fabricated physical materials referred to as the modern drumset. At that exact point in the decades-long process of this standardization, the drumsets were not considered revolutionary in terms of their designs, nor did they challenge a drummer to change their physical relationship to the instrument. This process towards a uniform instrument design was a necessary step in being able to realize what the drummer already wanted to do during live performance. However, the path leading up to this point in standardization included countless individual efforts of remarkable ingenuity and mechanical invention, each of them contributing towards the evolution of the instrument's construction, and by extension, its vocabulary.

The system presented in this paper, referred to as the *CV Drum Tracker,* is a cybernetic extension of this standardization, one which represents a singular effort towards reorienting the performer's physical relation with a hybridized version of the instrument. It encourages a potential user to think in terms of how computer programmers would conceptualize and procedurally apply a systems-oriented design method, which then emboldens their performance to explore the gestural possibilities and musical potentialities within a space that situates them as the mediator between the physical instrument and its cybernetic components. Through the design of computational systems, the implementation of multimodal data inputs into the system, and the leveraging of computer-vision technologies into a sensor-controlled visual interface, this approach to design can be thought of as a virtual augmentation of the drumset. This technological mediation, and the iterative nature of programming based on process-oriented outcomes forms the basis for what will be referred here to as *Procedural Aesthetics*. It is through this concept that the *CV Drum Track Tracker* exists in its current iteration. The desired outcome of the system is not focused on completing one particular piece of music, but on establishing a computational approach towards crafting an entire environment or infrastructure through which the combining of multimedia formats and multi-modal performance techniques could be achieved. The following sections will explore the design considerations encountered while programming performance systems for camera-controlled, computer vision technologies and the virtually augmented drumset.

2. DESIGN CONSIDERATIONS

2.1. Designing for Transparency

The drums are a physically demanding instrument. Players must possess coordination between four limbs, and utilize these skills according to the temporal and dynamic fluctuations occurring in the music. Depending of the musical style and the performance model of the ensemble, the drum set player may be responsible for outlining the structural form of the overall piece while simultaneously executing the micro rhythmic phrases that comprise a macro-musical interaction with a soloist. Within a free jazz context, these physical movements can be thought of as "hypergestures" [1] as each individual musicians' gestural activity can "invent their own creative musical trajectories" while simultaneously influencing the way in which other players in ensemble create trajectories of their own. The skill required to perform such a balancing act is premised on practice and experience of course, but can be accelerated through the means of acquiring tactile and kinetic muscle memory in combination with critical, audible feedback [2].

With that in consideration, knowing a physical gesture "feels good" (or physically familiar) is an important factor in having the confidence to perceive that a musical gesture "sounds right" within the context of a broader creative trajectory being created in real-time. If the drum surface is altered, or if the player is required to be tethered to some device that they are otherwise unaccustomed to wearing, this may alter the way the player moves during a performance. Moreover, placing nearly anything on the surface of the drum will change its natural resonance, timbre, and the tactile sensation of playing the instrument. Depending on the placement of these materials, the drummer may have to alter their physical approach to the instrument in meaningful ways [3]. This could dissuade drummers from experimenting with electro-acoustic musical practices altogether, as previous research has revealed that "improvisors who perform simultaneously on acoustic instruments and electronic devices are likely to bring different means to their use of electronic gestures" [4].

An indelible challenge in constructing an interactive system for the drum set is in designing it to be as transparent as possible during live performance. The system's design must function so as to not impede on the motions through which a drum set player executes a musical thought, nor on the sensory experience of playing the electro-acoustic instrument. In order to design an effective 2D screen-based musical interface, the programmer must apply their understanding of what perceptual psychologist J.J. Gibson refers to as his Theory of Affordances [5]:

"The *affordances* of the environment are what it *offers* the animal, what it *provides or furnishes*, either for good or ill. The verb to *afford* is found in the dictionary, but the noun affordance is not. I have made it up. I mean by it something that refers to both the environment and the animal in a way that no existing term does. It implies the complementarity of the animal and the environment."

This definition of affordances was made in the context of how mammals perceive the physical environment around them. Designer Don Norman coined the phrase "Perceptual Affordances" [6] to refer to the options unique to virtual, screen-based environments. To Norman, there is distinction to be made between the affordances provided by physical components that comprise the computer (or any real-world tool or environment) - the keyboard, the trackpad, built-in camera, to name a few - compared to the options provided to the user through the design of computer software. This distinction informs his approach to human-computer interaction, which he refers to as "human centered, natural-based design" [7]. This is an approach to designing environments where humans do not sense any type of resistance or struggle when interacting with a piece of virtual technology, and instead solely focus on achieving the desired end results of using any given tool. Often referred to as "natural design," Norman's design prioritizes the need to maximize the transparency involved in the interactions between humans and technology, to the point where humans ultimately forget that they are entering a technologically-mediated space at all [8]. Such design principles aim to enhance the transparency of use to the point where the experience feels unmediated through a particular technology at all.

As music technologist Thor Magnusson has stated, conceptual simplicity, and common use-functions are derived from an interaction model premised on transparency of use [9]. A well designed interface establishes the framework of an interaction mode that enables the user to recognize the gestural options and utility afforded to them. The affordances programmed into virtual devices are more imperceptible than those designed into physical tools [10], be it a saw, a steering wheel, a violin, or a snare drum. These virtual, screen-based interfaces also disembody the musicians from the tactile familiarity musicians acquire through years of development. In the case of the *CV Drum Tracker*, a clearly defined interaction model between subject (human) and object (virtual, screen-based software), is an absolute necessity.

2.2. Designing for Transparency

Ensuring that a piece of technology does not cause a severe disruption to naturally playing the instrument is a concern which exists at the forefront of designing the *CV Drum Tracker.* However, completely adhering to the principles of Natural Design can parameterize the creative potentialities of a particular technology, especially when it is being appropriated as the means for musical interaction. After all, enabling Facial Recognition features to log into a phone is a completely different relationship to Computer Vision technology compared to using it to gesturally manipulate incoming audio and visual signals in real-time.

In digital design, the counterpart to the affordances realized through the user are the constraints built into the system [10]. Constraints are established through parameter mapping, and the perceptual affordances of any system are realized through the user exploring the limits of its programmed constraints. Similarly, the physical and design constraints of any musical instrument (virtual or otherwise) define the way in which musicians can physically interact with its material dimensions. The expressive scope of this interactivity defines the constraints, which in turn, reveal the affordances in any system. This is to say that in any digitally-designed musical system, creative activity is assessed by how the users navigate its constraints while exploiting the affordances provided to them. Whether these features fall under Gibson's idea of "environmental" affordances or Norman's "perceptual" definition is determined by the constraints, not in spite of them.

Robert Rowe defines an Interactive Music System as a system "whose behavior changes in response to a musical or physical input" [11]. If a user does not change their behavior in response to the constraints and affordances in the system, then it is not truly interactive. Similar to human interaction within improvisatory musical environments, reciprocity must go both ways. Limiting the drummer through the principles of Natural Design alone would prevent the performer from realizing the full expressive, gestural, or musical potential that the system could afford them. This would limit the ways in which the system could react to user input, which would ultimately and severely parameterize the expressive scope of the instrument. Operating from such a stringent framework, the system designer would have to superimpose a layer of virtual technologies onto the drummer and the instrument in such a way that would negate the need for any interactivity during performance, thereby potentially eliminating the possibility of taking advantage of the efficiencies, constraints, and affordances provided by an interactive system.

Designing an interactive system that leverages buffer recording, machine listening and motion tracking technologies affords the performer access to musical material from a previous point in the performance. This temporally elastic, non-linear relation to their own performance affords the drummer to further process sounds by using expressive gestural motions that exist in contrast to the functional movement associated with playing an acoustic drumset vocabulary. Implementing this design consideration can expand the drummer's gestural motions from the instrument's acoustic timbre and material dimensions into a virtual space, permitting the performer to extricate themselves from learned rhythmic patterns, and to center their attention on deriving trajectories of motion intended for the explicit purposes of generating sustain on an instrument whose natural sonic profile mainly consists of short, densely layered and repeated impulses.

Simply stated, an approach to digital, screen-based instrument design based on transparency alone leads to a difficulty in perceiving affordances, while careless mapping leads to an inability to recognize constraints. From the user's perspective, ease of motion, flexibility, and clarity in design are of paramount importance as well. The inability to recognize constraints translates into a sloppily designed tool where its expressive scope is never fully realized. This makes style and creativity within a hybrid physical-virtual environment difficult to define, and challenging to evaluate.

3. MULTIMODAL DRUM EXTENSIONS.

3.1. Experiments in Creating a Virtual Drumming Environment with Motion Tracking

The *Virtual Drum Simulator* uses Computer Vision to build a "drum system that can be played using a webcam and a computer system alone," [12] by defining sensor zones and identifying the oft-changing contours of a drummer's hands while simulating a playing motion. The video feed acts as the interface for the user by highlighting every designed target with a colored frame, each one tethered to a distinct virtual drum or cymbal that would trigger if the user entered into its specified area. The OpenCV library was used to detect whether or not the contour of the hands inside the target rectangles was correct enough to trigger sound ("correct" being defined as whether the recognized position of the hands correspond to the motion of sticking that particular drum or cymbal in an acoustic setting). With such accuracy required to trigger each drum or cymbal, this software is intended to serve as a virtual replacement of an acoustic drumset, or an effective teaching or practicing tool.

Similar to the *Virtual Drum Simulator*, the *Air Drums* use Computer Vision to simulate the sensation of playing an acoustic drumset [13]. Using the same OpenCV library as the *Virtual Drum Simulator,* the *Air Drums* use color tracking for Object Detection/Tracking, Event Detection, and its subsequent Drum Synthesis. Makeshift sticks wrapped in colored paper, along with placing a color sticker on the user's left thigh substitute for the hands and bass drum, respectively. By using Blob Detection, *Air Drums* can use the largest blob to run a *By Points Comparison* and an *Acceleration Comparison* on a frame-by-frame basis, thereby triggering note onsets through a prediction model based on present stick position in comparison to the previous data acquired from the last two video frames.

In the tradition of incorporating a wearable sensor for the purposes (among many) of monitoring XYZ positional data - a concept similar to Max Matthews' Radio Baton [14], The *Airstick Drum* [15] integrates virtual percussion instruments alongside an acoustic drumset. Bluetooth sends data from the drummer's sticks to a computer which is then transferred into MIDI messages based on specific stick positions. Salient MIDI messages for note onsets, velocity, and duration are determined through attaching gyroscope accelerators to the sticks. In *Drum* [16], a Microsoft Kinect is used in conjunction with the sensing framework OpenNI to track drumming movements within specific sensing zones. Each sensing zone is mapped to a .WAV file that triggers whenever the amount detected activity within these regions exceeds a certain threshold.

3.2. Current Practices in Multi-Modal Augmented Drum Performance

Using the drums as an integral component in a multi-sensory, immersive experience is certainly not a novel idea, nor is the idea of using sensors to capture drumming gestures. Regarding the latter, this project distinguishes itself by the type of motion capture used and its subsequent artistic application.

From a design perspective, the conceptual approach most emulated in the *CV Drum Tacker* is a combination of the *Pragmatic Motion Capture System* [17] the *Digitally Active Drum* [18] and Pras's *Digital Musical Instrument* (DMI) for drummer Jim Black [4]. As designers Peter Williams and Daniel Overholt state, The *DAD* was constructed around the sentiment that the "natural resonances" of the head should be respected, that the drums should be designed for an allowance of "different techniques, nuanced control, and co-location of sound and instrument...digital augmentation should not obstruct choice of technique". Furthermore, the synthesis technique or degree of processing applied to the acoustic should not privilege any particular playing technique over another. The DAD assigned off-center locations on the snare drum to act as triggers for synthesis, where the audio amplitude tracking of each snare stroke is mapped to the amplitude envelope of the enacted subtractive synth sound. The snare drum head was separated into two primary regions: the Central and Accentric Regions. While the Central Region preserved the acoustic sound from the middle of snare drum, notes inside the Accentric Region triggered the aforementioned synthesis processed, among other user-specified, time-based audio effects.

Aptly named, The *Pragmatic Motion Capture System* [17] relies on a portable camera being angled to strictly capture only the drum strokes, drum surface and the neutral background of the wall. Simultaneously to this data acquisition, a dynamic microphone is used as a spot mic on the snare drum, quickly facilitating the designer to visualize drum gestures in two distinct mediums at once.

As varied as these methods are, nearly all of them attempt to capture the highly personalized and idiosyncratic nuances associated with drumming motions by closely tracking the variances in any combination of quantifiable attributes - timing, velocity, amplitude, and spectral centroid measurements - through modifying the drum's surface, body, or the drumstick [3]. Nearly all of the projects listed above simultaneously utilize multiple techniques and technologies to exact enough data in real-time to accurately account for the numerous physical and musical dimensions of a drummer's performance. Maintaining a sustained level of transparency in acquiring data is another factor contributing towards the frequent implementation of multimodal measurement systems, as they tend to be less intrusive to the performer [18].

When looking for similar projects to reference, the search included audio-visual experiences where the drums were to be conceptualized as a control source for sound-responsive data exchange. The artistic endeavors that are most aligned with the *CV Drum Tracker* can be found in Christos Michalakos's *Icarus* project [19]. *Icarus* is a hybrid interactive game/performance system designed for Michalakos's *Augmented Drumset* [20], an electro-acoustic drum set built from electronic drum triggers and contact microphones. In *Icarus,* the drummer has to navigate five distinct game environments, all of which are visualized through was Michalakos describes as "light art," [19] which is an interactive light system that alters its color, tone and direction based on the data acquired through actively running the acoustic audio signal through machine listening techniques. Audio signal processing and real-time performance tracking leverage the drum set into a controller for the video game, effectively improvising an electro-acoustic soundtrack that will differ upon each iteration of the experience.

The similarities between Michalakos's work and the *CV Drum Tracker* are primarily rooted in how the drums are positioned within their respective multimodal technologies, and in conceptualizing the instrument as transducer for these interactive experiences. There are also parallels between structuring the different levels of *Icarus* as distinct musical modes that the performer can autonomously navigate through and the different performance modes included in the *CV Drum Tracker* (these are discussed below). Of all the conceptual congruencies between *Icarus* and the *CV Drum Tracker,* the most consequential of them is the structural freedom the performer experiences when interacting with each system. While there are no gameplay consequences to the *CV Drum Tracker*, there exists a temporal elasticity that fuses the hybrid performance-installation into a dynamic experience that is at once emergent and indeterminate upon each engagement with the system.

From the plethora of projects and research listed above, it is obvious that the mere combined use of computer vision, machine listening, and multimodality with the drumset is not some sort of singular distinction for the *CV Drum Tracker.* However, the *CV Drum Tracker* distinguishes itself from the aforementioned projects by using transparent technologies of surveillance to preserve the act of playing the drums in a completely improvisatory context while also affording the performer to free themselves of these technical rigors in an effort to explore more elongated or alternatively expressive gestures. Based on the Free Jazz Performance Model [21] of Computer-Human Interactivity, this design consideration centers the compositional process around the performer itself, as their gestures become "the technical tool of communication and creative flow" [1]. Thus, the system can be considered a performance-driven software program, as there is no anticipation or realization of any preprogrammed musical score [11]. Transformative response methods process the incoming audio signal from the acoustically augmented drumset by simultaneously measuring pixel-to-pixel differentiation in the gestural movement monitored in the incoming input matrix.

While the process of data acquisition and feature extraction is completely virtual, the experience of playing the drums remains intact. In contrast to the *Virtual Drum Simulator* [12] or *Air Drums* [13] projects, computer vision techniques are not used to replace the drumset with a virtual facsimile of itself, nor it is meant as a practice replacement for the acoustic set, or to function as an educational tool for entry level drummers. Rather, that same transparency the computer vision tools provide in these projects functions as the same means to acquire gestural data in the *CV Drum Tracker*, guaranteeing that the necessity of measuring the drummer's movement during a performance does not impede on the tactile sensation of playing the acoustic instrument.

4. DESIGNING CV DRUM SYSTEMS

4.1. Phase One

The current design of *CV Drum Tracker* is a result of an iterative process, one which can be separated into three phases. Phase One represented the first attempt at designing the screen-based interface. The incoming video image was separated into smaller sub matrices, which were referred to as Target Sensors. The user was able to move four of the seven zones present in the camera feed: the Upper Left, Upper Right, Hi-hat, and Ride Zones. The user was not able to change the rate or range of their movement, but the Moving Target Zones (MTZs) could always be reverted to their original position. Saturation effects were applied to each submatrix as a way to contrast with the grayscale video feedback of the entire camera feed. This made a clear distinction between the motion occurring inside and outside the specified target zones. The Machine Listening techniques yielded amplitude tracking data that controlled the amount of feedback that was applied to the background video feed.

Computer Vision techniques of Frame Differencing and Centroid Tracking were used inside the Target Sensors to control audio processing in the signal chain. These mapping techniques were programmed into the system, unable to be changed by the performer.

Image 1. Video Screen Interface, Phase One[1]

The video feed is captured through a Logitech C920 Webcam. Using a camera detached from the computer enabled the performer to position the camera where it could best capture their own body position without manipulating the angle of the screen. All audio and visual processing software was built in Cycling 74's Max/Msp~/Jitter, using Jean-Marc Pelletier's cv.jit external package [22]

5.1.1. Parameter Mapping

Parameter mapping relationships could be established between the position of each MTZs and the gestures occurring inside of them. These relationships were referred to as Moving Target Mappings (MTM). MTM controlled the spatial and amplitude balance between dry and processed sounds. This is done by randomizing the position of the Upper Right or Upper Left Target Zones. Once this process is initiated, any movement of the Upper Right target zone along the horizontal axis controls the panning of four front speakers. While the horizontal movement controls the panning of dry and processed sounds, the vertical movement (when automated) manages the amplitude (level) balance between the individual effects, which include the Comb Filter, Bit Crusher, and Multi-Tap Delays. This is done by dividing the overall horizontal and vertical movements of the Upper Right (relative to pixel location) by half so that the overall video dimensions can be split into four individual quadrants. Each of these quadrants are assigned an audio effect. Once the Upper Right Target Zone moves into a quadrant, its gain level increases, just as it will decrease to zero as the zone transitions into another quadrant.

5.1.2. Evaluation

While these mapping constraints yielded some interesting sonic results, the affordances provided by these mapped constraints were a complete mystery to the user, which made them seem even more opaque to an observer. As Image 2 indicates, so little instruction was provided. There is no initial information provided on the user interface that indicates what these submatrices do, or how the user is supposed to interact with them. As a result, instead of interacting with the software as a musical counterpart the user has to develop these connections in real-time. While making connections between the gestures and sonic outcomes was supposed to be somewhat of an emergent process, the design simply proved to add to the difficulty of discerning the mapped relationships. The system afforded the performer very little in terms of exercising their own creativity within the very stringent constraints imposed upon them.

The MTZs were intended to extend the gestural possibilities at a drummer's disposal. However, since the gestural movement inside the submatrices was responsible for processing audio and not the movement of the matrices themselves, the user was forced to perform gestures that were completely separate from any physical motion required to play the acoustic drumset. This was especially true if the drummer wanted to augment the instrument's sound in real-time. This option to augment gestures was intended to be optional but by no means compulsory. There were far too many submatrices than were necessary, and the positioning of the sub-matrices made it difficult to expand gestural vocabulary beyond those motions inherent to playing the acoustic drums without a complete disruption of these drum-centric movements altogether. The drummer had to choose between one set of gestures or another. Furthermore, the performer was not able to designate any mappings between their own Moving Target Zones, gestures, and sonic outcomes. This proved to be too much of a constraint on a system which was capable of producing more outcomes than one specific mapping could possibly anticipate. In addition to a more flexible mapping strategy, more modularized processing software was needed to maximize the sonic potential of the system.

In summary, an ambiguous interface design lacking in any data or text-based information provided an interesting visual component, but it did not translate to the user having any sort of clarity in knowing how to interact with the software. The movement of the matrices produced too much of a game-like environment, where the user felt like they were competing against the software instead of mediating through it. The time it took to discover the few constraints and affordances of the system was unnecessarily long, and perhaps impossible to do if the user was not also its programmer and designer. Perhaps most crucially, the technological limitations of using only Frame

1

Differencing and Centroid Tracking as the means for audio processing produced results that were deemed to be sonically unsatisfactory. It became increasingly apparent that the amount of Computer Vision-based techniques in the system needed to be expanded while the interface itself needed to be clarified.

4.2. Phase Two

Phase Two has proven to be most crucial in determining the future development and design of the software, and focused on providing clarity to the user. Every submatrix was eliminated but one. No longer did multiple submatrices move across the screen, which eliminated the Moving Target Mappings from Phase One (along with the potential confusion that stemmed from their presence). The remaining single submatrix was still able to move around a section of the larger matrix.

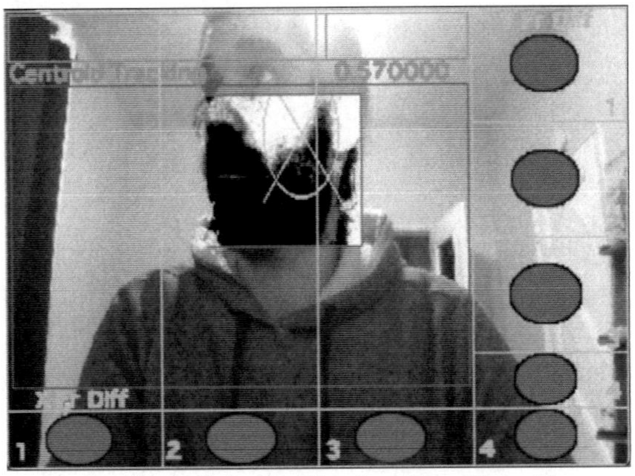

Image 2. Video Screen User Interface, Phase Two

The number of Computer Vision technologies at the user's disposal was expanded. These additions included Blob-Centroid Tracking and Optical Tracking. Rather than using Frame Differencing inside seven different submatrices, the performer could rely on other tracking techniques that provided more useful data for processing audio. Frame Differencing is effective for measuring extreme changes in motion on a frame-to-frame basis, but is not conducive for providing gradually changing data. In order to enact audio processing with Frame Differencing, either a very demonstrative gesture, long periods of complete inactivity, or increasing the distance between the performer and the camera feed, were required. Other techniques, such as measuring for concentrated areas of light inside the submatrix and tracking how these areas change over time, were more effective for generating data for processing audio over long periods of time. Switching to Blob-Centroid Tracking and Optical Tracking facilitated these subtleties in data acquisition inside the single submatrix, resulting in more fluid experimentation with gesture.

Frame Differencing was still used, although in a completely different manner than in Phase One. The video screen interface was separated into 16 sections (4 rows and 4 columns), all of equal size. Frame Differencing operations could be performed on each section. The incoming measurements were continuously evaluated against a set threshold, and virtual buttons were used on the video screen interface to indicate when a gesture exceeded this value. If the incoming motion exceeded the threshold, then the activity would trigger the process or event that was mapped to that particular region of the screen. For instance, Frame Differencing values on the rightmost column of the video screen would simultaneously trigger the playback of an audio file and switch between the primary camera view and feedback effect. The two leftmost, bottom regions triggered virtual synths.

The increase in computer vision technologies afforded the performer to use the software to both generate and process sounds. Virtual synths could be triggered by Frame Differencing, routed to an audio device, and processed with a mapped parameter coming from one of the video modules. The system was designed to afford the user to route any available video data point to a specified parameter in an audio processing device. Instead of having to discover these relationships in real-time during a performance, the user had to construct many of the constraints that they were to encounter. It became the standard practice to design this mapping procedure for each of the system's sound processing parameters.

5.1.2. Evaluation

The user interface on the video screen provided some salient measurements on the screen for the performer to reference. The options at the users disposal were far greater in Phase Two than in Phase One. While there were some data points provided on the video screen. The software required far more monitoring than before. This meant that the user had to perform with the interface on the video screen and simultaneously monitor the system's software in real-time. Experimenting with gestures became easier, but operating the software became increasingly difficult. Rather than freely playing the drums and interacting with the video screen, I often found myself thinking like a programmer or manager of the system during performance. Moreover, the buttons were placed in locations on the screen that made it nearly impossible to not trigger the processes associated with them. I could not simply put my hand into the submatrix to use these techniques of Optical Tracking and Blob Tracking without cueing a synth or triggering a visual effect. This made live performance quite difficult. It was decided that the complexities did not to be visible to the performer. Observing more than one screen during performance was superfluous and distracting. All of the information needed to monitor the data produced by the video-human interactions needed to be on the standalone video screen itself.

Additionally, the system had no way to organize time on a structural level. There was no way to transition to different presets or reconfigure the signal chain without manually clicking on the screen. Clicking on the screen proved to be incredibly difficult to do during performance, especially when the user was monitoring video data points from the software interfaces and their own motion in the video-screen interface. From a design perspective, this needed to be rectified. This design was also limiting the sonic capabilities of the system. At this point in development, the *CV Drum Tracker* represented a potentially interesting tool for generating and manipulating sound, but could not be considered an automated system for organizing improvisation any further than to interact with it through one preset. While the tool provided the user the affordance of generating and manipulating sound, the constraints built into the system did not make it a particularly effective tool for organizing time. Timed events were needed to both transition to a next signal chain of audio software, and to change the chosen presets for those modular devices. The user would have to compose the structure by thinking of each signal chain as a section of the piece and map the video data points to audio processing parameters for each device prior to the performance. Once this macro form was established, they could then improvise their way through each section by interacting with the video screen alone, without the need to organize time or create parameter mappings in real-time.

5.3. Phase Three

Phase Three represents the most technologically and conceptually sophisticated design of the system to date. More Computer Vision techniques have been implemented into the design, yet the complexity involved in monitoring the software during performance has been greatly reduced. The techniques of Blob Bounds Tracking, Blob Rotation Tracking, and Face-Tracking have been added into the system. This data provides far more control to the user and more options for parameter mapping. These measurement provide the size, movement, and rotation of each blob tracked in the submatrix. From a technological perspective these are the most consequential additions to the system to date, as the movement of this tracking data best resembles the way a performer would move a dial or slider on an analog interface.

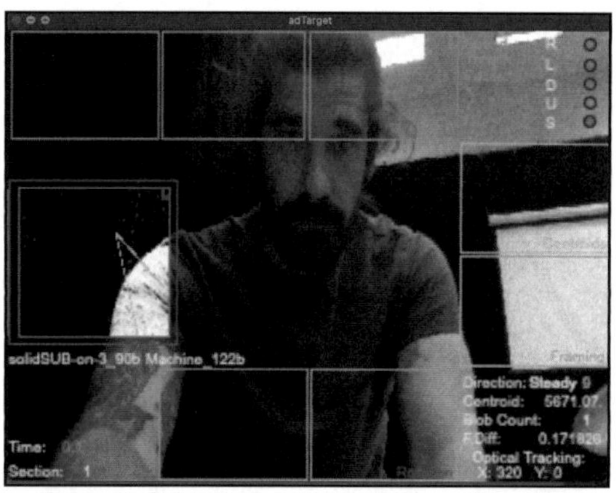

Image 3. Video Screen User Interface, Phase Three

Virtual buttons that were impossible to avoid triggering in the previous phase have been eliminated. Those spaces on the bottom left and right side provide a point of entry into the screen without enacting any musical or visual outcome. The submatrix no longer moves at all. This was a feature that was rarely used, so it seemed somewhat superfluous to keep including it. Eliminating the movement of the submatrix meant that there was more space to include salient data points that needed to be monitored. Instead of having to reference an expansive, complicated piece of software during performance, the user is provided the information for nearly all the CV techniques included in the design. The user can also now also monitor the direction of their motion and how long they have held steady in the submatrix. They are also able to switch between different tracking modes (which CV techniques can be monitored) by using the frame differencing techniques on the right of the screen. These buttons (which represent sections of the screen) were previously mapped to trigger visual effects and spoken word files.

Three more visual effects were added to the system: a texture generator, a color streaker, and a video glitcher. The visual effects were still triggered by the same technique, but the buttons and regions that cue these processes are located at the top of the interface. These buttons are placed in the topmost section of the screen, which virtually eliminates the possibility of the visual effects being inadvertently triggered. Situating these buttons at the bottom of the screen would make the user have to cross them to access any other part of the interface. This particular hindrance was discovered in performance during Phase Two and had to be corrected as soon as possible.

The updated design of the video interface meant that the need to click or touch the software at all during the performance had been nearly eliminated. In Phase Two, the user had to monitor up to 4 video images at once. Providing so much information on the video screen interface meant that there was no need to monitor a huge piece of software while performing, which led to an overall improvement and simplicity in the appearance of the user interface. This simplicity in design proved invaluable during performance. There was far less technology to be cognizant of while trying to play the drums, allowing the performer to simply focus on using the software as they desired during improvisation. No longer did the performer need to simultaneously assume the roles of "performing musician" and "system technician."

Turning the system on was now an automated process. Every component of the screen interface was automatically rendered without user input. All the performer would have to do was simply instantiate the software and the program ran by itself. Other new features in Phase Three included the ability to use a video as input source instead of the built-in video camera feed, and having the ability to choose between three main output modes for the matrix feed: the primary camera feed (or movie file), the Frame Difference Mode, and the Effects Mode. The Effects Mode had four different settings unto itself, giving the user up to 7 different visual outputs to choose from. The submatrix feed could be switched between 5 different outputs as well. Each video processing module has its own user interface embedded in the system. In order to access the individual CV modules, the user simply clicks (or assigns a MIDI controller to open them) on each individual button. However, this information does not necessarily have to be monitored by the performer, especially during improvisation.

In Phase Three, the system interface has been re-organized into two distinct sections. Any controls dealing with video input or data acquisition are located at the top of the interface. Any user-input that organizes audio processing is located at the button half. The most substantial addition to the software in Phase Three was the automated score control and audio signal routing system (and the addition of four more audio processors). This feature afforded the user to create audio signal routings that would change based on an automated timer. Each "section" of the performance can be thought of as individual signal routing. This timer feature manages the transition from one section to another without any user input during the performance. However, this automation is by no means compulsory, as the user does have the option to pause the timing of events, as well as skip to any of the pre-programmed sections (signal routings) during performance. Each audio processing module can be individually opened in the same manner in which each of the video modules can be accessed.

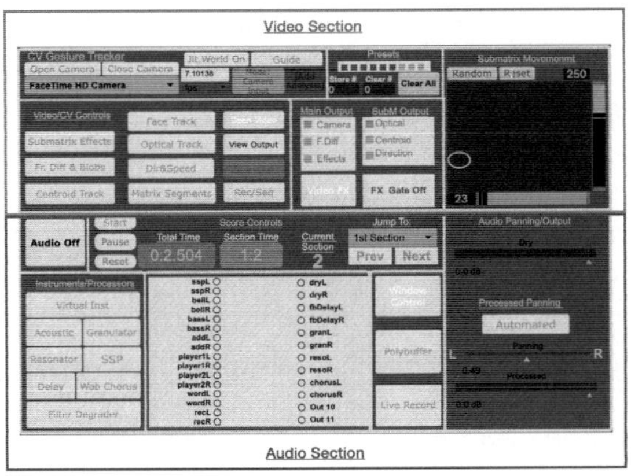

Image 4. Software User Interface, Phase Three

5.1.2. Evaluation

It is at this point in the development and creative process that the system represents a technology-mediated strategy for what composer and professor Sandeep Bhagwati refers to as "comprovisation" [23]. He describes his neologism as "An approach to creation in time-based arts predicated on an aesthetically relevant interlocking of context-independent and contingent performance elements. Comprovisation often uses unique constellations of oral, written, animated and interactive scores that can accommodate the scoring paradigms of many traditions and practices."

Musical form is decided by the transitions between user-defined signal routings, but the interaction model between the human and computer within these sections is based on the performer discovering these emergent gestural-to-sound (and visual) relationships through improvisation. Is it at Phase Three in the design process that the *CV Drum Tracker* represents an integrative approach to assimilating both its formal elements and indeterminate aspects into its technological infrastructure. The constellation of material that determines its multimodal output is embedded within the virtual machine itself. Far too often in electro-acoustic practices, the technology involved in the composition and improvisation is assigned a unidimensional, auxiliary, or tangential role in the creative process. The intention behind *CV Drum Tracker* is to conceptualize a musical process, evaluate its outcomes, and ultimately, define a personalized style through a holistic mediation with technology.

The design method described over the course of these three phases represents a procedural, systems-based, integrative approach to composition, where the comproviser is at once the programmer, designer, performer, listener, observer, and mediator of this hybrid environment. Such an orientation requires iterative prototyping, and the need to re-conceptualize the creative environment and the resulting aesthetic outcomes based upon the instant auditory and visual feedback yielded from the processes involved in this particular mediation with virtual and sensor-based technologies. Therefore, the term *Procedural Aesthetics* refers to both the iterative nature of how design choices are made and the dynamic, unfinished programming environment from which this technological mediation takes place. Time is organized and sound is generated and manipulated within a system made from an open programming environment (Max/Msp~/Jitter), not a Digital Audio Workstation. To hear the outcome of their design choices, the user does not have to play back a virtual tape machine, but has to rely on recursive operations that organize the playback of musical ideas. Observing musical and visual processes happening right at the point of programming changes the way the comprovisor evaluates and responds to the last decision that was made.The way time becomes organized and how sound is generated feels systematic in preparation, yet dynamic in performance.

5. CONCLUSIONS

Rowe distinguishes two types of computer-mediated interactive music systems based upon the degree to which the computer's output affects the actions of the human performer. The two classifications can be broadly determined by whether the objective is to either create a virtual musical instrument which acoustically augments a real-time performance by analyzing human gesture, or if the goal is to construct a cybernated improviser with their own performance behaviors that exist nearly independent from the user input [11]. The current design of the *CV Drum Tracker* clearly places it in the former category. Future development phases will be dedicated to leveraging more machine learning technologies so that the system interaction with the human improviser will exhibit the behavior of a semi-autonomous, cybernetic performer. This will be done by utilizing more computer vision techniques, such as Depth Data and Gesture Recognition, to construct histograms that analyze and subsequently respond to human activity.

Perhaps most important for the future design of the *CV Drum Tracker* is to distribute the technology into the hands of other drummers. Ultimately, the long term goal for the *CV Drum Tracker* is to construct a semi-autonomous, interactive environment that does not preclude the use of any current drumming vocabularies, but instead inspires a diverse range of drummers to explore the outer limits of their potential within this emergent physical and virtual assemblage.

6. REFERENCES

1. G. Mazzola and P.B. Cherlin, "Flow, gesture, and spaces in free jazz: Towards a theory of collaboration," *Springer Science & Business Media,* (2008).

2. B. Dolhansky, A. McPherson and Y. E. Kim, "Designing an Expressive Virtual Percussion Instrument," *Proceedings of the 8th Sound and Music Computing Conference,* Padova, Italy, Vol. 69, 2011, July.

3. A. Tindale, A., A. Kapur, G. Tzanetakis, P. Driessen, and A. Schloss, "A Comparison of Sensor Strategies for Capturing Percussive Gestures," *Proceedings of the 2005 Conference on New Interfaces for Musical Expression,* Vancouver, Canada, pp. 200-203.

4. A. Pras, M.G. Rodrigues, V. Grupp, and M. M. Wanderley, "Connecting Free Improvisation Performance and Drumming Gestures Through Digital Wearables," *Frontiers in Psychology*, vol. 12, 2021.

5. J.J. Gibson, J,"The Theory of Affordances," *Hilldale, USA*, vol. 1, no. 2, pp. 67-82, 1977.

6. D. A. Norman, "Affordance, Conventions, and Design," I*nteractions*, vol. 6, no.3, pp. 38-43, 1999.

7. D. A. Norman, T*he Design of Everyday Things: Revised and Expanded Edition.* Basic Books, 2013.

8. M. D'Errico, *Push: Software Design and the Cultural Politics of Music Production.* Oxford University Press, 2022.

9. T. Magnusson, (2006, October). "Affordances and Constraints in Screen-Based Musical Instruments," *Proceedings of the 4th Nordic Conference on Human-Computer Interaction: Changing Roles, Oslo, Norway,* pp. 441-444.

10. T. Magnusson, "Designing constraints: Composing and Performing with Digital Musical Systems," *Computer Music Journal*, vol. 34, no. 4, pp. 62-73, 2010.

11. R. Rowe, *Interactive Music Systems: Machine Listening and Composing.* MIT Press, 1992.

12. S. R. F. Bering, and S. M. W. Famador, "Virtual Drum Simulator Using Computer Vision," In *The 4th IIAE International Conference on Intelligent Systems and Image Processing,* Kyoto, Japan, 2016.

13. C. T. Tolentino, A. Uy, and P. Naval, "Air Drums: Playing Drums Using Computer Vision," *2019 International Symposium on Multimedia and Communication Technology,* Quezon, Philippines, 2019, pp. 1-6.

14. R. Boulanger, "The 1997 Mathews Radio-Baton and Improvisation Modes," *Proceedings of the 1997 International Computer Music Conference*, Thessaloniki, Greece, 1997.

15. H. Kanke, Y. Takegawa, T. Terada and D. M. Tsukamoto., "Airstic Drum: A Drumstick for Integration of Real and Virtual Drums," *Proceedings of the International Conference on Advancements in Computer Entertainment Technology,* pp. 57–69, 2012.

16. P. Sarang, A. More, A. Gaikwad, and T. Varma, "Air Drum Using Kinect and Arduino," *International Journal of Computer Science and Information Technologies*, vol.6, no.2, pp. 1153-1155, 2015.

17. R. Van Rooyen, and G. Tzanetakis, "Pragmatic Drum Motion Capture System," *Proceedings of the 2015 Conference on New Interfaces for Musical Expression*, Baton Rouge, pp. 339-342, 2015.

18. P. Williams and D. Overholt, "Design and Evaluation of a Digitally Active Drum," *Personal and UbiquitousComputing*, vol. 25, no. 1, pp. 783-795, 2021.

19. C. Michalakos, "Icarus: A Game/Performance for the Augmented Drum-kit," *8th Conference on Computation, Communication, Aesthetics & X,* Portugal, pp. 393-395, 2020.

20. C. Michalakos, "The Augmented Drum Kit: An Intuitive Approach to Live Electronic Percussion Performance," Proceedings of the *2012 International Computer Music Conference,* Slovenia, pp. 257-260, 2012.

21. T. Winkler, *Composing Interactive Music: Techniques and Ideas using Max.* MIT press, 2001.

22. J. M. Pelletier, "Cv.jit: Computer Vision for Jitter," Jean-Marc Pelletier. Retrieved March 10, 2023, from https://jmpelletier.com/cvjit/.

23. S. Bhagwati, "Glossaire Raisonné," *Circuit*, vol. 28, no.1, pp. 15–22.

基于 Max/MSP 的中国古代乐律学音律计算及可听化平台搭建

第一作者	第二作者			其他作者
翁若伦 allen1991shcm@gmail.com	贾云皓 1245899392@qq.com	逄居源 3248231449@qq.com	陈铭轩 1612789520@qq.com	秦毅 qinyi@shcmusic.edu.cn
作者单位：**上海音乐学院**				

摘要

对于传统的音乐学研究而言，中国历代乐律的系统性阐释藏于晦涩的古代史料文献：历朝历代的乐律系统，均涉及艰深的数理计算。本论文基于 Max/MSP 交互式编程语言与开发环境，探讨运用音乐科技手段初步搭建“中国古代乐律计算及可听化平台”的方法，促使抽象乐律知识的交互展示和体验变得简便。平台适用于教学、科普等多种场景，并探索音乐数据与声音处理新方法。平台以跨学科视角探索中国古代乐律创新性呈现与中国传统音乐文化创造性发展。

1、引言：中国古代乐律学研究现状及瓶颈

中国古代乐律学是一门研究中国古代音乐基本原理与技术理论的综合学科。从 20 世纪 80 年代起，学界开始使用“乐律学”这个概念。[1]自诞生起，中国古代乐律学始终与中国古代音乐史、古代声学、古代数学、天文历法等学科中的许多问题相互关联。就古代乐律学自身而言，它包含“乐学”与“律学”两个基本分支，[2]两者有千丝万缕的联系，“乐”是“律”的研究对象，“律”是“乐”的规范标准。律学理论在漫长的发展历程中，始终作为乐学理论的理论基础而存在，并与乐学形成互为表里的阐释系统。

无论是中国律制还是西方律制，律制的本质都是振动频率与音高之间的映射。即，律制是确定不同音高的真实物理频率的过程。律学作为处于物理学与音乐学之间的学科，也是“音乐声学”的组成部分之一，它依据声学原理，运用数理方法探究音乐中的音程关系及音高、音准的规定性。中国古代乐律学的研究对象，是音乐所用音律之间的音程关系，这一问题正是中国历代音乐的底层逻辑。中国古代乐律学，对于中国古代音乐乃至中国传统文化的传承与研究有着不言而喻的重要性。当前，在当代中国古代乐律学专家缪天瑞、黄翔鹏、陈应时、王子初、李玫等学者几十年的努力下，中国古代乐律学的学科建设已上升到新的高度，但仍面临一些难题：一、中国乐律学话语体系的建构不够完善。中国古代乐律学研究由于仍是“无声”的研究，它很难改变当下音乐实践理念并为弘扬中国音乐语汇贡献力量。二、中国古代乐律学数据库建设不足。目前中国古代乐律的整理、汇总和归纳仅停留于文集、索引等方面，尚未达到数据库的整合性和检索便利性等标准。

鉴于中国古代乐律学发展现状和瓶颈，本研究基于 Max/MSP 工程平台，借助跨学科的视角和方法，取音乐学—音乐工程双向视域，论述“中国古代乐律计算及可听化平台”的搭建原理，将乐律理论从纸笔、书堆中带出，以全新的媒介和音乐科技手段将它展示，探索中国古代乐律的创新性呈现。

2、音律计算及可听化平台的搭建

目前，运用 Max/MSP 交互式编程语言与开发环境进行的乐音体系计算、可视化处理以及跨学科研究尝试已经初具规模。[3]这使得 Max/Msp 运用于中国古代乐律学成为可能。“中国古代乐律学音律计算及可听化平台”基于 Max/MSP，使用计算机程序制作历代古代乐律系统的数理推导过程，使这一过程及其最终呈现简明易懂。用户可在应用程序中输入初始音律数值（如中国古人最常使用的“弦长数值”），通过简单

[1] 李玫. 中国传统乐律学[M], 北京：人民音乐出版社，2020, 第 1 页.

[2] “到了明代末期，朱载堉在《乐律全书》中正式将‘乐’、‘律’分开，各自独立成‘学’，其分篇分别为《乐学新说》和《律学新说》。”陈其射. 中国古代乐律学概论[M], 杭州：浙江大学出版社，2011，第 3 页.

[3] 参见范翎.交互式电子音乐研究[D]. 南京艺术学院, 博士学位论文, 2017; 宋伟明.基于物理运算引擎的可视化交互式电子音乐作品设计与实现[D]. 武汉音乐学院, 硕士学位论文, 2021; Manzo V J. *Max/MSP/Jitter for music: A practical guide to developing interactive music systems for education and more*[M]. Oxford University Press, 2016; Charles J F. A tutorial on spectral sound processing using Max/MSP and Jitter[J]. Computer Music Journal, 2008, 32(3): 87-102.

操作，即可了解各个音律系统的详细计算与推导步骤，以及各律的计算结果和具体弦长数值。同时，用户还可以利用该乐律平台的各个模块，在各音律系统内部拟合出基本的常用音列，并以可视化、可听化的方式进行感受。在平台界面中，用户可以直接调取所得律学数据，灵活运用至其他律学模块的计算过程。

“中国古代乐律学音律计算及可听化平台”主要功能在于计算与演示两个部分。基于 Max/MSP 的性能特征，它可以很好地兼顾演示与计算。其基础的视觉编程功能，能够确保在数学算式确定的前提下，计算结果的准确性与用户使用的便捷性。而其 DSP 信号处理的能力，能够提高声音演示的表现力，减少数据存储的负担。在乐律演示层级下，研究团队利用“时间长河”的外形与思路来构筑平台的二级目录，将古代律制按照时间断代分类，内含京房六十律、荀勖笛律、何承天新律、三百六十律等多个律制模块供用户选择使用。下面逐一展示各律制模块的搭建方式，以及平台搭建过程中数据与声音的处理方法。

2.1 “平台”音律计算模块的搭建

2.1.1 “三百六十律（含‘六十律’）”计算演示部分

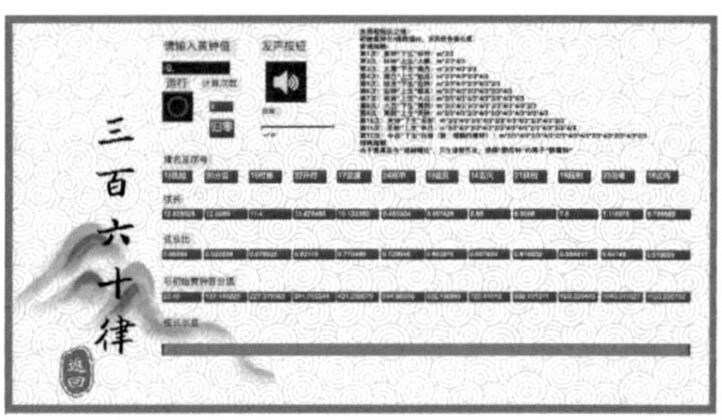

图 1：“三百六十律”主页面

“三百六十律”由南朝宋律学家钱乐之在刘宋元嘉年间（公元 424 年—453 年）创立。[4]“三百六十律”以三分损益法[5]以及汉代京房所创“六十律”为基础，将一个纯八度划分成区间不等的三百六十份。在生律过程中，钱乐之极力缩小三分损益法生还黄钟本律的音差，并将其命名为“一日”，现代律学称之为“钱氏音差”。这一音差值的发现体现出钱乐之在律学计算及“黄钟还原”问题上的可贵探索，为中国律学研究做出极大贡献。

“三百六十律”基本原理为，将三分损益律的运算按照不同的条件算法共计进行 359 次（第一律不用计算），由此得到更加接近初始“黄钟律”的弦长值。[6]研究团队先根据古籍，对“三百六十律”律学系统的运算公式进行推导，这一公式是搭建“三百六十律”模块的底层逻辑。现展示如下：[7]

设初始黄钟长/律数值 m，求其他各律长度：

【普通周期（以第一周期律名为例）】：

第 1 次：黄钟“下生”林钟：m*2/3 （1）

第 2 次：林钟“上生”太簇：m*2/3*4/3 （2）

第 3 次：太簇“下生”南吕：m*2/3*4/3*2/3 （3）

第 4 次：南吕“上生”姑洗：m*2/3*4/3*2/3*4/3 （4）

第 5 次：姑洗“下生”应钟：m*2/3*4/3*2/3*4/3*2/3 （5）

第 6 次：应钟“上生”蕤宾：m*2/3*4/3*2/3*4/3*2/3*4/3 （6）

第 7 次：蕤宾“上生”大吕：
m*2/3*4/3*2/3*4/3*2/3*4/3*4/3 （7）

第 8 次：大吕“下生”夷则：
m*2/3*4/3*2/3*4/3*2/3*4/3*4/3*2/3 （8）

第 9 次：夷则“上生”夹钟：
m*2/3*4/3*2/3*4/3*2/3*4/3*4/3*2/3*4/3 （9）

第 10 次：夹钟“下生”无射：
m*2/3*4/3*2/3*4/3*2/3*4/3*4/3*2/3*4/3*2/3 （10）

第 11 次：无射“上生”中吕：
m*2/3*4/3*2/3*4/3*2/3*4/3*4/3*2/3*4/3*2/3*4/3 （11）

第 12 次：中吕“下生”执始（新一周期的黄钟）：
m*2/3*4/3*2/3*4/3*2/3*4/3*4/3*2/3*4/3*2/3*4/3*2/3 （12）

【特殊周期】（音高发生“逾越错位”）：

1、沿用第 1 至第 5 次的公式，

2、令“应钟”=“新黄钟”，“新黄钟”的数据输入下一次普通周期的运算。

“三百六十律”的运算呈现周期性特征，因此平台中该律的程序设计以单独一次周期运算为主体，遍历运算一次过后，进行多次循环。在第一周期中，用户上一步输入的弦长值进入计算流程，每经过一次计算就将计算结果输出，并以此计算结果为初始数据进入下一计算公式中。由于在显示和操作时是以 12 个音为一组，计算程序最多一次计算 12 次。其计算展示界面如图 2 所示：

---

[4] 据《隋书·律历志》记载，钱乐之以《淮南子》“三百六十音，以当一岁之日”思想为本，在京房六十律的基础上，继续用三分损益法生满三百六十律，后人称“钱乐之三百六十律”。

[5] “三分损益法”是中国最常用的古老生律方法，在春秋时期《管子·地员》中已有记载。其大致原理为：将振动体减去或加上其三分之一长度，分别生成振动体原始频率的上五度、下四度，并按这种方法不断向下生律。三分损益法的具体运用在不同的律制系统中各不相同。文中所论“六十律”和“三百六十律”本质上就是基于三分损益法。

[6] 陈应时.“钱乐之三百六十律”中的三种音差[J]. 南京艺术学院学报（音乐与表演版）. 2009(2)；伍三土.汉京房六十律以来一脉相承的变律体系——要论三百六十律生律顺序的还原与多重错位逾越现象[J]. 中国音乐学. 2016(4).

[7] 中国古代基础的三分损益十二律名称（即“三百六十律”第一普通周期中的律名）以及大致相互关系如下：若设黄钟为 C，则 C—B 十二个半音可以按照从低到高的顺序对应黄钟、大吕、太簇、夹种、姑洗、中吕、蕤宾、林钟、夷则、南吕、无射、应钟。

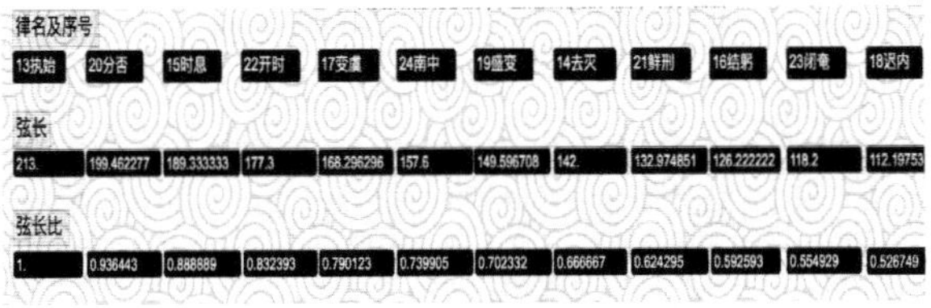

图 2：“三百六十律”模块普通周期计算数据展示界面

同时，由于特殊周期的存在，运算按键直接连接一个点击的计数器，并且通过 sel 物件筛选出特殊周期，遇到特殊周期时，便使数据进入专门针对这一周期、只运算 5 次的计算方法中（如图 3 所示）。最终，基于不同周期及音律序号，在对应信息框内显示音律名称。计算所得弦长在输出后，再次与用户输入的初始弦长相除，得到弦长比，并显示在对应音律之下，以供用户参考：

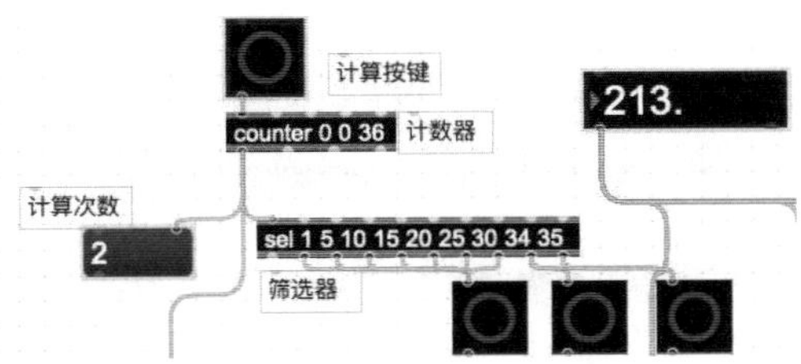

图 3：“三百六十律”模块特殊周期筛选流程

需要特别说明的是，由于钱乐之“三百六十律”是对汉代京房“六十律”的扩展且二者沿用同一套律名术语，平台的“三百六十律”模块可以轻松实现京房“六十律”的呈现。例如，“六十律”最具特征以及创新意义的音律是第 54 律“色育”至第 60 律“南事”。这七个音律的弦长数值和音分值等信息，可以通过“三百六十律”模块中第六周期的运算得出。

2.1.2 荀勖笛律计算演示部分

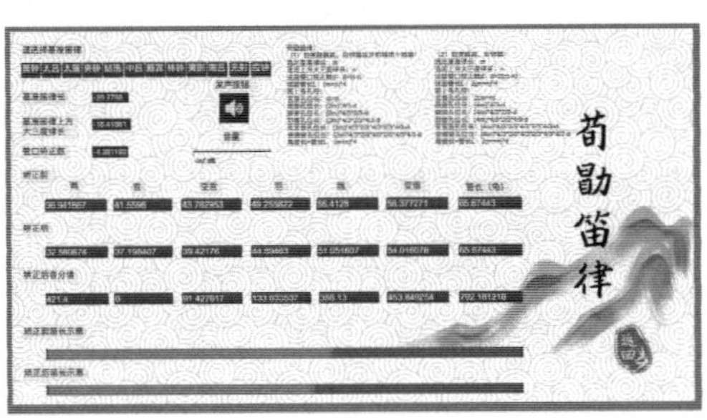

图 4：荀勖笛律主界面

“荀勖笛律”是一种用于乐器修造与定音的实践性律制。据《晋书·律历志》《宋书·律历志》记载，为解决笛定律的不准确性，荀勖[8]于泰始十年（公元 274 年）左右，创造性地将笛上的宫音与角音之差值作为“管口校正数”，以便更准确地确定笛上孔位，并使笛所奏音高贴近三分损益律的标准。[9]他据此方法制造十二支笛，分别以十二律为笛的基准“宫音”，构成一整套经校正后的笛律系统。荀勖笛形制如图 5 所示（横置展示）：

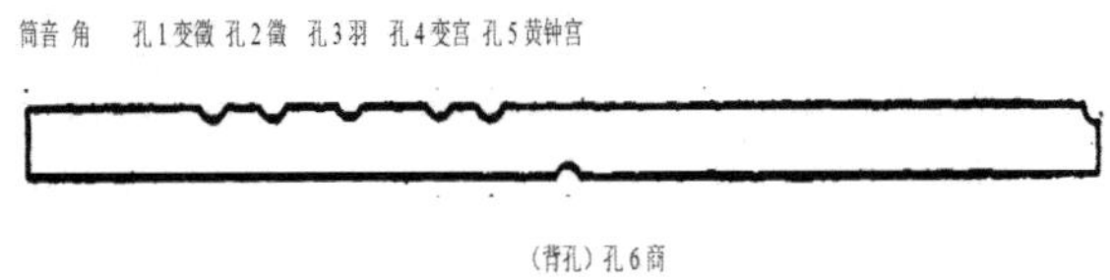

图 5：荀勖笛形制简图

荀勖笛律作为一种乐器修造律制，其拥有固定的初始基准笛律长，因此用户的输入操作变更为直接点击基准笛律名称。点击基准笛律名称后，对应的基准笛律长被输入进计算程序。研究团队根据已有史料文献，将荀勖笛律计算公式推导如下：

1）如求除蕤宾、应钟笛以外的其他十根笛：

选定基准律长：m

选定上方大三度律长：n

该笛管口校正数 d：d=m-n （1）

该笛管长 L：(m+n)*4 （2）

【笛上各孔位】：

宫音孔位长：m+n （3）

徵音孔位长：(2m)*4/3-d （4）

商音孔位长：(2m)*4/3*2/3-d （5）

羽音孔位长：(2m)*4/3*2/3*4/3-d （6）

变宫音孔位长：(2m)*4/3*2/3*4/3*2/3*4/3-d （7）

变徵音孔位长：(2m)*4/3*2/3*4/3*2/3*4/3*4/3-d （8）

角音长=管长 L：(m+n)*4 （9）

2）如求蕤宾、应钟笛：

选定基准律长：m

选定上方大三度律长：n

该笛管口校正数 d：d=2(m-n) （10）

该笛管长 L：2(m+n)*4 （11）

【笛上各孔位】：

宫音孔位长：2(m+n) （12）

徵音孔位长：(4m)*4/3-d （13）

商音孔位长：(4m)*4/3*2/3-d （14）

羽音孔位长：(4m)*4/3*2/3*4/3-d （15）

变宫音孔位长：(4m)*4/3*2/3*4/3*2/3*4/3-d （16）

---

[8] 荀勖（xù）（？—公元 289 年），三国至西晋时音律学家、文学家、藏书家。

[9] 具体可参见王子初. 荀勖笛律研究[M]. 北京:人民音乐出版社. 1995；陈正生. 荀勖的音乐声学研究[J]. 南京艺术学院学报：音乐与表演版, 2020(2).

变徵音孔位长：(4m)*4/3*2/3*4/3*2/3*4/3*4/3-d （17）

角音长=管长 L：2(m+n)*4 （18）

根据此算法，荀勖笛律模块的搭建首先需要设计条件判断，用以判断用户选项是否为“蕤宾笛”或“应钟笛”。这一过程在此模块中通过 gswitch 物件来实现。若用户选项为“蕤宾”“应钟”笛，则在所有运算前*2。

图 6：“上方大三度律长”和“管口矫正数”计算模块部分组件

接下来，按照上述公式，根据三分损益法的计算方法，先由基准笛律长计算出其上方大三度律长。如图 6 所示，之后可根据上述公式，计算其管口矫正数，以此为基础计算量计算出管口矫正前后的笛身定律位置管长值，供用户比较参考，并据此了解荀勖笛律原理下笛身各孔的定律位置（如图 7 所示）。

图 7：管口矫正前后的笛身定律位置管长值展示

2.1.3 何承天新律计算演示界面

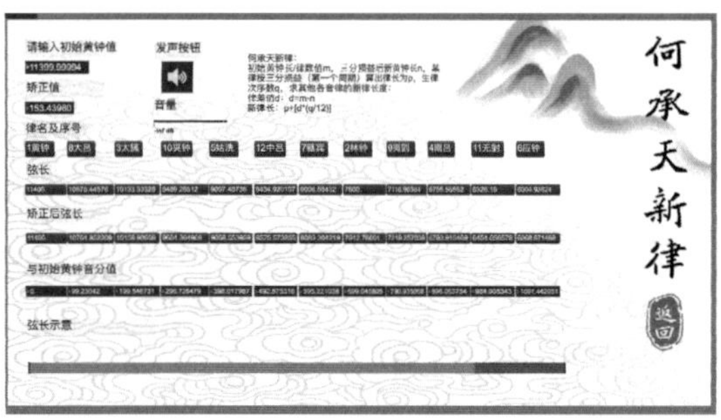

图 8：何承天新律主界面

何承天新律是南朝乐律学家何承天（公元 370 年—447 年）所创律制，《宋书·乐志》中称其为“新律”。为了实现古人“十二律旋相为宫”的理想，何承天没有延续汉代京房使用三分损益继续向下生律的方法。他在传统三分损益十二律内部进行调整，使其律长成为等差数列。[10]虽然这种律制并非真正的十二平均律，但其听觉效果已与之十分接近。

对于“何承天新律”的计算，设初始黄钟长/律数值 m，三分损益后新黄钟长 n，某律按三分损益（第一个周期）算出律长为 p，生律次序数 q，求其他各音律的新律长度：

律差值 d：d=m-n （1）

新律长：p+[d*(q/12)] （2）

平台中何承天新律在程序设计上沿用三百六十律的计算思路，将用户输入的数据代入程序进行计算。有所不同的是，由于何承天新律是在一个八度内进行等差数列的调和，不会涉及周期运算，只需要在单次运算周期中，按顺序加入矫正值（d*（q/12）），以此来显现原计算方式。图 9 展示了上述界面所计算的何承天新律各律弦长校正前后的数据：

图 9：何承天新律各律弦长校正前后计算数据展示

2.1.4 音分值计算系统设计

音分值（cent）是一种用以清晰描述音与音之间距离关系的数据。它以十二平均律为基础，将一个八度的音高距离设为 1200 音分。由于平均律一个八度内十三个音（含起始音的高八度音）频率呈等比数列且相邻半音之间音高距离相等，任意两个相邻半音间距离便为 100 音分。音分值对于描述音符之间的距离关系具有直观性，是各类律学研究必须使用的数据。

然而，由于不同律学研究者所处时代以及所用的计算工具不同，任意二音音高频率与其音分值之间的函数表达式长期没有统一，更没有现成可直接用于计算机以及 Max 这一特定编程平台的音分值表达式。因此，团队通过梳理历来乐律学成果，在此基础上进一步推导、总结出两种音分值计算公式。

公式（1）使用常用对数：音分值 C=

$$3986 \times \log_{10}\left(\frac{f2}{f1}\right) \quad (1)$$

[10] 参见陈应时. 十二平均律的先驱——何承天新律[J]. 乐府新声：沈阳音乐学院学报, 1985(2); 缪天瑞. 律学:第三次修订版[M],“何承天新律”部分, 北京:人民音乐出版社. 1996.

公式（2）不用常用对数：音分值 C=

$$\left|100\log_{2^{\frac{1}{12}}}\frac{f2}{f1}\right| \qquad (2)$$

研究团队在“中国古代乐律学音律计算及可听化平台”搭建过程中做了大量数据测试，发现在使用公式（1）进行参数运算的过程中，由于浮点数取舍以及二进制运算过程中存在的限制，平台计算结果难免会与科学计算在万分之一位的层级出现微小幅度的数据误差。这可能是由于在 Max 中，float 数据类型和 MSP 中的数据类型在计算方式上基本相同，但它们的内部实现原理却有很大不同。在 Max 中，float 类型利用 32 位二进制浮点数实现，然而 MSP 中的数据类型可以使用 float 类型或 64 位浮点数 double 类型，具体取决于所使用的对象或算法。由于 float 类型只有 32 位，因此它的表示范围比 double 类型要小，精度也相应较低。另外，在使用公式（2）进行运算的过程中，由于 Max/MSP 中对数运算的自身局限性，无法进一步保证计算结果的准确性。

最终，团队设计出一种全新的音分值计算方式，将误差最小化：如图 10 所示，利用 Max/MSP 中的 DSP 信号处理运算，将原有方程内的所有常量及变量都转化为数字信号，再接入对数函数中进行非线性函数处理，最终通过[snapshot～]组件将信号实时转化为常数，进行后续运算与输出。这种新颖算法尝试了 Max/MSP 数字信号处理的新用途，以弥补 Max 对数计算功能不足的先天缺陷，使得在乐律呈现时音分值计算的准确性大幅提高。

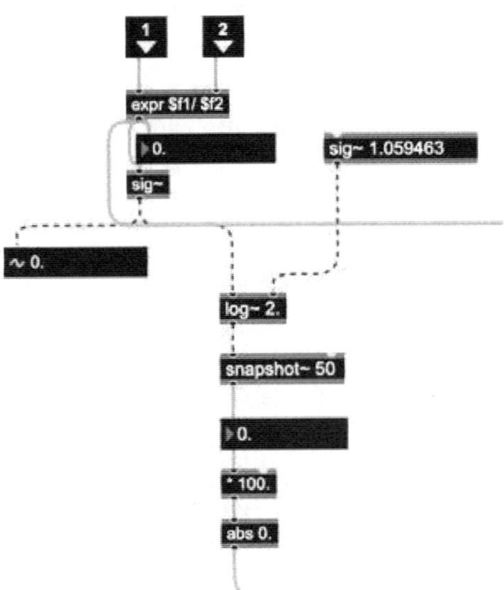

图 10：利用 Max/MSP 中的 DSP 信号处理机制进行音分值计算的程序架构

2.1.5 实验数据验证

在“中国古代乐律计算及可听化平台”完成后，研究团队针对平台所得数据进行了实验及验证。针对程序内数据运算的实验及验证，团队分批次在弦长值、弦长比、音分值、发声频率及发声稳定性等方面做对照验证。下面展示具有代表性的验证过程。

以“三百六十律”模块为例，繁复的传统乐律学研究方法得出在进行 359 次运算过后，第 360 个音与初始黄钟律之间音分值应当为 1.845310674082970270737052719 0324 音分[11]（在十二平均律中，一个半音为 100 音分），最终平台计算值为 1.845314 音分，与学术研究数据的误差值约为 0.0000033259170297，误差率约为 0.000180236156244%。第 54 个音与初始黄钟律之间音分值在学术上称为“京房一日音差”，具体数值应当为 3.615045865533140457796835081 1297 音分，最终平台计算值为 3.615051 音分，误差值为 0.000005134466859542203164918 8703，误差率约为 0.000142030476252%。“三百六十律”模块音分值误差率基本控制在 0.0002%以内。

再以何承天新律模块为例，根据传统的乐律学研究，加入矫正值[d*（q/12）]之后的林钟新律应约为 699.07 音分，[12]与十二平均律所需的音分值相差约 0.93。现用平台计算后得出的林钟律为 699.045805 音分，与十二平均律所需音分相差 0.954195。比较学术研究和平台所得音分值数据，误差值约为 0.024195 音分，误差率仅约为 0.0034610267927%。综上，按照计算结果与学术研究结论及科学计算结果对照验证，平台计算所得音分值误差极其微小，整体误差率基本控制在 0.0035%以内，完全不会影响平台使用者或研究者对于各音律音高的辨析和后续计算。

2.2 平台可听化部分搭建及音频处理

“中国古代乐律计算及可听化平台”的发声系统设计分为两种模式，一种是针对理论律制的纯音比较听辨，另一种是针对器乐律制的模拟声音。

第一种声音设计以“三百六十律”为主要运用。由于该律制仅为理论律制，历史上并无明确的实践运用记载，研究团队采用正弦波直接发出音律音高。程序使用中，用户点击音名时，会发送该音与基准音频率比，并使该频率比与基准音相乘。所得频率继续输入进正弦波振荡器程序中，用户点击音名按钮时触发该振荡器 ADSR 包络并发声。为更加凸显对比听辨的

[11] 此数据来源于陈应时.“钱乐之三百六十律”中的三种音差[J]. 南京艺术学院学报（音乐与表演版）. 2009(2).

[12] 此数据来源于李玫.中国传统乐律学[M]. 北京:人民音乐出版, 2020, 第 112 页。

功能，该发声程序首先会同时发出初始音与当前音，形成双音合奏。合奏持续一定时长后，再分别发出初始音与当前音，突出两音之间细微的音程距离关系。在三百六十律和六十律模块的使用过程中，用户极有可能感受到拍音的存在。但对于该平台而言，拍音正能帮助听众感受乐律系统两音之间细微的音程关系。

第二种声音设计以荀勖笛律为主要运用。由于该律学体系实际应用在乐器修造中，其音响的展示需要尽可能还原声学乐器本身的音色及频响特点。同时，此类程序的发声频率同样皆为实时可变的浮点数，若直接使用已公开发布的采样音源，几乎无法将音源中已有的采样音频实时进行以音分（或更小单位）为单位的细微调整。因此，在原本常规的声音生成逻辑的基础上，研究团队将正弦波振荡器生成的音色，更换成通过物理建模生成的合成音色。这种新颖方法一方面能够还原原声乐器音色，另一方面避免了采样合成器音高固定、无法根据不同频率值调整音高的弊端。团队在当前研究阶段主要致力于录制竹制笛子、古琴等乐器的音色，并进行相应的频谱分析，通过物理建模等技术手段进行音源插件的制作。当然，由于荀勖笛年代已久，其音色频谱细节、响度、动态范围等因素均不可探，因此本平台先竭力营造竹制笛子的基本音色。

为保持发声系统效果的整体性，所有律制频率计算均使用同一发声系统。在用户点击音律名称时，向下传输其弦长值，并调用初始弦长值与之相除，所得即与基准律长之频率比。之后，平台将频率比与预设好的基准频率相乘，得到每个音的发声频率。最后，将频率浮点数常数通过 MSP 处理成数字信号，输入相应发声单元。基准频率的设定，以人耳最为敏感的1000—3000Hz 频率范围为准。团队将该律制最低、最高音限制在这一范围中，以提高人耳听觉辨析度。

3、结论及平台未来发展

“中国古代乐律学音律计算及可听化平台”以 Max/MSP 为媒介，通过跨学科合力，初探中国古代乐律的可视化、可听化呈现，为改变中国音乐“无声的音乐史”之困境贡献力量，为中国音乐创造性研究提供新工具，同时推动中国古代乐器的修造、复原以及舞台演绎实践。该研究开发 Max/MSP 新运用的同时，使得中国古代乐律学能够走出书本、归于声音、走向舞台，为建设中国乐律学学科话语体系添砖加瓦。该平台也是中国古代乐律学数据库建设之路上的铺路石，能够提升检索、分析中国古代乐律信息的效率，并防止中国延续千年的乐律学知识体系的散失。

此外，本平台可以为高校教师提供合适的教学工具，为乐器博物馆、展览馆、文化馆等场合提供演示工具，将晦涩的乐律学知识，以生动形象的方式传播给学生与广大音乐爱好者，帮助人们对中国古代乐律理论建立感性认识，赋能中国古代乐律理论的传承。当前，本平台的探索仍在继续，着力实现先秦钟律、历代琴律的呈现。综上，“中国古代乐律学音律计算及可听化平台”探索中国古代乐律的创新性呈现，对于中国古代音乐文化延续具有深刻意义。

备注：本文为以下项目阶段性成果并受其资助：

中宣部“宣传思想文化青年英才”项目——“基于中国传统文化与音乐的创新思维研究”

上海市“晨光计划”项目（编号：21CGA78）——“中国当代跨媒介声音艺术的创新表达研究”

4、参考文献

[1] 李玫.中国传统乐律学[M]. 北京:人民音乐出版, 2020.
[2] 陈其射.中国古代乐律学概论[M]. 杭州: 浙江大学出版社, 2011.
[3] 范翎.交互式电子音乐研究[D]. 南京艺术学院, 博士学位论文, 2017.
[4] 王俊.基于 Max/MSP 平台的流行风格打击乐应用程序设计[D]. 武汉音乐学院, 2018.
[5] 宋伟明.基于物理运算引擎的可视化交互式电子音乐作品设计与实现[D]. 武汉音乐学院, 硕士学位论文, 2021.
[6] Manzo V J. *Max/MSP/Jitter for music: A practical guide to developing interactive music systems for education and more*[M]. Oxford University Press, 2016.
[7] Charles J F. “A tutorial on spectral sound processing using Max/MSP and Jitter”[J]. Computer Music Journal, 2008, 32(3): 87-102.
[8] Jensenius A R, Godøy R I, Wanderley M M. “Developing tools for studying musical gestures within the Max/MSP/Jitter environment”, project: “Musical Gestures (2004-2007)”, 2005.
[9] 陈应时.“钱乐之三百六十律”中的三种音差[J]. 南京艺术学院学报（音乐与表演版）. 2009(2).
[10] 伍三土.汉京房六十律以来一脉相承的变律体系——要论三百六十律生律顺序的还原与多重错位逾越现象[J]. 中国音乐学. 2016.
[11] 王子初. 荀勖笛律研究[M]. 北京:人民音乐出版社. 1995.

[12] 陈正生. 荀勖的音乐声学研究[J]. 南京艺术学院学报：音乐与表演版, 2020(2).
[13] 陈应时. 十二平均律的先驱——何承天新律[J]. 乐府新声：沈阳音乐学院学报, 1985(2).
[14] 缪天瑞.律学（第三次修订版）[M]. 北京:人民音乐出版社, 1996.

基于计算机技术的中国传统乐器数字化转型案例与对中国传统音乐发展的意义：以古琴为例

李宁
深圳大学音乐舞蹈学院
ron916@naver.com

摘要

本文以古琴为例探讨了使用计算机技术对中国传统乐器进行数字化转型案例及其对中国传统音乐发展的意义。首先，介绍了古琴数字化转型的各种案例，如虚拟古琴乐器的开发、古琴减字谱输入法应用的开发以及古琴数据库的建立，并阐述了古琴数字化转型的基本技术框架和应用情况。其次，分析了古琴数字化转型对中国传统音乐发展的意义，包括保护和传承传统音乐文化、扩大古琴传播范围、进传统文化与现代科技的融合以及推动中国传统音乐的数字化转型和创新型发展等。本研究旨在推动中国传统音乐的数字化发展，并为中国传统音乐的传承和创新提供新的思路。

1. 引言

古琴是中国传统音乐中最具代表性的乐器之一，具有悠久的历史和深厚的文化意义。如今，中国古琴在全球范围内越来越受到关注和认可，对音乐演奏、教育和文化交流起着重要作用。[1] 自 21 世纪以来，古琴艺术被重新评估为非物质文化遗产。2003 年，联合国教科文组织正式将古琴艺术列入“人类非物质文化遗产代表作名录”。[2] 2006 年，中国国务院将古琴艺术列入首批“中国国家级非物质文化遗产名录”。随着计算机技术的不断发展，越来越多的研究人员开始探索中国传统乐器的数字化转型以适应现代音乐发展的需求。同时，中国政府也积极推动“国家数字文化战略”，推动传统文化的数字化转型和发展，发布了《关于推进实施国家文化数字化战略的意见》等各种政策文件。[3] 在这些政策的大力推动下，出现了越来越多的古琴数字化转型案例，如数字虚拟古琴乐器、古琴减字谱输入法应用和古琴电子数据库等，为中国的传统音乐从业者和爱好者提供了许多便利。

作为中国传统文化的重要组成部分，包括古琴在内的中国传统乐器代表了自古以来中国音乐艺术的高度发展水平，蕴含非常丰富的演奏技巧和音乐表达。随着科技的发展，计算机技术也为包括古琴在内中国传统乐器的传承和发展提供了新的机遇和思路，中国传统乐器数字化转型的相关研究也有望实质性地推动中国传统音乐的发展和传播。本文以古琴为例，阐述了基于计算机技术的中国传统乐器数字化转型的技术框架和应用案例，并分析了中国传统乐器数字化转型对中国传统音乐发展的价值和意义。

2. 基于计算机技术的古琴数字化转化案例

2.1 古琴数字虚拟乐器开发与应用案例

古琴数字虚拟乐器的开发技术架构主要包括硬件和软件两个方面。在硬件方面，开发初期应使用高质量的录音设备对古琴进行录音和采样。由于来自不同琴派的古琴乐器自古以来没有统一的制造标准，所以每件保存下来的古琴的琴身和琴弦的结构、材料、制造年份和制造规格都不完全相同。此外，每个古琴琴派都有着独特的演奏技巧和指法特点，导致古琴在不同演奏状态下的音调、动态、谐波、共鸣频率和泛音也都不同。因此，用于古琴数字虚拟乐器采样的对象通常是不同琴派中具有代表性的保藏乐器在演奏过程中的各种参数和音频数据，如弦音、共鸣（泛音）、拨弦声、摩擦声、推弦声和共鸣箱的共鸣声等。

在软件方面，需要使用数字信号处理技术和人工智能技术对录制的数据进行处理和分析，以实现古琴演奏的实时模拟和还原。具体来说，需要采用声音合成技术、物理建模技术、神经网络技术等来对古琴演奏的各个方面进行建模，将建模结果与实时录制的数据融合，实现古琴演奏的数字还原和实时模拟。此外，还需要设计可视化界面，以便用户进行操作和控制。通过综合运用硬件和软件技术，可以实现高保真度的古琴演奏实时模拟，满足不同场景中的演奏需求。

古琴数字虚拟乐器开发的主要技术架构如下：

技术工具	实施内容
录音设备与古琴各琴派的代表性保藏乐器	录音与映射采样
数字音频工作站（DAW）	采样编辑/采样优化
	声音合成
虚拟乐器编程脚本（如KSP）	采样动态滤波
	映射变体编辑
	映射力度编辑
	虚拟声场设计
	界面视觉设计

表 1. 古琴数字虚拟乐器开发的技术架构

古琴数字虚拟乐器开发的代表性案例有很多，其中“Kong Audio-Chinee Gu Qin”是中国汕头市空音软件公司于 2008 年发布的基于采样技术和虚拟乐器技术构建的古琴虚拟乐器。该虚拟乐器在采样过程中，采用了高质量的采样技术，从真实的古琴演奏中录制并采集了大量的样本。数字建模过程中，使用 Kong Audio 自主开发的完整虚拟乐器引擎，该引擎支持多种声音模拟和处理功能，包括滤波、失真、混响、合奏等效果。该引擎还具有可调音高、可变速等功能，以便用户进行更多的音色探索和尝试。用户界面（UI）方面，Chinee Gu Qin 的用户界面被设计得直观、易用。它提供了各种可调参数的界面，例如音调、音量、衰减等。用户也可以轻松地进行对音色进行定制和调整，以实现所需的效果。兼容性方面，Chinee Gu Qin 支持多种音乐软件和操作系统，包括 Mac OS 和 Windows 操作系统，支持 AU、VST、RTAS、AAX 等插件格式，使用户可以方便地将其集成到各种数字音乐工作站（DAW）中进行音乐制作和演出。

此外，“Native Instruments Spotlight Collection-East Asia: Gu Qin”也是一个基于采样和模拟技术构建的虚拟乐器。该虚拟乐器在采样过程中，采用高质量的采样技术，使用了多个微调的麦克风在录制时捕捉古琴的不同细节和音色。通过这种方式，Gu Qin 提供了高度准确的声音再现，以及充足的音频素材供用户使用。在物理建模过程中，在采样数据的基础上进行了更深层次的数字建模和算法处理。这使得虚拟乐器能够更准确地模拟古琴的拨弦、音色变化和共鸣等方面的物理特性和声音表现。用户界面设计方面，界面被设计得直观、易用，具有高度的可调性和自定义性。用户可以通过控制不同的参数和效果器来实现所需的音色和效果，例如滤波、失真、混响等。界面还提供了可变速度、可变音调等功能，以满足用户的实际需求。兼容性方面，Gu Qin 也与 Kong Audio-Chinee Gu Qin 一样支持多种音乐软件和操作系统，包括 Mac OS 和 Windows 操作系统，支持 AU、VST、RTAS、AAX 等插件格式。这使得用户可以方便地将其集成到各种数字音乐工作站（DAW）中进行音乐制作和演出。

2.2 古琴减字谱输入法应用的开发与应用案例

减字谱是用于古琴的一种特定音乐记谱法，它有着悠久的历史。减字谱是基于汉字的简化形式来表示古琴曲中的每个音符，而不是表示音高或音程。[4] 减字谱还包括表示演奏技巧和情感的符号，帮助音乐家更好地传达音乐。随着时间的推移，减字谱逐渐演变成了一种独特的音乐记谱系统。由于它的简单性和易于记忆，减字谱在古琴音乐中被广泛使用。自 21 世纪以来，一些专业团队致力于减字谱的数字化工作。通过数字技术，传统减字谱的符号和音符可以转换为计算机可读的格式，实现数字化减字谱的制作和使用。减字谱输入法是一种基于计算机的工具，可以将通过键盘或其他输入设备输入的减字谱转换为可阅读的琴谱。以下图表是减字谱输入法应用开发的主要技术架构：

匹配系统语言
基于不同的操作系统平台构建不同语言下的设计架构

↓

输入法脚本引擎（如 IME）建模
进行用户输入识别，匹配录入的减字谱样本，并实现错误检查和纠正功能的设计

↓

音频引擎设计
该应用程序需要具备预览播放古琴音频的功能，因此需要集成相应的音频引擎。音频引擎需要支持实时合成和处理古琴音频，并提供高质量的音频输出

↓

适配输入设备
与该应用程序支持的特定输入设备，如键盘、鼠标、触摸屏、MIDI 键盘或者其他类似的音乐输入设备等，进行应用程序操作匹配

↓

用户界面设计
为了方便用户进行减字谱输入和古琴演奏，应用程序需要提供一个易于使用的用户界面。用户界面应该清晰明了，提供必要的功能和操作选项

↓

数据库建立
为了支持用户对古琴曲目的管理和检索，应用程序需要集成一个古琴曲目数据库。数据库应该包括古琴曲目的基本信息，如曲目名称、作者、曲谱来源等，同时还应该支持曲目检索和管理

表 2. 减字谱输入法应用开发的主要技术架构

减字谱输入法应用的开发案例有许多，本文以“古琴学习与教学系统”作为代表性案例介绍减字谱输入法应用开发的应用案例。“古琴学习与教学系统”是由浙江大学于 2018 年开发的古琴学习与教学的完整解决方案，其中包括减字谱输入应用程序。该应用支持拼音输入和手写输入，并具有减字谱符号的自动转换和播放功能。在“古琴学习与教学系统”中

开发的减字谱输入应用的技术架构主要包括以下几个部分：首先，使用 Web 技术进行开发，实现跨平台访问和无需安装的用户体验，前端技术采用 HTML5、CSS3 和 JavaScript 来实现页面设计和交互功能。其次，后端采用 PHP 进行开发，使用 MySQL 数据库实现数据管理和存储。前后端交互采用 Ajax 技术实现异步加载网页，无需刷新。再次，基于 MVC 架构设计，实现代码层的管理和解耦。最后，它集成了录音、播放、演示等各种功能，并提供丰富的古琴学习资源和互动社区。

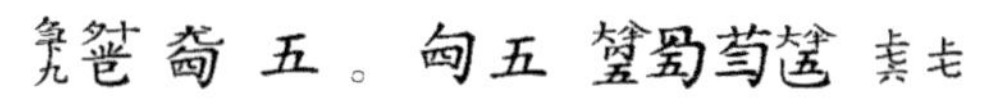

图 1. 由“古琴学习与教学系统”应用生成的减字谱

2.3 古琴电子数据库的建立与应用案例

古琴艺术相关的电子数据库是为了记录、收集、整理和传播古琴艺术文化而开发的一种信息系统。它可以包括古琴音乐、曲谱、演奏技巧、历史文化、乐器制作、表演艺术、艺术家传记等相关内容，以便于爱好者和专业人士的学习、交流和研究。古琴艺术相关的电子数据库是一个包含中国古琴音乐作品的数字化数据库，此类数据库的内容主要通常包括有古琴音乐理论资源、古琴音乐资源、古琴相关文化资源三大部分，一般情况下会涵盖丰富的古琴音乐作品，包括古琴演奏、古琴曲谱、古琴绘画等多个方面的内容。该类数据库的建设的目的是旨在推广和传承中国古琴音乐文化。该类电子数据库的技术构架如下：

前端	
Web 开发技术、HTML5、CSS3、JavaScript 等前端技术	
用户界面设计	用户交互实现
↓	
后端	
PHP 开发技术与 MySQL 数据管理技术、Ajax 技术与 MVC 架构设计技术、Java EE 技术和开源框架	
数据存储	数据管理和处理

表 3. 古琴电子数据库的技术构架

该数据库的技术架构包括前端和后端两个部分。前端主要负责用户界面的设计和用户交互的实现，后端则负责数据存储、管理和处理。具体来说，该数据库采用了现代化的 Web 技术和开源框架来实现前端和后端的功能。其中，前端采用了 HTML、CSS 和 JavaScript 等技术来实现用户界面的设计和实现；后端则采用了 Java EE 技术和开源框架来实现数据的存储和管理。数据库的底层采用了 MySQL 关系型数据库管理系统来存储和管理数据。

古琴艺术相关的电子数据库的代表性案例有“中国音乐学院古琴艺术电子资源库”“古琴图谱电子图书馆”等。其中，“中国音乐学院古琴艺术电子资源库”由中国音乐学院于 2012 年开发，内容涵盖古琴演奏技巧、古琴曲谱、古琴历史文化、古琴制作等方面的知识。它以图文并茂的形式呈现，包括了大量的图片、音频和视频资源。此外，该数据库还包括了一些对古琴演奏技巧进行分析和探讨的文章，为古琴爱好者提供了非常有用的参考资料。“古琴图谱电子图书馆”是上海音乐学院于 2015 年发布的，这个电子图书馆收录了众多古琴图谱，包括历代名家的图谱和现代制琴师所创作的新谱。这些图谱均以高清晰度数字图像的形式呈现，方便用户进行查看和研究。该电子图书馆的出现，让古琴图谱这一重要的古琴艺术文献得以更好地保护和传承。

3. 对中国传统音乐发展的意义

基于计算机技术的中国传统乐器数字化转型，例如古琴数字虚拟乐器开发、古琴减字谱输入法应用开发、古琴电子数据库建立等，对中国传统音乐发展具有重要意义，这些意义主要表现在以下几个方面：

第一，保护和传承中国传统音乐文化。随着社会的不断发展，传统音乐在现代社会逐渐失去了市场和关注，传统音乐文化逐渐被遗忘和淡化。通过数字化转型，可以更好地保存和传承传统音乐文化，让更多人了解和学习传统音乐，使传统音乐文化得到更好的保护和发扬。[5] 第二，提高中国传统音乐的演奏与创作效率。传统音乐演奏和创作通常需要很长时间的练习和琢磨，而数字化转型可以通过数字化技术提高音乐表现的效率，让音乐家更加专注于音乐创作和表现，提高音乐品质。[6] 第三，拓宽中国传统音乐的市场和受众。通过数字化转型，传统音乐可以更好地融入现代社会，拓宽传统音乐的市场和受众，使更多人了解和喜爱传统音乐。第四，促进中国传统音乐教育的普及和发展。数字化转型可以使传统音乐更加便捷地被传播和学习，[7] 提高传统音乐教育的普及和发展，培养更多优秀的传统音乐人才，推动中国传统音乐的发展。第五，满足当代人们的文化需求。数字化转型使得传统音乐更加便捷地接触和学习，满足了当代人们对音乐艺术的需求。[8] 数字化转型可以让人们在不同的场合和时间里欣赏到优美的传统音乐，满足了人们对音乐文化的追求。[9] 第六，为中国的传统文化交流提供新的方式和手段。通过基于计算机技术的中国传统乐器数字化手段进行创作数字音乐的方式可以更方便地将传统音乐文化传递到世界各地，进而可以增加更多的传统文化交流契机。[10] 第七，促进中国传统文化与现代科技的融合。基于计算机技术的传统乐器数字化转型开发可以促进传统文化与现代科技的融合，[11] 推动传统文化的创新和发展，同时也可以促进中国传统文化在创新型数字社会中的传承和发扬。

4. 结语

就基于计算机技术的传统中国乐器的数字化转型整体情况而言，古琴数字虚拟乐器的发展相对成熟。几家知名软件公司推出了多款古琴虚拟乐器，在呈现古琴音色方面取得了良好的效果。虚拟乐器的出现不仅为音乐家提供了方便快捷的演奏方式和更多的声音效果处理选择，还对推广古琴艺术和文化做出了重要贡献。随着计算机技术的不断发展，古琴虚拟乐器的发展将变得更加多样化和高端化。虽然这些虚拟乐器技术已经成熟，但仍存在一些问题。例如，虚拟乐器的音质与传统乐器之间仍存在一定差距，虚拟乐器的演奏风格也与传统古琴有很大的不同，这在传统古琴演奏者和古琴艺术传承者中引起了一些争议。

古琴减字谱输入法的开发始于上世纪 80 年代。[4] 在不断的改进和创新中，它已经成为一种成熟的数字化技术应用形式。不同的开发者和应用在实现方法上存在差异，但目标都是提供更方便、高效的减字谱输入方法。未来的古琴减字谱输入法将会进一步改进和创新，为古琴爱好者和实践者带来更便利的用户体验。随着数字技术的不断发展，与古琴艺术相关的电子数据库正受到越来越多的关注。这些数据库不仅可以记录和传承古琴艺术的丰富文化遗产，还可以帮助研究人员和爱好者更好地了解和学习古琴文化。

目前，古琴艺术相关的电子数据库已经涵盖了很多方面，包括历史、文化、演奏技巧、曲谱等。一些著名的古琴博物馆和研究机构，如北京中央音乐学院古琴研究所、上海音乐学院、台湾国立故宫博物院等，都建立了自己的古琴艺术电子数据库。这些数据库包含了大量珍贵的古琴文化遗产，如名家名器、珍稀古琴、古琴曲谱等，并提供了多种学习、研究和交流的途径。古琴艺术相关的电子数据库不仅可以满足古琴爱好者的需求，也对古琴文化的传承和发展起到了重要的推动作用。通过数字化技术的手段，可以更好地保存、保护和传承古琴文化遗产，也可以更好地传播和推广古琴艺术，促进古琴文化的国际交流和合作。同时，数字化技术的应用也为古琴研究者提供了更广阔的研究空间和研究方法，使得古琴研究和创新更加深入和广泛。古琴艺术相关的电子数据库已经成为古琴文化传承和发展的重要手段，可以为爱好者、研究者和文化工作者提供更加便捷、全面、准确的资源和信息。随着数字化技术的不断进步和应用，古琴艺术相关的电子数据库将会更加丰富、多样化和智能化，为古琴文化的传承和发展注入新的动力和活力。

本文结合计算机技术的中国传统乐器数字化转型案例分析得出，基于计算机技术的中国传统乐器数字化转型对于中国传统音乐的发展具有重要的推动作用，其可以保护和传承传统音乐文化，提高音乐创作和表现的效率和品质，拓宽传统音乐的市场和受众，促进音乐教育的普及和发展，满足当代人们的文化需求，为传统文化交流提供新的方式和手段，促进传统文化与现代科技的融合，有助于推动中国传统音乐的数字化转型与创新型发展。

5. 参考文献

[1] Zhang Y. “Digitization and Preservation of Traditional Music in the Digital Age,” *Journal of Culture and Art Education,* vol.18, no.3, pp. 80-85, 2020.

[2] Zhang W. “Digital Technology and Traditional Music: A Case Study of the Qin”, *Journal of Chinese Musicology*, vol.39, no.4, pp. 92-99, 2019.

[3] Zhang B, Xu P. “The Transformation of Traditional Music in the Digital Age: The Case of Chinese Minority Music”, *Journal of Music Research*, vol.1, pp. 91-100, 2020.

[4] Ding X, Ye X, Zhou C. “Coding and Compilatory Method in the Transnotation Jianzipu of Qin Zither”, *Musicology in China*, vol.2, pp. 93-96. 2008.

[5] Hofman A, Jovanović J. “Digital Transformation of Traditional Music and Dance in Serbia: New Forms of Cultural Preservation and Popularization”, *Science and Young Talents*, vol.1, pp. 25-34, 2019.

[6] Mukerji M. “The Role of Digital Technologies in the Preservation and Promotion of Traditional Music in India”, *Journal of World Popular Music*, vol.5, no.1, pp. 31-47, 2018.

[7] Johnson H. “Digital Technologies and Traditional Music Cultures: A Global Perspective”, *Journal of Folklore Research*, 2018, vol.55, no.1, pp. 1-14, 2018.

[8] Kearney D, Sweeney K. “The Impact of Digital Technologies on Traditional Music in Ireland”, *Journal of Music, Technology and Education*, vol.11, no.1, pp. 35-50, 2018.

[9] Dahlig-Turek E, Barda-Dworakowska E. “Digital Transformation of Traditional Music in the Age of Globalisation”, *Respekty Humanistyczne*, vol.5, no.17, pp. 35-48, 2019.

[10] Doherty L. “The Impact of Digital Technology on the Transmission of Traditional Music”, *Ethnomusicology Forum*, vol.25, no.3, pp. 360-375, 2016.

[11] Kholmirzaeva S. “Digitization of Traditional Music: Preservation and Promotion of the Intangible Cultural Heritage of Uzbekistan”, *Bulletin of the National Academy of Sciences of the Republic of Kazakhstan*, vol.1, no.449, pp. 96-103, 2020.

基于大规模预训练模型(GPT)和迁移学习的 AI 音乐生成

AI Music Generation Based on Large-scale Generative Pre-trained Transformer (GPT) and Transfer Learning

第一作者
朱春霖
湖南师范大学
575529721@qq.com

第二作者
田旭航
湖南大学
710980048@qq.com

摘要

ChatGPT 的出现让全世界耳目一新。ChatGPT 的核心技术是生成式预训练人工智能模型,它通过大规模样本的训练,能够生成符合人类逻辑和思想的高质量文本表达。音乐生成与文本生成在技术上有很大的相通之处,本文以GPT模型为基础,设计了一种基于迁移学习的音乐智能生成方法,将GPT 大模型包含的思维与表达"经验"用于指导音乐生成,实现了智能作曲。对比分析表明,本文方法较char-RNN、C-RNN-GAN、musicVAE 等方法在音乐生成质量等方面有着更好的技术指标。

1. 概述

音乐作为一种艺术形式,它涉及各种声音、音高和形式的自由相互作用,从而产生连贯的听觉体验。由于其复杂性,其特征往往较难捕捉。然而,随着深度学习的发展,这种类型的算法作曲任务,无论是国内还是都已有了许多有效的理论及方法。在相对早期的传统计算机音乐生成系统中,早已存在着许多的音乐的表示、记录及再现的方法。同自然语言数据一样,音乐也是一种时间序列,伴随着各类型序列建模算法的发展[1],计算机音乐生成研究也取得了长足的进展。

早期音乐生成算法,首先就生成规则制定了一定范围的音高、音名和时值,再用计算机在约束范围内随机生成旋律。后来,又有诸多浅层结构的音乐生成算法被提出,诸如条件随机场(Conditional Random Fields,CRFs)[2],隐形马尔科夫模型(Hidden Markov Model,HMM)[3]等 ,以替代随机生成过程实现更好的生成效果,但这类方法在音乐的连贯性上有一定的损失,因此,随后出现了基于深度学习的音乐生成方法。

近些年,随着深度学习技术的高速发展,以及其在自然语言处理等领域的突出表现,学术界开始关注将深度学习技术以及自然语言处理技术用于音乐生成。同自然语言数据一样,音乐也是一种时间序列,使用自然语言处理方法来处理音乐也是当下学术界最普遍的方向。现今的方法主要分为以下几类,第一种为基于递归神经网络 (Recurrent Neural Network ,RNN) 及其嵌套其他类型网络的实现 ,如 LSTM[4] 、 LSTM-RTRBM[5] 、 Char-RNN[6] 、 Folk-RNN[7] 、 C-RNN-GAN[8]等 ,这些模型主要通过网络学习到真实音乐中的音符特征之前的关系,而并非从整个曲子中学习和声以及作曲的一些规则;第二种为基于变分自编码器 (Variational Auto-Encoder,VAE) 的网络实现,例如musicVAE[9],通过分层的解码器对有长期结构的序列的建模进行改进;第三种为基于 Transformer 网络及其嵌套其他类型网络的实现,这部分的研究成果目前还相对较少,如 MusicBERT[10]。

本文也是研究使用 Transformer 类模型 GPT-2 实现自动音乐生成,由该模型生成的文本,目前在情感的表达以及上下文连贯性上超过了人们预期。通过对 GPT-2(Generative Pre-trained Transformer 2 ,GPT-2)模型进行迁移学习训练,得以将经过大量自然语言数据训练,具有 15 亿个参数的模型用于音乐生成,还设计了评估试验以对比了该方法同其他几个生成模型在音乐生产效果上有一定的提升。本模型生成的音乐过渡不突兀,整体风格一致,有着良好的通用性且生成的音乐自然。

2. GPT 大规模预训练模型

GPT 的全称为 Generative Pre-trained Transformer, 自 2018 年 6 月 GPT-1 的诞生起,至今已发布了 5代,分别为 GPT-1 ,GPT-2 ,GPT-3 ,GPT-3.5 (ChatGPT) ,GPT-4 。因为 GPT-3 ,ChatGPT ,GPT-4 的源代码没有公开 ,而 GPT-1 ,GPT-2 的源代码是开放的,所以本文以 GPT-2 为基础,来设计基于迁移学习的音乐智能生成方法。

GPT 使用的是将无监督的预训练与有监督的微调(fine-tuning)互相结合的训练策略,如此便能得到更适应下游需求的模型。相较于之前更为普遍的需要手动标记大量数据的方法,这种策略有效提高了模型在缺乏标注的资源的领域中的适应性[11]。在 GPT 的训练策略中，针对下游任务的微调与预训练均采用统一的框架， 而最后一层 Transformer 则直接连接到 softmax，使用 softmax 作为任务输出层，这可以有效减少计算复杂度。尽管 GPT 采用单向的 Transformer 进行编码，但是依旧可以很好的地捕获长距离语言结构。

GPT 的“半监督”训练方法涉及两个阶段：无监督的生成式预训练阶段，其中使用语言建模目标来设置初始参数，以及通过有监督的判别微调阶段这些参数适用于目标任务。

2.1 Transformer 特征提取器

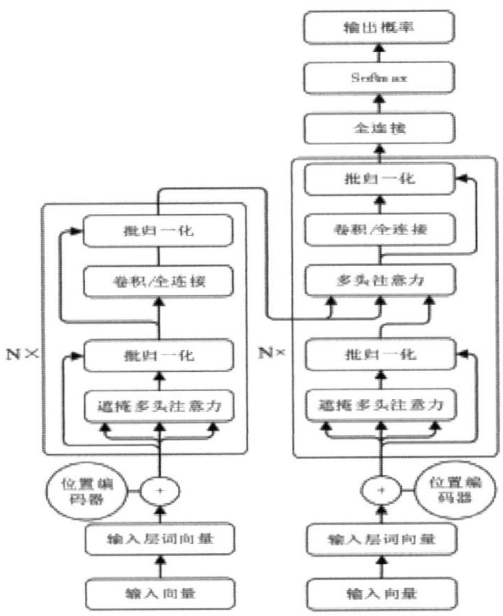

图 1 Transformer 模型架构

如图 1 所示，Transformer 特征提取器的整体结构由编码器和解码器构成。而其中编码器模块又由两类组成，分别为前馈神经网络层和多头注意力层。

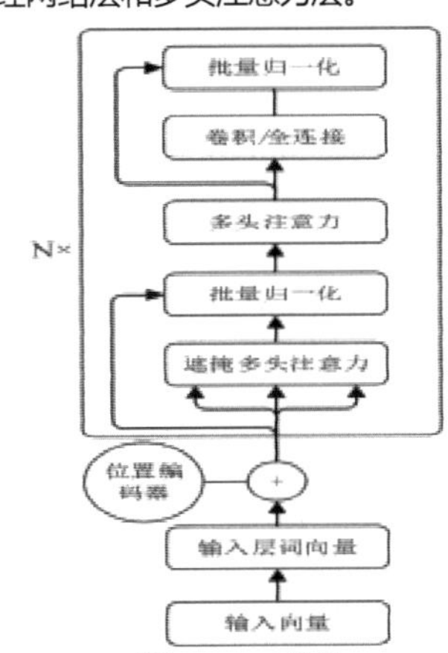

图 2 GPT-2 结构

如图 2 所示，不同于 Transformer 模型的构架，GPT-2 仅使用加有多头注意力机制的编码器模块堆叠而成。

OpenAI 发布了四种 GPT-2 模型，如表 1 所示，分别为 Base（模型参数数量为 117M），Medium(345M)，Large(774M)，XL(1.5B)。

表 1 四种 GPT-2 模型

模型	层数	Medium（355M）	注意力头数	参数量
GPT2 - base	12	768	12	117M
GPT2-medium	24	1024	16	345M
GPT2 - large	36	1280	20	774M
GPT2 - xl	48	1600	25	1558M

出于对被滥用的担心，OpenAI 仅分阶段开放了 124M 和 355M 版本[12]，仅向有限的机构提供 774M 和 1.5B 版本。本文根据实际情况，选择了 Medium（355M）。

2.2 位置编码器

如图 2 所示，GPT-2 中编码器模块为多层堆叠的结构，它的输入为原始序列片段，亦或是由上一层解码器解码后输出的向量。 在该模块中， 使用词嵌入（Word2Vec）[13]的方法对数据的维度进行压缩，使得高维的稀疏的词向量转换进入低维的空间中进行保存。

将词向量维度设为 d，在所有数据中存在 m 个不同的单词，便可以构造矩阵 $PE_{m\times d}$，矩阵中的元素为：

$$PE_{(pos,2i)} = \sin\left(\frac{pos}{10000^{\frac{2i}{d}}}\right) \quad (1)$$

$$PE_{(pos,2i+1)} = \cos\left(\frac{pos}{10000^{\frac{2i}{d}}}\right) \quad (2)$$

单词在句子中的位置用 pos 表示，分别采用正弦和余弦的方式对句子的奇偶部分进行编码。矩阵构造完毕后，One-hot 的表示向量为 $w_{l\times m}$，将单词的 $w_{l\times m}$ 与 PE 相乘，得到的编码 pr 即为该单词的位置。最后相加原始词嵌入向量 pe 与 pr，便可以得到经位置编码的词向量 p。

$$p_{1\times d} = pe + w_{l\times m} \times PE_{m\times d} \quad (3)$$

2.3 遮掩的多头注意力机制

多头注意力机制是一种用以适应对长期依赖的学习的机制，其实现过程如下。

首先，将每个经过位置编码的词向量 p 通过词嵌入矩阵进行变换，得到的三个向量，分别为 Q(Query Vector)，K(key Vector)，V(Value Vector)。由此经计算便可以得到每个单词的关注度得分，得分越高则得到“关注度”越高，反之亦然，该分数的计算为：

$$\text{score} = Q^T K \quad (4)$$

接下来为得分的标准化过程：首先假设 Q，K 中每一个元素是标准化的、独立的随机变量。

则其点积 $Q^T K = \sum_{i=1}^{d} q_i k_i$，均值为 0，方差为$d$。

再将该得分除以词向量维度的平方根，以得到其标准化表示。

$$\text{score} = \text{score} / \sqrt{d} \qquad (5)$$

对该得分还需要进行 softmax 归一化处理，其第 i 个词语的得分为：

$$\overline{score_i} = \frac{e^{\text{score}_i}}{\sum_{j=1}^{l} e^{\text{score}_j}} \qquad (6)$$

最后，将第 i 个词语得分 $\overline{score_i}$ 分别乘以向量 V 做加权求和，就可以得到对词语 i 的注意力。

$$\overline{score_i} = \sum_{j=1}^{l} V_i \cdot \overline{\text{score}_j} \qquad (7)$$

以上过程将重复多次，取多次结果的平均值，该机制便为“多头”。

遮掩机制，指的是在训练过程中，会随机的遮住原始语料中单词。这种机制可以有效增大分布的多样性，且在一定程度上防止过拟合。

2.4 批归一化

批归一化（batch Normalization）是一种深度学习中常见的处理机制，其作用为防止过拟合。

批归一化所作的处理为：

$$\hat{y}_i = \frac{y_i - \mu_B}{\sqrt{\sigma_B^2 + \epsilon}} + \beta \qquad (8)$$

在公式（8）中，$\hat{y}_i$表示第 i个词语批归一化后的词向量，y_i表示的是未经归一化的词向量，μ_B 为同一批输入的词向量的均值，σ_B^2 则为同一批词向量的方差，而 ϵ、β 则表示小的漂移量，其作用为防止出现分母为 0 的情况。

3. 复音音乐数据

复音音乐指同一个时间步内，乐谱能包含多个音符，比如在钢琴演奏中除主旋律外还能响起和声、和弦等伴奏便属于复音音乐特征。复音音乐被认为是单音音乐的自然发展，复音音乐乃至多轨音乐的生成也是当下音乐生成领域的主要的研究方向。

3.1 ABC 记谱法

ABC 格式的电子乐谱是一种简写形式的乐谱，是一种旨在使用纯文本标记音乐的格式，由 Chris Walshaw 等人拓展[14]，ABC 记谱法用“CDEFGAB”等字母记录音高，用“/[=”等附加符号配合，便能表示出音值、音调、降调、升调等音乐信息。

表 2 三种格式的电子乐谱比较（以欢乐颂为例）

比较项目	ABC	MIDI	MusicXML
力度	有	有	有
音高	有	有	有
音长	有	有	有
小节	有	无	有
房子	有	无	有
节拍	有	有	有
装饰	有	有	有
重复	有	无	有
多轨	有	有	有
歌词	有	无	有
表情记号	有	无	有
同音异名区分	有	无	有
文件大小/字节	736	1035	17158
冗余字符数	少	适中	多

ABC 记谱法基于美国信息交换标准代码（ASCII，American Standard Code for Information Interchange）实现，故可以使用任意文本编辑器进行编辑和存储，可以实现对齐到音符的歌词表示，对多声部旋律的表示，对多乐谱的标注，对指法谱、MIDI 以及多种其他音乐格式的转换[14]。

除了 ABC 格式，常见的电子乐谱格式还有 MIDI，MusicXML，这三种格式类型的电子乐谱在表示乐谱的结构、内容以及其他音乐信息上，有着一定的差异。作为用于乐谱建模和生成的数据，数据的格式应能够在更短的长度下表示更多的信息。

如表 2 所示，相较于其他两种类型[15]，ABC 在保证了能表示全部乐谱关键信息的同时，还有着冗余字符数少的优点。过长的字符数长度会增大模型的计算量，也会提高算法的复杂度，造成模型难收敛等问题，故采用 ABC 格式电子乐谱用于音乐的建模和生成工作。

3.2 基于 ABC 记谱法的复音音乐数据表示

表 3 ABC格式的《欢乐颂》

贝多芬《欢乐颂》
X:1 T:Ode to Joy By Ludwig Van Beethoven L:1/4 Q:90 K:C [c3/4e3/4C23/8G23/8]e3/4 f3/4 g3/4[g3/4G11/8]f3/4[e3/4G11/8]d3/4 [c3/4C23/8E23/8G23/8]c3/4 d3/4 e3/4[e9/8G11/8]d3/8 [B3/2d3/2G11/8] z/8 [c3/4e3/4C23/8G23/8]e3/4 f3/4 g3/4[g3/4G11/8]f3/4[e3/4G11/8] d3/4[c3/4C23/8E23/8G23/8]c3/4 d3/4 e3/4[d9/8G11/8]c3/8 [c3/2C11/8]z/8[d3/4G23/8]d3/4 e3/4 c3/4[d3/4G11/8]e3/8 f3/8 [e3/4G11/8]c3/4[d3/4G11/8]e3/8 f3/8[e3/4^G11/8]d3/4[c3/4A5/8] z/8[d3/4^F5/8]z/8[=G11/8z3/4][e3/2z3/4][c11/8z3/4]e3/4 [f3/4^A11/8]g3/4 [g3/4=A11/8]f3/4[e3/4=F11/8]d3/4[c3/4E5/8]z/8

[c3/4E5/8]z/8[d3/4G5/8]z/8[e3/4c5/8]z/8[d9/8G11/8]c3/8
[c3/2C11/8E11/8G11/8]

表 3 为《欢乐颂》的 ABC 格式表示。在 ABC 乐谱的开始通常为大写字母加冒号的形式，用以表示乐谱的基本信息，如“X:1”表示这是第一个旋律，“T:Ode to Joy By Ludwig Van Beethoven”表示乐谱的标题是“Ode to Joy By Ludwig Van Beethoven”，“L:1/4”表示默认音符长度是“1/4”，即为乐谱中的具体音符由一个字母表示一个四分音符，“Q:90”则表示一分钟 90 拍，“K:C”表示乐谱的调号是“C”，即 C 大调。

表 4 ABC 乐谱中部分符号表示规则

表示形式	表示信息	补充
英文字母	音高	小写字母为高音，大写字母为低音
'	音高	出现在小写字母后，表示更高的高音
,	音高	出现在大写字母后，表示更低的高音
数字	音符	出现在音高后，表示该音符的长度
z	休止符	
|	小节线	“|1”和“|2”即为 1 房子和 2 房子
|:	反复开始	
:|	反复结束	
|]	终止线	

乐谱中音高、音长等信息的具体表示如表 4 所示，还有更多的详细表示规则，在此不做赘述。

4. GPT-Music 模型

4.1 迁移学习

通常迁移学习用于解决数据获取限制，数据量不足的问题。通过迁移学习方法以将 GPT-2 在自然语言领域由巨量的数据和计算资源获得“经验”用于自动作曲领域[16]。

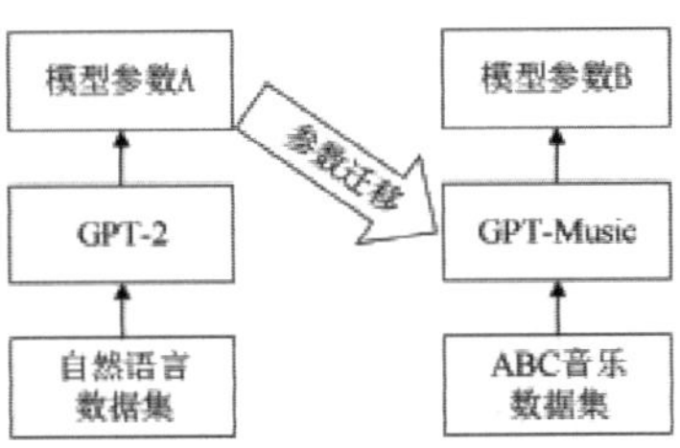

图 3 迁移学习示意图

音乐同文字一样，也在传达着情绪，情节等等的信息，也有着自己的语法规则。音乐与文字同属于时间序列，在数据的特征上也存在着一定的相似性。通过归纳式迁移学习中的参数迁移方法将 GPT-2 自然语言处理模型转换为 GPT-Music，以完成音乐生成任务。

4.2 注意力机制与词向量

同 1.3 所述，对于一个输入，音乐生成模型的注意力机制会先通过 Embedding 向量与随机矩阵计算乘积得到三个向量矩阵，分别为 Q（Query）、K（key）和 V（value）权重矩阵，之后根据这三个向量矩阵计算自注意力的分数值。具体公式如下：

$$\mathrm{Attention}(Q, K, V) = softmax\left(\frac{QK^T}{\sqrt{d_k}}\right)V \quad (9)$$

其中 Q，K 和 V 是由输入词向量构成的矩阵，dk 是输入词向量的维数。

本模型同样采用多头注意力机制，对于一个输入向量，会进行多组 Q、K、V 的矩阵的初始化，并最终得到多组向量矩阵，不同的头可以表示不同的语义信息。

词向量也可以根据下游任务“语境”的不同，而输出为不同类型的“语音”。将音乐也视为一种语言，得益于这种传递结构，便可以将模型在自然领域的“经验”在音乐生成领域进行输出。

4.3 GPT-Music 模型的训练

如图 4 所示，音乐生成模型的训练分为两个阶段[17]。首先为通过自然语言数据集训练 GPT-2-Medium 模型，这部分由 Open AI 公司实现。

$$L_1(\mathrm{U}) = \sum_i \log P\left(u_i \mid u_{i-k}, \ldots, u_{i-1}; \Theta\right) \quad (10)$$

音乐生成模型中使用的是 Transformer 模型的解码器部分，利用注意力机制获取词的向量分布。公式如下：

$$h_0 = UW_e + W_p \quad (11)$$

$$h_l = \mathrm{Transformer}_{\mathrm{block}(h_{l-1})} \forall i \in [1, n] \quad (12)$$

$$P(u) = softmax\left(h_n W_e^T\right) \quad (13)$$

其中，W_p 为位置信息的权重矩阵，W_e 为词嵌入的权重矩阵。

第二阶段为迁移学习阶段，训练 GPT-Music 模型。根据 ABC 音乐数据生成任务确定模型 Softmax 输出，之后利用 ABC 音乐数据对整个模型进行迁移学习。训练样本包括 ABC 段落序列 $[x_1, x_2, \ldots, x_m]$ 和类标签 y。根据 ABC 段落序列 $[x_1, x_2, \ldots, x_m]$ 来预测类标签 y。计算公式如下：

$$P\left(y \mid x_1, \ldots, x_m\right) = softmax\left(h_l^m W_y\right) \quad (14)$$

其中，W_y 为参数矩阵。损失函数如下：

$$L_2(\mathrm{C}) = \sum_{(x,y)} \log P\left(y \mid x_1, \ldots, x_m\right) \quad (15)$$

考虑预训练过程中的优化函数，音乐生成模型最终的损失函数为：

$$L(\mathrm{C}) = L_2(\mathrm{C}) + \lambda * L_1(\mathrm{C}) \quad (16)$$

其中，λ 为权重参数，用于控制预训练损失所占比重。

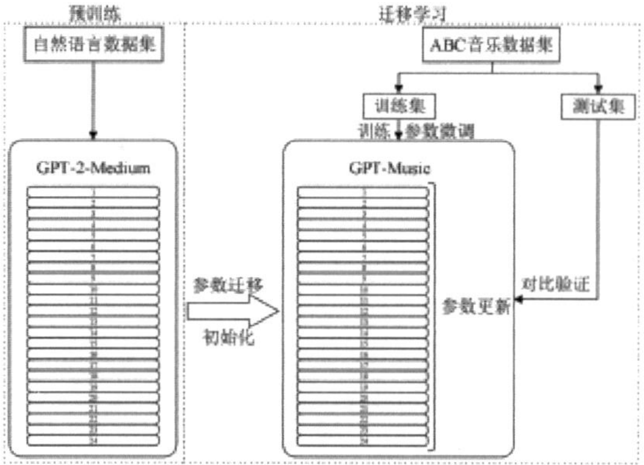

图 4 音乐生成模型结构

4. 实验

实验基于深度学习流行的 TensorFlow 框架实现，版本为 1.15，实验中所使用的服务器硬件配置为 Intel i7-8700K 3.7GHz 处理器，32G 内存和 NVIDIA RTX2080Ti GPU。

5.1 数据集

GPT-Music 模型使用 Nottingham 数据集进行训练和测试。它是一个包含 1200 首美国和英国民谣曲调的的开源 ABC 格式音乐数据集。在该实验中，经筛选后的数据被三组，分别为训练集、验证集和测试集，分别包含 694、173 和 170 首曲调。

5.2 训练实验

首先进行了训练实验，使用默认超参数，迭代次数设为无限，进行了 20 个小时的训练。

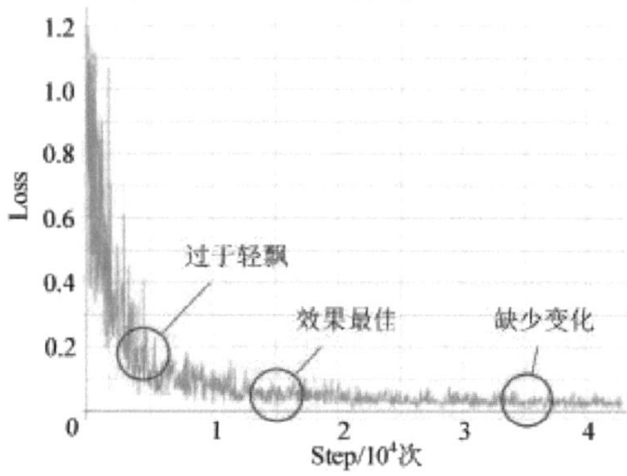

图 5 训练实验

在训练时，模型每学习一次数据之后，都会自我调整参数来使自己的输出更加接近数据集，这样一次模型自我调节的过程就叫一个 step。随着 step 的次数增多，模型会与数据集逐步拟合，生成的音乐效果也会大相径庭。分别使用多个 step 的模型检查点，对同一段旋律（来自验证集）进行续作，就主观听觉感受对其生成结果进行分析，如图 5 所示，5000step 时模型生成的音乐听感过于飘忽，35000step 模型听感缺少变化且衔接生硬，以 14500step 时生成的音乐最为流畅自然。

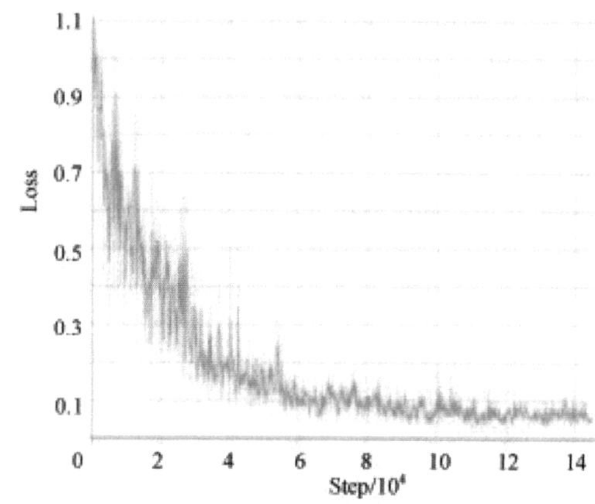

图 6 迁移学习中的训练损失

故将学习率从 1e-4 更改为 1e-5，以获得波动较小的损失曲线。将迭代次数设置为 14500 次，以避免后续的迭代可能带来的过拟合。训练损失的与 step 的关系曲线如图 6 所示，较低的学习率通常会导致较慢的收敛，但此时波动依旧已经接近稳定在 0.1 以内。

5.3 生成效果评估

在这一小节中，通过自动作曲任务来验证 GPT-Music 模型的生成效果。使用从 Nottingham 数据集提取的训练集来训练模型，并对乐曲生成结果的质量进行评价。

5.3.1 生成效果

为了得到尽可能长的乐曲片段，将 length 参数设置为最大值 1023，根据调参经验将 temperature 设置为 0.7，top_k 设置为 40，top_p 设置为 0。输出样本如图 7 所示。

```
<|startoftext|>--^--@
X: 16
T:GPT-M song
% abc-collection Database
M:4/4
L:1/4
K:Bb
P:A
F|:"Bb"B3/2c/2 d/2e/2f/2d/2|"Eb"e/2f/2g/2e/2 "Bb"d/2e/2f/2d/2|\
"Bb"e/2f/2g/2e/2 "F7"d/2e/2f/2g/2|"Bb"e/2d/2e/2f/2 "Eb"b3/2b/2|
"Bb"(3Bcd(3cBA "F7"F2ed|"Bb"d3/2c/2 d/2e/2f/2d/2|"Eb"e/2f/2g/2e/2 "Bb"d/2e/2f/2d/2|\
"Eb"e/2d/2c/2B/2 "F7"A/2B/2c/2A/2|"Bb"B3:|
P:B
|:"Bb"f3/2d/2 d/2e/2f/2d/2|"Eb"e/2f/2g/2e/2 "Bb"d/2e/2f/2d/2|\
"Bb"f3/2d/2 d/2e/2f/2d/2|"Gm"e/2d/2c/2B/2 "F7"A/2B/2c/2A/2|
"Bb"f3/2d/2 d/2e/2f/2d/2|"Eb"e/2f/2g/2e/2 "Bb"d/2e/2f/2d/2|\
"Bb"e/2f/2g/2e/2 "F7"d/2e/2f/2g/2|"Bb"e/2d/2e/2f/2 "Eb"b3/2b/2|
"Bb"(3Bcd(3cBA "F7"F2ed|"Bb"d3/2c/2 d/2e/2f/2d/2|"Eb"e/2f/2g/2e/2 "Bb"d/2e/2f/2d/2|\
"Eb"e/2d/2c/2B/2 "F7"A/2B/2c/2A/2|"Bb"B3:|<|endoftext|>
```

图 7 输出样本

通过 abcjs 库[18]可以将 abc 格式的音乐序列转换为 png 格式的五线谱图片，也可以将其装换为 wav 格式的音乐以方便播放。

图 8 生成音乐序列的五线谱表示

5.3.2 客观评价

对于音乐生成效果的评价实际较为困难，MuseGAN[19]的团队提出了一种数值化的评价标准，可以对复音音乐的生成效果进行评估，但仅适用于 midi 格式的音乐。本节结合 ABC 格式的特点并借鉴 MuseGAN 的标准并设计了 2 项客观评价指标。

如第 2 章中所述，ABC 格式有着自己的语法规则，根据 ABC 语法标准，设计了正确率（PC，percent correct）指标，用以检测模型是否能好的"理解"ABC 语法，其计算方式如公式（17）所示。

$$PC = \frac{\text{无语法错误的曲数}}{\text{生成的总曲数}} \times 100\% \quad (17)$$

在 MuseGAN 中，QN 指标表示"合格音符"数占总音符数的百分比，"合格音符"指超过设置时长的音符，它被设计用于检测生成的旋律是否过于碎片化，它的计算公式如（18）所示。

$$QN = \frac{\text{符合设置时常的音符数}}{\text{旋律的音符总数}} \times 100\% \quad (18)$$

而在 ABC 语法中，每个音符的时长与多个因素相关，与该音符是全音符还是几分音符、是否附点、是否具有延音线都有关系，故该标准不适用于 ABC 音乐。由于 ABC 音乐是由以 X 为开头表示全曲参数的"曲头"部分和表示旋律及伴奏音符的"曲身"部分组成，故模型在生成 ABC 音乐时，制定生成长度与单曲长度并不总是呈正相关，如果输出了多个"曲头"，便会产生小节数较少，听起来完整性较差的音乐。故设置完整性指标（PI,percent integrity）来检测模型整体音乐生成是否过于碎片化。

$$PI = \frac{\text{小节数大于4的曲数}}{\text{生成的总曲数}} \times 100\% \quad (19)$$

由于本模型使用 ABC 数据集，执行符号型音乐生成任务，故选用同样在该领域有着良好表现的模型来进行生成效果对比实验。

实验中对比了 Folk-RNN，Char-RNN，以及 GPT-Music 模型，三种模型均使用同一训练集训练，生成长度均被设置为 512 字节，各生成 100 首音乐进行比对，每组实验重复 5 次，取平均值。

表 5 各模型生成效果的对比

模型	PC	PI
Folk- RNN	53.6%	63.0%
Char- RNN	74.0%	82.4%
GPT- Music	88.2%	97.3%

对比结果如表 5 所示，在 PC 和 PI 两项指标的表现上，GPT-Music 都明显强于 RNN 及 LSTM 类的模型，这表明了注意力机制在很大程度上能比 LSTM 结构更好捕获符号型音乐类型时间序列的特征。

5.3.3 主观评价

设计了主观听觉评价实验来评价其质量，使用了和微软的小冰乐队[20]相同的指标，同时为了方便比对，一同展示了其复音生成能力。由于 Nottingham 数据集也存在 MIDI 格式版本，故加入 C-RNN-GAN、MusicVAE 模型一同对比，采用跟训练 GPT-Music 模型相同的训练集、验证集和测试集设置。各项指标的表述为：

- 节奏：音乐听起来是否流畅，停顿是否合适？
- 旋律：音符关系自然和谐吗？
- 完整性：音乐结构是否完整，不会突然中断？
- 复音：是否能够生成复音音乐。

表 6 各类样本主观得分

测试样本来源	复音	节奏	旋律	完整性	平均
测试集	是	3.79	3.71	3.79	3.76
GPT-Music	是	3.76	3.62	3.81	3.73
char-RNN	是	3.52	3.32	3.32	3.38
C-RNN-GAN	否	3.0	2.9	2.5	2.80
MusicVAE	否	3.1	3.2	2.8	3.03

根据测试结果，GPT-Music 模型的得分较其他几类模型有了很大提高，甚至已经较为接近真实音乐，这证明了 GPT-Music 模型在音乐生成上的有效性。

如表 6 所示，GPT-Music 模型可以生成复音音乐，且得分较 Char-RNN、C-RNN-GAN、MusicVAE 在节奏、旋律、完整性的平均水平上有了很大提高，甚至已经较为接近真实音乐，这证明了本音乐生成模型在音乐生成上的有效性。

生成 ABC 音乐的模型 ，在评分上都显著高于生成 MIDI 音乐的模型，这可能是由于复音音乐在听感上更为讨喜。较生成 MIDI 复音音乐需要按音轨进行划分，最后再进行音轨的合成并输出的生成思路 ，使用 ABC 语法能更容易的生成复音音乐，使用仅由 RNN 构成的 Char-RNN 模型也能获得较好的听感。

表 7 音乐图灵测试结果

测试样本来源	曲 1	曲 2	曲 3	曲 4	曲 5	平均
测试集	13	16	9	11	7	11.2
GPT- Music	12	17	9	13	17	13.6
Char- RNN	12	16	20	17	22	17.4
C-RNN-GAN	25	22	28	23	21	23.8
MusicVAE	19	22	21	18	24	20.8

同时还设计了音乐图灵测试实验，在测试过程中，提前告知了志愿者，他们即将听到的乐曲，部分为人类作曲，部分为模型生成，而要求他们就听到的乐曲是否为模型生成进行判断。统计结果如表 7 所示，分别从测试集和每个模型的生成样本中随机选取 5 首乐曲 ，统计判断该曲为模型生成的人数。

由测试结果可知，主观得分较高的乐曲通常也更容易被判断为人类作曲结果，然而即便是由人类作曲的音乐依旧会被认为是模型生成，本模型在结果上与测试集较为接近，志愿者并不能很好的区分出本模型生成音乐与人类作曲音乐。

5. 总结

不同于现有自动作曲方法常见的无法生成复音音乐、生成曲谱旋律性差、生成曲谱前后文关联性弱等问题。本文提出的 GPT-Music 模型很好的继承了 GPT-2 的各项优点：

1.本模型有着良好的通用性，进行复音音乐生成任务较单音音乐生成任务而言，不需要变动模型结构，也不增加计算复杂度，仅需调整音乐生成示例即可；

2.同 GPT-2 在自然语言处理方面的效果一样，GPT-Music 模型生成的音乐也使人感到自然，受试者无法准确区分生成音乐和真实音乐。

3.本模型生成的音乐过渡不突兀，整体风格一致。

在今后的工作中 ，将致力于探究以下几个方向：

1.探究不同大规模预训练模型在迁移学习后在音乐生成方面的效果，如 GPT-3[21]，BERT[22]等；

2.探究通过预训练模型的蒸馏策略来降低预训练模型的算力需求；

3.探究在迁移学习阶段如何进一步优化结构，以提高音乐生成效果，减少计算成本。

参考文献

[1] 柯登峰, 俞栋, 贾珈. 语音图文信息处理中的深度学习方法进展专刊序言[J]. 自动化学报, 2016, 42(6): 805-806. doi: 10. 16383/j.aas.2016.y000005

[2] Tseng H, Chang P, Andrew G, et al . A conditional random field word segmenter for sighan bakeoff 2005[C] . Proceedings of theFourth SIGHAN Workshop on Chinese Language Processing, 2005:168- 171.

[3] Baum L E, Petrie T, Soules G, et al . A maximization technique occurring in the statistical analysis of probabilistic functions of M ark-ov chains[J] . The Annals of M athematical Statistics, 1970, 41(1):164- 171.

[4] Nayebi A, Vitelli M. Gruv: Algorithmic music generation using recurrent neural networks[J]. Course CS224D: Deep Learning for Natural Language Processing (Stanford), 2015.

[5] Lyu Q, Wu Z, Zhu J, et al . Modelling high-dimensional sequences with LSTM- RTRBM: application to polyphonic music generation[C] . Proceedings of the 24th International Conference on Artificial Intelligence, AAAI Press, 2015:4138-4139.

[6] Sturm B L, Santos J F, Ben-Tal O, et al. Music transcription modelling and composition using deep learning[J]. arXiv:1604.08723, 2016.

[7] Karpathy A, Johnson J, Fei-Fei L. Visualizing and understanding recurrent networks[J]. arXiv:1506.02078, 2015.

[8] O. Mogren, C-rnn-gan: Continuous recurrent neural networks with adversarial training. arXiv:1611.09904, 2016.

[9] Roberts A , Engel J , Raffel C , et al. A Hierarchical Latent Vector Model for Learning Long- Term Structure in Music[J]. 2018.

[10] Zeng M , Tan X , Wang R , et al. MusicBERT: Symbolic Music Understanding with Large- Scale Pre- Training[J]. 2021.

[11] Choi K, Fazekas G, Sandler M . Text-based LSTM networks for au- tomatic music composition[J] . ArXiv :1604, 05358, 2016.

[12] Irene S, Jack C, Miles Brundage.GPT-2:1.5B Release[EB],https://openai.com/blog/gpt-2-1-5b-release/, 2019.

[13] Le Q, Mikolov T. Distributed representations of sentences and documents[C]//International conference on machine learning. PMLR, 2014: 1188- 1196.

[14] Almeida J J.Abcl:Abc music notation with rich chord support(Short Paper)[C]//7th Symposium on Languages, Applications and Technologies(SLATE 2018).Schloss Dagstuhl-Leibniz-Zentrum fuer Informatik,2018.

[15] 薛寒钰.基于递归神经网络的乐谱建模和生成[D].天津大学, 2017.

[16] 许敏, 史荧中, 葛洪伟, 等.一种具有迁移学习能力的 RBF-NN 算法及其应用[J].智能系统学报,2018, 13(6):959 －966.

[17] Radford A, Narasimhan K, Salimans T, et al.Improving language understanding by generative pre-training[J].2018.

[18] Paul R.abcjs[EB], https://github.com/paulrosen/abcjs, 2014

[19] Dong H W, Hsiao W Y, Yang L C, et al. Musegan: Multi-track sequential generative adversarial networks for symbolic music generation and accompaniment[C]//Proceedings of the AAAI Conference on Artificial Intelligence. 2018, 32(1).

[20] Zhu H,Liu Q,Yuan N J,et al.Xiaoice band:A melody and arrangement generation framework for pop music[C]//Proceedings of the 24th ACM SIGKDD International Conference on Knowledge Discovery& Data Mining.2018:2837-2846.

[21] Brown T, Mann B, Ryder N, et al. Language models are few- shot learners[J]. Advances in neural information processing systems, 2020, 33: 1877- 1901.

Devlin J, Chang M W, Lee K, et al. Bert: Pre-training of deep bidirectional transformers for language understanding[J]. arXiv:1810.04805, 2018.

A robotic environment for flute music performance and creation

Fernando Hurtado
Pontificia Universidad
Católica de Chile
fernandohurtado@uc.cl

Patricio de la Cuadra
Pontificia Universidad
Católica de Chile
pcuadra@uc.cl

Miguel Torres
Pontificia Universidad
Católica de Chile
mtorrest@ing.puc.cl

ABSTRACT

This article presents a robotic testbed to study the performance and sound generation of transverse flutes. The transverse flute is known for its complex mechanism that allows musicians to adjust various parameters dynamically, resulting in versatile and rich sounds. One important aspect of the transverse flute is that the musician's lips shape the channel, granting control over airflow, velocity, distance to the labium, inclination, and position.

The robotic testbed controls the key parameters of the sound-producing system and includes an artificial mouth and a motorized mechanism that adjusts jet length, incident angle and offset. Specialized software assists in route planning, visualizing and describing the trajectory of controllable parameters, and generating automatic parameter positions from a predefined dictionary.

Experimental results demonstrate the robot's ability to play a chromatic scale and achieve harmonically rich sounds within the desired range. Spectrogram analysis shows successful reproduction of intended pitches with slight detuning in the lower and higher notes. The robotic testbed provides a valuable tool to explore the interaction between musicians and transverse flutes, offering a rich platform for composers to create music that exceeds normal human capacities while contributing to the understanding and design of these complex instruments.

1. INTRODUCTION

The transverse flute consists of a very complex mechanism that allows musicians to obtain a rich and versatile sound by dynamically and simultaneously adjusting many control parameters. Like the recorder, its resonator is open on both of its ends, and the frequency depends strongly on the configuration of keys pressed and the velocity of the air jet, but unlike recorders, the channel is not predefined by the geometry of the instrument but is formed by the musician's lips, giving him or her the ability to adjust not only the velocity of the stream of air but also its distance to the labium, inclination, position, etc. This results in a wider operating range and a more flexible timbre.

Moreover, skilled flautists are not only concerned with specific configurations of variables to obtain a particular sound but also with how to plan a trajectory through them for a desired musical sentence. How to navigate the parameters they have at their disposal is in continuous dialogue with the flute geometry and tuning profile. It is therefore of great importance that flute designers consider the playability of the instrument, for which a good understanding of the musician's relationship with their instrument is needed. Regarding the traditional process, instrumentalists and flute makers have created a loop in which the evaluation of a flute serves as input for a new design, which after centuries of iteration has produced the optimal instruments we have today [1].

Nonetheless, this process is not only based on the evaluation of the latest designs; it also uses the knowledge obtained from the acoustic study of its mechanism to propose more adapted models. However the knowledge has grown significantly since its study began on the last century, the precise interpretation of some parameters, especially those related to the interaction between the musician and the instrument, remains unknown [2]. Therefore, a versatile testbed for experimenting with transverse flutes is proposed using a robotic environment, able to precisely and repetitively control the main parameters of the sound producing system.

Other artificial setups with the capabilities to obtain sound with flute instruments have been developed before. Most of the examples found in the literature have been used in laboratories to perform experiments with flutes [3, 4, 5, 6, 7, 8, 4]. A few examples have been created with musical intentions as Vaucanson's "Flute Player" [9] or Martin Riches's "Flute Playing Machine" [10]. A special mention must be made to Waseda Flustist Robot [11], an anthropomorphic robot with 41-DOFs designed to perform music with the transverse flute using a mechanism similar to that of humans. This impressive robot served as an important inspiration for the project.

2. GENERAL OVERVIEW OF THE ROBOT

In flute-like instruments, the sound is produced by the interaction of an intrinsically unstable air jet with a sharp edge called labium in the presence of an acoustic resonator. Therefore, the main parameters that determine the generated sound are both those that define the jet-edge interaction and those of the resonator geometry. The geometry of the resonator is mainly defined by the configuration of keys pressed, while the jet-edge interaction is more difficult to define. As a first approximation, this problem is addressed using three spacial parameters: the length of the jet before reaching the labium (l), its angle into the flute (θ), the jet's

[7]. These parameters are measured as seen in figure 1.

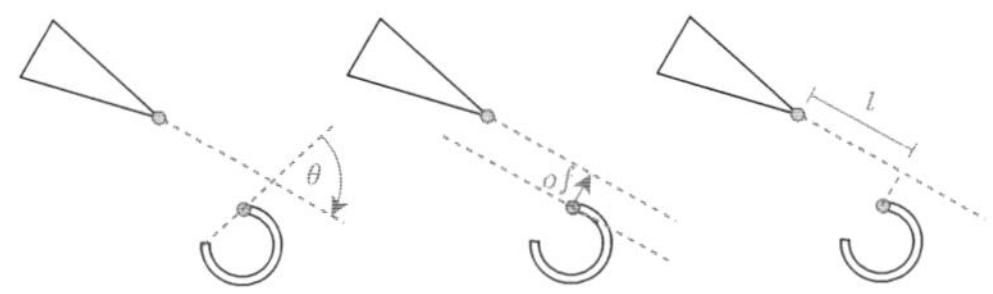

Figure 1. Graphical representation of the parameters that are used to characterize the jet-edge spacial relation

Control over these parameters is achieved by mounting a custom-designed artificial mouth into a 3-DOF mechanism operated with stepper motors. Figure 2 shows how the actuators are mounted. With this distribution, the artificial mouth, mounted in the third motor shaft, is moved around the flute to dynamically adjust the jet length, incident angle into the labium and offset. Each motor is controlled using a PID controller and feedback of the position is given by encoder readings.

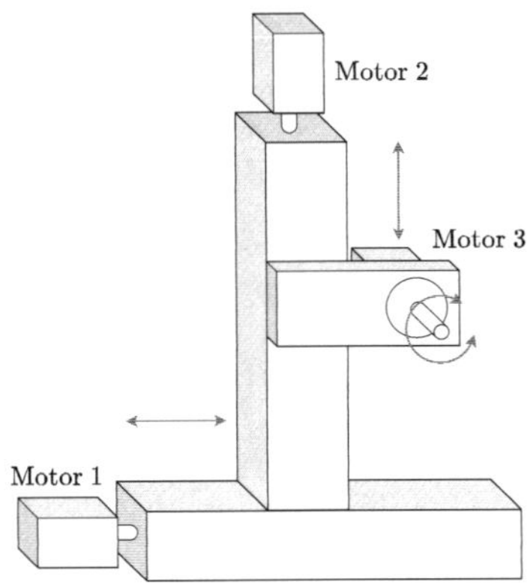

Figure 2. Robot's artificial mouth displacement system

As for the flow control, the system consists of an air compressor that feeds a mass flow controller through a regulator. The mass flow controller sets the aperture of an electric valve to obtain the desired flow. This is connected to an artificial mouth, where the pressure is measured, to end up forming the jet that will be blown into the instrument. Figure 3 depicts this situation. The artificial mouth was designed to emulate a real human mouth and its shape while performing with a flute. On its bottom, a soft elastic piece is attached to act as the lower lip, maintaining contact with the flute despite the position of the mouth.

Another robotic mechanism that can emulate finger action was implemented. It consist on nine linear actuators, each one responsible for activating a single key and mounted on an adjustable platform. This platform enables the adjustment of the angle, radial distance, and position along the flute to accommodate various flute geometries. The actuators were designed with a range of movement of 4mm, which can be traveled in less than 100ms with sufficient torque to press the corresponding key. This mecha-

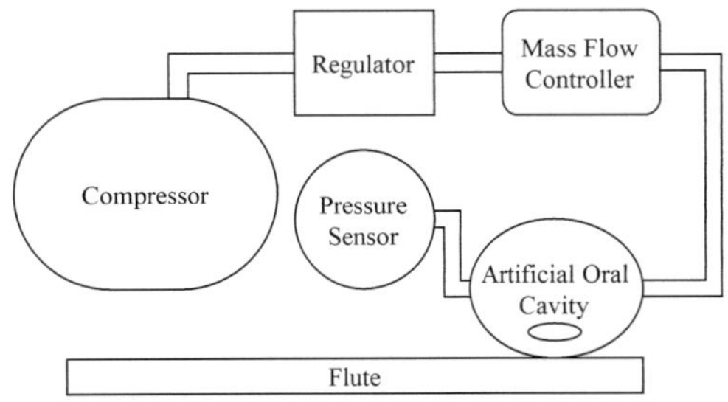

Figure 3. Set-up for the controlled air supply

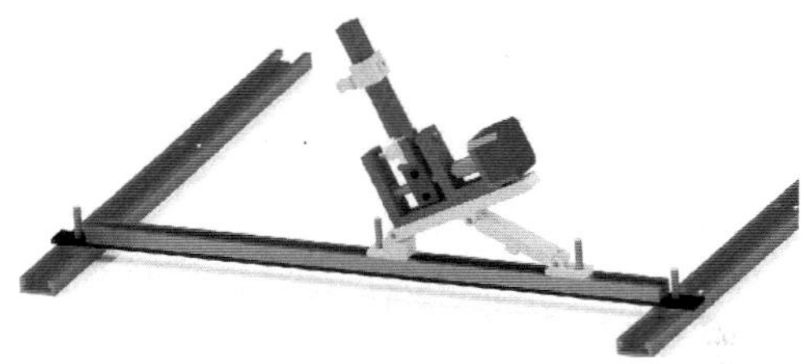

Figure 4. Finger actuator mounted on rails

3. ROUTE PLANNING

Specialized software was created to visualize the route and describe trajectories over time for the five controllable parameters: l, θ, of, Q_i, and finger positions for playing notes. (Note: Finger positions are manipulated as a whole to achieve the required configuration for each note.) The software enables the specification of points along the route for all these parameters by setting their time and value. The precise positioning of these points can be done through a dialog window with spinboxes, while rough positioning involves manually dragging them through the chart, easier for fast editing. Whenever a change occurs, a function is immediately generated to connect the points. For finger positions, a zero-order hold is applied, while for the other parameters, a first-order hold is used. The transition between two states of the finger positions occurs as quickly and synchronously as possible, considering their limited configuration space, which is treated discretely. If a sequence of finger positions is given, the software offers the option to automatically generate settings for the other parameters reading their values from a dictionary.

However, the initial path created by the first-order hold method contains discontinuities in the velocity and acceleration profiles at points where the slope changes. Therefore, a second stage is available (particularly for the parameters that control the position of the mouth for the motor movement they involve): the paths can be low-pass filtered, smoothing the signals and resulting in continuous speed and acceleration curves. The outcome of this step resembles that of a spline approximation, where the filtered function closely follows the points without necessarily passing through them exactly. The software provides different types of filters, and their parameters can be adjusted through the interface. Once the parameters are cho-

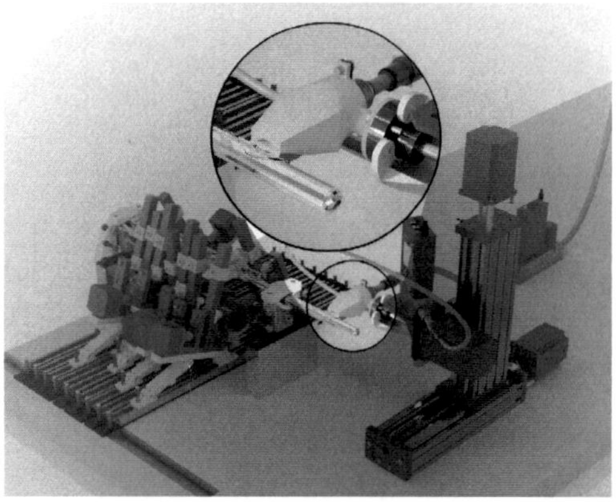

Figure 5. Render of the robotic system with the artificial mouth in position with the flute

position curve cannot be filtered. This step mimics what musicians do since When a musical phrase contains too many notes, performers cannot perfectly adjust the parameters for each note. Instead, they tend to interpolate and make smaller movements.

Finally, a third tool in the software allows the user to incorporate windowed sinusoids into the signal. This feature is especially useful for adding vibratos to the flow. With the window selection, it is possible to define different evolutions, and their amplitude, frequency and duration are also configurable. Just like the points, it is possible to precisely position the vibrato with a dialog window, or roughly by dragging it in the chart. Figure 6 shows these three tools used sequentially.

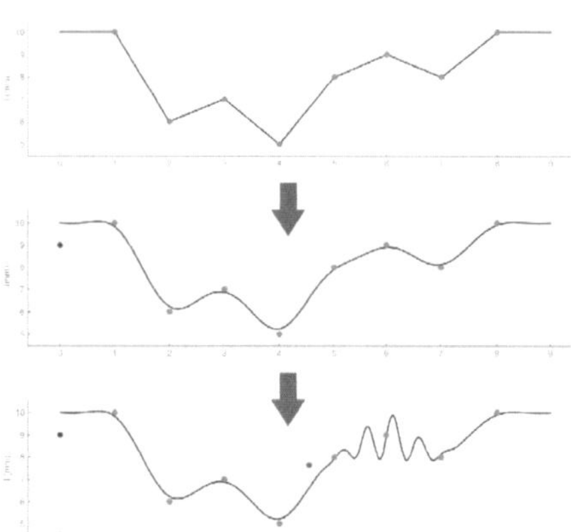

Figure 6. Optional tools for composing or describing a route, in this case for l. In the first frame a function is defined with points at certain times, in the second frame a filter is applied, and in the third frame a sinusoid windowed with a Blackman function is added.

Other functionalities of the software allow making generalized corrections to a function, e.g. moving the entire θ plot Δt in the time axis, or $\Delta\theta$ in the θ axis; and changing the tempo for the complete score by scaling the time axis.

4. INTERFACING WITH THE ROBOT

Two different ways to manipulate the robot were implemented, both through a graphical user interface (GUI). These are integrated with the route planning software, so only one program is required both for writing the trajectory (or composing); and for giving instructions to the robot.

The first way to interact with the robot is through the window presented in figure 7. Here, the state of the robot is directly accessed by altering the desired position of the mouth and flow. Whenever a change is submitted, the software calculates a straight-line trajectory and executes it. The speed of the trajectory is also configurable from the GUI. For moving the mouth, the instructions can be given in terms of l, θ and of, which is called "task space" or in terms of the position of each different motor, which is called "joint space". Also, the option to pivot around a certain point is available, which is especially useful when the point to pivot is the end of the mouth because this is a common movement in flute players. In the same window, an editable dictionary is available to reference each note to a mouth position and a flow dynamic. So then, when the finger configuration is changed, the robot can not only change the fingers to the new configuration but also adjust the mouth position and flow to the specified in the dictionary. This joint movement is optional, as the option of only moving the fingers and keeping the mouth position and flow is also possible.

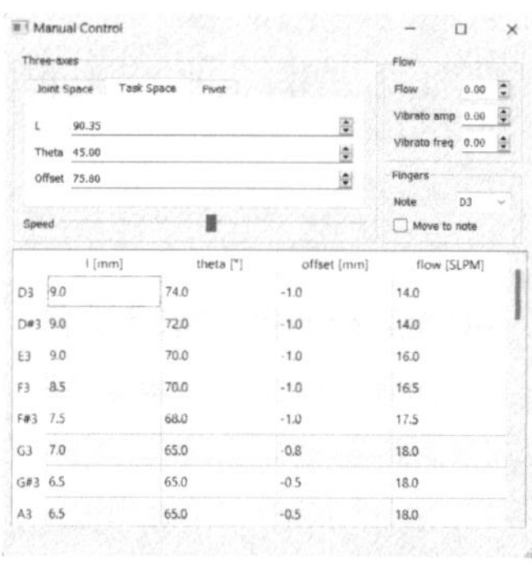

Figure 7. Interfacing with the robot through manual controls

The second way to interact with the robot is through the window presented in figure 8. In this case, the robot is instructed to follow a previously loaded score. This score can be written in the interface described in section 3. With a slider is possible to move a horizontal line, which will define the starting playing point. With a starting point selected, the robot can be moved to the state that defines it by clicking the button "go-to starting point". Once the robot reaches the starting state, the user can start playing the score. When the "Play" button is pressed, the robot will follow the instruction given by the score and will eventually stop if it finishes the score or if the user press the "Stop" button. While the robot is performing a score, the real measured values for each variable are plotted on top of the reference values. In the case of the notes, the detected pitch with a YIN algorithm [13, 14] is plotted.

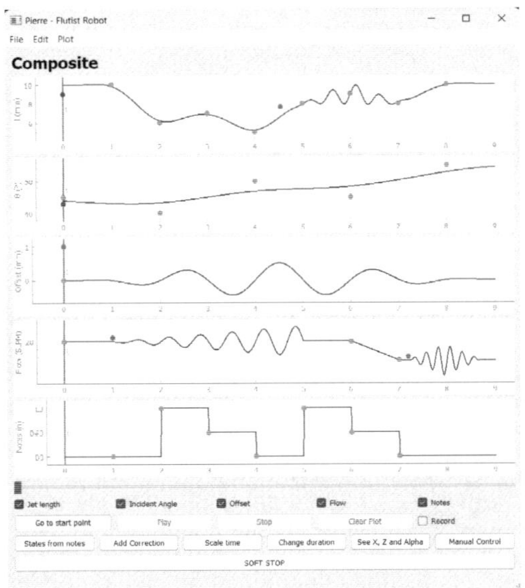

Figure 8. Interfacing with the robot through a score

5. EXPERIMENT AND RESULTS

Using the tools presented in sections 3 and 4, a dictionary was built to find reasonable combinations of parameters, or states, to play all the notes of the instrument. Then the trajectory for a chromatic scale, spanning from D3 (approximately 294 Hz) to A5 (approximately 1760 Hz) was written, and the states were generated from the dictionary. The robot was instructed to follow the scale while a microphone, 20 cm apart, recorded its performance. Figure 9 shows the spectrogram of the robot's performance, providing a visual representation of its harmonic structure and the homogeneity of the sound achieved by the robot. In Figure 10, a section of a melody shows the potential of the robot being able to emulate vibrato, dynamics and phrasing in a musical context.

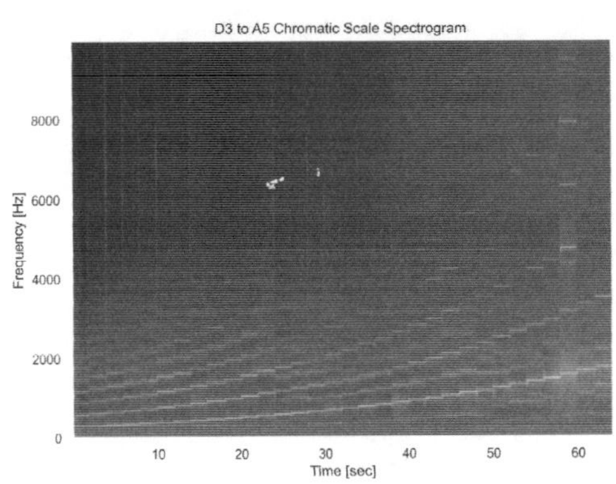

Figure 9. Spectrogram of the chromatic scaled performed by the robot

Two other scores were given to the robot as exercises to test its possibilities. In the first one, 'The Flight of the Bumblebee', the robot's dynamic response was tested along with the speed of the fingering system. The second

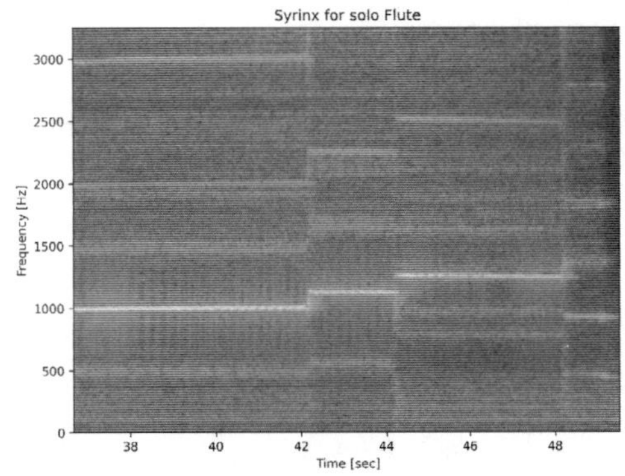

Figure 10. Close look to the spectrogram of the robot performance of Debussy's Syrinx for solo Flute, showing the robot ability to make vibrato.

score was some measures from Debussy's Syrinx for solo Flute. This time, the aim was to explore the robot's expressive possibilities with long phrases, vibrato, timbre modifications, and musical dynamics. A companion installation "Pierre, the flutist robot" is also presented at the conference, showcasing its ability to perform traditional flute music as well as some modern attempts to explore its potential.

6. CONCLUSION

A robotic system capable of performing music with the flute was presented. The system consists on a custom design artificial mouth fed by a controlled airflow and mounted on a 3-DOF platform with a finger mechanism to press the keys on the instrument.

Along with the robot, specialized software was presented. It enables the interface with the robot, allowing its manipulation through direct instructions or by automatically assigning the control parameters from a dictionary. It also facilitates route planning and trajectory visualization for parameters like jet length, incident angle, offset, flow, and finger positions. The software allows precise and rough positioning, interpolation, and filtering of trajectories. Optional tools like windowed sinusoids can be added for composing and adding vibratos. The software also enables generalized corrections, tempo adjustments, and file management.

Experimental results demonstrated the robot's capability to play notes accurately within the desired range. The spectrogram analysis showed a harmonious relationship between the intended and produced sounds. The robot's performance was further evaluated through the execution of challenging musical pieces such as 'The Flight of the Bumblebee' and Debussy's Syrinx, showcasing the system's flexibility and musical expressiveness.

As a beginner flutist who has to learn everything, we have presented a tool that allows researchers to explore the parameters that control the physical functioning of the instrument, but also to study the links between the construction of the instrument, its playing and its aesthetic sound. It will also enrich the study of historical instruments and analyze the evolution of instruments in relation to the evolution of music. Perhaps it will contribute to the reflection on the instruments of the future.

7. REFERENCES

[1] P. de la Cuadra, A. Ernoult, C. Balosso-Bardin, and B. FABRE, "Playability in flute-like instruments: Investigating the relation between flute making and instrumental control," *The Journal of the Acoustical Society of America*, vol. 141, no. 5, pp. 3874–3874, May 2017. [Online]. Available: https://doi.org/10.1121/1.4988664

[2] A. Chaigne, J. Kergomard, and B. Fabre, *Flute-Like Instruments*. Springer New York, 05 2016, pp. 559–606.

[3] K. Onogi, H. Yokoyama, and A. Iida, "Effects of jet angle on harmonic structure of sound radiating from the flute," *Acta Acustica*, vol. 5, p. 11, 2021. [Online]. Available: https://doi.org/10.1051/aacus/2021003

[4] Y. Ando, "Drive Conditions of a Flute and their Influences upon Sound Pressure Level and Fundamental Frequency of Generated Tone: An Experimental Study of a Flute I," *THE JOURNAL OF THE ACOUSTICAL SOCIETY OF JAPAN*, vol. 26, no. 6, pp. 253–260, 1970.

[5] A. Ernoult, P. de La Cuadra, and B. Fabre, "An Inclined Plane: A Simple Model for the Acoustic Influence of the Flutist's Face," *Acta Acustica united with Acustica*, vol. 104, no. 3, pp. 496–508, 05 2018. [Online]. Available: https://hal.archives-ouvertes.fr/hal-01943166

[6] R. Auvray, B. Fabre, F. Meneses, P. de la Cuadra, and P.-Y. Lagrée, "Specific features of a stopped pipe blown by a turbulent jet: Aeroacoustics of the panpipes," *The Journal of the Acoustical Society of America*, vol. 139, no. 6, pp. 3214–3225, Jun. 2016. [Online]. Available: https://doi.org/10.1121/1.4953066

[7] D. Ferrand, C. Vergez, B. Fabre, and F. Blanc, "High-precision regulation of a pressure controlled artificial mouth : the case of recorder-like musical instruments," *Acta Acustica united with Acustica*, vol. 96, no. 4, pp. 701–712, 2010. [Online]. Available: https://hal.science/hal-00445632

[8] Y. Sawada and S. Sakaba, "On the transition between the sounding modes of a flute," *The Journal of the Acoustical Society of America*, vol. 67, no. 5, pp. 1790–1794, May 1980. [Online]. Available: https://doi.org/10.1121/1.384200

[9] J. de Vaucanson, "Le Mécanisme du Fluteur Automate; An account of the mechanism of an automation: or, image playing on the German-Flute," *The Flute Library*, pp. 1–21, 1979.

[10] J. Solis and A. Takanishi, *Wind Instrument Playing Humanoid Robots*. Berlin, Heidelberg: Springer Berlin Heidelberg, 2011, pp. 195–213. [Online]. Available: https://doi.org/10.1007/978-3-642-22291-7_12

[11] ——, "An Overview of the Research Approaches on Musical Performance robots," in *International Conference on Mathematics and Computing*, 2007.

[12] P. de La Cuadra, "The sound of oscillating air jets: Physics, modeling and simulation in flute-like instruments," Ph.D. dissertation, Stanford University, California, Jan. 2006.

[13] A. de Cheveigné and H. Kawahara, "YIN, a fundamental frequency estimator for speech and music," *The Journal of the Acoustical Society of America*, vol. 111, no. 4, pp. 1917–1930, 04 2002. [Online]. Available: https://doi.org/10.1121/1.1458024

[14] M. Mauch and S. Dixon, "PYIN: A fundamental frequency estimator using probabilistic threshold distributions," in *2014 IEEE International Conference on Acoustics, Speech and Signal Processing (ICASSP)*, 2014, pp. 659–663.

Micro-variation of Sound Objects Using Component Separation and Diffusion Models

Philip Liu [1]
Korea Advanced Institute of Science and Technology
phplu@kaist.ac.kr

Youngjun Choi [1]
Korea Advanced Institute of Science and Technology
youngjun.choi@kaist.ac.kr

Jinjoon Lee [*]
Korea Advanced Institute of Science and Technology
jinjoon.lee@kaist.ac.kr

ABSTRACT

Micro-variation of sound objects stands as a cornerstone technique within the toolkit of practitioners spanning both the artistic and engineering domains engaged in sonic manipulation. It is often demanded to achieve musical repetitive patterns with slight variations or rich sound texture through layering. The 'micro-variation' denotes subtle variations in sound characteristics, while the 'sound object', as the term widely employed in music and sound art, refers to a fundamental unit of sonic material. Achieving the level of richness and diversity of a sound generated through physical vibrations in the digital domain is challenging, due to the deterministic nature of the digital domain. Several advanced techniques exist to overcome it, including physical modeling synthesis or sample-based generators with several types of pseudo-random algorithms implemented. In this regard, we introduce a novel approach to utilizing component separation techniques and deep neural networks (diffusion models) for the resynthesis of sound objects on par with the richness of the physical world in a digital environment: subtle yet sophisticated, non-deterministic variations in the phase, timbre, amplitude curve, and pitch of each instance of sound. By extending the applications of diffusion models, we provide a robust and efficient tool for generating an indefinite number of micro-variations, which has broad applications for constructing diverse patterns in samples and environmental soundscapes, hence expanding the potential of sound design and music composition.
Our project files and example sounds are available at https://github.com/youngjuene/microvar.

1. INTRODUCTION

Since the advent of the phonautograph, humanity has been endowed with the capability to capture and retain the ephem eral phenomenon of audio recordings. Nonetheless, an intrinsic fixity inheres within recorded sounds when in comparison to their manifestations in the actual soundscape. In particular, sounds emanating from a physical object ensure variability, within both analog and digital realms, all occurrences exhibit marginal variation. To replicate analogous outcomes within the digital domain, we suggest a resynthesis approach employing harmonic-percussive separation and diffusion models, aiming to reproduce audio samples highly similar to the original sample input, but with slightly different characteristics in their phase, timbre, amplitude curve, and pitch. With the implemented interface, our proposed method enables the reproduction of indefinite audio instances by recording or collecting desired audio samples and processing them through the system, without the need for specific mathematical models for each type of sound. For example, it is possible to produce organic environmental repetitive patterns or musical choir-like unison effects with layering, and utilize the result in a game engine or a digital audio workstation.

[1] Both authors contributed equally. [*] Corresponding author.

2. BACKGROUND

2.1 Existing concepts and methods

In the mid-twentieth century, Pierre Schaeffer accentuated the significance of sound repetition to craft a sound object, by diminishing the listener's attention to the source of the sound. The phenomenological connection between the sound and its origin is severed through repetition, transforming the sound into an autonomous object [1]. However, the inherent limitations of tape and other sample-based devices engender difficulties in achieving subtle variations with the same degree of sophistication and richness of physical vibrations. To illustrate, the act of striking a timpani in a comparable manner yields more elaborate diversities in the resultant auditory output, in contrast to the iterative results obtained from the majority of analog or digital (re)synthesis systems.
The nature of physical vibrational objects enables sophisticated repetitions with subtle variations and also permits the creation of an organic mass of sound through the application of layering techniques. This mirrors the manner in which choirs, strings, or oscillators play phrases in unison to imbue them with heightened expressiveness and emotional resonance. In this context, numerous analog or digital techniques have been explored to emulate the nuanced variations in sound produced by a physical instrument including its timbre, phase, amplitude curve, and pitch. There exist several analog and digital generators that partially mitigate the inherent weaknesses, one illustrative example is found in analog oscillators, which meticulously alter their attributes, including phase and fine-tuning. However, within the realm of fundamental synthesis techniques —such as subtractive, additive, or frequency modulation (FM) synthesis— attaining a faithful production of physical environmental or instrumental sounds remains an intricate undertaking. Moreover, the capacity for extensive

post-processing modifications becomes constrained after the sound is recorded. This limitation arises due to the fixed nature of a recorded sound, wherein a substantial portion of the requisite data to shape the sonic profile has already dissipated.
Upon delving into more sophisticated synthesis methodologies, it becomes evident that physical modeling synthesis presents a host of advantages [2] over the previously discussed techniques. This approach distinguishes itself by virtue of its remarkable flexibility and the achievement of an elevated degree of physical authenticity. However, it necessitates the formulation of distinct mathematical models tailored to each sound category, therefore, it becomes less efficient when confronted with a diverse array of musical sounds, entailing a substantial workload. For instance, the task of synthesizing the complete sonic environment of a virtual city with physical modeling would be exceptionally challenging when constrained by a limited amount of labor and mathematical models. On the other hand, a plethora of post-processing sound effects are available that possess the capacity to modify various attributes of a given sound, but these effects lack parity with the sonic intricacies engendered by the repetition inherent in a physical environment, which audiences are adept at discerning instances where two replicated sounds exhibit a semblance of similarity yet are imbued with nuanced distinctions is challenging to be replicated through conventional sound effects alone. Due to the limitations, sound designers frequently employ an assemblage of Foley [3] or field recordings when constructing virtual soundscapes, a choice motivated by the dual aims of enhancing generative efficiency and realism. However, real-world recording practices also demand a substantial investment of labor and time. In response to the multifaceted challenges elucidated by the assorted approaches, there are growing demands for a more expedient and potent 'in the box' solution without the need to grapple with the inherent limitations associated with traditional methods. Recent advancements in artificial intelligence (AI) audio technologies have significantly contributed to the gradual realization of this coveted objective, which will be explained in the next section.

2.2 Deep learning for sound design

The introduction of deep learning methodologies is considerably expanding the boundaries of traditional sound design. Starting from such successful results in the music and speech generation domain [4, 5], researchers achieved impressive results by applying neural networks for non-musical sounds such as material interactions [6], environmental sounds, and Foley sound effects [7], etc. More recently, diffusion models developed for raw waveform synthesis successfully captured significant data variations in both unconditional and class-conditional generation tasks [8]. By integrating text encoders with diffusion models, audio attributes could be flexibly controlled via prompting [9]. With the capability to accurately model fine details of audio samples, such models demonstrated strong performance in various tasks. While these advancements are promising, there still are a lot of undiscovered applications for both practical and artistic purposes.

3. IMPLEMENTATION

3.1 Datasets

We used two datasets to train our model, FSD50k [10] and a collection of license-free SFX (sound effects) Foley audio samples, the former dataset is mainly for environmental sounds(also contains some instrumental sounds) and the latter dataset is for Foley or rhythmic loop type of sounds.

3.2 Pre-processing

In our study, we adopted varied methodologies to pre-process the dataset by applying the following techniques:

1. Original datasets: As a foundation, we established a baseline by performing minimal pre-processing. We retained the original acoustic characteristics of the samples and simply resampled all audio files to a uniform sampling rate of 44,100 Hz. This standardization provided a consistent temporal frame of reference for our subsequent analysis and model training.

2. Machine learning-based classifications: We divided each dataset into harmonic and percussive/noisy groups (Table 1), through a machine learning-based audio classification application [11]. As a result, we aimed to train the total six resulting groups including the unclassified original set with diffusion models, ensuring that each resulting model is designed to handle the specific characteristics and complexities associated with arbitrary input sound type.

Group	FSD50k	SFX Foley	Harmonicity [%]
Full	51,197	6,053	0~100
Harmonic	24,140	3,859	50 >
Percussive	27,057	2,194	50 <=

Table 1: Types of dataset groups split by harmonicity

3. Harmonic-percussive source separation (HPSS): This method applies the median-filtering HPSS technique [12] to decompose each audio signal into its harmonic and percussive components (Figure 1). After the separation, we can compare the overall amplitude of the two resulting outputs. This comparison allows us to identify which component - harmonic or percussive - is more dominant. Once determined, we opt for the less dominant component and utilize our models to make micro-variations. Later, the processed output is merged with the original dominant pair. By separating the components instead of using the raw sample, we aimed to identify which component should be preserved to improve the final output quality by appropriately recombining it back with its paired component.

4. Spectral centroid separation: This method extracts the area around the spectral centroids to segregate the audio signal into two distinct bands: centroids and peripherals (Figure 2). The spectral centroid can characterize the "brightness" or timbre of a sound. Here, every frequency component of the signal is

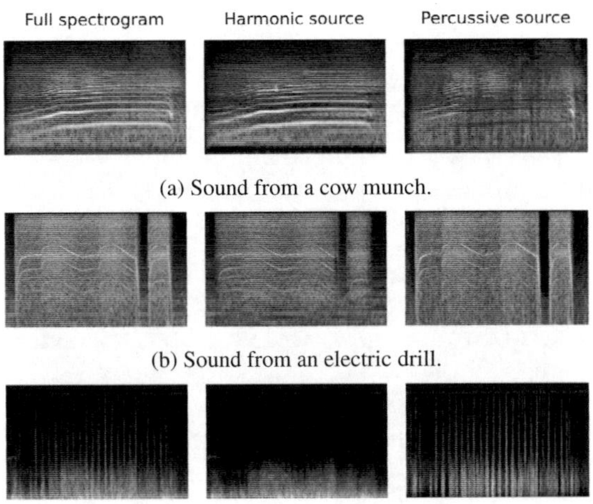

(a) Sound from a cow munch.

(b) Sound from an electric drill.

(c) Sound from a human walking on concrete.

Figure 1: Visualized spectrograms from samples after harmonic/percussion source separation. Examples from FSD50k (77241.wav, 71087.wav, 244592.wav) are placed in each row and different processes are aligned to each column.

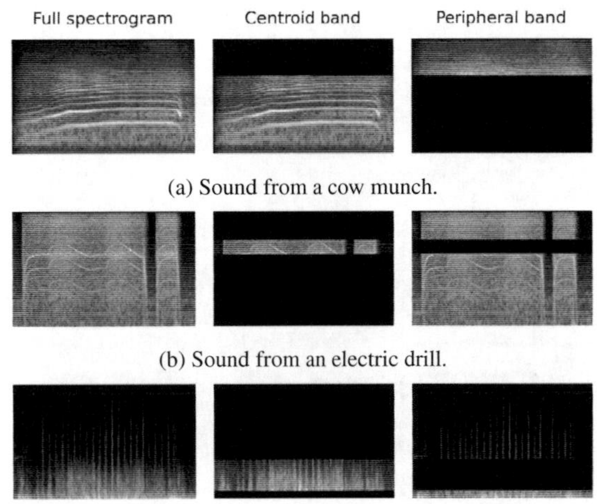

(a) Sound from a cow munch.

(b) Sound from an electric drill.

(c) Sound from a human walking on concrete.

Figure 2: Visualized spectrograms from samples after spectral centroid separation. Used same samples as Figure 1.

taken into consideration along with its corresponding amplitude. The calculation involves multiplying each frequency with its respective amplitude, and then summing these products. This total is then divided by the sum of all the amplitudes to get the weighted mean frequency. The centroid provides valuable insights into the frequency concentration of a sound, and it is often used in music analysis to compare different sounds. However, we observed several problems in some cases when attempting to apply the separation method of our pipeline. The most critical problem was the imbalance between two component-separated outputs. Depending on the characteristic of the input, the centroid output is often overly dominating, and peripheral output is close to silent, and vice versa. Consequently, we have decided to utilize the HPSS as our primary method of input component separation.

3.3 Diffusion model for audio synthesis

We implemented DiffWave [8] to produce audio samples with multiple variances. Diffusion models are engineered to create new data that mirrors the data they've been trained on. These models consist of a forward process or the diffusion process, where data is incrementally noised, and a reverse process, where this noise is converted back into a sample from the target distribution. Throughout the diffusion process, the model acts as a latent variable model by using a fixed Markov chain to map into the latent space. This fundamental operation involves systematically degrading the training data by repeatedly adding small Gaussian noise. Through this chain, noise is continuously added to the data, creating an approximate posterior (equation 1).

$$q(x_1, ..., x_T|x_0) = \prod_{t=1}^{T} q(x_t|x_{t-1}) \tag{1}$$

As a result, the data progressively transforms into pure Gaussian noise. The primary objective in training a diffusion model is to learn the reversal of the noising process, enabling it to generate new data by retracing its steps along the Markov chain (equation 2).

$$p_\theta(x_0, ...x_{T-1}|x_T) = \prod_{t=1}^{T} p_\theta(x_{t-1}|x_t) \tag{2}$$

Markov formulation stipulates that the distribution of each reverse diffusion transition depends solely on the previous timestep. Therefore the trained models can undo the diffusion process, generating new data.
We conducted our experiments by training the model on 6 dataset groups, each for 100 epochs. Following this, we investigated the model's capability to synthesize samples with variations.

3.4 Post-processing

Following the application of the diffusion model, a process of amplitude alteration of the resynthesized segment becomes crucial to sufficiently differentiate the amplitude envelope of the final output from the original. During this process, an envelope curve of the resynthesized, stronger component is extracted using a 6th-order Butterworth lowpass filter. Subsequently, a normalization procedure is executed, scaling the normalization target to a range between 1 and 3 based on the overall output level. Upon normalization, a multiplication operation is performed between the extracted envelope curve and the unaltered, comparatively weaker component. The choice of normalizing values exceeding 1 is strategic, designed to preserve the intrinsic dynamics of the weaker component post-multiplication. This approach is deliberately adopted to avert excessive alteration of the sonic character, as the preservation of the original sonic characteristics is also of paramount importance to the 'micro-variation.'

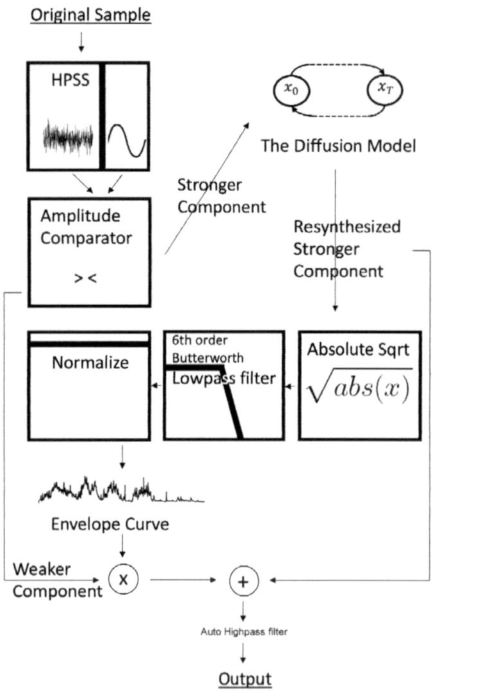

Figure 3: The entire pipeline including the post-processing.

3.5 Analysis of the result

With the proposed method, we have observed subtle yet discernible deviations between arbitrary original inputs and the corresponding resynthesized outputs. For instance, the original waveform of bird tweets in the FSD50k dataset is on the top of the three plots below (Figure 4), and the trained result of our training method using DiffWave with ML-based dataset classification(based on harmonicity) as the model along with the input component separation with HPSS is located in the middle. Lastly, the bottom is the result of the non-component-separated original sample going through the DiffWave with raw FSD50k model, and substantial differences between the original are observed in terms of both waveform and phase. The result of our method is different from the original in terms of amplitude curve and phase, yet maintains the characteristics of the original. We have also tested the system with audio samples that are not included in the training datasets and obtained similar results.

4. APPLICATION

4.1 Custom interfaces with server-client architecture

Aside from the Python side for all of the training and other processing mentioned, we have created a simple client-server architecture. In the custom-made client interface of

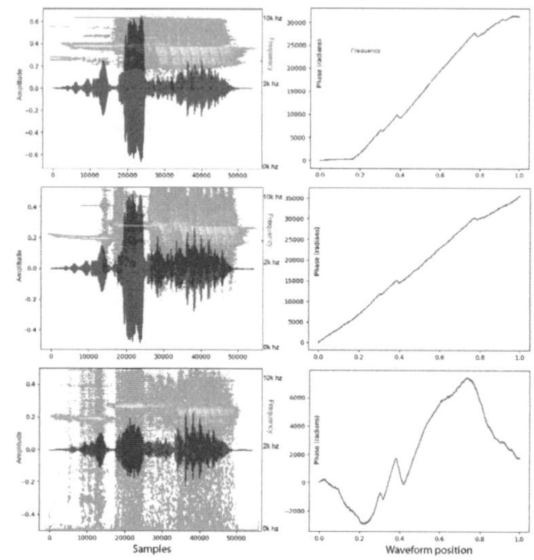

Figure 4: The waveform (blue), spectrogram (red) and phase plots (green) of outputs of the original (upper), our method (middle), and raw DiffWave (lower).

MAX/MSP or Unreal Engine, after selecting the desired 'Frequency', 'Density' and 'Length' of the sound pattern, by clicking the 'Load' button (Figure 5), a user can select any wave file in the storage and the entire information to execute the resynthesis process is sent to the server via UDP (User Datagram Protocol). Once the server finishes calculations, it sends an array of the paths of the generated samples back to the client. This architecture allows rapidly generating new sound patterns from the audio sample input, without needing to manually execute the code.

4.2 An algorithm for time distribution and practical results

We aimed at the two goals in the introduction: generating organic environmental repetitive patterns and a musical, choir-like unison effect. To achieve those, we have implemented a random impulse algorithm similar to Dust UGen of Supercollider[13], but improved in terms of controllability, to the two clients: MAX/MSP and Unreal Engine. By utilizing the algorithm, the client can distribute the generated samples, micro-variations, to the given length of the timeline that the user defines. Using the architecture, a soundscape of virtual birds in a virtual forest, generated from a single bird tweet sample was successfully created. Other successful experiments include generating patterns that consist of natural 808 kick drum variations out of only one 808 kick drum sample.

5. CONCLUSION

This study delved into a multitude of training pipelines aimed at enhancing the efficacy of the diffusion model, particularly focusing on DiffWave, alongside the application of post-processing techniques to engender micro-variations in the original input. The primary objective was to attain audio samples closely resembling the initial input while manifesting subtle differences in phase, timbre, dynamics,

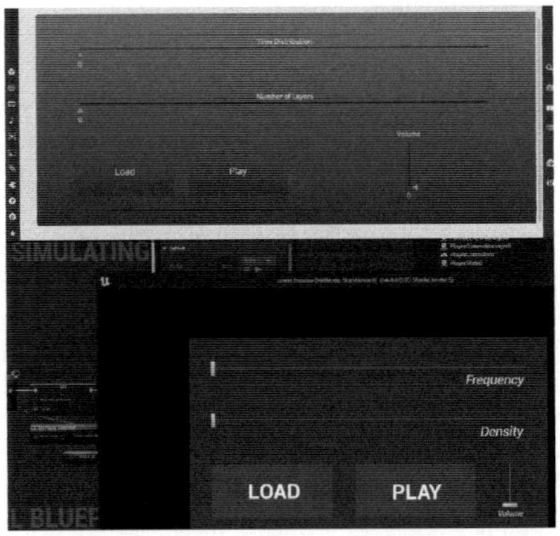

Figure 5: Two client interfaces for generating sound patterns: the MAX/MSP interface (upper) and Unreal Engine interface (lower).

and pitch. While our endeavors resulted in a partial realization of this objective, it was evident that DiffWave, when utilized in isolation, exhibited limitations in generating non-vocal sounds of commendable sonic quality. The most noticeable one is the inadequate reproduction of high-frequency components, particularly with regard to dynamics. With our proposed methodology, in most cases, we observed the characteristics of high-frequency components were well preserved compared to the exclusive usage of Diffwave, in terms of both magnitudes and dynamics. Moreover, the phase is also more akin to the original phase, which is beneficial as our purpose is to produce micro-variations, not radically resynthesized sounds. Nevertheless, instances were noted where sound quality degradation in high frequencies occurred when such frequencies predominantly resided in the weaker component after component-separated. In a comparative analysis between the outcomes of raw DiffWave and our approach, it was discerned that our method was more adept at generating natural and organic Foley, environmental, and artistic 'sound object' results. As a consequence, we contend that our proposed methodology is notably more suited for cases necessitating the creation of sophisticated and subtle variations out of an audio recording while preserving the sound quality to the utmost. We also posit that our method holds potential efficacy within specific contexts that demand the repetitive generation of richly textured, organic sound objects.

Acknowledgments

This work was supported by the National Research Foundation of Korea Grant (NRF-2023-RS-2023-00229653), and Institute of Information & communications Technology Planning & Evaluation (IITP) under the metaverse support program to nurture the best talents (IITP-2023-RS-2022-00156435) grant funded by the Korea government (MSIT).

6. REFERENCES

[1] P. Schaeffer, Treatise on musical objects: An essay across disciplines. Univ of California Press, 2017, vol. 20.

[2] J. Smith, "Physical Modeling Synthesis Update," Computer Music Journal, vol. 20, no. 2, p. 44, 1996.

[3] D. H. M. Kemper and D. Hug, "From foley to function: A pedagogical approach to sound design for novel interactions," Journal of Sonic Studies, vol. 6, no. 1, pp. 1–23, 2014.

[4] A. v. d. Oord, S. Dieleman, H. Zen, K. Simonyan, O. Vinyals, A. Graves, N. Kalchbrenner, A. Senior, and K. Kavukcuoglu, "Wavenet: A generative model for raw audio," arXiv preprint arXiv:1609.03499 , 2016.

[5] J. Engel, C. Resnick, A. Roberts, S. Dieleman, M. Norouzi, D. Eck, and K. Simonyan, "Neural audio synthesis of musical notes with wavenet autoencoders," in International Conference on Machine Learning. PMLR, 2017, pp. 1068–1077.

[6] A. Owens, P. Isola, J. McDermott, A. Torralba, E. H. Adelson, and W. T. Freeman, "Visually indicated sounds," in Proceedings of the IEEE conference on computer vision and pattern recognition, 2016, pp. 2405–2413.

[7] S. Ghose and J. J. Prevost, "Autofoley: Artificial synthesis of synchronized sound tracks for silent videos with deep learning," IEEE Transactions on Multimedia, vol. 23, pp. 1895–1907, 2020.

[8] Z. Kong, W. Ping, J. Huang, K. Zhao, and B. Catanzaro, "Diffwave: A versatile diffusion model for audio synthesis," arXiv preprint arXiv:2009.09761 , 2020.

[9] Z. Borsos, R. Marinier, D. Vincent, E. Kharitonov, O. Pietquin, M. Sharifi, O. Teboul, D. Grangier, M. Tagliasacchi, and N. Zeghidour, "Audiolm: a language modeling approach to audio generation," arXiv preprint arXiv:2209.03143 , 2022.

[10] E. Fonseca, X. Favory, J. Pons, F. Font, and X. Serra, "Fsd50k: an open dataset of human-labeled sound events," IEEE/ACM Transactions on Audio, Speech, and Language Processing, vol. 30, pp. 829–852, 2021.

[11] "Sononym." [Online]. Available: https://www.sononym.net/

[12] J. Driedger, M. Müller, and S. Disch, "Extending Harmonic-Percussive Separation of Audio Signals." in ISMIR, 2014, pp. 611–616.

[13] J. McCartney, "Dust UGen [Code]," in Supercollider. Code: in NoiseUGens.cpp of the Supercollider source code, 1996.

PATRICIA: a real-time singing synthesizer prototype for the Brazilian Portuguese language

Leonardo A. Z. Brum
Universidade Federal de Sergipe
leonardo.brum@dcomp.ufs.br

Eduardo A. L. Meneses
Société des arts technologiques
emeneses@sat.qc.ca

Edward David Moreno
Universidade Federal de Sergipe
edward@dcomp.ufs.br

ABSTRACT

This paper describes PATRICIA, a system that performs real-time singing voice synthesis (SVS) for the Brazilian Portuguese language. A technological mapping was conducted to study the latest industrial developments in real-time SVS and give directions for PATRICIA design and implementation regarding technical approach and phonetic input method. This mapping led us to choose the sample-based concatenative synthesis with text files providing the song lyrics in advance to perform the task. A proof of concept implementation of the synthesizer is presented. Future enhancements are pointed out to overcome the system's current limitations.

1. INTRODUCTION

The goal of singing voice synthesis (SVS) is to generate a singing voice employing computational methods. Some authors consider SVS as a branch of text-to-speech (TTS) technology [1, 2] since several singing synthesizers deal with textual input data, corresponding to the lyrics of the song to be synthesized. However, it is more accurate to classify this data entry as *phonetic* rather than *textual* because, as seen in this work, this kind of data can be provided by other means, like a voice audio signal. The other type of input data for SVS systems is the *musical* one, which provides sound qualities, e.g., pitch and duration, to the synthesized voice. Data formats like MIDI or MusicXML can provide these parameters.

Several techniques have been developed over the years to perform SVS. These techniques can be classified according to three main approaches [3]: rule-based approach, sample-based approach, and data-driven approach. The rule-based approach considers how sound is produced, generating voice employing physical models. It was initially developed by IRCAM with a system called CHANT in the early era of SVS [4]. In the sample-based approach, a set of pre-recorded sample voices is manipulated according to the phonetic and musical inputs of the system, as occurs in the Vocaloid [5] system engine. In a data-driven approach, statistical parametric models such as HMMs (Hidden Markov Models) are used to apply the behaviors of a given signal to the synthesized voice. The first system to use HMM to perform SVS was SinSy [6], developed by the Nagoya Institute of Technology.

In addition to the mentioned systems, all these approaches were employed to develop performative, real-time singing synthesizers [7]. In this kind of SVS, the voice is produced at the very moment the input data — phonetic, musical, or both — is provided by the user, which allows the use of the singing synthesizer as a musical instrument.

Beyond their intrinsic artistic purpose, these systems can be applied, for example, in music education, especially in the teaching of choirs. However, there is an absence of tools which perform SVS in the Brazilian Portuguese language. The prototype described in this paper is the first real-time singing synthesizer specifically designed to generate singing in this idiom.

This work is organized as follows: Section 2 presents the related work according to the results of a technological mapping, which establish the state of the technique of the real-time SVS area. Section 3 describes the design and implementation of PATRICIA, according to the systematic mapping previously discussed. Section 4 proposes an analysis and discussion of some technical aspects of PATRICIA compared to the related work. Finally, Section 5 presents a brief conclusion.

2. RELATED WORK

The present work performed technological mapping [8], which consists of a systematic research method. In the technological mapping, we searched for patents related to real-time singing synthesis to achieve a better comprehension of the state of the technique in this area. The research process is described below.

The search for patents related to real-time singing voice synthesizers was performed in the WIPO (World Intellectual Property Organization) database, called Patentscope [1]. The following search string was used:

```
FP:(FP:(("SINGING SYNTHESIS" OR
"SINGING VOICE SYNTHESIS" OR "SINGING
SYNTHESIZING" ) AND ("REALTIME" OR
"REAL-TIME"))).
```

This search provided eight patent deposits as a result. All of them were the property of Yamaha Corporation, from Japan, and had as objects an apparatus, method and storage medium for real-time singing synthesis. However, most patents were registered outside Japan, probably to warrant

[1] https://patentscope.wipo.int/

international legal protection. Figure 1 presents the geographical distribution of the patents.

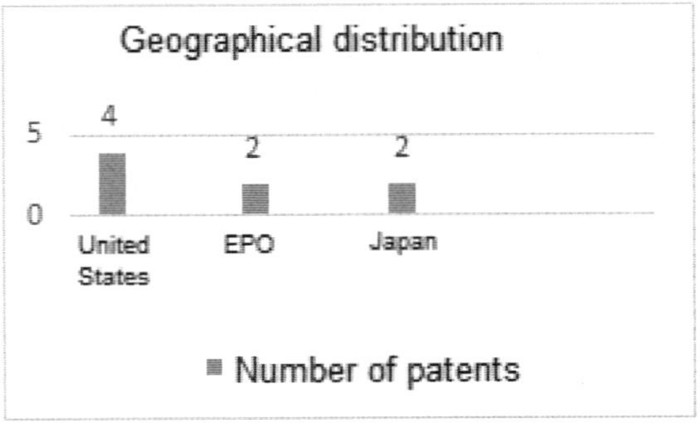

Figure 1. Number of patents found in each geographical region.

This product is denominated Vocaloid Keyboard and consists of a musical keyboard with an embedded singing synthesizer, allowing its user to make an instrumental performance. A prototype of the instrument, designed to synthesize singing in the Japanese language, was presented in a scientific paper in 2012 [9]. It has alphabetic buttons to the left, organized as follows: two horizontal rows with diacritical signs and consonants and, below them, five buttons with vowels, organized in a cross shape. With the left hand, the user could press these buttons to generate syllables; meanwhile, the musical keyboard could be played by the right hand to provide the musical notes. A display with *katakana* Japanese characters shows the generated syllables. Figure 2 presents the described prototype.

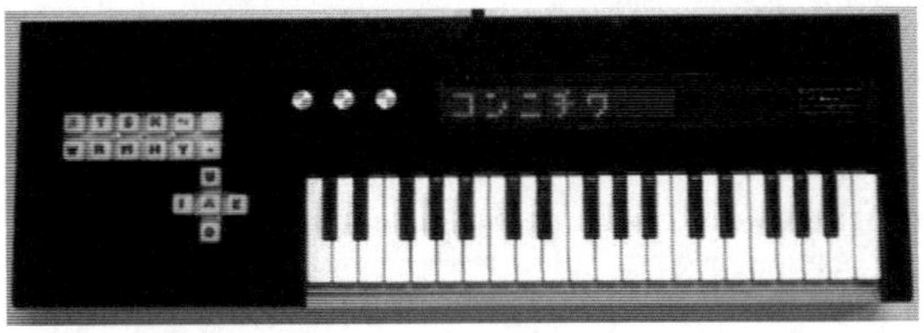

Figure 2. Vocaloid Keyboard prototype with letter buttons on the left side of its panel [9]

Nevertheless, the commercial version of the Vocaloid Keyboard, the VKB-100 keytar, abandons its prototypical phonetic buttons in favour of giving the song lyrics in advance instead of providing it in real-time [10]. The phonetic buttons were replaced by others, which add expression to the song, controlled by the left hand of the user.

3. PATRICIA

To the best of our knowledge, the system presented in this paper is the first singing synthesizer specifically designed for singing in the Brazilian Portuguese language. It retrieves phonetic data from a text file and musical parameters from a MIDI Keyboard to perform a concatenative synthesis with the aid of MBROLA [11] speech synthesizer, returning an audio file. This file is played in a loop while the respective MIDI note is kept active, providing real-time performance. The synthesizer is called PATRICIA, an acronym for *Programa que Articula em Tempo Real o Idioma Cantado Inscrito em Arquivo* (Portuguese for Program that Articulates in Real-Time the Singing Idiom Written in a File) and was implemented in SuperCollider [12], an environment and programming language for real-time audio synthesis. GitHub was used for version control.

The synthesis technical approach, phonetic input method, and audio output of PATRICIA will be discussed in the following subsections regarding the results of the technological mapping described in Section 2 compared with other real-time singing synthesizers.

3.1 Technical approach

Initially, PATRICIA was intended to be an embedded system which performs SVS in a MIDI Keyboard to provide real-time performance. This solution was already implemented and patented in the technological mapping process, resulting in Yamaha Vocaloid Keyboard [9]. Hence, a sample-based approach used both in MIDI keyboards in general and in the Vocaloid original system, was chosen for PATRICIA synthesizer.

In the proof of concept implementation of PATRICIA described in this paper, the complexity of the concatenative synthesis technique and the voice database construction were transferred to an already existing system, the MBROLA speech synthesizer. A similar architecture can be found in a tool called MaxMBROLA [13], but this system was designed to run in Max/MSP environment, which is proprietary software, while a free one, SuperCollider, was chosen for PATRICIA.

MBROLA performs a sample-based concatenative synthesis by unit selection. These units are diphones, i.e. a conjunction of two phonemes. A set of diphones of a given language is recorded and stored in a file that serves as a voice database for the system. For its turn, the speech to be synthesized can be stored in a text file with the *.pho* extension. Each line of this file contains a phoneme written in SAMPA notation [14], a duration in milliseconds, and a series of pitch targets composed of two numbers: the position of the target within the phoneme, which is a percentage of its total duration, and the frequency value in Hertz at this position. A command-line instruction invokes MBROLA, which performs the unit selection in the indicated voice database, concatenating the diphones according to the description within the *.pho* file and finally generating an audio file.

For each MIDI note and its corresponding syllable retrieved by PATRICIA, it is generated a *.pho* file. Thus, each line of this file contains these four parameters:

1. A SAMPA phoneme from the retrieved syllable (the *.pho* file will have as lines as phonemes in this syllable);
2. A phoneme duration, arbitrarily set as 50 ms for semivowels and consonants and 200 ms for vowels;
3. A pitch target position that is always 100%, which means that the pitch of the phonemes will be the same during all their duration;

4. A fundamental frequency to provide the pitch, calculated according to the MIDI note number.

Equation 1 shows the formula used to calculate the fundamental frequency f of each syllable, given its corresponding MIDI note number n:

$$f = \sqrt[12]{2^{n-81}} \cdot 440 \quad (1)$$

Once the *.pho* file was created, PATRICIA uses the SuperCollider engine to send to the operating system [2] of the host computer an MBROLA command line. This instruction references both the *.pho* file and the MBROLA Brazilian Portuguese female voice database *br4* [3] to create the corresponding audio file in *Au* format. A system diagram of PATRICIA is shown in Figure 3. The next subsections describe how PATRICIA retrieves the phonetic data and manages the mentioned *Au* files to generate the synthesized singing voice.

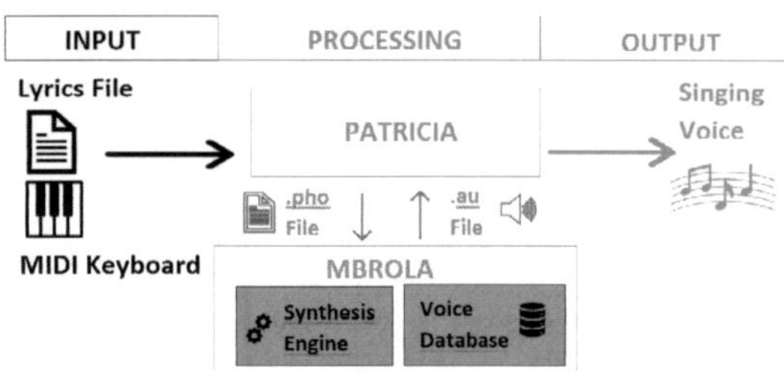

Figure 3. System diagram of PATRICIA.

3.2 Phonetic input method

As mentioned in Section 1, a singing synthesizer deals with two basic kinds of input data: the phonetic one, which comes from the song's lyrics to be synthesized, and the musical parameters, such as pitch and duration of the notes. Each syllable from the lyrics corresponds to a musical note.

The chosen diphone concatenative synthesis technique gives directions for selecting the phonetic input method. As PATRICIA counts on a pre-recorded sample voices database, it is neither intended to work as a vocoder, nor a training system that transforms a signal according to the characteristics of another voice as in [15, 16, 17, 18], so an audio signal as a phonetic input, used by other real-time singing synthesizers, was discarded.

Conversely, manual control of diphones using gestural controllers has limitations, as discussed in a paper describing a real-time singing synthesizer called T-Voks augmented theremin [19]. According to Xiao, "Diphone-based concatenative singing synthesis sounds very natural, but it can hardly be applied to real-time performative synthesis because it does not seem possible to select any arbitrary sequence of diphones on the fly". Indeed, if this task was shown to be possible by the Vocaloid Keyboard prototype, which presents buttons for the introduction of lyrics in real time [9], it happened on account of the more straightforward structure of Japanese moras, or prosodic units, most of them composed of a consonant and a vowel, in this order. Hence, when the user presses, for example, buttons "T" and "A" simultaneously in the Vocaloid Keyboard panel, the synthesis engine interprets this mora necessarily as a "TA" syllable since an eventual "AT" mora does not exist in Japanese language [20]. In contrast, Brazilian Portuguese has syllables like the last one in the word *"magistrais"*, whose structure is consonant-consonant-vowel-semi-vowel-consonant, a complexity that increases the challenges for using gestural controllers to map a real time, manual phonetic input.

However, as mentioned in Section 2, even the commercial version of Vocaloid Keyboard renounces this phonetic input method for giving the song lyrics in advance [10]. Thus, giving a previously prepared phonetic input in a text file appears to be the most suitable method for the current implementation of PATRICIA.

Once the phonetic input method is determined, it is necessary to discuss the format of this entry. The syllables could be written according to the Portuguese official orthography. Still, a phonetic notation was preferred to give the user two types of control over the voice synthesis: 1) The lyrics of the song are not a text in prose but in verses, so certain phenomena that occur in versification, such as elision, where two syllables merge into one, must be taken into account. The verse syllables do not necessarily coincide with the grammatical ones [21] and are better controlled at the phonetic level. 2) Brazilian Portuguese has several regional variants. For example, the first syllable of the word *"tia"* ("aunt") could be pronounced as [ti] or [tʃi] [4], depending on the region of the Brazilian speaker [22]. Therefore, the synthesis engine would transform an orthographic input syllable "ti" into an arbitrarily specific chosen phonetic variant, excluding other possibilities.

The solution, thus, is to give the phonetic input directly in a phonetic notation. SAMPA was chosen because it is based on ASCII characters, present in any standard computer keyboard, while the International Phonetic Alphabet (IPA) has many special characters whose entry is more difficult to do. Hence, PATRICIA retrieves phonetic data from a text file, which must be prepared before the beginning of the musical performance. Each line of this file must have a syllable written in SAMPA phonetic notation with its phonemes separated by hyphens. PATRICIA uses the same SAMPA characters adaptation for Brazilian Portuguese as MBROLA.

3.3 Audio output

Since each audio file generated by MBROLA has a constant duration, PATRICIA needs to extend it as long as the respective key is pressed in the MIDI instrument. To achieve this result, for each active MIDI note, the corresponding *.au* file is played into a loop. The start position of the loop is in the middle of the file in the time domain, where the vowel is, which is the periodic part of the syllable waveform. The ending position is calculated by adding the period in seconds, i.e., the inverse of the fundamental frequency, to the start position. The interval between the start and ending positions corresponds to one cycle or pitch period of the

[2] PATRICIA works in both Windows and Linux operating systems, provided that MBROLA and SuperCollider are properly installed.

[3] Available on `https://github.com/numediart/MBROLA-voices/blob/master/data/br4`

[4] The International Phonetic Alphabet (IPA) notation was used in these given examples.

waveform. This cycle is repeated while the corresponding MIDI note is kept active, extending the duration of the syllable. When a MIDI *Note off* message is received, the loop that corresponds to this note is released, and the rest of the *.au* file is played.

Figure 4 shows a partial view of a waveform generated by MBROLA for the first syllable of the word *"quando"* ("when") singing a G_4 note. The selected region in (a) is the pitch period calculated by PATRICIA, starting from the center of the sample. The repetition of this segment, which appears seven times in (b), prolongs the duration of the audio.

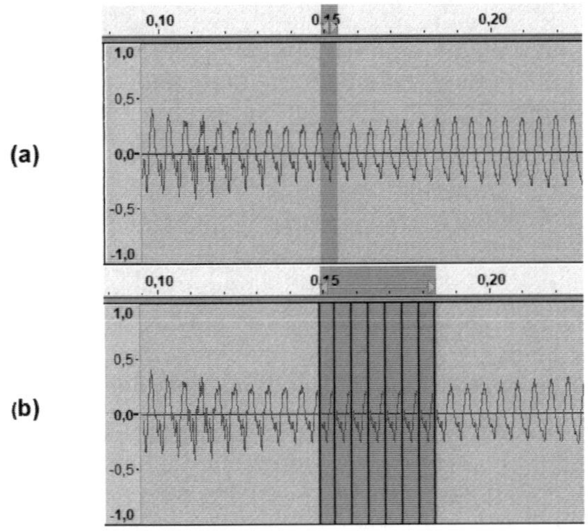

Figure 4. (a) Loop segment calculated by PATRICIA. (b) Repetition of the segment, extending the duration of the sample.

The differences between MBROLA and SuperCollider sample rates had to be considered for the audio to be correctly played. The successive repetition of the process described above results in generating a synthesized singing voice in the audio output of the host computer.

4. ANALYSIS AND DISCUSSION

As a proof of concept prototype, the singing synthesizer described in this work has minimal functional requirements. It only controls the pitch and duration of the synthesized voice in real time, while the phonetic data comes from a text file previously prepared. These functionalities were tested, and some conducted tests can be seen at `https://youtu.be/XK7y-mCw7KI`. The video presents the execution of PATRICIA in the SuperCollider IDE. At the same time, the picture-in-picture video shows the MIDI keyboard being played as Audacity records the generated audio. The chosen music was the popular Brazilian song "Asa Branca" by Luiz Gonzaga and Humberto Teixeira.

The tests reveal some limitations of the system. The first limitation is a certain lack of naturalness[23], whose main cause is probably PATRICIA's dependency on MBROLA, which was not designed to synthesize the singing voice. Other causes are the absence of expression control and a duration extension algorithm that generates a loop body too short [24], encompassing only one pitch period of the synthesized voice.

Furthermore, the expected phoneme-level control of the synthesized singing voice was not possible with the use of the *br4* voice database, since some diphones, like [ti] and [di], were already programmed to correspond to a particular variant of the Brazilian Portuguese language, resulting in the palatalized syllables [tʃi] and [dʒi], respectively.

Regarding input methods and gestural control, we believe a method to input diphones in real time would be beneficial to PATRICIA's flexibility and usage in more artistic settings.

However, as discussed in section 3.2, such implementation poses challenges, including interface design, mapping decisions, and issues related to the user's spare bandwidth [25]. Since the system needs phonetic and audio-related information, we expect a high level of complexity in the design, if desired to provide full control in real-time to a single user.

5. CONCLUSIONS AND FUTURE WORK

This work presented PATRICIA, a performative real-time singing synthesizer and the first SVS system designed to generate singing in Brazilian Portuguese. The project is still in progress, and the described synthesizer is a proof of concept implementation with a limited set of functional requirements implemented in SuperCollider language and environment.

Sample-based concatenative synthesis and song lyrics given in advance in a text file were shown to be, respectively, the most suitable technical approach and phonetic input method for the system, as discussed. The musical input is given in real time via MIDI, and the synthesis is performed by MBROLA, an adapted speech synthesizer.

In future versions of the system, its dependency on MBROLA is intended to disappear. It is desirable that PATRICIA may have its own voice library, initially built with the aid of MBROLATOR [5], a tool for creating MBROLA database files and, in the future, an independent wavetable with voice samples from a professional female singer, which will improve the quality of the generated singing voice.

It might also be useful to implement the concatenative synthesis algorithm into PATRICIA, in addition to treating MIDI velocity parameter, among others, and expression controls like vibrato. Ultimately, a single-board computer will be used to conduct the experiments on PATRICIA as an embedded system toward its final version, where it will run within a MIDI musical keyboard.

Issues about the patents of the Vocaloid Keyboard, which is a similar product and property of Yamaha Corporation, can emerge and will be discussed, as well as PATRICIA's eventual transformation into an augmented instrument with gestural control, in future research.

Acknowledgments

This work was supported by CAPES and CNPq, from Brazil and by SAT/Metalab, from Canada.

6. REFERENCES

[1] M. Alivizatou-Barakou, A. Kitsikidis, F. Tsalakanidou, K. Dimitropoulos, C. Giannis, S. Nikolopoulos,

[5] Available on `https://github.com/numediart/MBROLATOR`

S. Al Kork, B. Denby, L. Buchman, M. Adda-Decker *et al.*, *Intangible Cultural Heritage and New Technologies: Challenges and Opportunities for Cultural Preservation and Development.* Cham: Springer International Publishing, 2017, pp. 129–158.

[2] N. U. Khan and J. C. Lee, "HMM Based Duration Control for Singing TTS," in *Advances in Computer Science and Ubiquitous Computing*, D.-S. Park, H.-C. Chao, Y.-S. Jeong, and J. J. J. H. Park, Eds. Singapore: Springer Singapore, 2015, pp. 137–143.

[3] Y. E. Kim, "Singing Voice Analysis, Synthesis, and Modeling," in *Handbook of Signal Processing in Acoustics*, D. Havelock, S. Kuwano, and M. Vorländer, Eds. New York, NY: Springer New York, 2008, pp. 359–374.

[4] X. Rodet, Y. Potard, and J.-B. Barriere, "The CHANT project: From the synthesis of the singing voice to synthesis in general," *Computer Music Journal*, vol. 8, no. 3, pp. 15–31, 1984.

[5] H. Kenmochi and H. Ohshita, "VOCALOID - commercial singing synthesizer based on sample concatenation," in *Proc. Interspeech 2007*, 2007, pp. 4009–4010.

[6] K. Oura, A. Mase, T. Yamada, S. Muto, Y. Nankaku, and K. Tokuda, "Recent development of the HMM-based singing voice synthesis system—Sinsy," in *Seventh ISCA Workshop on Speech Synthesis*, 2010, pp. 211–216.

[7] L. A. Z. Brum and E. D. Moreno, "State of art of real-time singing voice synthesis," in *Anais do XVII Simpósio Brasileiro de Computação Musical.* Porto Alegre, RS, Brasil: SBC, 2019, pp. 50–57.

[8] A. Orjuela, J. M. Andrade, E. A. Cardona, R. Peralta, and J. J. Mendez, "Methodological proposal for the identification of incremental innovations in SMEs," *European Research Studies Journal*, vol. XXII, no. 4, pp. 199–214, 2019.

[9] S. Kagami, K. Hamano, K. Kashiwaze, and K. Yamamoto, "Development of realtime japanese vocal keyboard," *Information Processing Society of Japan INTERACTION*, pp. 837–842, 2012.

[10] K. Kashiwase, "An over-the-shoulder keyboard that extends the potential for VOCALOID performance." *Yamaha Corporation*, 2017, accessed: 2023-01-29. [Online]. Available: https://www.yamaha.com/en/about/design/synapses/id_104

[11] T. Dutoit, V. Pagel, N. Pierret, F. Bataille, and O. van der Vrecken, "The MBROLA project: towards a set of high quality speech synthesizers free of use for non commercial purposes," in *Proceeding of Fourth International Conference on Spoken Language Processing. ICSLP '96*, vol. 3, 1996, pp. 1393–1396 vol.3.

[12] J. McCartney, "SuperCollider: a new real time synthesis language," in *Proc. International Computer Music Conference (ICMC'96)*, 1996, pp. 257–258.

[13] N. D'Alessandro, R. Sebbe, B. Bozkurt, and T. Dutoit, "MaxMBROLA: A Max/MSP MBROLA-based tool for real-time voice synthesis," in *2005 13th European Signal Processing Conference.* IEEE, 2005, pp. 1–4.

[14] J. C. Wells *et al.*, "SAMPA computer readable phonetic alphabet," *Handbook of standards and resources for spoken language systems*, vol. 4, pp. 684–732, 1997.

[15] M. Dong, S. W. Lee, H. Li, P. Chan, X. Peng, J. W. Ehnes, and D. Huang, "I2r speech2singing perfects everyone's singing," in *Proc. Interspeech 2014*, 2014, pp. 2148–2149.

[16] K. Matsubara, T. Okamoto, R. Takashima, T. Takiguchi, T. Toda, Y. Shiga, and H. Kawai, "Full-Band LPCNet: A Real-Time Neural Vocoder for 48 kHz Audio With a CPU," *IEEE Access*, vol. 9, pp. 94 923–94 933, 2021.

[17] J. Tae, H. Kim, and Y. Lee, "MLP Singer: Towards Rapid Parallel Korean Singing Voice Synthesis," in *2021 IEEE 31st International Workshop on Machine Learning for Signal Processing (MLSP)*, 2021, pp. 1–6.

[18] C. Veaux, M. Astrinaki, K. Oura, R. A. J. Clark, and J. Yamagishi, "Gesture Control of HMM-Based Singing Voice Synthesis," in *Proc. 8th ISCA Workshop on Speech Synthesis (SSW 8)*, 2013, pp. 247–248.

[19] X. Xiao, G. Locqueville, C. d'Alessandro, and B. Doval, "T-Voks: the Singing and Speaking Theremin," in *Proceedings of the International Conference on New Interfaces for Musical Expression.* Zenodo, Jun. 2019, pp. 110–115.

[20] L. Labrune, *The phonology of Japanese.* Oxford University Press, 2012.

[21] M. Bandeira, "A versificação em língua portuguêsa," *Enciclopédia Delta Larousse*, pp. 3239–3249, 1960.

[22] T. C. Silva and C. Leite, "Padrões sonoros emergentes:(oclusiva alveolar + sibilante) no português brasileiro," *Caderno de Letras*, no. 24, pp. 15–36, 2015.

[23] S. Ternström, "Session on naturalness in synthesized speech and music," in *143rd ASA meeting, Pittsburgh*, 2002.

[24] C. Roads, "Sampling and Additive Synthesis," in *The Computer Music Tutorial*, C. Roads, Ed. MIT press, 1996, pp. 115–155.

[25] P. R. Cook, "Principles for Designing Computer Music Controllers," in *Proceedings of the International Conference on New Interfaces for Musical Expression.* Zenodo, Jun. 2001, pp. 3–6.

Melodic Constraint Satisfaction with a Generative Adversarial Network

Tsubasa Tanaka
Tokyo University of the Arts
tanaka.tsubasa@ms.geidai.ac.jp

ABSTRACT

Generative Adversarial Networks (GANs) are typically used in order to generate instances that resemble those in a data set. However, this study generalizes GAN so that it can be used as a method of constraint satisfaction. If GANs get the capacity to satisfy explicit rules that do not necessarily exist in the training data set, this may improve the controllability and trustfulness of generative AI. An experiment of a simple melodic generation suggests that the GAN can learn constraints from synthetic data sets for respective constraints and generate solutions that simultaneously satisfy all of the constraints.

1. INTRODUCTION

Deep generative models such as GANs, VAEs, and diffusion models have been extensively applied in artistic fields such as painting, photography, music, and poetry.

Among the deep generative models, GAN is a unique neural network structure that combines two different networks called a generator and a discriminator. While the discriminator tries to distinguish real and fake (generated) samples, the generator tries to convince the discriminator that the generated fake samples are real. In this way, both networks compete with and enhance each other.

This learning process of GANs is formulated as the following two-player minimax game [1]:

$$\min_{G} \max_{D} \left\{ E_{\boldsymbol{x}}[\log(D(\boldsymbol{x}))] + E_{\boldsymbol{z}}[\log(1 - D(G(\boldsymbol{z})))] \right\} \tag{1}$$

, where $\boldsymbol{x}$ is sampled from the data distribution and $\boldsymbol{z}$ is sampled from random noise.

After the emergence of the original GAN, many variants of GAN have been proposed. DCGAN (Deep Convolutional GAN) adopts a convolutional neural network (CNN) to generate clearer images [2]. Conditional GAN enables conditional generation by additional input information [3]. CycleGAN combines two GANs for image translation [2]. StyleGAN enables style manipulation using style vectors [4]. There are applications of GAN in the field of music generation such as [5].

In this study, we focus on GANs' mechanism of the discriminator and generalize it so that GANs can treat a wider range of tasks, especially solving constraint satisfaction problems.

2. PROPOSED METHOD

2.1 Generalizing GAN

The original GAN's objective is to make indistinguishable imitations from real data. In other words, the objective is to generate solutions that satisfy a criterion of genuineness that the discriminator has learned.

In analogy, we can imagine a generalization of GAN that have multiple criteria and target degrees of satisfying these criteria. In this case, we can introduce other criteria that are desirable to be realized instead of only genuineness. This is important because sticking to genuineness alone makes it difficult to deal with something more creative than imitating what already exists.

Therefore, the author proposes the following generalized formulation of GAN: the discriminator D learns to minimize the following loss function

$$L_d(\boldsymbol{\theta}_d) := E_{\boldsymbol{x}}\Big[\|R_{\boldsymbol{x}} - D(\boldsymbol{x})\|^2\Big] + E_{\boldsymbol{z}}\Big[\|R_{G(\boldsymbol{z})} - D(G(\boldsymbol{z}))\|^2\Big] \tag{2}$$

, and the generator G learns to minimize the following loss function

$$L_g(\boldsymbol{\theta}_g) := E_{\boldsymbol{z}}\Big[\|T - D(G(\boldsymbol{z}))\|^2\Big], \tag{3}$$

where $R_{\boldsymbol{x}} \in [0,1]^r$ denotes a vector that expresses how much $\boldsymbol{x}$ satisfies r criteria and $T \in [0,1]^r$ denotes a constant vector that indicates the target degrees of satisfaction of the r criteria. $\boldsymbol{\theta}_d$ and $\boldsymbol{\theta}_g$ are the parameters of D and G respectively.

Equation (2) means that D learns to accurately evaluate data X and generated samples $G(\boldsymbol{z})$ concerning the degrees of satisfaction of the criteria. Equation (3) means that G learns to generate samples that realize T, the target degrees of satisfaction of the criteria (rules or constraints), on the assumption that D can accurately output $R_{G(\boldsymbol{z})}$.

2.2 Implementation

The two minimization processes are implemented as iterative alternations of updating the parameters of D (Equation (2)) and those of G (Equation (3)) with backpropagation, as in the learning process of ordinary GANs.

3. APPLICATION IN MELODIC GENERATION

To verify the capacity of the proposed method, the author conducted an experiment on simple music generation with melodic constraints. For simplicity, this experiment only treats a minimum number of rules taken from music theory, although these are not sufficient from the viewpoint of musical quality. This Section explains these constraints and how there are formalized in the experiment, which is described in the next section.

3.1 Melodic Constraints

When creating melodies, there are rules that composers implicitly or explicitly obey. In counterpoint [6, 7, 8], which is a theory for composing Western polyphonic music, there are many explicit rules that melodies are recommended to satisfy or must satisfy. In the context of computer music research, counterpoint has been studied from various viewpoints including constraint programming [9, 10], stochastic models [11, 12], genetic algorithm [13], and integer programming [14].

From the rules of counterpoint, we adopt the following four rules in this experiment:

- Rule 1: basically, pitches are within a diatonic scale.
- Rule 2: specific melodic intervals should not be used.
- Rule 3: conjunct motion should be frequently used.
- Rule 4: turns should not be used too frequently.

3.2 Degrees of Constraint Satisfaction

To evaluate how much these rules are satisfied, we introduce a vector $R_{\boldsymbol{x}} = (r_1, r_2, r_3, r_4) \in [0, 1]^4$, which denotes the degrees of satisfying four rules for a melody $\boldsymbol{x}$. r_1 corresponds to the rate of pitches within a diatonic collection $\{C, D, E, F, G, A, H\}$ for the melody. For example, if a melody $\boldsymbol{x}$ only uses pitches within a diatonic scale, r_1 equals 1.0. r_2 corresponds to the rate of occurrences of melodic intervals recommended in counterpoint. In counterpoint, there are prohibited melodic intervals such as large leaps over an octave and dissonant intervals. Repetition of the same notes is also not recommended. Therefore, we set the recommended melodic intervals as $I = \{1, 2, 3, 4, 5, 7, 8, 9, 10, 12\}$ by semitone (both ascending and descending directions are possible). r_3 corresponds to the rate of conjunct motions between consecutive notes, namely the move of one semitone and that of two semitones. In counterpoint, conjunct motions are recommended to be used frequently. Therefore, the value r_3 should be large. r_4 corresponds to the rate of direction changes in the melody (from ascending to descending or vice versa). For example, if the melodic direction changes at every note, r_4 equals 1.0 (completely zigzag). In counterpoint, frequent changes of melodic direction are not recommended. This is because if there are too many direction changes, the unity of the melody is destroyed. Therefore, the value r_4 should be small.

Considering these four rules, we set the target rate T as $(1.0, 1.0, 0.66, 0.36)$. This means that melodies that G generate must strictly respect a diatonic scale and the recommended set of melodic intervals. Also, melodic motions must be musically well-controlled (conjunct motions are frequent, and turns are not too frequent).

4. EXPERIMENT

This section reports the result of the experiment to confirm that the proposed method works. This experiment aims to evaluate the capacity of the proposed variant of GAN to generate melodies with target vector T.

The role of discriminator D is to identify correct values of $R_{\boldsymbol{x}}$. Hopefully, D can identify $R_{\boldsymbol{x}}$ for any input melody $\boldsymbol{x}$ after learning. On the other hand, the role of generator G is to generate melodies whose $R_{\boldsymbol{x}}$ equals T. In this way, this GAN is expected to generate melodies that satisfy all of the rules.

4.1 Preparation of Synthetic Data Sets

To make a neural net learn the four melodic rules, the author prepared four synthetic melody data sets for respective rules $S_i (i = 1, 2, 3, 4)$. The strategy is to make the neural net learn each rule independently. It is not difficult to generate random pitch sequences specifying only one of the values of $r_i (i = 1, 2, 3, 4)$. However, generating random pitch sequences specifying all of the four values is difficult because the constraints become strict. This is why we use four different data sets.

The difficulty is that four synthetic data sets for respective rules, $S_i (i = 1, 2, 3, 4)$, do not necessarily contain ideal solutions whose $R_{\boldsymbol{x}}$ coincide with T. Therefore, solving the problem of extrapolation is necessary (G is expected to generate ideal solutions even if there is no such solution in the training data).

The number of samples in each data set S_i was set to 1300. These were generated by programming. When generating, the training data set i was only controlled to have every possible degree of satisfaction of the rule i in an equal frequency, and other rules than rule i were not controlled for data set i. The number of notes was fixed at 13. For simplicity, the durations of all 13 notes were set to a whole note. In the data sets, there was no melody whose $R_{\boldsymbol{x}}$ precisely coincides with T. The nearest sample to the target T had the values $R_{\boldsymbol{x}} = (0.92, 1.0, 0.58, 0.36)$).

Test data sets were also generated in a similar way. The number of melodies in a data set for rule i was set to 65.

4.2 Neural Network Structure

The proposed variant of GAN was implemented as follows. The discriminator D consists of four fully-connected layers. The first three layers have 256 nodes with Leaky ReLU activation function and dropout. The last layer has four nodes with sigmoid activation function. The four outputs correspond to the values of the four rules. The generator G consists of three fully-connected layers. The first two layers have 624 nodes with batch normalization and ReLU activation function. The third layer has $13 \times 24 = 312$ nodes. The output of the third layer is reshaped into a 13×24 matrix and output through a softmax function so that the final output becomes a sequence of 13 probability distributions of 24 classes. Each probability distribution corresponds to one note, and 24 classes correspond to the pitch range of 24 semitones (two octaves). The input of G is random noise of dimension 100. Adam optimizer with a learning rate of 0.01 is used.

When calculating $R_{G(\boldsymbol{z})}$, the output of G is converted into a melody (a series of one-hot vectors) by argmax decisions. Then, this melody is checked, and r_i is calculated. However, when calculating $D(G(\boldsymbol{z}))$, $G(\boldsymbol{z})$ is directly passed to D without converting to on-hot vectors.

4.3 Result

Figure 1 shows the transitions of losses in the learning process of the GAN. The losses of both D (Equation (2)) and

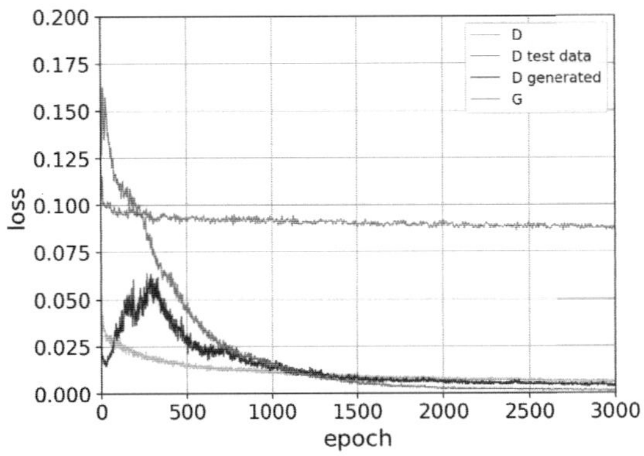

Figure 1. Transitions of the MSE in the learning process of D with both training data and generated data (Equation (2)), D with generated data (the second term of Equation (2)), D with test data, and G with generated data (Equation (3)).

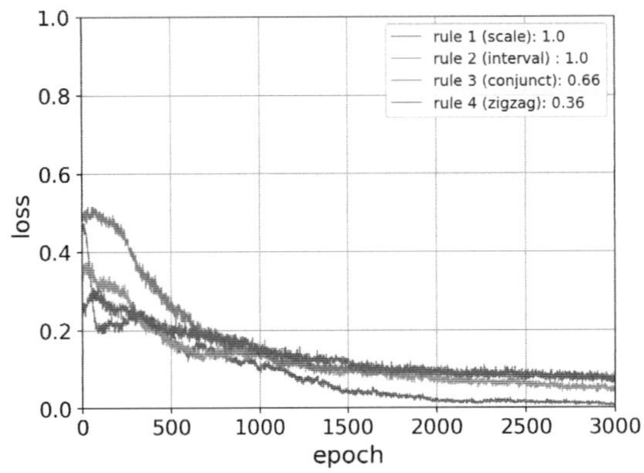

Figure 2. The transitions of the averages of $|r_i - t_i|$ for respective i ($i = 1, 2, 3, 4$). These indicate to what extent respective rules are satisfied.

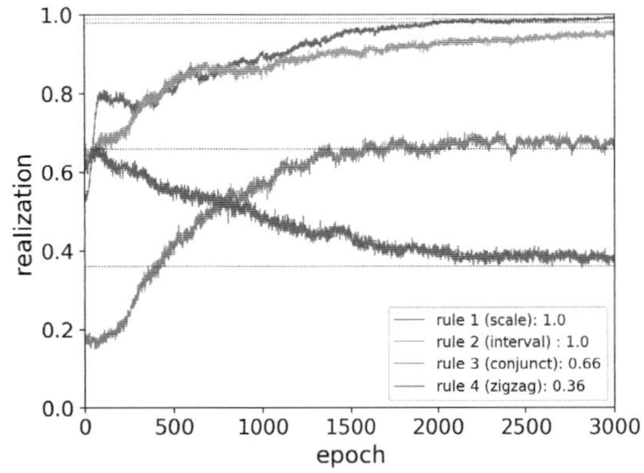

Figure 3. The transitions of averages of r_i for respective i ($i = 1, 2, 3, 4$). These indicate that $R_{\boldsymbol{x}}$ successfully converged to T (the horizontal lines).

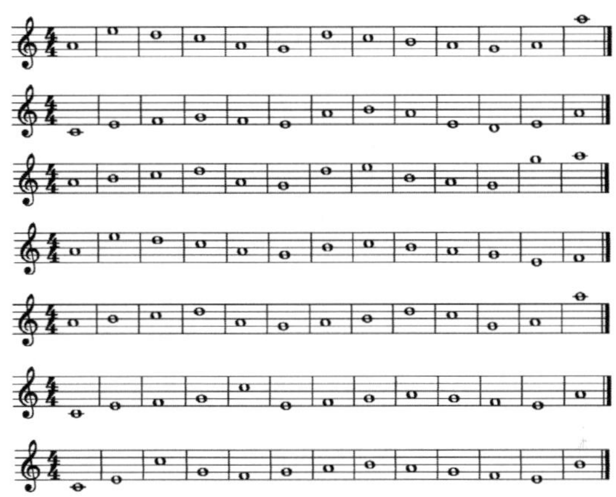

Figure 4. Some examples of generated melodies. These samples realize $R_{\boldsymbol{x}} = T$ $(= (1.0, 1.0, 0.66, 0.36))$, which means the constraints are perfectly satisfied. We can observe that there is no note outside of a diatonic scale, that all melodic intervals are included in the recommended set of intervals, that there are many conjunct motions, and that there are not too many direction changes.

G (Equation (3)) converged to 0.0, which implies that discriminations of both training data (D) and generated samples (D generated) were successful and G have acquired the capacity of satisfying the constraints (Equation (3)).

The loss of discrimination of the test data (D test data) continuously decreases, and the mean loss (MSE) is below 10%

Figure 2 shows the learning processes of respective rules (the transitions of the averages of $|r_i - t_i|$ for respective i ($i = 1, 2, 3, 4$). Figure 3 shows the transitions of averages of r_i for each i). This Figure indicates that all of the four elements of $R_{\boldsymbol{x}}$ converge to the target values of T. We can observe that r_1 converges more accurately than others, which is understandable. The satisfaction of Rule 1 is easier because whether a note in a melody is inside the scale or not is independent of other notes.

Figure 4 shows some generated melodies whose loss was almost 0.0 (optimal). We can observe that the contours of these samples are similar. This is probably because the generator lost its diversity through the learning process and focused on specific area of optimal solutions.

4.4 Discussion

From the result of the experiment, we have confirmed that the proposed GAN method has a capacity for constraint satisfaction. More precisely, the discriminator D could learn each rule "separately" from each synthetic data set and could teach the generator G to obey multiple rules simultaneously.

Although the author has conducted a preliminary experiment with another method based on a conditional VAE of which the target vector T is used as the conditional input, it was not successful. An important difference between this method and the proposed method is whether there is a mechanism of discriminator or not. In the case of conditional VAE, although the co-occurrence of the target vector and input melody is informed to the network, the binding force between them is not necessarily strong. On the other hand, in the case of the proposed method, the generator is forced to adapt to the "critics" from the discriminator. This mechanism of GAN's discriminator seems to contribute to the success of constraint satisfaction.

This capacity of constraint satisfaction suggested in this research may add another possibility of controlling the contents of generative AI by introducing explicit rules and degrees of satisfying constraints. It may also contribute to improving the trustfulness of generative AI, which does not yet have sufficient ways of regulating unwanted results.

As an extension of this research, there are remaining research issues. Although only synthetic data sets were used in this study, there is a possibility of combining real data in order to add the functionality of imitating real data as in the original GAN. In addition, the proposed method has a limitation that the target vector is fixed. If we change the target T, we must train the neural network from the beginning. To make the GAN possible to have more flexible controllability of the constraints, one imaginable modification is to add the target vector T as a conditional input.

5. CONCLUSION

This paper proposed a new generalized GAN variant designed to solve constraint satisfaction problems. The experimental result of the melodic generation task with some musical constraints shows that the proposed GAN can learn multiple rules separately from different data sets and generate instances that satisfy all the rules simultaneously.

There are some remaining research issues. An experiment of combining imitation with real data and constraint satisfaction with synthetic data should be done. This hybrid approach may lead to practical applications that need to respect some explicit crucial constraints when generating instances similar to those in real data. In addition, it is desirable to improve the proposed method so that it can change the target constraint values more flexibly.

Acknowledgments

This work was supported by JST, ACT-X Grant Number JPMJAX21AD, Japan.

6. REFERENCES

[1] I. Goodfellow, J. Pouget-Abadie, M. Mirza, B. Xu, D. Warde-Farley, S. Ozair, A. Courville, and Y. Bengio, "Generative Adversarial Nets," in *Advances in Neural Information Processing Systems*, Z. Ghahramani, M. Welling, C. Cortes, N. Lawrence, and K. Weinberger, Eds., vol. 27. Curran Associates, Inc., 2014. [Online]. Available: https://proceedings.neurips.cc/paper_files/paper/2014/file/5ca3e9b122f61f8f06494c97b1afccf3-Paper.pdf

[2] J. Zhu, T. Park, P. Isola, and A. A. Efros, "Unpaired Image-to-Image Translation using Cycle-Consistent Adversarial Networks," *CoRR*, vol. abs/1703.10593, 2017. [Online]. Available: http://arxiv.org/abs/1703.10593

[3] M. Mirza and S. Osindero, "Conditional Generative Adversarial Nets," *CoRR*, vol. abs/1411.1784, 2014. [Online]. Available: http://arxiv.org/abs/1411.1784

[4] T. Karras, S. Laine, and T. Aila, "A Style-Based Generator Architecture for Generative Adversarial Networks," *CoRR*, vol. abs/1812.04948, 2018. [Online]. Available: http://arxiv.org/abs/1812.04948

[5] L. Yang, S. Chou, and Y. Yang, "MidiNet: A Convolutional Generative Adversarial Network for Symbolic-domain Music Generation using 1D and 2D Conditions," *CoRR*, vol. abs/1703.10847, 2017. [Online]. Available: http://arxiv.org/abs/1703.10847

[6] J. J. Fux, *The study of counterpoint from Johann Joseph Fux's Gradus ad parnassum*. WW Norton & Company, 1965.

[7] Y. Hiroshi, *Traité de contrepoint d'après les méthodes du conservatoire de Paris*. Ongakunotomosha, 2012.

[8] G. Noël and B. Marcel, *Traité de contrepoint*. Durand, 1964.

[9] W. Shottstaedt, "Automatic counterpoint," in *Current directions in computer music research*, 1989.

[10] A. Torsten, C. Anagnostopoulou, and M. Alcorn, "Strasheela: design and usage of a music composition environment based on the Oz programming model," in *Proceedings of International Conference on Multiparadigm Programming in Mozart/Oz*, Charleroi, 2005, pp. 277–291.

[11] M. Farbood and B. Schöner, "Analysis and synthesis of Palestrina-style counterpoint using Markov chains," in *Proceedings of International Computer Music Conference*, 2001.

[12] T. Tanaka and et al., "Automatic Music Composition Based on Counterpoint and Imitation Using Stochastic Models," in *Proceedings of 7th Sound and Music Computing Conference*, Barcelona, 2010, pp. 213–218.

[13] D. Herremans and K. Sörensen, "Composing first species counterpoint with a variable neighbourhood search algorithm," in *Journal of Mathematics and the Arts 6.4*, 2012, pp. 169–189.

[14] T. Tanaka, "Formulating First Species Counterpoint With Integer Programming," in *Proceedings of 19th Sound and Music Computing Conference*, Saint-Etienne, 2022, pp. 601–607.

LaunchpadGPT: Language Model as Music Visualization Designer on Launchpad

Siting Xu*
SUSTech
xust2019@mail.sustech.edu.cn

Yunlong Tang*
SUSTech
tangyl2019@mail.sustech.edu.cn

Feng Zheng†
SUSTech
zhengf@sustech.edu.cn

ABSTRACT

Launchpad is a musical instrument that allows users to create and perform music by pressing illuminated buttons. To assist and inspire the design of the Launchpad light effect, and provide a more accessible approach for beginners to create music visualization with this instrument, we proposed LaunchpadGPT model to generate music visualization designs on Launchpad automatically. Based on the language model with excellent generation ability, our proposed LaunchpadGPT takes an audio piece of music as input and outputs the lighting effects of Launchpad-playing in the form of a video (Launchpad-playing video). We collect Launchpad-playing videos and process them to obtain music and corresponding video frame of Launchpad-playing as prompt-completion pairs, to train the language model. The experiment result shows the proposed method can create better music visualization than random generation methods and hold the potential for a broader range of music visualization applications. Our code is available at https://github.com/yunlong10/LaunchpadGPT.

1. INTRODUCTION

Launchpad is a popular musical hardware controller that allows users to create and perform music by pressing illuminated buttons or programming. It consists of 8×8 illuminated buttons, allowing users to trigger various musical elements like sounds, samples, and loops. Launchpad offers operations for music production and live performances. Due to the ornamental nature of Launchpad, enthusiasts frequently share their performance videos online, providing audiences with immersive visual experiences. Figure 1 illustrates a Launchpad [1].

By leveraging its illuminated buttons, Launchpad can generate synchronized visual effects that enrich the experience for both performers and audiences, which is an excellent form of music visualization. These visual effects can be programmed and customized to match the music's mood and style, resulting in audiovisual performances that fuse sight and sound [1].

Building Launchpad projects can be a complex and time-consuming task, particularly for beginners, for it involves multiple steps such as music production, programming, and designing intricate light effects. Besides, the design of light effects for Launchpad projects shares common ground with the broader field of music visualization, as it requires careful consideration of factors such as the rhythm and tempo of the music, the visual impact desired, and the synchronization with the audio.

* Equal contribution. † Corresponding author.
[1] https://www.ableton.com/en/products/controllers/launchpad/

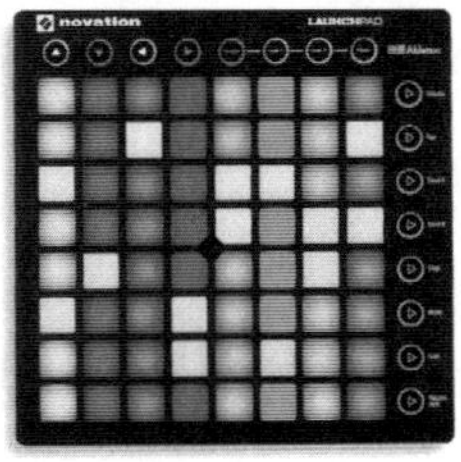

Figure 1: This is an illustrative figure of a Launchpad with 8×8 illuminated buttons from Novation.

To address these issues, we formulate the Launchpad visualization as translating a piece of music to a music visualization generation problem. Since language models show an excellent ability in cross-modal processing and the visual effects of music visualization can be encoded as similar semantic features as text information, we adopted the Generative Pre-trained Transformer (GPT) [2, 3, 4] and propose a language model-based framework for Launchpad-playing video generation, named **LaunchpadGPT**. Specifically, we first build a dataset of music-frame pairs by processing Launchpad-playing videos from the web to allow LaunchpadGPT to train and automatically generate music visualization. We then convert the Launchpad-playing frames into a textual representation of RGB values and button coordinates noted as X, followed by LaunchpadGPT to automatically generate Launchpad-playing videos. For the training and inference phase, the Mel-Frequency Cepstral Coefficients (MFCC) features extracted from audio act as prompt, and the corresponding RGB values with X coordinates act as completion.

Our model extends its ability to the domain of music visualization and video generation, enabling it to learn the complex patterns and structures of Launchpad-playing. It simplifies light design by providing automatic schemes based on inputted music. Additionally, it enables the creation of synchronized music videos showcasing Launchpad's performance and dynamic lighting effects, reducing production time. Experimental results demonstrate that LaunchpadGPT reveals the potential to extend its capabilities to other music visualization applications. Our envisioned applications contain a range of design possibilities within the realm of music visualization, including charting music game levels, LED screen designs for music performance venues, and devising captivating lighting schemes for music dance floors.

In summary, our contribution is twofold:

- We proposed LaunchpadGPT, a language model based on GPT, to generate music visualization on Launchpad automatically with given music.
- We collected a dataset of Launchpad-playing videos and construct prompt-completion pairs for training, which bridges the music and vision with texts.

2. METHOD

2.1 Overview

Figure 2 shows the framework of our LaunchpadGPT. Given a Launchpad-playing video, the video frames and music (audio) will be extracted respectively. For music, Mel-Frequency Cepstral Coefficients (MFCC) features will be extracted, whose number will be the same as the number of video frames so that the audio can be aligned well with the frames. The buttons' color information of the Launchpad keyboard in the frame will be recorded in text form called an RGB-X tuple. The X is the coordinate of one button on the keyboard. Then, we take the MFCC features as texts and concatenate them with the corresponding frames' RGB-X tuples (also in text form) to get the prompt-completion pairs.

In the training phase, the prompt-completion pairs are the input of a language model, which will be trained in a teacher-forcing paradigm. In the inference phase, the prompts (MFCC texts) will be the input to predict the completion (RGB-X tuples). The generated RGB-X will be used to generate the frames of the Launchpad keyboard.

2.2 Feature Extraction

In order to align the features of the music and the video frames, we set the audio frame length N_{af} and audio hop length N_{ah} as following:

$$N_{ah} = \frac{N_a}{N_{vf} - 1}, \; N_{af} = 2 \cdot N_{ah}, \tag{1}$$

where N_a is the audio sampling number, N_{vf} is the number of video frames. Then we will get N_{vf} MFCC features with the dimension of 128. For video frames, we represent them with (R, G, B, X) tuples, where the R, G, and B are the red, green, and blue channels of each button, and the X, ranging from 0 to 63, is the coordinate of one button on the Launchpad keyboard. Thus, we will get 64 RGB-X tuples from each frame.

2.3 Prompt-Completion Pairs Construction

With the MFCC features of music and corresponding frames' color-coordinate information, we can construct the prompt-completion pairs for the training and inference of the language model. Specifically, the MFCC features are transferred to texts directly as prompts with an additional prefix "prompt:". The corresponding frame's tuples of RGB-X are also transferred to texts with the prefix "completion:". Figure 3 shows a prompt-completion pair example.

2.4 NanoGPT

A language model refers to a probability distribution over sequences of tokens. A sequence is taken as an input for a language model and a probability performed as an assessment act as output, which can be denoted as $p(x_{1:L})$, with $x_{1:L}$ as a character sequence sampled by the language model, and p as the probability. The calculation of p is to use the chain rule of probability:

$$p(x_{1:L}) = \prod_{i=1}^{L} p(x_i \mid x_{1:i-1}). \tag{2}$$

Usually, conditional generation is to take a prefix sequence $x_{1:i}$ as input and sample the rest $x_{i+1:L}$ as output. The input is called **prompt** and the output is called **completion**. In our work, the MFCC features extracted from the music will be taken as prompt and a series of tuples representing the colors and coordinates of the buttons on Launchpad which is generated by LaunchpadGPT is the completion. Therefore, given a prompt $x_{1:i}$, an autoregressive language model will generate a completion $x_{i+1:L}$ accordingly.

The language model we use is NanoGPT [2], a medium-sized GPT [3] that tries to be smaller, cleaner, and more interpretable. With only a 6-layer Transformer [5] with 6 heads, it is very easy to hack it to our need, run on a single GPU or even CPU, and train it from scratch to fit our prompt-completion pairs data. As a GPT model, it decodes texts auto-regressively as Equation 2 shown.

2.5 Training

We train the NanoGPT with the prompt-completion pairs. Specifically, we combine all prompt-completion pairs into one corpus. The corpus will be sliced into contexts with a size of 256 characters, and each context will be tokenized into a feature with 384 channels. Then the NanoGPT takes the tokens as input to perform the next characters in a teacher-forcing paradigm [6]. The cross-entropy loss will be calculated to update the model parameters:

$$\mathcal{L} = -\frac{1}{N} \sum_{i=1}^{N} \log p(c_i \mid c_{<i}), \tag{3}$$

where N is the number of characters in the input sequence, c_i is the i-th character, $c_{<i}$ is the sequence of previous characters, and $p(c_i|c_{<i})$ is the probability of predicting the next character c_i given the previous characters $c_{<i}$. The cross-entropy loss $\mathcal{L}$ measures the difference between the predicted probability distribution and the true distribution of the next character.

2.6 Inference

In the inference phase, we can only use the music to get the prompt tokens. The trained NanoGPT will take the prompt tokens as input to predict the completion, i.e. the RGB-X tuples. With the RGB-X tuples predicted, a frame can be

[2] https://github.com/karpathy/nanoGPT/

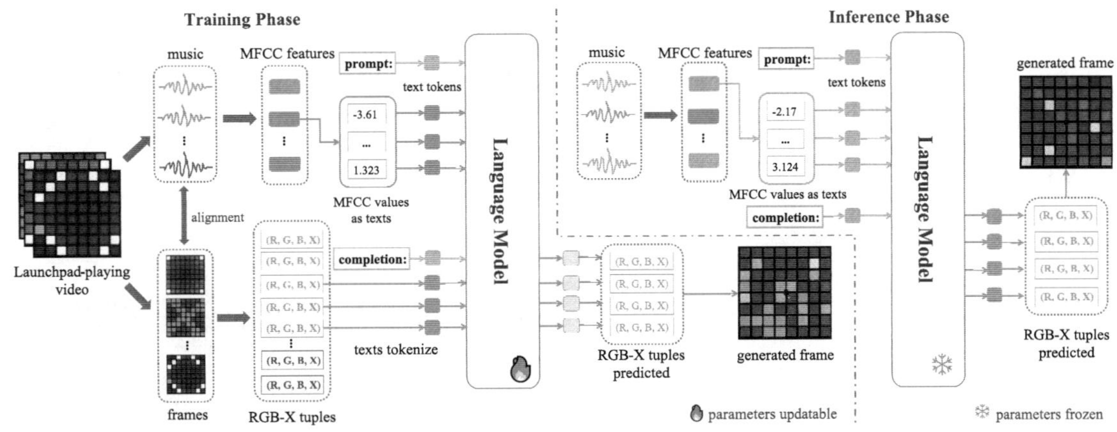

Figure 2: The framework of LaunchpadGPT. In the training phase, aligned music and frame information is extracted from the Launchpad-playing videos. MFCC features are extracted from the music, while the color-coordinate tuple (R, G, B, X) is obtained from the frames. The MFCC features to serve as the text prompt input for the language model, while RGB-X tuples are also tokenized as texts for "completion", training the language model in the teach-forcing paradigm. In the inference phase, the input music's features are extracted and transferred to text tokens, as prompt input for the trained language model, generating a series of (R, G, B, X) tuples as the "completion" output, and guiding the frame generation.

prompt	completion
[-29.44, 108.58, -15.65, 36.5, 2.3, 14.21, 4.92, 20.2, -2.59, 9.43, 10.56, 20.83, -0.24, 1.78, -12.75, 2.06, -4.75, 0.09, -4.64, -7.97, ..., 0.45]	[[245, 5, 169, 1], [242, 8, 13, 3], [89, 26, 161,16], [14, 5, 255, 28], [255, 8, 7, 50], [242, 15, 10, 51], [112, 6, 247, 59]]
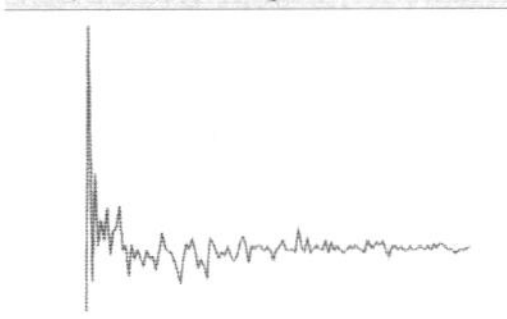	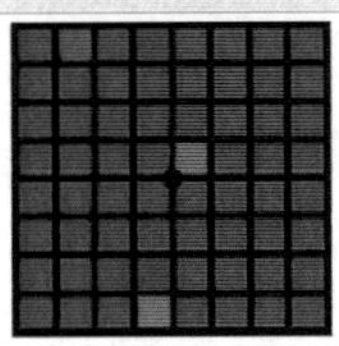

Figure 3: An example of prompt-completion pair. After the "prompt:" are the textual MFCC feature values, and after the "completion:" are the textual RGB-X tuples. The first RGB-X tuple (245, 5, 169, 1) denotes that the second button (the index of the first button is 0) on the Launchpad keyboard is purple.

generated by a post-process script, since a frame can be completely determined by a set of RGB-X tuples. Finally, the frames will form a Launchpad-playing video.

3. EXPERIMENTAL RESULTS

3.1 Dataset

We have collected 16 Launchpad-playing videos from the Internet, with a total duration of 3312 seconds. The frame rates of these videos are 25 Hz. Therefore, we have about 82800 frames in total. To ensure a uniform form, we concatenate all videos together to get a long video and crop each frame to 128×128 images. We cut the cropped long video into slices with a duration of about 10 seconds (250 video frames). Finally, the audio (music) of each video is extracted separately. These video frames and audio of music can produce about 82800 prompt-completion pairs, where 90% are for training and 10% are for validation.

3.2 Metric

We evaluate the performance of music visualization design on Launchpad with Fréchet Video Distance (FVD) [7] metric. FVD is a metric used to measure the similarity between the feature representations of real and generated videos. It is an extension of the Fréchet Inception Distance (FID) [8] metric, which is used to evaluate the quality of generated images. FVD uses a pre-trained neural network as a feature extractor to compute the distance between two sets of video features. The formula for FVD can be expressed as:

$$FVD(X,Y) = ||\mu_X - \mu_Y||^2 + cov(X,Y), \quad (4)$$

$$cov(X,Y) = Tr(\Sigma_X + \Sigma_Y - 2(\Sigma_X \Sigma_Y)^{\frac{1}{2}}), \quad (5)$$

where X and Y are the sets of feature representations of real and generated videos, μ_X and μ_Y are the mean feature vectors of X and Y, and Σ_X and Σ_Y are the covariance matrices of X and Y. The FVD score is calculated by comparing the distance between the mean feature vectors and the trace of the covariance matrices of the two videos. We represent the FVD score as FID$\downarrow$, which means the smaller the score, the better.

3.3 Quantitative Experiment

We use two random methods, *Random-RGB* and *Random-RGBX* as the baselines to compare with our proposed LaunchpadGPT:

- **Random-RGB.** The colors of the three channels of all 64 buttons are determined randomly.
- **Random-RGBX.** The buttons that will be activated are determined randomly at first. Then the RGB color of these selected buttons will be decided randomly.

The experiment results are shown in Table 1. It shows that the Launchpad-playing videos produced by our proposed LaunhpadGPT have the lowest FVD↓ among all the methods, meaning LaunchpadGPT can generate Launchpad-playing videos that are more similar to the videos produced manually by humans.

Method	FVD↓
Random-RGB	350.63
Random-RGBX	147.64
LaunchpadGPT (ours)	**75.22**

Table 1: The quantitative experiments. The result shows the Launchpad-playing videos produced by proposed LaunhpadGPT have the lowest FVD↓ among all the methods.

3.4 Result Visualization

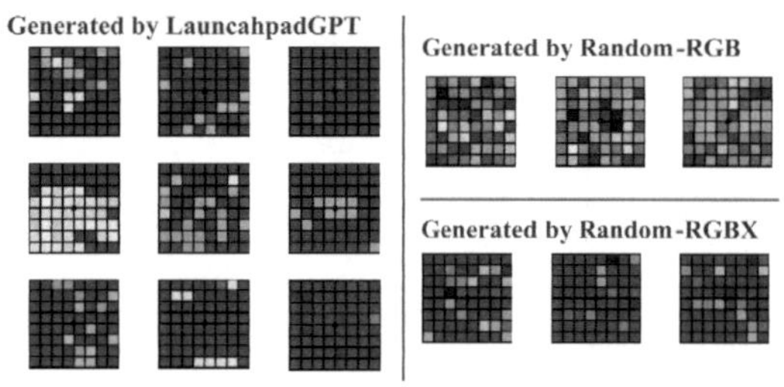

Figure 4: The outputs generated by LaunchpadGPT, Random-RGB, Random-RGBX respectively.

The language model output consists of RGB-X tuples and then be visualized as a colored Launchpad keyboard. As Figure 4 shows, we compare the output results from three different approaches: LaunchpadGPT, Random-RGB, and Random-RGBX. The observed results of outputs are illustrated as follows.

- **The outputs of Random-RGB** presents a chaotic and disorganized color effect on the Launchpad keyboard. As the colors are randomly generated, there is no discernible pattern or coherence in the color scheme.
- **The outputs of Random-RGBX** are random colors applied to illuminate specific button coordinates on the Launchpad keyboard. This results in a scattered pattern of randomly lit buttons, without any meaningful relationship between the colors and the button coordinates.
- **The outputs of LaunchpadGPT** presents similarities in color tones. The RGB colors tend to belong to the same color spectrum or display slight variations. This indicates that the language model has learned to generate RGB colors that are aesthetically coherent and reveal a level of color similarity.

The results show that LaunchpadGPT performs better than the random methods. This finding demonstrates the model's ability to capture and reflect the similarity in color tones, contributing to the generation of visually coherent RGB-X tuples. However, while LaunchpadGPT captures color similarities to some extent, it falls short in learning more structured patterns. We assume that the limitation lies in the representation of the RGB-X tuples, as the X component does not effectively convey the spatial relationships between buttons.

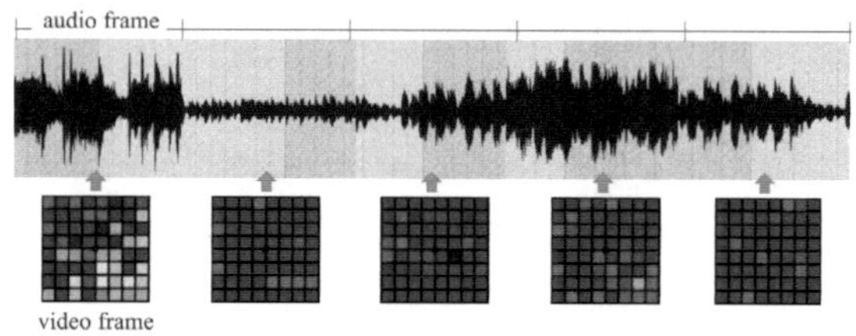

Figure 5: Results visualization aligning audio frames with corresponding generated video frames

In addition, we also discovered a positive correlation between the pattern activity of generated frames and the amplitude of the music's audio frames, which is shown in Figure 5. As the amplitude of the audio frames increases, the corresponding generated video frames exhibit higher pattern activity level. Conversely, when the amplitude is lower, the pattern activity level decreases.

The revealed ability of LaunchpadGPT opens up possibilities for task transfer in various music-related domains. The envisioned applications include designing music game charts, LED screen designs for music performance venues, and lighting schemes for music dance floors. By leveraging the model's ability to understand music-related patterns, designers, game developers, and lighting engineers can benefit from its generative capabilities to enhance the visual experience in music-related contexts.

4. CONCLUSIONS

We proposed LaunchpadGPT, a language model based on GPT, to generate music visualization on Launchpad with given music, assisting music designers in building Launchpad projects. LaunchpadGPT learns from Launchpad-playing videos to automatically generate synchronized light design schemes that enhance the visual experience. It simplifies the process of light design and empowers designers to explore different lighting schemes effortlessly, while also producing visually captivating playing videos showcasing the synchronized interaction between Launchpad, music, and dynamic lighting effects. The revealed potential of LaunchpadGPT in music visualization design can lead to a broader range of applications within the field of music visualization.

Acknowledgments

This work was supported by the National Key R&D Program of China (Grant NO. 2022YFF1202903) and the National Natural Science Foundation of China (Grant NO. 62122035 and 61972188).

5. REFERENCES

[1] H. B. Lima, C. G. D. Santos, and B. S. Meiguins, "A survey of music visualization techniques," *ACM Computing Surveys (CSUR)*, vol. 54, no. 7, pp. 1–29, 2021.

[2] A. Radford, K. Narasimhan, T. Salimans, I. Sutskever *et al.*, "Improving language understanding by generative pre-training," 2018.

[3] A. Radford, J. Wu, R. Child, D. Luan, D. Amodei, I. Sutskever *et al.*, "Language models are unsupervised multitask learners," *OpenAI blog*, vol. 1, no. 8, p. 9, 2019.

[4] T. Brown, B. Mann, N. Ryder, M. Subbiah, J. D. Kaplan, P. Dhariwal, A. Neelakantan, P. Shyam, G. Sastry, A. Askell *et al.*, "Language models are few-shot learners," *Advances in neural information processing systems*, vol. 33, pp. 1877–1901, 2020.

[5] A. Vaswani, N. Shazeer, N. Parmar, J. Uszkoreit, L. Jones, A. N. Gomez, Ł. Kaiser, and I. Polosukhin, "Attention is all you need," *Advances in neural information processing systems*, vol. 30, 2017.

[6] I. Sutskever, O. Vinyals, and Q. V. Le, "Sequence to sequence learning with neural networks," *Advances in neural information processing systems*, vol. 27, 2014.

[7] T. Unterthiner, S. van Steenkiste, K. Kurach, R. Marinier, M. Michalski, and S. Gelly, "FVD: A new metric for video generation," 2019.

[8] M. Heusel, H. Ramsauer, T. Unterthiner, B. Nessler, and S. Hochreiter, "Gans trained by a two time-scale update rule converge to a local nash equilibrium," *Advances in neural information processing systems*, vol. 30, 2017.

A Comprehensive Survey for Evaluation Methodologies of AI-Generated Music

Zeyu Xiong
Chilli Chicky Band
Computational Media and Arts Thrust
The Hong Kong University of Science and Technology (Guangzhou)
Guangzhou, China
zxiong666@connect.hkust-gz.edu.cn

Weitao Wang
Chilli Chicky Band
Earth, Ocean and Atmosphere Thrust
The Hong Kong University of Science and Technology (Guangzhou)
Guangzhou, China
weitaowangwtw@outlook.com

Jing Yu
Chilli Chicky Band
Carbon Neutrality and Climate Change Thrust
The Hong Kong University of Science and Technology (Guangzhou)
Guangzhou, China
jyu336@connect.hkust-gz.edu.cn

Yue Lin
Chilli Chicky Band
Computational Media and Arts Thrust
The Hong Kong University of Science and Technology (Guangzhou)
Guangzhou, China
ylin491@connect.hkust-gz.edu.cn

Ziyan Wang
Chilli Chicky Band
Computational Media and Arts Thrust
The Hong Kong University of Science and Technology (Guangzhou)
Guangzhou, China
zwang082@connect.hkust-gz.edu.cn

ABSTRACT

In recent years, AI-generated music has made significant progress, with several models performing well in multimodal and complex musical genres and scenes. While objective metrics can be used to evaluate generative music, they often lack interpretability for musical evaluation. Therefore, researchers often resort to subjective user studies to assess the quality of the generated works, which can be resource-intensive and less reproducible than objective metrics. This study aims to comprehensively evaluate the subjective, objective, and combined methodologies for assessing AI-generated music, highlighting the advantages and disadvantages of each approach. Ultimately, this study provides a valuable reference for unifying generative AI in the field of music evaluation.

1. INTRODUCTION

With the development of artificial intelligence generation technology, a large amount of work and applications have been generated for intelligent music generation [1, 2, 3, 4]. In particular, Music generation can be further divided into two types: the symbolic domain and the audio domain. Music generation in the symbolic domain is stored in MIDI format, and its textual and sequential data nature facilitates its applications (e.g., MidiNet [5], MuseGAN [6], BandNet [7] and TeleMelody [8]) in major deep learning models (e.g., LSTM [9, 10], autoencoder [11], RBM [12], and GAN [13]). For the audio domain, it is also possible for the analysis of the different bands according to the characteristics of the audio to obtain vectorized data for model training (e.g., Jukebox [14], WaveNet [15]). In addition to generating music from MIDI datasets or audio datasets, many works have started to look for connections between multimedia. For example, MusicLM [16] generates music from text, and BGT-G2G [17] generates music from images. All the above-mentioned works reach a certain level of accepted musicality. However, these ratings are either entirely referenced to parameters such as the accuracy of model training or are subjective ratings that rely entirely on user study.

Due to the different experimental processes and judgment criteria for subjective ratings, the objective model training metrics do not directly represent subjective feelings. There has not been a broad consensus on the evaluation of such generative models for a long time, resulting in a great challenge for music generation models in determining evaluation criteria [18, 19]. While subjective evaluation is usually better suited for evaluating generative models, it can be resource-intensive, and there are no uniform criteria. In contrast, objective methods, even if easy to implement, are usually less explanatory. To this end, we are dedicated to performing a survey for evaluation methodologies of AI-generated music and providing reference values for designing more scientific and effective evaluation methods in the future. Figure 1 shows the overview structure of this survey. We separate our survey into three main categories: (1) subjective evaluation, (2) objective evaluation, and (3) combined evaluation.

Our contributions to this work are listed below:

1. We provide a classification reference scheme of evaluation for creators in the field of AI music.

2. We provide a reference value for the unification of generative AI in the field of music evaluation.

2. RELATED WORK

In recent years, artificial intelligence (AI) systems have been increasingly involved in various applications of music composition, ranging from entertainment to therapeu-

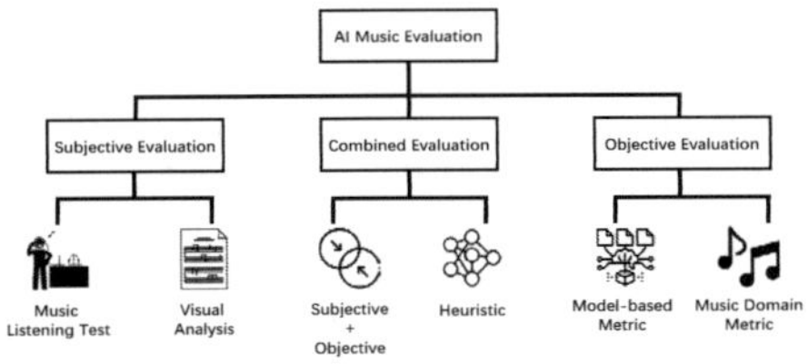

Figure 1. Overview Structure of The Survey: AI Music Evaluation Methods

tic uses. However, as the popularity of AI-generated music grows, an increasing number of issues have come to light (e.g., concerns about plagiarism in AI-generated music content [20], etc.). Therefore, to ensure the success of these applications, it is crucial to establish effective evaluation metrics.

Existing surveys on the evaluation method of AI-generated music predominantly categorize the evaluation methodologies into two primary classifications: subjective evaluations and objective evaluations. Subjective evaluation methods entail the solicitation of human listeners to provide ratings based on specific criteria, such as musicality, novelty, or emotional impact. Scholars such as Ji et al. [2] and Zhao et al. [21] have notably emphasized the use of listening tests as a widely employed approach to assess the melodic output of AI-generated music. Given the inherent subjectivity inherent in music appreciation, strict standardization of such evaluations remains a challenging endeavor, as noted by Yamshchikov et al. [22].

On the other hand, objective evaluation methods center on quantitative measurements applied to both the generated music and the underlying generative models. Ji et al. [2] elaborate on the objective evaluation as the quantitative measurement for both the generated music and the generative model. Notably, Theis et al. [23] conducted evaluations focusing on generative model performance from the perspective of log-likelihood, while Civit et al. [24] extended this evaluation to encompass considerations of dataset, code integration, and system structure. The selection of subjective or objective assessment methods often hinges on the specific purposes and criteria of measurement. Objective evaluation methods are commonly utilized in tasks such as classification, prediction, and recommendation, whereas subjective evaluations are more frequently employed to assess the quality of the generated musical content. In the following subsections, we delve into existing subjective and objective evaluation methods, and we also explore the amalgamation of these approaches. Furthermore, we analyze the application scenarios wherein each evaluation methodology finds relevance and effectiveness in the context of AI-generated music assessment.

3. SUBJECTIVE EVALUATION

Subjective evaluation of generated music is predominantly reliant on assessments provided by human listeners emphasizing their satisfaction. Due to the subjective evaluative nature of music in the real world, even though it tends to be more resource-intensive and less reproducible than objective evaluation, subjective evaluation is still an integral part of the process of AI music generation evaluation. Among the existing generative models, music listening tests and visual analysis are the two most important parts.

3.1 Music Listening Test

The music listening test is the most common method in subjective evaluation. Such evaluations are commonly conducted through two approaches: the musical Turing test or subjective query metrics based on modeled compositional theory [25]. Generally, a validated music listening test should require these conditions [26]: (1) The experiment was conducted in a controlled environment with specific acoustic characteristics and equipment, (2) The music knowledge level of subjects was evenly distributed, including both music amateurs who are lacking in music knowledge and experts in the field of music composition, (3) Each subject received the same instructions, and (4) Each subject received statistically significant results.

3.1.1 Musical Turing Test

Musical Turing Test measures the extent to which the generated music is indistinguishable from human-composed music. For example, Nadeem et al. [27] tested 28 users from the aspects of accuracy and preference to evaluate the generator output of a deep learning architecture combined with the proposed musical data. Although 57% of them correctly recognized that the music piece was generated by the computer, some claimed that the decision process was difficult. Ferreira et al. [28] invited 117 participants to differentiate the music composed by humans or five models (three transformers and two RNN models). What this study did good was that it divided all members into three groups according to their experience of classical music. It proved that people with better musical sensitivity had a higher correct rate of distinguishment.

To demonstrate statistically significant differences in evaluation results, hypothesis testing is usually performed (e.g., t-test [29], h-test [30], etc.).

3.1.2 Subjective Query Metrics

Nadeem et al. [27] and Ferreira et al. [28] also ask if the audiences love experimental music by a binary question. However, the answers cannot quantify the degree of their preferences with less representative. Therefore, more metrics should be considered during the evaluation of different models, which need to be specifically explained. In the study conducted by Chu et al. [31], 100 people participated in evaluating their interests in the music performed by different transformer models. This survey ruled out nine parameters (including overall creativity, naturalness, melodiousness, richness, rhythmicity, correctness, structures, and coherence) in a 7-point Likert scale. Take creativity as an example. It was described as the degree of novelty, value, and origin of the music pieces. In this way, participants can evaluate the music more specifically after a quantification process. Compared with the study, Hernandez-Olivan et al. [32] considered the melody, harmony, and rhythm of the music on a 5-point Likert scale. But they designed respective questions for different groups. Specifically, for people with less music knowledge, three parameters can be reflected by two questions. As for professionals with a solid foundation in music theory, they should answer six questions to determine those metrics. What's more, the experience of users should be paid more attention. Like the duration and the number of music pieces, these factors possibly make people fatigued, which may lead to a higher deviation in the results.

3.2 Visual Analysis

For visual analysis, the involvement of a music expert is often required. It is up to the expert to analyze the score, chord progression sheet, piano roll, etc., after visualization. For example, Dong et al. [6] analyzed the stability, fluidity, and musicality of melodies generated in chordal and rhythmic patterns in music. The waveform and spectrogram of the audio samples are also considered indicators for subjective evaluation. For example, Engel et al. [33] show each note as a "Rainbowgram", which is a visualization technique to show the relationship between time and frequency.

3.3 Summary

In conclusion, we believe that a good subjective evaluation should not only contain a precise design but also consider the users' characteristics. In this way, target metrics can be better determined while participants react in a comfortable environment, which can also contribute to the development of improved algorithms and models in the field.

Besides, although the subjective judgment is indispensable because of the artistic subjectivity of music, the resources expended behind it are enormous. At the same time, it is difficult to ensure the reproducibility as well as the stability of the experiments. Therefore, with the help of some objective quantitative indicators, it would be helpful to analyze the quality of music generation in a more scientific way.

4. OBJECTIVE EVALUATION

The objective evaluation involves using computational techniques to analyze the music and generate objective measures of its quality. Dong et al. [6] and Sturm [34] have used evaluation metrics based on probabilistic measures such as likelihood and density estimates (especially in the field of image generation [23]), yet whether there is a direct link between good or bad models and music quality is not yet known. Besides, metrics such as model metrics and music metrics are often used. For example, researchers may use metrics such as pitch entropy, chord progression complexity, or rhythmic variance to evaluate the music quality. We discuss the application of these metrics in detail in this section.

4.1 Model-based Metrics

Model-based Metrics refer to the general generative model evaluation metrics that do not contain music domain knowledge. Some common model-based metrics include *training loss*, *precision*, *recall*, *f1 score*, etc. Other metrics like the *chord prediction accuracy* [35], *style likelihood* [36], and *reconstruction accuracy* [37] are also applied for the objective evaluation.

Model-based evaluation methods are also limited to specific models or methods without strong universality because the methods and models of different generation systems are very different. Bretan et al. [11] considered a unit to be a variable length number of measures of music, and utilized objective metrics to assess the generative model, such as mean rank and accuracy, by evaluating the rank of the target unit. This is a specific evaluation metric based on model characteristics, not general metrics. Thus, a model-based metric inspired by domain knowledge is not universal but performs well on a particular task, even though its interpretability remains questionable in terms of music quality.

4.2 Music Domain Metrics

Music Domain Metrics (MDM) refers to the evaluation index under the domain knowledge of music, such as volume, pitch, chord, score, etc. Ji et al. [2] categorized these metrics into 4 categories: (1) pitch-related, (2) rhythm-related, (3) harmony-related, and (4) style-related.

4.2.1 Pitch & Rhythm Related Metrics

Widely-used pitch-related and rhythm-related metrics include scale consistency, tone spam, consecutive pitch repetitions, qualified rhythm frequency, rhythm variations, etc [38, 39]. For the state-of-the-art metric design, Yang and Alexander [25] propose a set of musicological objective assessment metrics, using which the output of the music generation model can be evaluated and compared. These metrics were validated in experiments and are reproducible. The proposed features include pitch counts, pitch category histograms, pitch shift matrices, pitch spans, average pitch intervals, note counts, average repetition intervals, note length histograms, and note length shift matrices.

4.2.2 Harmony Related Metrics

Harmony-related metrics focus on measuring harmonic consistency, chord histogram entropy, chord coverage, polyphony (how often two tones are played simultaneously), tone span, etc [40]. For example, C-RNN-GAN [38] and JazzGAN [39] used harmony-related metrics to measure the compatibility and musicality of generated outputs.

4.2.3 Style Related Metrics

In terms of style transfer, "Style Fit" (how well the generated music fits the desired style) and "Content Preservation" (how much content it retains from the original) are most commonly mentioned [41]. Cífka et al. [42] proposed a new set of objective evaluation metrics to be used alongside existing metrics. To capture the consistency in the harmonic structure, they preserve the content by calculating the frame-by-frame cosine similarity between chromatic features. For style fit, they collected so-called style profiles [43] to measure how well they are matched by the style transfer outputs.

4.3 Summary

In this section, we introduce model-based metrics and music domain metrics, as well as state-of-the-art innovative metrics. While the purpose of the above approaches is to reduce the workload of crowd-sourcing through scientific data, the interpretability of the above methods remains to be verified as the quantitative indicators do not fully represent subjective human perceptions. Therefore, studying the interpretability of objective evaluation indicators remains an issue worth exploring [44].

5. COMBINED EVALUATION

Combining subjective and objective evaluation methods can be an effective approach to evaluating AI-generated music. Recently, heuristic algorithmic frameworks have also emerged as important tools for combined evaluation. In this section, we discuss how the combined evaluation is performed and tested.

5.1 Subjective + Objective Evaluation

Subjective plus objective evaluation refers to evaluation methods that combine subjective user study and objective metrics, and a comparison between the subjective and objective evaluation forms the final conclusion. For example, Zhao et al. [45] evaluated the AI-generated music by combining objective musical metrics (polyphony, scale consistency, 3-tone repetitions, and tone span) analysis and subjective query metrics (harmonious, rhythmic, musically structured, and coherent) user study together. Huang et al. [46] trained a music mashup model and evaluated the outputs by combining objective evaluation (model-based metric plus music domain metric) and subjective listening tests (analyze mean of scores). The combined-style assessment of the above work intercepts the respective strengths of subjective and objective assessments and provides a more comprehensive assessment of the model's strengths and weaknesses in a broader dimension. However, the level of diversity in the database used above poses a challenge to the generalizability of the model. Besides, since the combination of the two also requires aligning final results, there is still no uniformity in the interpretable migration of the objective assessment compared to the subjective assessment.

5.2 Heuristic Evaluation Framework

Dervakos et al. [47] propose a heuristic framework to calculate the frequency of different features by using tools such as the "five-degree circle" to output quantitative scores for each metric. In this framework, the authors define four heuristic objective assessment attributes based on intuition and empirical observations as musicality. However, due to interpretability limitations, the authors still made a subjective assessment to prove the existence of the objective property was meaningful. In the subjective test, over 1,000 users participated in scoring three dimensions: 1) how much they liked the music, 2) how interesting the music was, and 3) the Turing test: whether the composer of the music was a human or a computer. The authors compared the final results of the user survey with the results of their proposed heuristic and eventually found a high degree of similarity in the results between the two, thus demonstrating the significance of the heuristic.

5.3 Summary

Subjective + objective evaluation is designed for learning the broad domain of the generated music. Through this method, many work evaluations become more robust. However, we have not yet found a unified assessment paradigm because of the different objectives of the different efforts. The heuristic evaluation framework seems to contribute significantly to mitigating the resource consumption of purely subjective evaluations. While subjective evaluation can provide valuable insights into the general public's perception of creative AI and the evaluation of music, heuristics can be used to evaluate specific features of AI-generated music without the need for comparison between generated and real data. However, the robustness of the method still needs to be compared in parallel with a purely subjective evaluation. This, in turn, gets caught in the trade-off between interpretability and experimental reproducibility.

6. DISCUSSION

As AI music generation continues to evolve, the methods of evaluating these generated outputs must also adapt to the increasing complexity and creativity of the models. There are several challenges and future directions that we have identified in this field.

6.1 Establishing Standards

At present, the evaluation of AI-generated music lacks standardization, which results in a process that is inconsistent and lacks a common reference point for stakeholders, including developers, musicologists, and audiences. The creation of a comprehensive, standardized evaluation system would streamline this process, benefitting all parties involved.

The envisioned system would include a set of standard metrics, incorporating both subjective and objective elements, applicable across various AI models and across different music genres. This is vital as different genres of music possess unique characteristics, influencing the type of metrics required for their evaluation.

For instance, the complexity of harmonic structure forms a critical component of classical music evaluation. In contrast, the "catchiness" or melodic hooks are often a major focus in the evaluation of pop music. This diversity necessitates the challenge of formulating genre-specific evaluation metrics, allowing for a fair and accurate appraisal of AI-generated music within the context of its intended genre.

In essence, the development of a standardized evaluation system that accounts for both general musical elements and genre-specific characteristics is a pressing need in the field of AI-generated music.

6.2 Bridging the Gap between Subjective and Objective Evaluation

As discussed in Section 5, one of the main challenges lies in bridging the gap between subjective and objective evaluations. While subjective evaluation considers the listeners' personal preferences and emotions, objective evaluation relies on mathematical and computational analysis.

The challenge is to find a balance and a correlation between these two methods. Future research could focus on developing methods that can effectively combine these two approaches to provide a comprehensive evaluation.

6.3 Interpretability of Objective Metrics

Although objective metrics provide a quantitative measure of the quality of AI-generated music, their interpretability remains an issue. Many of these metrics are based on abstract mathematical concepts that may not necessarily correlate with human perception of music quality. Therefore, it is crucial to develop objective metrics that can accurately represent subjective human perceptions and can be easily interpreted in terms of music quality.

6.4 Evaluating Creativity

Evaluating creativity in AI-generated music is a complex task as it involves assessing different criteria in different contexts. Some of these criteria are novelty, originality, and value. Novelty refers to the newness or uniqueness of a musical piece. A composition that sounds distinctly different from existing pieces can be considered novel. However, it's essential to remember that novelty alone does not equate to creativity. For instance, random notes played together might be novel but not necessarily creative or enjoyable. Another criterion is originality: it is closely related to novelty, but it adds an extra layer of refinement. An original piece of music introduces something new while also demonstrating an understanding of existing musical traditions and structures. It should show a level of sophistication and skill, breaking from the norm in a purposeful and artful way. Value is the third critical component of creativity. A creative piece of music should be novel and original with value, which can be emotional, cultural, aesthetic, or intellectual. It might be a piece that resonates deeply with listeners, offers a new perspective, or pushes boundaries in the music world. Current evaluation methods may not fully capture these aspects, and different audiences' definition of creativity varies. Therefore, developing methods to evaluate creativity effectively is a significant challenge. This could involve devising new metrics or modifying existing ones to measure these aspects.

7. CONCLUSIONS

AI music generation is a promising field with significant potential for both creative and technological advancements. The evaluation of AI-generated music, however, is still a challenging and complex task that requires both subjective and objective methods. In this paper, we discussed various evaluation methods, including subjective evaluations like music listening tests and visual analysis, objective evaluations like model-based metrics and music domain metrics, and combined methods. We conducted a comprehensive survey for the evaluation methodologies of AI-generated music; we separated these methods into three parts: (1) subjective evaluation, (2) objective evaluation, and (3) combined evaluation. We discussed in detail the advantages and disadvantages of various evaluation methods and provide a future perspective on the evaluation of generative AI in the music domain. This work also provided insights for the future release of a unified style of assessment method. We also outlined several future directions and challenges in this field, such as establishing standards, bridging the gap between subjective and objective evaluations, and evaluating creativity and different music genres. We believe that addressing these challenges will lead to more reliable and comprehensive evaluation methods for AI-generated music, contributing to the further development of this field.

8. REFERENCES

[1] M. Kaliakatsos-Papakostas, A. Floros, and M. N. Vrahatis, "Artificial intelligence methods for music generation: a review and future perspectives," *Nature-Inspired Computation and Swarm Intelligence*, pp. 217–245, 2020.

[2] S. Ji, J. Luo, and X. Yang, "A Comprehensive Survey on Deep Music Generation: Multi-level Representations, Algorithms, Evaluations, and Future Directions," 2020.

[3] Y. Cao, S. Li, Y. Liu, Z. Yan, Y. Dai, P. S. Yu, and L. Sun, "A comprehensive survey of ai-generated content (aigc): A history of generative ai from gan to chatgpt," *arXiv preprint arXiv:2303.04226*, 2023.

[4] S. Dai, Z. Jin, C. Gomes, and R. B. Dannenberg, "Controllable deep melody generation via hierarchical music structure representation," *arXiv preprint arXiv:2109.00663*, 2021.

[5] L.-C. Yang, S.-Y. Chou, and Y.-H. Yang, "Midinet: A convolutional generative adversarial network for symbolic-domain music generation using 1d and 2d conditions," *arXiv preprint arXiv:1703.10847*, vol. 32, 2017.

[6] H.-W. Dong, W.-Y. Hsiao, L.-C. Yang, and Y.-H. Yang, "Musegan: Multi-track sequential generative adversarial networks for symbolic music generation and accompaniment," in *Proceedings of the AAAI Conference on Artificial Intelligence*, vol. 32, no. 1, 2018.

[7] Y. Zhou, W. Chu, S. Young, and X. Chen, "BandNet: A neural network-based, multi-instrument Beatles-style MIDI music composition machine," *arXiv preprint arXiv:1812.07126*, 2018.

[8] Z. Ju, P. Lu, X. Tan, R. Wang, C. Zhang, S. Wu, K. Zhang, X. Li, T. Qin, and T.-Y. Liu, "Telemelody: Lyric-to-melody generation with a template-based two-stage method," *arXiv preprint arXiv:2109.09617*, 2021.

[9] D. Eck and J. Schmidhuber, "A first look at music composition using lstm recurrent neural networks," *Istituto Dalle Molle Di Studi Sull Intelligenza Artificiale*, vol. 103, no. 4, p. 48, 2002.

[10] J. Wu, C. Hu, Y. Wang, X. Hu, and J. Zhu, "A hierarchical recurrent neural network for symbolic melody generation," *IEEE transactions on cybernetics*, vol. 50, no. 6, pp. 2749–2757, 2019.

[11] M. Bretan, G. Weinberg, and L. Heck, "A unit selection methodology for music generation using deep neural networks," *arXiv preprint arXiv:1612.03789*, 2016.

[12] G. E. Hinton and R. R. Salakhutdinov, "Reducing the dimensionality of data with neural networks," *science*, vol. 313, no. 5786, pp. 504–507, 2006.

[13] I. Goodfellow, J. Pouget-Abadie, M. Mirza, B. Xu, D. Warde-Farley, S. Ozair, A. Courville, and Y. Bengio, "Generative adversarial networks," *Communications of the ACM*, vol. 63, no. 11, pp. 139–144, 2020.

[14] P. Dhariwal, H. Jun, C. Payne, J. W. Kim, A. Radford, and I. Sutskever, "Jukebox: A generative model for music," *arXiv preprint arXiv:2005.00341*, 2020.

[15] A. v. d. Oord, S. Dieleman, H. Zen, K. Simonyan, O. Vinyals, A. Graves, N. Kalchbrenner, A. Senior, and K. Kavukcuoglu, "Wavenet: A generative model for raw audio," *arXiv preprint arXiv:1609.03499*, 2016.

[16] A. Agostinelli, T. I. Denk, Z. Borsos, J. Engel, M. Verzetti, A. Caillon, Q. Huang, A. Jansen, A. Roberts, M. Tagliasacchi *et al.*, "Musiclm: Generating music from text," *arXiv preprint arXiv:2301.11325*, 2023.

[17] Z. Xiong, P.-C. Lin, and A. Farjudian, "Retaining Semantics in Image to Music Conversion," in *2022 IEEE International Symposium on Multimedia (ISM)*. IEEE, 2022, pp. 228–235.

[18] A. Borji, "Pros and cons of gan evaluation measures," *Computer Vision and Image Understanding*, vol. 179, pp. 41–65, 2019.

[19] A. Jordanous, "A standardised procedure for evaluating creative systems: Computational creativity evaluation based on what it is to be creative," *Cognitive Computation*, vol. 4, pp. 246–279, 2012.

[20] Z. Yin, F. Reuben, S. Stepney, and T. Collins, ""A Good Algorithm Does Not Steal–It Imitates": The Originality Report as a Means of Measuring When a Music Generation Algorithm Copies Too Much," in *Artificial Intelligence in Music, Sound, Art and Design: 10th International Conference, EvoMUSART 2021, Held as Part of EvoStar 2021, Virtual Event, April 7–9, 2021, Proceedings 10*. Springer, 2021, pp. 360–375.

[21] Z. Zhao, H. Liu, S. Li, J. Pang, M. Zhang, Y. Qin, L. Wang, and Q. Wu, "A Review of Intelligent Music Generation Systems," *arXiv preprint arXiv:2211.09124*, 2022.

[22] I. P. Yamshchikov and A. Tikhonov, "Music generation with variational recurrent autoencoder supported by history," *SN Applied Sciences*, vol. 2, no. 12, p. 1937, 2020.

[23] L. Theis, A. v. d. Oord, and M. Bethge, "A note on the evaluation of generative models," *arXiv preprint arXiv:1511.01844*, 2015.

[24] M. Civit, J. Civit-Masot, F. Cuadrado, and M. J. Escalona, "A systematic review of artificial intelligence-based music generation: Scope, applications, and future trends," *Expert Systems with Applications*, p. 118190, 2022.

[25] L.-C. Yang and A. Lerch, "On the evaluation of generative models in music," *Neural Computing and Applications*, vol. 32, no. 9, pp. 4773–4784, 2020.

[26] F. Ribeiro, D. Florêncio, C. Zhang, and M. Seltzer, "Crowdmos: An approach for crowdsourcing mean opinion score studies," in *2011 IEEE international conference on acoustics, speech and signal processing (ICASSP)*. IEEE, 2011, pp. 2416–2419.

[27] M. Nadeem, A. Tagle, and S. Sitsabesan, "Let's make some music," in *2019 International Conference on Electronics, Information, and Communication (ICEIC)*. IEEE, 2019, pp. 1–4.

[28] P. Ferreira, R. Limongi, and L. P. Fávero, "Generating Music with Data: Application of Deep Learning Models for Symbolic Music Composition," *Applied Sciences*, vol. 13, no. 7, p. 4543, 2023.

[29] C. Donahue, H. H. Mao, Y. E. Li, G. W. Cottrell, and J. McAuley, "LakhNES: Improving multi-instrumental music generation with cross-domain pre-training," *arXiv preprint arXiv:1907.04868*, 2019.

[30] W. Chi, P. Kumar, S. Yaddanapudi, R. Suresh, and U. Isik, "Generating music with a self-correcting non-chronological autoregressive model," *arXiv preprint arXiv:2008.08927*, 2020.

[31] H. Chu, J. Kim, S. Kim, H. Lim, H. Lee, S. Jin, J. Lee, T. Kim, and S. Ko, "An Empirical Study on How People Perceive AI-generated Music," in *Proceedings of the 31st ACM International Conference on Information & Knowledge Management*, 2022, pp. 304–314.

[32] C. Hernandez-Olivan, J. A. Puyuelo, and J. R. Beltran, "Subjective evaluation of deep learning models for symbolic music composition," *arXiv preprint arXiv:2203.14641*, 2022.

[33] J. Engel, C. Resnick, A. Roberts, S. Dieleman, M. Norouzi, D. Eck, and K. Simonyan, "Neural audio synthesis of musical notes with wavenet autoencoders," in *International Conference on Machine Learning*. PMLR, 2017, pp. 1068–1077.

[34] B. L. Sturm and O. Ben-Tal, "Taking the models back to music practice: Evaluating generative transcription models built using deep learning," *Journal of Creative Music Systems*, vol. 2, pp. 32–60, 2017.

[35] H. Lim, S. Rhyu, and K. Lee, "Chord generation from symbolic melody using BLSTM networks," *arXiv preprint arXiv:1712.01011*, 2017.

[36] G. Brunner, A. Konrad, Y. Wang, and R. Wattenhofer, "MIDI-VAE: Modeling dynamics and instrumentation of music with applications to style transfer," *arXiv preprint arXiv:1809.07600*, 2018.

[37] A. Roberts, J. Engel, C. Raffel, C. Hawthorne, and D. Eck, "A hierarchical latent vector model for learning long-term structure in music," in *International conference on machine learning*. PMLR, 2018, pp. 4364–4373.

[38] O. Mogren, "C-RNN-GAN: Continuous recurrent neural networks with adversarial training," *arXiv preprint arXiv:1611.09904*, 2016.

[39] N. Trieu and R. Keller, "JazzGAN: Improvising with generative adversarial networks," in *MUME workshop*, 2018.

[40] Y.-C. Yeh, W.-Y. Hsiao, S. Fukayama, T. Kitahara, B. Genchel, H.-M. Liu, H.-W. Dong, Y. Chen, T. Leong, and Y.-H. Yang, "Automatic melody harmonization with triad chords: A comparative study," *Journal of New Music Research*, vol. 50, no. 1, pp. 37–51, 2021.

[41] G. Brunner, Y. Wang, R. Wattenhofer, and S. Zhao, "Symbolic music genre transfer with cyclegan," in *2018 ieee 30th international conference on tools with artificial intelligence (ictai)*. IEEE, 2018, pp. 786–793.

[42] O. Cífka, U. Şimşekli, and G. Richard, "Groove2Groove: one-shot music style transfer with supervision from synthetic data," *IEEE/ACM Transactions on Audio, Speech, and Language Processing*, vol. 28, pp. 2638–2650, 2020.

[43] C. McKay, "Automatic genre classification of MIDI recordings," 2004.

[44] D. Castelvecchi, "Can we open the black box of AI?" *Nature News*, vol. 538, no. 7623, p. 20, 2016.

[45] K. Zhao, S. Li, J. Cai, H. Wang, and J. Wang, "An emotional symbolic music generation system based on lstm networks," in *2019 IEEE 3rd Information Technology, Networking, Electronic and Automation Control Conference (ITNEC)*. IEEE, 2019, pp. 2039–2043.

[46] J. Huang, J.-C. Wang, J. B. Smith, X. Song, and Y. Wang, "Modeling the compatibility of stem tracks to generate music mashups," in *Proceedings of the AAAI Conference on Artificial Intelligence*, vol. 35, no. 1, 2021, pp. 187–195.

[47] E. Dervakos, G. Filandrianos, and G. Stamou, "Heuristics for evaluation of AI generated music," in *2020 25th International Conference on Pattern Recognition (ICPR)*. IEEE, 2021, pp. 9164–9171.

Hypnagogia: An Autonomous Audiovisual Study

Jean-Philippe Jullin
Laboratoire Formes·Ondes – Faculty of Music, University of Montreal
jean-philippe.jullin@umontreal.ca

ABSTRACT

Hypnagogia is an audiovisual installation that explores the creative behaviours of autonomous algorithms. An immersive experience is offered through a dome of loudspeakers and video projection. It is inspired by the state of semi-consciousness known as hypnagogia, characterized by lucid dreams, hallucinations, and different forms of sleep paralysis. It is often associated with the onset of creative thinking and imagination.

This study uses machine learning techniques to generate complex audiovisual patterns. It creates a landscape with both supervised and unsupervised algorithms. The network of algorithms manages sound and video, continuously striving towards complete order or chaos. A regressor helped by a classifier attempt to find a balance between different forms of patterns. Hypnagogia offers an opportunity to explore autonomous systems' behaviour and reflect on their possibilities and limitations.

1. INTRODUCTION

Machine learning has given rise to new technologies that challenge traditional notions of creativity and aesthetics. It encourages a systemic approach to artistic expression, in which autonomous algorithms operate as agents within interactive ecosystems. The artist emphasizes a systemic approach to art, prioritizing the orchestration of interactions among diverse entities instead of perceiving tools solely from a utilitarian perspective. Donella Meadows notes that autonomous and self-organizing systems are highly unpredictable and that establishing a stable and sustainable relationship with them requires playful interaction [1]. We believe that what the author describes as "playful interaction" consists of the artist's creative input with the system's components, recognizing the mutuality between the different entities. The systemic art paradigm emphasizes the holistic treatment of objects in artworks. Sound is at the heart of "Hypnagogia," where agents exchange extracted audio features to influence each other.

"Hypnagogia" is inspired by the semi-conscious state of hypnagogia, the transitional state between wakefulness and sleep. Characterized by lucid dreams, hallucinations, and sleep paralysis, it is often associated with creativity. This study examines autonomous behaviours based on interactions between different entities and attempts to foster creativity in a system centered around the computer.

The installation uses techniques such as random audio corpus generation, descriptive analysis of corpora, concatenative sound synthesis, automatic dome spatialization and self-organizing maps to create a dynamic and evolving experience. The unsupervised generation of sound and visual patterns tends to induce a pronounced sense of synchresis - the psychological experience of linking what is seen with what is heard simultaneously, as Michel Chion described [2]. Its form remains in a state of continuous evolution, making it unpredictable yet organic.

This work combines artistic and technological elements through practice-based research. The installation fosters a systemic approach, viewing the outcome as an interactive ecosystem. This allows us to study the logic of exchange between various entities, valuing the agency of machines and humans. Exploring autonomous systems is essential to grasp the potential of machine learning and its value in artistic and musical creation.

This audiovisual installation offers a hypnotic experience that invites viewers to push the limits of their perception amid semi-chaotic exchanges. It represents a playground for engaging in systems characterized by dynamic relational states between sound and visual entities.

2. METHODS

This section will discuss the methods used in this study to explore machine creativity. We will focus on unsupervised learning and algorithmic processes to create interdependent audio and visual components.

2.1 Use of Machine Learning

Previous research, such as the "N_Polytope" installation by Chris Salter, Sofian Audry et al. [3] and "Performative Ecologies" installation by Ruairi Glynn [4], has demonstrated the potential of unsupervised learning in the generation of complex and innovative patterns in art and music. Both generate self-directed visual patterns and explore gestural dialogues between the audience and dynamic artworks. Unsupervised processes have been applied within installations to develop interactive and responsive displays that actively engage with viewers in real-time. At the origin of "Hypnagogia," we hypothesized that various machine learning processes could develop an ever-evolving and organic installation. We will explain the use of these processes in generating sound and video patterns in "Hypnagogia" and analyze the poiesis of the resulting artwork.

2.2 Audio Descriptive Analyses

In this installation, the musical agent relies on automatically generated audio corpora in Ableton Live. We recorded vast sound variations using custom racks by applying random envelopes on macros mapped to synthesizer and effect parameters. A selection process followed, retaining only the most intriguing sounds, resulting in a wide range from minimalistic tones to evolving noise textures. Initially, machine learning was attempted to record only exciting sounds, but the process was abandoned due to reduced variation.

After the initial sound corpora generation process, descriptor-based analyses were performed using the FluCoMa [5] library in the MaxMSP software environment. In these analyses, the entire corpus was first loaded into a single buffer and then split into 2,000 to 4,000 segments of equal duration. These segments were analyzed by Mel-Frequency Cepstrum Coefficients (MFCC), chromatic and spectral descriptors [6]. Those analyses organize sounds according to their timbral proximity, the relative strength of their pitch classes or characteristics such as their noise level. The dataset underwent robust scaling and normalization to reduce sensitivity to outliers. It was then segmented into distinct clusters using an unsupervised k-means algorithm to determine similarity. Each cluster was further reduced to two dimensions through principal component analysis (PCA) and uniform manifold approximation and projection (UMAP) before normalization (see Figure 1). A k-dimensional tree was trained on the dataset to facilitate sound access on a map.

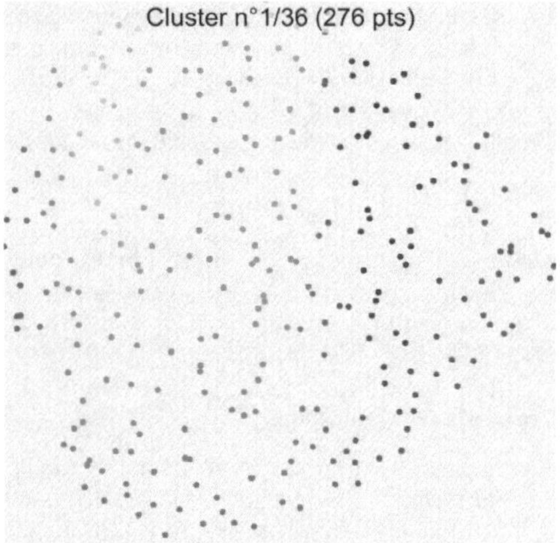

Figure 1. Normalized cluster of sounds.

2.3 Automatic Spatialization

Our program communicates with the SpatGRIS software developed at the University of Montreal [7] to spatialize the sound on a dome of loudspeakers. To position a sound, SpatGRIS requires a list of five data to be sent via Open Sound Control (OSC), consisting of the X, Y, and Z positions and the horizontal and vertical spread of each source. However, it was important that each sound was positioned in space based on its audio features, using solely an unsupervised algorithm. Therefore, a dimensional reduction process was employed on the clusters, each dataset being reduced to five dimensions that will control the position of sounds in a one-to-one mapping with SpatGRIS. It was achieved by passing them through a PCA and UMAP before normalizing them.

Using the minimum distance parameter provided by UMAP, we can obtain a relatively uniform distribution of the clusters. This uniform distribution creates synthetic spatial trajectories between sounds similar in timbre but distant in spatial planes.

2.4 Generative Video

The installation includes a video component created from a spectral analysis of the audio corpus. The spectrum is converted into a video matrix (see Figure 2) and transmitted to the Touch Designer video software.

Figure 2. FFT analysis converted to video matrix.

A patch based on video feedback was employed to automatically sort pixels, using blur to converge towards a single colour. It was inspired by the MaxMSP "Firefly Sync Simulation" patch by Robin Meier [8]. Although this simplification process is relatively fast, it has been extended with effects to slow it down and create complexity, such as noise reinjection, pixel warping, colour blending and various types of blur. The system's behaviour, whether towards total order (single colour) or chaos (random noise), depends on the selected parameters.

2.5 Regressor Helped by a Classifier

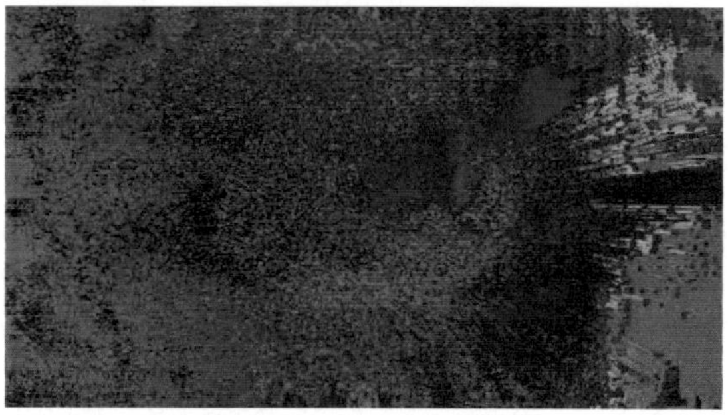

Figure 3. Example of generated output.

A multiple regressor was introduced to discover visually stimulating patterns. This regressor identifies areas where the video controls are most likely to yield captivating outcomes, aiming to balance different audio and visual patterns (See Figure 3).

However, as the regressor is designed to search for patterns continuously, it is supported by a multilayer perceptron classifier. This classifier is trained on hundreds of examples provided by the composer, enabling it to distinguish between uninteresting or noisy video input and potentially captivating patterns.

When the classifier recognizes input as noise, the multiple regressor is asked to establish parameters to generate a pattern. If the same pattern remains too long, the system resumes searching for a new one. This iterative process allows to maintain an element of unpredictability, generating an evolving display of patterns (see Figure 4).

Figure 4. Evolving visual pattern.

2.6 Self-Organizing Maps

As the video matrix undergoes processing in Touch Designer, every frame is sent back as a vector to MaxMSP. A self-organizing map from the ml.star [9] library is applied to reduce the image vector into two points. This neural network learns to map high-dimensional data onto a lower-dimensional space while maintaining the original data's topological structure. In this context, the self-organizing map helps to identify features from the video matrix and pick which sound to play, allowing an unsupervised mapping of video and sound gestures. Another self-organizing map chooses the cluster from which the sounds are selected, allowing for a lasting correlation between the audio and visual landscapes.

3. RESULTS

A recording was made during a public presentation in April 2023.[1] Additional excerpts are also available as supplementary material recorded afterward.[2][3][4][5]

3.1 Sound and Video Algorithms

This installation combines supervised and unsupervised machine learning algorithms to create audio and visual patterns that challenge and intrigue the audience. The soundscapes use concatenative sound synthesis driven by video patterns, resulting in musical structures that sometimes lack coherence in their overall form. While the self-organizing maps link visual forms with particular types of sound, there may not always be a clear underlying intention behind the resulting combinations, leading to a sense of detachment or impersonality in the installation.

Despite this, the installation showcases an intriguing form of "cold organicity," revealing complex, uncoded patterns emerging from the interaction of sounds and visuals. The generated video exhibits frequent colour changes and sudden shifts, evoking a sense of dynamic movement while imparting an impression of undesired randomness. While the regressor strives to sustain coherence by identifying equilibrium zones, it is constrained by the classifier's predictions, which can sometimes be inaccurate due to video vector compression during transfer between Touch Designer and MaxMSP.

Despite the potential lack of clear intent in the installation, some one-to-one mapping of live audio analysis to specific video parameters (such as monochromatic level or colour amplitudes) ensures clear points of interaction between the audio and visual elements (see Figure 5). These simple connections allow for a more cohesive and dynamic integration of the components, enhancing the overall impact of the installation.

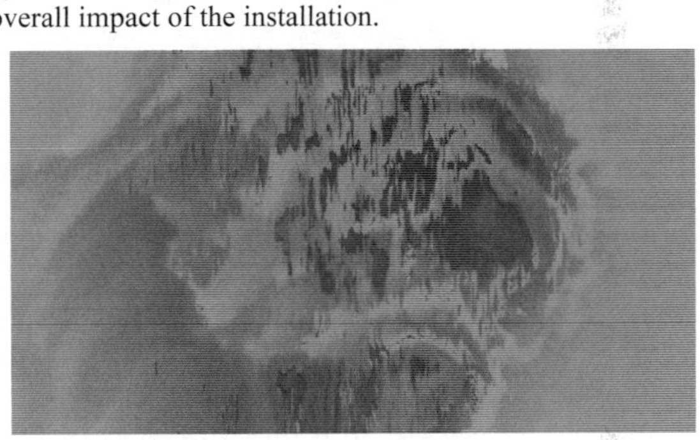

Figure 5. Monochromatic level mapped to noise.

3.2 Evolution and Complexity

Each time the system starts, the training data of the regressor is emptied, and it tries to find patterns from random conditions. If a pattern is found, its random vector is added to the dataset, which grows over time. The dataset's size is restricted to allow a continuous evolution, with older examples overwritten once the limit is reached. The lower the limit, the faster the model evolves.

Despite the seemingly chaotic appearance of the visual and sound patterns generated by the installation, their movements have a certain organic quality. Rather than being completely random, the patterns seem to flow and evolve in a way resembling some natural process. Indeed, the machine learning algorithms used in the installation are designed to adapt and evolve, learning from the patterns it generates and discovering new ways to create structures while forgetting previous ones.

Overall, the organicity of the installation reinforces the sense of machine improvisation and creativity at the heart of the project. They are essential to this study, as they challenge our notions of continuity and coherence and encourage us to see the world differently.

1 https://youtu.be/rtzXPYwynrY
2 https://youtu.be/OkNqfZZ9PMw
3 https://youtu.be/dGJGzkNMEik
4 https://youtu.be/mgeK1fg1kjs
5 https://youtu.be/zrfX4BItnLs

3.3 Aesthetics and Intrigue

Throughout the process, the goal is to create audiovisual components that go beyond mere visual and aural appeal. The intent is to produce something that challenges the viewer's interpretation while evoking a sense of wonder and intrigue. This installation creates evolving and unpredictable components by incorporating machine learning algorithms and unsupervised techniques. This approach can leave the viewer uncertain about the machine's perception and creative process, as well as the essence of the installation itself. This sense of uncertainty, ambiguity and intrigue is essential to the project's aesthetic design. The aim of keeping the viewer engaged and questioning what they are experiencing is to create a deeper level of engagement and immersion.

These components are also designed to be challenging from a machine perspective. The multiple layers of complexity built into the process make it difficult for the machine to predict and generate specific patterns. This aspect is crucial to creating an autonomous system that is not simply a chosen algorithmic product but a creative effort by the machine.

4. CONCLUSION

The autonomous installation described in this study showcases how machine learning algorithms can create unpredictable abstract patterns by shaping and moulding data, challenging our traditional understanding of coherence and continuity. This approach enables the system to adapt and evolve, continuously exploring the relationship between its senses.

In autonomous art, several innovative works already exist that use machine learning algorithms to generate new and unpredictable patterns, such as "N_Polytope" and "Performative Ecologies." These artworks, often created by interdisciplinary teams, explore the potential of machines in artistic expression and offer new perspectives on their relationship with humans.

"Hypnagogia" builds upon this tradition of exploring the capabilities of autonomous systems. The improvisational component of the system allows for a level of unpredictability that can lead to exciting and new artistic results. The ability of the system to learn and evolve is exciting in the context of interactive art installations, as it allows for a continuous and dynamic exploration of the relationships between the components and how they influence our perception of the work. However, the close but unsupervised relationships between audio and video can also create a sense of disorientation. The boundaries between the two media are blurred, and the fast pace of the patterns can create a confronting loss of reference. This loss can be a challenge while being an opportunity to explore how our perception of reality is influenced by the interconnection between different senses. It invites us to explore our limits and encourages questioning our notions of continuity.

This study showcases the potential of technology and machine learning in shaping our understanding of electronic art and human experience. As technology evolves and becomes more accessible, artists can explore new ways of creating engaging and immersive experiences for their audience. In electronic art, machine learning algorithms offer the potential for creating works that are dynamic, unpredictable, and responsive to their environment. Those algorithms create opportunities to explore the relationship between art, technology, and the audience.

Technology and machine learning can democratize art creation and consumption by providing accessible tools and platforms for electronic arts. Those tools allow more artists to participate and reach broader audiences, promoting a diverse and inclusive art scene and an informed public. This can lead to a more diverse and inclusive art scene, focusing on systems rather than single subjects.

Acknowledgments

We thank FRQSC for their financial support and our collaborators and friends whose contributions made this installation possible. We extend special thanks to Dominic Thibault and Jules Roze for their significant help and support, which was much appreciated.

5. REFERENCES

[1] D. H. Meadows, *Thinking in systems: A primer*, Chelsea: Chelsea Green Publishing, 2008.

[2] M. Chion, *Audio-Vision: Sound on Screen*, ed. C. Gorbman, New York: Columbia University Press, 2019.

[3] C. Salter, S. Audry, M. Baalman, A. Basanta, E. Bidinost and T. Spier, *N_Polytope*, Gijón: LABoral Centro de Arte y Creación Industrial, 2012. [Art].

[4] R. Glynn, *Performative Ecologies*, London: Bartlett School of Architecture, 2007. [Art].

[5] P. A. Tremblay, G. Roma and O. Green, "Enabling Programmatic Data Mining as Musicking: The Fluid Corpus Manipulation Toolkit," *Computer Music Journal*, vol. 45, (2), p. 9-23, 2021.

[6] G. Peeters, B. L. Giordano, P. Susini, N. Misdariis, S. McAdams, "The Timbre Toolbox: Extracting audio descriptors from musical signals," *The Journal of the Acoustical Society of America*, vol. 130, (5), p. 2902-2916, 2011.

[7] D. Ledoux, R. Normandeau, O. Bélanger and C. Lengelé, "Vers une approche immersive de la composition musicale par le développement d'outils de spatialisation sonore: ControlGRIS et ServerGRIS," in *Journées d'Informatique Musicale*, Bayonne, France, 2019.

[8] *Firefly Sync Simulation*. (2013). R. Meier. Accessed: May 2, 2023. [Online]. Available: https://robinmeier.net/?p=960

[9] B. D. Smith and W. S. Deal, "ML.* Machine Learning Library as a Musical Partner in the Computer-Acoustic Composition Flight," in *International Computer Music Conference*, Athens, Greece, 2014.

From Deep Listening to Aural Sonology: An Examination of the Dynamics of Electroacoustic Listening Practices

Xi Lu
DisPerSion Lab
York University, Toronto, ON, Canada
dmxilu96@yorku.ca

Doug Van Nort
DisPerSion Lab
York University, Toronto, ON, Canada
vannort@yorku.ca

ABSTRACT

This paper examines listening in electroacoustic music contexts from several perspectives. It provides an overview of electroacoustic music analysis and its relationship to scholarship on listening and embodied music cognition. Building upon previous research that has explored a listener-based approach to analyzing electroacoustic music, we investigate the audience listening experience and its relationship to the various sonic attributes that result from the creative process. We present a preliminary experiment that explores the dynamics of audience listening by designing both concert-based and online listening sessions that capture reflections from the audience's perspective. Through this work, we aim to broaden conversations around existing frameworks for electroacoustic music analysis to include an expanded understanding of listening – both in terms of composing and audience reception – as a holistic, embodied, and collaborative process.

1. INTRODUCTION

The term "electroacoustic music" or "electroacoustics" has taken on a number of meanings that more broadly place it as a branch of the art of sound organization [1]. The analysis of electroacoustic music has largely been established on one specific mode of listening – reduced listening [2]. Meanwhile, spectromorphology, developed by Denis Smalley, provides a distinct language and framework for describing and analyzing electroacoustic music. Coming from a different perspective, Deep listening, founded by Pauline Oliveros, articulates a practice that focuses on the awareness of listening in all of its dimensions, including the body, environment, self and others. This paper aims to provide an overview of electroacoustic music analysis and its relationship to listening and music cognition. Building upon previous works that have explored a listener-based approach to analyzing electroacoustic music, this study seeks to investigate the audience listening experience of electroacoustic music, and its relationship to the sonic attributes that result from the creative process. We present a preliminary experiment aimed at articulating the dynamics of audience listening by designing both concert-based and online listening sessions that capture unbiased reflections of people's experiences of listening to electroacoustic music. Through this work, we aim to broaden conversations around existing frameworks for electroacoustic music analysis to include an understanding of listening – both in terms of composing and audience reception – as holistic, embodied, and collaborative processes.

2. HISTORICAL CONTEXT/THEORETICAL FRAMEWORK

2.1 Electroacoustic Music Analysis

Electroacoustic music, as explained by Smalley, has admitted an "extensive range of sound sources into music", thus requiring new listening strategies to fully appreciate its originality and the imaginative revelations of human experience that result from this, as well as a new network of signs and meanings that expand and challenge the music-theoretical scheme of traditional Western music [3].

Electroacoustic music analysis is largely established on a specific mode of listening – reduced listening – proposed by Pierre Schaeffer, in which a given sound phenomenon itself is considered as a unit (a sound object) in the course of understanding or analyzing a piece of music [2].

Building upon this, Denis Smalley developed Spectromorphology in order to provide a language and framework for describing and analyzing electroacoustic music. This offers an extended structure for the typology of sound objects, based on a proto-type that was first proposed by Schaeffer, and introduces the duality of gesture and texture, the contrast between motion and growth, structural functions, and spatial motions among other definitions from which the analysis of electroacoustic music has benefited [4]. By adopting common terminology from existing terms both from music and from everyday life, mimesis and association are inevitably introduced into these interpretations [5]. This has been a common theme: whereas traditional Western music has been thoroughly studied as a carrier of messages, narratives, and means of communication with a well-established semantic system, electroacoustic music has "no score, no system, and no 'pre-segmented' discrete units like notes [6]," making formal analysis difficult.

In 2007, Lasse Thoresen proposed a revised version of TARTYP (Tableau récapitulatif de la typologies), which Schaeffer initially proposed as an all-encompassing typology that attempted to address and formalize all sound objects. Thoresen further expanded the existing typology and gradually developed it into a symbolic language that can be used for the graphic notation of any kind of sound phenomenon or "music-as-heard", called Aural Sonology [7]. Thoresen's typology categorizes sounding elements into a hierarchy of three levels: the sound-objects level, sound-patterns level, and the form-building patterns level, with each level corresponding to a different mode of listening. Based on Jakobson's model of communication [8], Thoresen proposed an adapted model of musical communication and the semiotics of music-as-heard, which provides a framework to examine which level, how, and under what mode of listening a given piece is interpreted by its listener [9].

The concepts of gesture and texture share a dualistic position in electroacoustic music, where the sonic/musical gesture is concerned with action and energy, related to the sense of progress and causality, while larger-scale gesturality in music is perceived as forward motion, linearity, and narrative [5]. The notion of a sonic gesture is often associated with music cognition and communication, as it is considered as the meaning-bearing unit [10] or even embodied meaning when the gesture perceptually evokes not only a sonic happening but also imagined physical movements of the human body [11]. Texture, on the other hand, emerges from a lack of gestural motion and is instead concerned with internal behaviour patterning, whose energy is directed inward and can be associated with the overall timbral identity, sense of time/timelessness, intrinsic context, and how these things can be related to extrinsic discourse ranging from a single sonic moment to the whole piece of music [12]. The interplay between the duality of gesture and texture in electroacoustic music is an important framing concept for this study and will be further elaborated in the following sections.

2.2 Deep Listening and Music Cognition

In the musical communication process, one's listening behaviour is an active part of what shapes the discourse. Listening itself has been the subject of extensive research in discussions focused on sound and other non-ocular-centric ways of representation, especially with the advancement of audio production technology and electronic music. Based on his four modes of listening (écouter, ouïr, entendre, comprendre), Schaeffer's theory of reduced listening advocates for focusing on the sonic attributes of any sound without indication of its source or meaning, which was further expanded upon by Michel Chion, who identified casual, semantic, and reduced listening in the context of audio-visual communication [13]. On the other hand, Smalley has emphasized the importance of considering technological listening, which is influenced by the methods and devices used in audio production [4].

The evolution of discourse around these different modes of listening highlights the importance of understanding the context in which the music is being heard and how it can affect the listener's perception of the sound. The embodied approach to music cognition emphasizes the multidimensional relationship between sonic gestures perceived in the music and imagined or real physical gestures of both the performer and the listener [14]. In a broader sense, Deep Listening, founded by Pauline Oliveros, is a practice that focuses on the awareness of embodied listening. By first separating active listening from passive hearing, this practice mainly involves balancing between two forms of attention, global and focal, as well as four modes of thought: sensation, intuition, feeling, and thinking. Adapted from Carl Jung [15], these modes of thought provide a framework that allows one to "listen to their own listening", so to speak, and to engage with music (or any soundscapes) with respect to how it can affect their emotions, thoughts, and perceptions.

The study of music cognition and communication in the context of electroacoustic music has adopted a listener-based approach with a lack of a standardized paradigm, as opposed to traditional Western music. By documenting and investigating listener responses to such music, composers and scholars have attempted to establish a pattern by which electroacoustic music functions as a medium of communication between composer and audience in a way that differs from traditional music theory. Both Delalande and Thoresen have proposed empirical approaches to musical semiotics and discourse; in Delalande's research, Taxonomic, Empathetic, and Figurative listening were identified [6], while Thoresen's model of musical communication couples different listening behaviours with semiotic functions. By introducing the semiotic functions into musical communication, Thoresen's approach provides a framework for analyzing the listening experience and its impact on the communication between the composer and the audience, the music and the listeners "with reference to the particular foci of attention" that occurs during the course, where the idea of sending a message to a receiver is not necessarily the main purpose, nor a one-way function [9]. We feel that combining these perspectives on listening helps to broaden the perspective; reflexive and embodied perspectives on listening can help to broaden the semiotic view on electroacoustic music listening, so that it is understood less as a linear flow of communication from composer intent to passive audience reception, and more of a relational co-construction of meaning.

2.3 Machine Mediation and Gestural Instrument Design

As mentioned earlier, there is an embodied perspective on the cognition of electronic music that considers the relationship between human physical gestures and perceived sonic gestures, both in terms of perceived performative actions and embodied movements that are induced in a listener. Such findings are often used to support and aid instrumental design and live electronic music. Gestures can act as a link between the human and non-human agencies that are at play in forms of technologically mediated music-making such as electroacoustic music [16], in addition to being a principle for interactive instrument design with the consideration of embodied creation and physicality of the human body [17], [18], [19]. In order to explore the role that such perceived gesturality had in the creation and reception processes, and how they relate to the various perspectives on listening we have discussed here, we developed a study in which a set of pieces were composed and listener responses were captured and analyzed. As part of this process, sound materials for the given pieces were generated with a custom-designed digital instrument created in Max/MSP that allowed the composer/performer to engage in gesture/texture relationships in an improvisational manner. While the design of the software is not the primary focus of this paper, its role in the broader context of the compositional process will be briefly noted in the following sections.

3. EXPERIMENT: EXPLORATION OF ELECTROACOUSTIC LISTENING PRACTICES

This study aims to explore the audience listening experience of electroacoustic music and its relationship with aspects of the creative process. By comparing the contextual meanings of both processes, we seek to improve our understanding of both composing and listening as a holistic, embodied, and collaborative process, extending the existing frameworks for the analysis of electroacoustic music and broadening the views on the role that listening plays in both processes. Beginning from the position that listening is an active part of meaning creation in the musical experience, we have designed a series of events that were part-concert and part-experiment in order to capture and investigate the unbiased reflection of people's listening experience of electroacoustic music.

3.1 Related Work

Previous studies have explored a listener-based approach towards the analysis of electroacoustic music, including classic works, ongoing compositions, and newly composed pieces. In early studies, Michael Bridger conducted group listening sessions with short excerpts of electroacoustic classics and analyzed the listeners' verbal discussions of the music from a semantic point of view based on Barthes' system of codes of meaning [20]. François Delalande observed the listening strategies reflected in the listeners' responses in free form to Pierre Henry's Sommeil and identified several modes of listening behaviour [6]. Andrea McCartney explored different interpretations and perceptions of Hildegard Westerkamp's soundscape works by collecting responses in the form of free writing with prompted questions [21]. Following on from the previous projects, the Intention/Reception Project developed a more systematic approach to collecting data on the reception process of electroacoustic music, where Leigh Landy and Rob Weale created a series of questionnaires and instructions for listeners, who were grouped by their age and experience with electroacoustic music. The project's findings shed light on the relationship between the composer's intention and the listener's perception of electroacoustic music [22].

In more recent studies, composer Roger Reynolds and researcher Steven McAdams collaborated and documented the compositional process with a score-based formal analysis of the *Angel of Death* [23] and audience response for analyzing the reception and perception of Reynolds' The Angel of Death piece [24]. The study spanned from the creation to the public debut of the piece in two separate concerts. During both concerts, participants were provided with an interactive device featuring two sliders indicating the "familiarity/resemblance scale" and "emotional force scale." Listeners' responses were captured as continuous input on each scale. At around the same time, another listener-based study on the same piece was conducted and reported by Lalitte et al. [25]. In this study, listeners were required to listen to excerpts from different themes throughout the piece and respond to questions based on how they perceived, memorized, and interpreted the thematic musical ideas. From 2012-16, Anıl Çamcı conducted a series of experiments aimed at investigating the narrativity of electronic music and how it is received by listeners. Participants were provided with an HTML-based interface for inputting responses during three repeated listenings of the selected musical work. They were asked to complete two different tasks: a general impression response to the piece after listening to it in full length, and responding with short descriptors in real-time while listening during a second round. The responses were then categorized by their meanings and compared with the composer's (Çamcı himself) intention throughout the timeline of each piece. Through this analysis, Çamcı concluded that "a gesture in electronic music is an intentional narrative unit", and that a gestural approach can be used to analyze the narrative structure of a work [10]. In a recent study, Jason Noble et al. investigated the perception of time and timelessness in electroacoustic music using an interactive system controlled by a joystick with a conclusion that electroacoustic music does relate meaningfully to perceived musical timelessness, with this being attributed to the role that technological processes play in allowing composers to extend sonic gestures beyond the limits of human bandwidth. Similar to Reynolds' study, the listeners' actions were continuously recorded, in this case, moving a cursor between temporal attributes. Listeners were divided into two groups, one of which was asked to rate the sense of time and timelessness expressed by the musical experts, while the other to rate the sense of time and timelessness induced in them by the musical experts [26].

Charles du Preez's recent doctoral dissertation in 2022 reviewed the analytical methods for electroacoustic music since Pierre Schaeffer and aimed to develop a systematic method for a listener-based approach for the analysis of electroacoustic music starting from Landy's Four-Part Question. Using Maximillian Marcoll's *Amproprification 1* (2016) and Jorge Vasquez-Solvagno's *Sorstalansag* (2016) as examples, du Preez provided a thorough schematic framework for analyzing electroacoustic music with a listener-based approach and suggested possible considerations [27].

We build upon these past studies, taking Çamcı's framing of musical/sonic gestures as an "intentional narrative unit", and broadening out our analysis from traditional electroacoustic music analysis to include perspectives from Deep Listening and embodied music cognition.

3.2 Participants

A total of 27 participants were recruited for the study from the York University community and online, with 15 attending in person and 12 participating remotely. Participants were recruited regardless of their age, gender, nationality, or educational background. Out of the total number of participants, 14 reported having experience with acoustic music, 14 with electroacoustic music, and 7 with Deep Listening training. Among those with experience, 9 reported having practiced for over 5 years.

3.3 Stimuli

The study employed three pieces of electroacoustic music by the first author, each lasting between 3 to 5 minutes, and composed entirely by digital means. The pieces were played to the listeners in random order during each listening session. They were created with consideration of balancing both gesture and texture. A primary agenda of the compositions was to present works that were either, as Smalley defined, a gesture-framing or texture-setting composition, or an even balance between these two. This a priori constraint was adhered to while otherwise maintaining a consistency in both the artistic style of the composer and their chosen way of utilizing both improvisationally-performed and algorithmically-generated materials. [1]

3.3.1 Piece 1 - Gesture-framing

With a total length of 4'47", the first piece was composed of thirteen improvised sessions generated with a digital instrument in Max/MSP. Framed with three main movements, materials were organized and arranged so as to preserve the real-time nature of sonic gestural actions and larger motions produced during each session. The piece features short gestures that indicate a clear trajectory of discrete, singular sonic units. Each gestural movement drives the progression of the entire piece and intends to motivate the listener's attention to focus along with this constant change of dynamic.

3.3.2 Piece 2 - Texture-setting

Using the same instrument for the generation of raw materials, with a length of 4'28", the second piece chooses to compose with longer and slower changes of content. By utilizing techniques such as layering and subtle modifications, this piece establishes an evolving soundscape-like aural space where the listening focus is intentionally guided away from the trajectory of single sonic units, but towards the inner change of each sound, where textural qualities can be registered and identified in a way that the evolution of changes will be perceived throughout the fullest timeline.

3.3.3 Piece 3 - In Balance

The third piece is the last to be composed and the shortest of the three, with a total length of 3'37". This piece recycles the improvisation sessions from pieces 1 and 2, which are then modulated, re-synthesized and layered along with new materials, in order to achieve a balanced entity of gestural and textural motifs. Piece 3 has three distinct movements that are segmented noticeably by recurrent sound units throughout the piece to achieve a sense of unity and to join sections and layers in time.

3.4 Apparatus

The in-person group listened to the music on two-channel speakers in a concert setting and played back from a Max/MSP patch that allowed for a time-tagged gathering of listener responses, entered via a web interface. This same interface was used for the online participants, whose initial prompts included a request to use high-quality over-ear headphones if possible. From the demographic questionnaire, their playback devices included Beyerdynamic Xelento Remote, Bose NC700, Sennheiser HD650, BeyerDynamic DT 770 Pro 80 Ohm, Kanto YU2, PreSonus Eris E5, UltimateEars UE 5 pro, AKG K240S, Beyerdynamic DT 990 Pro 250 Ohm, Air Pods Pro, and other inner ear pods. For both groups, the browser-based interface facilitated the gathering of demographic information, media playback, and text input. All the data was collected into a database through the internet and node.js-based integration.

3.5 Procedure

Prior to the listening, participants were not provided with any information about the pieces they would be listening to (beyond the composer and the number of pieces), whether they participated in person or online. The in-person group participated in three group listening sessions with 4, 7, and 4 people, while the online participants listened individually. Upon opening the website, participants were first required to sign an informed consent form and then complete a short demographic questionnaire that included questions about their experience with acoustic music, electroacoustic music, and Deep Listening, as well as the duration of their practice if applicable. Drawing from a method used in [10], participants were randomly assigned to one of two listening tasks: General Impression (GI) or Real-time Descriptor (RTD). Both groups listened to three pieces of music in random order and completed the same task for each listening.

For the General Impression Task (GI), participants were invited to relax, enjoy the listening experience as if it were a concert, and reflect on their experience after each piece with a passage of text, regardless of typos and grammar. They were permitted to take notes during the listening session if they desired. For the Real-time Descriptor Task (RTD), participants were asked to submit single words or short sentence fragments while listening to the piece at the moment when the inspiration arises and submit after each entry. They were encouraged to submit as many responses as they liked. In both cases, we asked participants to respond with answers that reflected what they *feel, imagine, or think* while listening. For both in-person and online responses, the choice of GI or RTD task was randomized for each participant.

3.6 Results

We collected 27 responses in total: 15 in person and 12 online. Among these 16 are GI responses, and 11 are RTD responses. Participants who performed the GI task submitted responses that ranged from 10-150 words, with an average word count of 69, while those in the RTD task submitted an average of 9 entries for each person during each piece (with the shorter piece 3 receiving fewer entries). As expected, the responses for the RTD task are usually single words or short sentences.

We noted that experience in electroacoustic music did result in a given participant leaning heavier on technological terminology. Additionally, there were several partici-

[1] Files can be found at: https://soundcloud.com/leaudeluhk/sets/ea-listening-study

pants who reported having taken an electroacoustic ensemble course during the twelve weeks prior to the listening session, where the Soundpainting language [28] was used for conducting live electroacoustic music. This resulted in a notable use of such language in their responses. Interestingly, the mode of playback (in-person/speakers vs. online/headphones) that the participants used for listening had no apparent significant impact on the result.

Examining across all response types for all pieces, we noted the emergence of keywords and descriptors that could be placed into the following six categories: Extrinsic Association, Gestural, Qualitative/Textural, Formal, Emotion/Sensation, and Judgement/Self-reflection.

- **Extrinsic Association**: These were related to Smalley's concept of the extrinsic matrix, which indicates a spectrum ranging from source-bounding behaviour to a more general imagination that the ambiguous sonic material may trigger [4], [12]. Extrinsic Association responses consisted of three main subcategories: source-bonding behaviour which identifies a source of a sound (e.g. 'water', 'airplane'); an imagined action, event or scenario that might have caused the sound (e.g. 'sounds like', or 'as if' followed by the description of an action, event or scenario); and the reference to a specific piece of music or cultural icon (e.g. 'Stockhausen', 'Wall-E').

- **Gestural**: These included descriptions of what we refer to here as sonic gestures, as well as more complex, potentially multi-gesture, actions over a small-to-medium timescale that Smalley would characterize as motions.

- **Qualitative/Textural**: This category contained two sub-types. Qualitative included reduced listening-type descriptions of the sound timbre/pitch/etc., while Textural comments focused on sonic layers, aspects of foreground/background, or what Smalley would call short-to-medium scale growth/evolution of sonic textures.

- **Formal**: The Formal category refers to comments on a larger timescale, such as a section of the piece, the whole piece, or between pieces. These comments have a tendency to refer to one's own memory of the previously heard context and how the perceived details integrate into and service the whole piece, thus they are more commonly seen in the GI responses and those who have a musical background.

- **Emotion/Sensation**: The Emotional/Sensation category of response focused on two sub-types: on one's emotional reactions, or their bodily feelings in the moment. These were either physical or mental, such as 'anxious', or 'my ears hurt'.

- **Judgement/Self-reflection**: The Judgement/ Self-reflection category describes responses wherein there was a clear indication of personal judgement either on the content of the piece or on one's own listening experience. These responses engaged some form of communication that was directed at the intrinsic musical context, such as suggesting an improvement to the composer, or reporting a shift of attention while listening.

The relative descriptor count for each of these categories is depicted in figure 1.

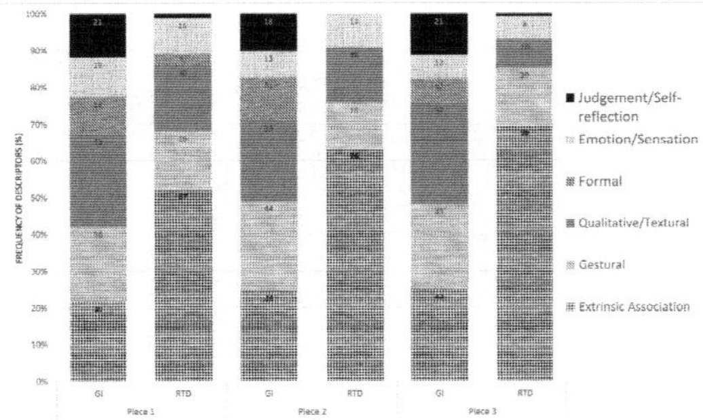

Figure 1: Frequency of Descriptors Per Piece and Per Task

A word cloud for the descriptors, as broken down by piece, can be seen in figure 2. The words "sound", "sounds" and "piece" occurred frequently and were removed. The word "like" was used in inconsistent ways: a transitional phrase often, as well as part of an analogy or in expressing affinity, and so that word was removed as well. The word "noise" was central in piece 1, even more dominant in piece 2, and was much less present in piece 3. These word clouds were formed by machine segmentation of the entire response texts, while our descriptor categories resulted from thematic analysis conducted by both researchers, which was then cross-compared for consistency.

4. DISCUSSION

4.1 Modes of Listening

We propose that the majority of studies on listening in electroacoustic music have tended to focus on reduced listening to intrinsic musical events, with extrinsic references being engaged relative to their narrative function, from a semiotic perspective. The attention to embodiment has tended to focus on gesturality in the sense of Smalley, and its role in this narrative-building process. We begin here by engaging more broadly with listening through the perspective of Pauline Oliveros' four modes of thought: Sensation, Intuition, Feeling and Thinking (which we capitalize to differentiate from the common usage in English). These introduce an awareness of listening context, environment and embodiment that we feel augments and enriches the aforementioned perspectives. One could argue that the majority of discussion surrounding modes of electroacoustic listening could be compartmentalized into the Thinking/analytic category. At the same time, while Deep Listening focuses on all manner of listening in all types of sonic contexts, our study does indeed look at the specific subset of the electroacoustic concert/presentation context, and so we look more closely at how this perspective on modes of thought can intersect with perspectives

(a) Piece 1 (b) Piece 2 (c) Piece 3

Figure 2: Descriptor Word Clouds For Each Piece

from the electroacoustic literature. In particular, returning to a Schaefferian point of view and the work of Thoresen and Delalande, we can identify six modes of listening behaviours that are implied by the results of the experiment: *Indexical*, *Taxonomic*, *Figurative*, *Empathetic*, *Judgemental* and *Reflective listening*. We relate these to the four modes of thought, whose action can be seen as being mediated by the processes of global and focal attention. This network of associations can be seen in the diagram of figure 3, which we detail below.

4.2 Perceived Gesturality

We did not observe a clear distinction between the pieces with regard to the amount of Gestural or Textural descriptors. However, with a high range of experience in acoustic and electroacoustic music among the participants, we did note a general trend towards a reduced listening behaviour that focused on describing the sound via abstract language. In particular, this was especially notable with the EA-experienced participants who contributed 74.53% of the Gestural and Textural descriptors, whereas the non-EA-experienced participants tended to report more of the Extrinsic Associations factors, contributing 60.83% of the total count in the category. Spectromorphological features were perceived as motions, such as the change of frequency, loudness, speed of movement, or the transition between sounds and spatial motions. As noted by Delalande, *figurative listening* commonly arises while focusing on such movements and motions, when the listener uses metaphorical imagination and "tends to find the 'figurative' in music, or, tends to think that certain sounds evoke something that moves, ultimately living [6]." We indeed found that motions were also perceived as imagined actions, such as 'laser circle', 'airplane tak[ing] off', 'robot autotuning', and 'monster breathing', which suggests these subjects imposed figurative descriptions onto the music, and that these were mediated by perceived gesturality. These figurative descriptors appeared across all groups, while abstract and taxonomic language was more present in the EA-experience group. In all groups, sudden changes or appearance of new materials were commonly detected and reported, as well as spatial movements, both in the cases of headphone and concert-based listening.

4.3 Perceived Timbral Quality and Textural Evolution

On the other hand, the two sub-categories of Qualitative/Textural descriptors commonly occurred together or in a complementary fashion. Participants described the quality or sonic identity of a sound, such as 'noise', or 'rough' in the course of noticing the interplay between layers of sounds, or referring to a multi-dimensional relationship such as 'background' and 'depth'. In contrast to piece 1, there is an increased use of the word 'morph' instead of 'turn' or 'transition', in pieces 2 and 3 when describing motion and growth, which indicates a perceived slow evolution of sound. Metaphors that do not indicate another object from one's life experience, again demonstrating figurative listening, are commonly used to describe a timbral or textural attribute, such as 'wet', 'sticky', or 'breath-like'. Mentions of noticing multiple layers also contribute to the description of textural changes, which implies participants (across all groups) maintained an awareness of the inner growth of juxtaposed and distinct sonic layers.

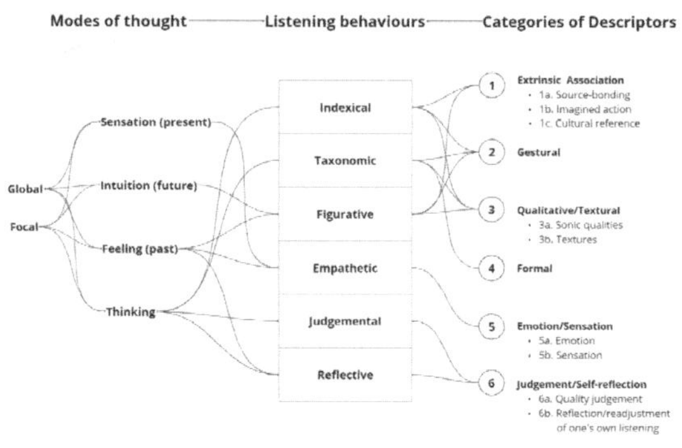

Figure 3: Relationship Between Modes of Thought, Listening Behaviours and Our Observed Categories

4.4 Emotion/Sensation and Self-Reflective Listening

Aside from the perceived gestural and textural functions, we noted instances in which embodied listening took place while listening to and reflecting on these pieces. In such cases, Sensation, Intuition and Feeling take over the attention and become the thing that the listener "holds onto" [22]. These modes of attention can be related to *figurative*, *empathetic* and *reflective listening* behaviours: in *figurative listening*, the listener focuses on an imagined mental state that exists outside of the musical world; *empathetic listening* suggests the physiological involvement of oneself in the dynamic of materials with one's focus on their feelings, either emotional or sensation-based [6]; while *reflective listening* shows a different mode of attention that focuses on the engagement of self-awareness either in terms of self-reflection or awareness of the composer. Description of one's own emotion triggered by the music is the most commonly seen, where the subject of attention becomes the listener themselves instead of the music or sound, such as being 'confused', 'anxious' or having an expression of affection. Not to be confused with an objective judgement with a clear reason (such as 'good use of sound' or 'works well') which implies an awareness of the composer and an analytical mindset; expressions of affection such as 'I enjoyed', and 'I like' indicate a centring of attentions on the self during the listening. Also part of an *empathetic listening* behaviour, Sensation reports are rare in the data but do exist, including descriptions such as 'my ears hurt' or 'like being popped on the head'. By contrast, responses such as expressing a sense that one was 'a part of the conversation' implies immersive attention into the music in a more self-reflective mode. In both cases, an Intuitive mode of thought is at play as the listener moves between figurative projections and self-reflexive engagement in an immersive, extra-musical imagined space that is not dominated by analysis and yet remains connected to the materials of the piece. Moving further away from this immersion in the sonic materials, there are some reports that reflect on one's own listening experience, such as 'found myself thinking of...', 'found myself focus on...', or 'found that I couldn't latch onto any...'. Some of these indicate a readjustment of listening modes, while others are direct reflections of one's attention mode at the moment, with an emphasis on Thinking as a mode of thought in this self-reflection process. This kind of *reflective listening* behaviour implies that one is aware of their situation and is listening intentionally not only to the exterior sound but also to one's own positioning in the sounding environment. Such listening behaviour is found across groups, regardless of their experience.

4.5 Analytical and Technological Listening

A number of the six categories involve analytical and technological listening, where the Thinking mode of thought dominated. These were often biased by musical or technological knowledge while listening and tended to reflect from a technical perspective. These tendencies can be found in the Extrinsic Association category, in cases where one focuses on *indexical listening* behaviour in which one intends to identify the source of the sound being heard. They can also be found in both Gestural and Qualitative/Textural categories when one focuses on naming the spectromorphological attribute or guessing the technique that produced the sound. This occurred most heavily in the Formal category from the GI responses, in cases where the listener focused on the entire piece and tried to find structural features, musical laws, or hidden narratives from their recollection of the piece. Aside from adopting a *reductive listening* and analytical mode of thought, these also show a tendency toward the *taxonomic listening* behaviour, where the listener tends to distinguish sound units by their spectromorphological traits, notice their sonic relationship with each other, and determine their functionalities within the whole piece. These modes of listening are more commonly seen within the experienced group. By the nature of the RTD task, there are fewer reflections on sounds from memory and on formal functions. However, comments on the repeated use of sound materials and feelings of anticipation were mentioned.

5. CONCLUSION

Drawing up and integrating several frameworks, we have profiled the listening behaviour of a group of people with various orientations towards – and backgrounds in – electroacoustic music. By reviewing previous studies on electroacoustic listening and the related theoretical background of electroacoustic music, this study seeks to offer a perspective on the connections between the intrinsic perceptions of such music and listening behaviour in a broader sense, where one might step away from the classic analytical and reduced frameworks of listening, and look at the musical context from an embodied, listener-centred perspective while still benefiting from the analytic rigour offered by these existing perspectives. From the results of this study, we can see that the interplay of sonic gestures, textural evolution and timbral quality, the main vehicle for musical communication in the electroacoustic world, can be perceived and reflected under different modes of listening, mediated by distinct listening behaviours and modes of thought. We offer this study and its analysis of how electroacoustic music is listened to, perceived and interpreted as one step towards offering a broader perspective on the dynamics of listening and its role for both the composer and the listener.

Acknowledgments

This research was supported by grants awarded to the second author from the Social Sciences and Humanities Research Council (SSHRC), The Canada Research Chairs (CRC) program, the Canada Foundation for Innovation (CFI) and an Ontario Early Researcher Award (ERA).

6. REFERENCES

[1] L. Landy, *Understanding the art of sound organization*. MIT Press, 2007.

[2] P. Schaeffer, *Treatise on Musical Objects: An Essay across Disciplines*. University of California Press, 2019.

[3] D. Smalley, "The listening imagination: Listening in

the electroacoustic era," *J. Contemporary Music Review*, vol. 13, no. 2, pp. 77–107, 1996.

[4] ——, "Spectromorphology: explaining sound-shapes," *J. Organised Sound*, vol. 2, no. 2, pp. 107–126, 1997.

[5] S. D, "Spectro-morphology and Structuring Processes," in *The Language of Electroacoustic Music*, S. Emmerson, Ed. Palgrave Macmillan UK, 1986, ch. 4.

[6] F. Delalande, "Music analysis and reception behaviours: Sommeil by Pierre Henry*," *J. Contemporary Music Review*, vol. 27, no. 1-2, pp. 13–66, 1998.

[7] L. Thoresen and A. Hedman, "Spectromorphological analysis of sound objects: an adaptation of Pierre Schaeffer's typomorphology," *J. Organised Sound*, vol. 12, no. 2, pp. 129–141, 2007.

[8] J. R, "Closing Statement: Linguistics and Poetics," in *Style in Language*, T. A. Sebeok, Ed. The MIT Press, 1960.

[9] L. Thoresen and A. Hedman, *Emergent Musical Forms: Aural Explorations*, ser. Studies in music from the University of Western Ontario. University of Western Ontario, 2015, vol. 24.

[10] A. Çamcı, "Imagining through Sound: An experimental analysis of narrativity in electronic music," *J. Organised Sound*, vol. 21, no. 3, pp. 179–191, 2016.

[11] R. I. Godøy, "Gestural-Sonorous Objects: embodied extensions of Schaeffer's conceptual apparatus," *J. Organised Sound*, vol. 11, no. 2, pp. 149–157, 2006.

[12] D. Smalley, "Defining timbre — Refining timbre," *J. Contemporary Music Review*, vol. 10, no. 2, pp. 35–148, 1994.

[13] M. Chion, C. Corbman, and W. Murch, *Audio-vision: sound on screen*. Columbia University Press, 1994.

[14] R. I. Godøy and M. Leman, Eds., *Musical gestures: sound, movement, and meaning*. Routledge, 2010.

[15] C. G. Jung, *Memories, dreams, reflections*, A. Jaffé, Ed. Vintage, 2011.

[16] I. Jarvis and D. Van Nort, "Posthuman gesture," in *5th International Conference on Movement and Computing*, Genoa, Italy, 2018, p. 3.

[17] D. Van Nort, "Instrumental Listening: sonic gesture as design principle," *J. Organised Sound*, vol. 14, no. 2, pp. 177–187, 2009.

[18] ——, "Human:machine:human: Gesture, Sound and Embodiment," *J. Kybernetes*, vol. 40, no. 7/8, pp. 1179–1188, 2011.

[19] D. Van Nort, M. M. Wanderley, and P. Depalle, "Mapping Control Structures for Sound Synthesis: Functional and Topological Perspectives," *J. Contemporary Music Review*, vol. 38, no. 3, pp. 6–22, 2014.

[20] M. Bridger, "An approach to the analysis of electroacoustic music derived from empirical investigation and critical methodologies of other disciplines," *J. Contemporary Music Review*, vol. 3, no. 1, pp. 145–160, 1989.

[21] A. S. J. McCartney, "Sounding Places: Situated conversations through the soundscape compositions of Hildegard Westerkamp," Ph.D. dissertation, 1999.

[22] L. L, "The Intention/Reception Project," in *Analytical methods of electroacoustic music*, M. Simoni, Ed. Routledge, 2005, ch. 3.

[23] S. McAdams, "Problem-Solving Strategies in Music Composition: A Case Study," *J. Music Perception*, vol. 21, no. 3, pp. 391–429, 2004.

[24] S. McAdams, B. W. Vines, S. Vieillard, B. K. Smith, and R. Reynolds, "Influences of Large-Scale Form on Continuous Ratings in Response to a Contemporary Piece in a Live Concert Setting," *J. Music Perception*, vol. 22, no. 2, pp. 297–350, 2004.

[25] P. Lalitte, E. Bigand, B. Poulin-Charronnat, S. McAdams, C. Delbé, and D. D'Adamo, "The Perceptual Structure of Thematic Materials in The Angel of Death," *J. Music Perception*, vol. 22, no. 2, pp. 265–296, 2004.

[26] J. Noble, T. Bonin, and S. McAdams, "Experiences of Time and Timelessness in Electroacoustic Music," *J. Organised Sound*, vol. 25, no. 2, pp. 232–247, 2020.

[27] C. du Preez, "du Preez, Charles. Listener-Based Analysis of Electroacoustic Music: A Selected Chronology of Methods as Applied to Amproprification 1 and Sorstalanság," Ph.D. dissertation, 2022.

[28] W. Thompson, "Soundpainting," Available at http://www.soundpainting.com/soundpainting/ (2023/05/04).

Generating Quadratic Difference Tone Spectra for Auditory Distortion Synthesis

Esteban Gutiérrez
Department of Information and Communications Technologies
Universitat Pompeu Fabra
egutierreo@mat.uc.cl

Christopher Haworth
Department of Music
University of Birmingham
c.p.haworth@bham.ac.uk

Rodrigo F. Cádiz
Music Institute and Department of Electrical Enginering
Pontificia Universidad Católica de Chile
rcadiz@uc.cl

ABSTRACT

Quadratic difference tones are one of a family of perceptual phenomena that arise from the neuromechanics of the auditory system in response to particular properties of physical sound. Long deployed as 'ghost tones' by improvisers, computer musicians and sound artists, in this paper we address the problem of creating quadratic difference tone spectra, where a QDT fundamental and harmonic overtone series is specified and the necessary acoustic components needed to evoke it are synthesised. A numerical algorithm for solving target distributions of amplitudes for the synthesis of quadratic distortion tone spectra is proposed. The algorithm aims to find a solution for a target distribution of amplitudes that matches the desired spectrum as closely as possible. The experiments were conducted using different parameter settings and target distributions. The results show that the algorithm is effective in solving the problem in the majority of cases, with at least 99% of the cases being solvable in real-time. The article also discusses the convergence of the algorithm and its potential mathematical properties. Additionally, audio examples implemented in Max are provided to demonstrate the synthesis of different quadratic distortion tone spectra using this approach.

1. INTRODUCTION

Auditory distortion products are perceptual illusions which arise from the neuromechanics of the auditory system. Often referred to as difference, sum or combination tones, these ghostly sounds have a long history as objects of musical intrigue, from their discovery by Giuseppe Tartini in 1754, to their contemporary use by improvisers, sound artists and computer musicians. In a hearing science context, evoked auditory distortion products have served as a key method used to probe the workings of the cochlea. Once believed to be caused when the otherwise linear mechanics of the auditory system were driven into a nonlinear region by high intensity sound, today they are understood to arise as byproducts of the active amplification process provided by the outer hair cells on the basilar membrane. Indeed, auditory distortion products are synonymous with the later-named 'evoked distortion product otoacoustic emissions' (DPOAEs) [1], so-called because the fluid disturbance in the cochlea backpropogates through the ear drum and middle-ear, and can be measured with a microphone in the ear canal.

Auditory distortion products (ADPs) have a rich musical history spanning experimental music, jazz improvisation, computer music, drone and noise music, and varieties of sound art. Their use varies between the fleeting, transient 'ghost' tones experienced in the improvisations of wind players like John Butcher and Evan Parker; to the disorienting, texturally dense static sound installations of La Monte Young and Catherine Christer Hennix; to the microtonal inner-ear counterpoint of Maryanne Amacher. In terms of ADPs relevance to computer music, a notable factor is their distinctive spatial imagery. When reproduced over loudspeakers, auditory distortion can be heard as a separate auditory stream localising close to the head, separate from the acoustic tones. This happens because the distortion tones are generated by the direct interaction of the acoustic components on the basilar membrane. Lateralization of the distortion tones is governed by Interaural Time (ITD) and Interaural Intensity Differences (IID) alone; head related transfers matter only insofar as they affect IIDs. Indeed, the closest comparable listening experience is headphone reproduction, where the auditory image appears inside and around the head, and is highly sensitive to head movements. But, crucially, this only happens when the acoustic tones are reproduced over loudspeakers. Over headphones, distortion tones can be difficult to hear as a separate stream.

Typical studies of distortion products deploy two sinusoidal signals (primaries) having frequencies f_1 and f_2, such that $f_2 > f_1$. In these conditions, the two most prominent tones that can be observed are the lower cubic difference tone (LCDT), which occurs at $2f_1 - f_2$, and obeys a cubic law distortion; and the quadratic difference tone (QDT), which occurs at $f_2 - f_1$, and obeys square law distortion. The LCDT is tuned, and to hear it requires that the ratio of the acoustic tones be in the range $1 < f_2/f_1 < 1.3$ [2, 514]. The highest level results from the lowest ratio, and it falls off quickly thereafter (Ibid). The level of the QDT, on the other hand, is only partially dependent on the ratio of the acoustic tones, and so retains its amplitude across large changes in interval size. Moreover, its distance from the primaries makes it much easier to perceptually segregate than the LCDT (see e.g. [3], [4] and [5].)

At the same time, audibility of the QDT is highly dependent on intensity. Greater than 50db spl is required for the component to be heard at all, and its amplitude grows proportionally to the level of the primaries, such that for every 1db increase the QDT grows by 2db [2, 514]. In [6], the authors described methods for ameliorating the listening fatigue caused by the high intensity needed to hear the QDT. Drawing on a method presented in [7], they utilised a sinusoidal complex with constant difference frequencies. They found that each adjacent pair of sinusoids produces the identical QDT frequency, adding linearly to its total gain, and thereby increasing the level of the distortion tone. On top of this, other QDTs are produced among the components, producing multiple harmonics of the fundamental (e.g. $f_2 - f_1, f_3 - f_1, f_4 - f_1$ and so on for all combinations). In [7], the authors reported that 'an harmonic complex tone . . . can produce a sizeable DS [distortion spectrum], even at moderate to low sound levels'. Thus, increasing the number of components, and spreading them out over a wider frequency range, permits the subjective level of the acoustic tones to be reduced, without compromising the audibility of the QDT.

This paper describes a method for direct synthesis of quadratic difference tone spectra (QDTS). We look at how to specify the fundamental frequency and relative amplitudes for an arbitrary number of harmonics, so as to generate complex QDT spectra. Through this, we are able to match the QDT spectra to a target timbre with considerable accuracy in particular cases. In section 2 the model used to synthesize QDTSs is explained. Section 3 contains a discussion regarding the well definition of the mathematical problem involved and a numerical procedure to solve it. Section 4 contains a brief discussion about the implementation of our algorithm in MaxMSP. Finally, Sections 5 and 6 discuss how the algorithm was adjusted and explain the examples included with this article respectively.

2. MODELLING THE QDT SPECTRUM

The problem of how to exert greater control of the timbre of the QDT spectra has been theorized in [6]. There it is stated that in order to generate a QDT from a complex of pure tones with frequencies $F, 2F, \ldots, (n-1)F$ and *target* respective amplitudes $t_1, t_2, \ldots, t_{n-1}$, it is necessary to have a *carrier* complex of n pure tones with the frequencies $C, C+F, C+2F, \ldots, C+(n-1)F$, where $C > 0$, and respective amplitudes $x_0, x_1, \ldots, x_{n-1}$, such that the following system of equations is satisfied

$$\begin{aligned} t_1 &= x_0 x_{n-1} \\ t_2 &= x_0 x_{n-2} + x_1 x_{n-1} \\ \vdots & \qquad \vdots \\ t_{n-1} &= x_0 x_1 + x_1 x_2 + \cdots + x_{n-2} x_{n-1} \end{aligned} \tag{1}$$

(for a graphic representation of this setting see figure 1).

Synthesising auditory distortion products using this approach is in theory capable of using QDTs to produce harmonic spectrums of arbitrary order, a result that goes beyond the 3-4 harmonics achieved in [6]. Because of the new control of timbre this affords, we have decided to call this method *quadratic distortion tone spectra* (QDTS) synthesis.

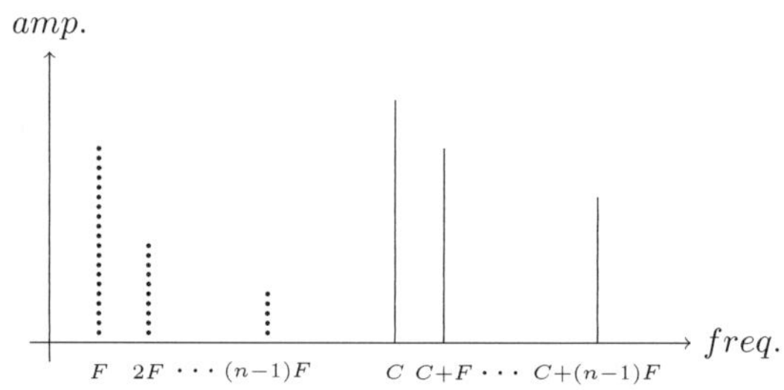

Figure 1. On the right, the amplitude and pitches of the *carrier* complex of pure tones are shown as continuous segments. On the left, the amplitude and pitches of the *target* complex of pure tones produced by QDT are shown as dotted segments. For comparison with the typical notation of combination tones used in the introduction, here $C = f_1$ and $C + F = f_2$, so that $F = f_2 - f_1$ symbolizes the difference tone.

Observe that the system (1) has $n - 1$ equations and n variables, so with the purpose of simplifying computations and using some particular numerical methods we decided to add an equation that fixes the amplitude of the first pure tone of the *carrier* complex to, let us say t_0.

Finally, and for the sake of order let us define the following n polynomials

$$\begin{aligned} p_0 &= x_0 - t_0 \\ p_1 &= x_0 x_{n-1} - t_1 \\ p_2 &= x_0 x_{n-2} + x_1 x_{n-1} - t_2 \\ \vdots & \qquad \vdots \\ p_{n-1} &= x_0 x_1 + x_1 x_2 + \cdots + x_{n-2} x_{n-1} - t_{n-1}, \end{aligned} \tag{2}$$

and the polynomials $d_j = p_j + t_j$ for $j = 1, \ldots, n-1$, and observe that:

1. The *distortion* function $D = (d_1, \ldots, d_{n-1})$ maps the amplitudes of the *carrier* complex into the amplitudes of the auditory distortion products as a result.
2. Solving the system (1) together with the condition $x_0 = t_0$ is, of course, equivalent to finding a root for the system $P = (p_0, p_1, \ldots, p_{n-1}) = (0, 0, \ldots, 0)$.

3. EXISTENCE OF SOLUTIONS AND HOW TO FIND THEM

In this section the existence of the *carrier* complex of pure tones together with some ways of finding such solutions are discussed.

3.1 About the existence

As seen in [6], finding a root for P can be done by hand for $n = 2, 3$ and 4, however after this point the problem gets increasingly complicated.

The problem of finding whether a system of polynomials in many variables has a solution is not trivial, and the state-of-the-art theory in this matter is known to be complicated and computationally expensive. The most widely used algorithm to solve this issue consists in finding a mathematical object called Gröbner basis, which strongly depends on the problem, and then use it to determine the number

of solutions of the problem (see for example [8]). Since we are interested in solving the system for any choice of *target* amplitudes $(t_1, \ldots, t_{n-1})$, it would be necessary to compute the Gröbner basis considering the constants t_j as variables, which is rather problematic, since this roughly duplicates the number of variables and the computational complexity of computing a Gröbner basis has been estimated to be double exponential in the number of variables (see [9] and [10]).
With the last being said, we have been able to compute a Gröbner basis for the system when $n = 2, ..., 6$ using an implementation of Faugère algorithm (for a brief summary of the results see 5.1), which has lead us to determine that in this cases there is always at least one complex solution and that the amount of solutions is always finite.
Proving only the existence of complex solutions is by no means our goal, however, one can prove by hand that if $(a_0 + ib_0, a_1 + ib_1, \ldots, a_{n-1} + ib_{n-1})$ is a complex solution for the problem, then

$$\begin{aligned} D(a_0, a_1, \ldots, a_{n-1}) - D(b_0, b_1, \ldots, b_{n-1}) \\ = (t_1, t_2, \ldots, t_{n-1}), \end{aligned} \tag{3}$$

that is, assuming that one can control the phase of the auditory distorted products, one could use phase cancellation to produce the *target* auditory distortion products by the superposition of two complex pure tones using the real and imaginary parts of the complex solution.
This approach has two problems:

1. little can be found in the current literature about determining the phase of ADPs, and
2. even though this could potentially generate the target auditory distortion products accurately, any implementation of this would still require to first compute the complex solution, which is in any case double as much work as finding a real solution provided that such solution actually exists.

To end this section, let us remark that discerning whether there are real solutions is an even more challenging problem than simply finding if there is a solution at all. Actually, even though such a problem can always be theoretically solved according to Tarski theorem (see for example [8]), the state-of-the-art algorithms used to solve this issue efficiently start by finding a Gröbner basis, which is still a problem. Moreover, we are already aware that not much more can be said in the general case since even when n is small, we have been able to find examples that do not have a real solution at all (*e.g.* consider $n = 5$ and $(t_0, t_1, t_2, t_3, t_4) = (1, 1, 1, 1, 1)$), so a reasonable goal would be to find a criterion that solves the question if there is a real solution or not before we even start looking for it.

3.2 Algorithm

The absence of real solutions for the system $P = 0$ appears to be a dead-end problem. However, we propose a workaround algorithm designed to avoid null returns. The algorithm first tries to find a solution for a given initial *target* distribution of amplitudes. Then, if it does not find it fast enough, it restarts the process with a new *target* that is chosen randomly in a small neighbourhood of the initial *target*, and repeats such process until a solution to the case with the new *target* is found.
An algorithm such as the one described before does not have any reason to converge in general. However, we have implemented it using the Newton-Raphson algorithm in the part where the solution is sought, and not even a single case where this does not work could be found in our experiments (see 5.2 and 5.3 for the details of the experiments), which gave us enough reasons to implement a solution for the problem using this approach.
Since we are interested in using this algorithm in real-time, we decided to try some other techniques in order to optimize the algorithm as much as possible. These techniques are described here:

1. The initial condition of the Newton-Raphson algorithm can be chosen to be:
   (a) the vector $(0.5, 0.5, \ldots, 0.5)$, since this is the average of the vectors in the ideal space of solution $[0, 1]^n$, or
   (b) a randomly chosen vector in the ideal space of solutions $[0, 1]^n$.
2. If a solution is not found using the Newton-Raphson algorithm, the process will restarts with a new initial condition (that has to be chosen randomly to avoids infinite loops) and a new *target* distribution of amplitudes, which can be chosen to be:
   (a) changed to a new *target* distribution of amplitudes that is close enough to the initial *target*.
   (b) changed to a new *target* distribution of amplitudes that is close enough to the **last** *target* used.

Every combination of techniques described was largely tested, and even though there was no objectively best option, we have decided to implement the combination of techniques given by 1.(b) and 2.(a), because of its speed and stability (see subsection 5.4 for the details of the experiments and results), giving algorithm 1 as a result.

4. IMPLEMENTATION IN MAX

In order to implement our algorithm in an efficient way and in a friendly environment, we decided to use the Min dev-kit, a software development kit containing an example package with the current best practices for package creation using modern C++ code. More precisely, using the Min dev-kit we were able to build an external object for Max that implements our algorithm in an efficient way and that can be freely downloaded from our GitHub repository [1].
The resulting external object was named `qdt.solver`, and its main utility is solving the system of equations (2) considering $x_0 = t_0 = 1$. `qdt.solver` has one input and two outputs: the input is a Max list of integer or floating numbers that represent the *target* distribution of amplitudes; the left output is a Max list containing the normalized estimation for the amplitudes of the *carrier* complex

[1] The GitHub repository can be accessed here `https://github.com/cordutie/QDTS`

Algorithm 1 QDT solver

Define the initial target $T_{\text{init}} \in \mathbb{R}^n$, the error tolerance $\varepsilon > 0$ and the number of iterations tolerance $N \in \mathbb{N}$

Define the initial conditions:

- $X =$ Random vector in $[0, 1]^n$
- $T = T_{\text{init}}$

while $||D(X) - t|| > \varepsilon$ **do**

  Run the Newton-Raphson algorithm on the function $D(\cdot) - T$ with intial condition X updating it in each iteration until either $||D(X) - T|| \leq \varepsilon$ or the number of iterations gets to N.

  if $||D(X) - T|| \leq \varepsilon$ **then**

    Redefine the initial condition

    - $X =$ Random vector in $[0, 1]^n$
    - $T = T_{\text{init}} + \varepsilon \cdot R$, where $R =$ Random vector in $[0, 1]^n$

  end if

end while

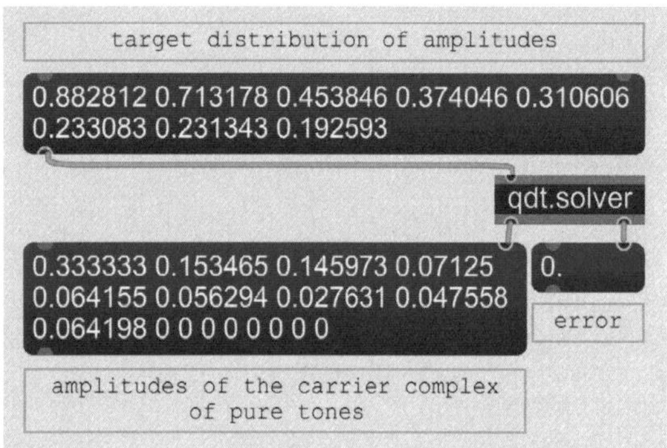

Figure 2. The `qdt.solver` object is used to find a solution for the *target* distribution of amplitudes at the top of the figure. At the bottom of the figure, the normalized solution together with the estimation error can be seen.

of pure tones necessary to generate the *target* distribution of amplitudes inputted; and the right output is a Max message containing a float number that represents the ℓ^2- error of the estimation, which can be thought as the energy of the difference between the targeted signal and the theoretical auditory distortion product described by QDT produced by the estimated *carrier* complex of pure tones (see figure 2). Additionally, whenever a solution could not be found in a reasonable amount of time, a message is sent to the Max console warning that experimental methods were used to approximate a solution in order to avoid Max from freezing.

Since most experiments were conducted using $n = 8, 12$ and 16, we also made three patches with a fixed amount of harmonics in the *target* distribution of amplitudes corresponding to these numbers. Such patches were made in a way that when loaded using the `bpatcher` object in Max, a simple but functional GUI is shown (see figure 3) whose main purpose is to make the usage of the external as simple as possible.

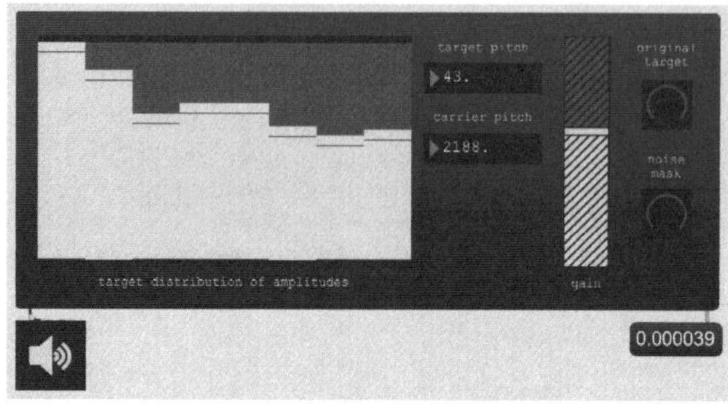

Figure 3. Example patch considering $n = 8$ loaded with the `bpatcher` object. In this example the patch is used to synthesize an Auditory Distortion Product with a frequency of 43Hz and a particular distribution of harmonics through a carrier complex of pure tones with frequencies 2188Hz, 2231Hz, 2274Hz, ..., 2489Hz and having an ℓ^2- error of 0.000039.

5. ADJUSTING THE ALGORITHM

In this section, the main experiments conducted to adjust the algorithm to its optimal form are described.

5.1 Experiment 1. Finding a Gröbner Basis

In order to find a Gröbner basis for the system of equations we tried several approaches. The following are some of the instances that we implemented.

1. Taking advantage of the fact that the computation complexity of a Gröbner Basis has been computed with accuracy in the case of homogeneous polynomials (see [11]), we homogenized the system by changing every t_j with t_j^2 and removing the polynomial p_0. This does not change the solutions of the system, since the targets are expected to be positive numbers, and one can simply add p_0 to the basis once it is computed to add conditions on x_0. This in fact works for the cases where we could find a Gröbner basis, and adding the polynomial p_0 is fundamental to reduce the dimension of the problem, that is, to make it a system with a finite amount of solutions.

2. Since in practice one can fix at least one variable, we tried $x_0 = t_0 = 1$. Also, since this implies that $p_1 = x_{n-1} - t_1$ and $p_2 = x_{n-2} + x_1 x_{n-1} - t_2$, one can easily replace $x_{n-1} = t_1$ and $x_{n-2} = t_2 - t_1 x_1$. This reduces the number of variables in 4 and does not change the total degree of the system, which is extremely useful since the complexity of computing a Gröbner basis has been estimated to be double exponential in the number of variables with base being the total degree of the system (see [9], [10]).

In both cases, we used the implementations of Buchberger and F5 algorithms in the Python package `sympy`, however after running every combination in parallel in the High Performance Computing Cluster at the School of Engineering of UC for over a couple of months, just the cases with $n = 2, 3, 4, 5$ and 6 have successfully finished. Moreover, the case $n = 7$ seems to be using a huge amount of ram, implying that the Gröbner basis for such a case is extremely large and making its use in real-time non-viable in a compact environment.

5.2 Experiment 2. Adjusting Newton-Raphson algorithm to the problem

The Newton-Raphson algorithm is known for its efficiency provided that it is known to converge, however since in our case we do not have certainty of its convergence, it is important to decide how many iterations will be tolerated before the process restarts with different initial condition and target.

In order to find a reasonable tolerance, we conducted an experiment that estimate the number of iterations needed for the algorithm to converge provided that it converges. For this task, we made a sample of 10^6 *target* distributions of amplitudes chosen at random in the space $[0,1]^n$ for each of the cases $n = 8, 12$ and 16. For each *target*, we tried the algorithm with random initial conditions chosen in the space of ideal solutions $[0,1]^n$ up to 10 times each, and for the cases that could be solved with these constraints, the number of iterations needed to find a solution was saved. A summary of these results can be found in table 1.

As a conclusion for the results found in this experiment,

n	mean $\pm$ sd	Percentiles $50, 90$ and 99
8	$12.55 \pm 12,9$	$(8, 26, 72)$
12	$17,41 \pm 15,92$	$(11, 38, 81.1)$
16	$21,26 \pm 18.21$	$(14, 47, 88)$

Table 1. In this table the results concerning the number of iterations needed to solve the problem provided that it could be solved in less than 10 tries are shown. In each case, a sample of 10^6 *target* distributions of amplitudes was used, and the number of samples that could be solved in less than 10 tries correspond to 99.46%, 99.89% and 99.98% of the total corresponding to $n = 8, 12$ and 16.

we decided that the tolerance will be fixed to satisfy at least 99% of the cases, that is, the algorithm will restart once it reaches the percentile 99 found in table 1 for each case. Finally, it is remarkable that with the data obtained and using a simple test of proportions, we can conclude that with a confidence of 99%, the proportion of the cases that can be solved in less than 10 tries (which is extremely fast and can be computed in real-time) correspond to at least the 99.45% of the cases.

5.3 Experiment 3. Empirical proof of conjecture

As discussed in subsection 3.2, the algorithm in this paper iterates until it finds a solution for a *target* distribution of amplitudes that is close enough to the actual *target* given. The fact that this algorithm actually converges is non-trivial, so before implementing the algorithm in Max we made some tests trying to find a case that is unsolvable. For this task, we fixed a maximum acceptable error corresponding to 2% of the energy of the signal to synthesize and ran the algorithm for 10^6 randomly chosen *target* distributions of amplitudes, saving the ones that could not be solved in less than 10 tries. Finally, we tried the algorithm again for the unsolved cases but this time adding a, small enough in magnitude, random vector and saved the ones that could not be solved again in less than 100 tries. These experiments was made for the cases $n = 8, 12$ and 16, and in each case, the result was the same: the set of unsolvable cases after considering the addition of a small random vector is empty.

Before going to the next experiment it is important to mention that the fact this algorithm converges could be explained by certain mathematical properties of the system, e.g. the set of unsolvable (in $\mathbb{R}^n$) cases could have an empty interior. However, we have not been able to prove this fact yet.

5.4 Experiment 4. Optimizing the algorithm

One can adjust the algorithm in at least two way: how to chose the initial condition and how to change the *target* at restart. The techniques that we considered for each one of these adjustments were described at the end of subsection 3.2, and the results for some testings made considering 10^6 *target* distributions of amplitudes chosen at random in the space $[0,1]^n$ for each of the cases $n = 8, 12$ and 16 can be found in tables 2 and 3.

n	Technique	mean $\pm$ sd	Percentiles $50, 90$ and 99
8	(a,a)	51.65 ± 721.47	$(7, 78, 438)$
	(a,b)	38.06 ± 176.04	$(7, 78, 459)$
	(b,a)	50.65 ± 944.41	$(8, 54, 427)$
	(b,b)	34.69 ± 175.26	$(8, 53, 437)$
12	(a,a)	34.19 ± 392.61	$(10, 87, 256)$
	(a,b)	31.36 ± 100.24	$(10, 87, 252)$
	(b,a)	$34,42 \pm 406.76$	$(13, 86, 246)$
	(b,b)	31.96 ± 93.71	$(13, 86, 248)$
16	(a,a)	35.49 ± 426.71	$(13, 97, 242)$
	(a,b)	33.79 ± 60.04	$(13, 97, 251)$
	(b,a)	36.84 ± 78.97	$(17, 98, 237)$
	(b,b)	36.83 ± 65.66	$(17, 98, 237)$

Table 2. Results concerning the **amount of iterations** needed to solve the problem. In each case, a sample of 10^6 *target* distributions of amplitudes was used. Technique (x,y) means that the techniques 1.(x) and 2.(y) were used in that case.

n	Technique	mean $\pm$ sd $(\times 10^{-6})$	Percentiles $50, 90$ and 99 $(\times 10^{-6})$
8	(a,a)	16.33 ± 23.89	$(2.96, 51.7, 95)$
	(a,b)	162.56 ± 2646.66	$(2.79, 69.1, 995)$
	(b,a)	14.65 ± 23.24	$(1.82, 49.2, 94)$
	(b,b)	160.69 ± 2610.3	$(1.88, 62.2, 813)$
12	(a,a)	15.79 ± 23.8	$(2.37, 50.85, 95.31)$
	(a,b)	51.55 ± 1032.92	$(2.39, 61.9, 242.39)$
	(b,a)	15.19 ± 23.48	$(1.94, 49.64, 94.31)$
	(b,b)	46.22 ± 1008.52	$(1.97, 58.56, 225)$
16	(a,a)	16 ± 23.87	$(2.26, 50.88, 95.04)$
	(a,b)	24.1 ± 410	$(2.31, 60.2, 171.83)$
	(b,a)	15.82 ± 23.82	$(2.11, 49.93, 95.31)$
	(b,b)	26.17 ± 443.42	$(2.16, 58.6, 160.05)$

Table 3. Results concerning the **squared error of the estimation** given by the solutions of the algorithm. In each case, a sample of 10^6 *target* distributions of amplitudes was used. Technique (x,y) means that the techniques 1.(x), and 2.(y) were used in that case. For comparison, an error of 400×10^{-6} corresponds to 2% of the signal energy.

6. SOUND EXAMPLES

Together with this article, we have created some videos [2] showing a series of sound examples that were built using the `qdt.solver` object. A brief explanation for each of the sound examples can be found in this section. In order to hear examples 1 to 5, any reasonable loudspeaker at a moderate level should work just fine, however example 6 will require to increase the volume a little further so that the QDTS is audible.

6.1 Example 1. Producing a sequence of pitches with the qdt.solver object

Example 1 consists of the synthesis of a little melody known popularly as *the lick* (see [12] and [13]) in the key of A. The audio example contains the melody synthesized using additive synthesis, the combination of the additive and QDTS synthesis versions, and the QDTS synthesis alone for comparison.
For the QDTS synthesis, the computations were made using the `qdt.solver` object together with a *carrier* complex of pure tones with $C = 2470$Hz.

6.2 Example 2. Masking the auditory distortion products with filtered noise

Example 2 consists of the synthesis of a single pitch overlapped with filtered noise. The audio example contains the single pitch synthesized using additive synthesis and QDTS synthesis first and then overlaps it with a high-passed filtered noise. The effect of the filtered noise with the synthesized pitch using additive synthesis is simply hearing both sounds, however, when the filtered noise is played together with the QDTS synthesis, the synthesized pitch gets muted because of the disorder around the *carrier* complex of pure tones.
For the QDTS synthesis, the computations were made using the `qdt.solver` object using a *carrier* complex of pure tones with $C = 2338$Hz in order to synthesize a single pitch with frequency $F = 55$Hz and a particular harmonic distribution. The noise was filtered muting all frequencies below approximately 1100Hz.

6.3 Example 3. Amplitude modulation and Auditory Distortion Products

Example 3 consists of the synthesis of an amplitude-modulated single pitch. The audio example contains the amplitude-modulated pitch synthesized using additive synthesis, the combination of the additive and QDTS synthesis versions, and the QDTS synthesis alone for comparison. It is important to note that since the Quadratic Tones arise from the Distortion function $D = (d_1, \ldots, d_{n-1})$ and such function is homogeneous of degree 2 one has that

$$D(\lambda x) = \lambda^2 D(x),$$

so in order to apply amplitude modulation, one has to use the square root of the usual AM carrier.
For the QDTS synthesis, the computations were made using the `qdt.solver` object using a carrier complex of pure tones with $C = 2338$Hz in order to synthesize a single pitch with frequency $F = 55$Hz and a particular harmonic distribution. The AM carrier used was a simple LFO of the form

$$L_1(t) = A\sin(\omega t + \varphi) + B,$$

for some $A, B, \omega, \varphi \in \mathbb{R}$ in the additive synthesis case, and the squared root version of the LFO

$$L_2(t) = \sqrt{A\sin(\omega t + \varphi) + B},$$

for its QDTS counterpart.

6.4 Example 4. Frequency Modulation and Auditory Distortion Products

Example 4 consists of the synthesis of a frequency-modulated single pitch. The audio example contains the frequency-modulated pitch synthesized using additive synthesis, the combination of the additive and QDTS synthesis versions, the QDTS synthesis alone, and a QDTS synthesis using frequency modulation on the *carrier* instead of the *target* for comparison. The result shows that frequency modulation is compatible with QDTS synthesis in certain ranges. Moreover, when the *carrier* complex of pure tones is frequency modulated, the auditory distortion product holds its pitch, since the difference of the frequencies of the *carrier* complex of pure tones holds the same, however, some amplitude changes can be heard in this case, showing the instability of the auditory distortion products with respect to the *carrier* frequencies.
For the QDTS synthesis, the computations were made using the `qdt.solver` object using a carrier complex of pure tones with $C = 2500$Hz in order to synthesize a single pitch with frequency $F = 55$Hz and a particular harmonic distribution. The FM carrier used was a simple LFO of the form

$$L(t) = A\sin(\omega t + \varphi) + B,$$

for some $A, B, \omega, \varphi \in \mathbb{R}$ in both the additive and QDTS synthesis case.

6.5 Example 5. Resynthesizing existing sounds with Auditory Distortion Products

Example 5 consists of the resynthesis of a real recording of a tuba through QDTS synthesis. The audio example contains the real tuba recording, a resynthesis of the real recording using a combination of 8 sinusoids with a pitch detector, a combination of the resynthesis made with the 8 sinusoids and with the QDTS synthesis, the combination of the real recording with the resynthesis using QDTS synthesis versions, and finally the resynthesis using QDTS synthesis alone. The results show that certain signals can be at a certain level be reconstructed using QDTS synthesis.
For the QDTS synthesis, the computations were made using the `qdt.solver` object using a carrier complex of pure tones with $C = 1979$Hz in order to resynthesize the recording of a tuba. The harmonic distribution was precomputed using the Discrete Fourier Transform of a small bin of the real recording. The pitch and envelope detection of the tuba recording were made in real-time using the

[2] All videos are available in the GitHub repository https://github.com/cordutie/QDTS

lope of the real signal was used in the QDTS synthesis as in Example 3 (see 6.3).

6.6 Example 6. Resynthesizing the same existing sound with different Auditory Distortion Products

Before start describing this example, it is important to mention that here we are resynthesizing a much higher in pitch signal than in the previous example, and hence to hear this Auditory Distortion Products it is required to increase the volume of the loudspeakers used.

Example 6 consists of the resynthesis of a real clarinet recording through various Auditory Distortion Products. The audio example contains the real clarinet recording followed by three resynthesis of it using three different QDTS synthesis settings. The results show that the same signal can be recreated using different QDTS synthesis settings allowing to have at least some control on the timbre of the *carrier* complex of pure tones.

For the QDTS synthesis, the computations were made using the `qdt.solver` object using a carrier complex of pure tones with $C = 2345$Hz. The computations were ran several times until three reasonably different solutions appeared. The harmonic distribution was precomputed using the Discrete Fourier Transform of a small bin of the real recording. The pitch and envelope detection of the tuba recording were made in real-time using the `sigmund` object. Finally, the square root of the envelope of the real signal was used in the QDTS synthesis as in Example 3 (see 6.3).

7. CONCLUSIONS

The results presented in subsection 5.2 show that, for each case (n = 8, 12, 16), we can conclude that with a confidence of 99%, the proportion of the cases that can be solved in less than 10 tries (which is extremely fast and can be computed in real-time) correspond to at least the 99.45% of the cases. In addition, experimental tests were conducted to find unsolvable cases, but in all cases (n = 8, 12, 16), the addition of a small random vector allowed the algorithm to solve all previously unsolvable cases. However, the mathematical properties of the system that explain why the algorithm converges have not been proven yet.

The algorithm presented can be optimized by adjusting the initial condition and the change in target at restart. Test results for these adjustments were presented in Tables 2 and 3, using 10^6 randomly chosen target distributions of amplitudes.

The audio examples provided in the paper demonstrate the synthesis of different target QDTS's using our algorithm. Overall, the experimental results suggest that the algorithm is highly effective in matching a target timbre to a QDTS. In particular, instrumental sounds having very low fundamental frequencies fare well with the method. In future, the algorithm could be expanded to incorporate live audio analysis and resynthesis of a sound signal.

Acknowledgments

This research was partially funded by ANID Fondecyt Grant #1230926, Government of Chile.

[1] D. T. Kemp, "Stimulated acoustic emissions from within the human auditory system," *The Journal of the Acoustical Society of America*, vol. 64, no. 5, pp. 1386–1391, 1978.

[2] W. M. Hartmann, *Signals, sound, and sensation*. Springer Science & Business Media, 2004.

[3] J. B. Dewey, "Cubic and quadratic distortion products in vibrations of the mouse cochlear apex," *JASA Express Letters 2*, vol. 11, no. 114402, 2022.

[4] E. Zwicker, "Different behaviour of quadratic and cubic difference tones," *Hearing Research*, vol. 1, no. 4, pp. 283–292, 1979.

[5] R. Plomp, "Detectability threshold for combination tones," *The Journal of the Acoustical Society of America*, vol. 37, no. 1110, 1965.

[6] G. Kendall, C. Haworth, and R. F. Cádiz, "Sound synthesis with auditory distortion products," *Computer Music Journal*, vol. 38, no. 4, 2014.

[7] D. Pressnitzer and R. Patterson, "Distortion products and the perceived pitch of harmonic complex tones," *Physiological and psychophysical bases of auditory function*, pp. 97–104, 2001.

[8] S. Basu, R. Pollack, and M. F. Roy, *Algorithms in Real Algebraic Geometry*. Springer-Verlag, 2005.

[9] T. W. Dubé, "The structure of polynomial ideals and gröbner bases," *SIAM Journal on Computing*, vol. 19, no. 4, 1990.

[10] A. R. Meyer and E. W. Mayr, "The complexity of the word problems for commutative semigroups and polynomial ideals," *Advances in Mathematics*, vol. 46, no. 3, pp. 305–329, 1982.

[11] J.-C. F. Magali Bardet and B. Salvy, "On the complexity of the $f5$ gröbner basis algorithm," *Journal of Symbolic Computation*, vol. 70, pp. 49–70, 2015.

[12] H. Judd, "Virals, memes, and the lick's circulation through online jazz communities," *Twentieth-Century Music by Cambridge University Press*, vol. 19, no. 3, pp. 393–410, 2022.

[13] C. Stover, "Dig that lick (dtl): Analyzing large-scale data for melodic patterns in jazz performances," *Journal of the American Musicological Society*, vol. 74, no. 1, p. 195–214, 2021.

特别鸣谢：
Special Thanks to:

深圳市龙岗区文化广电旅游体育局
Culture, Radio, Television, Tourism and Sports Bureau of Longgang District Shenzhen

香港中文大学（深圳）大学艺术中心
University Arts Centre, CUHK-Shenzhen

香港中文大学（深圳）行政事务处
Administrative Services Office, CUHK-Shenzhen

香港中文大学（深圳）学生事务处
Office of Student Affairs, CUHK-Shenzhen

香港中文大学（深圳）资讯科技服务处
Information Technology Services Center, CUHK-Shenzhen

香港中文大学（深圳）人文社科学院体育部
Physical Education Unit, School of Humanities and Social Science, CUHK-Shenzhen

香港中文大学（深圳）安保部
Security Office, CUHK-Shenzhen

中航物业港中大（深圳）服务中心
Service Center, Avic Property Management, CUHK-Shenzhen

深圳交响乐团
Shenzhen Symphony Orchestra

深圳市华韵民族乐团
Shenzhen Huayun National Traditional Orchestra

上海广远电子技术股份有限公司
Meyer Sound

深圳市数字创意产业协会
Shenzhen Digital Creative Industry Association

深海影业（深圳）有限公司
Seabed Pictures

美啊设计平台
Meia

International Computer Music Association
1819 Polk Street #330
San Francisco, CA
94109

ISBN 978-1-7138-8477-4

CURRAN ASSOCIATES INC.
proceedings.com